SPEAKEASIES to SYMPHONIES

American Made Music Series

ADVISORY BOARD

David Evans, General Editor
Barry Jean Ancelet
Edward A. Berlin
Joyce J. Bolden
Rob Bowman
Curtis Ellison
William Ferris
John Edward Hasse
Kip Lornell
Bill Malone
Eddie S. Meadows
Manuel H. Peña
Wayne D. Shirley
Robert Walser

SPEAKEASIES to SYMPHONIES

The Jazz Genius of James P. Johnson

Scott E. Brown

University Press of Mississippi / Jackson

The University Press of Mississippi is the scholarly publishing agency of
the Mississippi Institutions of Higher Learning: Alcorn State University,
Delta State University, Jackson State University, Mississippi State University,
Mississippi University for Women, Mississippi Valley State University,
University of Mississippi, and University of Southern Mississippi.

www.upress.state.ms.us

The University Press of Mississippi is a member
of the Association of University Presses.

"Hungry Blues" from *De Organizer* by Langston Hughes.
Copyright © 1940 by Langston Hughes. Reprinted by permission of
Harold Ober Associates and International Literary Properties LLC.

"You've Got to Be Modernistic." Words and music by James P. Johnson.
Copyright © 1930 UNIVERSAL MUSIC CORP. Copyright renewed.
All rights reserved. Used by permission. Reprinted by permission of Hal Leonard, LLC.

Any discriminatory or derogatory language or hate speech regarding race,
ethnicity, religion, sex, gender, class, national origin, age, or disability
that has been retained or appears in elided form is in no way an endorsement
of the use of such language outside a scholarly context.

Copyright © 2026 by Scott E. Brown
All rights reserved
Manufactured in the United States of America
∞

Publisher: University Press of Mississippi, Jackson, USA
Authorised GPSR Safety Representative: Easy Access System Europe -
Mustamäe tee 50, 10621 Tallinn, Estonia, gpsr.requests@easproject.com

Hardback ISBN 978-1-4968-5752-1 | Paperback ISBN 978-1-4968-5753-8
Epub single ISBN 978-1-4968-6064-4 | Epub institutional ISBN 978-1-4968-5755-2
PDF single ISBN 978-1-4968-5756-9 | PDF institutional ISBN 978-1-4968-5757-6

British Library Cataloging-in-Publication Data available

CONTENTS

Acknowledgments vii
Preface xi

Introduction 3
Chapter 1. New Brunswick, 1894–1902 9
Chapter 2. Jersey City, 1902–1908 23
Chapter 3. The Jungles, 1908–1913 30
Chapter 4. The Ticklers, 1913–1916 40
Chapter 5. First Publications and Recordings, 1916–1917 59
Chapter 6. The Giggin' Years, 1916–1918 71
Chapter 7. Toledo, 1919–1920 81
Chapter 8. New York Breakout Year, 1921 91
Chapter 9. Harlem Stride Piano 104
Chapter 10. James P. and Fats Waller 114
Chapter 11. Plantation Days, 1922–1923 121
Chapter 12. Runnin' Wild, 1923 139
Chapter 13. The Rent Party 159
Chapter 14. On Stage, 1924–1926 171
Chapter 15. Yamekraw, 1927 181
Chapter 16. Keep Shufflin', 1928 191
Chapter 17. St. Louis Blues, 1929–1930 212
Chapter 18. Changing Tastes, 1931–1935 232
Chapter 19. The Organizer, 1935–1940 250
Chapter 20. Spirituals to Swing, 1938–1939 269
Chapter 21. Café Society, 1939–1941 283
Chapter 22. Concert Hall Realized, 1939–1942 295
Chapter 23. In Demand Again, 1942–1943 306
Chapter 24. Recording Flurry, 1943–1944 317
Chapter 25. Pied Piper, 1944–1945 327
Chapter 26. The Slow Decline, 1945–1946 335

Chapter 27.	New Patrons, 1946–1949	344
Chapter 28.	*Sugar Hill*—The Last Innovation, 1949–1950	361
Chapter 29.	Final Years, 1950–1955	368
Epilogue		378
Notes		381
Bibliography		433
General Index		443
Show Index		460
Tune Index		461

ACKNOWLEDGMENTS

This book is the product of over forty years of research, and would not have been possible without the assistance, support, encouragement, and serendipitous interaction with many people. A number of those identified here have since passed on, and I may have missed some people who played a role in this effort. Any omissions are entirely my own oversight.

After several years of informal study and information gathering as a high school and college undergraduate student, I was fortunate to have been selected into an independent study program in my senior year at Yale University called the Scholar of the House program. This gave me the opportunity to spend my entire senior year researching and writing about James P. Johnson. The program supplanted all other undergraduate requirements and was considered a major course of study in itself. One might say I majored in James P. Johnson in college. For my work in that program, I was supported by Professor of Music Beekman C. Cannon, then chairman of the Scholar of the House program, and my advisor Frank Tirro, dean of the Yale School of Music. Dr. Tirro provided my first formal, robust influence and education regarding jazz music and its history and kept me on track during my work. William R. Bennett, head of Silliman College, and Elizabeth Sledge, the writing tutor in Silliman, provided valuable resources and review of the thesis. While working on his own biography of Langston Hughes, Professor Arnold Rampersad at Stanford University graciously allowed me access to the Hughes papers in the James Weldon Johnson collection at Yale. Others who assisted in my initial work and provided essential feedback included my thesis oral examiners pianists Anthony Davis and Joshua Rifkin, Yale Afro-American studies faculty member Henry Louis Gates, Derek Coller, Frank Trolle, Michael A. Lang, Willa Rouder, Mark Smith, Murray Stopol, Larry Thompson, and Johnson's youngest daughter Lillie Mae McIntyre who spent an afternoon with me sharing memories of her father. The great pianist Richard MacQueen "Dick" Wellstood helped me with understanding the musical details of stride piano and Johnson's style. I must especially thank my parents, Milton and Judith Brown, who understood my passion for jazz, James P. Johnson, and the opportunity provided by the Scholar of the House program. That I had already completed all of my medical school prerequisites helped in convincing them to support my decision to spend an entire year of college without classes.

Much of my research was done at the Rutgers Institute of Jazz Studies (IJS), and after graduation I brought a copy of my thesis to Dan Morgenstern, then director of the Institute. He, along with Ed Berger and Vincent Pelote, had guided me in the resources of the Institute. IJS had recently launched their Studies in Jazz book series with Scarecrow Press. Dan, along with the remarkable David Cayer, suggested adding my work to that series. David, a longtime Johnson scholar, was especially helpful with insights and information. I cherish my many conversations with him about Johnson and jazz. My text did not include a discography, so Robert Hilbert was engaged to provide one. Like David, he was a stalwart Johnson champion, and it was my honor to have him as co-author of my first book. I was fortunate to have the generous use of photographs from William P. Gottlieb, Duncan P. Schiedt, and the New York Public Library for that volume. And over the course of many years, Dan Morgenstern remained a critical contact both during and after his tenure as director of the Institute.

I am forever indebted to Maestro Marin Alsop and pianist Leslie Stifelman, who reignited the research flame and search for Johnson's lost manuscripts after my first book was published. Marin has continued to champion Johnson and these works, and they are available for rental. Their enthusiasm led us back to the Johnson family, his oldest daughter Arceola Glover, and his grandson Barry Glover. Any words cannot convey my immeasurable gratitude to them for trusting us and allowing us access to the many boxes of Johnson's personal papers, which are now safely archived at the Rutgers Institute. It is not too much to say that this book would never have been written without them. I continue to enjoy a close friendship with Barry.

The discovery of this material made it clear there was much more to add to the Johnson story, and it led me to resume additional research. In particular, I explored archival sources I had not examined when working on my thesis. I had expert assistance from: Dr. Robert Belvin and the staff of the special collections at the New Brunswick Free Public Library; Reverend Dr. Hartmut Kramer-Mills from the First Reformed Church, New Brunswick; Ron Becker, Dave Kuzma, Erika B. Gorder, Fernanda H. Perrone, and other staff at Special Collections and University Archives, Rutgers University, New Brunswick; Margaret M. Gurowitz, Chief Historian of Johnson and Johnson; Janice Greenberg, Cynthia Harris, and John Beekman from the Jersey City Free Public Library and their New Jersey Room; Lisa L. Jackson at the Bayview-New York Bay Cemetery; Barbara Hibbert at the New York City Municipal Archives;

Bruce Boyd Raeburn and the staff of the Hogan Jazz Archive (now the Hogan Archive of New Orleans Music and New Orleans Jazz); Donna Christian, Local History and Genealogy Department, Toledo-Lucas County Public Library; the staff of the New York Public Library, especially Paul Friedman at the Stephen A. Schwartzman Main Branch, as well as staff at the Billy Rose Theater Division and Schomburg Center for Research in Black Culture; Therese Dickman, Fine Arts Librarian, Lovejoy Library, Southern Illinois University Edwardsville; Mary Carter of the Pasadena Public Library; and Jeff Place of Smithsonian Music. I was ably assisted by researchers from ProGenealogists at Ancestry.com, including Paul Graham, Peter Marsch, Kerry Farnsworth, Karina Morales, Chloe Bailey, David Vance, and Melody Moore.

No jazz research can be pursued without the resources of the Rutgers Institute of Jazz Studies, to which I returned many times. In addition to those mentioned above, I am indebted to its other incredible staff, including Annie Kuebler, Tad Hershorn, Elizabeth Surles, Angela Lawrence, Adriana Cuervo, and Wayne Winborne, for their guidance, expert suggestions, and allowing me unfettered access to the Johnson papers. Vincent Pelote has made it possible to include images of items from the Johnson collection at IJS.

In 2018, I was able to pursue a Masters degree in Jazz History and Research at Rutgers-Newark. Thanks to Lewis Porter for conceiving the program, eventually opening enrollment to nonmusicians such as myself, and encouraging me to apply. Additionally, Lewis has been generous with information and insights into Johnson's music. A special thanks to Dr. Henry Martin, initially co-director with Lewis, and then director of the program after Lewis's retirement. Professor Martin taught many of my classes in the program and was my thesis advisor. Over the course of three years, my understanding of jazz history, historiography, music theory, Charlie Parker, and other critical aspects of jazz scholarship expanded enormously. By the time I enrolled in the program, I had written a nearly complete draft of this volume. A class on ragtime and stride piano was routinely included in the course offerings, and Henry suggested we use my draft as the text for that class. This provided a platform for feedback from him and my classmates. They contributed many factual elements and corrections, as well as their own observations and insights. I thank Tharien Karim Arnold, Peter Katz, Forrest Drennen, Jay Eisenberg, Leslie K. Haynes, Karuna Maddava, Saul Castellanos, Ricardo Cueva, and Ed Solomon for the invaluable experience of our robust discussions. Henry's encouragement, suggestions as a musician and author himself, and providing the opportunity to review my entire draft accelerated the completion of this book immeasurably. I must also thank him for working with me as a long-distance commuting student in the program, supporting me through some personal challenges along the way, moving the program into the virtual world as COVID-19 hit, and serving as advisor for my thesis on another great pianist, Jaki Byard. I would not have completed the program without him. Evan Spring and Sean Lorre were other exemplary instructors. They provided expert feedback on assignments I wrote that helped tie up Johnson research loose ends.

Special thanks to pianist Louis Mazetier and writer/blogger Michael Steinman for insights and research leads. Over the course of these many years, numerous others have contributed assistance, information, feedback, and insights. Thanks to Mike Stoller, Lorraine Gordon, Paul Nossiter, Jack Lesberg, Dick Hyman, Joe Turner, Siegfried Mohr, William A. Mays, Jon Milan, Susan Harman, Kevin Whitehead, Alex Hassan, Tom Roberts, Michael Montgomery, Floyd Levin, Jim Dapogny, Ed Berlin, John Edward Hasse, John R. T. Davies, Mark Berresford, Stephanie Trick, Ehud Asherie, Philippe Souplet, Marty Eggers, Hal Smith, Kris Tokarski, David Boeddinghaus, John Royen, Adam Swanson, Ethan Iverson, Tom Samuels, Phil Schapp, Artis Wodehouse, Marcello Piras, John Howland, Drew Lawhorn, Laurie Lawhorn, Michael Lacey, Jan Brown, Mark Cantor, Michael "Spike" Wilner, Terry Waldo, Bill Hoffman, Sam Carner, Sam Irwin, Michael Formanek, Rebecca Lantz, Alex Soudah, and my men's team Sherif Osman, David Jaffe, Lester Picker, and Terry Sexton.

This book would be so much the poorer and incomplete were it not for three people whose own Johnson scholarship adds immeasurably to understanding his story. Pianist Mike Lipskin has been playing Johnson's music for over sixty years. He graciously reviewed large sections of the text. Much of my essential understanding of what differentiates stride piano from other early jazz piano styles and ragtime derives from Mike's insights. Dr. Robert Pinsker has been studying Johnson and early jazz piano for as long as I have. He is an excellent researcher, pianist, and piano roll expert. Years ago Bob asked me to write an introduction to his Johnson piano roll transcription book. It is one of my most honored writing assignments. He has always been generous with details from his own research. Dr. Mark Borowsky, who has also been studying Johnson as long as I have, is my true alter ego in the Johnson universe. My friendship with him, and his activism in promoting Johnson through his own writing and advocacy efforts have been a crucial inspiration for me. He, too, has been generous over the years sharing research, rare recordings, and his own insights into Johnson and his legacy.

I'm honored to be a part of the University Press of Mississippi American Made Music Series, and I thank their expert staff and consultants that made this happen including Craig Gill, Katie Turner, Cassie Winship, David Evans, Amy Atwood, Shane Gong Stewart, Joey Brown, Pete Halverson, and Will Rigby.

And importantly, my wife Lisa has been there to support this life's work through many difficult personal circumstances, including illness and untimely death. I could not have done this without her.

PREFACE

My first biography of Johnson, titled *James P. Johnson—A Case of Mistaken Identity*, published in 1986 by the Scarecrow Press and the Rutgers Institute of Jazz Studies, was an outgrowth of my college thesis. Prior to that, aside from a series of interviews with writer Tom Davin, there had been only a few substantive journalistic pieces, and a discography with a brief biographical sketch. His most important contributions were known, but because much of his recorded and printed music was difficult to find, or thought lost, and many details of his life and activity were not well documented, music historians and writers acknowledged his importance in American music and jazz in an inconsistent manner. In my relatively brief period of time as a college student, I attempted to bring together information about Johnson's life and music in a more comprehensive manner. When I undertook that year of serious research, I was cautioned by more than one person that I might not find much more than was already known. I persisted, especially since I had a degree to complete, and, eventually, adding Robert Hilbert's discography, the breadth of Johnson's musical activity was better detailed. It was my hope that our book would provide a more robust basis for the chroniclers of the music to put him and keep him in what I thought the evidence clearly demonstrated was a prominent place as innovator, influencer, composer, and pianist.

Since that first book was published, it is clear this has not happened. Although my initial research added much important information, there were still substantial gaps that left many unanswered questions, and most of his music remained elusive. Shortly after my first book was published, I embarked on my career as a physician, and it seemed any further research to unearth the elusive details to answer the many lingering questions more fully would have to wait. The hiatus did not last long. Almost immediately after publication, I was contacted by conductor Marin Alsop, a Leonard Bernstein protégé, and her colleague, pianist Leslie Stifelman. Both were interested in jazz-inspired orchestral works. They had heard about Johnson's symphonic pieces and were eager to perform them. At that time, only his piano rhapsody *Yamekraw* was available. His other works went missing after their last performances in the mid-1940s. After several years of additional fruitless research searching for the lost music, we agreed to contact Johnson's oldest daughter Arceola Glover, and her son Barry Glover. As it turned out, they had carefully and lovingly preserved a trove of material previously only rumored to exist. Included were programs, letters, contracts, scrapbooks, music workbooks and sketches, and, most importantly, manuscripts of many of Johnson's symphonic pieces. Marin and Leslie had several of these pieces properly copied, and they were performed at Lincoln Center and recorded in the early 1990s. The discovery of his personal papers served as the impetus for me to pick up Johnson research again in earnest. Once I reengaged, seeking answers to the mystery of Johnson's obscurity, and attempting to further rectify it, became the focus of this new biography. I began by using this primary source material to fill in essential pieces in his story. It provided additional invaluable insights into Johnson the man and musician. It was clear this was only the beginning of completing the full Johnson picture.

The ensuing thirty years have enabled further research and assessment. Secondary sources have been rescrutinized. Many researchers have since investigated other musicians and business figures in Johnson's sphere whose stories bear directly on Johnson's. Additional archival research brought new details to light. Considerable effort has been made to investigate Johnson's genealogy. He offers intriguing hints about it in interviews and other documents. In addition to information available on internet databases, on-site archival research was required. These documents are fraught with contradictory information and inaccuracy. Nonetheless, this effort uncovered important details about his mother and her family, and, at least for the salient period of Johnson's childhood, details about his father, stepfather, and the Price family, after whom he is named.

The interviews conducted by writer Tom Davin with Johnson at his home, thought to have taken place in 1953, have been reassessed. By then, Johnson was significantly impaired from a severe stroke in 1951. This has led some to speculate that these interviews actually took place before his paralysis, since by 1953 his speech was slurred, he was confined to bed or wheelchair, and he often easily fell off to sleep. The detailed interviews took place in what must have been multiple exhaustive sessions. Davin took notes in his own personal shorthand and transcribed them later. They were serialized in the short-lived but highly regarded magazine *Jazz Review*. Five installments were published, the last in the March/April 1960 issue, just before the magazine folded. There were more interviews, but Davin apparently never found an outlet to publish the remainder of the series. He also never transcribed the remaining interviews from his notes before his death. The published installments constitute a detailed account from Johnson describing his earliest childhood memories up to his widespread success around 1921. Johnson recounts in uncanny detail the music, the people, and the places that had an impact on his development.

In my first book, most of the information about Johnson's early life was in large part taken from these interviews. As oral history, they must be interpreted with caution, but there wasn't time then to research corroborating information. In this new biography, I have attempted to verify the chronology, places, events, and characters that make up the early Johnson story. Memoir can fall prey to many pitfalls, including self-aggrandizement, hyperbole, revisionism, axe-grinding, and failed memory. Johnson certainly notes his own successes and importance but is respectful and complimentary toward the many others who were creating modern American music, highlighting their contributions as well. It reflects the personality recalled by the many who knew him—a gracious, thoughtful, and easygoing man. There are a few transcription errors, or perhaps errors from Johnson's impaired diction as a result of his stroke. With new corroborating information, it is clear that in very few instances is Johnson incorrect on his facts. At times events are mis-ordered or conflated, but all in all he and Davin produced an astonishingly accurate document. Included in the interviews, and not reproduced in detail in this book, are Johnson's descriptions of the physical characteristics, dress, and performance styles of many musicians and entertainers, as well as the details of the social milieu of the African American entertainment community during the first two decades of the twentieth century. He paints one of the most complete and compelling pictures of this era. The interviews are worth reading in their entirety.

Contemporaneous documentation was needed to fill in many gaps in his activity and the reception of his music. The internet has been an invaluable resource in this research. Many periodicals are now available in searchable databases, a process substantially more efficient than scrolling through microfilm reels. This was not without other substantial challenges, especially with a subject holding a common first and last name, and whose professional name varied, at times abbreviated according to conventions of the time. News accounts are themselves subject to inaccuracy, and the journalistic and editorial style of the early twentieth century could often be long on description and short on detail. Many thousands of citations were sorted through to determine if the subject was indeed this James P. Johnson. Corroboration often required assessment of other documents and sources. A book such as this can never be written in isolation, and invaluable information, insights, and research assistance was generously provided from many people identified in the acknowledgments.

A few words are indicated about how the unavoidable issues of race, racism, social inequities, and other disturbing aspects of our American history are handled. They cannot be shied away from, nor are they easily reconciled or dismissed by applying current sensibilities toward what are in many cases unquestionably abhorrent views and behaviors. It is not the intention of this book to engage with current scholarship on these aspects of social science, but, since they are so visible a component of Johnson's professional world, when appropriate and necessary, I attempt to give them context in that arena. This holds true for the actions of white figures as well as Black, as when addressing the vestiges of minstrelsy that persisted in African American stage productions. In examples where hateful language is quoted (in particular the N-word), the words are spelled out in their entirety. It is unsettling to read them, and to recognize the uncomfortable truth that this rhetoric and its practical effects were so blithely considered routine and acceptable.

Any reader familiar with the first book I hope will recognize that this retelling now brings nearly the complete Johnson story into even sharper focus, although frustrating contradictions and mysteries remain. There is a tendency to think of Johnson and others in his stride piano circle as a group holed up in rent parties who would only occasionally emerge to participate in jam sessions or to record. With substantial new information, we now know how deeply Johnson was involved in so many aspects of music, and that he interacted with just about everyone. To highlight this, the people and musicians he associated and played with, and the venues he played in, are frequently listed in detail. His musical theater work ran throughout nearly his entire professional career, and this book is as much a history of his contributions to the stage as to jazz. Inaccuracies in the first book have been corrected, and much more of his music is now available. It should be played more often and studied. I describe this work as a new biography, and not an update or second edition. I am hopeful that this accounting will leave little doubt about his rightful place in American music.

SPEAKEASIES to SYMPHONIES

INTRODUCTION

What to do with James P. Johnson? In American music, he has floated in, but mostly out of view for over a century. Situating his career, contributions, and influence has often been subject to the biases of partisan critics and flawed historiography, casting him as adjacent to, or a secondary figure in, the conventional telling of American music and jazz history. As early as 1941, writer and record producer Ross Russell, before he became better known as bebop and Charlie Parker champion, wrote the first feature article about Johnson in the jazz press. Although Johnson was still alive, Russell made a point of noting that he was "a discouraging subject for a biographer, which may explain why he has been overlooked so often by critics and historians of jazz." Johnson had been omitted from two early, important jazz texts—*Le Jazz Hot* penned by French critic Hughes Panassie in 1934, and *Jazzmen*, by Frederick Ramsey and Charles Edward Smith in 1939. His only mention in the latter volume is in the acknowledgments. In succeeding years, all three authors attempted to make amends for their slight. Even Johnson's good friend William "Count" Basie, who often acknowledged Johnson's critical influence, neglected to include him when asked in 1942 who his pick for the twelve greatest jazz pianists were. Twenty years after Russell's piece, the eminent writer and producer Stanley Dance, in the liner notes to the pivotal 1962 LP *James P. Johnson—Father of the Stride Piano*, in addition to coining this posthumous title for Johnson, reiterated, "James P. Johnson has never been accorded his due, yet it is not too much to claim that his was the first major influence on jazz piano." Forty years after Russell, Stanford jazz educator and Monterey Jazz Festival publicist Grover Sales wrote that Johnson "is still a leading contender for the dubious honor of America's most overlooked musical genius." And fifty years after Russell's comment, David Schiff wrote in the *New York Times* in the lead-up to the Lincoln Center performance of Johnson's symphonic works long thought lost, "Was James P. Johnson the invisible composer, the musical counterpart to Ralph Ellison's Invisible Man? Johnson, who died in 1955, holds the odd distinction of not being remembered as the composer of the 'Charleston.'"[1]

The reasons for Johnson's seemingly intractable obscurity in American music history are many. Russell offers one notable explanation—"the difficulty of tying him in with the tradition."[2] We might ask, then, which tradition? What has vexed writers and scholars of American music is where and how to situate Johnson in many traditions. He was much more than a one-dimensional jazz pianist. His peak decade, the 1920s—the "roaring twenties"—spawned dramatic cultural change and new music to go with it. Speakeasies, rent parties, lavish night clubs, Tin Pan Alley, musical theater, and the concert hall, all became the crucibles of invention that set the course for the succeeding century of music, from highbrow to lowbrow. And in each of these realms, Johnson's protean contributions, which include well-recognized benchmark examples of his work, are often marginalized as secondary to the work of more famous musicians or simply forgotten.

One of the most important cultural touchstones of the decade, and by which name it is often described, is the "jazz age." To the degree that Johnson is best known and acknowledged, it is for his contributions to the jazz tradition. In this context, Russell's reference to disconnection stems from the fact that Johnson was not born in New Orleans, and, for the most part, was not primarily influenced by those who were. The conventional history of jazz to this day remains tethered to the notion that jazz was born in New Orleans, made its way up the Mississippi River to Chicago, and was then disseminated around the world. There is likely some truth to the importance of New Orleans in establishing the sound of polyphonic, horn-based, instrumental jazz. But a separate, parallel migration happening along the East Coast set the course for the evolution of jazz piano as a distinct tradition. The alchemy Johnson wielded in melding ragtime, the blues, and the rhythms of a distinct dance form called the ring shout into the first identifiable jazz piano idiom, Harlem stride piano, inspired Stanley Dance to anoint him the father of the style. Johnson established its essential sound, composed its unavoidable test pieces, and was acknowledged as its preeminent player.

It would seem, then, that there should be no ambiguity about tying him in to this tradition. Yet, because his career began in the late ragtime era of the mid-teens, and continued until 1950, Johnson and stride piano have been ensnared in genre assignment arguments. Some writers soundly credit Johnson with the creation of a jazz piano style from its musical antecedents. Some consider stride piano a transitional style, and Johnson a transitional figure, a reflection of "the rather constricted canon of jazz piano history," wherein stride piano is considered merely "a necessary yet brief stop . . . as it moves from Joplin . . . to Tatum."[3] And still others hear stride piano only as a sophisticated offshoot of ragtime, somehow not worthy of inclusion in the jazz tradition. Tagging the style to the older form does not allow the possibility that Johnson could be an innovator, and, implicit in this sort of analysis, is the erroneous judgment that earlier music is in some way of lesser value and interest. Johnson started as a ragtime player and composer, but with his keen ear and prodigious talents, he moved the music in a new direction. He saw himself as a jazz pianist but loved ragtime and kept his earliest compositions in his repertoire throughout his life.

In assessing the distinctive features of Johnson's stride piano, identifying the parameters of demarcation between ragtime and jazz piano is possible without disparaging the beauty of the ragtime tradition. As pianist Mike Lipskin describes it, Johnson possessed a "monumental ability to string distinct variation sets that could go on and on."[4] This boundless capacity for inventive variation, in every way a method of improvisation, combined with his more "swinging" rhythmic sense, fulfill the essential elements of jazz. When Johnson burst on the scene in 1921, there was no question at that time that a new pianism had arrived, the ambivalence of some later generations of jazz writers notwithstanding. Stride piano was not the terminal phase for ragtime, but rather a vibrant, freestanding, stylistic outgrowth that also became the endoskeleton for a long line of jazz piano development. Ironically, in a piece devoted to Jelly Roll Morton, the eminent jazz writer Martin Williams notes that three greats of jazz piano form—Duke Ellington, Thelonious Monk, and John Lewis—were all influenced by Johnson, establishing that it is Johnson who anchors the history of jazz piano. Later in his book, Williams also includes Count Basie and Bud Powell as the beneficiaries of the impact of stride piano.[5] Directly and indirectly, he has influenced every subsequent pianist in the jazz tradition, ". . . whether they realize it or not."[6] Jazz piano as a discrete discipline begins with Johnson. The facts demonstrate that Johnson was as much a jazz innovator on his instrument as Louis Armstrong and Charlie Parker were on theirs, and not a footnote to Morton, Earl Hines, Fats Waller, or Art Tatum.

Within the domain of African American music traditions of the 1920s are the "classic" blues and jazz singers. Many dozens if not hundreds of primarily female vocalists moved away from the nasal belting or operatic delivery necessary in cabarets before amplification, to a richer, more nuanced delivery that needed accompanists to provide the same. This skill set is distinct from that of solo or band pianist. With his ability to find the spaces in the vocal line and deliver nuggets of improvisational brilliance that accentuated the imagery of the lyrics and complemented the inflections of the singer, Johnson was one of the most sought-after accompanists, backing more than thirty singers on record and on stage. He was the favorite accompanist of such differing vocal stylists as Bessie Smith and Ethel Waters. It is not a stretch to claim that Johnson established the essence of modern jazz piano vocal accompaniment, in evidence from his earliest recorded work backing singers in 1921.

With over five hundred openings, the 1920s has been called the first Golden Age of Broadway. Johnson as composer devoted nearly his entire forty-year professional career to writing for the musical theater. He scored all or part of more than forty stage shows for the most prominent producers including George White, Earl Carroll, the Shuberts, and Jules Hurtig, as well as those in the African American stage tradition. These productions played on and off Broadway and across the country. His music propelled two of the most successful shows on Broadway, and in Harlem his tunes were mainstays of floor shows at legendary venues like the Lafayette and Apollo Theaters, Smalls' Paradise, and Connie's Inn, often with Johnson leading the orchestra. It was in many respects the perfect medium for him. It allowed all aspects of his musical talent to flourish—composer, arranger, pianist, accompanist, and conductor. Yet, the history of African American musical theater in the first half of the twentieth century is akin to that of the Negro Leagues in baseball—fifty years of poorly documented exceptionalism that produced some of the finest work of its kind in a universe parallel to the white musical world. The genre was tied in its presentation to many requisite detestable cultural stereotypes. The demeaning artifice defined Black culture for much of the dominant white society. Despite that, and behind the mask, there were exceptional singers, dancers, actors, and musicians.

Johnson remains poorly appreciated as a composer for the stage, despite a prodigious body of work creating a portfolio of classics that have had timeless impact. As the reviews demonstrate, show after show, he contributed high-quality tunes in league with his white songwriting counterparts. Always looking to be the innovator, his last stage production in 1949, *Sugar Hill*, although still embedded in the "all-Black" format, included bold scoring for which he was criticized. Seven years later, in 1956, Frank Loesser was hailed for what was referred to as his groundbreaking expansion of the musical theater with his score for *The Most Happy Fella* using the same approach Johnson had used, and for which Johnson has been given no credit. Out of his first Broadway show twenty-five years earlier came the signature tune of the 1920s, "Charleston." In addition to composing for the stage, he added to the Great American Songbook with tunes like "If I Could Be with You" and "Don't Cry, Baby." What more need be said of him to secure a prominent place in the tradition of popular and stage composing?

The Harlem Renaissance, a time of intentional focus on African American artistic expression, was at its height during the 1920s. Although best known for the literary works produced by authors and poets such as Langston Hughes, the imperative of the Renaissance thinkers extended to music. Intellectuals such as Alain Locke envisioned the emergence of composers who would recast the folk and vernacular elements of African American music into forms that would garner serious attention—essentially the forms of Western art music. Johnson had incubated an interest in concert music as early as the late 1910s, and this aspiration for racial elevation or "uplift" as articulated by the Renaissance leaders provided the ideal route for him to achieve his own goals of becoming known as a composer not only of popular music but so-called serious music.

Toward this end, he studied with conservatory-trained musicians, white and Black, for nearly his entire adult life. From the mid-twenties through the early forties, he composed and orchestrated numerous symphonic works that would showcase the rich contributions of African Americans to American culture, society, and history. They saw limited performances and were perplexing to critics and academics who could not find a place for them in the acceptable art music tradition of the time. These works were unavailable for fifty years, hampering their subsequent assessment. Many of his pieces intended for symphonic performance, including his two symphonies, piano concerto, two one-act operas, and smaller works, have now been discovered, recorded, and are available for performance and study. They demonstrate Johnson's flexible incorporation of popular form and vernacular melodic, harmonic, and rhythmic elements into larger compositions that are now seen as genre expanding works that challenge conventional notions of what constitutes "serious" music.

With this portfolio of accomplishment in many traditions, why has recognition for him languished? There are other factors, some societal and some personal. Certainly, the pervasive racism that worked all too well in limiting his professional opportunities played a role. He navigated this minefield of racial subjugation and totemic stereotyping on the one hand by working within its confines, and on the other by seeking loftier planes of endeavor. With the former, he was attached to objectionable vestiges of hundred-year-old theater conventions that cast African Americans in spurious, defamatory, cultural cartoons. With the latter, opportunity was limited, and often nonexistent. But this was also true for his much better-known contemporaries.

In part, his general lack of broad recognition was the result of his introverted personality and some of the professional choices he made. He was not a uniquely colorful figure like many of his friends and protégés, such as Fats Waller and Duke Ellington. They eclipsed him in public recognition as performer and composer. In a tradition of nicknames, he had none. The details of his life are not an array of chimerical anecdotes around which a popular mythology can readily be built (like Morton), but there was certainly frustration and a tragic element to his story. Although for many years he was very active in after-hours Harlem nightlife, he also led a stable family life with his wife and three children. He was by nature taciturn, patient, considerate, and perhaps even too easily manipulated. He did not promote himself as readily as his contemporaries in building a national reputation as a performer, bandleader, and entertainer.

By the mid-twenties, when other now household names in jazz were establishing themselves with what are considered essential recordings, Johnson was out of the recording studio for over a year, on the road with stage work that brought him little national attention. It remains a mystery why he chose not to parlay his authorship of "Charleston," by then a worldwide hit, into greater public fame. He had no regular band, and his discography, while substantial, is spread across numerous labels and formats. For decades, there were no readily available compilations of his recordings. During the 1920s, there can be no question he was the preeminent jazz pianist, dominating at rent parties and cutting contests. When he was eventually toppled as piano king, it was at the hands of Art Tatum, perhaps the most intimidating pianistic phenomenon ever to have emerged in this tradition. As a result, to this day, the general public and many professed jazz, popular music, and musical theater aficionados are ignorant of his name. The extent of critical acclaim he has earned for his far-reaching contributions in these many facets of American music has been primarily limited to the traditional jazz community, and a relatively small group in scholarly and journalistic jazz circles.

This is not to suggest Johnson was a failure. He was a creative, stylistic exemplar. The success he achieved as popular composer provided him with sufficient financial security so that he never had to seek nonmusical work, as was the case with so many musicians who experienced early success only to die poverty-stricken. Johnson's story is that of a pioneer whose goals and dreams were often realized at the highest professional levels, if not always widely celebrated. He applied the African American experience to the broadest array of endeavors, from solo jazz piano to stage show, to symphony and opera. Maintaining the integrity of each of his musical endeavors was a deeply held priority. He knew when to be a virtuoso, and when to lay back and complement his band or a singer. He knew that both extraordinary keyboard technique and compositional skills required serious study. We might excuse the biased critics and flawed historiographers of the past for failing to place and keep Johnson positioned where he justly belongs. His biography had been challenging, as Russell observed, and for decades important details of his life and music were elusive. Now, this new biography of him presents a fuller picture. The more complete historical record, and the availability of so much more of his written and recorded music, should lead to the unsurprising realization that ". . . the slender threads in the disorganized pattern came to acquire lasting form and color after the rest of the picture had blurred off."[7] His milestone contributions gave structure, energy, meaning, and timelessness to the numerous musical traditions that accompanied the "roaring twenties," and this influence is still felt.

Chapter 1

NEW BRUNSWICK, 1894–1902

"THE HUB CITY"

In a brief, handwritten note on a small piece of paper retained for many years by his youngest daughter Lillie Mae Jr., James P. Johnson summarized his ancestry and birth. "On a cold morning in February 1894, I came into this world in a house in City Alley, an inconspicuous and plain dwelling in a section of New Brunswick, New Jersey, long ago torn down and now extinct as a living quarters and the neighborhood forgotten," he wrote.[1] An odd place, perhaps, to have produced one of the great pioneers of American music and "Dean of Jazz Pianists," the moniker he used to sign that note and others in later years. There would seem little about New Brunswick from which one could spin a compelling tale of a jazzman. Although a river city, it was far removed from St. Louis, the Mississippi delta, and New Orleans, where many histories would have us believe that at the turn of the twentieth century, they were the only crucibles of the burgeoning elements of American music that included ragtime, the blues, and jazz. New Brunswick could hardly be called a melting pot, but even in this small town whose population barely numbered five figures, there was enough musical activity to pique the interest of a youngster with a keen ear. James P. Johnson lived there for only his first eight years, but fifty years later, he could recall the impact on him of the local music scene and his first exposure to the religious and secular music of his own ethnic community. Some of these traditions had deep roots and came from afar, brought into their home by his mother and emanating from her rich background. As the new century approached, ease of mobility became a catalyst of social reconfiguration and cultural exchange. And Johnson's mother was an early example of one who risked leaving the comforts of her birthplace for a new life.

Of his mother, Josephine Harrison, Johnson wrote in that same note, "Mother's father was a Negro of half American Indian extraction who had bought his freedom. Mother was born in Petersburg, Virginia."[2] Nathaniel Harrison, Josephine's father, was born in Virginia in 1805. Little is known of his early upbringing and enslavement, or the circumstances of his emancipation. When and how he was able to purchase his freedom is missing from extant court documents, but he was no longer enslaved by the time he was fifty years old. His Native American heritage is unsurprising. The greater Petersburg region in Virginia was populated by thriving settlements of indigenous people, and comingling of African and Native Americans stemmed from sympathetic feelings for the suffering that resulted from respective injustices. Nathaniel worked as a waiter in Jarratt's Hotel. Jarratt's was the largest and one of the most elaborately appointed establishments in the city. It offered hot and cold baths, a billiard room, barber shop, and a private livery service for touring the city. Shortly after the Civil War, it promoted itself as a premier destination for touring the nearby battlefields. With its own railroad stop, it attracted visitors from Washington, Baltimore, and New York.[3] For Nathaniel, it was a stable job in a first-class hospitality center.

Josephine's mother, Frances Jones, was born around 1815. She was apparently born free in Greensville County, Virginia, near the North Carolina border. She is described as 5 feet 2½ inches tall and of dark complexion, physical attributes that would manifest in her grandson. Josephine was born around 1853 and had three older siblings, Martha twelve years older, John five years older, and William three years older. By 1870, only nineteen-year-old William, then working in a tobacco factory, remained at home with Nathaniel, who likely died around 1872 or 1873 since he is not listed in any subsequent tax records. Frances likely passed away before 1870. No death records could be located for either of Josephine's parents. Sometime before 1879 and before she was thirty years old, Josephine made her way north. A single woman who may well have had rheumatic fever as a child, she settled at 156 George Street in New Brunswick, New Jersey, a main thoroughfare in the heart of the city.[4]

New Brunswick was founded in 1681 when John Inian and a group of English settlers purchased a swath of land on the south bank of the Raritan River in Middlesex County in central New Jersey. The Raritan River empties into the lower region of New York Bay just south of Staten Island, affording easy access to New York, transatlantic crossing, and trade to the south. As in all of the original thirteen colonies, slavery was a legal enterprise, introduced by the Dutch to Middlesex County.[5] Unlike most of the other Northern colonies, New Jersey had a particularly conflicted and protracted course toward abolition. During the first decade of the nineteenth century, there were 164 slaves and 53 free Blacks in New Brunswick out of a total city population of 3,042.

The abolition movement began slowly in 1786, with a partial emancipation in 1805. New Jersey was the only Northern state not carried by Lincoln in 1860, and it failed to ratify the 13th, 14th, and 15th Amendments. Black men were enfranchised in 1870 only because a sufficient number of other states ratified the 15th Amendment to enact it as federal law. Life for African Americans was more hospitable in southern New Jersey due in large part to the strong Quaker influence there. Northern New Jersey, with a more substantial industrial base, maintained a stronger connection to the Southern states through their business interactions. Geographically, New Brunswick sits near the junction of northern and southern New Jersey. Although a few slaves were still held there into the mid-nineteenth century, it was an important stop on the Underground Railroad.[6] James P. Johnson's blended family can trace its beginnings to 1794, when Petrus Nevius Sr., a wealthy landowner and slaveholder, amended the inventory of his will to include valuation of his property. The Nevius family owned substantial plantations in Middlebush, just outside of New Brunswick. Included in the valuation statement was an itemization of "4 negroes."[7] Shortly after the 1805 emancipation in New Jersey, John Nevius was born free to these former slaves of the prominent Dutch family. He had four children—sons Peter and Richard, daughter, Sarah, and youngest son, provocatively named Freedom.[8]

Richard was born in 1837. In 1874, he and Peter, older by one year, were living in New Brunswick, Richard working as a clerk and Peter as a driver.[9] By 1879, however, Richard had moved back out to Middlebush and was working as a farmer when on March 16, 1879, he married Josephine Harrison. He was forty-two years old and had been married before, a circumstance that may have led to his move out of the city and back to the former plantation where his family had been held as slaves. In June 1880, they were living on the farm in Franklin Township in neighboring Somerset County with Richard's mother Mary, and Diana, Richard's daughter from his first marriage.[10] Johnson recalled he was the youngest of five children. His four half-siblings were born to Richard and Josephine. His oldest half-brother William Henry Nevius was born December 23, 1879, followed by Frank born October 25, 1881, and third son Clifford born October 15, 1883. Daughter Isabella, called Belle or Bella, was born around February 1886.[11] They would play a role in the upbringing of their much younger half-brother, including in his early musical life.

Shortly after Isabella was conceived in 1885, Richard became ill. Josephine's young family fragmented. She stayed in Franklin Township but moved in with the family of George Thompson, apparently without her children.[12] The Thompsons were also African American, and Josephine may have moved in to work and support her family. There is no record of her children or Richard in the 1885 New Jersey census. One can speculate that perhaps Mary and older daughter Diana, then twelve years old, were caring for Richard and the other four young children and were missed by the state census takers. Richard Nevius died June 2, 1887, the cause of death given as necrosis, a vague medical descriptor that implies a slow death due to multi-organ failure he probably suffered over the course of his two-year illness. Richard was buried in New Brunswick. By 1890, Josephine had moved back to New Brunswick and was living at 172 Albany Street, not far from her old residence.[13] Presumably, her four children were with her. The wealthy families of the expanding and thriving city created demand for the domestic work Josephine resumed.

The early and later years of William H. Johnson, James P. Johnson's father, remain mostly a mystery. Johnson wrote in his autobiographical summary, "My grandfather on father's side had been a soldier in the Civil War and, through some unexplained circumstance had lost his company papers and my father never received his pension. He was born in New Brunswick, New Jersey."[14] William was born in New Brunswick most likely in 1848 or 1849.[15] The names of William's parents and details of his early upbringing are muddled in a series of conflicting documents. For much of his first forty years, William seems to have moved from numerous households in and around New Brunswick, usually working as a laborer of some sort. William (noted with middle initial L.) married Harriet "Hetty" Francis on May 7, 1884. This is the same couple enumerated on the 1885 New Jersey state census with William's correct middle initial.[16] By 1888 and for the next twelve years, the William Johnson story is more certain.

By the late nineteenth century, New Brunswick was a formidable manufacturing, mercantile, and educational center for central New Jersey. The city produced rubber, shoes, wallpaper, musical instrument strings, and chemicals, amongst other products. Its most noted company, one that has maintained its world headquarters there, is pharmaceutical behemoth Johnson and Johnson, founded in 1886 as a maker of antiseptics and bandages. The center of commerce developed along the Raritan River on Burnet Street, with merchants supplying customers throughout the county. Queens College was founded there in 1766, eventually changing its name to Rutgers University after a major benefactor.

African American migration into New Brunswick was slow but steady through the nineteenth century. The Mt. Zion African Methodist Episcopal Church was founded there in 1827. It is the oldest Black church in the county and was established only a decade after the founding of the denomination. Well before the great migration north around World War I, African Americans came predominantly from the southeastern United States, especially Georgia and South Carolina. There were, overall, still relatively few African Americans in New Brunswick. In 1900, 3.7 percent of the state's inhabitants were African American. By 1910, there were 690 African Americans in New Brunswick out of a population of over 23,000 (2.9 percent).[17] New Brunswick became home to a much larger population of Eastern European immigrants, largely from Hungary.

New Brunswick, like most Northern cities, was a reluctantly tolerant but not especially encouraging town for African Americans. Although there was no distinct African American residential section of town at that time, segregation ran through many veins of society. Despite the burgeoning industrial activity, employment options for people of color were limited to menial positions. This was due both to the preferential hiring of European immigrants and the prejudiced and effectively segregated culture. Among the large industrial companies in New Brunswick, most would not hire Blacks, a practice intended to prevent "race mixing."[18] William, however, came to find steady work in a store owned by a prominent New Brunswick family named Price. In 1888, he was working for them as a driver, and, as was the case with many of his prior employers, living with them. The Price family lived at 255 Burnet Street in New Brunswick, a busy commercial district.[19] William soon developed new skills. As Johnson noted, "My father was a store helper and mechanic named William Johnson and worked for a man by the name of Price whom I was named after."[20] For at least the next twelve years, William would enjoy a productive employment and personal relationship with the Price family. They had been in New Brunswick for many years by this time and were established, well-connected, and respected merchants.

Family patriarch Caleb Price was born in 1788 and became a tinsmith,[21] moving to New Brunswick in 1829 to open his store. His son Henry M. Price, born 1818, joined him in the business in 1835. After the death of his father, Henry became sole proprietor in 1844.[22] Henry and his wife Abigail had many children, perhaps as many as eleven. In 1881, two of Henry M.'s sons took over the business, Henry C. (b. 1846) and William H. (b. 1855). William trained as a lawyer, acquiring skills that would prove useful in business and his future political pursuits.[23] When William and Henry took over, the business became known as H. M. Price's Sons. They expanded the business, carrying all manner of tinware as well as stoves, ranges, and heaters. They moved from 179 Burnet Street to a new, larger, three-story brick building encompassing addresses 249, 251, and 253 Burnet Street. Each floor measured 25 × 100 feet. The basement and third floor were used as storage, and the first floor was used as a showroom. It was one of the more prominent storefronts on Burnet St. The second floor housed the manufacturing space. The residence for Henry M., his two sons who were the principals in the business, and another son named James who worked as a clerk was next door at 255 Burnet. A fourth son, Benjamin, had established a very successful dry goods and carpet store at 257 Burnet.[24] Henry M. Price died January 30, 1889, after a two-month illness. William H. Johnson certainly knew the Price family elder, and, as a boarder in the home, may well have helped care for him as his health declined. Henry M. was eulogized as a generous, civic-minded, upstanding member of the community. He supported many initiatives for the poor as well as for the overall betterment of New Brunswick.

The Rev. P. T. Pockman performed the funeral service at the First Reformed Church in New Brunswick, the Price family's regular place of worship.[25] The family would call on Rev. Pockman again soon for another occasion.

William and Henry were very active in New Brunswick political and civic life, especially during the late 1880s through the turn of the century. At various times, William served as alderman for the 3rd Ward, postmaster, city tax collector, part owner of the *New Brunswick Daily Times* newspaper, and chairman of the local Democratic Party.[26] Henry served as alderman and as one of the city water commissioners.[27] The two brothers were held in high regard by the business community, and thought to have bright futures, with local writers noting, "They are prompt and reliable young men, active and enterprising, and are calculated to add additional lustre to the honorable business established by their father."[28] They employed a number of skilled workers, but it is not known if the Price brothers hired other African Americans. However, as Johnson implies in his note, and contrary to the practice and inclination of other New Brunswick employers, the Price brothers encouraged William. He advanced from driver to mechanic for their appliances. William Johnson worked for the Price family for at least twelve years.[29] Their personal support seemed a good reason for him to take their surname for his son's middle name. After the turn of the century, H. M. Price's Sons moved into the plumbing business. Henry C. Price died in 1920, and younger brother William H. in 1938. Older brother James, who worked as clerk in the business, died in 1896.

Josephine was doing domestic work, and we can speculate that she too may have been in the employ of the Price family at which time she met William. They were married on December 31, 1891. At the time of their marriage, Josephine had moved again, this time to 7 City Alley. Although Josephine was a Methodist, the Price family arranged for Rev. Pockman to preside over their ceremony at the First Reformed Church. At the time, the denomination was not especially welcoming to African Americans but was eager to evangelize them. Both William and Josephine are listed as persons of color in the church register, as are the official witnesses of the event, J. W. Jackson and William H. Russell. For reasons that remain a mystery, the man Josephine married on that date is called William H. H. Smith on the marriage certificate and in the church register.[30] Perhaps there was some irregularity from William's first marriage that necessitated using a different last name. In addition and unfortunately, the names of William's parents given on the certificate don't match names on older documents and census records. It seems clear though, that William H. Johnson and William H. H. Smith are the same person. On the marriage certificate, his address is given as 255 Burnet Street, where William H. Johnson lived. The age of forty-three is also consistent with William H. Johnson. There are no William H. or H. H. Smiths in any other documents from New Brunswick from that time period that in any way could match a spouse for Josephine.

Print advertisement for the appliance business of the Price family. The testimonial highlights the quality of the work of Johnson's father who assembled the stoves. (*Daily Times*, New Brunswick, New Jersey November 14, 1899)

Flooded Burnet Street with the H. M. Price's Sons storefront "Stoves" sign visible at upper left behind the lamppost. New Brunswick views, C3, Burnet Street, folder 2. Flood scene. (Special Collections and University Archives, Rutgers University Archives)

She and the man she married on December 31, 1891, would have a child in a short fourteen months, a time frame that would make it highly unlikely she married first a man named Smith, and within months remarry another man named Johnson who had been living at the same address.

William moved in with Josephine and her children at 7 City Alley. On February 21, 1893, their first child was born at their home. Dr. Arthur Leland Smith attended the birth of George Joseph Johnson, who was unnamed at birth. Unfortunately, Dr. Smith returned to the home in less than two months. George contracted mumps, from which he succumbed on April 7. The Johnsons were no doubt distraught, but in less than a year, they had their second child together. Dr. Smith returned, this time across the street to 6 City Alley where the Johnsons had moved. James Price Johnson, also unnamed at birth like his older brother, was born on February 1, 1894.[31] Arthur Leland Smith was a native of New Brunswick and become a distinguished physician in the community. He was dedicated to his patients, and later reluctantly agreed to take on the top position on the Board of Health.[32]

City Alley was a narrow, mixed-use, three-block stretch in the heart of downtown New Brunswick, four blocks from the Raritan River. Its eastern border was Albany Street, one of the city's major thoroughfares. Following west from Albany, City Alley's major intersections were Washington, Somerset, and finally Hamilton. Between Somerset and Hamilton, the Pennsylvania Railroad cut across City Alley at grade, with a freight depot at the intersection. Livery and boarding stables, hotels, and meeting halls comprised part of the commercial streetscape. One block south of the western stretch of City Alley, but a world away, was Rutgers College. Past the western border of Hamilton Street was the Johnson and Johnson plant. H. M. Price's Son's was only a half mile walk toward the east. At 6 City Alley stood the livery and carriage house of Patrick McCormick, situated at the corner of Washington Street and City Alley.[33] The Johnsons must have moved across the street after George died and were living either above the livery or in the attached carriage house. On the opposite side of Washington Street stood the Middlesex Shoe Company at 53 Washington St. Diagonally across from his birthplace at the same intersection of Washington and City Alley was a depot for the People's Brewery of Trenton. 54 Washington was occupied by W. S. Wylie and Co., a fertilizer company eager to pay up to $3 per head for "live horses" brought to them for cremation, the stench of which must have permeated the neighborhood.[34]

For residents, City Alley was a tough, forlorn neighborhood. City services such as trash collection were lacking.[35] Attacks were often noted in the press. Several months after Johnson's birth, the notorious murder of a teenaged white boy on City Alley by an African American man briefly raised racial tensions, culminating in the arrest of the boy's brother for assaulting another Black man.[36] Loitering youth sparked other violence as described in the press: "The police should take some steps to break up the gang of loafers who congregate in City Alley, near Somerset Street. Last night two boys who were going through the alley were stoned by these toughs, who take delight in annoying respectable people. The names of the gangs are known and if the police do not take steps in the matter complaints will be made by residents of the vicinity."[37] John Horan, a well-known mail carrier, "was held up on City Alley near his home early Sunday morning. He was severely dealt with and narrowly escaped with his life."[38] The western part of City Alley, from Somerset to Hamilton, was razed during the construction elevating the Pennsylvania railroad tracks shortly after 1900. The remaining section was later consumed by the expansion of the Johnson and Johnson complex. As Johnson put it, it is now "extinct."

In 1895, William and Josephine Johnson and all the children were living together on City Alley. There were African American as well as white residents living on City Alley, and the New Jersey census from that year erroneously identifies all the Nevius children with last name Johnson—William, Frank, Belle. Third Nevius son Clifford is also incorrectly listed as Stephen. All but Clifford are listed as white, while both William and Josephine and the rest of the immediate neighbors are listed as Black. William and Josephine separated before James was three, and Josephine married Perry Thompson in 1897. He was born in New Jersey of parents from Alabama. Thompson, who could not read nor write, worked as a hostler and later as a waiter. By 1900, the family had moved farther south to a more residential neighborhood at 71 Stone Street. Twenty-one-year-old William was working as a farmhand, and eighteen-year-old Frank and sixteen-year-old Clifford were working as waiters in a hotel. Bella was in school. James was not and spent his time soaking up the music around him.[39]

"My mother was a choir singer in the Methodist Church. She worked out as a maid and one day she got the chance to buy a big, ebony, 'flat-top' square piano from the people she worked for and she taught herself to play it," Johnson told writer Tom Davin more than fifty years later.[40] She sang at the Mt. Zion African Methodist Episcopal Church. Founded in 1827, the church built a permanent structure at 25 Division Street in 1881. Most of the African American community in New Brunswick was Baptist, and the church never had more than seventy-nine members until well into the twentieth century.[41] Despite the small numbers, it was an active congregation. As of 2022, the church is still in operation at a new location in New Brunswick, and the original Division Street building still stands. The religious services caught Johnson's attention, with him recalling, "In my mother's church the hymns attracted me—and they have ever since. Southern Negroes who came north carried their traditional music with them. You could hear real southern country church singing in New Brunswick around 1900."[42] The church sponsored many formal musical events

Mt. Zion A.M.E. Church where Johnson and his mother worshipped and attended many musical events. (New Brunswick views, Division Street. Mt. Zion A.M.E. Church, Special Collections and University Archives, Rutgers University Archives)

featuring their own Silver Leaf Singing Society, which were popular occasions in town. Young James may have participated in programs designed to include children: "Every seat should be filled in Columbia Hall tonight, when the concert and entertainment by the Silver Leaf Singing Society, of the Mt. Zion A.M.E. Church, begins. Great preparations have been made for this event and a programme of unusual merit is assured. It will include many novelties in drills and pantomimes in costume by children and young women. There will also be solos and choruses by sweet voiced singers, rendering all the popular songs of the day and instrumental selections by talented musicians."[43]

While Josephine taught herself to play church hymns and several other simple melodies on their square piano, Johnson played with the pedals. When he was four years old, he recalled, she began to teach him to play one of her favorite tunes "Little Brown Jug."[44] Meanwhile, his sister Belle evinced at best only lukewarm interest in her piano lessons. James, however, took a strong interest in the popular songs his sister and brothers brought home to play. By the time he was six years old, his high soprano voice was sufficiently good to wangle ten or fifteen cents from passersby on the street as he sang popular favorites like "There'll be a Hot Time in the Old Town Tonight" and "I'm Looking for That Birdie."

The marching, military-style brass band was especially popular at the turn of the century, many of them associated with local civic and fraternal organizations. New Brunswick counted its share of benevolent societies, Masonic lodges and temples, Independent Order of Odd-Fellows, and Knights of Pythias among others. The fire department had bands. Johnson recalled the Goodwill Band, founded in 1887. Other primarily musical units were the Connolly Fife and Drum Corps, James Parsons Drum Corps, the Third Regiment Fife and Drum Corps, and the Liberty Cornet Band. The Union Cornet band, organized in 1883,[45] promoted their annual minstrel show every April with a noonday parade of the twelve-piece orchestra.[46] Others preceded a traveling circus or vaudeville company. Johnson was an eager spectator but admitted that their playing was probably bad. As a child of six he was struck more by their fanciful uniforms and hats than by the music. Although he did not recall it by name when recounting his musical memories as a child in New Brunswick, on September 11, 1899, Johnson almost certainly enjoyed a visit from a young organization from Charleston, South Carolina, that would become one of the most famous training academies for jazz musicians.[47] What became known as the Jenkins Orphanage Band was founded in 1892 by Rev. Daniel Jenkins after finding four young children in a railroad boxcar. Two years later, as a desperate fundraising gimmick, Jenkins began teaching his children how to play music so they could entertain on street corners for the loose change of passersby.[48] Within a few years, the band had garnered a national reputation and was booking tours. On at least two occasions while Johnson lived there, they played in New Brunswick, appearances arranged by the Mt. Zion Church.

Johnson's mother and stepfather often entertained friends in their home. Many of their guests had recently arrived north from Virginia, South Carolina, and Georgia, bringing with them the country, set, cotillion, and "shout" dances, they exuberantly displayed in the Thompson parlor. Johnson recalled vivid memories of the proceedings: "The Northern towns had a hold-over of the old southern customs. I'd wake up as a child and hear an old-fashioned ringshout going on downstairs. Somebody would be playing a guitar or jew's-harp or maybe a mandolin, and the dancing went to 'The Spider and the Bed-Bug Had a Good Time' or 'Susie, Susie.' They danced around in a shuffle and then they would shove a man or a woman out into the center and clap hands. This would go on all night and I would fall asleep sitting at the top of the stairs in the dark."[49] Johnson describes in detail the figures called for in the square dances, the improvisations of the dancers, the costumes, and the prizes, usually liquor. This elaborate combination of music, dance, and theater made a big impact on him. At times, the alcohol got the best of the partiers and things got out of hand. He recalled, "Sometimes the men would get drunk and go out in the road to fight."[50] One night his stepfather became violent enough to warrant legal action, with the local press noting, "Perry Thompson was arrested, on Somerset Street, on Saturday night, on complaint of his wife

Josephine Thompson, who charged him with assault and battery. Perry in a fit of anger is said to have assaulted his wife with a razor." Perry was jailed for the episode.[51] The shout dances featured at these parties had undergone fascinating transformations by the time they emerged in the Thompson family parlor. Johnson frequently speaks of the deep impact the ring shout had on him. Their rhythmic complexity became the foundation of stride piano, the jazz piano style he later pioneered.

The ring shout is a complex amalgam of song, movement (dance), rhythm, worship, and ritual. Its origins before the Civil War are poorly documented, but by that time, it had evolved into a distinct African American idiom. Shouts were emotionally intense, highly rhythmic, communal activities, almost narcotic in their effect. The derivation of the genre is thought to be strongly African in origin, and, in the early days of slavery, before acculturation and attempts at Christian conversion, reflected African ceremonial practices. The use of the word *ring* references the characteristic circular movement of the participants. The earliest known use of the term *shout* to describe this ritual in slave culture dates from 1850.[52] The derivation of the word *shout* in this context is more complex. It has been attributed to Arabic, African, and European origins, and is associated with both a reference to movement, as well as the better-known use of the word to denote a loud cry. Henry George Spaulding was a Unitarian minister and a member of the US Sanitary Commission during the Civil War who visited the Sea Islands during a Navy stopover in 1863. His observations of the ring shout were originally published in the August 1863 issue of *Continental Monthly* as part of an article titled "Under the Palmetto." He wrote:

> At the "praise meetings" on the plantations, one of the elders usually presides and conducts the exercises with great solemnity. Passages of Scripture are quoted from memory, and the hymns, which constitute the principal feature of the meeting, are deaconed off as at church. Sometimes the superintendent or one of the teachers attends these meetings, and is then expected to conduct the exercises and make an address. After the praise meeting is over, there usually follows the very singular and impressive performance of the 'shout,' or religious dance of the Negroes. Three or four, standing still, clapping their hands and beating time with their feet, commence singing in unison one of the peculiar shout melodies, while the others walk round in a ring, in single file, joining also in the song. Soon those in the ring leave off their singing, the others keeping it up the while with increased vigor, and strike into the shout step, observing most accurate time with the music. This step is something halfway between a shuffle and a dance, as difficult for an uninitiated person to describe as to imitate. At the end of each stanza of

the song the dancers stop short with a slight stamp on the last note, and then, putting the other foot forward, proceed through the next verse. They will often dance to the same song for twenty or thirty minutes, once or twice, perhaps, varying the monotony of their movement by walking for a little while and joining in the singing. The physical exertion, which is really very great, as the dance calls into play nearly every muscle of the body, seems never to weary them in the least, and they frequently keep up a shout for hours, resting only for brief intervals between the different songs.[53]

The Union army captured many of the Sea Islands off South Carolina and Georgia early in the Civil War, and, in what became known as the Port Royal experiment, many northern, mostly white missionaries, health care workers, and observers, descended on the newly freed slaves, thinking they would need oversight and direction from them. *Slave Songs of the United States*, published in 1867, was the most famous publication to emerge from this social interaction. In it, William Francis Allan, Lucy McKim Garrison, and Charles Pickard Ware attempted to transcribe the spirituals and shouts they observed. They acknowledged the limitations of using European-informed musical understanding and notation in accurately conveying the complexities of what they heard. They noted that their work would only "convey but a faint shadow of the original. The voices of the colored people have a peculiar quality that nothing can imitate; and the intonations and delicate variations of even one singer cannot be reproduced on paper. And I despair of conveying any notion of the effort of a number singing together, especially in a complicated shout.... There is no singing in parts, as we understand it, and yet no two appear to be singing the same thing." They noted characteristics that today we would describe as heterophony, improvisation, call and response, note bending, perhaps blue notes, and even chord extensions, effects that produce, as they noted, "a marvelous complication and variety, and yet with the most perfect time, and rarely any discord."[54] Despite its limitations, the work of Allen, Ware, and Garrison preserved well over a hundred spirituals, shouts, and other songs from the midAtlantic through the Deep South, the bulk of which came from their firsthand observation on the Sea Islands. After the Civil War, the combined forces of European religious orthodoxy that spread in the Black church, a movement that frowned on the kinetics of the ritual, along with newfound leisure time that came with freedom, allowed new outlets for an evolving Black secular music. Although the ring shout had once been a vital part of the religious service, it became increasingly associated with nonreligious entertainment.

Shouts were once thought to be confined to South Carolina and Georgia, where the ring shout, as described by the observers of the Port Royal experiment, seems to have reached its most consistently identifiable form. But the notion of a shout in different formats was known in other regions.[55] Allen observed, "It is, however, an interesting fact that the term 'shouting' is used in Virginia in reference to a peculiar motion of the body not wholly unlike the Carolina shouting," again associating the term with movement rather than vocalization.[56] Johnson's Virginia-born mother certainly demonstrated her style of shouting in the family parlor. By the time the shouts had reached New Brunswick in the 1890s, so had other dances. Johnson gives us the flavor of the variety as he saw them, including what he called "real shoutings." "Real," as transcribed by Davin, was probably meant to refer to "reel," the Celtic dance form with set steps. What he observed in his parents' parlor was a transmigrated comingling of by then mostly secular entertainment, including the set or square dances and cotillion music of his Virginia-born mother and her friends from farther south. "These people were from South Carolina and Georgia where the cotillion was popular. . .," he recalled. He goes on to describe their specific choreography:

> One of the men would call the figures and they'd dance their own style of square dances. The calls were . . . "join hands" . . . "sashay" . . . "turn around" . . . "ladies right and gentlemen left" . . . "grab your partner" . . . "break away" . . . "make a strut" . . . "cows to the front, bulls stay back."
> When he called "do your stuff" or "ladies to the front," they did their personal dances. The catwalk [*sic*—cake walk?], for instance, was developed from the cotillion, but it was also part of the set dances.

"A lot of my music is based on set, cotillion and other southern dance steps and rhythms," he said, concluding, "I think the 'Carolina Balmoral' was the most spirited dance in the South. I find I have a strong feeling for these dances that goes away back—and I haven't found anyone else with it yet."[57] Johnson makes clear that among all the dances he was exposed to, the ring shout had the deepest impact on him. His parents' parlor would not be his last exposure to this unique cultural legacy from the Southeast. He would encounter it again in New York. Johnson's formulations that incorporated the rhythmic, expressive, vocalized, religious, secular, and folk features of the shouts would not mature until the late 1910s, and ultimately manifest in signal examples of a new jazz idiom, a worldwide popular phenomenon, and an art music.

Chapter 2

JERSEY CITY, 1902–1908

> But there is something else as well, and that's the direct influence
> of ragtime upon Harlem piano, particularly through the grand,
> impossible-to-over-estimate work of James P. Johnson.
> —CHARLES EDWARD SMITH

In 1902, when Johnson was eight, Josephine and her children moved to Jersey City. Perry likely followed a short time after, as he is still listed in the New Brunswick directory of 1903 working as a waiter and still living on Stone Street. Located on the banks of the Hudson River across from lower Manhattan, Jersey City was a growing industrial center like New Brunswick, only ten times its size. They settled at 60 Merseles Street, a four-block-long discontinuous stretch of mixed residential and industrial buildings. The dwelling is difficult to identify on early twentieth-century maps. The likely structure may have been attached to or over a garage nearly at the dead end of Merseles Street off of Bright Street. Johnson recalled it as a slum.[1] The immediate surroundings were comprised of mostly undeveloped plots or other structures, all likely owned by the Dixon Crucible Company, famous for its pencil factory.[2] There was only one nonindustrial property on Merseles Street listed on the tax rolls at that time. Dixon was growing quickly, and its sprawling industrial complex included multiple buildings a few blocks North on Merseles Street and three blocks west on Monmouth Street. As in New Brunswick, the family again found themselves near the Pennsylvania railroad that barreled by close to their home.

In the fall of 1902, when he was eight, Johnson was enrolled in the first grade. If he spent any time in school in New Brunswick, it was repeated in Jersey City. He was one of the oldest in the class but not the only eight-year-old. He attended

Public School # 9, five blocks from home and in easy walking distance. When School # 9 was built in 1896, it was a state-of-the-art facility. A few years later, a playground and park were built behind the school so that the complex occupied an entire square block on Brunswick Avenue bounded by Mercer and Wayne. The grand brick exterior housed a carefully thought-out design prioritizing the learning environment and safety of the children. Spacious classrooms occupied only the first and second floors, accessed by five wide fireproof staircases made of stone and iron to allow easy evacuation. Some of the technical features included internal fire hydrants, a pumping system for fresh air and heat, and cloakrooms designed to reduce the spread of communicable disease by keeping the children's clothing separated. In describing the details, the *New York Tribune* noted, "The building is a model structure, and is probably the most completely equipped schoolhouse in the state."[3] In addition to grammar and primary departments, a normal school for student teachers was integrated into the organization of the education program. The schedules and curricula for the youngsters were the training template for the aspiring teachers.

School # 9 replaced several other dilapidated schools in the area. Not only did their physical plant need improvement, but increased capacity for the rapidly expanding school-age population in Jersey City was necessary. When it opened in 1896, it had a capacity of over 1,100 students. By the time Johnson started first grade six years later, school # 9 was already overcrowded. From 1900 to 1906, the population of Jersey City increased by 15 percent, adding thirty thousand residents, the approximate entire population of New Brunswick.[4] From the start, Johnson's educational experience there was subject to the "Copenhagen" plan for handling the crowding. This approach relied on partial days and shortened terms. For his second grade during the 1903–04 school year, Johnson attended only from September through February. With plenty of time on his hands, (but not because of truancy—he missed only four days of school during the six-month term) Johnson explored the social and musical world of his older siblings to the extent any preadolescent could in their tough urban neighborhood. He recalled the numerous barrelhouses that dotted the streetscape near his home. Within ten blocks of their home, on Railroad Avenue and Monmouth Street alone, there were twenty-six saloons listed in the city directory of 1905–06. Johnson told of the non-pianistic musical exploits he practiced. Because he was still young and "in short pants," he was not allowed inside any of the saloons. Performing outside, he developed his buck-dancing, singing, and guitar playing. He listened to the music coming from inside, and picked up popular sporting house tunes, simple melodies that served mostly as vehicles for various versions of sexually suggestive lyrics. "Don't Hit That Lady (Dressed in Green)," "She Got Good Booty," and "Baby, Let Your Drawers Hang Low" were all popular tunes recalled by Johnson,[5] Willie "The Lion" Smith, and others. Johnson claimed to have used part of another suggestive tune, "Left Her on the Railroad Track," also known as "Baby, Get that Towel Wet," much later for his tune "Mamma's Blues." A piano was the focal point of entertainment inside the saloons, and the pianists were known as "ticklers." Johnson was taken with their glamorous lifestyles. In the days before the phonograph, radio, and television, a piano player was socially important, and always welcome. Through his young, romanticizing eyes, he recalled the social standing of the pianists: "They were popular fellows, real celebrities. They had lots of girlfriends, led a sporting life and were invited everywhere there was a piano. I thought it was a fine way to live, just as later kids would think singers like Crosby or Sinatra were worth copying."[6]

The term *tickler*, like the lyrics of the songs they played, was a double-entendre. Could the piano player handle the women as well as the ivories? When he was a little older, Johnson came into contact with many ragtime players who were friendly with his older half-brothers. The lives and livelihoods of most of these men were often not only tied to music, but gambling, drugs, prostitution, and various types of swindling, gouging, and hustling. Almost every American city had an area notorious for this type of activity, known as "the district." Probably the most famous district of this period was Storyville in New Orleans. In New York, the amalgam of legitimate and illegitimate entertainment and popular artistic activity was centered in an area that came to be known as the "Tenderloin," so named from the alleged comment of a corrupt police captain who said, because of kickback and protection money, he was able to afford tenderloin rather than chuck steak after being assigned to that precinct.[7] That moniker has been applied to similar districts in other cities. In the Davin interviews, Johnson details the social and economic stakes for the ticklers They did not make much money playing the piano, working twelve-hour days for ten dollars a week, perhaps with as much more in tips. There was more money in hustling, and women, Johnson observed, were attracted to musicians by their music and stature in the community. Once beholden to the musician pimp who managed their prostitution activity, the girls usually then traveled with them. The measure of a good girl, not surprisingly, was how much money she could bring in. The best were also thieves, but in smaller communities this often caused trouble. Johnson noted, "Sometimes, a girl would roll a live one and get $500 or $1,000. This usually brought a complaint to the police, so the girl and her tickler friend would have to leave town. They'd head north and east to New York, and the last stop on the railroad was Jersey City."[8] Unlike the larger tenderloins of New York, St. Louis, and New Orleans, the Jersey City district served as a temporary settlement for the tickler and his entourage as they moved north on their way to bigger scores in New York. Many of these players came from southeastern cities including Baltimore, Norfolk, Charleston, and Atlanta.

Jersey City at that time was one of the largest railroad hubs in the country. The waterfront was dominated entirely by the seven major railroad lines that terminated there and in lower Hoboken just to the north. The Central Railroad of New Jersey had the largest yard along the water in southern Jersey City and leased track to the Lehigh Valley, Reading, and Baltimore and Ohio railroads. Moving north, the Pennsylvania Railroad, New York, Lake Erie and Western Railroad, and finally the Delaware, Lackawanna, and Western Railroad in southern Hoboken brought thousands of passengers a day through their majestic terminals. In addition to local commuters to New York, they brought passengers from all over the Mid-Atlantic, South, and Midwest. There were no rail connections with New York at that time, but each of the rail lines operated ferries across the river to Manhattan. The first trans-Hudson rail tunnels were not built until 1908.[9] The jump to New York for a new tickler was a precarious proposition. The Black tenderloin in New York around 1905, situated downtown, was not a bustling community like Harlem, which was then in an embryonic stage of development as an African American community. Many of the established hustlers there paid protection to corrupt authorities and didn't abide transients who might attract attention from the police. The ticklers in Jersey City had to work their way slowly into the New York district. They played piano at night while their girls cautiously hustled.

Despite attentive teachers and a finely appointed building, school #9, with its overcrowding and fragmented scheduling, was no match for the allure of the life of the ticklers. Johnson and many of his contemporaries, however, began to see their musical careers as distinct from the criminal element. Although living in a slum (as Johnson described his home), Josephine continued to sing in the church choir and keep the faith at home. The family likely worshipped at the St. Mark's African Methodist Episcopal Zion Church on Monmouth Street, several blocks south of their home. In 1903, a firebrand of a new pastor arrived, A. P. Miller. Born in Mississippi and educated at Fisk University and the Yale University Seminary, Miller had traveled extensively in England, Africa, and the United States.[10] He was a highly respected clergyman and thinker in the Black community nationally. In his 1899 broadside titled *The Black Man's Burden*, he argues that for the Black community to develop the greatest degree of "race pride," education and exercise of the franchise were vital. He recognized, however, barriers existed to both, and it was essential to eschew low morals and embrace a force of character to overcome them. In his seminal work he concluded that "even as slaves, our fathers and mothers knew that character in this world was the pearl of great price, in comparison with which the wealth and learning of all ages were as nothing."[11] This was a message young James embraced. While many older players were involved in some kind of illicit activity, Johnson's generation began to legitimize the image of the "tickler." The burgeoning world of popular music catalyzed the transition from criminal to artist, while the social status of the piano player remained an integral part of the Black community for many years, serving as the backbone of rent parties before and during the Depression.

Josephine had sold the piano to pay for their move from New Brunswick. Although in some statements, Johnson recalled that he didn't touch a piano until they moved to New York in 1908[12] (other recollections include at least some piano playing while still in Jersey City). Johnson recounted the amusing story of his first job us a "tickler." When he was eight years old, shortly after moving to Jersey City, a woman approached him and asked if he was interested in making a quarter. Anxious for the extra spending money, he agreed and followed the woman into a parlor. She had heard that the youngster could play the piano, which he did for a few hours playing simple variations on "Little Brown Jug" and nursery rhyme tunes. He was instructed not to turn around so that he wouldn't see the people entering and those seated at a few tables. In what was certainly a bordello, Johnson did not consider this experience to be a professional job, saying "it didn't count."[13]

By age thirteen, after five years with little opportunity to play piano, he began picking up tunes by ear. Through his older brothers, Johnson encountered players in Jersey City who offered him the benefit of their knowledge and experience. "I guess at times there were more good ragtime players in Jersey City in those days than any other place in the United States," he recalled.[14] One such player, Claude Grew, bore the distinguishing mark of a good cabaret player. He could play any tune in any key, a requirement, Johnson noted, for accompanying singers. He later developed this skill and was renowned for his facility in transposing and modulating through many keys. He also recalled tutelage from George Perry, and a player named Floyd Keppard, who he described as "a Creole with French background, sharp features and thick, good hair."[15] The repertoire of the Jersey City ticklers was in large part ragtime, but Johnson was quick to point out that this was not the music of written scores, the format that years later was regarded as the quintessential example of the genre. The tickers at that time, he recalled, played "mostly popular songs with a strong rhythm and with syncopated vamps, not a whole composition or arrangement."[16] The rags of Scott Joplin, too, he recalled, were played piecemeal as part of this aural tradition. Ragtime dominated the popular music market and entertainment culture internationally for twenty years, with remnants of its influence clearly evident as the music transformed into jazz. Ragtime was the early template for Johnson as composer and player. As he notes in his extensive recollections, ragtime playing became a style that could be applied to any music—unsyncopated music, lightly syncopated ragtime songs, and added to more sophisticated piano ragtime compositions. Later, when he was more accomplished, Johnson created versions of a rag he called "Imitator's Rag," playing "Dixie" in the right hand and the "Star Spangled Banner" or "Home Sweet Home" in the left. It was one of his dazzling show numbers he used to win ragtime contests.[17]

If ragging is in some way improvising, is ragtime, then, the first form of jazz? The legacy of ragtime has primarily been the published body of work of the serious (and some popular) ragtime composers, music to be played as written and not improvised upon. Composed and printed ragtime that began in the 1890s broadly preserved the circulating aural traditions of playing from earlier decades. But it likely did not capture the nuances that so many different musicians brought to it. Instruction books add some insight, but with little recorded documentation of what the performed piano music sounded like until the 1910s, we can only speculate. Ragtime surely gave American music an American identity. The word jazz supplanted it, and has remained the designated descriptor of improvised music, despite the dramatic variation that has blossomed under this rubric. Ragtime as a performance tradition has, for the most part, been thought of as a jazz precursor. It loosened the Victorian imprint on sentimental songs, marches, and country dance tunes, but even Jelly Roll Morton, looking back toward the end of his life, commented on what he thought of as ragtime's limitations. He told Alan Lomax, "Ragtime is a certain type of syncopation and only certain tunes can be played in that idea. But jazz is a style that can be applied to any type of tune."[18] At the time he made that remark, ragtime had fallen dramatically out of favor, so Morton's agenda in distancing himself from the music of his youth is fraught with the same conflicts and contradictions that plague Johnson in threading this nomenclature needle. As Berlin succinctly notes: "Ragtime is properly viewed not as a single unified tradition, but as two commingling and cross pollinating traditions: one, a commercial, notated music, developed to a sophisticated level by some composers, well known today because of its ample representation in surviving sheet music; the other, a more complicated improvised music—essentially a jazz piano in every respect except name—but lost to us for the lack of recordings."[19]

James P. Johnson saw no conflict between these two conceptions of the music. He lived through the ragtime era, absorbed the brilliant, individualized, and often idiosyncratic performance lessons from the older musician ticklers he idolized, and learned the compositional form from published ragtime. Early in his career he composed ragtime compositions and, when performing, ragged everything. By 1921, his conception had evolved into the realm of a recognized jazz style, and in later years, he took great pride in his stature in the pantheon of jazz pianists. But he never abandoned his love for ragtime. He contributed to its canon, and throughout his career, demonstrated its musical relevance in all of its expressions when others thought it passé. He defended ragtime and scoffed at the writers who dismissed it as old fashioned. He advocated for its most important composers and their innovative contributions. Johnson maintained the highest regard for Joplin as a composer. Late in life, he remarked to Rudi Blesh and Harriet Janis, "Scott Joplin was a great forerunner. Joplin was fifty years ahead of his time. Even today, who understands 'Euphonic Sounds'? It's really modern."[20] Johnson was the first to record this Joplin masterpiece as a piano solo—in June 1944.[21] He follows the printed score for much of the rendition, reflecting his respect for Joplin's composition.

American music and jazz historians have perpetually entangled Johnson in the lingering murkiness around distinctions between ragtime and jazz. He is usually assigned to one of three camps in a mutually exclusive manner—ragtime player, transitional figure, or jazz musician. Typecasting him into only one of these categories, as if music historiography can abide only one characterization, should finally be put to rest. In a career that spanned nearly forty years from 1912 to 1951, he was all three. As Johnson scholar Mark Borowsky puts it, he could arguably be considered the last great ragtime composer, and, as we shall see, at the dawn of the jazz age, the first great jazz pianist.[22] The Thompson/Johnson family made their own move across the river to New York in 1908. The abundance of musical and cultural influences awaiting him there fed his ingenious creativity and soon produced his own innovations.

Chapter 3

THE JUNGLES, 1908–1913

> "San Juan Hill" has unique institutions.
> —*NEW YORK AGE*

In 1908, when Johnson was fourteen, Perry Thompson moved the family to 152 West 62nd Street in the San Juan Hill section of New York, west and north of Columbus Circle.[1] This area, also known as the Jungles, constituted the northern end of Hell's Kitchen, the notorious tenderloin district which ran from about 30th to 70th Streets, between Eighth and Tenth Avenues. San Juan Hill was one of the largest African American neighborhoods in the city. Johnson describes the Jungles as "the Negro section of Hell's Kitchen and ran from 60th to 63rd St. west of Ninth Ave. It was the toughest part of New York. There were two to three killings a night. Fights broke out over love affairs, gambling, or arguments in general. There were race fights with the white gangs on 66th and 67th St. It was just as tough in the white section of Hell's Kitchen."[2] Clashes with police were not uncommon. Most of the housing stock consisted of run-down and overcrowded tenements. Despite the violence and poverty, it had a thriving business district centered on West 63rd Street. Black-owned grocery stores, barbers, coal and wood dealers, restaurants, as well as physicians, photographers, and tailors could be found doing solid business. Historic congregations such as the St. Cyprian Episcopal Church and the Union Baptist Church, along with the Lincoln Day Nursery supported by its anonymous endowment, and the soup kitchen at the Henrietta Industrial School, were social anchors in the otherwise distressed neighborhood.[3]

Johnson's family was somewhat better off than most. There was once again a piano in the home. While attending P.S. 69, Johnson played for school

The tenement in the San Juan Hill section of Hell's Kitchen where Johnson and family first lived after moving to New York from Jersey City. The neighborhood was razed in the 1950s to make way for Lincoln Center. (New York City Department of Records and Information Services, 1940s Tax Department photographs, Collection REC0040 - RG 035. Department of Finance. Courtesy Municipal Archives, City of New York)

assemblies and minstrel show productions. Johnson's voice hadn't yet changed from impending adolescence, and he was very proud of his singing abilities. In his recollections years later, he conflates two events that remained prominent in his memory, telling Davin, "I had a high soprano voice yet, so I was put into the school chorus. Once, Frank Damrosch (Walter Damrosch's brother) auditioned us for his production of Haydn's *Creation*. He used one hundred boys in sections. I remember that he personally complimented me because I was singing so strong. We all got a bronze medal for taking part."[4] Damrosch had been director of music for the New York City Department of Education from 1897 until 1905. Godson of Franz Liszt and a member of a distinguished musical family, he founded the Institute of Musical Art in 1905, which later became the Juilliard School. His brother Walter was a noted composer and the conductor of the New York Philharmonic and New York Symphony. Frank Damrosch felt strongly that the most effective way to develop an appreciation of "good" (read classical) music was through sight singing.[5] Damrosch formed the People's Choral Union to engage amateur and avocational singers in performing classic oratorios. The People's Choral Union performed at Carnegie Hall, the Manhattan and Metropolitan Opera Houses, as well as the Hippodrome Theater. For many years he arranged for public schoolteachers to attend rehearsals of large-scale vocal works so they would inspire their students.[6] Although he had left his position in the school system by the time Johnson arrived in New York, Damrosch continued to work with schoolchildren. In 1907, 1908, and 1909, he presented young people's concerts of primarily instrumental music but on at least one occasion children were invited to sing.[7] The *Creation* was part of Damrosch's active oratorio repertoire. The specific performance of the *Creation* that included schoolchildren where Johnson may have attended and sung has not been specifically identified.

Around this same time, the City of New York planned and executed a citywide celebration for the one-hundredth anniversary of the birth of Abraham Lincoln in February 1909. Musical and other events were planned throughout the city, including morning and evening activities in the schools on what had already been designated a school holiday. On February 12, assemblies started at 10:30 a.m., followed by a reading of the Gettysburg Address in every school at noon. In the evening, one school in each of the city's forty-six districts with a large enough auditorium was chosen to host a community meeting for celebration that included a chorus of two hundred schoolchildren at each school. Johnson's school, P.S. 69, was not one of the schools chosen, so he likely attended the festivities and sang at the High School of Commerce, West 65th Street west of Broadway.[8] As part of the Lincoln commemoration, thousands of medals were struck in bronze and silver by several organizations. By far the largest run was commissioned by the New York City Centennial Committee. They arranged for forty thousand silver and bronze medals in four sizes, sold as inexpensively as twenty-five cents. The biggest demand was from the public schools. Johnson, along with most other children, received a bronze medal for his participation in the Lincoln Day festivities.[9] It seems likely, therefore, that his performance of the *Creation* with Frank Damrosch was a separate occasion from the Lincoln Day festivities for which he received his bronze medal. He was proud of his "high soprano voice," and his singing performance for Damrosch as well as the Lincoln Day tribute were clearly both memorable events he conflated forty years later in his recollections. Very soon after these concerts, his voice changed. Whatever striking quality of voice he possessed as a child vanished with puberty.

In 1910, Perry was working as a porter in a theater. Josephine continued to take in wash. Brothers William and Clifford, working as drivers, and sister Belle, who was working as a maid in a hotel, were all still living at home.[10] "In New York I got a chance to hear a lot of good music for the first time," Johnson recalled. A friend of one of his older brothers worked as a waiter and was offered symphony tickets from conductor Josef Stransky, who frequented the restaurant. Stransky was a German-educated Czech who, after the untimely death of Gustav Mahler in 1911, succeeded him as conductor of the Philharmonic-Symphony Society of New York. When it merged with the New York Symphony Orchestra in 1928, it become the New York Philharmonic. It was Johnson's first exposure to orchestral music. According to Davin, Johnson said of attending the concerts, "I didn't get much out of them, but the full symphonic sounds made a great impression on me."[11] He was seventeen years old when he attended the symphony and would soon develop a keen interest in composing symphonic music based on African American musical themes.

In New York, Johnson heard better-schooled pianists, observing, "When you heard the biggest ragtime specialists play, you would hear fine harmony, exciting touch and tone and all the themes developed."[12] A perhaps apocryphal story recounted by Johnson in the late 1930s describes an encounter that inspired him to begin serious study of music. Johnson was very highly regarded at the keyboard but was still playing by ear, relying on his perfect pitch. One day he confronted a man who was whistling off-key. An interviewer took down the story:

> He [Johnson] appointed himself a committee of one to correct the whistler, but the whistler didn't take kindly to the advice and promptly squelched him with this one: "Jimmie, as a man who can only play by ear, I think you are less competent to judge good singing or good whistling than a man who knows absolutely nothing about music, because any lead you would give would be contrary to the books. I would advise you to learn something about the music scale before you try to correct anybody." The laughs that went up at this remark served as the spark that fired Jimmie Johnson's ambition. From that day on he has been studying music.

Around 1909, Johnson began his first serious piano lessons, recalling, "At the age of fifteen I began to learn how to play the piano by note under the tutelage of a young lady named Marie Howell."[13] Although starting formal study somewhat late, within four years his remarkable talent would earn him the respect of the Harlem musical elite.

Perry Thompson died in July 1910. He had purchased a plot at Bayview-New York Bay Cemetery in Jersey City and was buried there on July 25. In 1911, Johnson's family moved farther uptown to 99th Street. Johnson was still in school and not quite old enough to patronize the cabarets of Hell's Kitchen or the few establishments in the nascent entertainment district that was developing in Harlem. An Irish Society Hall called McFarland's (also known as the 100th Street Hall after its location at 100th Street and Third Avenue) was approachable territory for Johnson. Run by a heavy drinker from Jersey City named Harry Souser, this basement dance hall featured four- or five-piece orchestras such as the New Amsterdam Orchestra and Hallie Anderson's Orchestra. After the band played, Souser rolled an upright piano onto the floor and displayed his own ragtime stylings. When he was through, Johnson and other pianists played until four or five o'clock in the morning. Johnson kept his books in the coal bin, and, after a few hours of sleep, went on to school. Around this time Johnson recalls he first met Jelly Roll Morton. Not exactly a meeting, as the seventeen-year-old Johnson rolled down his short pants and snuck in to Barron Wilkins's famous club in Harlem where Morton was playing. "He had just arrived from the West and he was red hot. The place was on fire! We heard him play his 'Jelly Roll Blues.' I was able to appreciate him then, but I couldn't steal his stuff. I wasn't good enough yet," he admitted. By this time, he was certain music would be his career. He was waiting for the right opportunity, which came the next year, revealing, "My mind was made up. I was going to be a pianist as soon as I felt I was good enough to get a job. That came next year in 1912, during vacation from school."[14]

Johnson made his way out to Far Rockaway, a beach resort near Coney Island. He found a job in a place run by a shady character named Charles Ett. His experiences there enticed him to leave school, recalling, "It was just a couple of rooms knocked together to make a cabaret. They had beer and liquor, and out in the back yard there was a crib house for fast turnover. It was a rough place, but I got nine dollars and tips, or about eighteen dollars a week over all. That was so much money that I didn't want to go back to school."[15] Far Rockaway had its own notables. At a place called The Cool Off, one could find various Clef Club members, musicians who belonged to the Black musicians union established by James Reese Europe in 1910. Now-forgotten characters like Kid Sneeze and Dude Finley were among those who played alongside Johnson in the Rockaway dives. Johnson recalled Finley's rag in D minor that was based on a common musical theme floating through the African American aural tradition.

"That fall, instead of going back to school, I went to Jersey City and got a job in a cabaret run by Freddie Doyle. He gave me a two dollar raise. In a couple of months, Doyle's folded up, and I came back to Manhattan and played in a sporting house on 27th St. between 8th and 9th Avenues, which was the

Tenderloin then. It was run by a fellow named Dan Williams, and he had two girl entertainers that I used to accompany," said Johnson of his first gigs as a professional musician.[16] They sang the popular "Indian" songs as well as most other popular hits of the day, and Johnson developed his skill as accompanist. Johnson played instrumentals, semi-classics, and rags—his own and others. Besides Joplin, he recalled playing "Maori" by Will Tyers (published 1913), and "The Dream" and "Peculiar Rag" made famous by the legendary pianist Jack the Bear. Around this time, Johnson was still working out his first rags and had yet to learn musical notation. Although Johnson recalled interest from Gotham and Attucks in publishing his music, he could not write it down and he knew no one who could take the time to do it for him. Gotham and Attucks was the preeminent Black music publishing company in New York around 1912. Many great Black musicians and performers gathered around the firm—Bert Williams, Scott Joplin, Will Marion Cook, Joe Jordon, Tim Brymm. The company, with offices at 136 W. 37th St, was run by its president, Cecil Mack (whose real name was Richard C. McPherson), and Will Marion Cook.[17] Both of these men would feature prominently in Johnson's life in later years.

Johnson remained at Dan Williams's place for only a few months. During the winter of 1912–13 he held several jobs, "playing movie piano at the Nickelette at 8th Avenue and 37th Street. They had movies and short acts for short money. Many vaudeville acts broke in there. Florence Mills first sang there I recall. . . . In the spring, of 1913, I really got started up in the Jungles." Johnson was hired to play at Jim Allan's place at 61st Street and Tenth Avenue in Hell's Kitchen. When he was younger, he used to sneak into Allan's by rolling down his knickers, same as he had done to see Jelly Roll Morton at Baron Wilkens's place. Johnson painted a vivid picture of Allan's:

> I'd wear my knickers long so they wouldn't notice that I was a short-pants punk. After they heard me play, they would let me come when I wanted. So, in the spring of 1913, I went uptown and got a job playing at Jim Allan's. It was a remodeled cellar, and since it operated after hours, it had an iron-plated door—like the speakeasies had later. There was a bar upstairs, but downstairs there was a rathskeller, and in the back of the cellar there was a gambling joint. When the cops raided us now and then, they always had to go back to the station house for axes and sledge hammers, so we usually made a clean getaway.[18]

Writer and composer James Weldon Johnson, in his book *The Autobiography of an Ex-Colored Man*, which was published anonymously in 1912, describes the reaction of the novel's protagonist upon his first encounter with a cabaret that might easily have been patterned after Jim Allan's. It is an early reference to Black music in Black literature and, in many ways, foreshadows similar references in Harlem Renaissance literature of the 1920s.

> We at length secured places at a table in a corner of the room and, as soon as we could attract the attention of one of the busy waiters, ordered a round of drinks. When I had somewhat collected my senses, I realized that in a large back room into which the main room opened, there was a young fellow singing a song, accompanied on the piano by a short, thickset, dark man. After each verse he did some dance steps, which brought forth great applause and a shower of small coins at his feet. After the singer had responded to a rousing encore, the stout man at the piano began to run his fingers up and down the keyboard. This he did in a manner which indicated that he was master of a good deal of technique. Then he began to play; and such playing! I stopped talking to listen. It was music of a kind I had never heard before. It was music that demanded physical response, patting of the feet, drumming of the fingers, or nodding of the head in time with the beat. The barbaric harmonies, the audacious resolutions, often consisting of an abrupt jump from one key to another, the intricate rhythms in which the accents fell in the most unexpected places, but in which the beat was never lost, produced a most curious effect, and too, the player—the dexterity of his left hand in making rapid octave runs and jumps was little short of marvellous [sic]; and with his right he frequently swept half the keyboard with clean-cut chromatics which he fitted in so nicely as never to fail to arouse in his listeners a sort of pleasant surprise at the accomplishment of the feat.[19]

One night a week, Johnson played for Drake's dancing class on 62nd Street between Ninth and Tenth Avenues.[20] Johnson noted at that time it was easier and cheaper for a Black-owned establishment to get a dancing school license than a dance hall license. Also known as the Jungles Casino, it was another basement establishment. There were no decorative fixtures, and it came complete with furnace and coal bin, where patrons could hide their liquor. When it rained, the dancing had to be interrupted periodically so that the cement floor, with poor drainage, could be mopped. Willie "The Lion" Smith recalled that the piano was surrounded with candles to keep it dry in the dank atmosphere.[21] There were no dance teachers. People came to dance as they pleased to the piano accompaniments of Johnson and the other ticklers. Two-steps, waltzes, schottisches, and the latest popular dance craze, "The Metropolitan Glide," were all "taught" to anyone who cared to watch. At various points in his playing, Johnson incorporated ragtime. The older dancers, he said, didn't care for it, but the young arrivals from the South enjoyed it, and displayed their own dance styles. Many were Gullahs and Geechies from the Georgia and South Carolina Coast and Sea Islands who had come north to work as longshoremen. Their dancing, as with his parents' friends he encountered in New Brunswick, retained the essence of the ring shout. As Johnson recalled:

> The dances they did at the Jungles Casino were wild and comical—the more pose and the more breaks, the better. These Charleston people and the other southerners had just come to New York. They were country people and they felt homesick. When they got tired of two-steps and schottisches (which they danced with a lot of spieling), they'd yell: "Let's go back home!" ... "Let's do a set!" ... or "Now put us in the alley!" I did my "Mule Walk" or "Gut Stomp" for these country dances.
>
> Breakdown music was the best for such sets, the more solid and groovy the better. They'd dance, hollering and screaming until they were cooked. The dances ran from fifteen to thirty minutes, but they kept up all night long or until their shoes wore out—most of them after a heavy day's work on the docks.

"Mule Walk" and "Gut Stomp" are Johnson compositions. He described them as ragtime arrangements of set dances. They are also, as he conceived them in 1913, the origins of the stride piano idiom. Other cotillion steps gave rise to the "Charleston." As he noted, "The Charleston, which became a popular dance step on its own, was just a regulation cotillion step without a name. It had many variations—all danced to the rhythm that everybody knows now."[22] Johnson said he composed eight "Charlestons" at the Jungles Casino, claiming one became the famous "Charleston" a decade later. Johnson's playing at this time was still very much a ragtime style, although the Jungles Casino provided ample opportunity for him to develop his facility as an improviser.

The vernacular blues was alien in New York before its commercial debut. Johnson cited the blues of W. C. Handy as his first significant exposure to the form.[23] Ragtime was ubiquitous, but the blues was beginning to have a substantial impact on the development of music in the Northeast, first as a composed, commercial form, and eventually also as a folk idiom. Johnson recognized the communicative power of the blues musically and as a verse form, observing, "The blues are the feelings of people, their protests, hopes, loves, hates; a mingling of feelings all rolled together."[24] The social mores of northern African American communities resisted the folk blues in the same way the ring shout was considered lowbrow. Reed player Garvin Bushell gives some indication of the attitudes of the Black community around 1910-15:

Most of the Negro population in New York then had either been born there or had been in the city so long, they were fully acclimated. They were trying to forget the traditions of the South; they were trying to emulate the whites. You couldn't deliver a package to a Negro's front door. You had to go down to the cellar door. And Negroes dressed to go to work. They changed into work clothes when they got there. You usually weren't allowed to play blues and boogie-woogie in the average Negro middle class home. That music supposedly suggested a low element. And the big bands with the violins, flutes, piccolos didn't play them either.[25]

As the United States began to accelerate industrial production in anticipation of entry into World War I, the demand for labor was made more acute by the limitation on immigration as a result of anti-German sentiment and general suspicion of foreigners. Employers in the North sent agents south to recruit workers, hastening what had been the slow influx of people. Those who had already moved north wrote home describing job opportunities, and in some respects, a more hospitable racial climate. The onset of what has been called the Great Migration began in earnest around 1916. This first phase lasted approximately two years until 1918, by which time about half a million African Americans resettled in the North.[26] The new arrivals brought their folk, religious, and entertainment music with them, including the folk blues. With newfound industrial and maritime jobs, they were a growing class of paying and drinking customers. Gradually, venues were more receptive to providing entertainment for them. Garvin Bushell described the transformation: "You could only hear the blues and real jazz in the gutbucket cabarets where the lower class went. . . . Gradually, the New York cabarets began to hear more of the real pure jazz and blues by musicians from Florida, South Carolina, Georgia, Louisiana, etc. What they played was more expressive than had been heard in New York to that time."[27] James P. Johnson called this music the "natural blues."[28]

The older, established musicians in New York were catering not only to their own community but also to mainstream white society. Men like James Reese Europe, Will Vodery, and J. Leubrie Hill were working diligently to restore African American music to Broadway and wouldn't risk their efforts by adopting elements that would provoke a backlash. Johnson, too, was aware of the standards demanded of pianists in New York. The less schooled approach to the piano would never be accepted. He recounted this expectation:

The other sections of the country never developed the piano as far as the New York boys did. Only lately have they caught up. The reason the New York boys became such high-class musicians was because the New

York piano was developed by the European method, system and style. The people in New York were used to hearing good piano played in concerts and cafes. The ragtime player had to live up to that standard. They had to get orchestral effects, sound harmonies, chords and all the techniques of European concert pianists who were playing their music all over the city.[29]

At the same time, the blues had become the new commercial music powerhouse. As ragtime waned, and before jazz took the country by storm, popular composers, white and Black, cranked out hundreds of blues tunes. Following Handy's model, they incorporated elements of ragtime, popular song, the by then standardized twelve-bar blues format and three-chord harmonic platform. Gunther Schuller observes that one of the innovations in James P. Johnson's music was the incorporation of various elements of the blues.[30] Others, like Max Harrison, take an opposing view, claiming, "For the New Yorkers it involved almost everything except the blues. . . ."[31] Ethnomusicologist Harold Courlander points out that "in reality, there are few individual elements found in the blues that may not be found somewhere else, in other kinds of Negro singing."[32] These elements include call-and-response patterns, blue notes (the flatted third and seventh major scale degrees), pitch bending, and other expressions of rhythmic and melodic elasticity. When these characteristics were reflected in instrumental music and melded with features of ragtime, the hallmarks of jazz were created. James P. Johnson held the older musicians in the highest regard, but also recognized the value in the folk forms, and made a conscious effort to assimilate the qualities which were scorned by others. Johnson expanded the expressive possibilities of the piano by introducing the blues feeling and rhythmic vitality of the ring shout into his music.

Chapter 4

THE TICKLERS, 1913–1916

> From the outset of his first regular cabaret job, at Barron's [sic—Leroy's],
> James P. Johnson was a hit with everyone who heard him.
> —ED KIRKEBY

In 1944, Johnson and his New York Orchestra recorded what he considered to be a sampling of the music heard in the Jungles around 1913. Ragtime was still king, and the group recorded Joplin's "Euphonic Sounds" from 1909. The blues, in its commercial incarnation, was just becoming popular, and the group waxed Handy's "Hesitation Blues," which dates from a little later in 1915. They also recorded a legendary tune from the annals of early ragtime, "The Dream—Slow Drag." Authorship has variously been attributed to pianists Jess Pickett and John "Jack The Bear" Wilson. Pickett is the likely composer, but "Jack the Bear" made it his signature piece. It has come to represent the sound of early East Coast ragtime. Its habanera bass line is evidence of the influence of Latin-inspired (and perhaps African derived) rhythms that bring to mind Jelly Roll Morton's requirement that jazz must have the "Spanish Tinge," although the tune likely predates anything of Morton since Pickett and Wilson were probably born in the 1860s.[1]

Virtually nothing is known of Pickett, who was a notorious gambler and died around 1920. "Jack the Bear" Wilson may have hailed originally from Pennsylvania or Ohio. He supplemented his income from music with work in the coexistent underworld of gambling and drugs and was known to have suffered from addiction himself.[2] While many pianists of this generation were never able to climb out of the grip of illicit activities in the tenderloin, Wilson worked for four years on the Black vaudeville circuit with Lawrence Deas, from 1896 to 1900. The pair composed a number of songs and were thought to be the first Black duo performers to sing their own songs with piano accompaniment on stage, certainly with Wilson playing.[3] Deas would go on to work in musical theater and play a pivotal role in *Shuffle Along* as choreographer and on stage as performer. When the pair split in 1900, Wilson began long residencies playing piano in Hell's Kitchen at places like Charles H. Moore's Little Douglass Club and later at Walter Herbert's.[4] His last sighting in the mid-1920s was reported by stage pioneer Salem Tutt Whitney in the *Chicago Defender*, describing an appearance by the ailing Wilson at Tom Smith's cabaret in Baltimore. Wilson was working at a malt syrup factory. Whitney, the renowned showman, paints a dramatic picture of the legendary but at that point forgotten pianist sitting in during a break for the band and wowing the crowd despite his crippling arthritis. In his heyday, around 1900, he is recalled as one of the best pianists, playing astonishing versions of "Stars and Stripes Forever" and his specialty number, "The Dream."[5] The piece goes by a number of different titles, including "The Ladies Dream," "Digah's Stomp," "Digah's Dream," "The Bowdiger's Dream," and "The Bull Diker's Dream." Wilson's version began at a breakneck tempo and concluded with a very bluesy slow drag. Willie "The Lion" Smith recalled Wilson's treatment of the concluding section as "mean and dirty."[6] The tune was written as an appreciation for lesbians, who found some refuge for their sexual identities at that time in houses of ill repute. Places like Jim Allan's and George Lee's, where Johnson often played from 9:00 p.m. until 7:00 a.m., provided just the forum for the mix of music he recorded years later.

Johnson recalled playing his first "Pigfoot Hop" in 1913. At Phil Watkin's place on 61st Street he was paid $1.50 to play for the night, plus all the gin and chitterlings he could consume. It was his introduction to a social event that was becoming an urban necessity in Northern cities as housing conditions began to tighten with the influx of many Southerners. Johnson looked at it as a career boost, noting, "This was my first 'Chitterlin Strut' or parlor social, but later in the depression I became famous at 'Gumbo Suppers,' 'Fish Fries,' 'Egg Nog Parties,' and 'Rent Parties.' I loved them all. You met people." The generous hospitality offered at these events had their detrimental side effects. With a regretful tone, Johnson noted, "At an all-night party, you started at 1:00 a.m., had another meal at 4:00 a.m., and sat down again at 6:00 a.m. Many of us suffered later because of eating and drinking habits started in our younger socializing days."[7]

Johnson soon had the opportunity to engage in serious musical training. He had become friendly with pianist Ernest Greene (Johnson spelled his name with an e, but it is often spelled Green). Greene was a child prodigy. His mother, Alma T. Jupiter Greene, was a highly regarded opera singer. They had been studying with an Italian music teacher named Bruto Giannini at least since 1906. On February 28, 1907, Alma and Ernest were featured in a recital at Majestic Hall. Although sparsely attended, the *New York Age* reviewer had this to say about mother and son:

> I have attended a great many recitals and consider it one of the best I ever attended for the small admittance fee. The musical part of the program was under the direction of Prof. B. V. Giannini, one of the best vocal teachers of grand opera in this city; also a composer, and the teacher of Mme. T. J. Green. Master Ernest Green, the child pianist, was excellent. His execution was great; he should be encouraged to continue his musical education. Mme. T. J. Green is one of the best grand opera singers of our race. All of her selections were from grand opera. She sings as fluently in Italian as in English: the grand aria from *La Traviata*, rendered by Mme. T. J. Green was magnificent.[8]

The Greenes were very active in the Mother Zion Church and performed there often. Willie "The Lion" Smith and Johnson[9] recalled Greene's virtuoso renditions of the *William Tell* and *Light Cavalry* overtures, and Smith credited Greene as the most influential in recommending the two young pianists incorporate concert pieces into their performances. Greene began playing professionally at least as early as 1909.[10] With aspirations dashed for a concert career, he worked as a cabaret and movie house pianist. He was working at Baron Wilkins's club in Harlem around 1913 where Luckey Roberts was the featured pianist. Johnson recalled it was Greene who introduced him to Roberts.[11] Alma encouraged Johnson to study formally with Giannini. Johnson recalled, "Ernest's mother got opera lessons from old professor Giannini by doing his housework, and she got him to teach me my harmony and counterpoint for just a dollar a lesson. I had to throw away my fingering and learn to put the right finger on the right note. I was on Bach, and double thirds need good fingering."[12]

Bruto Giannini, long a mysterious but important figure in Johnson's early development, has been well researched by music scholar Marcello Piras.[13] Bruto Valerio (or Valerico) Giannini was born March 28, 1848, in Ascoli Piceno, Marche, Italy. His father Palemone was a physician whose distinguished career was disrupted as a result of his liberal political views and support of Garibaldi, the famous military leader who unified Italy. Bruto's older half-brother Stanislao also became a physician, and older brother Valfredo a mathematician. Bruto and Valfredo fought with Garibaldi in 1866. Bruto studied music at the elite Bologna Conservatory, graduating in 1868. Although details of his formal studies are few, in later years it was clear Giannini was a highly proficient pianist and conversant in several foreign languages. After several teaching appointments in Italy, Sardinia, and the Greek island of Corfu, Giannini, his wife Nazzarena Battistoni, and their two daughters Corcira and Roma moved to the United States around 1890.

Shortly after their arrival, Giannini began advertising piano and singing instruction at his Union Square office in 1891. He and Nazzarena had a third daughter, Ameriga, in 1894. Giannini's stature continued to build. He was endorsed by Luigi Mancinelli, conductor of the Metropolitan Opera. He was often called on by society patrons to perform, culminating in a performance for President William McKinley at the White House in 1897. By then he had moved his studio to Carnegie Hall. The Gianninis apparently traveled back to Italy for three years, at which point Bruto's personal life began to come apart. As his profile with high society waned, his long-held liberal inclinations began to manifest more openly. His letters to *The New York Times* were virtual rants about repressive regimes in Europe and anti-Italian sentiment in the United States. By 1906, he had moved his studio to the Lincoln Square Arcade at 1947 Broadway, between 65th and 66th streets, room 322, only a few blocks from the Greene home. Giannini's barter arrangement with Alma Greene of domestic work for lessons engendered a deeper personal relationship. In the society notes of the *New York Age* on September 25, 1913, the following appeared: "Alma T. Jupiter Greene, 234 West 63rd Street, has returned to the city after a pleasant vacation at Saratoga. On Saturday [September 20] she entertained Prof. B. V. Gianinni [sic], Scott Joplin, his pupil, and Henry Pleasant at dinner." Like the Damrosch brothers and Johnson's later teacher Edward E. Treumann, Giannini, in keeping with his world view, prioritized opportunities for aspiring African American musicians. He is here socializing with three accomplished Black musicians. The mention of Scott Joplin is a revelation. By 1913, Joplin had long been known as the king of ragtime writers but was engaged if not engrossed in preparing his second opera, *Treemonisha*, for performance. As it would turn out, his career was in descent as he battled illness that compromised his musical abilities and hastened his death in 1917. Pleasant was a noted classical tenor.[14] And thanks to Alma Greene, Johnson was added to Giannini's roster of students. There is no indication, though, that Johnson ever met Joplin, despite their shared teacher.

Giannini certainly put Johnson through his paces, rigorously working on technique with Kohler-Bertini's Etudes, Clementi's Preludes, Exercises and Gradus Ad Parnassum, Handel's Fughetles, Bach's little Preludes and Exercises. He took two lessons a week with Giannini studying Brahms, Beethoven, Bach, and Liszt.[15] In two interviews in the late 1930s, Johnson confirms his start with Giannini around 1912 or 1913. He studied with him for perhaps as long as six years. Johnson likely first met Ernest Greene when he moved to San Juan Hill

Bruto Giannini, Johnson's first serious teacher during the 1910s. (Courtesy of Marcello Piras)

The Lincoln Square Arcade, built in 1906, stood at the intersection of Broadway, Columbus Avenue, and 65th Street. It was known as the "Bohemia of the Upper West Side," and was home to many, mostly immigrant artists, writers, and musicians, including Giannini, where he had his studio. (New York City Department of Records and Information Services, 1940s Tax Department photographs, Collection REC0040 - RG 035. Department of Finance. Courtesy Municipal Archives, City of New York)

in 1908, but Giannini had returned to Italy at that time, not returning to the United States for several years, delaying Johnson's introduction to him.[16] One interviewer attributes to Johnson the goal of becoming a concert pianist, but Johnson never articulated this aspiration.[17] Johnson was engrossed in the burgeoning Harlem entertainment world, and his goal was to be featured in it. Johnson studied with Giannini perhaps as late as 1918, when he was offered opportunities to go on the road. By 1922, Giannini and his studio are no longer listed in the New York City directory. He published a few additional compositions, and passed away on September 25, 1931, at age eighty-three.[18] One can wonder if he was aware in his later years of the success of one of his last students.

Johnson was eighteen or nineteen years old when he began his study with Giannini and had to abandon his bad habits. Johnson's ultimate success speaks to his innate genius, talent, perfect pitch, and determination—determination to outdo his competition. He developed his own practice technique, playing "in the dark to get completely familiar with the keyboard. To develop clear touch and the feel of the piano, I'd put a bed sheet over the keyboard and play difficult pieces through it." He intimated Giannini's exercises bored him, saying of his lessons, "... I got tired of the dull exercises. However, he taught me a lot of concert effects."[19] Johnson's attitude toward the classical repertoire he learned during this time seems more utilitarian than artistic. He speaks about how he used these "concert effects" to enliven his arrangements of other tunes:

> I played rags very accurately and brilliantly running chromatic octaves and glissandos up and down with both hands. It made a terrific effect.
>
> From listening to classical piano records and concerts, from friends of Ernest Greene such as Mme. Garret, who was a fine classical pianist, I would learn concert effects and build them into blues and rags.
>
> Once I used Liszt's *Rigoletto Concert Paraphrase* as an introduction to a stomp.
>
> When playing a heavy stomp, I'd soften it right down—then I'd make an abrupt change like I heard Beethoven do in a Sonata. Some people thought it was cheap, but it was effective and dramatic.[20]

> I used to like to rip off a ringing concert-style opening using Liszt's "Rigoletto Paraphrase for Piano" that was full of fireworks in the classical manner and then abruptly slide into a solid, groovy stomp to wake up the audience and get a laugh.[21]

If Giannini thought it was cheap, it doesn't seem he dissuaded Johnson from commingling popular and "classical" ideas in his playing. During their six-year association, Johnson achieved ever greater success in popular, ragtime, blues, and ultimately jazz music. He must surely have discussed his extracurricular and professional musical activities with Giannini. It seems unlikely Johnson would never have displayed his nonclassical playing styles for his teacher. As Marcello Piras observes, "Bruto was a *Garibaldino*; hence his approach was one of respect for all identities, be they natural or local. Wherever he went, he developed an interest for the music of the lower classes, listened, learned, and tried to create art music rooted in local traditions, all regarded as carrying some sort of basic people's truth."[22] Rather than rap Johnson's knuckles when a little ragtime snuck into the assignment, Giannini more likely encouraged his pupil, as he must have done with Joplin. But unlike Joplin, who was in the midst of writing his opera *Treemonisha* when studying with Giannini, Johnson was not quite ready to transform his creative efforts into an art music. That notion would start to take shape at the end of his tutelage with Giannini. Starting with him, however, Johnson had begun what would turn out to be a nearly unbroken course of private study with a string of conservatory-trained musicians over the next thirty years.

Johnson continued to listen to, admire, and steal the tricks and effects of other players. Most of these players never published or recorded. Their names linger only in the recollections of their more famous contemporaries. There were some highly trained, serious musicians among them. Sam Gordon played at the Elk's Cafe at 137th Street and Lenox Avenue, an early Harlem club. Johnson recalled he was classically trained in Germany and picked up syncopation in the United States, noting, "He was a great technician who played an arabesque style that Art Tatum made famous later. He played swift runs in sixths and thirds, broken chords, one-note tremolandos and had a good left hand." "Fred Bryant [*sic* Bryan]," Johnson recalled, "from Brooklyn was a good all-around pianist. He played classical music and had a velvet touch. The piano keys seemed to be extensions of his fingers. Incidentally, as far as I know, he invented the backward tenth. I used it and passed it on to Fats Waller. It was the keynote of our style."[23] Willie "The Lion" Smith also recalls Bryan invented the backward tenth, a left-hand figure whereby the upper note of the interval of a tenth is struck slightly before the lower root. Bryan had many nicknames. He was known as "The Harmony King" and the "Jazz Sousa."[24] Frederick M. Bryan was anything but a sporting house drifter. Bryan was a serious musician, composer, and conductor. He played in London in 1914 and was already a member of the Clef Club and became its musical director by 1916. He conducted their "A" section (of five sections) of touring singers and instrumentalists in 1918,[25] and appeared with W. C. Handy on a number of occasions at the Selwyn Theater, with Bryan conducting the Clef Club Orchestra and as featured piano soloist.[26] In 1927 he won first prize in a composition contest sponsored by the National Association of Negro

Pianist, composer, and Clef Club conductor Frederick Bryan. (*New York Age*, June 14, 1919)

Musicians (underwritten by the Wanamaker family of Philadelphia) for a lullaby.[27] Bryan was one of the first African American pianists to record on piano roll in 1912, and later worked as a copyist for the Pace and Handy Music Company.[28] He lived in Brooklyn at 136 Lefferts Place and was devoted to his family and active in the bridge Street A.M.E. church. He died of gangrene in 1929, a complication of diabetes he had struggled with for several years.[29] Bryan was an important figure in New York African American musical circles, and a prominent influence for Johnson and others.

Other players Johnson remembered included Fats Harris, who played in Chelsea. He had an original stomp tune called "Fats Harris Rag" that especially struck Johnson. Bob Gordon played at Allan's before Johnson. He was called the March King. Johnson recalled Gordon wrote "Oh, You Drummer," a popular tune published in 1911, but J. Leubrie Hill is listed as the composer. Freddie Singleton relieved Johnson at the Jungles Casino occasionally. One of the most cryptic but nonetheless original players was Kitchen Tom. Johnson did not recall his real name during the interview with Davin, but years earlier he had written the name Eddie Bosso next to Kitchen Tom on a list of early pianists who had influenced him.[30] Kitchen Tom (or Bosso) played quadrilles, set dances, and rags. Johnson remarked he had heard Kitchen Tom play an original left-hand rhythm that was later named the walking, Texas, or boogie-woogie bass years before it became popular in the Midwest. The playing of

Richard "Abba Labba" McLean had a profound influence on Johnson. The two had met in Chelsea in late 1914 where Abba Labba played. He was a favorite with many laundresses and cooks who supplied him with fancy clothes (pilfered from their customers' laundry) and good food, called cold kina (or keena), the leftovers taken after serving their employers. Living so well off his women friends, Abba Labba never took a steady job. He often made only a brief appearance, played just long enough to impress everyone, and then left. Johnson recalled, "Abba Labba had a beautiful left hand and did wonderful bass work. He played with half-tone and quarter-tone changes that were new ideas then. He would run octaves in chords, and one of his tricks was to play "Good Night, Beloved, Good Night" in schottische, waltz and ragtime. I fell on his style and copied a lot of it."[31]

"One-Leg" Willie Joseph was a brilliant player. Born in Boston, he lost his leg in an ice-skating accident as a child. Eubie Blake, who worked with Joseph in Baltimore in 1908, recalls Joseph's early experience as a prodigy:

> He was a concert pianist. You see, his mother had worked for some rich white people and they came home one day and heard young Willie playing their piano. So they sent him to the Boston Conservatory, where he majored in music. Now according to what Willie told me, when they had the commencement, he was one of the five top pianists in the class. They had them play in competition in cubicles where they could not be seen by the audience. Well, he won by the audience applause. So he came out—and he was black—and the man that was the head of the panel to give the awards told him, "I'd like to give you first place, but you being a Negro, I can't; I'd lose my job."[32]

Joseph had aspirations for a career as a classical concert musician. Like Will Marion Cook, a classically trained violinist, Joseph became very bitter, feeling that his vision was thwarted by the racial barriers preventing African American musicians from careers as classical musicians. Blake recalled him as moody and volatile, but able to mesmerize his audience and fellow musicians. While Blake was frequently in the habit of bestowing the title of "greatest piano player I ever heard" on many worthy musicians, "One-Leg" Willie was frequently referred to with the title. Luckey Roberts thought the same, and Blake recalls James P. Johnson said Willie was "the only piano player I'd pay to watch."[33] With his command of the classical repertoire, he was one of the first to rag the classics. "He was the most uncanny piano player you ever heard," Blake observed. "He had terrific technique. You'd walk into a room and he would be playing; he'd reach up and shake hands and keep right on playing everything with his left hand."[34] "One-Leg" Willie won many ragtime competitions, and claimed to have bested the prominent white pianist Mike Bernard in a famous contest at Madison Square Garden in 1900 sponsored by Richard K. Fox and his *Police Gazette* magazine. Joseph was denied the title, and an upset victory, since the contest was controlled by Tony Pastor, proprietor of the famous vaudeville theater on 14th Street, who rigged the outcome in Bernard's favor.[35] He played the "Stars and Stripes Forever" in march time, ragtime, and sixteen, a boogie-woogie, barrelhouse type bass line.[36] Willie "The Lion" Smith recalled, "Yeah, Joseph was one of the best of the old-time ragtime players. He had original ideas and never played the same number the same way twice; the melody would stay the same, but he would always vary the harmony. He was fast, real fast, and his fingers and brain seemed to be working together like a flash of lightning."[37]

Bob Hawkins was one of the first to play at Barron Wilkins's new location in Harlem at 2275 Seventh Avenue around 1914. He organized the first jazz band there after Luckey Roberts and Ernest Greene moved out of the solo piano positions.[38] Willie "The Lion" Smith notes, "He was famous, very fast, a good reader, good improviser, and the style that you hear—well, I'd say the bass that you hear myself and Jimmy and Fats play, that's the way Hawkins played. He had a terrific left hand, I mean beautiful." Smith recalls both he and Johnson thought highly of Mike Jackson from Louisville, who was also featured at Barron Wilkins's Club. Jackson had a modest radio and recording career during the 1920s, especially with Victor Records. He played with Mamie Smith, Alberta Hunter, Perry Bradford, Thomas Morris and others, as well as recording a few solos and piano rolls. He had a knack for composing clever and humorous tunes and was popular on the radio. After a brief move to Canada in the late 1920s, he returned to New York in 1929 and quickly regained his club popularity playing and singing his clever lyrics to such tunes as "Candy Lips." Other players Johnson recalled included Lester Wilson, Ralph Ralston, Willie Sewell, Thad "Snowball" Wilkinson (who could play only by ear in the key of B natural), Bubba Lee, Rock Island Red, and Dickie Huff from Newark, New Jersey. Willie "The Lion" Smith recalled Huff was his chief rival in Newark. Smith noted he "could sing, dance and play a lot of piano. He kept me on the jump, but he had one bad habit that gave me an advantage—Huff was a dope addict and would disappear for long periods of time."[39]

In an apartment building at 8th Avenue and 41st Street lived a remarkable array of piano talent. Alberta Simmons, as a woman in the otherwise male-dominated New York ragtime and jazz piano world, established herself as a matriarchal figure. Johnson recalled that "Snowball" Wilkerson taught her to play rags.[40] Simmons went on to instruct the next two generations of New York jazz pianists. Although only two years older than Johnson,[41] he acknowledged she was "kind enough to teach me the full Joplin rags that she played so well: 'Frogs Legs' [*sic*, composed by James Scott], . . . 'Maple Leaf Rag' . . . and the

'Sunflower Slow Drag.'" He noted that her musicianship as "a fine instrumental pianist" enabled her to play with Clef Club bands.[42] She played professionally in clubs such as the Wilhs' New Café in San Juan Hill on West 53rd Street.[43] A decade later, she tutored another youngster from the neighborhood in the rhythmic complexities of New York piano, Thelonious Monk.[44] As late as 1940, she was still remembered as a fixture at rent parties.[45] Below her lived Willie Gant, who, born in 1899, was already a very talented young teenager. Gant was one of Johnson's first students, apprenticed under him for five years, and credits him as his major influence. He noted Johnson's ability to slow down his playing so Gant could learn his complicated pieces but acknowledged no one could play them as well as Johnson.[46] Gant vividly recalled when he first met Johnson and started his lessons:

> There was a piano contest around 47th Street. I went up there—me and my little bunch of boys. We went up there so I says "who's Jimmy Johnson?" [Someone] said there he is. So he asked me to play. I had nerve. He said play one, so I got down there and I played the "Junk Man Rag." When he got down there and played, it brought a new life to me. It was something new. I'd been wanting, and here he'd had it. He had it!
>
> It was something my brain craved for. I couldn't get it from them other guys, but he had it. So then I said to him, "Can I come up to your house?" He says "yeah." I says "Well how can I get up there? I go to 41st Street School. How can I meet you and then you'll bring me up to your house." He says, "Ok you'll meet me at 59th St at the Circle." Where the Coliseum is now [demolished in 2000], that's where James used to meet me everyday, and take me on over to his house.
>
> I used to watch him, watch him, and used to teach me, teach me. He used to show me these things, and oh boy I was gone. He gave you the basics, not everything he knew.[47]

Gant was an early witness to Johnson's innovation and supremacy among pianists during this early time in his career. "James was just naturally a natural. James was born a natural. See Jimmy was, Jimmy at that time, he was the greatest. It was him and Luckey," he concluded.[48] Gant made only a handful of vocal accompaniment recordings in 1921, but fronted a popular band during the 1920s, and eventually settled into long residencies at various New York establishments playing solo piano. Other pianists who lived in the building at that time included Russell Brooks and Raymond "Lippy" Boyette. Seven or eight years later, Brooks would introduce Fats Waller to Johnson. During the Depression, Boyette served as a rent party impresario for Johnson and the other pianists. Simmons's home was a gathering place for pianists, and others

Johnson recalled there were Corky Williams, also a Harlem fixture in the 1930s, Dick Turpin, and Virginian Nat Stokes.[49]

Johnson met three men in 1913–14 who were not only great inspirations to him but who became his close friends and well-known figures in their own right. In 1913, while Johnson was playing at Allan's, he met "Luckey" Roberts. They were introduced at a party by their mutual friend Ernest Greene. Charles Luckeyth Roberts was born in Philadelphia in 1887. He began piano study at age five but spent a large part of his youth touring with vaudeville and minstrel shows, performing as singer, dancer, and expert tumbler. Born a Quaker, Roberts stayed clear of alcohol, tobacco, and drugs all his life. He did have his vice, however. Much to the chagrin of his friends, Roberts was a pool shark who hustled many Harlem thugs and gangsters. Like Johnson, in addition to possessing superlative keyboard technique, Roberts composed rags and the music for many stage shows and revues, had several popular hits, and scored fully orchestrated symphonic works. Unlike Johnson, one of Roberts's most successful ventures was the society orchestra he led during the 1920s. Roberts and his orchestra were the favorite entertainers at private parties on Fifth Avenue, in Palm Beach, and Newport. Among his clientele were the Astors, the Warburtons, the Wanamakers, the Goulds, and the Vanderbilts. Roberts commanded fees of a thousand dollars and more a night, a sizable jump from ten dollars a week in the dives of Philadelphia and Baltimore where he started. With World War II came the end of the big parties. Roberts bought the Rendezvous restaurant in Harlem in 1942 featuring singing waiters and his own occasional piano playing until his retirement in 1954.[50]

Eubie Blake recalled that early in his career, Roberts "could only play in one key, F sharp. He used to play for a singer; they'd say it was too high and he'd play the same thing an octave down."[51] By 1910, Roberts had become New York's premier player, holding the piano chair at Barron Wilkins's club. He was unusually short, only four feet ten inches, but had large and powerful hands that could stretch an interval of a fourteenth on the piano. Johnson recalled that "... he played tenths as easy as others played octaves. His tremolo was terrific, and he could drum on one note with two or three fingers in either hand. His style in making breaks was like a drummer's: he'd flail his hands in and out, lifting them high. A very spectacular pianist."[52] He was capable of playing lightning fast chromatic runs stretching several octaves, a trick no one else seemed able to copy. Roberts has the distinction of being the first New York ragtime pianist to have a composition published—"Junk Man Rag," published in 1913. His "Pork and Beans" was a favorite with eastern players. Johnson studied his playing and the two became lifelong friends. Abba Labba, who later worked for Roberts playing in one of his society orchestras,[53] and George Gershwin, on his frequent trips to Harlem, were also "students" of Roberts.

During the summer of 1914 in Atlantic City, Johnson first met Eubie Blake, who along with Roberts, was one of the most prominent East Coast ragtime pianists. Johnson stopped in at a place called the Belmont where Blake was playing and recalled how he "caught" one of Blake's rags on this visit. Blake is a little more dramatic in his account of their first encounter:

> And James P. Johnson! Black James we called him. I wrote "Troublesome Ivories" to have a number to cut everybody with. It was even hard for me to play. Black James, he was only sixteen years old, he came by where I was workin' in Atlantic City and he heard me play the piece twice and he had it. Only sixteen! He was still drinkin' sarsaparilla then. Greatest piano player I ever heard. I let him sit in for me for twenty minutes while I took a break. I come back and he's playin' "Troublesome Ivories" without no mistakes. I make mistakes, but not him.[54]

If the meeting described by Blake occurred in 1914, Johnson was then twenty years old, not sixteen. He must have still seemed like a kid to the twenty-eight-year-old Blake. James Hubert Blake was born in Baltimore in 1886, although all his life he used 1883 as his date of birth. He began organ and piano lessons at an early age and, like Johnson, listened attentively to the syncopated sounds emanating from local saloons. As he practiced, he experimented with his own syncopated variations. His religious mother was not amused by his modern sounds that were associated with brothels and saloons. He recalled, "One day my mother came home from work early and heard me playing like that. She said, 'Take that ragtime out of my house!' That's the first time I ever heard the word ragtime."[55] Blake was especially impressed by English light opera, including such works as *Florodora* by Leslie Stuart. The show featured music that moved through many different keys, a characteristic Blake incorporated into his own playing and composing. As his mother feared, by the time he was as adolescent, Blake was playing at Aggie Shelton's bawdy house. He then moved into prizefighter Joe Gans's Goldfield Hotel in Baltimore in 1907. From 1910 to 1915, he spent his summers in Atlantic City, and the remainder of the year in New York.

In 1915, he teamed with lyricist/singer Noble Sissle. Their traveling act, "The Dixie Duo," was very popular and played top-rank vaudeville theaters. The two worked closely with James Reese Europe and the Clef Club. In 1921, the team of Sissle and Blake (along with the comedy team of Miller and Lyles, who later also worked with Johnson) produced the most successful all-Black musical of the decade, *Shuffle Along*. "I'm Just Wild About Harry," one of Blake's greatest song hits, came from the show. Blake continued to compose, going in and out of retirement several times through the years. Before his success as a popular songwriter he was, as Johnson put it, "one of the foremost pianists of all time." Rudi

Blesh commented that in the course of research for his historic book *They All Played Ragtime*, he was not aware that Eubie Blake had ever been a preeminent "tickler." It was James P. Johnson who mentioned Blake's piano skill to Blesh, a tip-off that helped initiate Blake's return to an active career performing ragtime.

In early August 1914, Johnson scored the plum position as pianist at Leroy Wilkins's Café.[56] During that summer, he won a piano contest in Egg Harbor near Atlantic City. He played his own "Twilight Rag" and "Steeplechase Rag." The title "Steeplechase" may have been a reference to either the great rollercoaster at Coney Island, called the Steeplechase, or the Steeplechase amusement pier on the Boardwalk in Atlantic City. Johnson had by then played in both seaside recreation destinations. The death of George C. Tilyou in 1914, founder of the popular Coney Island roller coaster, was widely covered in the newspapers, and perhaps Johnson named his composition to capitalize on the press. The piece was published in 1939 with the title "Over the Bars," the sheet music cover depicting a steeplechase horse race rather than a roller coaster. Both pieces remained in Johnson's active repertoire. Johnson mentioned another of his compositions, "Night-time in Dixieland," which was never recorded or published. After his short stay at Leroy's, Johnson began traveling with a singer-dancer he had met at Jim Allan's club, Lillie Mae Wright. Her first husband, whom she married in 1911, was a piano player named Fred Tunstall, also known as "The Tonsil." At that time he was a pimp who preferred to live off his girls rather than take a steady job. "He was a sporty dresser: green ties, high stiff collars, and a Norfolk coat with pleats that spread out when he took his seat at the piano. He was a piano player worth hearing if you could catch him when the mood was on him," recalled Willie "The Lion" Smith generously. Tunstall was a fixture in the Jungles and later in Harlem, playing venues including the cabaret of "Handsome" Harry Pyle and Fred Laurie in 1920. Pyle's attracted the "sports with middle-class bankrolls," recalled Ethel Waters.[57] Tunstall served as music director for Mamie Smith during her 1925 tour,[58] and found his way into travelling editions of Johnson's shows in the mid- to late 1920s. Lillie Mae Wright was not partial to Tunstall's assertive manner, and left him for the more easygoing Johnson.

After a brief return to New York, Johnson and Lillie Mae crossed back over the Hudson River to Newark, New Jersey, in the late fall of 1914. There they met Willie "The Lion" Smith, who was playing at a place called Randolph's, located in the tough section of Newark known as the Coast. The two hoped to find jobs working together. She was hired as an entertainer, but the manager insisted he already had a piano player, Willie Smith (he was not yet known as the Lion). As Smith recalled, "Lillie figured the way to get Jimmy in on the deal was to give me a hard time." This she did by singing in the wrong key. She and Smith argued, and Lillie started hollering for a pianist who could accompany her properly, all the while motioning Johnson to the piano. Willie refused to concede, recalling, "After she ran out of excuses I said, 'Come on, what can you sing'? She said she'd like to do 'That Funny Man from Dixieland' and this time we really got together and had all the customers clapping their hands right along with us." After her first set, Lillie introduced the two pianists. Smith recalled, "Although Johnson was actually a shy, retiring type, we immediately hit it off. In later years I did a lot of his fighting for him as he never seemed to want to bother. That is, I helped him out in the brawls around the saloons.... Back in 1914, Jimmy and I were just two young boys who played piano by ear. We couldn't read or write music, but we were to both learn very soon. As the years went by we became like twins and came up together."[59] Johnson was able to get a job at the Kinney Hall. When Smith left Randolph's (renamed Lewis's Saloon), Johnson took his place at the piano.

William Henry Joseph Bonaparte Bertholoff Smith, born in 1893 (he gave 1897 as his birth year throughout his life) in Goshen, New York, was a colorful personality. He, like Johnson and many other jazz musicians, was given instruction by his mother on the piano and organ at an early age. Much of his childhood was spent in Newark and the surrounding area. In his autobiography, *Music on My Mind*, written with George Hoefer, Smith tells many of the same stories that Johnson did about the early days of Black music in New York. He was a fixture in the cabarets of the Jungles and Harlem. In 1917, Willie Smith enlisted in the army and sailed to France with the all-Black 92nd Division, 153rd Brigade, 350th Field Artillery, Battery A. True fighter that he was, Smith volunteered to fire the French 75s, huge cannons perched at the front line. It was during the war that he acquired his nickname. He relates, "I shot those 75s at the Fritzies for forty-nine days without a break or any relief. Word got back about the several hits I had to my credit and a colonel came up and said, 'Smith, you're a Lion with that gun.' Before long everyone was calling me 'Willie The Lion,' a name that has stuck with me ever since."[60] Willie "The Lion" Smith had a long and active career in music. He recorded first in 1920, as part of the accompaniment to the first vocal blues recording by a Black singer, Mamie Smith. He had an unusually inquisitive mind, broadly assimilating disparate ideas about topics from music to religion. Smith, who credited the strength of his left hand to playing Bach, also played ragtime, developed into a superb stride player, and became a prolific and original composer. Many of his works exhibit impressionistic and romantic melodic and harmonic ideas. His biological father, who abandoned the family when Smith was young, was Jewish. Smith embraced Christian and Jewish theology, wearing both a St. Christopher's medal and a Star of David. He was opinionated, fancying himself as a fighter, an intellectual, an all-around entertainer, and a first-rank piano player who was always ready to prove it.

"Willie Smith was one of the sharpest ticklers I ever met—and I met most of them," Johnson said of his close friend, who he privately nicknamed "Cuz." "He was a fine dresser, very careful about the cut of his clothes and a fine dancer, too, in addition to his great playing. . . . When Willie Smith walked into a place, his every move was a picture." A rehearsed entrance had become an important part of a musician's identity, as Johnson noted, "every move we made was studied, practiced, and developed just like it was a complicated piano piece." Johnson recounted a lengthy, detailed description of the stylish clothes and show business mannerisms of the highest-class players. The following is his description of a tickler's routine from the time he entered a place to the completion of his performance:

> When you came into a place you had a three-way play. You never took your overcoat or hat off until you were at the piano. First you laid your cane on the music rack. Then you took off your overcoat, folded it and put it on the piano, with the lining showing.
>
> You then took off your hat before the audience. Each tickler had his own gesture for removing his hat with a little flourish; that was part of his attitude, too. You took out your silk handkerchief, shook it out and dusted off the piano stool.
>
> Every tickler had his special trademark chord, like a signal . . . players would start off by sitting down, wait for the audience to quiet down and then strike their chord, holding it with the pedal to make it ring.
>
> Then they'd do a run up and down the piano—a scale or arpeggios—or if they were real good they might play a set of modulations, very offhand, as if there was nothing to it. They'd look around idly to see if they knew any chicks near the piano. If they saw somebody, they'd start a light conversation about the theater, the races or social doings—light chat. At this time, they'd drift into a rag, any kind of pretty stuff, but without tempo, particularly without tempo. Some ticklers would sit sideways to the piano, cross their legs and go on chatting with friends nearby. It took a lot of practice to play this way, while talking and with your head and body turned.
>
> Then, without stopping the smart talk or turning back to the piano, he'd attack without any warning, smashing right into the regular beat of the piece. That would knock them dead.
>
> After your opening piece to astound the audience, it would depend on the gal you were playing for or the mood of the place for what you would play next. It might be sentimental, moody, stompy, or funky. The good player had to know just what the mood of the audience was.

At the end of his set, he'd always finish up with a hot rag and then stand up quickly, so that everybody in the place would be able to see who knocked it out.

Every tickler kept these attitudes even when he was socializing at parties or just visiting. They were his professional personality and prepared the audience for the artistic performance to come. I've watched high-powered actors today, and they all have that professional approach. In the old days they really worked at it. It was designed to show a personality that women would admire. With the music he played, the tickler's manners would put the question in the ladies' minds: "Can he do it like he can play it?"[61]

At the outset of the twentieth century, a group of thoroughly schooled musicians in New York undertook the difficult struggle of moving Black music beyond the denigrating image of the Black performer as an untrained, primitive talent. One early organization called the Frogs, which took its name from the Aristophanes play, was dedicated to the advancement of African American arts, both musical and theatrical. Its members included Alec Rogers, J. Rosamond Johnson, Jesse A. Shipp, R. C. McPherson (Cecil Mack), and James Reese Europe, many of whom would later work with James P. Johnson. In 1910, these same men, led by Europe, organized the Clef Club. The organization was established primarily as a booking agency to represent and promote the interests of Black musicians. Working within the framework of an organization like the Clef Club, Europe was able to make dramatic changes in the working conditions for Black entertainers. His orchestras played only in finer establishments, with wages and hours set by contract. Europe rejected the notion of the Black musician as a foolish bumpkin and insisted on proper deportment of the members. The Clef Club had a central office where musicians could gather, eager to be sent out on a "quick call" assignment. The Club maintained several orchestras, any of which could be sent to play for the parties of the very rich in Newport or on Park Avenue, or for an Ivy League prom. Europe paved the way for Luckey Roberts's success in the same market after the demise of the Clef Club in the early 1920s. Europe assembled large orchestras for big events, often with somewhat unusual instrumentation including mandolins, violins, banjos, harps, and as many as ten pianos. They often played without written music, since their employers expected them to be musically illiterate. Europe was not fond of improvisation or exploring folk musical materials like the blues. He resigned from the Clef Club in the fall of 1913 after a dispute with other musicians, and formed a rival organization called the Tempo Club. He was murdered by his drummer Herbert Wright in 1919. James P. Johnson played on many Clef Club dates perhaps as early as the late 1910s, and into 1921.

In 1914, Johnson was still playing regularly at Allan's and, as he says, "visiting around." He said, "From 1914 to 1916, I played at Allan's, Lee's, the Jungles Casino, occasionally uptown at Barron Wilkins', Leroy's, and Wood's [run then by Edmund Johnson]. I went around copping piano prize contests and I was considered one of the best in New York—if not the best. I was slim and dapper, and they called me 'Jimmy' then."[62] New York ragtime had taken on a distinctive character, an amalgam of classic ragtime, popular semi-classics, the harmonic feel of the musical theater, and the rhythmic vitality of the southeastern seaboard. The playing tradition in the East required far more of the performer than playing from the published score. As Johnson put it:

> New York developed the orchestral piano—full, round, big, widespread chords and tenths—a heavy bass moving against the right hand. The other boys from the South and West at that time played in smaller dimensions—like thirds played in unison. We wouldn't dare do that because the public was used to better playing.
> We didn't have any instruments then, except maybe a drummer, so we had to use a solid bass and a solid swing to get the most colorful effects. In the rags, that full piano was played as early as 1910. Even Scott Joplin had octaves and chords, but he didn't attempt the big hand stretches. Abba Labba, Luckey Roberts and later ticklers did that.[63]

The solid bass line in the left hand working as the rhythm section supporting a thickly textured melodic right hand made full use of the keyboard, leading some writers to describe this style as "orchestral piano." In 1915, Johnson was apparently still taking lessons from Giannini and continued to explore the blues and the ring shout. He imposed on himself the strict discipline of the trained musicians. He would "woodshed" the tunes of others, playing them in every key, and experimenting with substitute chords and harmonies. He described his approach:

> I was starting to develop a good technique. I was born with absolute pitch and could catch a key that a player was using, and copy it, even Luckey's.
> I did double glissandos straight and backhand, glissandos in sixths and double tremolos.
> These would run other ticklers out of the place at cutting sessions. They wouldn't play after me. I would put these tricks in on the breaks and I could think of a trick a minute. I was playing a lot of piano then, travelling around and listening to every good player I could. I'd steal their breaks and style and practice them until I had them perfect.

Sometimes I would play basses a little lighter than the melody and change harmonies. Another time, I'd use pianissimo effects in the groove and let the dancers' feet be heard scraping on the floor. It was used by dance bands later.

I had gotten power and was building a serious orchestral piano. I did rag variations on "William Tell Overture," Grieg's "Peer Gynt Suite," and even a "Russian Rag" based on Rachmaninoff's "Prelude in C-Sharp Minor," which was just getting popular then.

In my "Imitator's Rag," the last strain had "Dixie" in the right hand and "The Star-Spangled Banner" in the left. (It wasn't the National Anthem then.) Another version had "Home Sweet Home" in the left hand, and "Dixie" in the right.[64]

Years later, he told Will Marion Cook and his son Mercer that he had acquired the skill of rapidly learning a tune on the spot by working as an accompanist in talent shows. He was often unaware of what tune a contestant might sing until he was on the stage.[65] While Johnson continued to work at developing his playing ability and the orchestral sound he desired, he began to view composing and songwriting more seriously. By 1915, he had arranged several "homemade blues" tunes for the piano from vocal renditions he had heard. One of these, "All Night Long," he recalled, was later made into a song by Shelton Brooks, another popular Black composer. Brooks's tune by that name was published in 1912, so it seems unlikely Brooks picked up a melody line from Johnson. The ragtime instrumentals he formulated won him piano contests, but he could not write them down. That was about to change, and an opportunity for popular composing and playing soon arose in association with one of the most popular and important stage shows of the decade.

Chapter 5

FIRST PUBLICATIONS AND RECORDINGS, 1916–1917

> Just like those songs came to Gershwin,
> that's how them things came to Jimmy.
> —WILLIE GANT

In 1916, Johnson noted he "did the music" for a tab show called *The Darktown Follies*. He recalled working with J. Leubrie Hill and Frank Montgomery on this production.[1] The original production was the work of Hill, a well-known and extremely talented singer, comedian, and pianist born around 1867 in New Orleans. By way of Memphis and Cincinnati, he came to work in musical theater with Williams and Walker and Ernest Hogan, after whose death he began work on his own productions. His comedic specialty was playing a "mammy" character in drag. Hill wrote the book, music, and lyrics and staged the original edition of the show which was subtitled *My Friend From Kentucky*. He took the leading part and toured with the show from 1914 through 1916, making its way from New York to Chicago and elsewhere.[2] After the death of Bob Cole, Ernest Hogan, and George Walker within the span of two years from 1909 to 1911, for the remainder of the decade, African American musical theater on Broadway had fallen out of favor. Hill, however, had great aspirations for his production, and was looking aggressively for a white patron to bring it to Broadway. A very successful run at the Lafayette Theater in late 1913 drew white patrons from downtown to the emerging African American entertainment center of Harlem. James Weldon Johnson described the appeal of the show, noting, "*Darktown Follies* drew space, headlines and cartoons in the New York papers; and consequently it became the vogue to go to Harlem to see it. This was the beginning of the nightly migration to Harlem in search of entertainment."³

One of the first to seek out talent in Harlem was famed producer Florenz Ziegfeld, who, while recognizing the originality, vitality, and commercial potential in African American music and dance, wasn't quite prepared to support Hill's work as a stand-alone production. Ziegfeld bought the rights to the finale of *Darktown Follies*, a number titled "At the Ball, That's All," along with two other song hits, "Rock Me in the Cradle of Love" and "Dear Old Dixie," all of which he incorporated into his own *Ziegfeld Follies of 1914*.⁴ James Weldon Johnson describes the impact:

> The Finale to the first act of *Darktown Follies* was one of those miracles of originality which occasionally come to pass in the world of musical comedy. Its title was "At the Ball," the tune was the sort of melody that, once heard, is unforgettable, and words and music were combined into a very clever piece of syncopation. But it was the staging that made it so striking. The whole company formed an endless chain that passed before the footlights and behind the scenes, round and round, singing and executing a movement from a dance called "Ballin' The Jack," one of those Negro Dances which periodically come along and swept the country.⁵

J. W. Johnson also highlighted the fact that "Rock Me in the Cradle of Love" was indeed a love song and sung that way by the lead African American tenor to his love interest. Johnson proudly noted that the tune was rendered "in a most impassioned manner, demonstrating that the love-making taboo had been absolutely kicked out of the Negro theatre."⁶ Hill worked tirelessly to secure exposure in a "legitimate" downtown theater, and managed to arrange an opening of a pared-down tabloid production that opened at Hammerstein's Vaudeville Theater on June 1. The condensed production, without its most humorous and popular turns, was lost on the audience and the show closed after a week.⁷ It was the only fleeting presence for Hill and for Black musical theater on Broadway during the decade.

The full production remained popular on tour, and Hill revised it several times with the large cast changing over time, at one point swelling to seventy-five performers. The show continued to run in 1915, with Alex Rogers joining Hill in 1915 to revise and revitalize it. Hill and Rogers wrote a new score and book, recruiting a new cast and renaming this edition of the *Darktown Follies*, calling it *Here, There, and Everywhere*.⁸ After a stay in Philadelphia, the full company of seventy-five began a three-week run in Washington, DC, on March 13, 1916. At a meager twenty-five to fifty cents a seat, financial pressures mounted in supporting its three acts, fourteen scenes, and twenty-five music and dance numbers. Hill closed it in DC, and returned to New York to trim

Post card of the famous Luna Park amusement center at Coney Island, Brooklyn, New York. At far right is the marquis for *Darktown Follies*, the first stage show Johnson toured with. (Author's collection)

it down. Hill was once again forced to condense it into a tabloid version that opened at the Coney Island mega amusement center Luna Park in early July 1916.[9] The *Darktown Follies* franchise name was retained, but this edition was called *From Speedville to Broadway*. Leubrie Hill was recognized as a workaholic, but not as an astute businessman. The stresses of managing financial headwinds, and some bad luck, took their toll, aggravating smoldering health issues with which he had struggled for several years and hastening his death at age forty-nine on August 30, 1916.[10] Hill had been in failing health for some time, and his death was not unexpected. After Hill died, Frank Montgomery, another veteran stage producer and known as "The King of Funmakers," took over the show.

The various editions of *Darktown Follies* were an influential franchise. The tabloid version, by definition a platform designed for ongoing modification, gave Johnson the opportunity to compose new tunes, at times on a moment's notice. The *Darktown Follies* played at Coney Island for the 1916 and 1917 summer seasons. Since Johnson recalled working with both Hill and Montgomery, he likely joined the show with Hill playing Coney Island in 1916 and stayed on with Montgomery on tour under the new name into the fall. It was his first experience in a major stage show, the first in a long list of revues and musicals that became his primary outlet for popular composing, and as a platform for him to demonstrate his innovative ideas and musicianship at the piano. But Johnson was still unable to write his musical ideas down on paper, and without that skill, publication was impossible. That year, he came under the wing of a musician who would teach him, get him published, and recorded.

William Henry Farrell was born June 27, 1885, in Bayonne, New Jersey. His father was born in the West Indies and worked as a laborer, and his mother Anna was born in Virginia and worked as a domestic.[11] His father was adept on the concertina and instilled in William an early appreciation for music. He worked in the law office of W. D. Salter primarily doing chores but gained an appreciation for the protections afforded by the legal system.[12] Farrell became an actor, songwriter, and pretty fair pianist. His experiences in the law office inspired his activism in the movement to unionize performing artists. In 1911, he became recording secretary for the Colored Vaudeville Benevolent Association.[13] Founded in 1905, it was the first organization devoted to the protection of African American vaudeville performers' rights. He was one of the founding members of the Clef Club, played piano in their inaugural concerts in 1910 at the Manhattan Casino, and was honored by them in 1915 for his efforts working on behalf of African American performers.[14] In 1916, Farrell was chief deputy organizer of an organization called the White Rats Actors' Union. The White Rats was up until that time a restricted vaudeville actors trade organization prohibiting African American members.[15] With increasing pressure on trade unions of all sorts, they were eager to expand their membership. Farrell placed ads and wrote letters to the editor in the major Black papers recruiting members and offered discounted membership in the White Rats for $1.00 instead of the usual $15.00 dues.[16] Working with the executive director of the organization, Farrell was successful in enticing his colleagues to join.

How Johnson and Farrell became acquainted is unclear, although Johnson was already friendly with other musician members of the Clef Club who may have made an introduction. Since Johnson was especially interested in writing for the theater, he hoped to capitalize on Farrell's substantial connections in the entertainment field. They formed a partnership and launched into popular songwriting. It was Farrell who taught Johnson how to notate his compositions. The two worked out of Farrell's office on the twelfth floor at 145 West 45th street. By 1916, Farrell was promoting himself as "music publisher," and used the office for his work as secretary of the "Colored Branch" [author's quotes] of the White Rats.[17] "Mama's Blues" (also known as "Mamma's and Pappa's Blues" or "Mama and Papa Blues") was their first composition together. Farrell had had his own songs published by the well-established music publisher F. B. Haviland, and they published the Farrell/Johnson collaboration in May 1917. Johnson recalled the origins of this tune noting, "There had been a piece around at the time called, 'Left Her on the Railroad Track,' or 'Baby, Get That Towel Wet.' All pianists knew it and could play variations on it. It was a sporting house favorite. I took one opening strain and did a paraphrase from this and used it in 'Mamma's and Pappa's Blues.' It was also developed later into 'Crazy Blues,' by Perry Bradford."[18] Willie "The Lion" Smith also recalls Johnson

Advertising card for William H. Farrell, Johnson's first partner, and his late-in-life playing engagement. (Author's collection)

claiming he used a common blues strain that Mamie Smith later used for her "Crazy Blues," confirming that the melody may have come from the old bawdy house tune, "Baby, Get That Towel Wet."[19] Johnson and Farrell composed the World War I–inspired "Boys of Uncle Sam" and "Stop It" (later titled "Stop It, Joe"), both also published by Haviland in July and August. They apparently sold the tunes outright for $25 apiece. Giving up royalty potential seems an odd move for Farrell. By that time he had had many tunes published and was at the forefront of the fight for performer's rights. Johnson, on the other hand, was at the beginning of his songwriting career. And Johnson had another motive for quick cash—he needed a piano. He put the money from the sale of their tunes toward a down payment on a baby grand piano.[20] When President Wilson announced his "Preparedness" campaign, Johnson wrote a second patriotic number, a March Fantasia called "Liberty." He dedicated it to James Reese Europe's 369th Infantry. In 1941, Johnson scored it for full orchestra.[21]

Haviland was eager to promote these latest additions to their catalogue. They published notices about "Mama's Blues" and "Stop It" in *Billboard*. Wilbur Sweatman, one of the few Black bandleaders making records at that time, was said to be featuring "Mamma's Blues" in "his ragtime act," and was planning a recording to be promoted as a fox trot.[22] The popularity of the tune continued into the next year. It was included as one of "Haviland's Hits for 1918" and played by "all the big orchestras."[23] In 1918, at least two phonograph recordings of the tune were made, and Pete Wendling, a prominent pianist at the QRS Music Company, recorded it on piano roll.[24] The sheet music cover of "Stop It" includes a prominent picture of Sophie Tucker, describing the tune as her "sensational song success." She did not, however, record it. Johnson recalled he and Farrell composed and performed for a variety of musical productions. He described the common practice of producers who "would round up a couple of clever girls, work up an act with scenery and costumes, promote the music, and then try to sell the whole unit to a circuit. We'd get paid for performing (not for composing). It would get our songs heard—and maybe published. All composers and lyric writers started out that way then, even those that became the biggest in their field." Through their office, and with Farrell's connections in Vaudeville, they were approached to write for a wide variety of settings. They wrote music for social club shows, industrial and convention shows, and topical songs to advertise first production numbers in revues. They played one-night shows and dances as well as weeklong engagements at the Lincoln or Crescent Theaters in Harlem. Several contracts included road tours. Johnson paid particular attention to the audience reaction to his music, noting "We'd get the Negro reaction in the South and the opera house, white reaction in upper Pennsylvania, Connecticut, and New York State. I was learning how to do show music, and it was all a new experience."[25] The details of these productions are unknown, but the two were likely active in this way in the latter part of 1916 after Johnson left *Darktown Follies*, and into the first half of 1917, their experiences culminating in the three published tunes.

Johnson recalled that he received a message to see a Mr. Fay at the Aeolian Company to make ragtime piano rolls. It was most likely in the early part of 1917, and no doubt arranged by Haviland. In 1916, the Vocalstyle Company of Cincinnati developed a process for printing the lyrics to songs on the piano roll so that their customers could sing along as the roll played.[26] The publishers expected these so-called "word rolls" to hurt sheet music sales and were wary of allowing release of their tunes on piano roll. Word rolls became enormously popular, and roll sales dramatically increased. But rather than hurt sheet music sales, this too ballooned. The publishers took notice. Not only were sheet music sales increasing, but the publishers could exact a royalty payment as well from the roll makers. The Universal Music Company, a subsidiary of the Aeolian

Company, actively courted music publishers to promote the printed lyrics on their rolls.[27] By 1917, jazz had exploded on the music scene, but the demand for ragtime continued. Haviland saw the opportunity to partner with piano roll manufacturers as another outlet to promote their popular music as well as ragtime numbers in their catalogue. In Johnson they had the complete package—composer and virtuoso player of popular songs and instrumentals. From the spring of 1917 until late 1917 or early 1918, Johnson recalled he made one or two rolls a month for Aeolian at their New York laboratory,[28] ten in all. He also recorded for three other roll makers: four rolls for the Standard Music Roll Company in Orange, New Jersey; three for Bennett and White in Newark, New Jersey, on their "Artempo Record Rolls" line, which they promoted as "music as actually played"; and two for Rhythmodik in Belleville, New Jersey, a subsidiary of the American Piano Company. In addition to their flagship line Perfection, the Standard Music Roll Company released the same recording on several labels including Singa Word Rolls, Arto, and the Supertone label sold by Sears Roebuck. Universal (Aeolian) did the same with releases on their Metro-Art and Angelus labels.[29]

To record a hand played piano roll, the pianist plays through the desired piece on a special marking piano. The hammers draw marks on a roll of paper pulled through the mechanism, afterward cut to form notched holes, varying in size depending on the duration of the note. This master roll would then be used to produce copies. Johnson recalled the process of "recording" a piano roll at that time required him to write out everything that was played, the skill he had recently learned from Farrell, so that mis-punched holes could be corrected. Notes could appear "played" on the marking roll when the markers recorded a key brushed by or partially depressed and not usually heard. If marked and not corrected, they would be punched and the spurious notes would then be reproduced on the master.[30] The finished product could be considered a "hand-played" piano roll, and advertisements and roll labels bore the subscript "Played by James P. Johnson."

Johnson's first roll was a tune of Farrell's, published by Haviland, called "After Tonight." They played it as a duet for Universal and it was released around May 1917, followed shortly after by two Johnson rags, "Caprice Rag" and "Steeplechase Rag." "When It's Cherry Time in Tokio [sic]," another Haviland tune, followed on the Perfection label. Remarkably, of the nineteen known rolls Johnson made during this period, sixteen are of his own compositions and include a number of instrumentals.[31] He believed himself to be the first Black composer to record his own compositions on piano rolls, but several pianists predate Johnson's efforts including Blind Boone, Fred Bryan, and Scott Joplin.[32] Johnson recalled that he had written rags in every key of the scale, a claim supported by the piano rolls that include compositions in the keys of

B-flat, D, E-flat, E, F, F-sharp, and G, seven of the twelve major keys. Three rolls remain unaccounted for, their existence substantiated only by listings in catalogues and advertisements. These include two versions of "Mama's Blues" and one of "Stop It," but the Aeolian versions are well known. The dates associated with rolls in discographies represent the date of release, not of recording. The actual recording date was not kept as part of the cataloguing files. It is safe to assume that rolls were cut at least two months prior to the release date to allow for editing, reproduction, and distribution arrangements. Release dates have generally been determined by compiling information from catalogues, promotional materials, and advertisements in trade journals.

Three of the rolls released during these years were duets. In addition to "After Tonight" with Farrell, Johnson also made two rolls with Edwin E. Wilson, who was not a collaborator of Johnson's, but a member of Aeolian's recording and editing staff. His name appears frequently in Aeolian listings both in combination with other artists, including George Gershwin, and as a soloist and arranger.[33] The remainder of the rolls are Johnson solos and include instrumentals and songs. Johnson recorded four pieces specifically identified as rags in the title—"Caprice" (copyrighted by Haviland in 1917 but not published), "Steeplechase," "Daintiness," and "Twilight." All were kept in his active repertoire and recorded in the 1940s. Another instrumental, "Fascination," Johnson also later recorded in the 1940s. The provocatively titled "Innovation" was never published or further recorded, but the theme became the third movement of Johnson's *Harlem Symphony*, completed in 1932.

His last two rolls from this period, released around February 1918 on Artempo, are two unique compositions. "Eccentricity" is Johnson's syncopated waltz. It did not get wide recognition. The other is the first recorded version of "Carolina Shout," the composition that would become the model of stride piano, later versions studied by the first generation of jazz pianists. Although he adopts the sixteen-bar structure of ragtime, Johnson clearly strives to convey a feeling different from the classic ragtime of Joplin as well as the more theatrical feel of Eubie Blake and Luckey Roberts. Except for the A strain, "Carolina Shout" is overall much less melodic in conception than the other rags he recorded. The A strain employs a descending melodic line reportedly known for years as a folk paraphrase. It appears in many notable compositions before and after Johnson's use of it. Ted Synder's popular "Wild Cherries Rag" from 1908 makes use of this phrase, as does Jelly Roll Morton in his "Perfect Rag," King Oliver in "Buddy's Habits," and years later Joe Sullivan adapted it in his "Little Rock Getaway." The B strain invokes Will Vodery's 1914 tune "Carolina Fox Trot," a ragtime piece he was hoping would channel some essence of the music newly arrived from the Southeast. The remainder of the composition emphasizes powerful rhythmic figures, inspired by the ring shout and other dances brought north by the Gullahs and Geechies. Johnson attempts to capture with music the rhythmic urgency of the terpsichorean gyrations and the bite of the vocalizations he had been absorbing since his days at the bottom of the stairs in his mother's home in New Brunswick, and later during his accompaniments in the Jungles Casino in Hell's Kitchen. The frenzied sound and jolting rhythms come to life as he employs pianistic techniques such as clusters, grace notes, shuffle rhythms, and dissonances. The emotional intensity of the ring shout is revealed with call-and-response phrases and register changes.

The 1918 "Carolina Shout" is a notable stylistic break from his other compositions, and the rags of his contemporaries. Unfortunately, the piece, as recorded, seems hampered by some of the inherent shortcomings of the piano roll as a medium of musical reproduction. Although the number was hand played, and despite Artempo's claim their rolls conveyed "music as actually played," the final product sounds choppy and at times uneven, an outlier performance compared to his other rolls of this time. There are a number of possible explanations. Artempo's hole punches were not in fact single holes for each note, but rather a series of discontinuous small holes. In playback, it does not reproduce nuanced rhythmic phrasing. The roll would have also been subject to the whims of editing, a process that could entail adding notes, removing notes, repeating sections and, as it seems for this version of "Carolina Shout," creating phrases of odd lengths. These aberrations, completely out of Johnson's phrasing character at this time, could have been the result of careless and/or hurried editing. There may be another explanation for what challenged the editors. Throughout the performance, we hear Johnson turn the beat around with back beats disrupting the steady oom-pah flow. Other rhythmic devices he uses include call-and-response phrases, triplet figures, off-the-beat block chords in the right hand, broken backward and walking tenths in the left, and shuffle rhythms between both hands. These devices, at the time alien to the musical conventions of popular song and ragtime, may simply have thrown off the post-production roll editors. Perhaps they, not knowing quite what to make of the rhythmic disruptions, cropped out what may have sounded like aberrant beats, or failed to properly accommodate for the asymmetries produced by a marking piano. We can only speculate, but this latter theory is an intriguing reinterpretation of what many perceive as a flawed roll.

Johnson reveals himself to be a pianist of great skill on these early rolls. His style is beginning to break from East Coast and classic ragtime. The "Carolina Shout" is an interpretive instrumental rendering of a century-old cultural legacy, and a fascinating harbinger of what would become the underpinning of the long line of solo jazz piano. Its geographical (Carolina) and cultural (shout) roots are explicitly broadcast in the name of the tune, long before jazz critics and scholars began to analyze jazz and ragtime for lines of origin and

The rare early piano roll of "Carolina Shout," recorded in late 1917. (Author's collection)

influence. With this title, Johnson is signaling the lineage of a jazz tradition that was born out of an ethno-geographic musical legacy far afield from New Orleans. We can't know for sure if this roll accurately represents Johnson's 1917 rendering of "Carolina Shout." The generally mechanical sound of the player piano, and the choppy, halting, post-edited result challenges the ear. Three years later, his next memorialization of this composition on piano roll left no doubt he had reconciled any lingering rhythmic and structural conundrums. But even at this point in 1917, his conception was already exerting influence on other players, including Charles Thompson and Willie Gant.

By the late teens, Johnson and George Gershwin were both emerging from the gestation of formal piano instruction, and forging their own paths in American music, but each in their respective parallel universe. Johnson was a performing pianist in the orbit of the Clef Club and Black vaudeville. Gershwin was a song plugger for the Jerome H. Remick publishing house and a rehearsal pianist on Broadway. The Black and white music worlds at this time intersected and clashed as they had always done, and so it is not surprising that the two aspiring composers would cross paths at some point. Johnson told Tom Davin that he had met George Gershwin in 1920 when they were both making piano rolls for Aeolian. Johnson recalled that his repertoire at that time included blues tunes, and that Gershwin was recording "Oriental" numbers. By the time they met, Johnson added, Gershwin had already composed "Swanee" (1919), and the two exchanged ideas and spoke about their mutual interest in the blues and other indigenous American music, including their "ambitions to do great music on American themes."³⁴ While Johnson is usually remarkably accurate in his recollections to Davin, his recounting of this intriguing first encounter with Gershwin raises questions. The two were in documented professional proximity in 1917 and again in 1923, so the 1920 date is curious.

Gershwin had been an Aeolian pianist since 1916, and Johnson began recording in the early spring of 1917. The two men were recording for Aeolian throughout the year, and their rolls are noted in the same listings.³⁵ Johnson's recollection that Gershwin was making rolls of "Oriental" numbers is partially substantiated when looking at the titles of the tunes Gershwin made for Aeolian during this time. "Chu-Chin-Chow" was a Gershwin duet with Edwin E. Wilson, and "Chinese Medley" included three tunes played by five pianists including Gershwin and Wilson. Although these are the only two such numbers representative of this disparaging genre, both were released in September 1917, the same month as two of Johnson's rolls—"Fascination" and his own duet with Wilson, "Mama's Blues." If Johnson's repertoire featured blues tunes, this was the only one. Most of his rolls were popular tunes or rags. Popularity of tunes with appropriation of Asian themes as exotic but which were more an expression of racist stereotyping remained popular into 1920, and three of Gershwin's own such tunes were released then—"Limehouse Nights" and "Poppy Land" around January, and "Idol [*sic*, Idle] Dreams" around June.³⁶ But Johnson was still in Ohio in January, and may only have been newly arrived back in New York by June. No Johnson rolls from 1920 are known from Aeolian or any other company, casting further doubt on a 1920 meeting. It is possible some were cut by him and not released, especially since he had recorded for Aeolian earlier, but this would be pure speculation. Johnson's focus on blues numbers was true for his roll making for QRS that began the next year, but Gershwin never recorded for QRS.

Johnson's recollection also puts their encounter after Gershwin had written "Swanee" in 1919, and that the two discussed their orchestral ambitions. In disturbingly racialized terms, Gershwin articulated his musical vision to an interviewer in 1920, saying, ". . . the darky is a very definite part of our life. His songs and spirituals, in my opinion, form the base upon which our permanent music will be built." "Operettas that represent the life and spirit of this country are decidedly my aim. After that may come opera, but I want all my work to have the one element of appealing to the great majority of our people."³⁷ Or did the two discuss their symphonic aspirations back in 1917? By then, Johnson was ending his formal study with Giannini, and Gershwin had quit his full-time job at Remick's to devote more time to serious music study.³⁸ It is also likely they discussed their lofty goals in 1923 in London when they were working on the same show, accounting for the placement of "Swanee" in the timeline. And finally, Eubie Blake recalled hearing about Gershwin from Johnson and Luckey Roberts while Gershwin was still plugging songs for Remick, telling an interviewer, "James P. Johnson and Luckey Roberts told me of this very talented ofay [white] piano player at Remick's. They said he was good enough to learn some of those terribly difficult tricks that only a few of us could master."[39] It seems more plausible, then, since there is no evidence of work together in 1920, that Johnson and Gershwin first met at Aeolian in 1917, given their well-documented time together there.

Other curious facts surround the Johnson-Gershwin time at Aeolian. Gershwin's role and rolls were very different from Johnson's. Although Gershwin had left Remick by the summer of 1917, he recorded very few tunes published by them, or of his own compositions. Gershwin made little fuss about his roll-making days, and there is no record of him discussing it. Some have speculated that as a freelance roll maker, he did it only for the quick and easy cash. At $5.00 a roll, it was great money for a kid.[40] Johnson, on the other hand, spoke of his piano rolls as a source of great pride. Of the nineteen piano rolls made by Johnson in 1917, all were either tunes of other composers published by Haviland (three) or were his own compositions (sixteen), including "Innovation," which was released on Universal (Aeolian) in October 1917. Gershwin was much busier, banging out whatever the Aeolian marketing team requested. Eight of his rolls were released in October,[41] and so he spent a fair amount of time in the New York office, where he likely encountered Johnson working on his latest composition. Johnson obviously thought "Innovation" was special, giving it a provocative title. It was never published, but Gershwin, a decade later, used the same harmonic progression and melodic shape, and was credited with an instant standard—"I Got Rhythm."

Farrell and Johnson split toward the latter half of 1917. Farrell would have several other songwriting successes. His tune "I Like You (Because You Have Such Loving Ways)" was published by W. C. Handy and recorded in 1921 by Eddie Gray and Lucille Hegamin. In 1929, the Ziegfeld production *Show Girl*, mostly a vehicle for the Gershwins, included Farrell's tune "Who Will Be with You When I Am Far Away." It received attention when featured by Jimmy Durante. Farrell worked with the comedian Billy K. Wells and then Ike Hatch and recorded for Black Swan Records.[42] His last partner was Sadie J. Chadwick, lyric soprano. She retired in 1932, and Farrell began a residency playing a miniature piano near the bar at the Place Elegante in the former Woolworth Donohue mansion. He remained there through 1940s.[43] His last engagement at the Cattleman restaurant in midtown Manhattan found him leading a sing-along in the "saloon." Johnson would soon strike out on the road, experiencing the rough-and-tumble world of show business touring, and absorbing firsthand music from locales other than the Northeast.

Chapter 6

THE GIGGIN' YEARS, 1916-1918

> The Smarter Set presenting a musical comedy entitled "Darkest Americans."
> Everything new and ahead of the times—Balcony reserved
> for the Colored people.
> —*MESSENGER-INQUIRER*, OWENSBORO, KENTUCKY, 1919

Johnson called the 1916–1918 period "The giggin' years." In addition to his first published compositions and piano roll recordings, 1917 proved to be a very busy year with other musical activity. The chronology of his activity in New York is difficult to pin down, and some of his recollections from the time around WWI may have occurred in 1920 and 1921. Johnson recalled working as an accompanist to a singer named Reece Dupree. They worked at the Crescent Theater, a "hole-in-the-wall vaudeville house" on 135th Street.[1] Known as "The Singing Cabereter," Dupree often worked with single piano accompaniment at theaters such as the Crescent and Lafayette, offering a mixed repertoire of popular tunes, ragtime, and blues.[2] Johnson wanted to be a leader and arranger. He rehearsed groups of three, five, seven, or fourteen players, experimenting with contrasting melodies and counterpoint. He played engagements through the Clef Club with Arthur "Happy" Rhone. Rhone was born in Wilmington, North Carolina, but the family soon moved to New York, where he began singing in church and eventually took up banjo and ultimately made his name as a drummer, vocalist, bandleader, and comedian. He became closely associated with Europe and the Tempo and Clef Clubs. In 1914, he performed at functions with Europe and Vernon and Irene Castle.[3] In 1918, two Johnson associates and mentors, Rhone as comedian and Fred Bryan as conductor, headlined at the Clef Club in Philadelphia. An eighteen-year-old local contralto named Marian

Drummer, actor, and bandleader Arthur "Happy" Rhone. (*New York Age*, March 22, 1919)

Anderson was invited to sing. The press noted "promise of creating a sensation in the musical world if she continues to improve."⁴ Like Luckey Roberts and Jim Europe, Rhone developed his own orchestra to provide entertainment for wealthy white society. He so impressed Broadway star Nora Bayes as an actor and comedian that she convinced her managers that an African American should play the role of Washington the butler in her 1919 show *Ladies First* rather than a white man in blackface. She made Rhone an offer he couldn't refuse, so he gave up his lucrative position leading his orchestra. He was a hit.⁵ In 1922, he opened his own club at 143rd Street and Lenox Avenue, where he featured his version of an oversized orchestra of eighty-six pieces.⁶ He is credited with designing a left-foot pedal for the sock cymbal, a drummer's innovation that was widely adopted.⁷

Rhone was an ideal role model and mentor for Johnson and his musical aspirations at this time. He formed his own group to play jobs arranged by Rhone, what Johnson referred to as "fast calls." The Jimmie Johnson Trio worked as often as three times a day earning eighteen to twenty-five dollars a gig. Johnson held his musicians in the highest regard, considering them all virtuosos. Nelson Kincaid, recalled Johnson, played sax and clarinet and "could reach E above altissimo" and "transpose from trumpet parts on sight." Shrimp Jones played violin, and Clarence Tisdale was their relief man on alto saxophone. All were well schooled and had no trouble learning the music Johnson prepared, with all the parts written out. They played arrangements of "The Crocodile," "The Vamp," "The Sheik," and "La Vida." In keeping with the image expected of white society, they memorized the music so that they would not be seen reading.[8]

The best Black band in New York in the late teens, according to Johnson, was Ford Dabney's orchestra. As with many other Black entertainers, Dabney secured his job with his orchestra of sixteen musicians at the Ziegfeld Roof with the help of Jim Europe. For the most part, they played straight Broadway, popular, and show tunes. The pianist and violinist with Dabney's group was Alfred W. "Allie" Ross. By 1920, Ross was conducting the proud New Amsterdam Musical Association Orchestra. Founded in Harlem, it was at first primarily a dance orchestra, but under Ross's direction, the organization strove for recognition as a concert orchestra. Only a few years older than Johnson, they were good friends. Ross had studied theory and harmony with E. Aldama Jackson, and he likely recommended that Johnson study with him. Johnson described Ross as a "very serious musician" who enthusiastically spoke of transcribing Johnson's piano pieces for chamber orchestra. These ambitions never materialized, however. Like other African American musicians with serious interest in concert music, Ross found that the only reliable living was in popular music and the musical theater. He fronted one of the first bands at Connie's Inn, one of the three legendary Harlem nightspots of the 1920s and '30s along with the Cotton Club and Smalls' Paradise, and in 1928 conducted the orchestra for the enormously successful Broadway show *Blackbirds of 1928* produced by Lew Leslie. He died of a massive stroke at age forty-one in 1933 while rehearsing another show for Leslie.[9]

When James P. Johnson returned from his road tour with Farrell in late 1916 or early 1917, the Original Dixieland Jazz Band had landed in New York from Chicago and were a big hit at Reisenweber's Café, located in midtown Manhattan near Columbus Circle. Their recordings, starting in early 1917, are considered to be the first jazz records by many aficionados and scholars. Johnson found the musical climate in a clamor after their arrival. The ODJB consisted of five instruments: cornet, clarinet, trombone, piano, and drums, and the polyphony of the cornet, clarinet, and trombone weaving their melodic lines in and around each other was an alien sound to New York. It was certainly very different from the arrangements used by Clef Club bands. Johnson recognized the appeal of this new and energetic style and tried to organize similar groups through the Clef Club. The older members would have none of this "lower class" music. They reflected the same prejudices against the New Orleans jazz style as had been used to thwart the blues influence. "They thought that kind of playing was vulgar compared to what they were trying to do. This experience, and others, was an example of their not encouraging the younger musicians. As a result, their membership fell off," observed Johnson.[10]

Meanwhile, Johnson continued to be an active part of the nightclub scene. The movement uptown of the New York Black community was proceeding at a much faster pace by 1917. The area around 135th Street between Lenox and Seventh Avenues had become a new residential and social center. One of the most famous of the early Harlem cabarets, recalled by several musicians, was called The Rock or The Garden of Joy. It was in fact, built on top of a shelf of rock in a vacant lot at 140th St. and Seventh Avenue. With a kitchen and dance floor and decorated with Japanese lanterns and cooled by breezes from the Harlem River, the Rock looked like a summer resort situated in the middle of the city. Johnson recalled:

> On weekends, the dictys would hold their socials, but on weekdays us musicians had it to ourselves. Piano players would come up there to improvise and show off their latest riffs afternoons and evenings: lots of small bands (many of them became famous outfits later) worked out their arrangements on The Rock, or sat in with us piano players developing new music. It was a lively little musical mountain, visited by all the talent in Harlem.
>
> Some years later, Willie "The Lion" Smith, Fats Waller, Willie Gant and myself hung out there regularly, knocking each other out with rags, stomps, shouts and every wild chorus and freakish break we could think of. It was an odd place for an academy of music, but very relaxing; and there was always an intelligent and appreciative audience to follow us.[11]

Another Harlem cabaret was the Livia on 139th Street. Many female vocalists were fond of the Livia and performed there at some point in their careers. The list includes Ethel Waters, Bessie Smith, Florence Mills, Gertrude Saunders, Adelaide Hall, and Martha Copeland. Below the Rock on 139th Street was the 101 Ranch. On 135th Street was The Hole in the Wall. Many small bands played at these cabarets, usually without written music. They ". . . just let go with natural blues, hot stomps and all sorts of wild rhythms and sounds that popped into their heads and right out through their instruments without the benefit of formalities," recalled Johnson.[12] Willie "The Lion" Smith recalled Lottie Joplin's boardinghouse at 163 W. 131st Street as another after-hours watering hole. Lottie Joplin continued to run the establishment after the death of her husband Scott in 1917. She allowed only musicians and theater people to stay there. "It was a common occurrence to stop in at six in the morning and see guys like Eubie Blake, Jimmy Johnson, and The Lion sitting around talking or playing the piano in the parlor," Smith recounted.[13]

Johnson called the superior technique and sophisticated use of classical themes by the better players "fancy piano." Willie "The Lion" Smith was known for his renditions of "The Sheik of Araby" or "Moonlight," using elaborate concert-style introductions based on classical themes like Schubert's "March Militaire." Donald Lambert, who studied Johnson's playing and became a legendary pianist in the style, was known for his use of passages from Grieg, Massenet, and Beethoven. Johnson made use of similar elements, derived from his lessons with Giannini and the New York concert scene. "I used to like to rip off a ringing concert-style opening using Liszt's 'Rigoletto Paraphrase for Piano' that was full of fireworks in the classical manner and then abruptly slide into a solid, groovy stomp to wake up the audience and get a laugh," he recalled, pointing out the importance of showmanship.[14]

Johnson did not have the pugilistic tendencies of his friend Willie "The Lion" Smith, of whom Johnson said, "He was always a fighter; and he fought a lot of my battles over the years. I remember the first thing he ever said to me when I met him and played after him on The Coast over in Newark. He said: 'Well, you may be able to play better than I can, but I'll bet I can beat you fightin.'"[15] During World War I, Johnson had no intention of enlisting in the army to go overseas like Smith. In June 1917, he registered with the draft board. Perhaps to avoid seeing action in Europe, he stretched the truth and indicated he was married, and that his wife was solely dependent on him for support. He and Lillie Mae didn't marry until two months later on August 6 in Newark, New Jersey.[16] Of his marriage he said, "Oh, I mustn't forget something important in 1917. That year I married Lillie Mae Wright, whom I met at Allan's in 1913. We've trouped together for years and have seen lots of things change."[17] James P. was twenty-three, Lillie Mae twenty-eight. She was from Braddock (or Coatsville according to her passport application), Pennsylvania. They would visit her family there frequently over the years. She was apparently using her mother's maiden name Wright, but would use Hughes, her father's surname, as a professional name. She was a dancer and occasional actress and appeared on screen in the 1920s.[18] For the war effort, Johnson was assigned a job in the Quartermaster Corps warehouse. The physically exhausting job pushing a one-ton hand truck didn't keep him from staying out all night playing piano. Johnson often misplaced his draft card, an oversight that almost cost him time in jail. "One night, when I didn't have my card on me, I was in a place when the MPs raided. I knew what it meant, so I just jumped out a window: It was only on the second floor."[19] The Johnsons were still living in the Jungles at 214 West 64th street. On his draft registration card, Johnson listed his occupation as "piano player," and place of employment as Douglaston, Long Island. Douglaston, situated on Little Neck Bay in northeast Queens, boasted some of the most desirable homes in New York with stunning views of the water.

Lillie Mae Johnson in the 1940s. (Reproduced with permission of Barry Glover, from the James P. Johnson collection [IJS.0111], Institute of Jazz Studies, Rutgers-Newark)

At that time it was becoming a popular residence for many in the arts and entertainment industry. He listed his employer as a Mr. Pearson, who perhaps engaged Johnson for an event, or was in the employ of Aeolian or Haviland.

Johnson went on the road in late 1917. George V. Hobart, sometime writer for Ziegfeld, wrote a comedic play titled *What's Your Husband Doing*. It began a successful nationwide run in the fall of 1916. A new cast was engaged to start the season in the fall of 1917, and in November returned to Broadway. In early December, Johnson was called to put together a five-piece band for the play, recalling, "It was my first five-piece band, and we had a five minute scene on stage."[20] *Variety* noted, "A colored jazz band was added to 'What's Your Husband Doing' at the 39th St [Shubert Theater] Monday by George V. Hobart. The idea was to create atmosphere in the [Honeysuckle] Inn scene in the second act."[21] After the run on Broadway, they took the play on the road to the Belasco Theater in Washington, DC to play Christmas week, and then moved to the Shubert Theater in Boston.[22] While in Boston after the show was over, Johnson played at Lucas' Place, a "hangout for professionals." He played with Louis Mitchell, a classical violinist from the Boston Conservatory. Johnson recalled meeting Flournoy Miller and Aubrey Lyles, a comedy team with whom he would later collaborate on many stage shows.[23] After stops at the Shubert

Majestic in Providence, Rhode Island, the Tech Theater in Buffalo, and the Wieting Opera House in Syracuse opening February 7, the play returned to New York City, playing the Bronx Opera House in early March,[24] and closed at the Teller's Theater in Brooklyn in mid-March. It is not known when Johnson left the play, and if he returned to New York before the performances in upstate New York. *What's Your Husband Doing* went on to have great success. In June 1919, the Lafayette Players, the house troupe at the theater, put on a production. Johnson was already on the road with another stage show and not part of this Harlem production.[25] A silent film version was produced in 1919, retaining the jazz band scene but without Johnson.

Johnson had occasion to work with the prominent vaudeville ragtime pianist Ben Harney "in a song and dance act."[26] Harney's race has been debated for decades, but it is unlikely he had any African American lineage. He insisted, with some historical truth behind the claim, to have been the first to introduce ragtime piano to New York on stage when he performed at Tony Pastor's vaudeville house in 1896. He went further, though, inaccurately claiming the title of originator of ragtime, a genre even then well recognized as in large part derived from African American musical roots. This conceit engendered substantial resentment in some quarters of the Black community. Johnson, however, recalled Harney's trick of playing two pianos at the same time, one with each hand, and considered him to be a great piano player and entertainer. His impressions of Harney, as he relayed them to Tom Davin, bear no tone of resentment, even while recalling Harney's claim as "the inventor of ragtime," a claim Johnson knew was untrue. Other than Johnson's mention of it, the time spent with Harney is not documented. William Farrell later played on some of the same bills as Harney,[27] and may have introduced them, or vice versa. By the late teens, Harney's career was on the wane, and bookings were sporadic. Most likely Johnson worked with him after returning to New York from touring with *What's Your Husband Doing* in early 1918. Harney was well known to have worked with African American musicians, including other pianists. An intriguing item in *Variety* from mid-January might well have been describing Johnson: "Ben Harney has what might be termed a 'jazz' specialty assisted by a negro [*sic*]. At the opening Harney is at the piano playing ragtime (which he claims to have originated). An assistant joins in the chorus from the gallery. From then on he is all over the house and finally lands before the footlights to take up the playing. The colored fellow can make the ivories talk and possesses the faculty of just making the audience like him. He is of huge aid to Harney. Mr. Harney returns for some semi-character dancing that gains big results. It forced them to take a well-deserved encore and a speech."[28] Harney's routine of having an associate make his appearance from the gallery dates as far back as his appearance at the World's Columbian Exposition in Chicago in 1893.

Harney played Baltimore in early March and then again in April, followed by Philadelphia in May 1918,[29] perhaps accompanied by Johnson on this Northeastern tour. Harney continued to play the vaudeville circuits as "the inventor of ragtime," but by the mid-1920s, with his health failing after a heart attack, he became another forgotten and neglected figure. Although Harney's career was on the decline, Johnson's was just beginning. Harney's good friend in later life, Roscoe Peacock, commented that Harney's style was like that of Fats Waller.[30] There is no evidence Harney and Waller ever met, but since Waller's style was heavily influenced by Johnson, perhaps Harney's was as well.

Johnson recalled that he made his first phonograph recording, "Caprice Rag," for a company that started in his office building, later becoming OKeh Records.[31] Its founder, Otto Heineman, had been in the United States since 1914 working as an advance man for the Carl Lindstrom Company's Odeon record label. With the outbreak of World War I, he was unable to leave the States, so Heineman cobbled together his own recording and recording supply companies that included what remained of the Rex Talking Machine Corporation after it was liquidated in bankruptcy in January 1917 and launched OKeh Records in 1918. The recording laboratory was located at 35–37 West 31st Street in New York City.[32] There is no indication that Johnson's recording was ever issued. Johnson commented that the recording companies did not yet have much confidence in recordings by Black musicians. There were very few making records. Bert Williams was the only Black singer in Columbia's catalogue. James Reese Europe's orchestra recorded for Victor in 1913–14, and again in 1919 after returning from the war. Wilbur Sweatman and W. C. Handy, recording with their orchestras, were slowly evolving lightly syncopated dance music by adding more jazz elements. The adoption of improvisation was true more for Sweatman than for Europe, who did not favor much individualization from his musicians.[33]

By the summer of 1918, Johnson was again enticed into touring with a musical stage production. Salem Tutt Whitney and J. Homer Tutt were veteran vaudeville performers who had assumed stewardship of the Smart Set production company, a popular Black touring vaudeville franchise created by Sherman S. Dudley a decade earlier. Salem and J. Homer claimed to be half-brothers. From around 1908, they wrote, produced, and performed as blackface comedians in yearly touring musical theater shows until the late 1920s. By the late teens, they were calling their company "The Smarter Set." In July, they were beginning rehearsals for their production in the upcoming season. The Tutt brothers had re-signed Luckey Roberts to write the score. They had had success the season before with music by Roberts for their 1917–18 production of *My People*. Roberts was musical director, and the cast also featured his wife Lena Sandford Roberts.[34] Johnson was probably pleased to work with his piano mentor in a medium he was only just learning. The new effort, in two acts and ten scenes, was titled *Darkest Americans*.[35] The story begins at Howard University, one of the best known and respected historically Black universities, where a fictious dean, Kelly Miller, embarks on an international archeological expedition. The African American newspaper *Philadelphia Tribune* summarizes the premise of the Dean's exploration: "Dean Kelly Miller of Howard University, goes upon a voyage of archeological research to furnish ocular proof, if possible, of the antiquity of the Negro races, to prove that the frequent allusions of the ancient historians and Greeks to the land of Ethiopia and its wonderful people were not founded upon fantasy but fact, that the black races have contributed their quota to the arts, sciences and religions of the world."[36] Whitney and Tutt, like many of their theatrical colleagues, took what little opportunity they had to introduce an element of community pride before the theatrics inevitably devolve into the type of theater expected of African Americans by society at that time. Many press reports noted the improved structure of this latest edition from the comedian brothers, relying less on "slapdash" bustle, and more on crafted plot development. Whitney and Tutt made specific mention in their ads that their production was not a minstrel show but a "colored musical comedy," in an attempt to redirect expectations away from century-old racist elaborations. Once the Dean's "straight" premise is established, the farce begins. Abe and Gabe Washington, played by Salem and J. Homer, are admitted to Howard under false pretenses. The Dean is reported missing, and Abe and Gabe are recruited to search for him. They travel the globe, finding themselves in all manner of suspense-filled comedic situations. They find Dean Miller, and all three return home to a glorious homecoming. Salem plays the comedy part of Abe, while straight man J. Homer plays Gabe. Auditions began in Philadelphia at John T. Gibson's New Standard Theater on August 4, with the opening planned for August 19. The costumes and sets were noted to be extravagant but tasteful and the opening week was attended by "gaily bedecked women and men in evening dress." The orchestra included cornet player June Clark, who was looking to make a career transition from working as a Pullman porter to full-time music. Gibson put up a substantial sum of money to float the Tutt brothers on their upcoming tour.[37] Benton Overstreet, composer a few years later of the popular tune "There'll Be Some Changes Made," was the director of the orchestra at the Standard for many years. Johnson recalled that another star was rising in the Philadelphia Dancing Class, a young girl named Ethel Waters who was thrilling audiences with her comic personality and dancing.[38] Waters would soon become one of the most sought-after singers and stage entertainers of the 1920s and later developed a successful dramatic stage and film career.

Johnson recalled *Darkest Americans* played a week in Philadelphia, and one and a half weeks in Wilmington, Baltimore, Washington, Norfolk, and Atlanta. After Philadelphia, the show went to Washington for the week of August 26 at the Howard Theater. They apparently circled back to Baltimore and then New Jersey, playing three days in Trenton at the Trent Theater the second week in September, and then the Lafayette Theater in Harlem the last week in September. The show returned to Pennsylvania playing at the Orpheum in Harrisburg but was then held up in Philadelphia for a time due to the impact on the cast of the flu epidemic. Eventually, the company headed south to Norfolk aboard the Chesapeake Bay Ferry. Lillie Mae accompanied her husband, but it does not appear she was in the show. Johnson told of an embarrassing incident that occurred on the boat, and how he and his wife made the best of the situation:

> I had a few drinks and dozed off. When I woke up, I found that somebody had taken all my money and my collar buttons, which were gold. Others had been robbed too, by the lush-rollers. We wouldn't have a cent when we got to Norfolk.
>
> There was a piano on the boat, so I sat down and started to play, and my wife, who was with me, began to sing and dance. Pretty soon money started dropping. When the boat tied up, we had enough to eat in Norfolk.[39]

The show made its way to the heart of the African American entertainment district in Atlanta, centered on Decatur Street.[40] The show played the 81 Theater, also known as Bailey's 81 Theater after its owner, Charles P. Bailey, who Ethel Waters described as "a Georgia cracker and a sort of self-appointed czar. You did what Mr. Bailey said—if you wanted to work for him. He even made all his performers on his bill live at Lonnie Reed's boardinghouse."[41] The neighboring theater at 91 Decatur was featuring Bessie Smith and her trio. At a party, she was introduced to Johnson, who accompanied her as she sang one of her homemade blues tunes, "Alcoholic Blues." The fine blues and ragtime pianist Eddie Heywood Sr. also played at 81 Decatur Street but was off during Johnson's stay and the two never met.[42] By November, the show was moving through the Midwest. In Indiana, they played at the Park Theater in Indianapolis, and the Nelson Theater in Logansport on November 20 and 21.[43] J. Homer Tutt was born in Logansport, and his homecoming was well received during the short two-day stay. "The beauty and richness of the scenery and costumes astonished the local people while the snappy dancing, singing and the clever jokes which were pulled over in fine style by the former local comedians, kept the audience in a continual uproar. Music for the comedy was furnished by a ten-piece orchestra," wrote a local reviewer.[44] By the end of November, the show was in Chicago for three weeks, opening at the Grand Theater. In mid-February 1919, the show was playing the Grand Theater in Cleveland, Ohio.[45] Johnson's tenure with *Darkest Americans* was his longest stretch away from the Northeast to date. It would end shortly, but not with a return to New York.

Chapter 7

TOLEDO, 1919–1920

> When I was a child I never realized how brilliant a pianist James P. was.
> —MAURICE WALLER

The Johnsons, cornet player June Clark, and trombonist Lee Baxter left *Darkest Americans* while playing in Chattanooga and settled in Toledo, Ohio, in early 1919. James P. and Lillie Mae, along with Baxter and his wife, stayed in a large rooming house on Erie Street. Lillie Mae was working in a theater, and her husband, the Baxters, and another musician in the house were working in a cabaret.[1] The African American entertainment section in Toledo centered around Canton Avenue and a four-block stretch of Lafayette Street. Johnson, Clark, and Baxter first worked at Benny Goldstein's Cabaret, then at Herman's on Lafayette. They were joined by another young trombone player named Jimmy Harrison. The new trio of Johnson, Clark, and Harrison became close friends. The symbiotic musical relationship of the two horn players has been described as akin to Armstrong and Oliver.[2] Both became highly regarded musicians, especially Harrison, for his lyrical, improvisational capabilities. He spent most of his last years with Fletcher Henderson. Illness would cut short these two individual early jazz voices. By 1931, Harrison was dead, and Clark had all but stopped playing. Johnson recalled playing a club called The Lion's Jaw, noting Art Tatum later told him that he had heard him play there and studied his style.[3] Tatum, the partially blind piano prodigy born in Toledo in 1909, would later unseat Johnson as reigning New York piano king. Tatum would have been only ten or eleven years old at that time. Although his parents held a somewhat liberal view of alcohol despite being well-respected churchgoing people, it seems unlikely he could gain entry to a saloon at that young age.[4] It is more likely Tatum heard

Johnson when he was back in town with his show *Plantation Days* in 1922. By then, Tatum's prowess on the piano was widely known locally, and he would have been openly invited any place there was a piano.

Johnson met a pianist whose name he recalled as Johnny Waters. Johnson recalled Waters's fine piano playing. Little is known of Waters. He traveled around the upper Midwest including stops in Pittsburgh and is also cited specifically by Earl "Fatha" Hines as an important early influence.[5] Johnson referred to him as a fine "natural" player, implying he was self-taught. Singer Lois Deppe worked with him briefly in Pittsburgh at the Leader House, noting, "They realized I was a drawing card, and all they had in there was a boy named Johnny Waters out of Toledo, Ohio, just playing piano. 'I can't work with him' I said. 'I tried to, but he only plays in two keys. They're both sharps, and he can't transpose.'" Hines, however, first making the rounds on the Pittsburgh scene, was inspired by Waters. Deppe noted, "Earl would stand around and dig him."[6] Johnson described Waters's piano as "Western" piano. He noted Waters played slow blues with tenths but doesn't specify whether Waters was using the much larger tenth intervals in the right hand or left hand. Johnson noted "Western" pianists generally used smaller intervals in the right hand such as thirds and sixths. Hines, however, emphasizes Waters's right-hand techniques, and adds that the tenths, which also impressed Johnson, were played in the right hand. He said: "Then a fellow came to town from Detroit, named Johnny Watters (*sic*?). Now he kept stretching the tenths with his *right* [emphasis in original text] hand, and it was the first time I saw that. His hand was so large he was playing the melody with his middle fingers and using his thumb and last finger for the tenths. He played some of the prettiest things I ever heard. He was very fast executing with his right hand, and this was fairly simple to me because of my classical training, but I couldn't make the tenths and use the middle fingers the way he did. Johnny was a guy who loved Camel cigarettes, and his beverage was gin."[7]

In addition to impressing two of the greatest jazz pianists of the 1920s in Johnson and Hines, Waters is cited as an important influence on a third important 1920s pianist, Roy Bargy. Born in Michigan, Bargy grew up in Toledo and was touted as a child prodigy. He managed to seek out the pianists in the Black tenderloin district while also playing for movie houses and at the country club. Johnson noted Waters taught Bargy a number of his "tricks." He would go on to make a name as a novelty-style pianist but also as pianist and arranger for notable bands including the Benson Orchestra, Isham Jones, Paul Whiteman, and Jimmy Durante.[8] Years later, Waters's influence on Bargy remained a point of pride in the African American music community. In his 1944 feature article on the contributions of African American musicians, William Grant Still, the "Dean of Afro-American Composers," referenced Waters's influence on Bargy.[9]

Johnny Waters traveled around the upper Midwest, including frequent trips to Detroit. The Wolverine barbershop there was a popular destination in the African American community for local and many itinerant pianists. The most prominent pianists in the country, while travelling through town, would stop in. African American sportswriter Russ J. Cowans wrote of his recollections of many great pianists who played there. He noted the playing of Waters and another pianist from Toledo, writing, "I took a real pleasure in contrasting the playing of Johnny Waters with that of Bart Howard, as did so many of the boys in the shop. Waters was from Toledo and would visit five or six times during the year."[10] Cowans also recalled Johnson passing through the famous barbershop, reflecting the likelihood he also traveled regionally during his stay in Toledo. Jelly Roll Morton, too, passed through Detroit before 1917. He composed "Wolverines," later renamed "Wolverine Blues," as an appreciation for the owner of the barbershop.[11]

The trail for Waters's whereabouts goes cold after the early to mid-1920s. Early jazz researchers speculated he may have been Ethel Waters's father or half-brother, also both named Johnny and both accomplished pianists, but this identification has been ruled out. While most of the audio and written references to the Toledo pianist clearly refer to him as Waters, he is likely the Johnny Walters (or perhaps Watters) who listed his occupation as musician on his 1917 draft registration card. Discovered by Dr. Robert Pinsker in 2007, the information includes his birth in Sidney, Ohio (about 100 miles south of Toledo), on November 11, 1887. In 1917, he was married and was residing in Toledo.[12] Walters or Waters was sadly known to be a serious alcoholic. Johnson told Davin he ". . . had a pint of whiskey every morning for breakfast."[13] Hines bought him gin and cigarettes for lessons, and Toledo horn player Russ McGowan implies Waters succumbed to alcoholism and perhaps sexually transmitted disease, recalling, ". . . the whores and bad liquor got to him."[14] It is intriguing to think of Waters as perhaps a missing link given his influence on the two great jazz pianists of the 1920s who themselves were enormously influential, not to mention his influence on Bargy and Tatum. It seems clear Johnson's sojourn through the south and lengthy stay in the Midwest had great impact on him. He further refined his heavily ragtime-influenced East Coast style by absorbing Waters's big stretches with internal voicings as well as blues characteristics different from Handy's composed formulations. Not only was Johnson influenced by the Midwest pianists he encountered, but he had an effect on them.

The prominent St. Louis ragtime composer and pianist Charles Thompson frequently cited the influence of Johnson's eastern rhythms on his own playing. He may well have met Johnson in Cleveland in 1919, as he told Rudi Blesh, or in Toledo around the same time.[15] Thompson had been integrating elements of the "eastern" ragtime style into his own playing since the early 1910s when he attended Howard University in Washington, DC. By 1912, the twenty-one-year-old Thompson, who had started playing at age eleven and was self-taught, travelled throughout the East and Midwest. Thompson credited his defeat of reigning Missouri state ragtime champion Tom Turpin in the famous St. Louis ragtime contest of 1916 to incorporating Eastern elements that were more virtuosic, improvisational, and off the beat rhythmically. Thompson may have met Johnson earlier than 1916, but not as early as 1911 or '12, as some have cited, when Johnson, three years his junior, was just embarking on his own professional career. Thompson must have learned the "Carolina Shout,"[16] earlier than 1916, likely on a trip east. Johnson had been working on it since 1913. Although the piece was still in a formative stage in Johnson's repertoire, his fledgling Harlem stride rhythms were clearly a departure from the Midwestern ragtime Thompson knew. Regardless of the date of their first association, they developed a close friendship. In an interview late in life, Thompson describes in detail the four-week ragtime contest at the Booker T. Washington Theater in St. Louis in 1916 when he bested sixty-seven other contestants before edging out the favorite Turpin. Thompson makes a point of telling the interviewer several times that James P. Johnson was his greatest influence.[17] Thompson's dominance at the piano among the Midwestern ragtimers is corroborated by S. Brunson Campbell (1884–1953), thought to be the only white student of Scott Joplin. Campbell said, when comparing Thompson to other renowned ragtime players including Louis Chauvin, Scott Hayden, and Tom Turpin, "Charley Thompson—he was the best of all of them."[18] Johnson's musical fingerprints were already making their mark.

Johnson's musical education continued beyond the tenderloin. He had given up his formal lessons with Giannini when he left New York to tour, but in Toledo, he found another resource for his serious study of the European classics. Bradford Mills, a newly graduated baritone from the Oberlin Conservatory in 1899, found his way to Toledo. Musical life there at the time was practically moribund, despite the construction of Collingwood Hall five years earlier to provide a suitable venue for performance. Mills was a determined man, intending to bring music to Toledo. In the fall of 1900, he leased space in Collingwood Hall, a beautiful Venetian Gothic structure with a sizeable auditorium and many meeting rooms, founding the Toledo Conservatory of Music. To attract top-level musicians, he created the Toledo Civic Music League. Over the course of the next two decades, Mills brought to Collingwood Hall the likes of Walter Damrosch, Vladimir De Pachmann, Sarah Bernhardt, Jan Kubelik, and the highlight of his efforts, Enrico Caruso in 1917.[19] By 1910, the conservatory boasted an enrollment of nearly five hundred students and fifteen full-time faculty, and was well respected in the highest musical circles.[20] Collingwood Hall was built in the well-to-do West End residential neighborhood, removed from downtown Toledo. Walking out its doors one encountered a serene, tree-lined street with large homes. In addition to the Conservatory, the Hall housed the Semple Sisters dancing school and the Misses Janes and Franklin School, a finishing school preparing the upper-class students of the city for boarding school in the East.[21] The Conservatory offered a four-year curriculum with a focus on attaining a teaching certificate as well as performance degrees. But it also served as a resource for the serious amateur. Their promotional literature proudly noted, "The Conservatory not only offers unrivaled advantages for those seeking a musical education for the purpose of entering upon a professional career but caters to hundreds who pursue some branch of the art as a means of self-culture or as an accomplishment."[22]

It had been more than a year since Johnson had his last lesson with Giannini. Despite his seemingly contradictory feelings about piano pedagogy, Johnson knew he needed to return to serious technical study of his instrument, and the Toledo Conservatory provided the perfect outlet. At night he thrived "in the alley," and during the day he made his way past the homes of Toledo's elite to take lessons next to their children. In many ways, Toledo was less segregated than New York. Formal music study for him in Toledo did not rely on the beneficence of a small group of broadminded musicians like the Damrosches and Giannini. The best musical education in the city at an institution with a national reputation was available to him for the asking. At the Conservatory, he worked with the pianist Jan Joseph Chiapusso (1890–1969), who was born in Java, Dutch East Indies, of an Italian father and Dutch mother.[23] His earliest musical training was in Holland, followed by enrollment at the Cologne Conservatory. After graduating in 1911, he studied in Berlin and Paris. He immigrated to the United States in 1916, fleeing the war in Europe where there were no longer concertizing opportunities.[24] Shortly after arriving in the United States, he started his new professional life as a teacher, with several academic affiliations including Shorter College in Rome, Georgia, and the Minneapolis School of Music. The Toledo Conservatory thought it a plus that they developed their faculty for its teaching skill rather than contract only with well-known performing musicians. They proudly noted, "The teachers in the Conservatory have been chosen for their capability and wide experience in teaching. It has not been the policy of the school to engage teachers whose names have been conspicuous for attainments in the concert field."[25]

Chiapusso was only in Toledo for a brief period, and traveled to teach, perform, and record. He is not listed in the 1920 catalogue as a faculty member and was more likely contracted as an adjunct instructor. He is listed in the 1920 Toledo phone book but not in any of the city directories. In addition to his work at the Conservatory, he was teaching privately in Detroit during this time.[26] He had not given up his aspirations to be a concertizing musician and

Jan Chiapusso, Johnson's teacher at the Toledo conservatory during 1919–1920. (Author's collection)

(Author's collection)

booked two appearances at Aeolian Hall in March and April 1919, and again in April 1920. He made several piano rolls for the Ampico label of works by Chopin, Couperin, and Liszt. His broad repertoire included Bach, Beethoven, Chopin, Debussy, Ravel, Balakirev, Liszt, Brahms, Hahn, Schubert, Albeniz, and Godowsky.[27] Johnson studied with him for perhaps as long as a year, when Chiapusso was in town. Judging from his playing on the Ampico piano rolls, which incorporated technology to reproduce touch and dynamics, Chiapusso had a bright, crisp attack with a bravura style. Critics described him as "a pianist of the grand style," with "Brilliant, assured and faultless technical disclosures." One critic described his attributes to include "powerful and reliable fingers and a brilliant tone that makes every note as he strikes it from the keyboard into a fragment of musical flint."[28] A *Detroit News* reviewer observed, "Jan Chiapusso is a pianist whose performance occasionally sounds like the outgivings of a symphony orchestra."[29] It would seem Chiapusso was the perfect teacher for Johnson, whose own style engendered similar descriptions, including the power of his playing, his brilliant tone, and his stride piano as "orchestral." Chiapusso left Toledo in 1921 for Chicago, where he headed the Bush Conservatory for ten years, ultimately settling in Lawrence, Kansas, where he had a long and distinguished academic career at the University of Kansas. In 1968, he published an influential book on Bach.[30] Mills also left Toledo in the early 1920s for the West. The Conservatory continued into the 1950s, then moved to downtown Toledo, becoming the Bach Conservatory. Collingwood Hall was demolished in 1939.

The Johnsons returned to New York from Toledo sometime in mid-1920. His sister Belle had married Moses L. Boyd, who worked as clerk. They had lived in the Jungles at 458 West 57th Street, not far from her brother and sister-in-law. By the time James P. and Lillie Mae returned to New York, Belle and her husband had moved uptown to 267 West 140th Street.[31] An invitation was extended by Belle to James P. and Lillie Mae to stay with them while they resettled. They had been out of the city for nearly two years. Johnson picked up any playing jobs that were offered, including Clef Club fast calls. He made the rounds of the clubs and cabarets, and landed work at Edmond Johnson's place, located at 132nd Street and Fifth Avenue. Johnson described it as a "black-and-tan place," a venue that catered primarily to the African American clientele but wasn't necessarily strictly segregated. A former boxer, Edmond "Mule" Johnson moved his midtown bar to this basement location in Harlem in 1915. The low ceiling was decorated with paper streamers and artificial chrysanthemums. Photographs of African American sports and entertainment figures lined the walls. A tiny dance floor was surrounded by closely placed tables that could seat two hundred patrons. E. Johnson featured singing waiters and the finest rising female singers. Despite the talent Johnson hired, it was a rough place, attracting gamblers, prostitutes, and other unsavory characters. Ethel Waters made one of her first appearances in New York there around 1919 or 1920 after several years on the road. She described it as "the last stop on the way down in show business."[32] She sang Johnson's "Stop It, Joe," with Johnson often accompanying her. Mattie Hite, whom Johnson remembered as one of the greatest cabaret singers of all time, and Josephine Stevens, a coloratura "able to hold a note while the rhythm strode through and then pick up the rhythm without a break," also sang there.[33] Other pianists who played there were Johnny Lee and Walter "One-Leg Shadow" Gould, who had been around since the 1890s and whose playing reflected an older blues-based ragtime style. Waters described him as a "one-tune piano player," who "didn't have a hell of a left hand," but "sure knew his blues."[34] His inability to read music ultimately led to his release by Johnson.

After moving to New York in 1917 from South Carolina, where he worked as an elevator operator, Edwin A. Smalls opened his Sugar Cane club at 135th Street and Fifth Avenue and became a legendary nightclub owner/operator. For forty years, he successfully managed to navigate the tumultuous and dangerous world of Harlem nightlife, remaining independent of the mob bosses who controlled many establishments. Most of the help was recruited from the old Jungles neighborhood. They worked as singing and dancing waiters who performed little side shows while they served the customers. Johnson described their entertaining ministrations: "One of the attractions at The Sugar Cane was the jive of the waiters, who sang, danced and carried on a separate sideshow of their own while they took care of the customers between the regular floor shows. Each waiter served drinks or set-ups to his tables with an original strut, shuffle, or tap, and then they'd cut away with a heel pivot and dip, spinning their empty trays over their heads like jugglers."[35] One of the most popular waiters was a man known as "Whistling Seath." He was able to whistle the blues through his teeth. Eventually, the Smalls waiters adopted the "Charleston" when that became the national fad. When June Clark and Jimmy Harrison eventually made their way back to New York, the two horn players remained playing partners and worked for Ed Smalls. In 1925, he moved to a new location at 2294½ Seventh Ave, also in Harlem, with a new club called Smalls' Paradise. It became one of the "big three" of Harlem's destination entertainment meccas, along with Connie's Inn and the Cotton Club.

Many musicians have recalled in memoirs and interviews the fast growth of Harlem nightlife. The environs of Harlem in 1920 were the area from 130th to 140th Street between Fifth and Seventh Avenues. 125th Street was still part of a white neighborhood. Many cabarets opened along 135th Street, Harlem's main artery, while the fashionable street to walk down was Seventh Avenue. Jerry Preston's The Orient on 135th between Lenox and Fifth Avenues, Leroy's down in a cellar on 135th and Fifth Avenue, and the Band Box on 131st and

Seventh Avenue, were all popular. Most cabarets featured a five-piece band and seven or eight singers. The pianists played long hours, and many of the dozens of spots that could accommodate a piano became impromptu sites for jam sessions and cutting contests. Black stage shows were featured at the Lincoln Theater on 135th Street, succeeding the older Crescent a few doors away. Johnson played there periodically, but in 1920, sixteen-year-old Fats Waller was the regular pianist and organist.

In July 1919, the National Association of Negro Musicians held its founding meeting, at which the delegates resolved to work for a "truer appreciation of Negro music."[36] However, their view of "Negro Music" did not include jazz, which they saw as destined to remain mired in lower-class vulgarities. Not only did the musicians disdain it, almost all Black intellectuals of the time did not see jazz as part of the high art form they hoped would emerge. Cultural observer Nathan Irvin Huggins describes the attitude and irony of their position:

> Harlem intellectuals promoted Negro art, but one thing is very curious: except for Langston Hughes, none of them took jazz—the new music—seriously. Of course, they all mentioned it as background, as descriptive of Harlem life. All said it was important in the definition of the New Negro. But none thought enough about it to try and figure out what was happening. They tended to view it as folk art—like the spirituals and the dance—the unrefined source for the new art. Men like James Weldon Johnson and Alain Locke expected some race genius to appear who would transform that source into high culture. It is very ironic that a generation that was searching for a new Negro and his distinctive cultural expression would have passed up the only really creative thing that was going on.[37]

Although jazz did not establish a foothold with the African American intellectuals, it was quickly becoming a popular sensation. Recording companies were still reluctant to record Black jazz artists as the decade began, but, in 1920, a record was made that opened up an as yet untapped market, the Black community itself. Perry Bradford, a Black songwriter and promoter originally from Alabama, had arranged for blues singer Mamie Smith to record several tunes for the General Phonograph Company, producers of OKeh Records, the same company that had recorded Johnson several years earlier without issuing his record. Mamie Smith recorded two popular songs, "That Thing Called Love" and "You Can't Keep a Good Man Down," with the Rega Orchestra, the company's five-piece house band. Although these recordings met with only marginal success, Bradford was able to secure a contract for a second session at which Mamie Smith recorded two Bradford compositions. In August 1920,

Mamie Smith and her Jazz Hounds, a Black group, recorded "Crazy Blues" and "It's Right Here for You." This record resonated, reportedly selling seventy-five thousand copies in Harlem within several weeks of its release. "Crazy Blues" is the earliest known blues recording by a Black vocalist.[38] This record became the first "race" record, aimed primarily at the Black music-buying public. Soon after, many record companies began to record Black jazz artists when it was clear there was a market.

Johnson's firsthand recollections as transcribed by Tom Davin end at this point. The last published installment concludes with a brief note about the upcoming segment, one that would never be published. At age twenty-six, Johnson was poised for his leap into prominence. His résumé at this point included formal study with two European trained musicians, high regard as a ragtime pianist, one of the first African Americans to record piano rolls, several published tunes, composer of tunes for stage shows, arranger and leader of small and mid-size orchestras, vocal accompanist, teacher to younger Harlem musicians, and stylistic influence during his time in the Midwest. There was no aspect of musical training, composition, or performance he did not aspire to cultivate and master. Opportunity was about to explode, and his imminent, ground-breaking musical contributions have come to define the decade of the 1920s.

Chapter 8

NEW YORK BREAKOUT YEAR, 1921

> To James P. Johnson—
> The greatest genius I've ever met and I knew Liszt.
> —WILL MARION COOK

In January 1921, Johnson was called to the office of the QRS Music Company in the Bronx, NY. By then, QRS had become the largest manufacturer of piano rolls in the country, if not the world, surpassing Johnson's old roll company Aeolian. The company began as the brainchild of Melville Clark, the gifted piano and organ entrepreneur and inventor. Born in upstate New York in 1850, Clark's early musical training led him into instrument production rather than performance. After founding several companies manufacturing reed organs, he partnered with the Story brothers in 1884 to found the Story and Clarke piano company. As his own creative designs accumulated, he founded his own company in 1900, the Melville Clark Piano Company. They manufactured the Apollo piano and, in 1901, the first eighty-eight-note player piano. Clark formed a subdivision to cut piano rolls that could be played on his instruments. By 1910, the eighty-eight-note player piano had become the standard and QRS was functioning as an autonomous subsidiary. In 1912, Clark unveiled their revolutionary marking piano that made hand-played rolls possible. Melville Clark recorded over 250 patents during his career as the most prominent designer of pianos and player pianos. Just before Clark's death in November 1918, Thomas M. Pletcher, who had been with the company since 1903, bought a controlling interest in QRS. He expanded its production of rolls worldwide and led QRS to enormous success during the 1920s.

Lingering mystery surrounds the meaning of the name of the company, forever known only by the famous initials. An exhaustive search of surviving company files decades ago gives no definitive clue, nor has any contemporaneous trade publication or catalogue been found thus far. "Quality Roll Supply" and "Quick Roll Service" were suggested by company employees nearly a hundred years after the company's founding, with no supporting documentation.[1] "Quality Reigns Supreme" has had greater appeal, but also has been emphatically rejected. Another story printed in a trade journal in 1926, almost certainly apocryphal, suggests that when piano roll orders exploded, the paperwork simply overflowed from filing under "R" into the adjacent letters "Q" and "S" in the filing cabinet. Pletcher, who was known to be a savvy marketer, filled in the acronym using "Quality Real Service" in print on catalogues at least as early as 1922.[2] Melville Clark's original explanation may be lost forever.

The QRS Music Company had a broad catalogue and featured many popular, novelty, and early white jazz players, one of whom was Max Kortlander (1890–1961). He eventually became general manager of the company's recording laboratories. In the era before electrical recording of phonograph records, the player piano was a mainstay of home entertainment. In 1921, two hundred seventy-five thousand pianos were made by two hundred manufacturers. Half of those were player pianos.[3] Like the explosion of ragtime songs a decade earlier, the late teens and early twenties saw the proliferation of blues songs. White players like Pete Wendling and J. Russel Robinson had recorded blues rolls for QRS, and Kortlander, following the lead of OKeh's great success with Mamie Smith, sought out Black pianists. On January 10, 1921, Johnson signed an exclusive contract with QRS for two years. To record two rolls per month, he was paid $125 per month for the first year, and $150 per month for the second year. In addition, he was paid royalties on his own compositions—three cents per roll for "word rolls," two cents per roll for instrumental rolls.[4] This remarkable business deal, as far as is known, is the first such exclusive contract between QRS and an African American pianist, and a good one at that. Johnson was guaranteed a retainer for two years with a second-year increase, and a royalty in excess of the usual two cents per roll. The non-compete was only ninety days, after which Johnson could place his tunes elsewhere for recording. It established him as the first African American staff pianist for the renowned roll maker. As was their practice, QRS wanted a publicity photo. Johnson sat at an upright piano, head turned toward the camera. His long spindly fingers, stretching across the keyboard, belie his somewhat diminutive stature of five foot, six inches. He signed at least three copies "James P. Johnson 1921." It has become an iconic image in jazz history, heralding the beginning of jazz piano. It is the image of him on the cover of this book.

Veteran QRS staff pianist J. Russel Robinson recalled Johnson's first recording session, telling an interviewer twenty-five years later, "I remember the first

QRS Music Company advertisement from January 19, 1921, noting Johnson's historic position as their first African American staff pianist. He can be considered along with Bert Williams and Mamie Smith as one of the earliest pioneers of the burgeoning market for African American "race" music. This ad promotes the upcoming availability of his piano rolls at prominent Chicago music stores. (*Chicago Defender*, January 29, 1921)

time James P. Johnson came to QRS. He was making his first piano roll, and nervous as hell. They asked me to calm him down, so I talked to him for a while, and set the machine going to record Johnson's first piano roll, 'Carolina Shout,' his own tune."[5] Johnson acknowledged Robinson's instruction in "how to run the piano roll cutter,"[6] but Robinson's description of Johnson as "nervous as hell" seems an exaggeration. Robinson's interview is filled with self-congratulation. By the time Johnson arrived in the QRS recording lab, he already had experience with the world of mainstream, white-controlled music publishing and piano roll manufacturing. He had also negotiated himself a lucrative contract. If he were nervous at all, it may have been due more to his new stature as the first Black man recording rolls for the preeminent roll company, which was big news. Before any rolls were released, a syndicated column in the African American press highlighted that QRS was releasing a roll of W. C. Handy's then very popular tune "Loveless Love," and that it was recorded by their first Black staff recording artist.[7] Advertisements touted Johnson's relationship with the Clef Club. Johnson recorded five rolls in January, but they were not issued until May.[8] Luckey Roberts joined the staff soon after. QRS looked to promote the music of the new African American pianists not only to Black audiences but also to the broader public. They advertised widely, reproducing Johnson's publicity photo in the ads. QRS had manufacturing plants and distributors throughout the United States and internationally, including Buenos Aires, Sydney, and London. QRS continued to build on the success of the rolls by engaging a master arranger.

Jean Lawrence Cook was born on July 14, 1899, in Athens Tennessee. He was a classically trained musician with aspirations of becoming a composer. He studied music at Haines Normal Institute in Augusta, Georgia and, after coming to New York, studied with E. Aldama Jackson.[9] Jackson also taught Johnson, who probably introduced the two. Cook became fascinated with the player piano. He bought a unit he saw advertised in *Etude* magazine for home piano roll making and started experimenting with arranging and embellishing techniques, eventually hoping to interest the roll manufacturers in his work. He recounted his big break, noting, "I came to New York in 1920, and with some homemade rolls under my arm, started making the rounds of different instrument companies looking for a job. My reception was less than enthusiastic until I met James P. Johnson who was just hitting the big time with his music on piano rolls. He was working for QRS and though they didn't show too much interest in the work I had done in my home workshop, they let me fool around with some of Johnson's numbers."[10] Although QRS made no formal offer, the United States Music Company in Chicago showed interest and hired Cook. His rolls for them soon drew some attention. He continued, "Q. R. S. Music Company investigated the success of the rival company, and after finding out that I was one of the main cogs in the wheel, they called on me quick. Finally, on May 1, 1923, I signed a contract with QRS . . ."[11] Although formally an employee of US Music Company until May 1923, Cook had already been doing some arranging for QRS as a sideline. Their advertisements from the year before include rolls "played" by Cook, and the trade journals noted he was under contract as early as March 1922.[12]

It was, however, Johnson's advocacy for Cook at QRS that propelled the career of the most legendary piano roll arranger in the history of the medium. The *Music Trade Review* of April 1922 noted that Johnson's and Cook's rolls were met with "enthusiastic reception," and commented, "Mr. Johnson particularly is recognized as one of the leading negro [sic] exponents of music and incorporates in his interpretation the characteristic negro [sic] influences."[13] Johnson recalled, ". . . my rolls were a sensation overnight."[14] It is not known which if any of Johnson's pre–May 1923 rolls were published with "arrangements" by Cook, although he admits they let him "fool around" with some of them. Durrell Armstrong, who worked with Cook at QRS in the 1950s, notes Cook was clear that he had simulated Fats Waller's style on a series of rolls listed as played by Waller, but as far as Armstrong knew, Cook did little editing of Johnson's rolls.[15] Some of Johnson's earliest rolls, such as "Loveless Love" (QRS 1340) and "Doctor Jazzes Raz-Ma-Taz" (QRS 1473), are clearly embellished with added notes. The extent to which any roll or part is a combination of hand playing or post recording arranging, including the addition of entire sections, remains an area of heated debate amongst scholars of mechanical music reproduction.[16] By

1926, QRS was increasingly criticized by the highbrow music-buying public for its focus on syncopated music in preference to "the better class of music." Their advertising manager noted, "Many people are much concerned over the state of music and of musical culture in the United States, and there are many ready to blame the music roll manufacturer for the present popularity of jazz. We hear criticisms to the effect that the jazz music roll hurts the player business, but the fact is that this popular stuff sells itself."[17]

In early April 1921, Johnson was the featured performer for an affair sponsored by the track team of the St. Christopher Club.[18] Johnson also renewed work with orchestra leader Happy Rhone frequently during this time, including a date on April 22 at the Manhattan Casino. For both appearances, Johnson is promoted as an exclusive QRS artist. He performed with four women pianists, described as his "Four Piano Fiends." Although the intent may have been more for novelty effect, their performance was very well received critically.[19] Also on the bill is William Farrell, Johnson's old partner. Farrell had since teamed with Ike Hatch to form a two-man vaudeville act. The first five Johnson piano rolls recorded in January were released in May: "Carolina Shout," "Eccentricity," "Don't Tell Your Monkey Man," "It Takes Love to Cure the Heart's Disease" (a tune for which Johnson composed the music and wrote the words), and "Loveless Love—A Blues Ballad." "Carolina Shout," a reworking of his 1918 version, had a much wider distribution than the earlier roll and became well known throughout the Northeast and beyond. It is considered the authoritative version of "Carolina Shout," and became the prototype for stride piano, just as "Maple Leaf Rag" had been for ragtime. In June, two remarkable rolls were released by QRS—"Doctor Jazzes Raz-Ma-Taz" and "Roumania." Increasingly, his reputation as a top pianist was a regular item in the press. On June 8, he was the featured musical guest for several hundred attendees for the Mi-Tee Monarch Marching Club of Monarch Lodge No. 45 Elks Ball shirtwaist dance at the New Star Casino, located at 107th Street and Lexington Avenue. He appeared with Fraction's Jazz Kings and was billed as "the well-known piano wizard."[20] On June 12, in a concert arranged by Will Marion Cook at the Winter Garden Theater, Johnson, with an orchestra, accompanied singer/comedienne Gertrude Saunders, then appearing as one of the featured performers in *Shuffle Along*, which had opened only five weeks earlier. *Billboard* noted she was the first African American woman to be featured at the Shubert-owned theater heading up her own act. Johnson, described as "the remarkable pianist," played a piano medley "with wonderful effect."[21] He continued formal piano studies at the Conservatory of Musical Art in Manhattan, earning a certificate for a third-level course in piano in June 1921.[22] Also in June, Johnson and his wife applied for a passport. They were living at 673 Lenox Avenue. His friend and ardent supporter Will Marion Cook witnessed the application, attesting to an exaggerated relationship of twenty years. They planned to travel to England and France, with his stated purpose the study of music. They were scheduled to sail on the *Imperator* on July 4 for a six-month stay. It does not appear they made the trip, because Johnson played at the Manhattan Casino on July 28 in a benefit for the Dressing Room Club, an organization supporting African American actors, authors, composers, musicians, and other theatrical "Allied Professions."[23] They were raising money for a new clubhouse. The organization's stated goals embraced an uplift sentiment, working to "impress the world with the dignity and economic value of the Negro element of the profession," while preserving "to posterity the history of the Negro in theatricals."[24] Johnson claims to have taken more of a leading role with Rhone's group, playing additional Clef Club jobs where bands ranged in size from trios to forty men. Johnson desperately hoped to conduct one of the concerts like his good friend Fred Bryan, but recalled, "In these days the Clef Club used to give big concerts in which all the good musicians played. I was ambitious to conduct one of these concerts and worked hard at it. But I didn't get it, and it broke my heart. I quit the Clef Club and returned to rehearsing my own group." Johnson continued to experiment with different breaks and instrumentation. He copied the "Dixieland" style in his arrangements as an attention-getter. Johnson composed "After Hours," a piece published in 1923, describing it as "a good instrumental that had a blues in the last strain with a slow, sobbing end that was muffled."[25] He took the piece to Columbia and Victor Records, who both rejected it, but he soon had another opportunity to record his first commercially released record.

In August, James P. Johnson accompanied singer Alice Leslie Carter with his group Jimmie Johnson's Jazz Boys. They recorded five sides for the Arto label, the phonograph division of his former piano roll company the Standard Music Roll Company out of Orange, New Jersey. Little is known about Carter. She had been working professionally since 1907, when she toured overseas with Henderson Smith's Fourteen Black Hussars.[26] With her partner Bert Titus, she was playing in Harlem at The Royal Café at 69 West 135th Street during the latter half of 1914, at one point along with the better-known Mattie Hite. Shortly thereafter, she may have moved to Paris and returned to the United States in 1916.[27] Arto had entered the vocal blues recording arena soon after Mamie Smith's success, signing Lucille Hegamin in November 1920. By the next summer, Arto was suffering financial and distribution problems despite deals to press their releases under dime-store labels such as Bell, which was sold by W. T. Grant.[28] In an effort to continue to ride the wave of vocal blues popularity, Carter and Johnson's group recorded another two sides in September and four more in November. Ten of their eleven sides were blues numbers, including some of the most popular blues tunes at that time in the W. C. Handy style of sixteen-bar song form with twelve-bar blues refrains. These included "Dangerous Blues," "Cry Baby Blues," "Aunt Hagar's Children Blues," and "Decatur Street Blues." The Carter sides were pressed on five different labels, including Hytone, promoted as "The Indestructible Phonograph Record Company." Over the next three months, Johnson also recorded with vocalists Eddie Gray and Lavinia Turner. Unfortunately, Johnson cannot be heard on the eleven Carter sides or the Gray side. In large measure, the arrangements on these recordings are likely the sort of things Johnson had been using with his Clef Club groups, a lilting but formal approach similar to his role models Vodery, Europe, W. M. Cook, and Handy. Although the Carter recordings have often been dismissed since Johnson's piano is inaudible, and Carter is an old-style vaudeville belter as a singer, on close listening, Johnson's arrangements often reveal a more adventurous polyphony.[29]

The six sides with Lavinia Turner are another thing entirely. They were made for the US division of the French label Pathé, and Johnson's piano is afforded a much more prominent role. Turner first recorded for Pathé in March with Harlem pianist and Johnson protege Willie Gant, accompanying her with a band. She recorded "Jazz Me Blues" with the Original Dixieland Jazz Band in May for Victor, but the major label was unwilling to gamble with a female blues singer on an interracial recording. Four tunes were recorded in September with Johnson, and he solos on three. In the November session, for the first time on record, he alone accompanies a singer on two tunes, "Watch Me Go" and "You Never Miss a Good Thing Till It's Gone." His debt to Luckey Roberts and Eubie Blake is apparent, but his rhythmic surety and astonishing creativity breaking from ragtime conventions complement Turner's vocal in new ways. Each vocal break is complemented with a unique idea, and his swinging feel propels the collaboration, demonstrating why he was to become the most sought-after accompanist of the "decade of the blues singer." Despite promotion by Pathé of her earlier recording "Can't Get Lovin' Blues" as the "greatest blues record ever made," Turner's vocal style soon fell out of favor. Unlike the blues tunes he recorded with Carter, the Turner sides are popular cabaret songs, three of them written by Original Dixieland Jazz Band pianist and fellow QRS musician J. Russel Robinson. Like Carter, Turner was a cabaret singer. Their vocal styles have the belting nasality needed to project over a crowd, rather than the resonant blues feeling of a Ma Rainey and the gold standard set by Bessie Smith a few years later. Turner made her last records the following year. Little is known about her life. She periodically made stage appearances, including in 1930 as part of an interracial cast in *Lily White* starring the social activist actress Helen Menken. She was a member of the Negro Actors Guild of America and by 1945 was quite sick and confined to Goldwater Memorial Hospital in New York.[30] The Johnson-Turner collaborations were waxed just before financial troubles mounted for American Pathé which, like many other record companies in the early 1920s, succumbed to overextended business operations just as the postwar recession hit. Bankruptcy proceedings ensued for Pathé, and they were successfully reorganized as a purely American company the following year focusing on the low end of the market, initially for department stores, and then dime stores and mail order. One of their new lines, the fifty-cent Perfect label launched in June 1922, included the rerelease of the Johnson-Turner sides.[31]

On the band side "He Took It Away from Me," Johnson alone accompanies Turner half way through the second chorus. He punctuates each break in the vocal with a different rhythmic and melodic statement, often complementing and accentuating the lyric or vocal inflection, a feature that would make him one of the most sought-after accompanists of the decade. Since quitting the Clef Club, he looked to offer "new effects" in his own groups by using the xylophone,[32] which can be heard on "If I Were Your Daddy," an early example of his penchant for incorporating interesting instrumentation. On "When the Rain Turns into Snow," he accompanies Tuner alone for most of the third chorus in what is nothing short of a rollicking, rhythmically complex romp.

In September, Johnson cut his first piano solo on 78 rpm record, his instrumental "Harlem Strut," issued on the Black Swan label. Black Swan was the product of one of the first all-Black-owned and -operated record companies, the Pace Phonograph Corporation. Harry Pace, W. C. Handy's former partner in the publishing firm of Pace and Handy, started the record company in 1921. Pace saw the need to record and promote music by Black musicians. Since Black music by Black performers was swiftly gaining in popularity, the advertisements for Black Swan Records emphasized that its recordings were made by Blacks and not whites attempting to imitate Blacks. Ironically, performances by white artists were nonetheless issued by Pace to fulfill a contractual agreement. In 1923, the Pace Phonograph Corporation expanded and changed its name to the Black Swan Phonograph Company. In April 1924, Black Swan was in serious debt and acquired by Paramount Records. Johnson accompanied singers Trixie Smith and Eddie Gray for Black Swan with his orchestra, but "Harlem Strut" was his only piano solo released by that label. On October 18, 1921, Johnson recorded again for the General Phonograph Corporation on its OKeh label. In 1918, he had recorded a presumably lost test of "Caprice Rag" for the same company. He waxed two more of his own compositions as piano solos, "Keep Off the Grass," and "Carolina Shout." About these two sides the great jazz pianist Dick Wellstood noted, "If he had recorded nothing else, these two sides would have established Johnson as the father of stride piano. All the essentials of his style are present.... What we are hearing is a fascinating example of the transition from ragtime to jazz...."[33] Indeed, the "Carolina Shout" had been in Johnson's arsenal since as early as 1916 if not earlier and comparing the two piano roll renditions already recorded by the time of the OKeh record release demonstrates that transition. By the end of 1921, along with "Harlem Strut," Johnson's three phonograph instrumentals might be considered a series of etudes exemplifying the mature stride piano style.[34] The "Carolina Shout" became the emblematic model for a new style, different from "ragging" music, thus making the OKeh version the first jazz piano solo on record. The origin of the title for "Carolina Shout" is identifiable, but where Johnson came up with "Keep Off the Grass" remains speculative. It may have been a humorous reference since he caps off the recording with the "good evening friends" coda. But Johnson had just left the Clef Club, and a comment by Eubie Blake about entertaining New York's upper crust with engagements arranged through the Club may give us a hint. Although Black musicians were in high demand, racial restrictions applied in many performance spaces, including private homes. Blake said, ". . . we didn't use the Steinway either. It was locked up and covered with velvet and flowers that said, 'Keep off the Grass!' There would always be a rented piano."[35] Perhaps the expression was well-known code for these indignities.

OKeh launched a new record series in August to specifically promote and identify its expanding roster of African American musicians, especially blues singers. They referred to their new line as the "Colored Catalogue." The new series numerically began with 8000. Although Johnson recorded his pairing in October, OKeh kept it in the standard catalogue with a 4000 number.[36] Johnson recorded a band version in August around the same time as the Alice Leslie Carter dates, predating his solo version.[37] No piano is audible on the band version of "Carolina Shout." H. Qualli Clark, owner of the Sphinx Music Publishing Company at 201 W. 136th Street, published an arrangement for orchestra. Clark was an accomplished arranger who had worked with P. G. Lowery and, after arriving in New York in 1914, with Will Vodery and eventually in 1918 with Pace and Handy.[38] Clark composed one of the tunes Johnson recorded with Carter, "You'll Think of Me Blues." The orchestrated version of "Carolina Shout" was publicized as "An Instrumental Fox-Trot" by Clark, perhaps at the urging of Johnson,[39] who was no doubt looking to expand the attraction of the number with the larger public, and a dance orchestration was essential. It is, however, his piano rendering of the tune that has had lasting impact. As jazz pianist and vocal accompanist, Johnson's first contributions to the musical underpinning of the "roaring twenties" had been established.

Johnson traveled up and down the East Coast promoting his piano rolls and records. He was often part of large-scale productions featuring numerous musical acts. Johnson accompanied Happy Rhone to New Jersey for a November 11 "Armistice Night" concert at Plainfield High School that included a "huge array of talent." Also on the bill was blues singer Lucille Hegamin, promoting her Arto recordings.[40] Johnson is noted as playing exclusively for the QRS

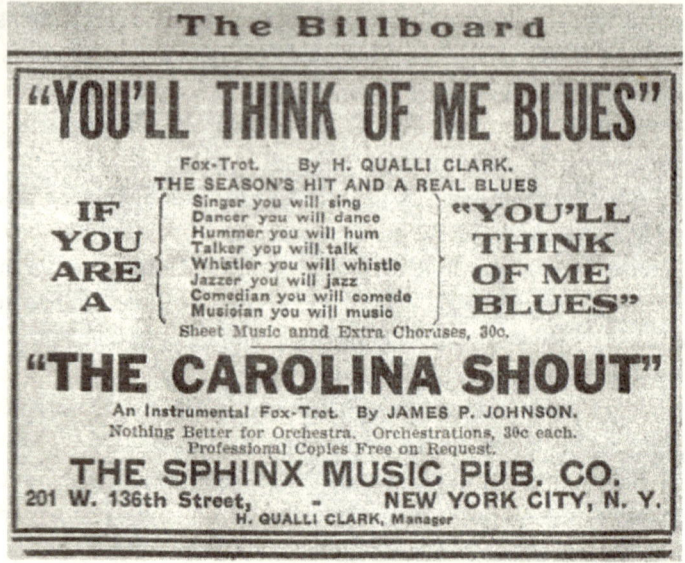

"Carolina Shout" is now thought of primarily as the exemplar of stride piano. In its day, nearly all music was promoted as dance music, as this advertisement from *Billboard* notes. (*The Billboard*, November 5, 1921)

Company, an association by then routinely referenced in his performance notices. A few weeks later he was in Washington, DC, at an event promoted by two local civic organizations whose efforts included sponsoring both small- and large-scale entertainment. J. H. Matthews and George H. Tucker of the "Orientals" and Alonzo Collins and G. Frank Jones of the "Stenographers" put on "The 20th Century Jazz Review" at Convention Hall on November 21, 1921. The *Chicago Defender* noted the featured stars included Hegamin and "J. P. Johnson, piano wizard of New York City." The moniker "piano wizard" by now was used routinely to describe Johnson in performance notices. The *Defender* reviewer listed the local artists who were performing, and as Duke Ellington biographer Mark Tucker observes, "captured the colorful flavor of jazz at the time."[41] Performing were, among others, Gertie Wells and her Jassimba Sextet, "Doc" Perry's Jazz Bandits, [Elmer] Snowden's Eccentric Serenaders, Branson's Hypnotic Arcade Hounds, and Duke Ellington's Wild Cats.

It was a memorable evening for the twenty-two-year-old Edward Kennedy "Duke" Ellington, who recalled:

> My first encounter with James was through the piano rolls, the Q. R. S. rolls. There was a drummer in Washington who told me about them, took me home with him, and played me 'Carolina Shout.' He said I ought to learn it. So how was I going to do it, I wanted to know. He showed

me the way. We slowed the machine and then I could follow the keys going down. I learned it! And how I learned it! I nursed it, rehearsed it. ... Yes, this was the most solid foundation for me. I got hold of some of his other rolls, and they helped me with styling, but "Carolina Shout" became my party piece.

Then James came to Washington to play Convention Hall. It holds maybe four or five thousand people. I was always a great listener. I'm taller on one side than the other from leaning over the piano, listening. This time I listened all night long. After a while my local following started agitating. "You got to get up there and play that piece," they said. "Go on! Get up there and cut him!" So you know, I had to get up there and play it. "Hey, you play that good," James said. We were friends then, and I wanted the privilege of showing him around town, showing him the spots, introducing him to my pals, the best bootleggers, and so on. That, naturally, meant more leaning on the piano. Afterwards, we were fast friends, and James never forgot.[42]

Tucker points out Johnson may have been in Washington before this, and he was back again on January 2, 1922. Johnson was clearly popular with the Black community in the District. J. A. Jackson in *Billboard* reported, "James P. Johnson, the piano wizard, of New York, who records exclusively for the Q. R. S. rolls, was the stellar attraction at a big concert in Convention Hall, Washington, DC."[43] The event was again sponsored by the "Stenographers," and concluded with a dance for the three thousand attendees. Johnson and Ellington likely spent time together again, and the next year were more regularly associated when Ellington moved to New York. For the next twenty years, the Ellington piano style was the stride piano he learned from Johnson—the style that defined jazz age rhythms, the style distributed widely on Johnson rolls and records, the style that influenced a generation of pianists—and, for many like Ellington, a style that influenced their approach to orchestral arranging. Willie Gant recalled the absolute necessity of having Johnson's recordings available, noting, "If you came through my house, or anybody's home, and if they didn't have Jimmy Johnson's records or piano rolls, well nobody would stay. He was a big wheel. He was the biggest thing that God gave."[44]

By the beginning of 1922, although Johnson had been accompanying singers for nearly a decade, his work the previous year had solidified his renown as a vocal accompanist. On January 20, 1922, the first Annual Concert and Ball of the 15th Infantry was held at the Manhattan Casino. Still holding their military ranks as lieutenants, Will Vodery and Noble Sissle led the sixty-seven-member band once fronted by the late James Reese Europe. Sissle sang some of his own songs from the smash hit *Shuffle Along* that was still running on Broadway. Several

(*New York Age*, January 21, 1922)

thousand people attended, with hundreds filling the dance floor. At midnight, a blues singing contest got underway. The previous year had seen a race to capitalize on the dramatic success of Mamie Smith. While the record companies marketed comparisons of their divas in print, the blues singing contest may have been the first heavily publicized, formal, head-to-head competition as a public exhibition. Six singers were scheduled to perform, but Edith Wilson and Mary Safford apparently did not participate. The four who squared off included Trixie Smith, the "Southern Nightingale," singing her composition "Trixie Blues" (some papers reported her tune as "Stingaree Blues"); Alice Leslie Carter, the "International Blues Singer," singing "Decatur Street Blues"; Lucille Hegamin, "Harlem's Favorite," singing "Arkansas Blues"; and Daisy Martin, "The Girl with a Smile," singing "If You Don't Believe I Love You (Look What A Fool I've Been)." "'Jimmie' Johnson's Syncopated Jazz Orchestra of QRS Fame"[45] (also referred to as his "Six Syncopaters") accompanied the singers. Carter had recorded with Johnson, and he had certainly accompanied Hegamin during their tour events together. It is possible, in the musical crucible that Harlem was fast becoming, that Smith and Martin had also been backed by Johnson at one time or another. All four of the contestants were seasoned vaudeville singers and performers who had traveled cross country for at least a decade prior to this event.

The *Chicago Defender* reported that the judges would include Irene Castle of the famous dance team, Irving Berlin, Al Jolson, and Bert Williams.[46] Of these, only Castle appeared, but Governor Nathan Miller made an appearance, and a last-minute judge included the former president of the Board of Aldermen also holding his military rank (and future mayor of New York City), Major Fiorello H. La Guardia. Colonel Charles W. Anderson and the editor of the *New York Age* Fred R. Moore served as the other judges. After each contestant sang, Sissle led them back to the stage for the audience to register their appreciation. The judges took note and were charged with gauging the audience preferences.[47] Smith and Hegamin closely vied for the top spot, but in the end Trixie Smith edged out the others for the silver loving cup top prize.[48] She, too, would soon be accompanied by Johnson on record.

Chapter 9

HARLEM STRIDE PIANO

> Analyzing hot piano playing like this seems to reduce it to
> such simplicity but executing it amounts to genius.
> —MURIEL REGER, *JAZZ QUARTERLY*

The term *Harlem stride piano* to denote the style played by Johnson and those influenced by him was applied many years after its wide dissemination that began in 1921 with the "Carolina Shout." Some consider stride piano to be a type of ragtime, the final extension of the East Coast style epitomized by Eubie Blake and Luckey Roberts. Indeed, when the term *stride* was mentioned to Eubie Blake, he replied, "My God, what won't they call ragtime next?"[1] In large part this view is based on the retention of the oom-pah left hand found frequently in both genres. Willie "The Lion" Smith, in his inimitable manner, claims ignorance of the term (beyond his comment that "shouts are stride piano"): "The writers who make up titles for the ways of playing music have called our piano style here on the eastern seaboard Harlem Stride Piano. I am not very sure I know what they are talking about. I do know how we played here in the east. A good pianist had to be able to play with both hands, performing in perfect unison. It was like learning to walk correctly. Some people just lope along while others walk like they are crippled, while a good walker goes forth with balance and dignity."[2] Smith's analogy with gait implies the term was probably used to describe the motion of the left hand, appearing to walk or "stride" up and down the lower end of the keyboard. Smith prescribes correctly that this walking motion must be carried off with "balance and dignity." Before the music was widely referred to as stride, its utilitarian functions were incorporated into the nomenclature, with such terms as parlor social or rent party piano used to describe the style.³ Some simply called it Harlem piano.

The first documented use of the term *stride* appears on a recording from December 4, 1935, by Fats Waller and his band playing "I Got Rhythm." Waller is joined on this record by another fine pianist fully conversant with the style, Hank Duncan. After the band plays and Fats sings, Duncan launches into a solo with Fats commenting, "Oh, there's brother Duncan. He's getting smart, too. Look at that cat stridin' over there. Looks like he's trying to get something from me." A band member encourages Duncan, saying, "Show him how to swing, Hanky." In what may be the first recorded depiction of a piano cutting contest, Fats retorts with "Oh I ain't gonna have that. I've got him son. He belongs to me. He's mine. There he is." Fats then plays his solo in response.⁴ Pianist Joe Turner claimed Johnson first applied the term, noting, "James P. Johnson called it stride. I don't know why. I guess because it's just like striding down the avenue."⁵ The term was more widely encountered by 1944. Pianist and newspaper editor Dan Burley offers a definition of "striding" in his 1944 treatise *Dan Burley's Original Handbook of Harlem Jive*, as "playing ten key stretches in bass on piano." Here Burley is referring to the left hand substituting a stretch of an interval of a tenth for the more routine octave found in ragtime. In the same year, the term stride piano can be found in *Metronome* describing the non-boogie woogie playing of Freddy Slack (ironically best known for his boogie woogie style) on one chorus with his orchestra on a tune called "Furlough Fling." The next month, the magazine rightly but disparagingly used the term in reviewing a Johnson recording.⁶ Later in the year, *Metronome* lauded Alberta Simmons, Johnson's old teacher from Hell's Kitchen, commenting, "Alberta Simmons, from down in the Jungles, could beat the average man's striding."⁷

Another term for the predominant "oom-pah" of the left hand came into more common usage around the same time, referring to it as a "Boston." Pianist Herbie Nichols, who for most of the 1940s was a regular columnist for several Harlem-based newspapers and music periodicals, used the term in print in August 1944 when writing about Thelonious Monk. Although Monk was already gaining attention for his unusual modern approach, Nichols expresses his personal preference for Monk as a stride player, noting, "Thelonious Monk is an oddity among piano players. This particular fellow is the author of the weirdest rhythmical melodies I've ever heard. They are very great too. (Don't ever praise Monk too much or he'll let you down.) But I will say that I'd rather hear him play a 'boston' than any other pianist. His sense of fitness is uncanny."⁸ Dick Wellstood referred to the "boston" as an oom-pah accompaniment behind a band or other musicians rather than as a synonym for stride in general. The origin of this term is even more obscure than stride, although there are hints from a tune in Johnson's ill-fated show *Sugar Hill* from 1931 that closed after only eleven performances on Broadway. One of the dance numbers titled "Boston" was scored to include a string accompaniment playing alternating quarter notes and quarter rests on various beats of each measure. He subtitles the section "stop-time chorus," but the effect is that of a back-beat infused, oom-pah stride accompaniment.[9] While the score for *Sugar Hill* was orchestrated by William Grant Still, no doubt Johnson had specific ideas he wanted realized for this number. A few years later, Johnson, to indicate that the third movement of his *Harlem Symphony* should be rendered with this oom-pah support, writes "Boston Effect" on the score.[10] It is not likely the term is related to the original Boston popularized as a social dance in the early 1900s which was in waltz (3/4) time. Johnson's dance was in 4/4 time, like a fox-trot. Although Johnson's "Boston" dance from *Sugar Hill* may not have amounted to much since the show failed so quickly and the tune was never published, using the title as descriptor for an oom-pah accompaniment seems to have stuck.

In the 1950s, music writers began to assess the style more critically, offering technical descriptions that focused in more detail on the left hand. "The stride effect is produced by the left hand hitting a single note on the first and third beats and a chord of three or four notes on the second and fourth beats" was a commonly cited definition, but does little more than describe the mechanics of an oom-pah.[11] A marginally better description a few years later includes the role of the right hand: "Stride piano is characterized chiefly by an oom-pah left hand (a two-beat seesaw, whose ends are a powerful mid-keyboard chord and a weaker single note played an octave or a tenth below) and by an arabesque of right-hand chords and arpeggios, fashioned in counter-rhythms."[12] James P. Johnson has also stressed the importance of both hands in making a distinction between ragtime and stride, noting "The difference between stride and traditional piano ragtime was in the structure and the precise bass played in a rag style by the left hand, while the characteristic strides were performed by the right hand."[13] Johnson's definition, attributing the stride patterns to the right hand, might at first seem to confuse the analysis. However, as pianist Mike Lipskin, a student of Willie "The Lion" Smith, has noted, the essential sound of stride piano derives from the interplay between the right and left hand, not one hand alone. An array of pianistic devices in both hands create "various critical rhythmic tension and releases," the underpinnings of "a rocking, swing beat."[14] Stride piano often retains the oom-pah also found in ragtime, but the overemphasis on this feature has clouded an appreciation for the complex rhythmic interplay between the two hands. It is this rhythmic tension that propels stride out of the lilt of ragtime and into the swing of jazz. Even the great ragtime documentarian and activist Rudi Blesh noted the striking rhythmic differences between the "Eastern shout" and "classic Midwestern ragtime," writing, "The two beats set up far different rhythmic tensions with the conventional ragtime bass. For this reason, a shout is infused with a different spirit and has a different emotional effect from the classic ragtime of Scott Joplin and the other Missouri masters."[15] Documenting this transition has been hampered to some degree by the dearth of solo piano recordings from the late 1910s and early 1920s.[16] A closer look at some of these rhythmic tensions helps illuminate why they sound so different.

Stride piano and ragtime share the traditional "oom-pah" marchlike pattern of alternating strong and weak beats of the bass rhythm played by the left hand. The strong beats are thought of as the "oom" beats, and the weak beats are thought of as the "pah" beats. In most ragtime, the oom beats consist of single notes or octaves. The stride players introduced more complex combinations. In stride playing, the oom or strong beat may include single notes, octaves, broken octaves, tenths, broken tenths, and tenths played with other interval notes. While there is virtually no written evidence of tenths in ragtime, Johnson noted a number of New York pianists were using tenths before the terms jazz and stride were adopted. In a melodic reduction of stride bass lines, the strong oom notes tend to move in scalar and chromatic patterns that set up a melodic line of their own, complementing or contrasting with the melody line being played by the right hand. In stride, the melodic line of the oom beats are supported by more frequent chord changes for the pah beats. Stride is best played with near equal emphasis of ooms and pahs, a characteristic of the "balance and dignity" referred to by Willie "The Lion" Smith.

Although the placement of an "oom" and a "pah" falling on the expected strong and weak beats of the measure is common in stride playing, other combinations of strong and weak beats are frequently used by stride players to disrupt the regular two- or four-beat pulse. This rhythmic disruption often gives the impression of having turned the beat around, introducing a triple (3/4) rhythmic feel in the midst of a duple (2/4 or 4/4) performance. This left-hand device, known as "change-step"[17] or "backbeat," is a notable bass characteristic employed by most stride pianists. The wide stretch between the oom bass notes and pah chords gives stride its full sound, and enables the player to activate the overtones of the piano by specific pedaling techniques.[18] Louis Mazetier, a jazz pianist fluent in many styles and the stride style in particular, remarks that the earliest stride masters increased the distance between the oom and pah beats by playing the pah cord with inversions higher up on the keyboard, enhancing the feeling of swing, and further distinguishing the sound of stride from ragtime.[19] Traversing the distance between the bass note and chord in the course of playing stride creates a strong feeling of propulsion. This is especially noticeable when single notes are used in the bass, since the momentum is maintained with more of a springing than pounding feeling. The various bass patterns and countermelodies employed by the left hand give it a more independent feel. As one writer notes, when "the left hand began to develop its own cohesive line, the beat began to be felt independently between the two hands."[20] Pianist Henry Francis notes, "The oom-pah-oom-pah left hand is merely necessary, not sufficient, for stride piano. No ordinary left hand will do, for stride must swing. Rather, if it does not swing, it is not stride."[21]

While the rhythmic phrasing of the left hand can often create very complex patterns, the time of the performance must always be kept by the left hand. Dick Wellstood, a second-generation master of stride piano, reminds us of this important function: "To a non-performer, the left-hand dominance probably seems either unimportant or self-evident, but it is the crux of a successful stride performance. If, in the heat of battle, the time switches to the right hand (because perhaps of a series of heavily accented figures), leaving the left hand merely to wag, then the momentum goes out the window. The left hand must always be the boss and leave the right hand free to use whatever vocalized inflections the player desires." He expands on the notion of the right hand in stride playing, echoing the statements of Johnson and Lipskin about the importance of the interplay between the hands, observing, "... the characteristic rhythms of stride are provided by the right hand, not the left. It is possible to play an otherwise impeccable stride bass and ruin it by playing inappropriate right hand patterns. By pulling and tugging at the rhythms of the left, the right hand provides the swing."[22] Francis builds on this analysis, noting, "... [W]hile the striding left hand defines the beat, the right hand leads or lags it and in so doing creates in effect another beat of the same tempo but displaced in time." The right hand is free to approach the beat, established by the left hand, from any rhythmic angle: before it, with it, or after it. The use of riffs, triplet figures, chromatic runs, and dramatic register changes reaching the upper end of the keyboard, and especially the call-and-response pattern adopted from the ring shout, create a rhythmic tension distinct from ragtime. The stride right hand weaves in and around the pulsating left hand, which itself is shifting rhythmic emphasis from a two to three beat feeling and back again. Subtle phrasing shifts began to loosen the pulse of the right hand, and Johnson was at the forefront of this transition to a more swinging feel by loosening the strict "straight" eighth note at one rhythmic extreme, and smoothing out the halting dotted eighth at the other. All of this combines to create "perhaps the most earthy non-blues piano style in the history of jazz."[23] The expressiveness of the blues enters into stride playing through use of touch, attack, dynamics, note "bending" with clusters and other devices giving the music an expressive quality simulating vocal or other instrumental effects.

Improvisation, along with swing, is a defining feature of most jazz. Blake, Smith, Johnson and others frequently comment on the individuality of their obscure colleagues from the early part of the twentieth century. Analysis is hampered by there being virtually no recorded examples, although early piano rolls of the 1910s help corroborate the notion of a rudimentary improvisation. The classic ragtime composers in particular frowned on deviating from the score by adding notes, a tactic seen as sloppy and imprecise. Both Scott Joplin and Artie Matthews admonished players not to "fake" the music. The stride pianists, however, incorporated "improvisation within a broad compositional frame of reference."[24] But they are often criticized as a group as not being great improvisers. Wellstood himself observes, "The idea with them was to compose an original piece or perhaps make an arrangement of current show tunes, and then to wow the folks with it, night after night."[25] The musical vocabulary that came to characterize stride piano incorporated a wealth of material from which the pianists drew. These elements in themselves provided the framework for individualized interpretations, and so it is notable that the various stride pianists can be distinguished by their individual style.

Johnson developed a particular skill at variation. His early piano rolls reflect this, as he rarely incorporates typical ragtime devices despite his substantial admiration for the work of Joplin and others. Most accounts of his contemporaries highlight how Johnson's playing set him apart from other pianists. He had a consistent ability to work out original and inventive ideas. In his own words, "I could think of a trick a minute." The technical virtuosity he had developed enabled him to project a broad array of variety from the shout dances, concert music, and other sources. The rhythmic soul of stride piano derives from the shout dances. Adapting the short rhythmic statements of the shouts into instrumental form was one route toward the development of the riff. Certain attributes of Johnson's playing make it distinctive. He took advantage of the upper end of the keyboard, where his riff figures take on a ringing or chiming character. His touch varied from light and springy in the upper register to rather heavy-handed. Johnson was a master at devising new and startling rhythmic fragments with which he reshaped a tune. Several scholars have noted Johnson's use of such figures. "Many of his [Johnson's] 'melodies' are essentially rhythmic figures that happen to have pitches attached to them," notes Gunther Schuller.[26] Newberger notes his ". . . improvised figures gravitate about small discrete snatches from the melody."[27] Wellstood observes, "He keeps repeating little figures or riffs, especially ones that center around one particular note, so that the momentum builds through repetition over changing harmonies."[28] He goes on to offer a fitting metaphor, describing Johnson's approach as "an almost architectural way of handling rhythm, of placing pulses like building blocks, and a wonderfully subtle manner of allowing different rhythmic conceptions to exist simultaneously in both hands."[29] The "Carolina Shout" recordings include most of these devices and constitute the musical vocabulary that became the stride style. With them, Johnson increases tension and forward pull throughout the five distinct strains. From a compositional standpoint, the use of riffs, shuffle rhythms, call-and-response patterns, and other devices are worked into what jazz theory scholar Henry Martin calls a thematic block that serves as the framework for Johnson's future performances.[30]

Johnson's crystalline, staccato attack of precisely placed off-beat rhythmic figures played by his right hand pull and tug at the regular pulse of the left, propelling the listener along. At times the right hand seems uneven, but this is merely a Johnson deception. Johnson was very proud of the accuracy of his playing. "Listen to Jimmy Johnson today—and watch his fingers..." writes one observer; "... abandon and rubato there are, in abundance; but every finger at every note knows just where it is going. The blending of the improvisatory spirit with the precision of the virtuoso makes for a delicious uncertainty that at no moment slips out of control."[31] Overall, his playing reveals the "... crisp delicacy and incomparable imagination of a playing that, like the ring-shout, sang while it danced," noted Rudi Blesh, who frequently sponsored Johnson in performance and on record.[32] In many instances, Johnson seems to unleash these features more boldly when caught in "live" settings (radio broadcasts, concerts, private recordings, and so on) than were captured in the recording studio. Critics, writing while he was alive and in his prime, noted this, and encouraged firsthand observation in person rather than only through studio recordings.

Some writers have overemphasized the comments by Johnson, Blake, and Smith of their use of breaks, concert effects, and other novelty elements. These critics incorrectly assign these devices as defining features of the stride style. They are not. They are more appropriately thought of as part of the broad performance practices of ragtime and early jazz, before the music migrated more toward an art music rather than as a popular medium. However, even in this early period, the compositional arm of Joplin and others with classic ragtime, and the works of Blake, Luckey Roberts, and Johnson, highlight the serious intent of their work product. The "Carolina Shout," in fact, is an art music transformation of vernacular and cultural ritual devoid of novelty and triviality. Appreciating its full essence requires performance. Johnson's recordings demonstrate this, in addition to his ability to improvise on them as evidenced by the differences heard in the January 1921 piano roll and the October 1921 78 rpm recording. Similarly, while stride piano executed in its most codified form is a vibrant, identifiable idiom, the underlying force of the stride style, and the root of its longstanding impact, is the tension and release created by the rhythmic phrasing. This distinguishes it from other idiomatic styles such as boogie woogie and may at least in part explain why many of the stride pianists did not have much use for boogie-woogie.

During the 1920s, Johnson was broadly acknowledged as the piano king. Reed player Garvin Bushell, who regularly worked with Johnson, notes, "James P., due to the influence of Abba Labba and his own capacity, was one of the few great pianists in New York. . . . When you heard James P. at his best, that was Abba Labba, except that James P., who had studied, played with a little more finesse and taste." Bushell was well aware of the impact Johnson's piano rolls were having, and noted, "When Ellington came to New York with Elmer Snowden's band, he was playing like James P. He'd apparently heard the QRS rolls."[33] Pianist Joe Turner, from Baltimore, recalled the first time Johnson's name was mentioned to him: "Frank [Johnson] was the first one, too, who mentioned the name of James P. Johnson to me, making clear that James P. was known, in fact, as the greatest jazz pianist in the world. That happened in 1923."[34] New Orleans bassist Pops Foster compared Jelly Roll Morton's style to Johnson's playing, observing, "It didn't swing like most jazz and wasn't up to date like James P. Johnson's." He also compares Willie "The Lion" Smith, stating, "Willie could play in more keys than anyone except James P."[35] Bushell adds, "Willie 'The Lion' played more ragtime than James P. Johnson. James P. was cleaner and more inventive, as those early QRS rolls demonstrate. He played things that were very close to what pianists in Ohio and the West were doing. He was getting away too from the ragtime of Joplin, adding to what he retained, and expressing himself."[36]

Any pianist who made their way to New York during the twenties could not avoid the impact of Johnson's style, including unlikely musicians such as New Orleans pianist Walter "Fats" Pichon. He told an interviewer many years after the fact, "Like all the other pianists in New York during that period, my playing was strongly influenced by that grand gentleman, James P. Johnson."[37] Ethel Waters offers her observation on Johnson's influence, relating "I was learning a lot in Harlem about music and the men up there who play it best. All the licks you hear, now as then, originated with musicians like James P. Johnson. And I mean all of the hot licks that ever came out of Fats Waller and the rest of the hot piano boys. They are just faithful followers and protégés of that great man, Jimmy Johnson." When Harry Pace pressured Waters to undertake a tour in the fall of 1921 to promote her and his Black Swan record label, she was irritated that Black Swan music director Fletcher Henderson was to accompany her. His more conservative style, the result of his classical piano training didn't have "the damn-it-to-hell bass, and that chump-chump stuff that real jazz needs," she said. After numerous arguments with him, she devised a crash course for Henderson: "All during the tour I kept nagging at him. I said he couldn't play as I wanted him to. When we reached Chicago, I got some piano rolls that Jimmy Johnson had made and pounded out each passage to Henderson. To prove to me he could do it, Fletch began to practice. He got so perfect, listening to James P. Johnson play on the player piano that he could press down the keys as the roll played never missing a note. Naturally, he began to be identified with that kind of music, which isn't his kind at all."[38]

Before amplification, pianists had to compete with other players, dancers, rowdy crowds, and poor acoustics. They developed performance practices that were intended to be heard and marveled at. Teddy Wilson commented on the power of the pianists who influenced him and how they developed their styles, noting, "[Earl] Hines came along before microphones, and so he played with great strength and power. He spread his right hand out to an octave so that he got the whole hand behind his fingers. James P. Johnson did the same thing, and I've seen him play so hard that the piano actually bounced."[39] Hines is usually acknowledged for developing his "trumpet" style of right-hand figurations and veering away from the ragtime/stride tradition. Although his formative years were in Pittsburgh, he too was influenced by Johnson's stride style, saying, "That's what I learned to do first!"[40]

Virtuosity was an important component of the stride player's musical expression. One critic noted, "For Johnson and the other most advanced New York pianists, as for Liszt, Alkan, Chopin and the other Romantic piano composers almost a century before, the point of virtuosity was not the chances it offered for display but that it was a catalyst, a means of extending the instrument's scope and hence their music's range of expression. The audience could be dazzled if it liked, yet what mattered to the pianists was bringing fresh resources—rather literally—into play."[41] Stride piano need not be, and is not always, a freewheeling, breakneck avalanche of sound. In fact, subtlety, nuance, inflection, and, as Willie "The Lion" Smith used to say, "beautification" were as or more important. At its most aggressive, it surges furiously like a raging bull or a barreling freight train. But it can also be delicately expressive, proving that swing and lyricism need not be mutually exclusive. Johnson, along with the other accomplished pianists in New York, make up the first generation of true jazz virtuosos. Johnny Guarnieri, an avowed Waller disciple and exceptional pianist who mastered the stride style, noted in an interview, "After James P. Johnson had written his 'Carolina Shout,' he was regarded as the father of the style. Maybe James P. Johnson deserves the most credit if you talk to the old people."[42] Pianist Billy Taylor, who adopted a catholic view of the jazz piano tradition as both a player and academic over his long career, had heard the early greats and concluded, "James P. Johnson: He was the greatest stride piano player I ever heard."[43] There is sufficient primary source material with early recordings, printed sheet music, and especially piano rolls to conclude that the essence of stride piano and its break from classic, advanced, and novelty ragtime was Johnson's innovation. He certainly "borrowed" from his outstanding predecessors including Blake, Roberts, Bryan, Abba Labba, and the other obscure ticklers he encountered. But it was Johnson who most completely melded and enhanced the nascent tensions in the styles of these other players

Although his original contract term had lapsed by the end of 1924, Johnson was still clearly the preeminent piano roll artist for QRS. With references from him, QRS added his teacher Luckey Roberts, his student Fats Waller, his publisher Clarence Williams, and his arranger J. Lawrence Cook. (Courtesy of the Afro-American Newspapers Archives, November 22, 2024)

into a new, identifiable conception that moved the rhythmic center of gravity, and represents ground zero for the jazz piano tradition.

Schuller contends that "the solo piano style Johnson brought to its finest flowering was made obsolete by orchestral developments in jazz...."[44] Johnson's style, however, fostered many of these orchestral developments, most notably the application of tension and release using off-the-beat contrasts and other devices, as well as the "thematic block" structural approach. The case seems clear when one considers that many of the leaders of New York orchestral jazz were stride pianists themselves, most notably Duke Ellington and Count Basie. Stride piano was often referred to as "orchestral piano," so the leap from keyboard to orchestration wasn't a big one. Further, with such a statement, Schuller fails to acknowledge the notion of a continuous solo jazz piano tradition, built on Johnson's innovations. One can easily follow this legacy through generations of subsequent pianists such as Fats Waller, Duke Ellington, Count Basie, Art Tatum, Erroll Garner, Thelonious Monk, Jaki Byard, and many others. Obsolete is the wrong word, as the adoption and transformation of the foundational rhythmic voice of stride piano by this group of pianists attests.

Chapter 10

JAMES P. AND FATS WALLER

> Some little people has music in them, but Fats, he was all music,
> and you know how big he was.
> —JAMES P. JOHNSON

The "Carolina Shout" had particular influence on mostly African American pianists, notably but not exclusively in the Northeast. It "was a best-seller immediately [after] it was issued and quickly became the popular hit of the day in the race market," with Johnson "quickly [becoming] their leading race artist," recalled Ed Kirkeby, who would famously manage Fats Waller in the 1930s.[1] For this up-and-coming generation of pianists, Johnson's new sound was an approach different from the ragtime that dominated until that time. And they had best learn it. There was a distinct advantage to learning a piece from a piano roll rather than from a phonograph recording, which at that time could not be slowed down without distorting the music. A roll can be slowed down without changing the pitch of the notes, and a piece could be learned by following the keys as they are depressed in slow motion. Many pianists learned to play Johnson's "Carolina Shout" and other tunes by placing their hands into the correct position of the depressed keys as the roll advanced, the approach used by Duke Ellington and Johnson's most notable student, Thomas "Fats" Waller. Waller would ultimately gain worldwide fame with his ebullient personality and comic showmanship, features that masked his thorough mastery of Johnson's stride piano style.

Thomas Wright Waller was born in New York City in 1904. His father, Edward Martin Waller, was a minister and eventually became an associate pastor of Harlem's most famous church, Abyssinian Baptist. The congregation was founded in downtown Manhattan in 1808 and moved several times including to Greenwich Village and eventually to Hell's Kitchen at 242 West 40th Street where it was located at the time of Waller's birth. His mother, Adeline, was also religious and encouraged her son to play hymns and other church music, since he had taken to music at an early age. By 1920, Fats Waller (a nickname applied to him from elementary school days) had developed limited but sufficient proficiency on both piano and organ to play the film accompaniments at the Lincoln Theater. The man responsible for introducing Johnson and Waller was a fellow Harlem pianist, Russell Brooks. Waller was a friend and schoolmate of Brooks's younger brother Wilson, so Russell had a passing acquaintance with Waller, who was very anxious to learn the new music developing in Harlem. Waller approached Brooks most likely sometime in late 1920 while Brooks was playing at a dance on Lenox Avenue and 140th Street. The "dance hall" was merely a tent and Waller had no trouble sneaking in under a flap and talking to Brooks on the bandstand. Waller confessed his desire to learn to play rags and shouts. Brooks did not consider himself to be a teacher and half-heartedly promised to arrange an introduction to a friend of his who might be able to help, James P. Johnson. Johnson's reputation was already great, and Waller idolized him as Johnson had idolized older players in his youth. Waller raced out of the tent elated. Before he could escape cleanly, he managed to catch his foot in a supporting rope and brought down the whole tent. Neither Waller nor Brooks followed through on a meeting with Johnson, and nothing came of it.[2]

Waller's life changed dramatically with the death of his mother Adeline from a massive stroke on November 10, 1920.[3] Waller was particularly close to his mother and was devastated by her death. He had always been on poor terms with his father and argued bitterly with him after his mother's passing. He left home and went to stay with his friend Wilson Brooks. Brooks's mother recognized Waller's talent and had some sympathy for his aspirations since her own son Russell was a musician. She tried to soften Edward Waller's rigid and stifling control over his son. A compromise was struck, and Waller's father registered no objections to his son's new residence with the Brooks's, which became permanent. The Brooks family had a player piano, an instrument Waller had never worked with.[4] By the late spring of 1921, the QRS rolls of James P. Johnson, and soon after Luckey Roberts, became available and were acquired by the Brooks family. Waller began to learn them and often practiced late into the night. Adman, impresario, and jazz concert MC Ernie Anderson recalled Waller's dedication to studying Johnson's rolls:

> Fats's easy virtuosity was breathtaking. No musician could ever resist his graceful flowing improvisation. It was hard to believe that such talent could have evolved without the customary academic training.

He insisted that he learned the rudiments by studying the movement of the keys of a player piano as James P. Johnson's piano roll of "Carolina Shout" turned. His ambition to play like that inspired a relentless determination. No one will ever know how many days, nights, weeks, months, he sat in study at that keyboard as that roll revolved. In the end he played it exquisitely and he played it that night as I listened. The fact is he continued to play it as long as he lived. It became one of his show stoppers.[5]

Russell, who had since married and moved out, heard Waller playing Johnson's "Carolina Shout" one day during a stop home to visit his family. This rekindled Brooks's interest in the youngster's music. He remembered his earlier promise and soon mentioned the boy to Johnson.[6]

Johnson knew of Fats Waller as the organ player at the Lincoln but did not know him personally. He recalled Russell Brooks's introduction:

A friend of mine who used to hang out with me—his brother used to bring Fats to his house—he and Fats went to school together. My friend came around one day and told me about this Waller kid who was coming to their house to play the piano. So I went down there—they lived on 131st St.—and he played a couple of things. He had fervor—he was the son of a preacher, you know—but he didn't have any swing then.

My friend's father said Fats had to stop coming there because he worked nights and couldn't sleep with all the noise going on every afternoon. I was living with my sister at 267 W. 140th Street. She had a piano and I brought mine there, too. Then I took Fats home. I'd get on one piano, he'd get on the other, and we'd work together. This went on for a couple of years, steady. He picked up all the stomps and rags I knew and that walkin' bass, too.[7]

Waller's son Maurice relayed how he had heard the story of the legendary meeting from all three pianists, and, in what is likely paraphrased dialogue, tells of his father's reaction to the first meeting:

I've heard the story of that encounter between my father and James P. hundreds of times from both of them, and from Russell Brooks.

"The first thing I noticed," dad told me, "was that Jimmy had two pianos, a baby grand and an upright. I never played on a baby grand before." He sat in the parlor in awe of the man, his home, and his pianos, waiting for James P. to make his appearance. Johnson was only twenty six, a mere ten years older than Dad, and already had a vast reputation.

"At first James P. didn't say much. He just let me play. Then he'd tell me to do this, or try that, and I did. Before I knew it, he was sitting on a stool next to me, making that piano rock. He'd play trills and strong bass figurations. He taught me more in an afternoon than I had learned in ten years."

But what most surprised the student was that James P. kept on emphasizing the importance of scales, pointing out that the root of Fats' difficulties was his inability to move adeptly through those same rudiments that Miss Perry had stressed ten years earlier. Miss Perry's instructions were one thing, but James P. Johnson's were like the law of God.[8]

As his private student, Johnson taught Waller the essence of stride piano, introduced him to other great New York musicians, and made it possible for Waller to record his first piano rolls and phonograph records. Through Johnson's tutelage, Waller became the third pianist in what has been referred to as the triumvirate of great Harlem stride players: Johnson, Willie "The Lion" Smith, and Waller. The Johnson household became a second home-away-from-home for Waller, with Lillie Mae Johnson, his surrogate mother, making sure that he did not lose too much sleep practicing the piano. She gave him his first pair of long trousers. She recalled a slightly different version of their meeting:

> Right after James P. heard Fats Waller playing the pipe organ, he came home and told me, "I know I can teach that boy." Well, from then on it was one big headache for me. Fats was seventeen, and we lived on 140th Street, and Fats would bang on our piano till all hours of the night—sometimes two, three, four o'clock in the morning. I would say to him, "Now go on home—or haven't you got a home?"
>
> But he'd come every day and my husband would teach. Of course, you know the organ doesn't give you a left hand and that's what James P. had to teach him.[9]

Ed Kirkeby recounts in his biography of Waller many of the same stories. The "Carolina Shout" was the test piece, and he noted, "It was a show piece and his great stand-by at parties for years, and it was lifted and borrowed by countless others in their time. But although others played this piece, the buoyant stride which James P. applied to its performance and his great technique made him absolutely invincible."[10] In late 1921 or early 1922, Waller won a talent contest at Harlem's Roosevelt Theater by playing "Carolina Shout," the result of regular lessons with Johnson, practice with the piano rolls, and his own burgeoning pianistic buoyancy.[11] Indeed, Russell Brooks later told Maurice Waller after hearing his father, ". . . maybe I should take lessons from James P.

I never saw anyone improve so much in such a short time. I couldn't believe this was the same Fats Waller who slept on the sofa in my mother's parlor and practiced fingering on the player piano."[12]

Johnson made sure Waller was properly introduced and exposed to the other great pianists in Harlem. The most notable was Willie "The Lion" Smith, who had established a formidable reputation. He was the featured pianist at Leroy Wilkins's club, still a favorite hangout for the Black celebrities of the day. Smith recalled his initial encounters with Fats Waller:

> James P. Johnson brought him down one Sunday afternoon. We were all dressed in full-dress suits and tuxedos and in comes this guy with a greasy suit on, walks down to the bandstand, and says, 'Hello there, Lion, what do you say?' He made me furious. I turned around to Jimmy and said, 'Get that guy down, because he looks filthy. Get them pants pressed,' I said. 'There's no excuse for it.' From that day on, I called him Filthy.
>
> So he sat down until I got finished and when I got finished he was insistent, very persistent. He insisted he wanted to play Jimmy's "Carolina Shout" and when I got through he sat down and played the "Shout" and made Jimmy like it and me like it. From then on it was Thomas Fats Waller.
>
> I gave him a listen and made my famous prediction: I said to James P. Johnson, who was in the house again that night, "Watch out, Jimmy, he's got it. He's a piano-playing cub!"[13]

A short time after, Smith left Leroy's and Johnson arranged to have Waller take his place. However, Waller would now have to accompany singers, a new challenge that frightened him. With the help of James P. and Lillie Mae Johnson, who was one of the singers at Leroy Wilkins's club, Waller started his career performing in the better-known establishments. Johnson recalled, "When Waller got his first job, as accompanist at Leroy Williams' [sic] cabaret at 135th and Fifth, he got stage fright and wouldn't go. We sat him down at home, my wife sang the songs and I played the backgrounds to show him he could do it, too. After that, he started going up."[14] Johnson also introduced Waller to the rent party circuit in 1921. At his first outing booked as a featured player by "Lippy" Boyette, he played alongside "Corky" Williams and Russell Brooks at the Lenox Avenue Apartments on 141st. Although Johnson could not attend the party, Waller made a fine debut.[15] With Johnson's help, Waller made his first phonograph recordings in October 1922—"Muscle Shoals Blues" and "Birmingham Blues."[16] Through Johnson he was introduced to Max Kortlander, J. Lawrence Cook, and others at the QRS Music Company. His first roll was released in March 1923.[17] By January 1926, both men were hailed as piano sensations.[18] Johnson and Waller only recorded together commercially from 1927 through

1929. They cut two piano roll duets, "If I Could Be with You" (QRS 3818) and "Cryin' for My Used to Be" (QRS 3800), both released in 1927. Between March 1928 and November 1929, they recorded twelve commercially released 78 rpm sides on which they both play.

Johnson, Smith, and Waller, the "big three" of the 1920s Harlem piano giants, were in demand not only at the rent parties but also in the homes of white, socially connected society. They frequented the renowned Harlem nightspots but desired to bring the talent downtown into their private residences. Many of the well-to-do wished to flout the presentation of star performers as emblematic of a broad-minded, socially progressive image. More often than not, however, the hosts were patronizing to the Black artists, and the invitation into their homes was merely artifice. From their performer guests, they expected reenactments of stage show antics and stereotypes rather than abiding unmasked presentation of their artistry. It was the next incarnation of the same conceit demanded when Clef Club musicians played without music to reinforce the notion of them as natural rather than schooled performers. Only now the charade was veiled in the trappings of some element of social conscience, often referred to as "taking up the Negro." The pretense was not lost on the uptown guests, and many played along with the deception expected of them. But not Johnson. Ed Kirkeby recounts Willie "The Lion" Smith's recollection of a party at the Upper West Side home of steel magnate Charles M. Schwab during the mid-1920s: "James was always so modest. He wouldn't act funny at all, just always relied on his playing. He always used to say, 'What do I have to do for them besides play?' That was enough for him and I guess it was enough for the customers, him being James P. But I had my own act, and I poured it on 'em, even as I still do now. When Fats came along, he took that West Indian dialect from James and ran away with it."[19]

Willie "The Lion" Smith commented on Johnson's artistic evolution:

It is my opinion that James P. was a better composer than Fats, although Waller's tunes have had much more success.

James P. started to devote most of his time to writing show scores during the early twenties. He also got on an arranging and conducting kick. It was his hope he could become a symphonic conductor. From then on, he had no eyes for clowning or showmanship. I used to tell him that when we ran into pianos with the keys broken you had to mug your way to entertain the people. His reply was, "Lion, it just ain't dignified."[20]

Dick Wellstood compared Johnson and Waller as musicians, noting, "James P. was not Pete Johnson, nor a mere 'teacher' of Fats Waller. He was a much more interesting musician than Waller. His bass lines are better constructed, his right hand is freer and less repetitive, his rhythm is more accurate, and his playing is not so relentlessly two-beat as that of Fats."[21] Eubie Blake sums up his feelings in three lines: "Fats Waller knew how to hold an audience, and he could really play too. Between you and me, though, he wasn't no James P. But he learned a lot from Black James."[22] Waller came to admire many pianists over the years, including those who claimed him as a major influence. His favorite, however, always remained James P. Johnson. He recognized his debt to Johnson and often attributed his stalwart faith in maintaining melody in music to his mentor, saying "You got to have melody. Jimmy Johnson taught me that. You got to hang onto the melody and never let it get boresome."[23] Even Luckey Roberts, whose influence on Johnson was well known, acknowledged the Waller style was based deeply on Johnson's, and remarked, "Fats Waller got all his stuff from Johnson, so that makes me his grandfather, I guess."[24] The mutual admiration and friendship between Johnson and Waller marked one of the most famous teacher-pupil relationships in jazz history. They teased each other with derogatory nicknames, with Johnson adopting Willie "The Lion" Smith's nickname for Waller and adding an adjective to make it "Big Filthy," and Waller referring to Johnson as "Jackanapes."[25] Smith called Johnson "the brute" or "the bear cat," ironic nicknames given Johnson's genial manner. Johnson called Smith "cuz."[26] Waller cultivated a popular persona and performing style enriched by his vocal skills and a natural feel for comedic turns that often thinly veiled his ironic commentary. He reached widespread success in the 1930s recording hundreds of sides with his group, "Fats Waller and his Rhythm." He is the best-known stride pianist and a colorful figure in jazz history. Waller had substantial appetites for food, alcohol, and women. A grueling touring, performing, and socializing schedule took its toll on his obese and often intoxicated frame, and he died from pneumonia on a transcontinental train near Kansas City on December 15, 1943, at age thirty-nine.

Chapter 11

PLANTATION DAYS, 1922-1923

Music by James P. Johnson, America's Greatest Jazz Pianist
—LAFAYETTE THEATER ADVERTISEMENT, *NEW YORK AGE*

On the heels of her success at the blues singing contest, Trixie Smith, who was little known in New York and had yet to be recorded despite her work as a performer on various vaudeville circuits for almost a decade, came under contract to Black Swan and recorded exclusively for them, and subsequently Paramount after their purchase, for the remainder of the decade.[1] On her first release, Johnson led the orchestra for her pairing of his tune "Desperate Blues," and her prize-winning number "Trixie's Blues." Her victory at the blues singing contest with this tune is written on the record label, but Johnson is not credited. His orchestra, James P. Johnson's Harmony Eight, is credited on Smith's second release. Aside from one other session for Victor in January producing only a single unissued piano solo, and the eleven piano rolls released by QRS during 1922, he made no other trips to the recording studio that year. Although his contract with QRS required him to cut two rolls a month, he recorded them all in the first six months before leaving New York to pursue his musical theater ambitions. His experience in *Darktown Follies* and *Darkest Americans* whetted his appetite for the many benefits of such work. He saw the adulation bestowed on the Tutt brothers and Luckey Roberts, and more recently the success of Sissle and Blake. He was now ready to advance his own profile as a stage composer and orchestra leader. And compared to the fledgling recording industry, which in 1922 was struggling to emerge from its own financial challenges, work in the musical theater paid well. Johnson devoted a great deal of time to composing for the theater during the 1920s. His output was enormous, a good portion of it unpublished and lost in the miasma that surrounded the meager operating infrastructure of the Black theater during this time. Most tunes penned by even the biggest names in popular composing met with little success beyond the stage performance. But there were also blockbuster hits that established Johnson as a major figure in American theater composing.

Johnson put together an orchestra to play for the Colored Vaudeville Benevolent Association celebration for their new club location at 424 Lenox Avenue on March 10. The featured entertainment was "a veritable kaleidoscope of vaudeville" that included, among many notables, Maceo Pinkard and his wife, Johnson's wife Lillian, and dance duo Leonard Harper and Oceola Blanks. Harper was also serving as one of the hosts of the evening.[2] Harper was born in Birmingham, Alabama, in 1899. He eventually married his partner Oceola Blanks. Harper and Blanks had been touring for five years before the CVBA event and had become well known and highly regarded. The year before, they leapt from the Black vaudeville circuit onto the Broadway stage in Irvin C. Miller's production of *Put and Take*, one of the first African American productions to follow *Shuffle Along* into a so-called "legitimate" theater. The duo caught the attention of the Shubert brothers, who had been intrigued by the newly available Black talent now more visible to them in the higher-profile venues of Broadway. Harper and Blanks were hired as the first African American performers to play the white Shubert vaudeville circuit, which included a run at the Winter Garden Theater. After a tour of the Northeast and Midwest, the couple returned to New York. Their brief time with the Shuberts was not without a dose of racial contention. Despite acclaim for their work by reviewers, their stage time was cut after protestations by other white performers.[3]

Like Johnson, Harper was eager to lead his own production. Shortly after meeting at the Vaudeville Benevolent event, Johnson and Harper collaborated on their first effort, *Harper and Blanks Revue*, which played as part of the Grand Spring Carnival Week at the Lafayette Theatre the week of May 15. Johnson was musical director, his first known production as leader.[4] Jimmy O'Neal, a Chicago booking agent, had come to New York like so many others in search of the next big hit using "racial performers and musicians." He secured the services of Lawrence Deas, who had had a part in staging the dances for *Shuffle Along*, hoping to replicate that theatrical success.[5] O'Neal also struck a deal to act as personal representative for Harper, and gave him the enormous sum of $20,000 and artistic freedom to put together a show.[6] After their success at the Lafayette, Harper engaged Johnson to work with him on this new show for O'Neal to open in Chicago.

Around the same time, promoter Lew Leslie, at the beginning of his career, spotted a young performer in *Shuffle Along* who had broken out of obscurity in that production as an understudy to land a starring role. Her name was

Florence Mills, and, over the course of the decade, she and Leslie would make theatrical history. The cabaret space above the Winter Garden Theater, once owned by Harper's former employer the Shuberts, had been reenvisioned by its new owner Sam Salvin at the urging of Leslie. The original Folies-Bergère setting was converted to a plantation. While plantation themes were not new as the backdrop for Black productions, this new "Plantation Room" magnified all the antebellum and Jim Crow racist tropes in its décor and production effects. Leslie enticed Mills away from *Shuffle Along* to star in his "new" concept at the Winter Garden. He called it *Plantation Revue*, and, despite the regressive nature of the performance construct, was a hit with Black and white audiences.[7] Harper and Johnson, like many others, took notice, and they named their new production *Plantation Days*. Initially hoping to capitalize on the reenergized antebellum genre, their production would have staying power and impact for the remainder of the decade.

Just before leaving for Chicago, Johnson and his vocalist recording partners from the year before, Alice Leslie Carter and Eddie Gray, played for the *Original Spring Revue* of the "July Club" at the Manhattan YWCA on May 25. Johnson was no doubt engaged for the production through the efforts of the Club's chairperson of the program committee, Mrs. James P. Johnson, and the financial secretary, Mrs. Eubie Blake.[8] Johnson and Harper's show *Plantation Days*, produced by Greenwald and O'Neal, opened at the Green Mill Gardens in Chicago in June, and was slated for a twelve-week engagement. The Green Mill was a multi-venue supper club that featured entertainment from "dusk till dawn." Their food specialty was a southern chicken dinner.[9] They promoted the best dance floor in Chicago in a sunken outdoor garden encircled by a terrace of flowers and climbing vines. The building spanned an entire city block on the North side of Chicago. Built in 1907, it had been owned by Tom Chamales since 1910 and by the early '20s was managed by Henry Horn. During the 1910s, The Green Mill had been a favorite of many celebrities and actors from nearby Essanay movie studios, including occasionally Charlie Chaplin. With the advent of Prohibition, it was also a favorite watering hole for Al Capone and other mobsters. The place was so well connected, when Chamales and Horn were arrested by federal marshals for violations of the Volstead Act while *Plantation Days* was playing, Chamales brazenly reassured his patrons in an item in the *Chicago Daily Tribune* that no liquor had been confiscated during the arrest.[10]

The show was a vaudeville-style pastiche of individual performers loosely tied together by its plantation theme, but rather than being presented in a typical theater, it was performed in a casual, supper-club atmosphere. Harper and Blanks were featured with their dancing and singing of "old time songs." Other holdovers from the *Harper and Blanks Revue* included comedian Eddie Green and husband and wife dance team Dave (Stratton) and Tressie (Mitchell). Their dance specialty included "novelty turns," described as acrobatic, eccentric Russian dances. Stratton was well known for his precision and regular, often sudden tempo shifts, a challenge for many of the musicians playing for their act. It would take a musician like Johnson to skillfully keep up. When they left the show later that year, Dave and Tressie found another capable musician in Fess Williams and toured with him. Also in the show were song and dance team Joyner and Foster, dancer George (Stamper) Pasha, and the versatile comedian Blondi Robinson, who sang and danced. Soprano Marjorie Sipp, reported by the *Chicago Daily Tribune* as the only Black graduate of the Conservatory of Music in Milan, sang ballads and syncopated songs with piano backing by Johnson including several numbers from *Shuffle Along*, a segment of the show that would soon explode in controversy. "Strut in with Jerry," a Johnson tune, was sung by Sipp and a chorus of "eight girls dressed in black silk coats, white trousers and straw hats." One of the chorus girls soloed on the song to great applause. The Plantation Four, also soon to be embroiled in controversy, sang "old jubilee songs in harmony." Along with the chorus, Harper and Blanks featured Johnson's tune "International Vampire Babes," and Dave and Tressie rendered his "Ukulele Blues." The finale featured Johnson's "Broadway Glide."[11]

The orchestra for the production, which also played for dancing, is variably listed as Elgar's band as well as The Plantation Days Syncopated Orchestra. Johnson, who had established his reputation as a formidable pianist the year before, was billed as "World's Greatest Jazz Piano King." He was musical director and led Elgar's Syncopated band.[12] Lawrence Deas's staging called for six costume changes. A slow start quickly matured into a must-see ticket. "The revue was not a riot at the opening, but well received and grows in favor steadily," noted *Billboard*.[13] The dancing was singled out by the *Chicago Daily Tribune*, observing: "To these is added a group of principles [sic] notable chiefly for their skill in dancing. The best of them are two amazing hoofers identified in the playbill only as 'Harper' and 'Dave.'"[14] The show apparently did not complete its full twelve-week run at the Green Mill, as Harper needed to refresh the chorus in August.[15] Johnson took advantage of the break to return to New York. On August 21, he played in a large dance production at the Manhattan Casino arranged by Jack Hatton, a showman who billed himself as "the original creator of jazz music" with his Novelty Band. Hatton had formerly worked with Happy Rhone, where he was likely introduced to Johnson.[16] By this time the Johnsons had moved into their own apartment at 269 West 141st Street.[17]

In September, *Plantation Days* reopened at the Avenue Theater on the south side of Chicago. It was very successful and held over an extra week. Johnson was referred to as "the king of syncopation."[18] *Variety* gave a glowing assessment.[19] During the Chicago run, Ethel Waters was added as a special attraction for two weeks. Before embarking on the road tour with *Plantation Days* and

The Johnson home in Harlem from 1922 until they moved to Jamaica, Queens, in 1930. (New York City Department of Records and Information Services, 1940s Tax Department photographs, Collection REC0040-RG 035, Department of Finance. Courtesy Municipal Archives, City of New York)

looking to parlay the talent they had assembled in town when *Plantation Days* left the Green Mill for The Avenue, Greenwald and O'Neil prevailed on Harper to stage a new show to open at the Green Mill. The new show, *Bandanna Land*, featured some of the same cast members as *Plantation Days* but with different musical numbers directed by Johnson. A different "Plantation Four" had been recruited from the production *Strut Miss Lizzie* for the new show, but the male quartette by the same name with *Plantation Days* filed a protest. Why the *Plantation Days* group wasn't used for *Bandanna Land* is a mystery.[20] As Johnson would do frequently in subsequent stage shows, he featured his piano playing. The program noted, "In accord with the Public Demand James P. Johnson presents Chicago's Favorites."[21] Johnson's tune, "Desperate Blues," was featured by George Pasha (Stamper) and Baby Mack "in which a sensational dance of the Apache type is done."[22] This tune, recorded by Johnson the year before, was copyrighted by Sphinx in November but not published. After two weeks at the Green Mill, *Bandanna Land* ran for two weeks at the Avenue behind *Plantation Days*, closing when the latter left town with much of its shared cast. Before leaving town, the local Appomattox Club sponsored a members-only cabaret and smoker in honor of the composers of *Strut Miss Lizzie*, Henry Creamer and Turner Layton. Johnson was engaged for the entertainment accompanying Marjorie Sipp.[23] Creamer and Johnson collaborated on a few tunes copyrighted the following year, "Hot Diggity Dog" and "You Said You Wouldn't But You Done It." Six years later they reunited in a productive songwriting partnership that produced one of the most enduring tunes out of the Great American Songbook, "If I Could Be with You."

Plantation Days toured much of the upper Midwest. It received enthusiastic receptions, noting record-setting runs in Detroit at the Orpheum in October where 1,500 people, mostly white theatergoers, were turned away at a midnight showing.[24] The mainstream press reviews were uniformly positive.[25] They next played the Shubert-Park and then the Shubert-Murat Theaters, both in Indianapolis during the first two weeks of November, where it was reported artists playing at all the other theaters in town were expected to pay a visit.[26] Johnson was billed as "The World's Greatest Jazz Piano King."[27] The Prospect Theater followed in Cleveland for the last two weeks in November.[28] In December the show was playing in Toledo, where it was praised for its outstanding musical numbers and the performances of its leading duo, Harper and Blanks. Charles Elgar's Chicago-based orchestra that included future jazz notables Joe Sudler, trumpet, Bert Hall and Harry Swift, trombones, Darnell Howard, violin, Wellman Braud, bass, and others, continued under Johnson's direction.[29] Johnson's "Ukulele Blues" was again singled out.[30] Johnson recorded it the year before and it was copyrighted in April 1922. Art Tatum likely first met Johnson during this brief stay when Tatum would have been thirteen years old. One performance in Cleveland on December 9 again featured Ethel Waters. One performance in Youngstown was followed by three days at the Grand Theater in Canton. The company returned to Cleveland by popular demand for two weeks at the end of December playing the Globe Theater.[31] During that run, Osceola Blanks and Ethel Waters played a special performance at the Carlton Terrace restaurant.[32] By early 1923, the company played a return engagement of two weeks at the Orpheum Theater in Detroit, followed by Columbus and then Pittsburgh in early February to continued stellar reviews.[33] *Plantation Days* was an unqualified hit, selling out its performances and adding matinees and midnight shows whenever possible.

While in Chicago on nights off and after the show, Johnson sought out the thriving nightlife that rivaled any in the country. Jelly Roll Morton had returned in June from the west and began his own string of legendary orchestra and solo recordings. Johnson had seen Morton in New York a decade earlier, when Morton's reputation as pianist was already recognized and Johnson was beginning his career. Ed Kirkeby describes their meeting in Chicago:

> James P. entered a club one night. As usual, he was greeted with enthusiasm by everyone present. He played a couple of numbers and then joined some friends at their table for a drink. Presently, in walked Jelly Roll, as large as life, and twice as natural. Acknowledging the applause, he sat down at a table, until someone came over and pleaded with him to play. He consented and had just got to his feet when, across the room, he spotted James P. Suddenly he changed his mind. No, he wouldn't play—he wasn't feeling too good. However, after much persuasion, during which it was pointed out to him that it might look as if he was scared, Jelly's pride got the better of him and he rose, ceremoniously folded his coat and laid it on the piano top. Then he sat down, rolled off a terrific "Pearls" and immediately afterwards grabbed his coat and dashed out of the club, saying he had another appointment. This was one battle of music lost by default before it had begun.[34]

Years earlier Morton, as Johnson had described him, was "on fire." Now it was Johnson's turn, and Morton knew it. What he probably did not know was that while many of the Harlem pianists looked down on him, Johnson was one of the few who made no secret of his admiration for Morton.

Johnson recalled in written notes made in the late 1930s that his tune "Ivy, Cling to Me" was used in *Plantation Days*.[35] However well received Johnson felt his first published songs "Mama's Blues" and "Stop It, Joe" had been, "Ivy, Cling to Me" became his first widely popularized and recorded commercial success. Unlike with the earlier two tunes, he secured some financial stability with the provision of a royalty agreement. These benefits enured to Johnson through an association with one of the most prominent white bandleaders of that time. When *Plantation Days* opened, Chicago nightlife was already a cauldron of entertainment activity. In particular, the city had become the dance band capital of the country, and its king was Isham (pronounced Eye-shum) Jones. Born within hours of James P. Johnson on January 31, 1894, in Coalton, Ohio, Jones rose from an upbringing of hardship in the mines of Saginaw, Michigan, to lead Chicago's premier dance band. He trained as a pianist but fronted his band with a saxophone, the instrument he took up after World War I, recognizing its potential as the replacement for the violin in dance band arranging. By 1922, he had secured a national reputation with a successful record contract with Brunswick, which the year before produced a multi-million-selling record, "Wabash Blues." "He was an irascible man with a trigger temper and an utter contempt for his audience," noted writer Gene Lees, also pointing out, "Along with his touchy temper, Jones had an astute sense of business." By June 1922, Jones had reportedly made $800,000 from composer royalties and by commanding performance fees of $3,500 a week.[36] Even more remarkable is that his most popular tunes were still ahead of him, including "It Had to Be You" and "I'll See You in My Dreams." During the early years of the success of his band, Jones's music was often characterized as jazz, perhaps an inevitable descriptor at the advent of the "jazz age." Scholars continue to debate the nature of his music, attempting to situate it somewhere along the continuum from straight popular music to hot jazz. While Jones himself acknowledged no pretense toward the latter, he knew a good thing when he heard it and took the opportunity to absorb its lessons. Around the same time *Plantation Days* opened, Joe "King" Oliver and his Creole Jazz Band had returned from a California tour and reopened at the Lincoln Gardens on Chicago's south side. Not only was Jones often in attendance to hear Oliver, but Jones insisted his whole band do so. Black and white patrons, many of them musicians, filled the dance floor at the Lincoln Gardens, and it was the New Orleans trumpet king's masterful dance band presentation that Jones most admired, perhaps even more than the small group jazz Oliver had brought "up the river."[37]

No doubt Jones also investigated the latest hit show at the Green Mill, at some point connecting with Johnson. "Ivy" is listed on a *Plantation Days* program from its run in Chicago but is not mentioned in the early reviews. Years later, James Breyley, Jones's manager from the 1930s, recalled to journalist James T. Maher that when Johnson played his tune for Jones, he suggested adding his name to boost recording potential, implying Jones had no actual role in the composing. Breyley also recalled Jones took no cut of the royalties, insisting Johnson (and presumably lyricist Alex Rogers) receive 100 percent of the profits.[38] On October 16, Johnson, Jones, and Rogers signed a contract for publication of a song titled "Carolina Ivy" with Irving Berlin's publishing company. In early November, Berlin copyrighted the tune with the truncated title "Ivy," the listing now excluding mention of Jones with words and music by Jimmy Johnson and Alex Rogers. Ultimately, Berlin published the tune with the title "Ivy (Cling to Me)" but with restored composer credits shared between Johnson, Rogers, and Jones. Composer royalties were included for Johnson in the deal with Berlin. Despite Jones's volatile personality and reputation for frugality, he was also known to have a warm heart and on many documented occasions helped other musicians get published and recorded.[39] Jones had worked with Berlin earlier in the year, co-composing the music for Ernie Young's *Passing Parade*,[40] and likely recommended the Johnson number for publication to the emerging music mogul. Jones merely as composer figurehead is certainly possible. This is substantiated by the initial credits sans

Jones, but the Berlin contract makes it seem less likely Jones ultimately gave away his share. With the title simply "Ivy," an arrangement of the tune by H. Qualli Clark was copyrighted in early November by his Sphinx Music. Clark also copyrighted "Ukulele Blues" and "Desperate Blues" from *Plantation Days* but did not publish them. Clark had arranged Johnson's "Carolina Shout" for orchestra the year before, which was included as an overture in *Plantation Days*. By November, *Plantation Days* was as solid a hit on the road as it had been in Chicago. True to his word, Jones recorded "Ivy" on December 30 on a "special release," as did Paul Whiteman, whose recording was also specially issued on February 15, 1923, and advertised as far away as India well into 1923. Jones's version was advertised as "the biggest hit since Dardanella."[41]

In April 1923, QRS released a piano roll of "Ivy," listed as played by J. Russel Robinson. Because of his affinity for more complex syncopations and jazz, he was often called "The white man with the Colored fingers," and, after 1921, assimilated much of Johnson's pianistic revelations. As is true of many rolls, the exact recording date is unknown but was likely several months before the release date. Johnson was in New York very little if at all during the fall of 1922 and early part of 1923. His last QRS roll was released in September. His absence may explain why he did not record his own composition or at least was not slated to record it and ride the wave of popularity already generated by Whiteman, Jones, and a number of others who had recorded it in late 1922. But the last chorus of the roll sounds so much like Johnson some piano roll scholars believe it was actually played by Johnson, either at the time Robinson was cutting it, or at a later date and then added in the editing process.[42]

For the most part, the cross-racial reception to *Plantation Days* and the collaboration with a prominent white bandleader were in large part positive experiences for Johnson. A large white audience was clamoring to see African American talent, at least in the North. The press reported no racial incidents during performances. And with "Ivy," Johnson found himself and his music associated with the biggest names in white entertainment—Jones, Berlin, and Whiteman. He was widely praised and acknowledged as the king of jazz pianists, a musical genre not yet six years old. A triumphant run in New York was waiting, but by early February, both opportunity and trouble were brewing. *Plantation Days* was scheduled to open at the Lafayette Theater in Harlem the week of February 25, 1923. After their week at the Lafayette, the company was scheduled to sail for London. The British agent Sir Alfred Butt engaged the company to come to England after the week's run in Harlem. He pitched to producer Albert De Courville the notion of incorporating some of *Plantation Days* into a larger show being written by George Gershwin. Harper and Blanks wished to break the contract with the Lafayette to expedite their transatlantic venture. But *Plantation Days* was prevented from leaving for Europe by an injunction successfully sought by the travelling *Shuffle Along* company. The 1923 edition of the still popular show, while on their own cross-country tour, had not been receiving the enthusiastic response they expected. As it happened, they were following *Plantation Days* through the larger cities. Eventually, the *Shuffle Along* company was informed that *Plantation Days* was registering big success with musical numbers taken from their show. They engaged the services of the Keystone National Detective Agency of Chicago (a Black agency) to work on stopping *Plantation Days*.[43]

The three numbers used by *Plantation Days* were the hits "Gypsy Blues," "I'm Craving for That Kind of Love," and "Bandanna Days." Many of the *Plantation Days* cast had once performed in *Shuffle Along*, including Marjorie Sipp, Sydney Grant, the Plantation Four, and the Creole Flappers.[44] That the problem centered on "borrowed" musical numbers perhaps does not reflect favorably on James P. Johnson, since he was musical director. It didn't seem, though, that he or anyone in the production was looking to disguise the inclusion of the successful numbers. At least as far back as its run in Chicago, and into November on tour, programs and many advertisements specifically noted "Shuffle Along Hits" were performed by Marjorie Sipp and Johnson.[45] The Black press noted, however, "We understand that the colored people in the show had no choice, as they are under contract to white men behind the company."[46] Grant Harper Reid, Leonard Harper's grandson and biographer, suggests the malfeasance was perpetrated by Lawrence Deas under false pretenses. Reid contends Deas falsely advertised his connection to *Shuffle Along* as its producer, and that he thus had the rights to include the tunes in *Plantation Days*. He took credit in many of the advertisements from the Midwestern tour of *Plantation Days* touting himself as the producer, upstaging the spotlight from Harper. A Chicago program lists both Deas and Harper as producers. Deas did, in fact, help stage the dances for *Shuffle Along*,[47] and he appropriated the same routines and numbers for *Plantation Days*.[48] Leonard Harper assured the *Shuffle Along* principals that they would no longer use Deas's staging of the three numbers. By the time the show reopened in Chicago at Gibson's New Dunbar Theater in mid-February,1923, the tunes from *Shuffle Along* had been deleted.[49] Despite the absence of the contested musical numbers, the show, and especially Johnson, garnered ebullient reviews in the press, which noted, "Jimmy Johnson's Plantation Orchestra is a nifty one, but they hold the stage too long in doing their specialty. Jimmy sure does spank wicked ebonies and ivories. The accompaniment throughout the show is perfect."[50] Johnson continued to use the stage as more than a platform for his composing and conducting. The nightly (and often daily) capacity audiences were given ample exposure to his new jazz piano sound. He had programmed in "Carolina Shout" as an overture to the production, with one reviewer noting, "... there is in the rhythm the beat of a triply syncopated tom-tom."[51]

Harper had untangled the problem with the musical numbers from *Shuffle Along* but now needed to extricate the show from its commitment to the Lafayette so they could pursue the enticing opportunity to play alongside George Gershwin in London. The company was hailed as the first large-scale Black musical theater company to go abroad in nearly twenty years, none since the days of Williams and Walker. Harper renegotiated the contract with the Coleman brothers, proprietors of the Lafayette Theater, to allow a "new" *Plantation Days* company to play there. Harper and Blanks, Johnson and Lillie Mae Johnson, and the original *Plantation Days* company sailed for England on the Red Star Steamer *Finland* out of Pier 58 in New York on March 3. A hastily reconstituted alter ego *Plantation Days* company finally opened at the Lafayette Theater on Monday, April 2. The cast retained Eddie Green and the "Plantation Four," adding Adams and Tunstall (Lillie Mae's ex-husband Fred Tunstall), Julian Mitchell, Smith and Deforrest, Ida Roley, a "Peppy Chorus," and Sam Wooding's Famous Syncopated Orchestra as an added attraction. Daisy Pizarro staged the dances. The reviews were generally only fair, likely the result of the absence of the dancing of Harper and Blanks, the piano of James P. Johnson, and the crowd-pleasing numbers from *Shuffle Along*. The *New York Age* noted, "*Plantation Days*, now playing at the Lafayette, is only a group of vaudeville acts hurriedly gotten together. Although most of the cast possess talent, none stood out and the show as a whole failed to go over."[52] Other critics cited two bright spots, however: the performances of comedian Eddie Green, and the "Hawaiian Number." While he was off to Europe, Johnson's "Ukulele Blues" had apparently been retained in the new show, preserving some small semblance of musical value.

Harper, Johnson, and others from the original company, as well as new cast members, arrived in Plymouth on March 12 to begin rehearsals in London for inclusion of their part in the larger production written by George Gershwin titled *The Rainbow*. Gershwin was offered $1,500 and a round-trip ticket to write it. In three days, he produced a score that he later considered to be his weakest effort.[53] *The Rainbow* opened at the Empire Theater on April 3. The Plantation segment depicted life along the Mississippi and was positioned between the two acts of Gershwin's contribution. There were two shows each night. James P. Johnson and his Syncopated Orchestra remained mostly intact, with Bert Hall, Wellman Braud, Joe Sudler, and Darnell Howard making the trip, and led off the intermezzo with an opening chorus that included the entire company of thirty-two. The tune "Simply Full of Jazz" featured Harper and Blanks with the Pepper Chorus. This may have been another tune borrowed from *Shuffle Along*, the full title being "I'm Just Simply Full of Jazz." They were followed by the Four Cracker Jacks with a Ragtime Jubilee, the Silver Tone Four with barbershop harmony, and a "Plantation Days" act. George (Pascha) Stamper and Josephine Stevens preceded the finale, which highlighted Harper's staging and Johnson's music.[54]

In addition to their performance during the main production, Butt had intended for the *Plantation* company to stage a cabaret show at the Empire after regular theater hours. The troupe brought along Wilhemena Steptoe, renowned for her New Orleans–style cuisine, to cook for the company. To entice theatergoers to linger for the cabaret nightclub performance after the show, Ms. Steptoe provided authentic Southern food for the patrons. Harper reported the simulated restaurant/cabaret occupied more of their time than their segment in the show. Butt intended to modify the front entrance to the theater, designing a Plantation motif whereby the members of the company could also intermingle with potential patrons on the sidewalk and draw them into the theater.[55] The expanded role would mean work and publicity, but on arriving in England, Harper and Johnson, having survived their legal vexations in the States, unexpectedly found only more contention. Both white and Black American performers were accused of taking work from British performers. American jazz was quickly gaining in popularity around the globe, and African American musicians were more frequently seen in British venues, engendering increased racial prejudice. The prospect of Black performers and white patrons mixing caused a scandal. When the prospect of licensing the proposed cabaret of all-Black performers at the Empire came before the London County Council, Albert Voyce, chairman of the British Variety Artists Confederation, protested on all accounts: "We think it would be a disgrace if permission were granted to exploit imported black men and women in this way, while hundreds of talented British artists are on the verge of want for lack of engagements. We have no objections to American artists coming to England. In fact 90 percent of those who come here join our federation and are welcome. There are also in England Negro turns, most respectable and most decent, who behave themselves and keep their place. But we view with the greatest apprehension a cabaret where black artists would actually mix with the white folk at the tables."[56]

Sir Alfred Butt, himself a member of Parliament, had the ear of English aristocracy. At a meeting of the Variety Artists Benevolent Fund shortly after the *Plantation* company arrived, Butt vigorously defended the American performers before Lord Chamberlain and other well-connected entertainment and political figures. His arguments were well received.[57] Nevertheless, the local political threat was real, and Butt proposed a compromise. He would erect a railing around the section of the room where the Black company would perform so that it would not be physically possible for the audience to meld with the players in the cabaret. The entryway redesign was also scrapped. The Empire's locale in Leicester Square had at times, most notoriously twenty years earlier, been a gathering spot for local prostitutes, the recurrence of which was irrationally thought more likely if Black performers were mingling with white theatergoers. Despite continued opposition with attempts to invoke fire code violations as a veiled rationale to refuse it, the license was granted.[58]

Often confused with *Plantation Days*, producer Lew Leslie's *Plantation Revue*, starring Florence Mills, ran for several months at the Plantation restaurant on Broadway to great acclaim in early 1923. Leslie had initially approached Butt regarding a London production, but Sir Alfred balked at Leslie's fee of 1,300 British pounds weekly. So Leslie engaged British producer Charles B. Cochran as his second choice to contract for Mills and the *Plantation Revue* to appear in a larger show in London. When Butt became aware, he quickly made arrangements with O'Neill and Greenwald to do the same with the *Plantation Days* company headed for New York after its sensational run in the upper Midwest. Ethel Waters recalled Greenwald's attempts to recruit her for the overseas tour. Greenwald was equally eager to scoop Leslie in bringing African American talent to audiences in the UK. Waters had reservations about making such a commitment to white producers, and found an excuse for not going, recalling, "Greenwald had already signed up James P. Johnson and said Jimmy would be my accompanist. I told Greenwald I wouldn't take Johnson and insisted I must have Pearl [Wright, her regular accompanist at that time]. But this was only to get out of going, because the one and only Jimmy has always been one of my idols."[59] Waters's concerns proved correct. Cochran and Butt sparred legally over the use of the word *Plantation* in the title. Beaten to the London West End, Cochran sued Butt over the name. A London court threw out the suit, partly a result of Butt's connections, as well as representations he made in court agreeing to change the name of his show, commitments that would soon prove to have been duplicitous.[60] Harper was convinced a smear campaign propagated by Cochran ignited the simmering anti-American and especially anti-Black sentiment that bubbled over in the London press. The *Plantation Revue* didn't open in London until May 31, after the *Plantation Days* company had already returned to the United States. The *Plantation Revue* became part of a larger production called *From Dover Street to Dixie* opening at the Pavilion Theater. The "Dover Street" section was made up of white English actors and actresses who appeared in the first part. The "Dixie" section followed, and featured Mills, the company, and Will Vodery and his orchestra. The revue scored as big a success in England as it had in the United States. Unfortunately, box office receipts notwithstanding, the Ministry of Labor, in response to the continued antagonistic sentiment of English performers toward alien entertainers, subjected the Black members of this company to the same restrictions and insults they had inflicted on the cast of *Plantation Days* who had preceded them on the London stage. The *Plantation Revue* was prematurely withdrawn and its members set sail for the United States in September.

Much of the anti-American and especially anti-Black frenzy was fomented by the prominent London newspaper columnist Hannen Swaffer. In the most opprobrious manner, Swaffer fanned the flames of racism and xenophobia, writing such overtly hateful comments as, ". . . while the actors and actresses of England are concerned about their bread and butter . . . Sir Alfred Butt and C. B. Cochran are quarrelling apparently about which niggers they have got."[61] Artist Robert Law, who painted the scenic backdrops for the *Plantation Days* segment, was quoted using the most vile, racially disparaging terms about his feelings for the Black actors as well as their cook Ms. Steptoe.[62] The controversy spilled over into the show itself. On opening night, British comedian and female impersonator Jack Edge, who felt his part had been sizably and unfairly cut, delivered an impromptu protestation on stage just before the finale. He spoke of the poor treatment afforded English performers, and how they were in his view superior to Americans. Edge was physically removed from the stage.[63] There were cries from some in the audience to "send the Negroes home."[64] Even Gershwin was not immune from harsh criticism and accusations of displacing English actors and musicians, the latter reportedly numbering two thousand without work. He was booed off stage during the final scene and made plans to return to the United States three days later. In attendance that night, at the invitation of Sir Alfred Butt, were Fred Astaire and his sister Adele. They were in London starring in the musical *For Goodness Sake* (retitled *Stop Flirting*). Astaire's biographer Bob Thomas describes this experience, noting, "During their early period in London, the Astaire's had an alarming experience at the Empire Theatre. They attended the opening night of a revue that failed to find favor with the audience. Patrons in the gallery talked back to the actors, boos and whistles punctuated the performance. The curtain brought a chorus of disdain. Fred and Adele stared at each other with trepidation. . . ."[65] The Astaire's production opened on May 30, the day before Florence Mills and *Dover Street to Dixie*. The Astaires were enthusiastically received and stayed in the UK for well over a year. Perhaps, for the London audiences, the absence of any Black performers was enough to forgive and ultimately embrace exclusively white American productions, even if there were still unemployed English actors.

Already stoked by the popular and political circus replete with resentment and bigotry, the theatrical reviews of the *Plantation Days* segment were viciously derisive. The *London Observer* suggested the Black performers should "come under the Performing Animals Act," and that the performance was "stupid, vulgar, and dreadfully ugly." *The Sunday Times* of London acknowledged that much of the opposition was unreasonable but thought deleting entirely the truncated "Plantation" segment would not be much of a loss. They complained, ". . . the character of dances and the noises made is the reverse of pleasing."[66] Not everyone was reviled by the Americans, including Elaine Lettor, one of the premier dancers with *The Rainbow* portion of the show. She was the daughter of the wardrobe manager to his Majesty King George V, and goddaughter of Queen Mary. An array of royals and their high society entourage attended the opening, but rather than succumb to the poison of the hecklers and race baiters, they were thrilled by the energy and talent of the *Plantation Days* performers. In attendance were Queen Alexandra, Lady Patricia Ramsay, the Grand Duchess Marie, the Princess Royal, the Duke of Connaught, Prince George, Prince Henry, and the Duke and Duchess of York. Their approval encouraged a large segment of the theater going public to ignore the political and racial attacks and attend the production.[67] The royal family was well known to be receptive to "roaring twenties" American culture, and, in a few years, would adopt the dance craze from Johnson's pen that swept the world, the "Charleston."

While in England, members from *Plantation Days* and the newly arrived *Plantation Revue* productions were honored by a Black social club called "The Coterie of Friends." According to the program of the event, the club was "started by a small group of Students [sic] with the object of creating a social vehicle whereby the much isolated population of serious minded people of colour may come into contact at frequent intervals." On the evening of May 13, 1923, the guests of honor included Florence Mills, Will Vodery, and Shelton Brooks, all from the rival production *Plantation Revue*, which was still in rehearsal, along with Johnson and members of the West Indian cricket team. The program credits Johnson and his orchestra "who have kindly taken charge of the Musical Program," and Harper, who served as master of ceremonies. One of the principals of the Coterie was Edmund Thornton Jenkins, son of the founder of the legendary Jenkins Orphanage. The younger Jenkins had had formal musical training and aspired to be a serious composer and musician. Ironically, he left the United States because of the segregated music world. He continued his serious musical education in England from 1914 as an expatriate.[68] This was a serious-minded group whose honorable intentions were not taken seriously by the media, now in full froth with racist sentiment. The event was dismissed in the local press with the same racially charged mockery used in reviews of the theatrical production. The event was open to club members and a select group of 150 prominent Londoners who received a mailed flier. There was a notice posted at the Empire Theater. A few notable American entertainers in London at the time attended, including Nora Bayes and Paul Whiteman, the two unswayed by the vitriol in the press and who had a native understanding and appreciation for their American theatrical and musical brethren. Other high-profile English guests, intrigued by the novelty of Black American entertainers and inspired by the positive reaction of the royal family, also managed to gain admission to the social affair. Johnson and his orchestra were to be paid for their performance out of the door receipts. The price of admission was five shillings, but many of the guests found entry without paying. Jenkins, while grateful for the "personal enjoyment" of Johnson's music, apologized to him for the meager take. Along with his note of explanation, he included a box of cigarettes for each member of Johnson's orchestra which he hoped would be taken as, ". . . a very small mark of my personal appreciation."[69] Johnson and the other African American talent did their best, at least for an evening, to retreat from the toxic buzz of controversy in the London theatre. The audience that night was surely appreciative of the distinguished guests.

Upon their return to the United States, Harper and Blanks declared their British engagement to have been a great success, despite the various social and contractual problems. Perhaps the royal imprimatur and the audiences who followed were enough for Harper to overlook the barrage of disrespect. The restaurant/cabaret, where they were to have spent most of their time, never did open. The roped barriers were positioned anyway. Left with only a brief spot in the larger production when their stage time was cut from thirty minutes to about twelve minutes, the producers could not justify the expense of retaining them and subsequently cut their pay. Their dressing rooms were moved to the water-logged basement. After their despicable treatment in London, some of the cast was gun-shy about further travel to Europe, so, despite Harper's negotiations for a run on the continent, the company returned home after six weeks. With two shows a day, *The Rainbow* ran for 113 performances.[70] Alfred Butt, in a final turn of ignominy, paid only for passage in steerage for the *Plantation Days* company, despite assurances otherwise. Although the disgrace of third-class accommodations was reported in the press, Harper noted that, in addition to financial help from Florence Mills, the cast members themselves made up the difference in fare to travel in second class.[71] Johnson returned to New York with the others out of Liverpool on the SS *Cedric* on May 19, arriving on May 28.[72] On the crossing, he was already at work on his next endeavor.

Back in the United States, Lew Leslie, the original producer of the *Plantation Revue*, had already put together a new *Plantation Revue* that was playing on Broadway. This production initially featured "Hamtree" Harrington and Cora Green. Upon her return to New York, Florence Mills was added to the cast. When they returned from England, Harper and Blanks produced their own *Plantation Revue* at the Lincoln Theater. The hastily cobbled together alternate production of *Plantation Days* that had opened at the Lafayette starring Eddie Green was beginning to gain traction and embarked on an extended tour playing through the summer. When it disbanded, Lawrence Deas, who had left the original production after the *Shuffle Along* music scandal, assembled a new production that opened in Chicago in July.[73] They embarked on an extended tour through the Western United States and Canada in the fall and winter. Deas, ever the promotional manipulator, again advertised a self-described inflated role in *Shuffle Along* as well as a fictitious role in the London production in which he played no part. Back in Chicago by spring 1924, Earl Dancer and Ethel Waters rejoined the show alongside Chappelle and Stinnette, whose own reputation had broadened such that they chose to leave the show shortly after to become a featured act.[74] On May 24, some of the original cast including Dave and Tressie and George Stamper, along with Lena Wilson (sister of singer Edith Wilson), and Honey Brown, known as the "Chocolate Pavlova," joined the production at the Olympic theater in Chicago. Johnson reportedly wrote a special score for the show and personally conducted the orchestra.[75] In 1925, the show was playing the Pantages circuit. It was cut from its original two hours to ninety minutes but remained popular. Wen Talbert, who would later conduct the first performance of Johnson's *Harlem Symphony*, was musical director.[76] In the fall of 1925, future groundbreaking bandleader Blanche Calloway joined the show, left in early 1926, and rejoined it in the fall of that year. Calloway was a well-known veteran of the vaudeville stage and had been touring since 1921. In March 1927, her twenty-year-old younger brother Cabell (better known as Cab), by then already a popular, local entertainer in Baltimore, joined his sister in the show as part of a male quartette when it played at the Royal Theater in Baltimore.[77] Blanche was featured in a "speedy hula number."[78] Brother and sister toured with the company until the show closed in Chicago in late 1927.[79] Johnson's old songwriting partner William Farrell joined the show in 1925 with his new partner Sadie Chadwick.[80] Blues singer Ida Cox was also a headliner, and noted that *Plantation Days* was "the biggest Negro road show going at the time. . . . " She said that the run at the Grand Theater in Chicago was one of the highlights of her career. "That's when I first got my name in lights," she recalled fondly. Shortly after, she organized her own touring show called *Raisin' Cain*.[81] 1927 saw further cast changes. When singer Ada Brown joined the show, she brought along her accompanist Harry Swanagan, who served as musical director.[82] A *Plantation Days* company continued touring until at least 1930. It is difficult to know how much of Johnson's music remained after 1925 as new musical directors took the helm, but the musical underpinning of the *Plantation Days* franchise always remained inseparably associated with him.

The impact of *Plantation Days* cannot be overstated, notwithstanding the earlier success of *Plantation Revue* with Florence Mills. From its opening in mid-1922 until the end of the decade, it was the epitome of touring Black vaudeville. The show launched and advanced the careers of many talented performers including the Calloway siblings, and its attraction to mixed-race audiences provided broad exposure. It propelled Johnson and Harper, whose stature was already building, onto another level in the entertainment world, positioning them as two of the most sought-after African American musical theater performers. Leonard Harper became one of if not the most important dancers and musical production choreographers during the heyday of Harlem and Black Broadway stage shows. By 1924, he was advertising his studio on Broadway in the Navex building at 225 W. 46th Street, suite 309. Like Johnson, Harper was highly sought-after by white performers. Fred Astaire, among others, was known to seek him out at his studio. In addition to teaching, he staged musical comedies and revues, and served as a booking agent for bands, orchestras, and music arrangers. Billy Pierce was his general manager then,[83] but the flurry of activity he would sustain for the next twenty years required training many other assistants. Before *Plantation Days* opened in London, Johnson had been engaged to bring his musical theater composing talent to Broadway. Working with the most prominent blackface comedy team of the time, he wrote music for what would become his most successful stage show and give the world one of the greatest pop culture phenomena in history.

Chapter 12

RUNNIN' WILD, 1923

> Last September, fourteen plays opened in New York. When May came around this year Miller and Lyles merry musical revue was still running strong at the Colonial Theater, and was the only survivor; many discriminating theatergoers were seeing "Runnin' Wild" for the third and fourth time.
> —*THE BRIDGEPORT TELEGRAM*

After his return from London, Johnson dove into a busy schedule of composing and recording. In July he signed an exclusive contract with the Jack Mills Publishing Company as songwriter. Mills had seen the success of tunes by Black writers and decided to embrace African American music, signing a number of writers.[1] Johnson made monthly trips to the recording studio for three different record companies. He recorded six piano solos, four of them his own tunes. All were well received and when released in the fall had national radio play, especially the two tunes he had not written, "Bleeding Hearted Blues" and "You Can't Do What My Last Man Did." The latter number was composed by Perry Bradford, who also likely arranged for the record date and its marketing. The famous music house Philip Werlein in New Orleans prominently introduced Johnson's new association with Victor, a major label, but incorrectly claimed him as a native son, calling him "New Orleans famous Colored pianist."[2] The record sold well and was advertised nationally into 1924.[3] At least in the North, its radio play was often broadcast alongside a wide array of music including Hawaiian numbers, Will Rodgers comedy sketches, and dance bands.[4] The Johnson instrumental originals "Scouting Around" and "Toddlin'" were recorded for OKeh in August. It was enthusiastically described by Abel in the *New York Clipper* as "A brace of hot rags by an expert ivory tickler," adding,

"The instrumentalization [sic] is snappy and wicked."[5] The OKeh date was Johnson's last trip to the recording studio for more than two years. During this time, he was working on a show planned for Broadway that paired him with the most famous Black comedy team in the country.

As students at Fisk University around 1905, Flournoy Miller (1889–1971) and Aubrey Lyles (1882–1932) were campus hits with their comedy routines. Forsaking their studies, they left school and headed for Chicago and the legendary Pekin Theater where they were hired as playwrights. Their 1905 musical stage show *The Mayor of Dixie* was a big success. The pair worked with many then current and future leaders of the African American musical theater, including Will Marion Cook, who was composing for and leading the orchestra at the Pekin by 1906.[6] By 1910, Miller and Lyles struck out on the vaudeville circuit and for at least six years were stars on the popular Keith circuit. As Black vaudeville historian Henry T. Sampson observes, "Their act was unique in that, unlike other comedians of the period, Miller and Lyles did not sing nor dance. It consisted of ten minutes of patter which bristled with wit and humor followed by an original acrobatic boxing exhibition."[7] As was standard practice then, they performed in burnt cork blackface makeup. During this same time period, Eubie Blake and his songwriting partner and singer Noble Sissle had been touring on the white vaudeville circuit and playing society jobs arranged by James Reese Europe. Remarkably, these two premier stage duos had never crossed paths until a meeting at an NAACP fundraiser in Philadelphia in 1920. As recalled by Blake, when they met again serendipitously on the streets of New York, Miller, impressed with Sissle and Blake's musical style, proposed that the four work to produce a show robust enough to attract backing for a run on Broadway, where there had been no all-Black production in over a decade.[8]

Based on their Pekin comic sketch *The Mayor of Dixie*, a large-scale production renamed *Shuffle Along* opened on the outskirts of the Broadway district on May 23, 1921, at the 63rd Street Theater. The company limped into town after near financial collapse on the road. The show broke with several conventions to which previous Black shows felt compelled (or required) to adhere. The majority of the dramatic cast did not wear burnt cork. The light-skinned female chorus, in the tradition of white shows like the *Follies* or *Vanities*, presented a line of precision dancers in semi-suggestive garb. During the first heyday of Black musical theater in the first decade of the century, expression of romantic affection on stage was forbidden.[9] *Shuffle Along* broke with this taboo by including a serious, romantic love scene without parody or satire. Sissle and Blake's tune, "Love Will Find A Way," was the featured number, notably without comic or childlike portrayals. But as the title of the show suggests, much remained of the old depictions of African Americans. From a twenty-first-century vantage point, the changes bravely wrought by Miller and Lyles and Sissle and Blake may seem marginal. Yet *Shuffle Along* established a new and urbane standard for Black musicals that had broad appeal while at the same time presented the humanity of African Americans and not merely caricatures.

Shuffle Along ran for an astounding 504 performances on Broadway before embarking on a cross-country tour. The two comedians, who did not accompany the road production, quickly looked to further capitalize on its success. Their opportunity came when producer George White sought them out to write a book for a new show where they would also play the leading roles. George White (1891–1968), famous for his series of productions called the *Scandals*, was himself a trained dancer and at one time a star of the *Ziegfeld Follies*. After a split with Ziegfeld about salary in 1916, White formed another dancing team and shortly thereafter began producing elaborate miniature revues. He produced his first *Scandals*, patterned after the more famous *Follies*, in 1919. These fast-paced song-and-dance stage shows catapulted him to the top of the entertainment world, helped substantially by the addition in 1920 of a new, young songwriter named George Gershwin. White was an aggressive, hands-on producer. Although he had his own firm conceptions, he was always looking for a new angle and new talent. The success of *Shuffle Along* and the potentially lucrative market for "race" entertainment was not lost on him, and now he wanted in. His clout could easily bring a new show to Broadway. Miller and Lyles were more than eager to construct what in many ways constitutes a sequel. Others from the *Shuffle Along* cast were recruited for the new show.

White's plan to title the show *Shuffle Along of 1923* was quashed with a lawsuit filed by the producers of the original show.[10] Other tentative titles included *George White's Black Scandals* and *Miller and Lyles Cakewalkers*.[11] *Runnin' Wild* was eventually agreed upon, but not because it represented anything particular about the show. It was a frequently used descriptive image of the day. The enormously successful popular tune by that name, written by A. H. Gibbs, Joe Grey, and Leo Wood, had been published the year before. Authorship is often incorrectly attributed to Johnson, although the song was, during the out-of-town run of the show, included as an encore in the second act. While White's new show was playing, there was also an unrelated movie and a white burlesque travelling show each named *Runnin' Wild*. Miller concocted a story around two deadbeats from the southern town of Jimtown. They skip on their board bill and go to the frigid climate of St. Paul, Minnesota. After a fill of the cold, they return to Jimtown as spiritualistic mediums. As was typical of this genre, the shallow story line served as the framework for a series of song-and-dance numbers and comedy sketches. This included Miller and Lyles's well-known boxing and arithmetic sketches, and a séance for the "Ghost Society."

Johnson was already at work writing numbers for *Runnin' Wild* during his trip to London with *Plantation Days*. Other songwriting opportunities could not be turned down. He wrote a score for a short-lived show titled *Raisin' Cain—A Cyclonic Musical Comedy*, starring the popular duo of Buck and Bubbles. It ran for two weeks in mid-July at the Lafayette Theater in Harlem before reduction to tabloid size, which then toured the Fox circuit. Rehearsals for the as yet unnamed White show began July 10 in Bryant Hall in New York.[12] A brief tour through other eastern cities was planned before opening in New York, the common practice then as now for shows headed for Broadway. *Runnin' Wild* opened on August 25, 1923, at the Howard Theater in Washington, with Will Marion Cook leading the orchestra. Cook had returned from his extended stay in Europe in March 1923, and shortly after returning began work on his own stage musical titled *Cotton Blossoms*. He recruited old friends Alex Rogers, Luckey Roberts, and Johnson to collaborate on the score. It does not appear the show was completed or produced.[13] Cook tried desperately to keep his good friend Jim Europe's Clef Club orchestral legacy alive. Under mounting expenses, Europe's once mighty presentations of fifty or more musicians had winnowed to a dozen. Gigs were more infrequent,[14] and Cook was looking for work. It is likely either Miller, with whom he had worked twenty years earlier, or Johnson, recommended him to lead the fifteen-piece orchestra for the out-of-town opening. Johnson was at the piano for the opening, and in a newspaper interview in July, Cook declared him to be the most versatile pianist of the race.[15] George White accompanied the show and was personally involved in last-minute changes.[16] The racial mix of the audience was three-fourths white, "which is unusual for Washington," noted the reviewer from *Variety*. Miller and Lyles, Johnson and lyricist Cecil Mack's tunes, and the chorus were cited as standouts in the early reviews. "Of the musical numbers, which are the work of James Johnson while the lyrics are by Cecil Mack, there isn't one but that will register. The 'love number' is the theme song and will undoubtedly be one of the big sellers of the coming season," wrote Meakin in *Variety*.[17] Jonesy, in *Billboard*, was even more taken by the tune, writing, "Ina Duncan, Adelaide Hall and Arthur Porter put over the biggest song hit of the show, 'Old Fashioned Love.' It was indeed one of the more tuneful and bewitching numbers I've ever heard."[18] Another reviewer further praised the music, writing, "The song numbers are very tuneful and there are more hits in *Runnin' Wild* than is heard in two or three of the average musical comedies."[19] The dancing was singled out as "a revelation," and "handled by some clever artists and most of them young showfolk."[20] Of the dance feature "Charleston," Jonesy in *Billboard* noted only, "Elizabeth Welch and chorus with 'Charleston' and 'Juba Dance' were well received."[21]

The show appeared to have a successful start at the Howard with sellout crowds for its first week of ten performances grossing $8,000, but financial pressures and a salary dispute threatened to scuttle the whole venture. It was an elaborate production. The fifteen-piece orchestra cost $1,200 a week, and the headlining comedians commanded $2,000 a week, in addition to the over sixty others in the cast and supporting staff. With a top ticket price of one dollar, White predicted a loss, and Miller and Lyles agreed to waive salary for the first week. They also assured White that the others in the cast would do the same. Whether they were misrepresented or had a change of heart, as the show began its second week, the cast demanded their pay. When threatened with closure by White, Miller and Lyles made good on waiving their salary, and the other cast members accepted partial payment.[22] The show survived its close call and completed a second week, moving on to New England with an even higher bar to jump.

The show opened in Boston at Selwyn's Theater on Labor Day. George White attended the opening there as well. As the sole owner of the show at that point, he monitored (and meddled with) its progress with intense scrutiny.[23] He had good reason. By the early 1920s, Archibald "Arch" Selwyn was the owner of a vast network of theaters and had been one of the founders of Goldwyn pictures, later to become Metro-Goldwyn-Mayer. (The "wyn" half of the name is derived from the latter half of Selwyn.) Selwyn knew well the potential of an all-Black show. After its New York run, Selwyn had booked *Shuffle Along* in Boston for only two weeks, but it ran for fifteen. The extended stay ran him afoul of his other contracted bookings. With *Runnin' Wild*, even before a run in New York, he was ready to commit to a longer stay. Selwyn booked the show for an unlimited run, but, cautious to protect his interests, insisted on a gross revenue clause—the show would close if it grossed less than $10,000 a week for two consecutive weeks.[24] White would see to it that did not happen.

Reviews in Boston were uniformly very favorable. *The Boston Globe* noted, "'Runnin' Wild' is full of dancing and singing, and both are excellently done. New comedy business by the stars, Miller and Lyles, adds a generous amount of riotous mirth so that throughout the audience is constantly entertained. Of the musical numbers 'Old Fashioned Love' seemed to make an undisputed hit." *The Boston Telegram* noted that "'Old Fashioned Love' runs through the show at intervals in a most pleasing manner." They further proclaimed, "By a long shot a better show than the famous 'Shuffle Along,' the all colored musical sensation *Runnin' Wild* with Miller and Lyles doing the comic, opened what should be a highly successful engagement at the Selwyn Theater yesterday, with a popular matinee and a capacity evening house." *The Traveler* praised the show, its music and dancing, noting, "There is a hit in every song in the show," and "The song hit of the show is 'Old Fashioned Love.' You may expect to hear this jazzed by every phonograph and piano, but never again will you hear it jazzed as these singers and the 'Runnin' Wild' orchestra jazz it." *Billboard* noted Will Marion Cook was still with the show as choral director, and that the "modest" scenery and costumes were more than made up for by the comedy,

CHAPTER 12.

"SEASON'S GREETINGS"

dancing, and the "outstanding song hits" that included "Open Your Heart," "Gingerbrown," "Old-Fashioned Love," and "Log Cabin Days."[25] None of these reviews mentioned the dance number "Charleston."

Financially, the show had a solid but not spectacular start. After a disappointing first week with gross receipts of $11,000, well behind the pace of *Shuffle Along*,[26] things picked up and for its first five weeks in Boston grossed over $12,000 a week. By mid-October and despite the glowing reviews, maintaining this level of revenue came at great cost to the cast. Miller and Lyles, still pursued legally by the original backers of *Shuffle Along* who claimed them as their exclusive promotional property since the pioneering show was still on tour, won a court victory in early October allowing them to advertise themselves in *Runnin' Wild* as the same pair who had made *Shuffle Along* a great success. But their fifth-week gross barely hit $12,000, and only because of add-on matinees and midnight shows. At one point there were four shows in twenty-eight hours, accounting for an additional $1,500 for the week.[27] In its final week, the show grossed $11,000 and closed in Boston on October 20 after sixty-three performances.[28] This was a respectable showing but not spectacular and well behind the pace set by *Shuffle Along* at $15,000 a week. Nonetheless, White was convinced it would be a winner in a "legitimate" Broadway theater. The trouble was finding one. There was little if any interest by the managers and owners of the major Broadway theaters to extend a lease, despite the rising appeal of African American musical theater productions to a broad audience. Eventually, White landed on the Colonial Theater. Built in 1905 as the Colonial

Music Hall, it featured musicals for a brief two months when it was sold. Its subsequent owners were a string of vaudeville producers including the famous B. F. Keith in 1912 and in 1917 E. F. Albee. Although physically sitting on Broadway, with its uptown address at 62nd Street and vaudeville as its entertainment fare, it was not thought of as a mainstream or "legitimate" Broadway theater.[29] White convinced Selwyn to buy an interest in the show, and secured a one-year lease for the Colonial for $35,000, excluding Sundays, which continued to be reserved for its local vaudeville clientele.[30] The old vaudeville house reclaimed a place in the new world of legitimate Broadway musical theater, albeit with an all-Black "cut rate" show, the official terminology used for shows whose seat prices were lower than high-profile productions farther downtown. Before leaving Boston, the exhausted cast had nine days before opening in New York and found the time and energy to sing for the Masons and for a sacred concert at Shawmut Congregational Church, a white congregation, with proceeds going to the African American St. Marks Congregational Church.[31]

The show opened at the Colonial Theater on October 29, 1923. In New York, John T. Ricks' Orchestra replaced Will Marion Cook in the pit. A teenage John Hammond, later to become a prominent record producer and patron of jazz, was sneaking home Johnson's 78rpm recorded piano solos and piano rolls and recalled meeting him for the first time when he was playing in the orchestra at the Colonial Theater.[32] As was true for most highly promoted productions, opening-night attendance was dominated by "music publishers, critics, and regular first nighters" such that it seemed the audience was "all white."[33] White hoped to cash in by asking an ambitious $5.00 a seat. The strategy backfired and the opener did not sell out. Prices were cut for night two, which grossed an additional $2,000.[34] The reviews were highly favorable. Most of the cast members were veterans of *Shuffle Along* and had established their reputations in that show. The feature number "Old Fashioned Love" was presented by three such veterans: Ina Duncan, Arthur Porter, and Adelaide Hall. This number continued to be singled out above all others by the reviewers as the overwhelming hit of the show. Gordon Whyte wrote in *Billboard* there is "good comedy, tuneful music, spirited playing and fast dancing. The key song of the piece, 'Old Fashioned Love,' was particularly well done and seems destined for great popularity." Johnson had worked on this tune (and probably others) on the trip back from England in May, but he had worked out the theme two years earlier. In one of his first piano rolls from early 1921, he inserts what would become the chorus of "Old Fashioned Love" into his rendition of Lukie Johnson and Ted Koehler's tune "Don't Tell Your Monkey Man."

Whyte's astute eye noticed that in the scenery backdrop for the Minnesota scenes were advertisements for New York businesses. He concluded this was a lack of attention to detail. More likely it was recycling of old scenery as a move to keep costs low, but one wonders whether it was intentional as part of the humor. Whyte singled out the acrobatic tap dancer Tommy Woods and the Song Birds female quartet but incorrectly attributed the "lazy dance" to Ralph Bryson. This slow-motion dance feature, including kinesthetically perfect splits done in a manner later made famous by the Nicholas Brothers, was performed by George Stamper.[35] Woods and Stamper were singled out for praise by Alan Dale in the *New York American*.[36] *Billboard* highlighted Mattie Wilkes. Known as the "Dean of Colored Actresses," she was also a veteran of *Shuffle Along* and the widow of Ernest Hogan.[37] *The American Stage*, along with *Variety*, singled out "Old Fashioned Love" and "Open Your Heart," with the Miller and Lyles arithmetic comedy routine "13 is 1/7 of 28" as "the humorous high spot."[38] Another of their comedy routines titled "Can't Do It," during which Lyles tries to convince Miller that he could not have been jailed although it has already happened, was recorded by the duo the year before for OKeh Records.[39] *The New York Times* noted the dancing and their reviewers felt it was a better and more successful show than *Shuffle Along*, commenting, "As a matter of fact, one who was not particularly moved by 'Shuffle Along'—and who remained unimpressed as its various imitations took the boards—was vastly entertained last night at the first performance of *Runnin' Wild*."[40] The paper went further in its praise, noting "George White has rung the bell squarely with his new Negro revue, *Runnin' Wild*. Although quartered as far north as sixty-third Street, it has been packing its theater (the Colonial) since the opening. It has begun at a pace that seems to stamp it as a much bigger success than *Shuffle Along*."[41] *Runnin' Wild* was the chic experience. Everyone wanted to be seen with the cast of this new hit. The granddaughter of cosmetics tycoon Madame C. J. Walker arranged a prenuptial party at the theater with the cast as part of what was hailed as the largest African American wedding in history.[42]

Of the lead stars, Aubrey Lyles was flamboyant, mercurial, and at times loose-mouthed. Flournoy Miller was the opposite. He was judicious, thoughtful, and recognized the responsibility of his position as an African American leader. "Miller also felt that the only way to put Negro performers into white theaters with any kind of dignity was through musical comedy, where they could run their own show unhampered," concluded Sissle and Blake biographers Kimball and Bolcolm.[43] Through his dedication against long odds, he developed his comedy sketch *The Mayor of Dixie* into the musical theater juggernaut of *Shuffle Along* and its offspring, realizing the ambition of J. Leubrie Hill, Tutt and Whitney, Jim Europe, and others in reestablishing African American performers in mainstream Broadway theaters after more than a decade in exile. *Runnin' Wild* proved to be another successful demonstration of Miller's talents. "He is a fine example of the quiet, forceful characters that accomplish things . . ." for the "future betterment of the race," wrote

J. A. Jackson in *Billboard* in its section dedicated to African American arts.[44] Miller was eager to chip away further at the virulent stereotypes embedded in post-minstrelsy entertainment genres that for most whites defined African American society and culture. Alongside his blackface comedy sketches with Lyles, Miller was writing dramatic works for artists such as the acclaimed actor Charles Gilpin, which he intended for production in Black theaters for Black audiences.[45] Flournoy Miller became one of Johnson's closest friends.

The comic technique mastered by Miller and Lyles, although often erroneously ascribed to them as their invention, has been called "indefinite talk." Its origins date to the nineteenth century heyday of minstrelsy. At its most effective and in purest form, it requires precise, well-rehearsed verbal persiflage between two performers who perpetually interrupt each other before completing a statement. In an act of mind reading, they finish each other's sentences, incompletely conveying the details of the story they are telling. The blanks are left to the audience to fill in, relying on their own experiential notions of the minstrel-derived, racialized actors before them. That is, if they catch on at all. As perfected by Miller and Lyles, their complete synchrony of communication, delivered in cryptic drollery, incorporates touchstones of cultural practice identifiable to their Black audiences, but for most of the white audiences, appeared as nothing more than the ranting of two hapless buffoons. This is all there was for white onlookers, unaware of the signifiers familiar to Black audiences that include oral traditions, storytelling, call and response, and street-corner repartee. That the messengers perform in blackface complicates critical assessment of the content. Certainly, in the 1920s, one did not buck these conventions easily, and did so at one's peril, personally and professionally. When asked why he and other Black ragtime composers wrote so many pieces in difficult keys with many sharps and flats, Eubie Blake quipped, with his inimitable wry humor, that they played on all the black keys because they were afraid to play on the white keys.

By the time the all-Black musical had its rebirth in the 1920s, it was essentially only the comics who maintained the blackface ritual. The singers, dancers, and musicians did not wear the burnt cork, unlike the white blackface singers such as Al Jolson and Eddie Cantor. Miller and Lyles dominated Black musical theater for the entire decade because they were creative, expert showmen. As writers Yuval Taylor and Jake Austen note, the potency of indefinite talk demonstrates "that stereotype-burdened minstrelsy spawned innovative black brilliance...."[46] The incremental evolution Miller was forging for Black performers before mixed audiences was not lost on the unidentified opening-night reviewer in the *New York Times*, who observed, "*Runnin Wild* follows the general pattern of the negro [sic] show fairly closely, but there is an inventiveness in many of the comedy scenes that has not been evident in these entertainments in the past. For this the Messrs. Miller and Lyles are responsible, for they are their own authors. There is, to be sure, the traditional superstition scene, but there is not so much as a line about shooting craps, and ham replaces chicken as the most desirable of all dishes."[47] *The Globe and Sun* noted that *Runnin' Wild* is "a rather dignified rewriting of the immortal *Liza*," the 1922 all-Black Broadway show produced by Flournoy Miller's brother Irvin C. Miller.[48] While the comedy retained some of the familiar uncomplimentary racial conventions, the singing adopted the high art presentation of the prominent Black choirs of the day that performed in venues such as Carnegie Hall. In an otherwise negative review that devoted significant space to comparison with white performers, the *New York Tribune* reluctantly noted, "Anyway the audience . . . had an exceedingly good time" and ". . . didn't leave its seats until the last negro [sic] tenor in evening clothes had sung his last song in a highly cultured voice without a trace of dialect."[49] The dancing included plenty of "acrobatic" technique to satisfy the expectation of a "fast" show, the adjective that had been used as the yardstick of quality for all-Black productions for years, but there was at least one segment that drew comparison to the best of Ziegfeld, known for dramatic dance numbers. Highlighted by another reviewer, "It comes at the end of the first act. Its title, according to the program, is 'Finale.' Six or seven of the loveliest of the chorus participate. It is a frame, even as the whites have shown, of brownish girls, which the whites would never have shown, reclining in postures which, for want of a better term, might be called artistic. . . . It is very, very beautiful."[50]

Gross receipts surpassed White's and Selwyn's expectations. In the weekly tallies reported by *Variety*, it grossed as much as $20,700 and never less than $17,400 in its first six weeks. A minor legal tangle for Miller and Lyles didn't derail the momentum when Harry Bestry sued them for claimed uncompensated managerial services.[51] Bestry was a New York agent who, when the show first opened in Washington, had claimed ownership along with company manager Clarence Gray. The two insisted White had only assisted with the production, and that he was not entitled to any financial interest.[52] This was clearly untrue,[53] and when the show's success was evident, Bestry, who may have had some role in casting, looked to recoup on his trumped-up grievance. His attempt failed. Although the pace slowed somewhat through the winter holidays and into January, by the end of February, *Runnin' Wild* was reported to have outgrossed *Shuffle Along* and in a shorter run.[54] Seats were reportedly selling eight weeks ahead.[55] At the height of its financial heyday in December and riding "the wave of public enthusiasm," Selwyn announced he was looking to take the show to London in May,[56] but erosion of receipts by late winter scuttled those plans. Competition was stiff. Broadway was booming with the fifty-five "legitimate" theaters (the Colonial included) grossing a record breaking $1 million at that point in the season. Repeating his strategy to bolster the return on his investment, which seemed to be flagging, White added

Flournoy Miller and Aubrey Lyles in full blackface makeup and costume from *Runnin' Wild*. (Photo by White Studio © New York Public Library for the Performing Arts)

Miller and Lyles with the chorus of *Runnin' Wild* in the St. Paul, Minnesota, scene. (Photo by White Studio © New York Public Library for the Performing Arts)

performances in late February.⁵⁷ In March, with receipts sinking to $10,000, new musical numbers were added and cast changes were made.⁵⁸ The changes were euphemistically described as the opening of a spring edition.⁵⁹ White was hoping to run out the season and had already planned a Chicago opening in early summer. There was still some steam remaining, as the quality of the show continued to be acknowledged. "Miller and Lyles are witty and jovial as ever, and the olive chorus girls dance, sing and frolic throughout the show to rival the animation of any picked chorus of white entertainers. On the whole, the show is not unlike the former edition, but it reminds us that as time goes on we can afford less and less to disregard the sparkle and the wit of the folk from Harlem," acknowledged the Brooklyn paper.⁶⁰

White continued to be hounded by the principals of Shuffle Along, Inc., who were determined to keep Miller and Lyles their exclusive domain. He finally had to settle with them out of court.⁶¹ Another scandal briefly plagued the production, inferring a scheme to provide discounted tickets to white patrons while excluding working-class Blacks and keeping the theater segregated. In this impropriety Miller and Lyles were themselves accused of complicity.⁶² The blatant racial motivation of the Theatre Cooperative and Recreation Service and the Colonial Theater management who hatched the plan seemed to work, as the "overwhelming part of the audience is white," noted one correspondent.⁶³ If the intent was to increase ticket sales, it had limited effect. One further attempt at cutting expenses and making revisions did little to prop up attendance, and receipts fell further from $9,000 a week, a level reportedly still profitable, to a low of $8,000 before the show closed on May 3.⁶⁴ Just before closing, the *Runnin' Wild* company performed a matinee benefit for the Tuskegee Institute on April 30.⁶⁵ Although far behind the staggering 504 performances of *Shuffle Along*, *Runnin' Wild* ran for a very respectable 220 performances on Broadway. It was enough to put it in the top 10 percent of openings for the entire decade, a period of time that would become known as the first golden age of Broadway.

Runnin' Wild was a hit, and even before its popularity began to flag, Johnson began work on another theatrical songwriting venture. His commitment to the new effort may explain perhaps why songs by other composers including Porter Grainger and Turner Layton were added to the "spring edition" of *Runnin' Wild*. On the other hand, Johnson was a songwriting machine and was frequently juggling the compositional demands of multiple commitments. Will Marion Cook had long aspired to present the cultural and musical legacy of African Americans on stage in a manner different from the vaudeville/tabloid format typical of Black (and much of white) musical theater at the time, but he recognized there would be limitations to how far he could go. In a show titled *Negro Nuances*, Cook traces through music a history of Black people from Africa, arriving in the New World on slave ships, living through the years of slavery on the plantation, adopting minstrelsy during reconstruction, culminating in a frenzied jazz finale comprising the last twenty-two minutes of the production. He subtitled the production "the soul of a race, told in song and dance." Cook was a conservatory-trained musician, not a comedian, and with loftier aspirations for his creation, he added "novel historic and patriotic effects accurately reproduced," in a production he was "determined shall be his masterpiece."[66] The book was written by Abbie Mitchell, Cook's wife, a prominent singer and dancer who had recently concluded a three-year European tour. Since early January, Cook and Johnson, after concluding his Broadway responsibilities each evening, were working late hours together on the music in a studio the two shared for the project at 232 West 138th Street.[67] The score was written primarily by Cook, except for the jazz finale he called "The Land of Jazz," which was composed by Johnson with additional material from Sidney Bechet.

Cook planned to line up the cream of Black stage entertainment. In addition to his wife, he planned to include Gertrude Saunders, Alberta Hunter, Lucille Handy, his daughter Marion Douglas, and son-in-law Louis Douglas, who had made a name for himself in Europe with his dancing. Leonard Harper was engaged to stage it with additional dance training for the chorus from a student of the noted Russian dancer/choreographer Michel Fokine.[68] On January 27, Cook managed a preliminary performance at the Times Square Theater under the auspices of a new promotional organization he created called the Negro Folk Music and Drama Society. In addition to Saunders, Hunter, and Mitchell, other notables who reportedly performed included Paul Robeson, Edith Wilson, and members of the *Runnin' Wild* company including the ladies quartet and dancer George Stamper. It was to be the first in a series of performances. Cook led the orchestra of twenty-five along with Edmund T. Jenkins, expatriate son of the renowned Jenkins orphanage founder Reverend Daniel Jenkins.[69] Cook and the younger Jenkins had first met when Cook was in London in 1919 with his Southern Syncopated Orchestra. Johnson had also met Jenkins when he was in London with *Plantation Days*. Edmund Jenkins had studied in Europe and was an accomplished musician and composer. Cook sent specially for him to assist with the music, and at great personal expense Jenkins came from Paris, where he was making significantly more money.[70] No further Sunday performances followed, and Cook attempted to regroup. He advertised for chorus girls in February[71] and planned for initial out-of-town trials in Jersey City and Newark, New Jersey. In early March he planned performances in the larger eastern cities of Philadelphia, Washington, and Baltimore, the traditional pre-Broadway tour.[72] Cook concluded that a jazz finale would not be enough to draw an audience, and during rehearsals in February, he drew further from *Runnin' Wild*, adding comedy sketches by Miller and Lyles. J. A. Jackson of *Billboard*, who had been following the progress of the show and saw some preliminary sketches in the Cook/Johnson studio, observed that the levity was added so that the seriousness of Cook's music and Mitchell's narrative would be "relieved" by the two comedians. Of Johnson's association with Cook, Jackson further commented, "James P. Johnson, if he does nothing more (and the boy has just arrived) than to have written the tuneful melodies of 'Running [sic] Wild,' current Broadway success, he will have a lifelong claim to an honored place among the composers of this age."[73] An initial opening for the revised show was scheduled for March 4 but was delayed, and a new opening was set for Easter Monday, April 21, at a Shubert Theater on Broadway. Instead of his own orchestra, Cook sought out Ohio bandleader Sammy Stewart, whose style was more dance band than jazz.[74] By this point, Cook's artistic vision had been badly diluted, and the product was likely a fragmented production little different from other Black theatrical offerings. Cook was planning much more, and in what must have been a bitter disappointment for him, the show apparently never saw any further performances.

♪

Plans were underway for publication of songs from *Runnin' Wild* well before the Washington, DC, opening. The behemoth publishing firm Harms had published many numbers from George White's *Scandals* annually since 1919. By early September, they had copyrighted and published five of Johnson's musical numbers: "Ginger Brown," "Love Bug," "Old Fashioned Love," "Open Your Heart," and "Charleston." "Love Bug" was eventually dropped from the show during the New York run. Johnson had composed his "Worried and Lonesome Blues" earlier in the year, and had recorded it in June. By the New York opening of *Runnin' Wild*, he had incorporated it into the show. It was positioned as the musical backdrop for George Stamper and his "lazy dance." Stamper and Johnson had worked together on several prior occasions as far back as 1916 with Frank Montgomery and the *Darktown Follies*. Stamper had gone to London with Johnson in *Plantation Days*. Perry Bradford copyrighted it, along with Johnson's "Weeping Blues," in July and published it with the title "Worried Lonesome Blues" in November.[75] The sheet music features a cartoon depiction of Stamper in a "lazy dance" pose, noting its status in "Broadway's Biggest Hit." Stamper's slow-motion performance backed by Johnson's "pleading" blues tune was noted by the critics, igniting Stamper's career as a sought-after dancer and choreographer. For Johnson, Bradford's publication and Stamper's performance propelled the release of his recording of the tune to very healthy sales for a piano solo. Stamper and Johnson would be associated again a decade later on film.

Unlike Eubie Blake, who recorded many of the musical numbers from *Shuffle Along* during its run, Johnson made no phonograph records of the tunes from *Runnin' Wild* during the height of its popularity. The tunes from the show were enormously successful. By February 1924, *Variety* reported a Columbia Records release of "Old Fashioned Love" was one of the six best sellers for January. Of production music, which "was selling better than ever," "Old Fashioned Love," "Charleston," and "Open Your Heart" were tops in popularity. There were at least ten jazz and jazz-oriented recordings of one of these three tunes cut from October 1923 through February 1924. The reviewer Abel, in the *New York Clipper*, commented, on the Victor release of "Old Fashioned Love" and "Charleston" by Arthur Gibbs and His Gang, that Johnson was "already a jazz pianist of much ability," and predicted "Charleston" would be very popular on the dance floor.[76] Since phonograph recording session fees did not pay as well as the composing and performing opportunities that were increasingly coming his way, and since he was receiving composer royalties on the sales of the recordings of his tunes by others, Johnson had little incentive to record his own tunes. In March 1924, Harms published a thirteen-page "Selection" folio of Johnson's tunes from *Runnin' Wild*. The famous Broadway arranger Robert Russell Bennett (listed as Russell Bennett on the music), who had joined the staff at Harms in 1919, strung together "Ginger Brown," "Old Fashioned Love," "Charleston" (spelled incorrectly as "Charlestown" on the sheet music), and "Open Your Heart." Although Johnson's contract with QRS had expired, he continued to cut piano rolls for them. While a record session might only pay $30, he would make $100 for each of his piano rolls. The same month as the Harms "Selection" sheet was published, QRS released Johnson's piano roll medley that included "Charleston," "Old Fashioned Love," "Open Your Heart," and "Love Bug." Throughout his recording and performing life, Johnson seemed eager to promote his own tunes, and he started this musical self-promotion from the outset of his recording career. Almost all his earliest piano rolls from 1917–18 were his compositions. Four of the six spectacular 78rpm solos he recorded in 1923 were his tunes. The enthusiasm for African American material in print and on record showed no sign of slowing and ignited opportunity for both the older generation of composers as well as a new generation. With *Runnin' Wild*, Johnson was acknowledged as the leader of the latter group in the mainstream trade magazines, with *Billboard* noting, "The wave of public enthusiasm for 'blues' and the scramble of the recording companies for material with which to meet the demand has been the avenue thru [sic] which many names have crept into the list of Negro composers. Those known to earlier fame have continued, many becoming the publishers of their own numbers. Perhaps the most prolific and most successful of the new school is James C. [sic] Jimmie Johnson, the young pianist who wrote the music for the numbers in the 'Runnin Wild' show, this after he had done more than a score of other melodies for publishers and recording concerns."[77] It seems odd that Johnson did not pursue recording his hit tunes. He had had success at convincing the recording companies to include many of his other compositions in both record and piano roll sessions. As *Runnin' Wild* was wrapping up, he organized a performing orchestra, but they did not record. Harms was probably satisfied with the recordings of others and the sheet music sales. Johnson's lapse in not recording his own tunes from his most successful show would prove to be the first misstep in derailing an opportunity for broader national recognition.

♪

In September 1923, Elmer Snowden and his Washington Black Sox Orchestra began a six-month contract to play at a Broadway restaurant/nightclub newly renamed the Hollywood Inn (previously the Palais De Dance). Duke Ellington was the pianist in the band led by banjoist Snowden. Leonard Harper had been engaged to stage a show at the Hollywood titled *Harper's Dixie Revue*,[78] and he may have been the catalyst for the Black Sox Orchestra's appearance since Ellington was boarding with Harper at the time. The Hollywood was a small, dank, physically unwieldy but well-located dive in the epicenter of the Broadway district at 203 West 49th Street and Broadway. Leaky pipes from the low ceiling overhung the crowded stage. Its limited capacity of one hundred people frequently left it in financial straits.[79] By February 1924, Ellington had become the leader of the band. Most of the members hailed from Ellington's hometown of Washington, DC, and from that point they were known simply as the Washingtonians. The "Charleston" was then gaining momentum with the public, prompting Harper to add it as a dance specialty to the spring production of the *Dixie Revue*.[80] Ellington and the Washingtonians played at the Hollywood (which changed its name to the Club Kentucky in 1925, but more often referred to as the Kentucky Club. They then established a policy of allowing white patrons only) for forty of the next forty-eight months. During those eight months off, the band traveled, usually out of town, as they did starting in April 1924, to New England.[81] The tour was necessitated by the closure of the Hollywood for a month because of a fire.[82] When the club reopened in May, the management contracted with Johnson to bring in a band. Fresh off their failed collaboration with Cook, and as *Runnin' Wild* was coming to a close, Johnson included Bechet in the band along with a sixteen-year-old Benny Carter. At this stage in his career, Johnson, like Ellington, was inclined more toward an arranged sound for his band, an approach that rankled the mercurial Bechet who, in a small-group setting, much preferred to play in his native

New Orleans Creole style rooted in collective polyphony. Johnson claimed the manager of the club was more in favor of his own approach, a likely notion since Johnson was following Ellington's band. In a rather disdainful tone, Bechet commented, "James P. was trying to make it almost like one of those big swing bands—hit parade stuff."[83] Their stylistic disagreement quickly led to Bechet's departure from the group.

Harper put together a new floor show with a new score written by Johnson that debuted in early May. Old colleagues from *Plantation Days* were featured including Dave and Tressie and George Stamper along with singer Lena Wilson and dancer "Honey" Brown.[84] Noted burlesque producer Jules Hurtig was a frequent patron at the Hollywood and admired Harper's work. With his partner Harry Seamon, Hurtig and Seamon had been theatrical giants for two decades. They had established a reputation early on as white producers who were not afraid to support African American stage shows. They sponsored Bert Williams and George Walker, including their European tour. In 1913, they built Hurtig and Seamon's New Burlesque Theater on 125th Street in Harlem. Two decades later, it became the Apollo Theater. Hurtig engaged Harper to stage a series of productions. Harper saw it as an opportunity to open the door to the white theatrical world. Their association rekindled at the Hollywood, Harper brought along Johnson to do the music. One wonders if Ellington had any trepidation about his idol and mentor spelling for him while he was out of town. He needn't have worried. Johnson's interest was not the development of a carefully crafted orchestra. As a result of their renewed association at the Hollywood, Harper and Johnson were soon back on the road collaborating on other stage productions.

After *Runnin' Wild* closed in New York, White and Selwyn arranged a road tour. The company maintained most of its New York cast and continued to attract a mixed-race audience and favorable reviews. Its ancestor *Shuffle Along* was also still touring, but one reviewer noted that "certain touches make it more interesting than any of its predecessors, including *Shuffle Along*, which set the pace for works of its kind." "Open Your Heart" and a new tune written by Jo Trent and Porter Grainger titled "Heart Breakin' Joe" were singled out.[85] Miller and Lyles, who did not tour with *Shuffle Along*, did so with *Runnin' Wild*, accounting for much of its success well into 1924. The duration of Johnson's role with the company is not exactly known. He was tied up with Harper and a succession of other stage shows which were playing in Chicago while *Runnin' Wild* was playing there. Programs of the road tour name only the orchestra director (which was not listed as Johnson) or make no mention of the musical accompaniment at all. A gossip page item from September 1924 makes reference to Johnson as a member of the *Runnin' Wild* company,[86] but this seems unlikely since at the time the show was on a three-week tour of Manitoba,

Minnesota, and Wisconsin.[87] Miller and Lyles continued to lead the company and were a huge draw on the road. The tunes were still mostly Johnson's, with a new number of his titled "Sun Kist Rose" noted as one of the most popular.[88] In mid-1925, Irvin C. Miller, Flournoy Miller's brother, took over producing *Runnin' Wild*. Perry Bradford managed to place a number of his own tunes in the revised show, including "Hydrant Love," "I Ain't Gonna Play No Second Fiddle," and "Lucy Long."[89] The featured comedian in the show was now Eddie Lemons, who was replaced in February 1926 by Albert Jackson.[90] In May 1928, a traveling company took the show to London.

Runnin' Wild's greatest and most important legacy sprang from one song and dance. One would be hard pressed to identify one song and dance that came to symbolize a worldwide cultural phenomenon so completely as did the "Charleston." Its three component parts—the dance, the rhythm, and the tune—came together with a spell-binding synergy in *Runnin' Wild*. The penetration and ultimate dominance of the "Charleston," to the virtual exclusion of others, has rendered it the signature performing arts emblem of the decade—the "roaring twenties." Its future historical importance was well recognized by the height of the "Charleston" craze in 1925. "The Charleston, an All-American dance recently evolved and so characteristic of young America today that it is apt to go down in dance history as typifying this particular period," noted the *Kenosha Evening News*. The dance, in some form as an offshoot of the ring shout, filtered its way from the Georgia and South Carolina Sea Island Gullah and Geechie communities to the city. Starting just before the turn of the twentieth century and continuing into the 1920s, migration up the Eastern Seaboard brought these dances into Harlem, where James P. Johnson observed them and composed for them. He recalled:

> The people who came to The Jungles Casino were mostly from around Charleston, South Carolina, and other places in the South. Most of them worked for the Ward Line as longshoremen or on ships that called at southern coast ports. There were even some Gullahs among them.
>
> The Charleston, which became a popular dance step on its own, was just a regulation cotillion step without a name. It had many variations—all danced to the rhythm that everybody knows now. One regular at the Casino, named Dan White, was the best dancer in the crowd and he introduced the Charleston step as we know it. But there were dozens of other steps used, too.
>
> It was while playing for these southern dances that I composed a number of Charlestons—eight in all—all with the same rhythm. One of these later became my famous *Charleston* when it hit Broadway.[91]

Jack Mills copyrighted one of Johnson's versions of a Charleston, "The Charleston Dance," in June, before *Runnin' Wild* was in rehearsal. It was never published, was not the version included in the show, and did not include the famous rhythm as we know it.

Harms seemed to have been dragging its feet in promoting "Charleston." However, most of the reviews singled out the song "Old Fashioned Love" as the number most likely to catch the public's favor, not the "Charleston." Abel, in *Variety*, had predicted the popularity of the dance only a month after the opening of *Runnin' Wild*. As late as May 1925, he made note of the publisher's hesitation to review a recording of the tune by the Golden Gate Orchestra, observing, "Why 'Charleston,' the original creator of the Charleston dance craze hasn't happened sooner has given rise to no little wonderment. Only lately has Harms, Inc. music publishers, gotten behind it seriously, and there is little doubt this corking tune will click at this comparatively late date."[92] By July, Harms hired a special Midwest sales representative to specially promote Johnson's tune.[93] Harms finally embraced the popularity of the tune, and by 1925 sheet music printings included pictorial instructions on the back cover for mastering the dance steps. On the front cover they declare clearly their tune is, "The original of all Charlestons first introduced in 'Runnin' Wild.'" Johnson's tune has been recorded in a jazz setting nearly 250 times,[94] not to mention the pop and dance band versions. The "Charleston" had become the most popular dance and song America had known.

For most of the Broadway run of *Runnin' Wild*, "Charleston" was featured as the finale of the first act. It was acknowledged first by the African American press as a phenomenon to reckon with. In early 1924, the *New York Age*, one of Harlem's important newspapers, took note of the dance, reporting, "'Runnin' Wild' has one ensemble number that's a wow. It is the finale to the first act. Here Broadway is given an exhibition of a chorus that can both dance and sing. Lyda Webb, Alice Allison and associates are versatile chorus girls among whom symmetry of form and comeliness of face are generously distributed, and how they can 'Charleston'!" Shortly after the tour began in late spring, the *Pittsburgh Courier* commented on the dance specifically as a highlight.[95] Through its tour cross country in the latter half of 1924, however, little mention is made of the dance in the mainstream press. By 1925, the "Charleston" craze had reached its zenith across America and the world, and the show, still on tour, responded. The dance number was placed before the finale of both acts and was choreographed to include the entire company. Although versions of the dance and rhythm were known for decades in the African American community, the now codified version with its namesake city attached to Johnson's tune and rhythmic construction was quickly adopted.

Chorus line of *Runnin' Wild* dancing the "Charleston." (Photo by White Studio © New York Public Library for the Performing Arts)

Once the dance became a worldwide sensation, just about everyone took credit for it. While Johnson may not have reaped accolades from white society as the composer of the hit tune, his royalty agreements were bearing financial rewards. For the three months ending December 31, 1925, the height of the Charleston craze, Johnson took in nearly $4,000 in mechanical royalties alone from record and piano roll sales. The tune sold over one hundred fifty thousand records on ten different record labels, this during a slump in the recording industry in general.[96] A nice sum, but very small compared to what white bandleaders and composers were making. Johnson didn't help himself in this regard. He never commercially recorded the "Charleston" on record. He recorded two piano roll versions for QRS, the first as part of the *Runnin' Wild* Medley released in March 1924, and a stand-alone version released in June 1925. Johnson was never interested in leading a touring band other than with the orchestras he led for his stage shows. Rather than front a dance band and record, he spent most of his time during the peak of "Charleston" popularity composing and playing for the musical theater, and for much of the later part of 1924 and 1925, he was out of New York. He and Cecil Mack wrote a sequel titled "Everybody's Doin' the Charleston Now" copyrighted in September 1925 by Irving Berlin Music, Inc. which appeared in their short-lived show *Mooching Along*. It attracted only modest attention. The "Charleston" craze seemed to pass him by, but other great successes lay ahead.

Chapter 13

THE RENT PARTY

> This would be 3 or 4 a.m. People stuck their heads out of windows, ready to throw a pot. "Who's that down there," they'd growl. "This is Lippy," the answer would be. "I got James with me." Those doors flew open. Lights switched on. Cupboards emptied, and everyone took a little taste. Then it was me, or maybe Fats, who sat down to warm up the piano. After that, James took over. Then you got real invention—magic, sheer magic.
> —DUKE ELLINGTON

The slow, steady stream of African Americans who moved from the largely rural South to the cities in the North that began after Reconstruction became a turbulent rapids with the Great Migration that started just before and accelerated during World War I. It transformed the American social landscape. This mass movement of people was first catalyzed by the decline in European immigration due to wartime restrictions, creating serious unmet demand for labor in the North. Over the next half century, as life in the South for Black Americans became increasingly intolerable, some six million people, a number that is likely underreported, sought opportunity for a new life, one that seemed worth the risk of abandoning the devil they knew for the devil they didn't.[1] In many cases, life in the North was marginally better, presenting new internal and external pressures. Within their own community, well-settled middle-class African Americans scoffed at the newly arrived southerners who they perceived as unsophisticated and crude. The influx put pressure on housing as demand outpaced supply. Apartments intended for single families needed to accommodate many more people, and unscrupulous landlords gouged the new residents with rents they could scarcely afford. Although jobs were available, they were primarily the lowest-paying work. The combination of cultural marginalization and financial necessity led many to embrace a customary tradition of creating a social environment of self-help. One concrete need, paying the rent, was met with neighborly assistance.

In the African American community, the phenomenon of community outreach to raise money to pay the preacher or help a needy congregation member was nothing new. Back home, a church group might arrange such an event in a parishioner's home. Guests paid a nominal admission charge at the door, usually twenty-five or fifty cents. Food and drink were plentiful along with musical entertainment. The take was used to cover expenses and finance whatever cause prompted the occasion. They went by numerous names—Chittlin' Struts, Gumbo Suppers, Fish Fries, Egg Nog Parties, Saturday Night Functions, Buffet Flats, and Parlor Socials. In the northern cities, these social events developed into a distinct phenomenon that came to be known as the rent party.[2] Appearances may have suggested a variety of reasons for arranging a rent party, but the necessity of communal support was the common, underlying motivation. Rent parties predominated as middle- to lower-class private entertainment during the 1920s, although they had existed in recognizable form as early as 1913 and continued into the Depression. Despite the cramped space in the overcrowded tenements, rent parties could draw large crowds. Since most homes had a piano, and with little room for a large band, pianists dominated as rent party entertainment, and their music became known as rent party or parlor social piano.

The rent party phenomenon could be found in many Northern cities, with music reflecting regional styles. On Chicago's south side, a hybrid form that became known as barrelhouse, skiffle, or south-side piano predominated. It was a cross between Midwestern ragtime and blues-based boogie-woogie styles. In the 1920s, one could find both ragtime-oriented players such as Jimmy Blythe and Clarence Johnson, as well as boogie-woogie pianists like Clarence "Pinetop" Smith and Meade Lux Lewis playing for rent parties.[3] Many of these pianists had themselves migrated from the South and brought with them their earthier conceptions of blues piano. In the Midwestern cities, the pianists cut across multiple styles and varied skill levels and often considered themselves a part of the community of newcomers. At the rent parties in Harlem, one heard stride piano, played by highly respected, established musicians. This was the product of the Northeast, and its players were the most sought-after musicians, not only for the parlor, but also the stage, recording studio, and publishing houses. Years after the heyday of this phenomenon, Dan Burley, newspaperman and player of "skiffle" piano who had moved from Chicago to New York, recalled:

Research by the eminent folklore specialist Kenneth Bright brings out the fact that when we were skiffling in Chicago, James P. Johnson, Fats Waller, Willie (The Lion) Smith, Lucky Roberts, Donald Lambert, J. C. Johnson, The Beetle Henderson and others were playing for "Parlor Socials" in Harlem where the lights were low and the wrinles [sic] came out on plates at 75 cents per and the King Kong flowed like Muda Grass Wine. Here, you had to be an expert on the 88s and the great technicians of the house party pianoers [sic] today are the masters. But at the skiffle all you had to play was one or two chords, simple and with a solid beat to get your whiskey and all you could eat.[4]

Duke Ellington recalled the singular sociocultural environment that was Harlem during the 1920s, noting, "Harlem had its own rich, special folklore, totally unrelated to the South or anywhere else. It's gone now, but it was tremendous then."[5] Northern urbanity absorbed the Southern custom of the parlor social, its cuisine, and elements of its music into what became an integral part of Harlem social life and a distinguishable phenomenon within this folklore. Traditional Southern dishes became the standard bill of fare. The rent party also provided an easy outlet for illegal alcohol during Prohibition. During the 1920s, admission was usually one dollar. Sometimes a hundred people would crowd into a seven-room railroad flat, with the furniture stored in another apartment. The kitchen was always active, as was the bedroom for serious gambling or casual sex. The rent party was the place to pick up the latest news, jokes, and gossip.[6] Although many middle-class African Americans disdained the perceived debauchery they saw at the parties, the fashionable section of well-to-do Harlemites residing on 139th Street between Seventh and Eighth Avenues often featured rent parties. James P. Johnson recalled, "It was called Striver's Row because people strived like hell to pay the rent and taxes. They were the days of bathtub gin and corn whisky and stills in the apartments and Jimmy Walker was Mayor. The parties attracted a lot of people, many white folk who were taking up the Negro."[7] Some of these curious elites from white society (whose liberal-minded intensions varied in their sincerity) included Carl Van Vechten, John Hammond, George Gershwin, and Dudley Murphy. In addition to the wave of immigrants from the South, an international wave of immigrants, especially from the West Indies, added additional cultural diversity to the Harlem social milieu during the twenties. James P. Johnson found the West Indian accent a source of amusement. He embedded their sing-song prosody into his own pidgin language that was understood only by his close circle including Fats Waller, Andy Razaf, and a few other Gaiety Building and rent party regulars.[8]

Perhaps as much as the alcohol and food, the attraction at the parties was the entertainment. The big three on the rent party circuit were James P. Johnson, Willie "The Lion" Smith, and Fats Waller. Another player named Lippy Boyette acted as a booking agent. He contracted several pianists for each party, sometimes lining up as many as three parties in one night for the same players. They would make the rounds, starting in the afternoon and continuing until late the next day. Tickets printed to advertise the performers were sold in advance on the street. Some of the colorful language used to promote the events included:

> Hey! Hey! Come on boys and girls let's shake that thing. Where? At Hot Poppa Sam's West 134th Street, three flights up. Jelly Roll Smith at the piano. Saturday night.... Hey! Hey!
>
> Fall in line, and watch your step, for there'll be Lots of Browns with plenty of pep at a social whist party.... Refreshments just it. Music won't quit.
>
> Shake it in the morning. Shake it at night at a social matinee party.... music too tight. Refreshments just right.[9]
>
> If you're looking for a good time, don't look no more, just ring my bell, and I'll answer the door. Southern barbecue given by Charlie Johnson and Joe Hotboy, and how hot![10]

To be included in a particularly good lineup, a player would arrange for a substitute to take his place at his regular job for the evening. The tradition of deportment combined with a dose of flamboyant theatrics that had been a crucial part of pianist's performance practice in rathskellers and other "joints" was maintained at a rent party.[11] The musicians knew well that their performance at the piano determined the success of the party.

In spite of the image of tasteful stylishness the players hoped to convey, the picture painted of the rent party among many in the middle class and highbrow cultural elite was one of decadence. Harlem Renaissance novelist Wallace Thurman, in his controversial 1929 novel *The Blacker the Berry*, depicted unsavory images of the rent party, the vulgarity of the participants, and the unappealing image of the pianists, images that were part of intraracial perceptions. He wrote:

> When they returned to the room, the pianist was just preparing to play again. He was tall and slender, with extra-long legs and arms, giving him the appearance of a scarecrow. His pants were tight in the waist and full in the legs. He wore no coat, and a blue silk shirt hung damply to his body. He acted as if he were king of the occasion, ruling all from his piano stool throne. He talked familiarly to everyone in the room, called

women from other men's arms, demanded drinks from any bottle he happened to see being passed around, laughed uproariously, and made many grotesque and ofttimes obscene gestures.

Emma Lou could not keep her eyes off the piano player. He was acting like a maniac, occasionally turning completely around on his stool, grimacing like a witch doctor, and letting his hands dawdle over the keyboard of the piano with agonizing indolence, when compared to the extreme exertion to which he put the rest of his body. He was improvising. The melody of the piece he had started to play was merely a base for more bawdy variations. His right punished the piano's loud-pedal. Beads of perspiration gathered grease from his slicked-down hair, and rolled oleagenously down his face and neck, spotting the already damp baby-blue shirt, and streaking his already greasy black face with more shiny lanes. . . .

A sailor had suddenly ceased his impassioned hip movement and strode out of the room, pulling his partner behind him, pushing people out of the way as he went. The spontaneous moans and slangy ejaculations of the piano player and of the more articulate dancers became more regular, more like a chanted obbligato to the music. This lasted for a couple of hours interrupted only by hectic intermissions. Then the dancers grew less violent in their movements, and though the piano player seemed never to tire there were fewer couples on the floor, and those left seemed less loathe to move their legs.[12]

The rent party often became a musical battleground. The partygoers, especially after several drinks, did not hesitate to express their opinions about whose playing they appreciated most. The contests between pianists were, in many instances, taken more seriously by the audience than the performers, for whom the spirit of professional but friendly competition prevailed.

There was a semi-official pecking order for playing time at the larger affairs as well as the clubs, cabarets, and saloons where cutting contests would break out at a moment's notice. One player would sit down and "warm up" the piano with several choruses of a particular song. After a while, another player would slide in on the piano bench next to the first player, relieving him one hand at a time. This procedure continued until everyone had played. Then, only the best players (or the most daring) would vie for the support of the audience. The competition often grew heated. Willie "The Lion" Smith described his approach:

We would embroider the melodies with our own original ideas and try to develop patterns that had more originality than those played before us. Sometimes it was just a question as to who could think up the most patterns within a given time. It was pure improvisation.

You had to have your own individual style and be able to play in all the keys. In those days we could all copy each other's shouts by learning them by ear. Sometimes in order to keep the others from picking up too much of my stuff, I'd perform in the hard keys, B major and E major.[13]

By nearly all accounts, the acknowledged piano king at the rent parties was James P. Johnson. "James, for me, was more than the beginning. He went right on up to the greatest," remarked Duke Ellington. "You know, he ordinarily played the most, and in competition a little bit more."[14] Garvin Bushell described Johnson's preeminence:

There'd be more controversy among the listeners than the participants. There was betting and people were ready to fight about who'd won. Jimmy played with the most originality. He'd create things the other guys hadn't thought up.

Jimmy was on top most of the time. You got credit for how many patterns you could create within the tunes you knew, and in how many different keys you could play.[15]

Boston-born Tom Whaley was a pianist on the rent party scene in the twenties. He became a mainstay of the Ellington organization in the early 1940s as copyist and arranger and remained with Ellington for thirty years. Whaley observed the Johnson inventiveness in competition, noting, "Every Monday night was a piano contest night at the Hole in the Wall on 129th Street. James P. would play thirty-two choruses in a row, and never one the same."[16] Johnson's stride compositions often served as the test pieces. All the stride pianists mastered "Carolina Shout" or "Harlem Strut." For any player to develop credibility within the guild, these had to be performed convincingly with the right dose of originality.

In addition to the stories of Ellington and Waller's first meeting with Johnson (see chapter 10), pianists Cliff Jackson and Joe Turner, whose styles were also heavily influenced by Johnson's, told of the first time they played for the composer himself. Jackson recalled:

It was during the prohibition. I was making a lot of money on liquor, and I walked into the room at this big party and told the guys to set everybody up. I had noticed a big fellow sleeping on a couch in the corner, but I didn't pay him much attention until after someone asked me to play the piano. I started playing 'Carolina Shout' and this fellow, without moving, opened one eye and asked: 'Who are you?' I got pretty mad, because I was quite well known in Washington and I figured this guy had some nerve asking who I was! So I answered him with the same question, but when he told me he was James P. Johnson I couldn't play anymore. He asked me to continue, but I just couldn't.[17]

Joe Turner relays a similar experience upon his initial arrival in New York:

> I asked the first person I met where I could find the colored people in town. I was told to take the L-train to 130th Street in Harlem. There I asked where the musicians were hangin out. They told me that it was a place called the Comedy Club.
>
> Going there, I had a drink, set my bag down, and noticed that anyone who wished could go to the piano and play. Realizing that none of the pianists who had performed before me had done anything special, I walked over to the piano and started to play. After a warm-up number, I went into the "Harlem Strut," and then I went to the climax with the "Carolina Shout."
>
> When I had finished, people swarmed around me and wanted to know where I came from. After I told them, someone in the crowd reminded me that the composer of the last two numbers I had played was in the room—James P. Johnson! Of course, you can imagine how I felt! I must have impressed him, however, since he left his table, came up to the piano, and played the same two numbers as nobody in the world could![18]

Sonny Greer, born in Long Branch, New Jersey, first met Ellington in Washington around 1919 and became the rhythmic anchor of the Ellington band for thirty years as drummer/percussionist. Greer recalled the piano contest scene in Washington at places like the Dreamland Café, Ellington's proficiency with Johnson's style, and his own role in giving his boss the edge:

> Duke wasn't a professional then, but he would come in and play his "Carolina Shout." He was a great admirer of James P. Johnson, and he had got his Q. R. S. piano rolls down fine. He really idolized James P. and he was the only man I ever knew who could play "Carolina Shout" equally well.
>
> In those days, they would have piano contests as an attraction to get people to go to dances. Cliff Jackson was around and so was Claude Hopkins. Claude's father was a professor and his mother a librarian at Howard University, and he was born and raised on the campus. He was ahead of Cliff Jackson then in terms of finish and experience. Thanks to me, Duke had a cheering section of seven or eight with their noisemakers. So Duke

would be all set to play his "Carolina Shout," and I would be there to play the drums, and Toby [Hardwick] the bass, so we couldn't lose. We won all kinds of things—suitcases, and I don't know what. We'd keep them overnight, sell them next day, and go have a ball again.[19]

After 1940, Ellington's piano style migrated away from a striding left hand, but he never abandoned his affection for Johnson and the style. At live performances into the 1960s, he would play the "Carolina Shout" when he amusingly introduced himself as the band's pianist.[20] For Billy Strayhorn, as he lay dying of esophageal cancer in 1967, Ellington arranged for a group of pianists working in France to tape record some solos. The group included French pianist Claude Bolling, with expats Joe Turner (Ellington's stride piano compatriot from Washington), and Strayhorn's former lover Aaron Bridgers. Bolling asked what they should play, and Ellington responded, "Give him some James P.," with Bolling noting how much Ellington loved James P. Johnson.[21]

Pod's and Jerry's was the shorthand name for the Catagonia Club, a speakeasy on West 133rd Street well known as a haven for pianists. It was run by Charles "Pod" Hollingsworth and Jeremiah "West Indian Jerry" Preston, a notorious gambler who had started his nightclub career with another legendary Harlem spot called The Orient on West 135th Street. Eddie Condon was a frequent visitor to Pod's and Jerry's, noting that the place "specialized in fried chicken and piano players." Condon had an affinity for the Harlem pianists and was often an eager spectator of the piano battles. Willie "The Lion" Smith was one of the first pianists to hold down a residency at Pod's and Jerry's after it opened in 1925. Condon recalled some of the other pianists' comings and goings: "The Negro Joe Sullivan had a powerful unique style. After his night's work at the Cotton Club was done Duke Ellington dropped in to hear him. James P. Johnson was often in the place, eating fried chicken, listening and beating time. It was a 'cutting joint'—by five o'clock in the morning pianists from all over town were taking turns at the keyboard, each trying to outplay the others."[22] Canadian-born pianist Louis Hooper was never introduced to Johnson, but he was a spectator at a cutting contest he vividly recalled:

> One night at the Hoofer's Club . . . I just wandered in to fill a bit of time . . . it was a place underneath the Lafayette Theatre where all the professional people gathered. . . . Gradually people started to wander in a few at a time . . . a few young fellows were playing . . . I didn't know them. Then Lucky [Roberts] came in . . . Fats, James P., Willie the lion . . . they all came in separately. . . . When Lucky sat down . . . he had a style of playing themes like almost Debussy . . . very long fingers and big hands . . . played real powerful rags too. More than one player would

play the same tune. Of course Willie, when he first sat down, had to use his slogan "Get up, you can't play that piano . . . I'm the Lion"! It boiled down to Fats and James P. Finally Fats got up and made that very famous statement . . . he stopped everybody, stopped the music and said . . . "Ladies and Gentleman . . . here is an artist." James took a bow and the session broke up. I've always thought how fortunate I was just to have been there.[23]

Rex Stewart, trumpet star with Duke Ellington and Fletcher Henderson, was also a keen musical observer and wrote about it extensively. In *Down Beat* in 1967, he published his recollections of the great cutting sessions he attended, including an unforgettable piano battle at the Rhythm Club in Harlem. Jelly Roll Morton strolled in, and, with his usual bombast, proclaimed his keyboard superiority. He played a few tunes, and Willie Gant, thinking greater keyboard firepower was needed to respond to Morton, called Willie "The Lion" Smith. He and Morton traded verbal and pianistic barbs as a larger crowd gathered. Fats Waller was not to be found, but the grapevine apprised Johnson of the brewing musical showdown. Stewart completes the story:

Just then, the all-time boss of the Harlem stride piano players, James P. Johnson arrived. James P., who sometimes stuttered, said, "Jelly, come on, l-l-let's go down to the Hoofers. They have a b-b-better piano there, and I'll en-entertain you."

Jelly agreed, and everybody followed. As I recall, there were about sixty or seventy cats in the "second line" on that occasion. History was made as James P. wiped up the floor with Jelly Roll. Never before or since have I heard such piano playing![24]

Clarinetist Milton "Mezz" Mezzrow, in his autobiography *Really the Blues*, told the story of a fantastic "cutting contest" at a rent party. This particular incident took place sometime during the Depression, probably the mid-1930s. Johnson had moved out of Manhattan, but Harlem nightlife continued to draw in the keyboard king. Mezzrow recalled:

One morning a sensational cutting contest took place, just between piano players.

Corky [Williams] sat down and started to play "Tea for Two," a number that Willie The Lion could give a fit. All of a sudden Willie jumped up and said to Corky, "Git up from there you no-piano-playin' son of a bitch, I got it," and with that he sat down next to Corky. As Corky slid over, Willie started to play just the treble, while Corky still kept up the bass, and then he picked up with his left hand too, the tempo not even wavering and without missing a beat. Willie played for a while and then Fats took over, sliding into the seat the same way Willie had done. He played for a while, looking up at Willie and signifying every time he made a new or tricky passage. It went on like that, the music more and more frantic, that piano not resting for even a fraction of a second, until finally Fats said "I'm goin' to settle this argument good." He went into a huddle with his chauffeur, who left and returned about an hour later, but not alone. Fats had telephoned to Jamaica, Long Island, and woke up James P. Johnson out of his bed. When the chauffeur brought Jimmy in he was still rubbing his eyes, but as soon as he sat down at the piano that was all. He played so much piano you didn't have to yell "Put out the lights and call the law," because the law came up by request of the neighbors. "We been sittin' downstairs enjoying the music," the cops told us, "when we got a call from the station house to see who was disturbing the peace around here. Some people ain't got no appreciation for music at all. Fats, just close them windows and pour us a drink, and take up where you left off." So for the rest of the morning the contest went on, with these two coppers lolling around drinking our liquor and listening to our fine music. It was great.[25]

Willie "The Lion" Smith also recalls the police joining in the parties.[26] Raucous or illegal activity at rent parties might range from disturbing the neighbors and serving alcohol, or more serious violations of drug dealing and prostitution. Noise and liquor seemed innocuous enough, especially if the police were complicit, a far from unusual circumstance during Prohibition and the Depression. This image was romanticized in the 1933 Vitaphone film short *Underneath the Harlem Moon*. It features the Mills Blue Rhythm Band, and purports to depict the band first in a nightclub and then at a rent party. The dance team of the Three Dukes play three police officers who are asked if they are part of a raid. They immediately dispel that notion and quickly join in the party with their dance feature. This scenario is immortalized in Fats Waller's 1941 soundie *The Joint Is Jumpin'*. The police first barge into the party as if executing a raid but quickly begin dancing with the girls.

Around 1933, a sixteen-year-old youngster named Thelonious Monk joined the rent party circuit. He told an interviewer, "They used to have what they called rent parties and they used to hire me to play when I was very young. They'd pay you about three dollars. And you'd play all night for 'em. And they'd charge admission to people who would come in and drink. That's the way some people used to get their rent together, like that."[27] Stride piano was still the predominant music of pianists at that time, and it became an elemental

A mid-1920s "slim and dapper" Johnson sporting all the trappings of his success. (Reproduced with permission of Barry Glover, from the James P. Johnson collection [IJS.0111], Institute of Jazz Studies, Rutgers-Newark)

building block of Monk's style that he never exorcised. His solo piano recordings from the 1960s and 70s are replete with examples of the essential stride components—a regular alternating left hand and rhythmic tension and release between the right and the left—while putting his own unique stamp on it.[28]

A far cry from the rent parties of Harlem were the fashionable and often elaborate cocktail parties taking place in the homes of white, socially connected society. New York's upper crust, while continuing to frequent the renowned Harlem nightspots, often desired to bring the talent downtown and into their private residences. Johnson's white counterparts in the music world, men like Harold Arlen, George Gershwin, Vernon Duke, and Roy Bargy, requested his presence at these formal affairs. One such event in particular was the celebration of the success of Gershwin's *Rhapsody in Blue* in 1924, to which Johnson, Smith, and Waller were invited.[29] If his white colleagues hoped to pick up new ideas from Johnson, they would have to rely on the sharpness of their ears. Willie "The Lion" Smith and Pops Foster recalled that Johnson explained very little of what he was doing. There was another agenda for inviting Johnson and the others. While most of society harbored deeply held racist views, some of the social elite hoped the presence of Black musicians in their homes would serve as evidence of a broad-minded, socially progressive image many of them wished to promote. Often, however, the hosts betrayed their patronizing attitudes, expecting reenactments of the stage show rather than abide unmasked demonstration of their guest's artistry. It was a new incarnation of the same conceit from the prior decade when Clef Club musicians were required to perform without music to substantiate the notion of them as natural rather than schooled performers. Only now the charade was veiled in the trappings of some element of social conscience. The pretense was not lost on the uptown guests, and many played along with the deception expected of them. But not Johnson. Ed Kirkeby recounts Willie "The Lion" Smith's recollection of a party at the Upper West Side home of steel magnate Charles M. Schwab during the mid-1920s: "James was always so modest. He wouldn't act funny at all, just always relied on his playing. He always used to say, 'What do I have to do for them besides play?' That was enough for him and I guess it was enough for the customers, him being James P. But I had my own act, and I poured it on 'em, even as I still do now. When Fats came along, he took that West Indian dialect from James and ran away with it."[30] Johnson would remain the reigning piano king until Art Tatum showed up in 1932, unseating him and blazing a new path for jazz piano. Tatum, however, didn't abandon the foundation Johnson had set, but integrated it into his own style and built on it.

Chapter 14

ON STAGE, 1924–1926

> A production far removed from ordinary Burlesque is
> "Step on It," the Hurtig and Seamon production
> which ranges from musical comedy to light opera in scope.
> —*PHILADELPHIA INQUIRER*

Josephine Harrison Thompson passed away after a long illness on May 14, 1924. A brief obituary in the *Chicago Defender* noted, "She was the mother of James P. Johnson, the famous pianist, and was herself an accomplished musician."[1] The cause of her death is noted to be chronic valvular heart disease and kidney failure, perhaps as a result rheumatic fever as a child, and diabetes, and/or high blood pressure accounting for her kidney failure. She was living with her daughter Isabelle who made the burial arrangements. Josephine was laid to rest in the same grave with her husband Perry in Jersey City.[2] On May 24, after concluding his run at the Hollywood, Johnson was back in Chicago for what would be an extended stay, working extensively with Leonard Harper. Johnson wrote a new score for a revitalized *Plantation Days* and led the orchestra at the Olympic Theater. During the summer, he wrote the score for the 1924–1925 edition of a recurring Hurtig and Seamon production called *Hollywood Follies*, with dances staged by Harper. In typical burlesque fashion, it was described as a "gay, girlie musical riot."[3] As was their bent, Hurtig and Seamon frequently produced mixed-race shows, a practice that generated as much controversy as it did revenue. *Hollywood Follies* ran at the Columbia Theater and featured Gertrude Saunders in the leading role. Saunders was a veteran stage actor and singer who had played in *Shuffle Along*. Although much lesser known today than her contemporaries Ethel Waters and Florence Mills, during the mid-1920s she was considered a star of the first order. She was recruited out of the cast of *Shuffle Along* by Hurtig, just as Harper and Johnson were recruited out of the Hollywood. When the show first opened, Johnson accompanied Saunders on stage as well as performing his own solos.[4] Johnson wrote fifteen musical numbers for the eight stage settings that included a rainstorm, the interior of an artist's studio, the exterior of a California bungalow, a comedic courtroom scene, and a movie studio scene that demonstrated the making of a motion picture. Twelve costume changes were required.[5] The revue came east without Johnson. After a few performances in New Jersey, it opened at the Columbia Theater at 47th Street and Broadway in Time Square on June 23.[6] Two African American jazz bands were included, the Hollywood Serenaders and Dewey Weinglass and His "16 Colored Syncopaters."[7] It received rave reviews by the New York papers,[8] and was held over for four weeks closing July 27.[9] Johnson's tunes, none of which are known, were described as "extremely catchy."[10]

Johnson wrote for another Jules Hurtig recurring seasonal production called *Step on It*. It was also a burlesque show with a book, such as it was, written by Hurtig himself with Allan Tenney. It toured on the Columbia circuit in tandem with *Hollywood Follies*. Harper staged the dances and Johnson wrote the music, described as "crisp and snappy."[11] Although no music is known, the scenes Johnson wrote for included a New York roof garden at night, a California lifeguard and bathing beach, a country sanitarium, a cabaret, a rowboat, and the interior of a streetcar on Broadway. Flesh and titillation were plentiful, and, as one reviewer observed, "Just how certain indiscreet portions of the Life Saving Station scene got past the Columbia circuit's censor is more than we know."[12] *Step on It* was promoted to celebrate the fiftieth anniversary of burlesque as an American entertainment format. The typical burlesque template was patterned off the minstrel and variety show, but Johnson left his mold-breaking imprint on it by including musical forms described as ranging from musical comedy to light opera. In what would otherwise have been a typical burlesque, Johnson introduced a more ambitious musical palate. And it was well received.[13] For *Step on It*, alongside the white cast, "Naomi and the Brazilian Nuts" was promoted as "the premier Colored act of America."[14] Both *Hollywood Follies* and *Step on It* ran well into 1925.

Producers Will Morrissey and Harry Bestry, who, the summer before, had nearly tanked the inclusion of the "Charleston" in *Runnin' Wild*, lined up Johnson and Cecil Mack to do the music for their new effort called *Watch Out*. Harper staged the dances.[15] It opened in Boston at the Selwyn Theater on August 1, and was scheduled to open in New York around September 1.[16] There is no further evidence of it and it was likely scuttled by an Actor's Equity dispute.[17] Morris Cain of Cain and Davenport engaged Harper and Johnson to provide lyrics and music for *Harry Steppe and His Big Show*. Steppe, born

Abraham Stepner in Russia in 1888, came to the United States in 1892 and became a popular comedian and singer on the vaudeville, burlesque, and variety show circuits. He often performed in Jewish/Yiddish dialect and was known as "The Hebrew Gent." He was one of Bud Abbott's first partners and had a tremendous influence on many subsequent comedians including Phil Silvers, The Three Stooges, and Lucille Ball.[18] Johnson and Harper provided "snappy musical numbers and delicious dance diversions . . . generously sprinkled throughout the performance. . . ."[19] Cain and Davenport's production introduced "novel mechanical as well as artistic effects" to support numerous elaborate scene changes, eleven in all, with a "bewildering array of special costumes," all set to sixteen Johnson numbers.[20] The show was highly praised and ran for the entire burlesque season, from August through April.

Johnson continued to work with Harper and original *Plantation Days* producer Jimmy O'Neil in late 1924 for the revue *Cottonland*, a restaging of Harper's production that had run at the Cotton Club in New York. The show continued to feature the Cotton Club Chorus.[21] The show opened in Chicago the week of November 4 at the newly remodeled Plantation Café, formerly Al Tearney's,[22] and moved to the Grand Theater on December 8, 1924. The pastiche of song, dance, comedy, and musical numbers were loosely fit around a levee front backdrop and a riverboat labeled *Robert E. Lee*. Gertrude Saunders was featured on several musical numbers that included "Promise Me Blues" and the Johnson tunes "Desperate Blues," "The Love I Crave," and "Love Bug," with Johnson accompanying her on piano. In his *Chicago Defender* review of opening night, Tony Langston noted, "Jimmie stopped things himself with a set of solos and was finally forced to play unprogrammed numbers for the enthusiastic ticket buyers. It is a red hot spot."[23] After the two-week run at the Grand, the show moved to St. Louis and played the Booker Washington Theater.[24] The show was very well received.

Except for a piano roll medley of tunes from *Runnin' Wild*, no recordings were made by Johnson in 1924. In 1925, the "Charleston" was released as a single on piano roll. Johnson was, however, continually in demand as composer and performer. He returned to New York in 1925 after nearly eight months in Chicago and the Midwest, and remained active playing in numerous jam sessions, after-hours parties, sitting in with various groups, and no doubt leading some of his own bands in Harlem clubs. He continued his formal piano studies and had started instruction with concert pianist and teacher Edward Emil Treumann. E. E. Treumann, as he was known, was born in Vienna in 1875 and immigrated to the United States at the age of eight in 1883.[25] The musically precocious Treumann returned to Europe for his musical studies. He studied with Emil von Sauer and Julius Epstein in Vienna, where he had his concert debut. He toured throughout Europe, Central America, and the United States.[26] He settled in New York in 1895 and, like Damrosch and Giannini, was part of the European-trained musical elite of New York who were especially enlightened regarding music education for the underclass and ethnic minorities. He ran in the highest circles of the European classical music tradition and considered himself a colleague of Josef Hofmann and Vladimir de Pachmann. After building a successful career as teacher and concert pianist, by the 1920s, he focused his attention on promoting his two studios on 86th Street in Manhattan and in Brooklyn. He was eager to attract African American students, and by 1925, was delighted to count Johnson as one of them. In an advertisement in the *New York Amsterdam News* for his teaching studios, he made prominent note of his successful pupil from the neighborhood, albeit with some factual errors: "Mr. Treumann is the Instructor of James P. Johnson, pianist, composer of 'Shuffle Along' and 'Runnin' Wild,' musical comedies, also the 'Charleston,' and many other concert pianists of note" noted his ad.[27] Treumann offered scholarships and maintained close ties to the African American community. He was associated with the Carnegie Hall Studios and also continued to appear in Harlem into the 1930s, with notices in the *New York Amsterdam News* that continued to mention that "Mr. Treumann is a master teacher and pianist. Numbered among his many artist pupils is J. P. Johnson, brilliant pianist and composer."[28] Treumann died in 1958.

During this time Johnson was also studying with Professor Eugene (E.) Aldama Jackson (1886 or 1887–1965). Jackson was the organist and choirmaster for the St. Marks African Methodist Episcopal Church in Harlem from 1914 until 1932. A Juilliard graduate, he was the third African American admitted to the American Guild of Organists. As a religious institution in Harlem society, St. Marks A. M. E. Church was second in prominence only to the Abyssinian Baptist Church. Jackson brought his renowned choir to Carnegie Hall first in 1919,[29] and continued yearly for seven consecutive years.[30] By 1915, he had started advertising his teaching availability,[31] and by 1922 established the Jackson School of Composition and Music.[32] In 1928, he started the Jackson Music Shop to sell arrangements, especially to other church choirs.[33] Johnson probably started his studies with Jackson around 1921.[34] The two may have met at St. Marks, where Josephine, maintaining devotion to her Methodist faith, may have worshipped. They may also have been introduced by Will Marion Cook or by Allie Ross. Jackson had known Cook since 1913, when Jackson led a one-hundred-voice choir for Cook's landmark concert at Carnegie Hall commemorating the fiftieth anniversary of the Emancipation Proclamation,[35] and Allie Ross had studied with Jackson. Jackson noted his capabilities as "teacher of theory and piano," the instruction including "elementary and advanced harmony and counterpoint."[36] With Jackson, Johnson studied Percy Goetschius's *Theory and Practice of Tone Relations, The Homophonic Forms*

Edward E. Treumann
Artistic Piano Instruction

Highest Testimonials and Indorsements from Emil von Sauer and Josef Hofmann

Studios: 110 West 86th Street   Phone Schuyler 2753

One Free and Six Partial Scholarships
Teachers Post Graduate Courses a Specialty
Interview 9-12 Daily or by Mail Appointment

(unidentified clipping; Author's collection)

EDWARD E. TREUMANN
CONCERT PIANIST AND ARTIST PEDAGOGUE

Highly Recommended by Prof. Emil von Sauer, Director of the Master School of Vienna, and Josef Hofmann, the World-Famous Virtuoso

Artistic Instruction—Repertoire, Interpretation, Technic and Preparation for Public Recitals

Mr. Treumann is the Instructor of James P. Johnson, pianist, composer of "Shuffle Along" and "Running Wild," musical comedies, also the "Charleston," and many other concert pianists of note.

One free scholarship awarded to an exceptional talent without means, also six partial scholarships to talented students showing promise. Applications by mail.

STUDIOS
110 West 86th Street, N. Y.   Tel. Schuyler 2753
2152 78th Street, Brooklyn.   Tel. Beachview 6096
30th Season Opened September 15th.   Booklets.

(*New York Amsterdam News*, September 23, 1925)

of *Musical Composition, Counterpoint Applied in the Invention, Fugue, Canon and Other Polyphonic Forms*, and his *Larger Forms of Musical Composition*. Jackson had been a student of Goetschius. From 1927 to 1929, Johnson studied Ebenezer Prout's *Instrumentation* and *Counterpoint: Strict and Free*, and Ernst Richter's *Manual of Harmony* with a Mr. Furgieule (the spelling may be incorrect).[37] There have been some references to Johnson studying with Leopold Godowsky.[38] There is no primary reference supporting this, and Johnson does not list Godowsky as one of his teachers, but Johnson did work with lyricist Stella Unger, who worked with Godowsky. It is possible Johnson met Godowsky through her.[39]

Johnson was sporting all the trappings of 1920s success. He was fond of wearing his raccoon coat and drove a Cadillac roadster. The Johnsons took time to visit Lillie Mae's family in Pennsylvania, sometimes accompanied by her brother, trap drummer William J. Wright. In 1924, Lillie Mae landed a role in Oscar Micheaux's silent film classic *Body and Soul*, which was filmed in the Bronx and released in late 1925. She played "Sis" Caline, a pious woman in the congregation of Reverend Jenkins, who was played by Paul Robeson. It was

CHAPTER 14.

E. Aldama Jackson (*New York Age*, May 25, 1916)

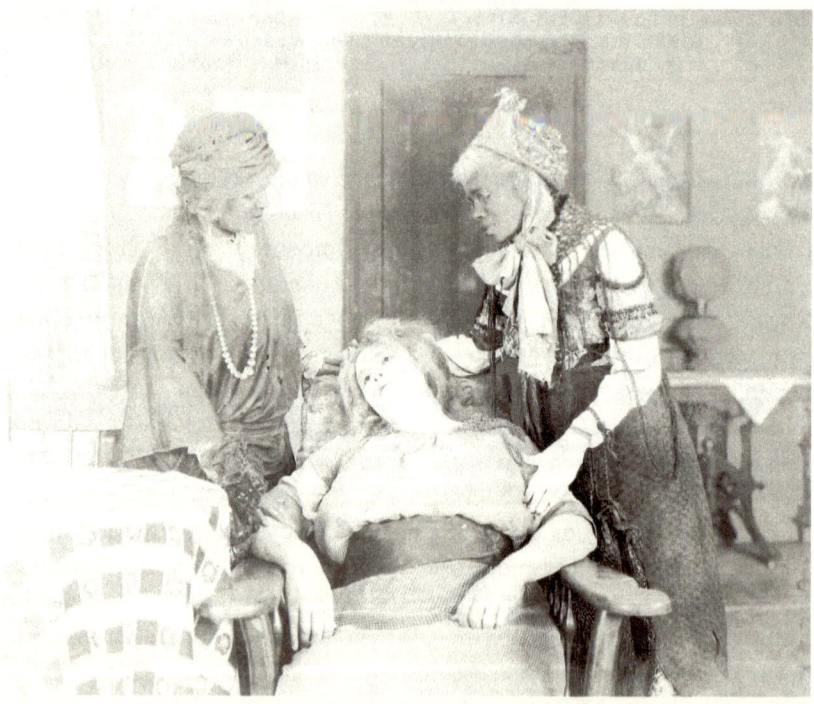

Film still from *Body and Soul*. Lillie Mae Johnson plays the pious congregant "Sis" Ca'line (left), Mercedes Gilbert as "Sis" Martha Jane (center), and Madame Robinson as "Sis" Lucy (right). (Reproduced with permission of Barry Glover, from the James P. Johnson collection [IJS.0111], Institute of Jazz Studies, Rutgers-Newark)

his first screen role. Also in the cast was Mercedes Gilbert. First educated as a nurse, she found limited opportunities for herself in health care. The booming market for African American music provided a more lucrative outlet for her talents as a writer. James P. Johnson had known her at least since the early part of 1923. The two had composed two tunes together then, and another in 1924.[40] By June 1924, Gilbert had become manager of the Down South Publishing Company.[41] She was a multitalented writer, poet, and actress in film and on Broadway, and became one of the few women active in the Harlem Renaissance. She would remain lifelong friends with the Johnsons and collaborate with James P. again in the 1940s. *Body and Soul* was a hit for Micheaux at the time, and is considered one of his best films from a cultural and technical standpoint. It gave a boost to Gilbert's career, but Lillie Mae chose to settle in to her life as wife, and very soon, mother.

In the summer of 1925, plans began for a Broadway show to include in the featured role the child actor Ernest Morrison, whose stage name was "Sunshine Sammy." He was the then eleven-year-old star of the *Our Gang* comedies. His father had formed a production company in 1924 to feature the boy in a tour of the country. By June 1925, he had performed in New Orleans, Atlanta, and Nashville to great reception. He was reported "to uncork a 'wicked' Charleston."[42] Initially, the project was tentatively titled *The Whirl of Dixie*, with music and lyrics by Johnson and his *Runnin' Wild* partner Cecil Mack. Will Marion Cook was to lead the orchestra, and an opening at one of the Shubert Theaters was planned. Comedian John Rucker was slated to co-star. He and Sammy's father, Joe Morrison, were writing the book.[43] Producer Will Morrissey, in association with Abe Feinberg, planned two weeks out of town on the Loews vaudeville circuit for the show. Jesse Shipp, the "Dean of the Colored Theatrical Profession," was added to rewrite the book and model it after the "operetta style" of the Williams and Walker shows of twenty years earlier, which Shipp had helped to write.[44] The show was in rehearsal in August. Leonard Harper was brought in to stage it. He added half a dozen other children to the cast. The show was retitled after the young actor, and simply called *Sunshine Sammy*.[45] But Johnson's show was bogged down in rewrites, and, by the end of September, little Sunshine Sammy was again on the road with a different show staged by Leonard Harper and a mixed-race cast.[46] The new show played in St. Louis, Chicago, and Baltimore.[47] By this point there was little hope of salvaging the original collaboration with "Sunshine" Sammy Morrison. His participation in the Johnson/Mack/Shipp show was then recast as a rumor.[48] It is not known if Johnson contributed material to Sammy Morrison and Harper's touring show, but Johnson, Mack, and Shipp did finally open a show of their own one month later. *Moochin' Along*, in two acts and ten scenes, opened prematurely at the Lafayette Theater on December 7, 1925. An out-of-town trial upstate was originally intended.[49] Reviewers made note of the "wholesome" nature of the show, with "the discard of every semblance of smut and an entire absence of any vulgar display of near-nudity."[50] Several reviews criticized its lack of cohesion, but praised the music, noting, "It is rather hard to comment upon the show as a finished product, for there is much to be done to it yet. The music was excellent, and the book, with a few minor changes, should please."[51] After the week at the Lafayette, the show went on the road, first to the Howard Theater in Washington.[52] A planned opening at the Royal Theater in Baltimore[53] was scuttled by Jesse Shipp, who felt the production never came together to meet his expectations. *Moochin' Along* finally closed in late January at the Dunbar Theater in Philadelphia.[54]

The precarious world of the stage show business consumed six months of work on this ill-fated project. A year and a half of activity in burlesque and vaudeville nearly came to naught. Gertrude Saunders, who had also hitched her wagon to Hurtig and Seamon, suffered a career setback from the association. For Johnson, too, even highly acclaimed activity with white producers for white entertainment did not immediately translate into greater mainstream opportunity beyond the lowbrow theater. Yet, in the fall of 1924, there were at least five stage productions with scores written predominantly by Johnson widely touring the country—the Broadway hit *Runnin' Wild*, the "all-Black" vaudeville franchise *Plantation Days*, and the three white-produced burlesque shows. Add in the dominating presence of the "Charleston" in nearly every other facet of entertainment, and one would think Johnson's name would be on every tongue. That was his goal, to be recognized as a composer. What press there was that referenced him, and there was some, in both the African American and mainstream papers, was certainly glowing about him as a composer and pianist. Despite this, his name garnered little public attention. Johnson's contemporaries, like Ellington, Henderson, Armstrong, and Jelly Roll Morton, were beginning to attract substantial attention from their recordings and with their orchestras. Johnson made only two trips to the recording studio in 1925 to cut the same two tunes on each occasion. An October 7 date with Perry Bradford's Jazz Phools waxed two Bradford tunes, "Lucy Long" and "I Ain't Gonna Play No Second Fiddle" using members of the Fletcher Henderson orchestra, which at that time included Buster Bailey, Don Redman and Louis Armstrong. These were rejected and the same group returned on November 2 for a second try that was issued. These are marvelous, swinging, somewhat freewheeling sides, generously infused with a Charleston rhythm. Bradford later claimed they were so relaxed because the group was under the impression they were only cutting test records.[55] Although he was more likely recalling the first rejected session, the issued takes still fit his description. The year was partially salvaged for Johnson the composer with the publication of three Johnson/Mack collaborations, two in September 1925 and one January of 1926. They were likely part of the score for *Mooching Along*. By then, the Charleston craze was in full tilt. Many dozens of tunes were written incorporating the Charleston rhythm and/or including the name in the titles. The songwriting team responsible for the music behind the original dance couldn't resist a follow-up number of their own. The title of their tune, "Everybody's Doin the Charleston Now," fittingly sums up the international state of affairs in popular entertainment.

The new year brought a reversal of fortune for him that continued through the end of the decade. On January 19, 1926, Johnson was elected to membership in the American Society of Composers, Authors and Publishers (ASCAP). Johnson's total copyrighted output increased steadily through 1925, 1926, and 1927. Several of his earlier instrumental pieces, including "Eccentricity Waltz" and "Keep Off the Grass," were finally copyrighted and arranged for publication, as well as newer pieces like "Jingles" and "Scalin' the Blues." Clarence Williams had assumed the rights to "Carolina Shout" and promoted it heavily in advertisements noting Johnson's piano roll and disc recordings from five years earlier.[56] Despite his invisibility as composer for work he had committed himself to since the New York closing of *Runnin' Wild*, Johnson continued to concentrate on writing for the popular and theatrical market. Johnson reconnected with seasoned songwriter Henry Creamer. The two had written one tune together in 1923 but, starting in 1926, worked together regularly. Creamer had worked with some of the biggest names in both the Black and white music world including Ernest Hogan, Alex Rogers, Al Jolson, Fannie Brice, Sophie Tucker, and Florenz Ziegfeld. Creamer was at the center of efforts to revive high-profile African American theater during the decade of the 1910s. He and Alex Rogers organized the Negro Players in 1913 for such purpose, responding to the backlash against the Black stage successes of the previous decade that kept African Americans off Broadway. The Black press noted, "Messrs. Rogers and Creamer assert that the only hope for the Negro to 'come back' in the show business is through his own people; that in order to do this he must write plays that will have real human interest—playlets that will show that the Negro can love, hate and display the same kind of sentiment that other people feel; in fact, to show that we have hearts."[57] That effort would fail, but beginning in 1918, with songwriting partner J. Turner Layton, Creamer today is recognized for many outstanding tunes that at the time suffered from underexposure, including "After You've Gone," "Dear Old Southland," "Strut Miss Lizzie," and "Way Down Yonder in New Orleans."[58] Creamer and Johnson were prolific. Like Flournoy Miller, Creamer never abandoned his desire to write more serious dramatic works. With music by Johnson, two stage shows were written and copyrighted in 1926 but not produced—*Chicago Loop: Musical Comedy in Two Acts* and *Geechie: Dusky Romance in Three Acts*. *Geechie* in particular dealt with material devoid of the typical stereotypes that continued to characterize Black stage shows. Johnson would later blame himself for sabotaging its production.

Johnson wrote the music for Leonard Harper's 1926 *Creole Follies*. Orchestrations were handled by William Grant Still, Russell Wooding, Izzy Myers, Joe Jordan, and Maceo Jefferson and performed by "Leroy Smith and his incomparable Creole Follies Orchestra." Eddie Green and Blanche Calloway were featured. The show was a nightclub revue that opened at the fashionable Ciro's on West 56th Street at the end of February to favorable reviews.[59] Ciro's had opened the year before and was patterned after the famous club of the same name in Paris. Johnson's "Chicago Stomp Down" and a novelty derivative of the "Charleston" titled "Charlestonovitch" were featured by the ensemble.[60] In mid-April, it moved to the Lafayette Theater for a week.[61] Soon after, his continual work in the musical theater began to bear fruit for him professionally. Johnson was called on for work in major white Broadway productions. His tune "Alabama Stomp," written with Creamer, was featured in the fifth edition of Earl Carroll's *Vanities* in mid-1926. *Billboard* singled out the tune and noted it "originated a new style of dance."[62] *Dark Secrets of 1926* was written by Johnson, Creamer, Maceo Pinkard, and Roy Turk. Leonard Harper staged the dances. The show did well on the Black vaudeville circuit and ran for 154 performances, closing in early January 1927.[63] Producer Fred Fisher was hoping for a Broadway opening that never materialized.[64]

Johnson had only one record release during 1926, a vocal accompaniment behind the obscure Sadie Jackson from November. It is a fine session and sold reasonably well. In November 1926, "If I Could Be with You (One Hour Tonight)" was copyrighted.[65] It became his most popular song hit, and a staple of the Great American Songbook. The song had a slow start on the popular charts. George Randol and Andy Razaf featured the tune in an edition of Irvin C. Miller's *Brownskin Models*. Ruth Etting, the famed star of the *Ziegfeld Follies*, introduced it to the majority of the white music-buying public in 1930. Her recording boosted it to the top of America's popular song market. Louis Armstrong recorded it in the same year, as did McKinney's Cotton Pickers. Once again, while Johnson frequently advocated for recording his own tunes, he recorded this chestnut only twice, once as a piano roll duet with Fats Waller in early 1927, and again in 1944. Second only to the "Charleston," it remains Johnson's most recognized tune. Johnson and Creamer composed and copyrighted "I Need Lovin'," which garnered reasonable popularity for a number of years and became a theme song for Blanche Calloway. Unlike so many other Johnson tunes, neither song was associated with a stage show. In November, Johnson was one of numerous performers who played a benefit at the Lafayette Theater for Salem Tutt Whitney, his former employer from the Smarter Set company tour of 1918. Johnson accompanied singers Henri and LaPearl.[66] Before the end of the year, the Johnsons added their first child to the family, James P. Jr. Early the next year, Johnson began another legendary association.

Chapter 15

YAMEKRAW, 1927

> Listen to Jimmy Johnson today—and watch his fingers—as he plays his
> rhapsody on themes from the music of the Georgia Negroes
> entitled "Yamekraw." Abandon and rubato there are, in abundance; but
> every finger at every note knows just where it is going.
> The blending of the improvisatory spirit with the precision of the virtuoso
> makes for a delicious uncertainty that at no moment slips out of control.
> —ISAAC GOLDBERG

By 1927, the presence of African American–owned publishing, booking, musical, and related arts businesses in the Broadway district was substantial. In less than ten years, to satisfy the thirst of the general public for popular and show music, the initial foray into the Gaiety building by W. C. Handy and Harry Pace, who first sublet desk space around 1918, was followed by many other prominent musicians and entertainment entrepreneurs. Perry Bradford was one of them, and after his success with Mamie Smith in 1920, fancied himself as the axis around which most of the Black entertainment industry revolved at that time. Bradford's publishing, composing, and marketing business was at its height. There can be no question his output and influence were significant, and especially so for Johnson. They were good friends. The intimate business dealings around these Broadway offices spawned a social set Bradford coined the "Joy Club." After concluding the business day, Bradford, Johnson, Fats Waller, Andy Razaf, Spencer Williams, Willie "The Lion" Smith, and others congregated at various establishments, from private homes to the lowliest dives. This extraordinary coterie of Harlem's entertainment elite was a hard-partying group. Bradford restated their motto in several ways: "We never let business interfere with our pleasure," or "Whenever business mess up with pleasure, then cut out the business and let the pleasure roll on."[1] As a boy and young man, Johnson was tantalized by the perks bestowed on the "ticklers" in the old tenderloin. He was now the premier tickler, and, at least in the African American community, Broadway royalty, but the allure of carousing, drinking, and heavy eating continued to be a central but ultimately destructive element of this culture.

One of the most notorious hangouts for the Joy Club was the Daisy Chain, a bordello run by famed Harlem madame Hazel Valentine, who frequently relocated it to various homes in the West 140s to stay one step ahead of the law. Perhaps the most popular brothel in the city, according to Ed Kirkeby, its name derives from the appropriation of the legitimate usage of the term referring to a series of connected events or objects, to a slang description of multi-person sexual acts. Her establishment was memorialized in music by two of Valentine's stride pianist associates—Count Basie in "Swingin' at the Daisy Chain," and Fats Waller in "Valentine Stomp." At Waller's birthday party in 1937, he recorded his brief patter with his guests, including a suggestion to Johnson that they meet at the Daisy Chain, to which he enthusiastically responds, "right on!" Waller and Valentine enjoyed joy-riding in Johnson's Cadillac until it was repossessed one day while they were in it. Waller and Johnson would often disappear for days at a time, sometimes with Johnson's wife Lillie Mae in hot pursuit. To retrieve him, she knew the likely hangouts, knew his piano style as it rang out from the open windows of un-air-conditioned apartments, and at times spotted his car parked out front.[2]

The vitality of the African American influence on popular entertainment in the 1920s was not lost on a multitude of white musicians, entertainers, producers, and publishers. They eagerly sought it out, and the four blocks around Broadway where African American musicians had their offices were a frequent destination. Bradford recalled, in his apocryphal storytelling style, of a visit from Mae West's assistant, none other than Charleston champion dancer Bee Jackson. In perhaps a violation of their motto, business did intrude in the Joy Club:

> [The party] was still going strong at 3 g-m (which means good morning), when who should buzz in but Bee (hot story telling) Jackson, Miss May [sic] West's personal maid. "What brings you here so early?" I asked. "Miss West told me to drop by here and get a copy of some man song that you published before I left the theatre last night."
>
> I don't know what man song she wanted, because we had three men songs: "He Used to Be Your Man—But Now He Belongs to Me," "He's A Mean-Mean Man—But He's So Good to Me" and "He May Be Your Man But He Comes to See Me Sometimes."

Jimmy Johnson played "He Used to Be Your Man" until it soaked in good, but when he played "He May Be Your Man But He Comes to See Me Sometimes," Bee folded up the two songs and said, "That'll get it," because she remembered the last song from a phrase that Miss West made famous in later years, "Come up and see me sometime."[3]

The wealth of talent was not squandered in late-night revelry nor focused only on generating an immediate Broadway hit. The African American community relied on its musical celebrities for charitable, promotional, and celebratory events. On January 11, 1927, Johnson made a surprise appearance at the Lafayette Theater to support a fundraiser for a Harlem foot clinic, with the press noting, "A delightful surprise was the appearance of Jimmy Johnson who obliged with a piano jazz classic and also furnished an accompaniment for two 'Black Bottom' dancers from the Cotton Club."[4] Johnson attended the annual ASCAP dinner at the Ritz-Carlton on March 30, 1927, the first year after his induction into that organization. African American members at that time included Nathaniel Dett, Will Marion Cook, James Reese Europe, Will Tyers, James Weldon Johnson, W. C. Handy, Clarence Williams, Maceo Pinkard, Chris Smith, Henry Creamer, Cecil McPherson (Cecil Mack), and Jo Trent.[5]

Johnson's published output in 1927 highlights the diversity of his efforts as composer. Rather than forsake any one aspect of his compositional identity to pursue another, he worked on many forms concurrently. Tin Pan Alley and show tunes, ethnic descriptive songs, jazz instrumentals, and an extended piano rhapsody were all added to his portfolio. He maintained numerous roles as performer—virtuoso soloist, orchestra leader, vocal accompanist. He saw himself as a craftsman in each area and did not see work in disparate musical forms as requiring artistic compromise. His work product stands as an estimable contribution to the greatest music of that era. Many examples of his work from this time have become timeless classics. To some degree, however, the loss of professional focus distracted him from creating an identity readily recognizable to the general public. In assigning composer or performer credits, he vacillated between using Jimmy Johnson for his popular work, and James P. Johnson for jazz and his "serious" compositions. A seemingly small difference, but decades later, libraries and museums would have materials filed separately under these names as if they are two different people. In some ways they are. There were many sides to James P. Johnson during the 1920s, and beyond. But except to those specifically aware of his skillful contributions, broad popular recognition always eluded him.

His collaboration with Henry Creamer gained steam. At least sixteen Johnson popular songs were copyrighted and/or published in 1927. His popular composing sustained him while attendance at Black theaters ebbed substantially during 1927. There were no new Johnson stage shows produced for the Black vaudeville circuits that year. He was, however, sought after for white mainstream Broadway productions. Johnson contributed three numbers to Rosalie Stewart's revue, *A la Carte*. "I'm Stepping Out with Lulu," written with Henry Creamer, was one of the featured tunes from the show and did well commercially. Most of the score was written by Herman Hupfeld, later famous as composer of "As Time Goes By." Perry Bradford published three folios of music, each characteristic of a different genre other than popular song. Folios of this sort were becoming a popular publishing trend. Among them was a collection of "Five Descriptive Negro Songs," given the title "Dixieland Echoes." Bradford wrote a foreword to the collection explaining the nostalgic images and meanings of each of the tunes:

"Echoes of Ole Dixieland"

We picture a log cabin scene in Alabama, with Fathers, Mothers, Sons and Daughters after their evening meal at sundown.

"Honey"

A crooning Negro lullaby, with love for its theme.

"Mississippi River Flood"

A Negro Musical Poem, of the Mississippi River Flood, with style descriptive.

"Cotton Pickin'"

A descriptive gem, telling how the Negroes celebrate the event by singing, dancing, banjo playing and giving thanks to the Lord for their good crops.

"Liza Jane's Weddin'"

A Terpsichorean Jazz Classic, with words that describe the happenings at a Negro Wedding.

The nostalgic effort played on the romanticized images of Black life in the rural South that many white and even some Black folks clung to. At its worst, this sort of depiction fed the longing among many for an antebellum society of

African American subjugation. In Bradford's hands, it was a marketing gimmick, his Alabama roots notwithstanding. Although countless popular songs had beaten to death many of these same images, Johnson's use of descriptors such as, "Crooning Negro Lullaby," "Negro Musical Poem," and "Terpsichorean Jazz Classic" convey an attempt to use these folk materials as more than stereotypical pandering. Johnson would use the material from this folio in a later symphonic reworking, *Mississippi Moan: Symphonic Poem*.

Another folio was titled "Jazzapation—A Study in Jazz by the Masters," and included "Six Hot Piano Solos," two each by Johnson, Bradford, and Fred Longshaw. Longshaw, a pianist from the Midwest, is best known for his work accompanying Bessie Smith and other blues singers through the 1920s. He recorded "Chili Pepper" and "Tomato Sauce" in 1925 before their inclusion by Bradford in "Jazzapation." His recorded versions reveal an interesting blend of blues, ragtime, and novelty effects. "Toddlin' Home" and "Scoutin' Around" are the two Johnson contributions. He had recorded them for the OKeh label in 1923, the former with the title listed simply as "Toddlin'." As a collection of "jazz" piano solos by three composers, "Jazzapation" was probably more of a success than "Dixieland Echoes" was as an ethnic song collection.

Johnson's longtime ambition of utilizing African American folk materials in symphonic music using western concert forms rather than jazz or song formats was first achieved with *Yamekraw: Negro Rhapsody*. His greatest desire was to be considered a serious composer, and the road he followed to achieve that recognition was to actualize the vision of the Harlem Renaissance thinkers in elevating the roots of African American culture into so-called higher musical forms. This is his first and what some consider his best work in this regard. Johnson completed it in early 1927, and it was published by Bradford that summer in folio format for solo piano. Noble Sissle recalled Johnson's work and progress on this piece:

> When James P. Johnson got to kicking around the idea of composing a Rhapsody he first tried to use an original theme. In fact he was quite on the way with the first movement when he dropped in to Perry Bradford's office and asked a group of fellow musicians to listen to his efforts. Among the listeners was Will Vodery and Will Marion Cook both of whom were great musicians and knew construction of the classics whereas Johnson was doing a good technical job.
>
> Both Will Marion Cook and Vodery suggested to the young composer that rather than trying to compose an original theme why not get one of Perry's Spiritual and Blues and use them as to themes. Because as they both pointed out that an American Rhapsody would have to include those great elements. And they called attention to how Dvorak used the

Spiritual melody of "Going Home" in order to set the mood for his "New World Symphony." And thus this great work ["Yamekraw"] was created.[6]

The foreword to *Yamekraw* describes the intent of the work as "A genuine Negro treatise on spiritual, syncopated and 'blue' melodies by James P. Johnson, expressing the religious fervor and happy moods of the natives of Yamekraw, a Negro settlement situated on the outskirts of Savannah, Georgia."[7] The foreword also hints at a comparison with Gershwin's *Rhapsody in Blue*, which had already received worldwide acclaim as an important contribution to American music. In the segregated world of 1920s America, Johnson and his community saw his career as parallel to that of Gershwin and, with closer links than Gershwin to the African American experience and musical tradition, perhaps even better qualified to redefine "American Music" utilizing this material.

Many other Black composers of the period with similar aspirations, like J. Rosamond Johnson, W. C. Handy, Will Marion Cook, and William Grant Still (who orchestrated *Yamekraw*) may have had more formal training, but Johnson had closer ties to the musical vernacular. Who among all these musicians heard the religious music of his mother's church *and* the bawdy secular tunes popular in the tenderloin, studied Bach *and* played at the Jungles Casino for the migrant Gullahs and Geechies from the coastal Southeast, wrote hit tunes for Broadway *and* was the king at Harlem rent parties, and who was both the most sought-after vocal accompanist for the female blues singers of the decade *and* stylistic inspiration for a whole generation of pianists? These experiences came together in Johnson with *Yamekraw*. Johnson's pioneering effort expresses the range of emotion and vitality in Black music. The piece incorporates jazz, stride, ragtime, blues, and the spiritual. Johnson intended to use these elements of Black folk, religious, and composed musical traditions, as Sissle pointed out, in the same way that European masters had used Black American folk material. Cook had been a Johnson booster for a number of years. His feedback regarding the use of an extant "roots" theme, even one of Bradford's, was in line with his insistence that the music of African Americans must reflect their navigation through history in an involuntary homeland. Any composer looking to create an art music must celebrate the roots of their inspiration, not cast it off in favor of strictly European aesthetics.[8]

Bradford outlined what he thought served as the thematic material which Johnson used for the four movements of *Yamekraw*. The first is based on "Every Time I Feel the Spirit Moving in My Heart" and "Sam Jones Done Snagged His Britches." The second movement includes "Brothers and Sisters," a melody separately published as a song. The third and fourth movements include a theme that was used separately in a later show, "Mississippi Roustabouts." "You Can Read My Letters, But You Can't Read My Mind" and "We Are Leaving for Yamekraw" constitute the closing sections.⁹ Johnson scholar and pianist Dr. Robert Pinsker has found fragments from other Johnson pieces including sections of the first theme of the piano roll version of "Stop It" from 1917, and elements of the main theme of a Johnson instrumental piece from 1923 titled "After Hours."¹⁰ John Howland finds hints of other Johnson pieces, including "Caprice Rag," as well as elements from his good friend Eubie Blake and, interestingly, from Rube Bloom's "Soliloquy."¹¹

After publication, Johnson and Bradford began to publicize it aggressively.¹² At the time the piece was highly praised in the African American musical community, with sentiments acknowledging its importance to the Harlem Renaissance, including less than subtle comparisons with Gershwin and hailing Johnson as the musical beacon for "race pride." Andy Razaf wrote in the *New York Amsterdam News*:

> Hats off to Jimmy Johnson, the master pianist and rhythm king. We predict that George Gershwin and the rest of his tribe will bundle up their little blue rhapsodies and make it for the tall timber when they hear Jimmy's "YAM-E-KRAW," a rhapsody in black—and all that the name implies. At this particular time, when so-called white authorities on jazz, blues, and spirituals are climbing to wealth and fame on the backs of their colored brothers, Jimmy Johnson rises like a Negro Moses to deliver us out of musical bondage. Wish I was able, I'd soon be "hiring a hall" and inviting H. L. Mencken and the rest of his crowd to come and hear Jimmy play his "Yam-E-Kraw," America's first genuine blues rhapsody.¹³

Similar feelings were expressed by pianist Dave Peyton in his regular column for the *Chicago Defender*: "Several months ago this writer asked the question why do not some of our composers write a syncopated opera, a jazz opera or a syncopated classic on the order of Gershwin's 'Rhapsody in Blues' [*sic*]? This question has been answered in the release of the Perry Bradford Music Company's 'Yamekraw,' a Race rhapsody by the well-known composer, James P. Johnson.' This composition by J. P. Johnson will lend encouragement to our other composers to follow Mr. Johnson. There is something in the score that is admirable. It is the introduction of the spirituals. They are well treated in paraphrased form and well colored with variable harmonic figures."¹⁴ All three folios were recognized in the press, likely through the promotional efforts of Bradford: "Perry Bradford's tunes will bring good results to singers and musicians. 'Dixieland Echoes,' five classic descriptive melodies composed by Perry Bradford and James Johnston [*sic*] in book form, which sell for a dollar, are in demand and is proving itself one of the best works of these composers. Another of their famous works was 'A

Negro Rhapsody.' Another real American syncopation in jazz, blues and spirituals is 'Yamekraw' from the pen of James Johnson. Another instrumental of six red-hot piano solos is in book form and is entitled 'Jassapation.'"[15]

Like *Rhapsody in Blue*, *Yamekraw* was played in the movie houses, usually as an overture to the feature presentation.[16] The following year, in 1928, Bradford sold the piece to Alfred and Co., which published the piano solo as well as William Grant Still's orchestrations for small orchestra, theater orchestra, and full orchestra. Jazz and blues "rhapsodies" had become a new popular genre, and Alfred put substantial resources into promoting Johnson's work with large orchestras.[17] Their efforts paid off. Nat Shilkret's Victor Recording Orchestra, Don Voorhees' Columbia Orchestra, and the Phil Spitalny band with forty-eight voices included it in their books. In July, the Mediterraneans, led by Hugo Mariani, along with the Jubilee Singers, broadcast it over WJZ in New York and over thirty-eight other ABC network stations nationwide. The *Palmolive Hour* planned a broadcast. Mariani was born in Italy in 1899 and moved as a young boy to Buenos Aires, where his father directed an orchestra. He came to the United States in the mid-twenties, became a naturalized citizen, and ultimately director of the National Broadcasting Company Orchestra. He eventually settled in Costa Rica, where he established their National Symphony. To capitalize on the success of the nationwide broadcast of *Yamekraw* that demonstrated an audience for symphonic jazz, Alfred published two new "miniature" rhapsodies before the end of the summer.[18] The Mediterraneans repeated their successful broadcast in December.[19] They were then tapped to play it in a Warner Brothers movie short based on the piece as part of their Vitaphone series of short subjects. It was released in June 1930. The film was directed by Murray Roth and the cast included Louise Cook, Margaret Sims, Ernest Taylor, Dickie Wells (not the future trombone player with Count Basie), and Jimmy Mordecai.

In the film, the composition is the musical backdrop for a love story written by Stanley Love portrayed with singing but no other spoken dialogue. The plot situates poor Southern, rural, African American farm dwellers (depicted with the typical derisively intended images of watermelons, pickaninnies, and a ramshackle cabin) in conflict with Northern, urban, modernized, amoral sophisticates.[20] The program for the New York premiere on August 1, 1930, at the Warner Brothers Strand Theater at Broadway and 47th Street, described it as "A Rhapsody of the Black men's blues, by the noted composer James P. Johnson. It presents the emotional mood of the Negro, amid swiftly changing camera angles and unique lighting effects."[21] It had a favorable run at the enormous Hollywood Theater also on Broadway.[22] Warner Brothers distributed it widely in the North.[23] Reviews were positive and included comparison to the work of Dudley Murphy, who had directed *St. Louis Blues*, with Bessie Smith backed by Johnson's piano and orchestral direction, and Duke Ellington's *Black and Tan*, both released in 1929. *Billboard* made note of its artistic qualities as "one of the most artistic shorts yet given to sound pictures and stamps Roth as a director out of the ordinary," and ". . . the musical accompaniment being a feature of the film as well as the photography." They concluded, "The entire picture is beautifully done, pictorially imaginative and directorially perfect."[24] By late August it was playing in Harlem at the Lafayette Theater. Its reception there seemed to be much less objectionable than Murphy's *St. Louis Blues* had been, despite depiction of some of the usual degrading stereotypes. The *New York Age* called it "sensational."[25] Perhaps the attachment of serious art pretentions affected the critical reception in the African American community. After all, Johnson's own intentions were to reach for a highbrow aesthetic. The retained racist conventions as part of the "white projection" of cultural notions of that time that inform the visual, narrative and character elements require particular effort at contextualization in order to best appreciate Johnson's music and the art film conventions of the day.[26]

Several years later, Alfred looked to further parlay the popularity of the piece by extracting segments for publication as individual tunes. "Hot Curves" (© 1930) incorporated material from *Yamekraw* and was promoted as a fox-trot with the subtitle "A Flaming Outburst of Negro Syncopation."[27] "Yamekraw Blues" (© 1931) was published as part of their "stomp series." Both were arranged by future Fats Waller arranger Ken Macomber. Recordings of *Yamekraw* continued to receive radio play as late as 1933, and at stations far from New York.[28] In 1938, it was used as an overture to Orson Welles's production of *Macbeth*. Joe Jordan conducted the Negro Unit Orchestra of the Federal Theater Project for the production which opened at the Lafayette Theater. Years later Johnson attached lyrics to at least part of the work. *Yamekraw* has posed aesthetic and analytical dilemmas for cultural observers, music scholars, and historical academics looking to tie Johnson's work into one tradition or another. Some writers have dismissed it as lacking in the typical thematic development expected of Western art music, noting, "What emerges is a collage of short themes that seem to be lifted out of context and lose all sense of spontaneity. It's like seeing scenes from a movie in the form of 'previews of coming attractions'—intriguing, but somehow incomplete."[29] A more nuanced analysis holds that what emerges, as Howland suggests, is a complex and unique combination of source elements—some folk, some commercial, some jazz—cast in a vehicle conceived with aspirational intentions driven by a highbrow cultural imperative, but manifesting as a fluid array of "serious," commercial and "roots-based" strophic compositional and performance practices. Johnson had his musical fingers in many pots, and *Yamekraw* reflects a confluence of many of those influences. In its time, it didn't quite make the leap, as he had hoped, from middlebrow symphonic jazz to the high art designation required by major symphonies. Like Gershwin's rhapsody, as time has gone on, Johnson's original intent has been more broadly respected. It took thirty years, but since the early 1960s, it has been performed many times not only by solo pianists in concert settings but also by small and large symphony orchestras.

Chapter 16

KEEP SHUFFLIN', 1928

> The jazzy and peppy musical score has been composed by Jimmy Johnson, who will conduct his own colored orchestra for the performance, a feature which goes far in making it the liveliest of all Miller and Lyles productions.
> —*THE ENGLEWOOD TIMES*

The first half of 1928 proved to be a signal time period in the professional relationship between James P. Johnson and Fats Waller. Johnson was already a towering figure in the African American musical community, and Fats was fast becoming one. Their relationship as teacher and pupil, and then good friends, matured into successful collaborators. Together, they wrote music for one of the decade's most popular Black musicals on Broadway (and one of the most popular of any show on Broadway), set down more than half of their total recorded output together, and furthered each other's career. The spark for this flurry of collaborative activity was a new show proposed by Miller and Lyles in late 1927. Six years after *Shuffle Along* first opened, enthusiasm for Black shows on Broadway was beginning to wane, although they were not uniformly unsuccessful. Miller and Lyles were continued sought-after headliners. Their effort during the summer and fall of 1927 was a show called *Rang Tang*. It has often been characterized as a failure, but the music of Ford Dabney and lyrics of Jo Trent powered Miller and Lyles's still enormously popular comedy style to over one hundred performances. By September, the show was grossing $16,000 a week, a considerable sum by this standard benchmark of Broadway success.[1] Within a month, however, things began to unwind. Pay disputes with the rank-and-file performers, and perhaps with Miller and Lyles as well,[2] were apparently resolved, but dwindling audiences on tour in November soon spelled the end.³ Financial irregularities were nothing unusual in the business, and Miller and Lyles seemed to have come out solvent enough to contemplate opening a nightclub in Harlem at the prime location of 147th Street and Lenox Avenue. The club didn't materialize, which was just as well for the pair as they embarked on their next idea for the stage. Increasingly, white and Black talent were working together on Broadway, and some heavyweights were eager to collaborate with the comedy duo.

Con Conrad was a well-trained pianist and spent his entire life in music and show business. Born Conrad K. Dober in New York in 1891, he began his professional career playing piano for silent pictures. He toured the vaudeville circuit in the United States and Europe and went on to apply his musical abilities as a popular composer for Tin Pan Alley, the musical theater, and ultimately Hollywood. He dabbled with limited success in other aspects of the business tangential to his composing, including as publisher and producer. He died in 1938 in California at the young age of forty-seven, but not before registering with a number of well-known and successful tunes. In 1920, his songwriting collaborator was pianist J. Russel Robinson. They produced three tunes that year which, at least in jazz circles in large part due to notable recorded versions, have had substantial continued renown: "Margie," "Singin' the Blues," and "Palesteena." He also scored when Eddie Cantor adopted his tune, "Ma, He's Making Eyes at Me." Conrad's greatest commercial hit was "Barney Google," from the successful musical comedy of 1923 *Barney Google and Spark Plug*, based on the enormously popular comic strip of the same name. His collaborator on this tune was a young Billy Rose, just breaking in to the entertainment industry. Conrad continued to contribute to Broadway productions through the middle twenties with some success. He was known as an impetuous practical joker who, despite ASCAP membership since 1920, tended to squander his royalties.⁴ 1927 was a particularly lean year for him. His string of earlier successes had not lifted him to a sustained level as major commercial or theatrical composer. He was now looking to cash in on the often more lucrative but also risky production end of musical theater. Up to that point, he had not had any formal, professional association with the African American musical community. He saw an opportunity in the Broadway winning streak of Miller and Lyles, by then numbering two blockbuster shows and the solid result from *Rang Tang*. As 1927 came to a close, Conrad had had only one inauspicious tune placed in the show *Take the Air* earlier that year. *Rang Tang* was winding down for Miller and Lyles, and Conrad likely sought them out, hoping to convince the comedy team he was the right man to produce their next effort.

With his fortunes waning, Conrad found his way into the employ of one of the leading figures of New York's underworld, mobster and gambler Arnold Rothstein.⁵ Rothstein was alleged to have fixed the 1919 World Series between the Chicago White Sox and Cincinnati Reds but was never convicted. He was involved in crap games, card games, and horse racing at the well-known tracks in Saratoga Springs and Belmont in New York, and was part owner of the track at Havre de Grace, Maryland, known as "The Graw." He was the first major crime figure to appreciate and capitalize on the opportunities presented by Prohibition. The entire New York political machine of Tammany Hall was in his pocket. Rothstein held court at the famous Lindy's deli in the heart of Broadway. "Rothstein's table was sacrosanct," one writer has noted. "It was right near the cashier's booth, and after 9 PM no one else was allowed to occupy it but Rothstein himself. He conducted business over cups of coffee and a danish." Writer Damon Runyon coined for him the nickname "the brain" for Rothstein's legendary ability to keep track of numbers in his head. In outward appearance and casual interaction, he appeared a mild-mannered, sympathetic, soft touch. In some cases he was. His empire, however, was held together by a stable of protégés that included some of the era's most notorious and brutal gangsters—Jack "Legs" Diamond, "Dutch" Schultz, Charles "Lucky" Luciano, Meyer Lansky, Frank Costello, Lepke Buchalter.[6] They were all beholden to Rothstein.

The underworld and entertainment communities in the 1920s were intimately connected. For Rothstein, the potentially lucrative world of show business provided a ready means of laundering money made in his protean illegal pursuits. His first foray into supporting theatrical productions was bankrolling the first edition of *George White's Scandals* in June 1919. In 1922 he helped bolster Anne Nichols's struggling *Abie's Irish Rose*, which would run for an unprecedented five years. Rothstein was known for welching on his debts and borrowed $20,000 from Irving Berlin in 1922 and never repaid it. He later proposed a partnership with Berlin, who boldly turned him down. Conrad approached his boss about financing the new show he planned with Miller and Lyles. Rothstein was certainly aware of Miller and Lyles's successes. He had a piece of several Harlem nightspots, including the Cotton Club. Rothstein saw the opportunity and agreed, including in the deal his usual substantial cut of the profits.[7] His involvement was no secret. *Billboard* reported Conrad's role as producer with his office at 45 West 57th Street, a building owned by Rothstein, and that Rothstein was bankrolling the production.[8] Rothstein insisted his money provide for the best musical talent, and Conrad struck out to recruit it.

Perry Bradford, in his rambling, stream-of-consciousness memoir, contends Conrad first approached him, suggesting he, Bradford, write the score with Henry Creamer. Conrad, according to Bradford, called on him with a desire to return a favor Bradford had done for him several years earlier in mediating a publishing dispute with W. C. Handy.[9] Conrad also boasted he was expecting a musical contribution from George Gershwin for the new production. This was not so outlandish a notion. Their paths had crossed two years earlier when

Gershwin had contributed one song to the successful revue *Americana*, for which Conrad had composed most of the score.[10] Bradford spins his role into that of lynchpin for the whole effort. But Bradford and his office was indeed a nexus for cross-cultural musical interaction. Bradford suggests he talked Conrad out of Gershwin in favor of James P. Johnson, telling Conrad, "'George Gershwin would be a knockout man for a white show—but for a Negro show you should have Negro music. I know a good man who plays a hand-full of piano keys with every note by the name of Jimmy Johnson.'" Conrad confessed that he had never heard of Johnson, and Bradford reminded Conrad of Johnson's qualifications. Bradford pointed out Johnson's role in *Runnin' Wild*, especially as composer of the "Charleston." He encouraged Conrad to check Johnson's bona fides with Miller and Lyles, but Conrad had a flash of recollection, saying to Bradford, "Yes, I was there, Perry, on the opening night at the Colonial Theatre and I'm glad to learn that Jimmy Johnson was the man who played so much piano mess. So Jimmy is in. Thank you Perry, for this Johnson man, because he may be our key-man to put in the orchestra pit to send our singing and dancing chorus to 'Hitland.'"[11]

The deal, however, was not yet done. Bradford needed to mend fences between Johnson and Miller and Lyles. The previously successful association of the *Runnin' Wild* foursome including Cecil Mack had, according to Bradford, become strained over a royalty dispute while the show was on tour in Pittsburgh. Flournoy Miller, whose relationship with Johnson was warmer, agreed to a renewed endeavor with him. Aubrey Lyles, profligate spender and more worried about the effect any financial deal would have on his own pocketbook, reluctantly agreed. "I don't like to put bread in that guy's [Johnson's] mouth—and I ain't gonna take none out. So tell Con it's ok and also tell him that I'm hoping that the same bee don't sting me twice."[12] In reality, the "bee" that stung Lyles was his own financial mismanagement that led to his personal bankruptcy in December 1925. Lyles was well known for his conspicuous consumption. He was a spectacle parading through Harlem first in his custom-built Pierce-Arrow and then Rolls Royce. The major creditors in his bankruptcy filing were automobile related, followed by Mrs. A. L. Lyles, the Shuffle Along Co., and Flournoy Miller's brother Irvin C. Miller, who had taken over producing *Runnin' Wild* in 1925, all of whom had loaned Lyles substantial sums during the preceding three years.[13] Johnson and Mack are not listed as creditors in the bankruptcy filing. If there was contention between Johnson and Lyles, it did not seem to interrupt the production in Pittsburgh. There is no mention of internecine financial problems in the press, usually attentive to reporting this sort of scandal. Any role Lyles might have had in royalty arrangements is unknown. It is not a stretch, however, to think Lyles did somehow manipulate *Runnin' Wild* payouts to bolster his own financial situation.

Maurice Waller, in his biography of his father, suggests it was Miller and Lyles who prevailed upon James P. Johnson to write the score.[14] Ed Kirkeby writes in his Waller biography that both Rothstein and Conrad were longtime admirers of Miller and Lyles. This was likely true, but he erroneously characterizes Conrad as a "Harlemite" and as having traveled to Europe with Miller and Lyles in 1921. Kirkeby contends Conrad first came to Johnson,[15] contradicting Bradford's recollection. Although Johnson was eager to find another Broadway outlet for his commercial composing since the short-lived *A La Carte* closed in September, he was also busy with his rhapsody *Yamekraw*. The piano score had already been published by Perry Bradford. He was now working with William Grant Still on the orchestrations that were ultimately published in 1928 by Alfred Music. Johnson may also have started work with Bradford on another show titled *Messin' Around* that did not appear until 1929, but one of the numbers that ended up in the show, "Skiddle-De Scow," was recorded by Johnson and Bradford in September 1927. After that recording, Johnson was absent from the recording studio for five months until February 1928. But he had a reliable and deep portfolio from which he was drawing royalties. In April 1927, he had recorded his tunes "Sweet Mistreater" and "Lock and Key" with Bessie Smith. From the recording mechanical rights alone, Johnson was paid $75.00 for sales during the last quarter of 1927.[16] As a small piece of his very productive output over the prior few years, including "If I Could Be with You," Johnson had a steady income from royalties. He was busy and comfortable and was now pondering the task of composer and music director for Conrad's ambitious proposal.

Bradford takes credit for suggesting Fats Waller as co-composer and pianist along with Johnson in the show. Says Bradford about his conversation with Conrad, "Just as I was getting ready to go the thought came to mind of how Fats Waller and Jimmy Johnson had murdered the piano the night before in our 'Joy Club' jamboree and Fats and Jimmy had asked me to see what could be done to use both of them in the Miller & Lyles show. So I suggested: 'Here's a natural for the show. Fats Waller and Jimmy Johnson playing two pianos in the orchestra pit. Man, you should hear those two crazy piano cats spanking two baby-grands.'" According to Bradford, he and Conrad arranged for Johnson and Waller to audition for Rothstein, who was very favorably impressed, and signed them both.[17] Waller had spent the summer and early fall of 1927 in Chicago playing with Erskine Tate at the renowned Vendome Theater where Louis Armstrong was also in residence. Waller was summoned back to New York for delinquent alimony payments to his first wife Edith, but dodged a legal bullet, avoiding jail time. His Lafayette Theater job playing the organ came to an abrupt end in September when his then wife Anita joined him at the organ to celebrate the birth of their new son Maurice. After an argument with the management over her presence, Waller reportedly quit.[18] He could hardly afford the loss of income now with two children and legal obligations. Regular recording for Victor and his few royalties were not sufficient to sustain him financially. Johnson, who likely knew of Waller's predicament, was juggling several other endeavors. By most accounts then, since Johnson was first approached, it was likely he played a significant role in suggesting that Waller share composer responsibilities. He had good reasons to suggest bringing on his friend and his lyricist partner Andy Razaf. It turned out to be a very good decision.

Rehearsals began in earnest. The early promotion of the show noted there would be tunes contributed by George and Ira Gershwin and Cole Porter.[19] Conrad had promised at least the Gershwin inclusion to Bradford. *Keep Shufflin'* opened at the Gibson Theater in Philadelphia on February 13, 1928. There was one Gershwin song included on opening night, "The Man I Love."[20] It was written in 1924 for the show *Lady, Be Good*, but dropped before the Broadway opening. In 1927, the Gershwins placed it in *Strike Up the Band*, but the show (and the song) never made it to Broadway at all. One more attempt was made to place it in Ziegfeld's *Rosalie* that began rehearsals in late 1927, and despite several successful recordings of the tune by that time, once again it failed to secure a place beyond the tryouts.[21] Conrad, trolling around theatrical society since the fall, came upon the opportunity to include it, but for the fourth time, this Gershwin masterpiece was not destined for the Broadway stage. By the time of the New York opening, no Gershwin or Porter tunes were included. Will Vodery, a musician of great stature best known as writer and arranger for Flo Ziegfeld's *Follies*, contributed the orchestrations. The published sheet music of the tunes from *Keep Shufflin'* credits Leonard Harper with staging the dances and ensembles, but the newspaper notices and reviews credit his onetime assistant Clarence Robinson. Joe Jordan conducted the orchestra for the opening in Philadelphia,[22] although advertisements noted the music was performed by "Will Vodery's Symphonic Band." The early reviews from Philadelphia highlighted the frenetic pace of the routines and musical numbers, with praise overall.[23] Tap dancers Eveleyne Keyes and Byron Jones were singled out for praise, as was Jean Starr, singing a wide variety of material including the upbeat but plaintive Johnson number "Give Me the Sunshine," which recurred throughout the production. Popular dances of the decade including the "Charleston" and "Black Bottom" were revisited in the choreography.

It was a huge production. During the course of its run, the number of cast, orchestra, and chorus members ranged from sixty to ninety. It opened at Daly's 63rd Street Theatre on February 27, 1928. This was the outer edge of the Broadway Theater district but had been home to the successful Black shows *Shuffle Along* and *Liza*, as well as productions featuring Antoinette Perry, Basil Rathbone, and Mae West. In 1922, the interior was redesigned with a bright red and gold color scheme.[24] Johnson apparently led the orchestra for the New

York opening.²⁵ A month before, Johnson was scheduled to play for a fundraiser the same night as the opening. Zora Neale Hurston, among others, was sponsoring a scholarship barn dance at the Renaissance Casino in Harlem.²⁶ Johnson clearly could not miss the New York opening of his highly anticipated show, even for a worthy cause with such august Harlem Renaissance sponsorship. The barn dance could also have been scheduled after his show at Daly's, as "midnight shows" were often the custom. Whether Johnson fulfilled the fundraiser is unknown. Throughout the Broadway run, Joe Jordan's role was interrupted by contract disputes with Conrad, and also perhaps with Lyles. As a union member, Jordan had negotiated a handsome weekly salary for his conducting responsibilities. On several occasions in March and April, he was conspicuously absent from the conductor's position. Opening night may have been another occasion. By the end of April, the show was without a standing orchestra director. Johnson assumed the role while he continued at the piano.²⁷

The return of Miller and Lyles to Broadway was highly anticipated. A banner welcoming them was strung across 63rd Street. The duo reprised their successful characters and locale from *Shuffle Along*, *Runnin' Wild*, and *Rang Tang*. As usual, the paper-thin plot primarily serves as a scaffold for a series of comedic sketches, song and dance specialties, and novelty acts. Over time through its run, these constituent pieces were revised with additions and deletions. Miller plays Steve Jenkins, described as a "lazy husband." Lyles again plays Jenkins's unappreciated friend Sam Peck. With a group of other "malcontent" townspeople, once again set in Jimtown, they plan to rob a bank. In preparation for handling their spoils, they form the "Equal Got" League. The "League" is intended to divide the money so as to enrich all those involved in an equitable manner. Sam objects to the name, insisting it should be named the "Equal Git" League since "we isn't got but we're gonna git" the money. The League meets in Sam's Garden with Miller and Lyles engaging in comedic speeches arguing over their positions as secretary and treasurer. To decide who should place the dynamite for the robbery, they arrange a "battle royal" boxing match. Miller's character Jenkins is knocked unconscious. In his comatose state, he envisions the effects of their distribution scheme. The residents of Jimtown first destroy all their possessions and then go on a spending spree that ends in economic catastrophe. He awakens just in time to scuttle the disastrous plan.

The opening night program lists sixteen musical numbers in what seems like a round robin of pairings of its composers—Johnson, Waller, Conrad, Vodery, and Clarence Todd (a longtime collaborator of Clarence Williams)—with lyricists Creamer and Razaf. Todd also directs the "Jubilee Glee Club" embedded in the story. The reviews of the opening were mixed. About half a dozen reviews found little to recommend, but at least ten other reviews were complimentary. The quality of the libretto/book was left to the eye of the beholder—it either clearly transcended the fragmentation of the typical revue and was a solid book musical, or it was "ragged" and weak without structure. Some of the white mainstream papers lamented ". . . the comparative lack of essentially Negro character and comparative prevalence of the manner and matter of conventional white vaudeville and musical comedy." The reviewer in *The American Stage*, while noting parallels with past all-Black shows, went so far as to comment that *Keep Shufflin'* had much in common with mainstream white theatrical entertainment, and that, "in general the score, contributed by four colored composers and Mr. Conrad, smacks far less of Dixie that it does of Tin Pan Alley."[28] This was of course the intent of Miller and all the contributors. With what seemed at first glance to be a succession of carbon copy remakes of the same basic theater piece based on *Shuffle Along*, Miller gradually evolved away from the harsh stereotypes, dashing expectations of some that each of their efforts would continue to portray the same demeaning images of African American culture. The reviewer from the African American *Pittsburgh Courier* was relieved that some of the more egregious bits of minstrel mockery did not emerge. Some found deeper social commentary in Miller's writing, noting that the "Equal Got" league was seen as a veiled comment on socialism.[29] The vignettes around the dancing and music began to break through the residual veneer of the minstrel show. If some in the white audiences were disappointed that nineteenth-century Zip Coon and Jim Crow characters and behavior were fading with each successive show, others were impressed with the quality of the entertainment that filled that void. But the stereotypes weren't all expunged. Levee scenes were retained, the title of the show perpetuated the imagery of a lazy man's gait, and Miller and Lyles continued to wear blackface.

The reviews made much greater reference to the orchestra than usual. The quality of this particular pit band was quite remarkable. Three members are listed on the program: "On the White Keys . . . Fats Waller—On the Black Keys . . . Jimmy Johnson—Behind the Bugle . . . Jabbo Smith." Cladys "Jabbo" Smith (1908–1991) was born in Georgia, and learned music at the renowned Jenkins Orphanage School. Before playing in the pit of *Keep Shufflin'*, Smith's jazz credentials included several years at Smalls' Paradise with Charlie Johnson, and recording with Duke Ellington. He was a highly skilled player with a brilliant, inventive style. Some have argued that he equaled Louis Armstrong in technical skill and imaginative interpretation. His name on the program speaks to his reputation at that time. Of Johnson and Waller, Smith remarked: "When I first went to New York, James and Fats was the thing. Gone. I was just a lucky guy, getting with those cats. He was something else, that Fats. He was something special. A showman. James P. wasn't a showman, but he was with that piano. He was something else. With that piano that cat was something else. James and Fats used to run together. I guess James did as much partying as Fats but it just

Miller and Lyles with the chorus of *Keep Shufflin'* (1928) in the levee scene. (Photo by White Studio © New York Public Library for the Performing Arts)

didn't look that way. You see Fats and everyone is laughing and carrying on."[30] "They were beautiful people, they were like brothers, just fabulous people."[31]

Another highly acclaimed member of the orchestra was reed player Garvin Bushell (1902–1991). Bushell had worked with Mamie Smith and Ethel Waters, and toured Europe with Sam Wooding. He would later play with many bands in the 1940s and then led his own groups. Other members included: Joe Lyman and Wesley Howard, violin, Marion Cumbo, cello, Brown and Ramsey, cornet (first names unknown), Rudy Jackson and Herb Johnson, saxophone, Harry Hull bass, Carl "Battle Axe" Kenny, drums, and Bert Hall, trombone.[32] Kenny was well known as the house drummer at Leroy's, the fabled Harlem nightspot where Johnson and Waller enthralled the lucky patrons with their piano tandem. E. Bert Hall, from Baltimore, came to New York around 1920 and opened the Rhythm Club, also known as the Bert Hall Rhythm Club, Inc. The great but mysterious pianist Paul Seminole got his start there.[33] Hall was dedicated to advocating for the rights of Black musicians, arranged bookings, and was active in the musician's union. His wife, Josephine Hall, was in the cast of *Keep Shufflin'*. Bert Hall died in 1932.[34] Rudy Jackson had played with Carroll Dickerson, King Oliver, and had recently been replaced in the Ellington band by Barney Bigard. Herb Johnson and Garvin Bushell had worked together in Sam

Wooding's band in 1923. Bushell recalled, "Herb was from Boston [sic, he was born in Hartford, Connecticut] and had studied at the conservatory there. He also played bassoon, and I liked that. So when a guy came along and offered to sell me a bassoon, I bought it and asked Herb to teach me. We had a thing at the Nest [Club in Harlem] where we used two bassoons, which was unheard of."[35] H. Johnson's tutelage of Bushell on bassoon would bear its greatest fruit in a few months. Harry Hull had recorded with Mamie Smith, Johnny Dunn, and with James P. Johnson and Perry Bradford. Marion Cumbo was a top-tier trained musician. A native New Yorker, he graduated from the Institute of Musical Art (the Juilliard School) and also studied in Chicago. He was an original member of the Negro String Quartet in 1919. He and his wife devoted their careers to Black and integrated symphonic organizations.[36] I. Wesley Howard was a prominent violinist. He served as assistant band master of the 809th Infantry band in France during World War I,[37] taught at Howard University, and later the Hampton Institute.[38] Bushell recalled another band member at the outset of his career, eighteen-year-old and future Ellington tenor saxophone player Al Sears (1910–1990). Sears joined the touring production later in the year. The backup pianist was nineteen-year-old Samuel C. Allen from Middleport, Ohio. He had moved to New York to study with Johnson and would later record with Teddy Hill, Slim Gaillard, and Stuff Smith, among others.[39]

Johnson's music, as was often the case, was praised.[40] *Variety* noted, "the score is as good as that of the first named success," referring to *Shuffle Along*. Jean Starr was acclaimed singing "Give Me the Sunshine." "Sippi," put forth by Mabel Russell, was "even more catchy."[41] Another reviewer singled out "Give Me The Sunshine," noting, "It's such a good song in itself, and it is sung with such contagious good humor by the vivid Miss Jean Starr, that it's quite worth sitting through duller parts of the show for; indeed, almost worth going up to sixty-third street for an evening, even if there were nothing else."[42] Other tunes singled out in various reviews were "How Jazz Was Born" by Waller and Razaf and "Charlie, My Back Door Man."[43] The Waller/Razaf tune "Willow Tree" was added to the production after its opening week. It is not listed in the original program, but it too became a popular hit. Harms published eight tunes from the show.

There was unanimity in the press about the two pianists—Johnson and Waller were a hit. Even before the Broadway opening, a Philadelphia paper noted, "Fats Waller and Jimmy Johnson at the pianos in the orchestra pit attracted as much attention as the company of footlight performers. Throughout the performance the rippling crescendos and diminuendos of these two pianists added an undercurrent of foot-moving music that was irresistible."[44] With Johnson and Waller each at his own piano, the *Keep Shufflin'* Orchestra astounded audiences night after night. Bushell recalled in his autobiography, "Jimmy conducted the pit orchestra, and Fats played piano. They had a two-piano thing where they played some of the same things they did down at Leroy's. The show could hardly go on after they got through."[45] The Johnson-Waller piano duo was so popular they continued playing during intermissions. One of the acclaimed hits from the show was a tune written by Johnson, Creamer, and Conrad called "Sippi."[46] Between acts, Johnson and Waller used the tune as musical artillery for their piano tandem of which only brief glimpses remain on their few recordings together. By May, word of their two-piano intermission show had reached Europe. Writing from Paris, columnist A. F. Rosemond said, "There is a piano act [Wiener and Doucet, white] which is headlining the music halls of Europe and receiving a very large income therefrom. The act is undoubtedly good. However, if Messrs. Jimmy Johnson and Thomas ("Fats") Waller would make a tour of the European halls (after finishing their engagement in "Keep Shufflin'") they would create a furor."[47]

True to their operating principle, the "joy club" trumped the demands of a successful Broadway run. Garvin Bushell recalled, "Some Monday Nights we'd have to send someone out to find James P. and Fats, since they'd have been out at parties since Friday night, playing piano, spending money, buying liquor, they'd just close the places up. Monday night they'd be ossified and you couldn't get them on. That was living in the fast lane then."[48] Flournoy Miller lamented that even the responsibilities of performance couldn't attenuate the distracting behavior of the two men. Maurice Waller writes, "Miller noted the popularity of the two men and thought it would be a fine idea to have them play at intermission. They enjoyed the opportunity but would race back to their dressing room each night for some refreshment. Years later Miller recalled how he had to push James P. and Dad out into the theatre pit every night to make sure they would play."[49] Voracious eating was as important as the drinking. After moving out of the city, Johnson and Waller continued to find iceboxes to empty. Johnson's neighbor, Clarence Williams, knew how to keep his friends close; as Ed Kirkeby recalled, "At Clarence's house one afternoon [in the 1930s], they cleaned out the ice-box, the winner consuming ten pork chops. Eggs were eaten as if they were grapes. . . ."[50]

Filtered through the long lens of history, their insatiable appetites have become romanticized images of that time of excesses. In truth, they were both headed down a tragic path of self-destruction that robbed their families and the music world of two giants. Johnson's predilection for the lifestyle romanticized by the early ticklers he encountered and looked up to as role models was part of his undoing. Willie Gant observed that Johnson's association with people Gant called "bums" was more of a barrier to a successful breakout in the mainstream music world than the generalized racial discrimination so common at the time. He said, "He had everything. He was equipped with everything, with the muscle and the bomb. I've heard people say they wouldn't have accepted him because he was a Negro. That's pushing it. Had he gone to the whites right ... James could have been accepted more then than he could have been at any time."[51] Why Johnson's attraction to this element and lifestyle should have been the primary factor hindering acclaim for him, but not for Waller or Bessie Smith, casts doubt on attributing this degree of importance to his carousing. But Johnson was not the performer/personality of a Waller or Smith, and other aspects of his personality and career choices had much to do with his invisibility. The drinking certainly played a part. Decades later, Johnson reflected on the destructive effect of his drinking. In 1926, he wrote a show with Henry Creamer titled *Geechie*. Creamer died suddenly in 1930, and in a letter to Flournoy Miller from October 1950, Johnson expressed his regrets about his behavior and its consequences:

> You sure tickle me to death when you say that you have a swell idea for Creamer's book. Because now I will be able to do something for his boy and ex-2nd wife. That is almost a pledge on my part because you remember when I used to drink so! I gummed up the works & stopped Arons and Freedly from putting it on because I was off on a binge & could not be found to play the audition which I am sure that would have gone over, & this is one of my past indiscretions which has caused me much mental grief and suffering I truly confess to you.[52]

On March 26, 1928, Johnson, Waller and Bushell found time to record two sides for Vocalion, a date arranged by Bradford that included his tune "What's The Use of Being Alone." They recorded under the leadership of Johnny Dunn (1897–1937), a popular and influential trumpet player before the emergence of Armstrong. With Johnson and Waller at two pianos behind Johnson's "theater style" orchestrations, we can listen in on the type of music that stirred the *Keep Shufflin'* audiences. The next day, Johnson, Waller, and Bushell were joined by Jabbo Smith and traveled to Camden, New Jersey, to record for Victor. The group was given the mysterious name Louisiana Sugar Babes, but no one recalls who suggested it. The group used unorthodox instrumentation: Johnson, piano; Fats Waller, pipe organ; Jabbo Smith, cornet; Garvin Bushell, clarinet, alto saxophone, and bassoon. Bushell recalled:

> That was probably some of the first jazz bassoon was ever on Victor records. I didn't play bassoon in the show, just alto and clarinet. But James P. had heard me playing the bassoon someplace—I think I played it in his *Yamekraw*—and he wanted me to do it, so I carried the bassoon with me to Camden. I got this baritone sax sound on the bassoon;

that's why I could play jazz on it. I didn't sound like a bassoon. I used a different type of reed. I had used bassoon in Europe with Sam Wooding's orchestra, and there I was mainly playing from written out parts. I never took a bassoon solo with Sam. I was featured in some of the arrangements—"Covered Wagon," and a couple of Indian melodies I used to play—but those records with James P. and Fats, that was the first time to my knowledge that anybody played jazz bassoon on records. There's a kind of an Adrian Rollini influence on that bassoon solo. He played bass sax. I was always fascinated with that.[53]

They recorded at the former Trinity Baptist Church on North Fifth Street in Camden, New Jersey, which Victor had purchased in 1918. It was nearby Victor's other main offices, laboratories, and studios where the company was founded in Camden in 1901. An upper floor of the church was the first space used as a recording studio. The church hall itself, while it had desirable acoustics, was difficult to record in. When the Western Electric recording system supplanted the old acoustic method, the original upper floor became studio #2. On the other side of the church, "Studio No. 1, Church Building" was created. Contrary to some sources, the organ was not installed until after Victor purchased the church building in 1918. The Estey pipe organ they purchased had been rebuilt twice by the time Waller recorded on it first in 1926. With the second rebuild in 1926, a lighted console organ was installed in the studio that remotely controlled the pipes in the other room.[54] The recording sheet indicates at least the first title recorded was directed by Nat Shilkret.[55] The organ-piano pairing could have been Shilkret's idea, since he had recorded the Rhyth-Melodists only three weeks earlier with the combination of a pianist and Waller on organ.[56] This time, Johnson was at the piano. The other instrumentalists were gathered around the console organ attempting to time Waller's playing with the delayed sound emanating from the adjoining room housing the pipes. Bushell recalled "The organ pipes were in one room, and we were in another. The piano and the organ manual were together, but since the pipes were in the next room Fats had a real job, because the organ always sounded a fraction of a second late. It was quite a thing. And it was hard keeping time because we had no drums or bass. That morning, Fats didn't drink his fifth of gin until after we got through recording."[57] He went on, "We rehearsed over there. We'd been playing it, so we knew the tunes, so as far as getting it together, all we had to do was figure out how the routine was going to be. Jabbo would do anything on trumpet, but we had a hard time keeping together." Waller, however, had had many prior outings on organ in Camden before this date. Most of them either had a drummer to help keep time or were vocal accompaniments. Recording the organ with a small group and no rhythm section other than the piano was challenging for the engineers. The group recorded four titles: "Willow Tree" and "Sippi" from *Keep Shufflin'*; "Thou Swell" from *A Connecticut Yankee* by Rodgers and Hart; and "Persian Rug" by Gus Kahn. Bushell noted, "James P. was in charge of the date. He was conductor of the pit orchestra, so naturally he was the leader. Maybe Jimmy picked out the tunes from the show that he wanted to record. Victor must have picked out those two Broadway show tunes 'Persian Rug' and 'Thou Swell.'"[58] Multiple takes were recorded of each tune. The recording sheet indicates both studio 1 and 2 were used, but this is unlikely. Studio 2 was in a different part of the building and did not house the organ. That the musicians were in one room and organ pipes in another may have led to some confusion, even on the part of the Victor staff. The recording was scheduled for the morning and early afternoon to allow the musicians to get back to New York for the evening performance.[59]

The Louisiana Sugar Babes session was fraught with hazards. The four musicians were on an early train from New York to Philadelphia, no doubt after a late night. Three of the musicians had been in the recording studio the day before. For what were, for the time, mainstream jazz musicians, the instrumentation is odd, and not what they were playing every night in the pit of *Keep Shufflin'*. As leader, Johnson needed to keep the arrangements from derailing as a result of the organ timing problem and lack of a rhythm section. As pianist, the potentially overpowering organ threatened his contribution. Musicologist and Waller scholar Paul S. Machlin, in a detailed analysis of all takes of the recordings, makes the following observations about Johnson and the level of musical excellence achieved by the Louisiana Sugar Babes." In "Willow Tree" he notes:

> Johnson's piano constantly shifts ground, moving between melodic prominence and background chordal and rhythmic support for the other instruments. Johnson carefully includes a sophisticated musical commentary on the melodic material as well: Waller outlines a motive in the soprano range of the organ, which Johnson echoes, mid-phrase, in the piano's baritone register. Johnson's highly decorated line and the improvised chordal fragment he adds at the close of the phrase provide an ornamental veneer to the simpler melodic shape Waller outlines. Johnson's barrage of ornamentation on the piano helps foster the illusion of a continuous stream of melody, thereby overcoming the inherent handicap facing the pianist who has to compete simultaneously against an organ.

Machlin notes that the final choruses of "Willow Tree," "Persian Rug," and "Thou Swell" each begin with two eight-bar piano-organ duets. He observes: "These passages demonstrate the different but extraordinarily compatible styles of Waller and Johnson on their respective instruments. The degree of interdependence between these simultaneously improvised solos bespeaks an intuitive response in both performers to each other's music, style and approach. There can be no doubt that both performers were improvising: the parallel passage in the second take of 'Thou Swell' is substantially different. To improvise a coherent solo is difficult enough; to improvise keyboard duets that are coherent, exciting, and musically satisfying represents a significant—indeed, an astonishing—achievement not often duplicated in the annals of early jazz."[60] These recordings have attained legendary status on nearly every level. The Victor Church building, long ago razed, is a fabled recording studio in league with an Abbey Road and Muscle Shoals in later times. With "Sippi" and "Willow Tree," we have tunes from a successful Broadway show recorded during the run of the production, and not just by the orchestra members, but by the composers themselves. The instrumentation is odd, and in a sense experimental, perhaps foreshadowing a "third stream" notion incorporating two instruments more associated with symphonic and church music. The extraordinary capabilities of the four musicians, however, mold the combination into a cohesive jazz sound. The spectacular music of the group, and the Johnson-Waller pairing in particular, provides a timeless and scintillating listening experience.

At the height of its popularity, those involved in *Keep Shufflin'* took every opportunity to celebrate their success. On April 3 after the show, drummer "Battle Axe" Kenny sponsored a chicken dinner at Rose's dining room for Miller and Lyles and the orchestra musicians.[61] Miller and Lyles produced a silver jubilee concert at the Manhattan Casino in Harlem on April 14, celebrating the twenty-fifth year of their association as performers. Johnson and Waller played with the *Keep Shufflin'* band alongside Fletcher Henderson for the gala attended by three thousand guests.[62] The entire *Keep Shufflin'* company was in attendance, along with other celebrities such as prizefighter Jack Dempsey, who paid tribute to the legendary comedy team.[63] By this time, Conrad was promoting himself as Miller and Lyles's manager, and presented the comedy duo with a "loving cup" to commemorate their successful quarter century in show business.[64] Conrad too, led a band called the "Cotton Pickers," and Miller and Lyles, along with former Jim Europe drum major J. Mardo Brown, bedecked in his colorful uniform and expertly wielding his baton, led a "grand march around the floor."[65] White society was also eager to avail their charity events of the hot, Harlem-style entertainment fashionably presented on Broadway. On April 21, the Debutante Committee held its annual charity Rainbow Ball benefit for the Association for the Aid of Crippled Children at the Ritz-Carlton. The multicultural cabaret entertainment during dinner included Miller and Lyles as well as Johnson and Waller playing duets, the Hawaiians from the Heigh-Ho restaurant, Margot Zolnay and Cesar Romero performing specialty dances, and

Barbara Stanwyck and Hal Skelly who then were playing in the show *Burlesque*.[66] On April 23, *Keep Shufflin'* moved farther downtown to the heart of the theater district, opening at the Eltinge Theatre on 42nd Street west of Broadway. The Eltinge, operated by the well-known theater and burlesque house Minsky family, was smaller than Daly's by one hundred seats. *Variety* reported that business had dropped off at the uptown venue. From its height of $14,000 the first few weeks, it took in only about $7,500 in its last week there, below what was needed to cover expenses. With its better location and cheaper seat prices attracting more patrons, the Eltinge averaged receipts around $10,000 a week.[67]

In the meantime, W. C. Handy was working on an ambitious project. Handy had met Robert Clairmont, whom Handy described as "a hatless bohemian from the 'Village.'"[68] Clairmont was one of the vivid characters of the 1920s. High school friend and author Tom Boggs wrote a partly fictionalized biography of Clairmont called *Millionaire Playboy*. Under mysterious circumstances, Clairmont inherited $350,000 from Sellers McKee Chandler, a Pittsburgh businessman, in 1925 while working for Chandler as a lifeguard. Clairmont enrolled in the Columbia School of Journalism. He also began speculating in the stock market, making enormous returns during the height of the boom. He spent his money freely, mostly supporting other people and artistic ventures that appealed to him. He was known both as the "Otto Kahn of Greenwich Village" (after the noted financier philanthropist) and the "last of the Bohemians."[69] Handy and Clairmont became good friends, and it was Clairmont who suggested to Handy that he produce a concert at Carnegie Hall to demonstrate the evolution of Black music. Clairmont had laid out $5,000 to support the production, so Handy could contract with top-tier talent. The date chosen also marked the twenty-fifth anniversary of the publication of Handy's "Memphis Blues."[70]

It was a large production. A chorus of sixty voices and an orchestra of thirty musicians led by Handy, along with a number of featured soloists, performed a wide range of music. In accordance with Clairmont's suggestion, Handy strove to demonstrate examples of the complete African American musical repertory to that point. He included examples of blues, jazz, spirituals, plantation songs, work songs, "character" songs from Bert Williams and Ernest Hogan, piano and vocal art songs, the cakewalk, and ragtime. The program included a number of spirituals arranged by Handy and J. Rosamond Johnson. Handy conducted the orchestra and chorus on his arrangements, while J. R. Johnson played piano and sang with his duo partner at the time, Taylor Gordon. Katherine Handy sang several of her father's more famous blues compositions ("Yellow Dog Blues" and "St. Louis Blues"), and W. C. Handy Jr. performed a xylophone solo of Scott Joplin's "Maple Leaf Rag." Tenor soloists Russell Smith and George E. Jackson sang several "plantation songs" written by the prominent nineteenth-century ballad composer James A. Bland. Works of Coleridge-Taylor, Nathaniel Dett,

Harry T. Burleigh, Will Marion Cook, Ford Dabney, Clarence and Spencer Williams were included. Soprano Josephine Hall, who had recently departed *Keep Shufflin'*, sang Dabney's "Africa." Not on the printed program but mentioned in the review of the concert was a composition by Fred Bryan titled "Santanna."

Under the heading of "Negro Rhapsody," Handy included James P. Johnson's *Yamekraw*. It was the first performance of William Grant Still's orchestration. Handy directed the orchestra using a manuscript copy, saying, "Still's pencil score was so fine that I had to stoop over, bending my knees to see it."[71] Handy implies it was his intention from the beginning to line up Waller to play both organ and piano, including the part for *Yamekraw*. Waller is listed on the program as pianist for *Yamekraw*. Maurice Waller and Ed Kirkeby, in their books, tell a different story. They write that Handy hoped to arrange for James P. Johnson to play the piano part. He was, after all, the composer and a good friend held in high regard by Handy. Johnson, however, was under contract to lead the orchestra of *Keep Shufflin'*, which had moved into the Eltinge Theater only four days earlier. Now truly in the heart of Broadway, Miller and Lyles, and likely Conrad, were unwilling to waive Johnson's commitment for the night. The conflicting concert occurred on a Friday night, an important evening in the theater, and Johnson's presence was that important. Johnson suggested that Waller lead the band for that one performance, but Miller and Lyles were adamant. Prevented from performing the debut of his most ambitious work in one of America's most prestigious concert halls, the disappointment must have been deep. It became necessary to arrange for a substitute pianist at Carnegie Hall, and Johnson recommended Waller. Miller and Lyles did agree to allow Waller to take Johnson's place at the concert, a comment on their relative importance to the show. According to Kirkeby, the promoters of Handy's production, having never heard Waller play, suggested an audition. Waller played both piano and organ and was so impressive that a set of Waller organ solos was programmed for the concert in addition to his part in *Yamekraw*.[72]

The concert took place the evening of April 27, 1928, and Anita Waller, Fats's second wife, recalled, "It was a Friday night, and the city was hit with a wild, spring storm. It rained all day, and the streets were so windy you couldn't walk around. With all that bad weather you'd think no one would go out and I was surprised to see that hall filled to capacity."[73] Overall the program was well received. Waller played the "Beale Street Blues" on organ as a solo followed by a piano encore. "Waller's torrid interpolations at the ivories stopped everything . . . ," noted *Variety*.[74] *New York Age* reviewer Lucien H. White was also taken with Waller, noting "Mr. Waller is familiarly known as 'Fats,' and his virtuosity as a jazz pianist quickly won favor with the large audience," but he found *Yamekraw* to be "pretentious."[75] Six years earlier, White had expounded on many occasions his dislike for jazz. He especially despised composers and performers who appropriated the ethnic roots of Black music for jazz arrangements.[76] He must have softened his views, at least regarding jazz, in acknowledging Waller's ability, no doubt recognizing the audience reaction to Waller's infectious presence and performance but didn't see equal merit in *Yamekraw*. Waller may have been the perfect choice to play it, other than the composer himself. In addition to the obvious reasons as Johnson's protégé, Waller had been playing *Rhapsody in Blue* as an overture to the productions at the Lafayette Theater the year before. If Johnson hoped for a sensitive reading of his work that would register in the same manner as Gershwin's, Waller would have certainly known how to do it.[77] The next month, White and his wife found themselves in the company of James P. Johnson at the birthday party in Harlem for Mrs. Peach Goodridge. Johnson played solo piano later in the evening, and one wonders if he and White discussed White's dismissal of Johnson's artistic vision.[78]

After its debut at Carnegie Hall, Johnson programmed *Yamekraw* into the score of *Keep Shufflin'*.[79] The Louisiana Sugar Babes records were available by the second week of May, but the show soon closed at the Eltinge on May 26 after a respectable 104 performances. Stiff competition opened across the street the week before, with Lew Leslie's *Blackbirds of 1928* starring Adelaide Hall and Bill "Bojangles" Robinson,[80] and with the opening of DuBose Heyward's play *Porgy*. *Keep Shufflin'* was reported to have closed abruptly, with Miller and Lyles telling their company "they were tired and simply wished to close."[81] An attempt had been made by producer Louis Isquith to remove the show shortly after it opened at the Eltinge. Isquith claimed that a lease had already been signed for his new show, *The High Hatters*, to begin at the theater on May 1. The lease was to run until September 1.[82] Isquith's show opened on May 10 at the Klaw Theater, his legal wrangle for the Eltinge unsuccessful thanks in part to a high-priced Wall Street lawyer representing Miller and Lyles.[83] Isquith would not have needed the four-month lease at the Eltinge. His show ran for only twelve performances.[84]

Perhaps Miller and Lyles were weary from the string of legal challenges, continual revisions, and grueling schedule of add-on midnight and matinee performances, but certainly falling box-office receipts as well as the personal and financial troubles of Rothstein, Conrad, and Waller played a role. Arnold Rothstein had overextended in building his latest criminal enterprise, the heroin trade, and had gone deep into hock with some very high-profile gambling losses. Rothstein was habitually slow to pay his obligations, including late payments to the show well before it closed. Not long after the move to the Eltinge, Waller left the show. His legal troubles were mounting. In early April, he was arraigned again for delinquent child support and alimony payments. Waller had endeared himself to Rothstein, and although there are several stories of

Rothstein handing him as much as $500 for cab fare, when Waller failed to show up in court and produce $400 owed in back payments, a bench warrant for his arrest was threatened.[85] By late June, with Waller squandering whatever money was coming in, he moved to Philadelphia to take a job playing organ at the Grand Theater. Waller's move was precipitous, as he was a no-show at a scheduled appearance for a Hill's Social Club event on June 21.[86] In arrears with his alimony payments, by the fall he could no longer evade a three-month stint in jail from September to December.[87] Con Conrad's fortunes also suffered. With the finances of *Keep Shufflin'* foundering, he inexplicably bankrolled a show for his fiancée, who then walked out on the act. The lawsuit that followed was the final blow for him, and Con Conrad, Inc., the production company he formed specifically to run *Keep Shufflin'*, filed for bankruptcy.[88] In 1929, Conrad sought his fortunes in California writing for Hollywood, as so many songwriters for the stage did. In a stunning mid-Depression comeback, his tune "The Continental" from the 1934 movie *The Gay Divorcee* was awarded the first Academy Award for Best Song. He died only four years later at age forty-seven.

Johnson and Waller, on the heels of their success on stage and probably to promote their recent spate of recordings together, appeared on radio as a piano duo.[89] And before Waller's move out of town, Waller, Johnson, and Bushell again recorded together on June 18 on a Bradford Columbia date with a different group under Johnson's name, Jimmy Johnson and his Orchestra. On "Chicago Blues" and "Mournful Tho'ts," the two tunes recorded, they both play on one piano. Waller and Johnson complement each other so well that it is difficult to distinguish them. On this outing they are joined by a rising trumpet star, Charles Melvin "Cootie" Williams (1911–1985). He had just arrived in New York, and this was his first recording session. Williams became one of the most prominent players of the swing era, making his name with Duke Ellington. Reviews of the record were positive.[90] Johnson spent the summer and fall sporadically in the Columbia recording studio, almost exclusively as vocal accompanist. He cut sides with Martha Copeland in June, a session with Clarence Williams, one with Ethel Waters, and at least three unlikely sessions with white "yodeling" singer Roy Evans.

Evans burst onto the yodeling scene in 1928 with eleven recording sessions, heavily promoted by Columbia. Evans is a mysterious figure. Some have suggested he was African American, and perhaps passing as a hillbilly star, making records that positioned him across genres with the discs issued in Columbia's popular, hillbilly, and race record catalogues, often with the same disc issued in more than one series. He was managed during his brief recording career by African American agent and publisher Harrison Smith, who wrote of his experiences with him. Roy Evans was born in Evanston, Indiana, and was the nephew of the noted Welsh-born minstrel George "Honey Boy" Evans, most famous for his troupe the Honey Boy Minstrels, and as composer of "In the Good Old Summer Time." Roy came to New York in 1928 to work in clubs and on Broadway when he was discovered by Columbia, who promoted him as their answer to the popular yodeler Jimmie Rodgers, the "Singing Brakeman," on rival Victor Records. Smith recalled, "He made loads of records for Columbia, with James P. Johnson and many all-star groups. His records were advertised in 367 newspapers & at the time were the companies [sic] best sellers. His most talked about record was: 'Georgia's Always on My Mind,' prior to [Hoagy] Carmichael's of the same title. Roy and James P. were a terrific combination and loved to work together. The records sold big in England. . . ."[91] Their first session in June included Garvin Bushell on clarinet and bassoon, likely added given the success of the Sugar Babes session for Victor. Ellington cornet player Arthur Whetsol joined them for one of the sessions. Whetsol was well established with Ellington's band, at the time ensconced in their second Cotton Club revue. They had been friends since childhood in Washington, DC.

The highlight of Johnson's accompaniments that summer was his one and only session with Ethel Waters, who had by this time established herself as a star of the first order. She and Johnson had crossed paths many times by then. They recorded four tunes on August 21, all with lyrics by Andy Razaf, and three with music composed by J. C. Johnson—"Lonesome Swallow," "Guess Who's in Town," "Do What You Did Last Night," and Razaf's tune "My Handy Man." With her theatrical style and crisp diction, Waters swoops and scats through these classic double entendre songs. Waters was glowing about Johnson as accompanist. He perfectly times his musical gesticulations to complement Waters's vocal accents of the lyrics. Johnson was renowned for lobbing the melody to his partner without competing for it or intruding. His solos range from emotive lyricism to exuberant stride. These are four of the greatest vocal accompaniments on record from any era.

Toward the end of the summer, *Keep Shufflin'* was reorganized and embarked on a road tour. Conrad was gone, but Rothstein kept his hand in it as Miller and Lyles were still a draw. Dancer Byron Jones, who had distinguished himself with Florence Mills several years earlier with her *Dixie to Broadway* show, had been with *Keep Shufflin'* since the beginning. He was now credited with staging the dances and ensembles. Johnson stayed on directing the orchestra. The flexible scaffold of Miller's plot was now partnered with a score of nearly all new tunes. Of sixteen musical numbers on the program from opening night in New York in February, only five appear as the show started its road tour in September—"Chocolate Bar," "Where (How) Jazz Was Born," "Give Me the Sunshine," "Sippi," and "Keep Shufflin'." "Willow Tree," added shortly after the New York opening, was also maintained, as was "Exhortation," a spin-off from *Yamekraw* and initially credited to Conrad and Creamer in February, but published in May by Perry Bradford crediting Johnson and Creamer. "Skiddle de Skow," a tune recorded the year before, was now included. It is a reflexive dance number with descriptive but not instructive lyrics by Bradford, who also managed to incorporate a *Yamekraw* reference into it. Johnson and Bradford looked for any opportunity to promote the rhapsody. Most of the new numbers for the touring production were Johnson's. The notices during the tour highlight Johnson as orchestra director and often mention only him as composer of the score. On occasion, Gershwin contributions continue to find mention in the newspapers, but there is no evidence they were included for the touring production. In addition to his fee as orchestra director, he was clearly looking to the stage as a vehicle to promote his tunes. "Give Me the Sunshine" and "Sippi" are consistently mentioned as the show's hit numbers.

The revised production first opened in the outer boroughs of New York, then headed west.[92] Many of these engagements were brief, including a three-day stint at English's Theater in Indianapolis the third week of October,[93] and the Shubert Pitt for one week beginning November 5.[94] Blanche Calloway was added to the cast in Pittsburgh, and was exuberantly applauded by the audience for her blues singing.[95] Garvin Bushell, who stayed with the show, recalled playing in Michigan, Ohio, and St. Louis.[96] The company then moved on to the Erlanger Theater in Chicago beginning November 18.[97] It closed suddenly in Chicago after only one week of the scheduled two-week run. Arnold Rothstein's underhanded dealings finally caught up with him when he was murdered on November 4 for failing to pay a gambling debt, so the story goes. Despite positive reviews and solid box-office receipts, additional financial backing dried up with Rothstein's death. To keep everyone busy, Johnson moved the orchestra to a club run by Bert Hall in the Musician's Union building until the group returned to New York at the end of the month.[98]

Keep Shufflin' would breathe one more breath on stage with a brief revival in April 1930, when it was staged at the Lafayette Theater. It was not the same successful outing. By then, Lyles had gone to Africa, and Miller was laying low recovering from a severe bout of pneumonia. Reportedly, most of the original cast was included with a new pair of comedians. Notably, the female lead was played by singer and trumpeter Valaida Snow.[99] Waller would go on to compose some of his most popular songs for one of the last African American blockbuster shows on Broadway the next spring, *Hot Chocolates*. Johnson would have three more stints on Broadway over the next ten years, all unsuccessful. His musical theater successes for the next decade, though, came in Harlem.

Chapter 17

ST. LOUIS BLUES, 1929–1930

> Of eleven pianists who accompanied her on records, Johnson was unquestionably the best. None of the others could begin to approximate his invention and sophisticated musicianship. His richly embroidered, two-fisted style embellished and complimented Bessie's voice in much the same manner as Louis Armstrong had done two years earlier.
> —CHRIS ALBERTSON

During the 1920s, the busiest years in the recording studio for James P. Johnson were from 1927 to 1930. He was involved in sixty recording sessions. Recording had become a much more profitable venture in the latter half of the decade. Trumpeter Louis Metcalf, with whom Johnson recorded during this time, recalled the situation, noting, "It happened overnight and it just boomed—records, records, records. We used to make so many records during the day that we didn't feel like working at night. That's where the money was and for at least three or four years I didn't bother about taking a steady job at night."[1] New Orleans–born bassist George "Pops" Foster recalled what it was like accompanying Johnson and Waller in the recording studio:

> in New York going to a recording session was like going on a picnic. The most fun was with Fats Waller. He'd pack up a suitcase like he was going on a trip but it would be full of whiskey. When he'd get to the recording studio he'd pass bottles out to the guys. Then Fats would sit at the piano with his bottle and a big glass to drink out of. Him and James P. Johnson would sit down and fool around on the piano. They'd write and arrange the number right there in the studio. Then Fats would say something like,

"Let's time this chorus." He'd have them time one chorus of what he was doing. As fast as Fats would play it, Jimmy would write it out. When Fats finished he'd go get a drink. Jimmy would write the music out and pass it around to the guys. Sometimes if Jimmy needed a note he'd go over to the piano and find it. Fats would sit down and say, "OK, fellas, b-flat we're gonna do this in." And off we'd go.

Jimmy always talked very soft and tried to help guys with their music. Jimmy would tell you when you were wrong, but if he told you, you were wrong. Then he would tell you when you were right.

Jimmy always wanted someone to come to the studio with him when he cut piano rolls or made records just to have some company. He'd want you to go out and get his booze and you'd sit and drink and joke. He used to come by the house and get me when he was going to the studio. . . . Sometimes Jimmy would bring four or five people with him.

Foster commented further on Johnson's skill as an arranger, noting, "Jimmy could write music very fast. He's the fastest one I know of. If you told him to arrange something, when you finish playing he'll sit down at the piano and play it and say, 'this what you want?' Then he'd write it out."[2]

Bessie Smith, the "Empress of the Blues," is the most celebrated member of the juggernaut of female vocalists of the 1920s who sang what was later called "classic blues." She had a distinctive, deep, heavily resonant voice that set her noticeably apart from the others. Her interpretation of the blues fit somewhere between the earthy sound associated with the blues from the South and the more polished "pop" blues styles. She began recording for Columbia in 1923 for their race record catalogue and recorded exclusively for them through 1931. She was their biggest seller. Although she and Johnson had met in 1918 or 1919 in Atlanta when Johnson was on tour with Tutt and Whitney's musical comedy *Darkest Americans*, they had never recorded together. Johnson was ensconced in the musical theater and often on the road by the time Smith made her first recordings. Smith, too, had a heavy touring schedule, so no opportunities arose during the mid-1920s. Johnson's acclaim as accompanist was well known to Columbia, and, finally, on February 17, 1927, Bessie Smith and James P. Johnson made their first records together with Johnson alone accompanying Smith on two blues tunes, "Preachin' the Blues," and "Backwater Blues." Over the next three years, they collaborated on twelve recordings that included traditional blues tunes, many of them Smith originals, and non-blues Johnson originals. All are classics of the genre.

But what genre exactly? The nature of their musical efforts together has confounded writers, critics and historians. On the one hand, Johnson was undoubtedly Bessie's finest accompanist on piano, his work thoughtfully constructed, highly musical, and precisely executed. He stays out of her way during her singing, and, as was his practice and innovation, fills the vocal breaks with unique, improvised, complimentary musical statements. On "Backwater Blues" in particular, Johnson creates a musical backdrop reflecting the mood set by Bessie's lyrics. Yet, Johnson's effectiveness as an interpreter of the blues has been questioned by some. It is a criticism leveled at many of the northern pianists arguing that they had little exposure to the more earthy blues of the Deep South, accounting for the dearth of traditional blues piano figures in their playing. The reality is that Johnson and his circle could certainly play them but considered these traditional blues figures simple and unchallenging. His playing purposely avoids what would be considered by some the clichés of traditional blues piano style. But not all the tunes they recorded are blues, and the interplay between these two musical giants on varied material seems to transcend defining them only as singer and accompanist. Perhaps they are more duets, but this designation, too, doesn't quite capture the essence of their collaboration.

Bucking the trend of many critics who dismiss Johnson's approach to the blues, dancer and writer Roger Pryor Dodge, one of the earliest to assess jazz critically, had little use for stride piano, but was highly complimentary about Johnson as a musician and his playing on "Backwater Blues." He wrote, "James P. Johnson is a great pianist. His piano accompaniment of Bessie Smith on the recording of 'Back Water Blues' alone is enough to prove his superiority. . . ."[3] In 1929, on a short list of musicians Dodge credited with producing "virile, non-emasculated jazz . . . ," both Smith and Johnson were included.[4] Johnson's influence as a blues interpreter was acknowledged by pianists who cut their own teeth on purportedly more authentic Southern and Midwestern blues styles before hearing Johnson. Texas-born pianist Sammy Price, who began his professional travels touring on the famous (or infamous) Theater Owners Booking Association (TOBA) show circuit in the spring of 1927, described the impact of the Smith-Johnson recordings. He recalled, "When George Williams and Bessie Brown came out to sing one of those songs, or Ida Cox had a solo, or Bessie Smith was singing the *Back Water Blues*, there was no place for an instrumental soloist, because James P. Johnson had set the precedent, on records. Very rarely did people stray from that original format."[5] Jay McShann, born in Oklahoma and highly regarded for his territorial-infused deep blues style, recalled his first exposure to Smith and Johnson on records he found in the bed of his father's truck. He told an interviewer, "That was the 'Back Water Blues' by Bessie Smith and James P. Johnson. After I heard that, I was hooked on the blues."[6] Whatever it was Smith and Johnson were doing—blues, vaudeville, singer with accompanist, or duet—they made a clear, trend-setting impact.

The "Backwater Blues" is Smith's most famous composition, although Johnson likely had a hand in composing it. Her lyrics portray the events of a great flood. Smith's sister-in-law relates an episode while they were on tour in Ohio that served as inspiration. Bessie's show had left Cincinnati and arrived in a small town nearby that had flooded. Bessie's entourage, along with other passengers, were taken off the train into rowboats, and her troupe was escorted to an undertaker's parlor next to the theater where they were to stay. A group of other guests asked her to sing the "Back Water Blues." Bessie had never heard of a tune by this name. Her sister-in-law relates that when Bessie returned home, she wrote such a tune based on her flood experience in this small town. The release of the recording several months after it was made in February coincided with the great Mississippi River flood of April 1927, the event often erroneously credited as her inspiration for the song. Nonetheless, the coincident timing thrust her song into an association with what has been described as the worst natural disaster in American history. The African American community was especially devastated. Smith and Johnson's recording depicted their plight, a coincidental connection that drove robust sales.[7] The pair recorded two other songs in April, "Sweet Mistreater" and "Lock and Key," both Johnson tunes. In March, Johnson recorded two other classic solos, one of which was his first recording of his famous instrumental "Snowy Morning Blues."

Before the end of 1928, the Johnsons added another member to the family, adopted daughter Arceola. After returning to New York when *Keep Shufflin'* closed suddenly in Chicago, Johnson again joined with Miller and Lyles as well as Fats Waller, recently out of jail, for a Christmas week show at the Lafayette Theater in December 1928. This was reported as the first appearance for Miller and Lyles at a Harlem theater in fourteen years.[8] The group was reportedly scheduled to tour on the Keith circuit after leaving the Lafayette.[9] If so, Johnson's travel was brief, as he was back in New York by the end of January for another solo recording session that produced the moderate tempo "Feelin' Blue" and stride tour de force "Riffs." Three more sessions, one arranged by Clarence Williams in February and two by Perry Bradford in March, are band sides. The March 5 Bradford date included "Put Your Mind Right on It" and "Sorry," both tunes soon to be included in Johnson and Bradford's next Broadway venture, which was already in rehearsal.[10] Although they had released Roy Evans's version backed by Johnson titled "So Sorry" the summer before, Columbia chose not to issue "Sorry" this time around, even after three takes. Perhaps vocalist Gus Horsley (Bradford's office manager) did not have nearly the appeal of Evans.

Johnson and Bradford had been writing tunes and recording together for several years. They were planning a vehicle to introduce several of the tunes they had been working on to the Broadway Stage. *Messin' Around* was scheduled to open on the road first in Baltimore for a week beginning on April 8 at the Embassy Theater but was delayed by a week.[11] Bert Hall's orchestra was noted as providing the music for the out-of-town opening, and one report noted Fats Waller was in the pit playing piano and organ.[12] If Waller was in the show his presence was brief, because the next month he opened his own new floor show, *Hot Chocolates*, at Connie's Inn in Harlem. It soon moved to Broadway and became Waller's greatest musical theater accomplishment. *Messin' Around* opened on Broadway at the Hudson Theater, 44th Street east of Broadway, on April 22, 1929. Unlike the venues available to all-Black productions earlier in the decade, the Hudson was one of the premier theaters in New York. Built in 1903 by Henry B. Harris, it could seat 1,100 patrons. Sandwiched between neighboring brownstones, the somewhat plain Renaissance-style façade belied the spectacular décor inside that included a marble box office with four bronze heads of Hermes, a hundred-foot-long lobby with a triple-domed ceiling of Tiffany glass, and direct and indirect light in the auditorium highlighting the silk velour curtains and mosaic panels with iridescent glass. In 1912, Henry Harris and his wife Rene were returning to New York on the RMS *Titanic*. He went down with the ship, and his wife was reportedly the last person to be rescued to a lifeboat. She ran the theater from that time on.[13]

The production was conceived and staged by Louis Isquith, whose relationship with Johnson had ranged from the success of *Runnin' Wild* to the legal acrimony of *Keep Shufflin'*. The dances were staged by the renowned tap dancer Eddie Rector, and the orchestra was directed by Johnson. The cast included Arthur Porter and Josephine Hall, Broadway veterans of many prior hits, as well as singer Monette Moore, who had recorded well-received blues numbers. Despite the contributions of Johnson, Rector, and the others, the show received mixed and some poor reviews and ran for a little over a month. It was positioned as a follow-up to Lew Leslie's enormously successful *Blackbirds of 1928*, structured more like a Harlem stage show rather than the Miller and Lyles–driven musical comedy that was loosely held together by a story line, albeit the thinnest of ones. One review noted, "'Messin' Around' is one of those amorphous affairs that are neither revue nor musical comedy. . . ." It meanders "from Harlem to the South and then to a carnival and back to a Harlem nightclub."[14] The result was a seemingly random sequence of vaudeville acts without the benefit of Miller and Lyles. The comedy of Billy McLaurin and James (Slim) Thompson was universally panned. Virtually the only aspect of the show most reviewers praised was the music. One song in particular was singled out as a certain hit, "Your Love Is All I Crave." Reviewer M. W. in the *New York Sun* went so far as to title his review, "Song Saves A Show." John C. Fitzgerald in the *New York Evening World* was enthusiastic, calling it "A lilting, captivating, all-satisfying smash hit," and described the songs as "sizzling," singling out "Your Love Is All I Crave" and generally complimenting Johnson as composer. *Billboard* commented, "As far as the material goes Jimmy Johnson has made the most successful contribution. His music is tuneful and rhythmic."

Particular note was made of "Your Love Is All I Crave," "Put Your Mind Right on It," and "Get Away From My Window."[15]

Williams G. King, writing in the *New York Evening Post*, noting Johnson's quality stage composing and its importance to this effort, wrote, "The music of the piece is better than usually is found in revue scores, and that helped a very great deal."[16] *Variety* observed "Put Your Mind Right on It," sung by Monette Moore and Joseph Willis, was "one hot number" and "scored strongly," and "Your Love Is All I Crave," sung by Hilda Perlino and Sterling Grant, was "rather pretty, partly reminiscent."[17] "Get Away From My Window" was a comedy number, and "Skiddle-De-Skow" was intended to spark enthusiasm for the dance described in the lyrics. The first act included "Spiritual-like numbers" such as "Shout On," which Johnson recorded later in the year. He worked *Yamekraw* into the show, although it did not make it into every performance. The incremental attempts to introduce artistic content divorced from the minstrel ancestry of Black stage shows did little to change most perceptions of the genre as anything other than a distinctly ethnic vehicle anchored in the old stereotypes. Charles Bracket in *The New Yorker* thought it a "third rate colored show."[18] Richard Watts Jr. attempts to find redeeming features in the show, but ultimately casts both his criticisms and kudos in predictably patronizing terms, writing in the *Herald Tribune*, "Where most of the Negro revues have managed to capture that grand quality of excitement that is their chief virtue, it is entirely lacking from 'Messin' Around.'" "These Negro offerings, however, even when inexpertly done, manage to possess a liveliness and an unpretentious gayety that make them worthy of a certain friendliness. . . ."[19]

Watts, however, went on to give a rather lengthy, perceptive, and ultimately complimentary description of Johnson as orchestra director. One gets the impression that Watts spent more time watching Johnson in the pit than the show itself. He wrote:

> In its composer and orchestra leader, Jimmy Johnson, it has a figure with enough instinctive showmanship to make it seem unfortunate that he is not placed upon the stage, rather than obscurely in the pit. The rest of the players are, however, without the ability to make themselves inherently interesting to the expectant paying guests.
> If a really adept showman had been in charge of 'Messin' Around,' he would certainly have made more use of the unconscious histrionic ability of Jimmy Johnson, though perhaps, in the process, the excellences of that ebony gentleman would have been diluted. A placid, lethargic band leader, with an apparent gift for restfulness, he seems to grow more and more excited as he leads his own compositions to victory. Beginning with a calm crouch, he suddenly starts to expand until at the climax of his melody he

seems fairly leaping upon the stage in his enthusiasm. He is a good revue composer, an excellent leader and a marvelous instinctive showman.

Most of Mr. Johnson's music is pleasant, but certainly undistinguished, but in at least one number he has scored that ambition of his profession—he has written an authentic song hit. It is called, "Your Love Is All I Crave." It is more than a bit reminiscent, but it has the stuff of which triumphant Broadway melodies are made and its future radio popularity is more than ordinarily deserved.[20]

The Black press was only slightly more generous overall, with the *New York Age* noting Johnson and Bradford's music and lyrics were good.[21] The *Pittsburgh Courier* summarized the opinion of the Broadway critics with an article entitled "'Messin' Around' Makes Debut—New Musical Comedy Faces Fire of Gotham Critics; Johnson's Music Lauded. . . ."[22]

Messin' Around might have survived the initial mixed reception in the press. In its first midnight show it sold out the house and showed some promise for an extended run,[23] but controversy plagued it from the outset. Pre-Broadway orchestra leader Hall, who had strong union ties, was owed $500. Union members threatened to boycott the opening, but, after assurances were made to them, they didn't scuttle it.[24] Louis Isquith again found himself embroiled in legal straits. The show's management was accused of misusing dramatic editor John Bryamn's *New York Times* review in promoting the show. For one show, at the urging of the musicians' union, the orchestra was pulled just before curtain but reopened the next night. In an attempt to draw theatergoers, welterweight boxing champion and future actor Canada Lee appeared on stage to referee the novelty female boxing scene between Aurelia Wheedlin and Emma Maitland.[25] Their four rounds of one minute each was the highlight of the series of novelty bits that made up the carnival scene after intermission. Others included Frank Lloyd's strong man act with a large dumbbell, Bamboo McCarver's buck dance on roller skates, and DeWayan Niles's circus scene. Although the review in *Variety* had praised the music, there was little complimentary they had to say about the rest of the show. In addition to commenting on the poor comedy, monotonous dancing of the chorus, and incessant encores, they disparaged the physical appearance of the chorus and other female cast members. With a poor attempt at discretion, they commented that the "women performers run to plumpness," and that the show was "better suited to Harlem than to Broadway."[26] Ironically, Josephine Hall, recruited late in an attempt to salvage the show, had been bringing down the house up at the Cotton Club before making her way downtown for this debacle. Criticism of the physical appearance of the cast was not limited to the white media. Geraldyne Dismond, writing in the *Baltimore Afro American*, pulled no punches, warning, "Positively we can't ask the au faits to pay a three or four dollar top to look at bad hair, big feet, ugly legs, funny shapes and sad faces. No amount of the pep of hoofing will make up for a preponderance of a plain homeliness. And 'Messin Around' is weighed down from the start to finish by too many ugly women." But Dismond did note the following: "The program announced that Jimmy Johnson, who wrote the score, would play his Negro jazz symphony "Yamekraw." That alone would have been worth the price of a front row seat, but he didn't."[27]

Johnson and Bradford finally pulled their music out after a "misunderstanding" with the producer. The show closed May 20.[28] Eleven tunes from the show were published by M. Witmark and Sons. "Your Love Is All I Crave" was used in *Show of Shows*, a very early colorized film version of a straight revue with an all-star cast. The tune had some popularity. Johnson never recorded it, and it seems to have faded from memory. Johnson and Bradford regrouped despite the limited success of *Messin' Around* and the morass of legal issues surrounding it. They promoted a new office together at 153 West 45th Street, moving from 1547 Broadway.[29] They reworked the show, gave it the new title *Stoppin' Traffic*, and planned for a tour playing Philadelphia and Chicago.[30] It is not known whether the revised show was ever mounted. Fats Waller followed Johnson into the Hudson with his enormously successful show *Hot Chocolates* that ran from the middle of June through the middle of December. Rene Harris turned down an offer of $1,000,000 for the Hudson Theater in 1929, but in three short years, at the depth of the great Depression, she lost it in foreclosure, settling for one tenth that price.[31]

In June, Johnson recorded the soundtrack to one of the most important short jazz films, *St. Louis Blues*. The film starred Bessie Smith and captured what would be her only on-screen performance. The director, Dudley Murphy, was the son of two artists, and, after service in World War I and a brief foray into electrical engineering, was drawn to Hollywood. "As a filmmaker," observes his biographer Susan Delson, "Murphy was something of a provocateur—erratic, messy, even irritating, but an envelope pusher nonetheless. Formulated at the height of the silent era, Murphy's aesthetic was visually oriented and musically inspired." His concept centered on "relating moving image to music." One of his early films, *Ballet Mecanique*, completed in 1924, remains a touchstone of avant-garde cinematic art. Unlike his previous films, the musical inspiration for *Ballet Mecanique* is jazz. One of its notable scenes highlights a pair of mannequin legs dancing a stop motion "Charleston." The film was conceived and completed while Murphy was in France. For inspiration, he drew upon French and white American expatriate intellectuals as well as the growing Black American musical community there. When he arrived back in New York for its premiere screenings in the spring of 1926, Murphy gravitated to the roiling explosion of African American entertainment in the city. Its center was Harlem, and Carl Van Vechten became his guide. In his memoir, Murphy recalls an early screening of *Ballet Mecanique*: "There being no score to accompany the film, I got a Negro drummer from Harlem, who played on drums, tin washpans and washboards, and who would watch the film as he played interpretations in his own far-out manner, to the images which excited him on the screen. The audience at these showings got so excited that they would create near-riots in the theater."[32] Murphy then spent two years in Hollywood, without success, in mainstream commercial cinema. He returned to New York, at which point RCA employed him to write and direct sound shorts promoting their Photophone system for talking pictures. He rekindled his acquaintance with Van Vechten. Smalls' Paradise in Harlem and Van Vechten's West Side apartment, among other venues, became the trough that fed Murphy's appetite for urban ethnic nightlife and the intellectual discourse that accompanied it. After two relatively successful nonmusical shorts for RCA, a musical theme captured his attention for the third.

The original idea for a film based on the "St Louis Blues" is claimed by both the tune's composer, W. C. Handy, and also Murphy. Handy, in his autobiography, insists he, along with Kenneth W. Adams, wrote a story conveying "a serious picture of Negro life." They offered it to RCA Photophone who agreed to make the film with Dudley Murphy directing the two-reeler.[33] Murphy recalled it was he who initiated the proposal and wrote the script, writing, "I approached WC Handy, who sold us the rights and who did a special arrangement of his classic piece. I got Bessie Smith, the greatest blues singer of all times, to play the part of the St. Louis woman, and wrote a story for the film, suggested by the lyric."[34] Murphy is credited as writer and director on the film credits, and Handy with the special musical arrangement. Murphy may have met Bessie through Van Vechten, but her biographer Chris Albertson credits Handy with the introduction.[35] It remains unclear how Johnson was recruited. It had been two years since he last accompanied Smith on record, but she may have suggested him. Certainly Handy, whose admiration for Johnson was boundless, may have offered his name, especially if he had suggested Bessie. Van Vechten certainly knew of Johnson, but perhaps the most likely recommendation at this time came from Fats Waller. Murphy was living in a penthouse apartment on East 41st Street atop an office building. With no nocturnal neighbors, his place was frequented by many musicians and party-seekers. "My apartment, being close to the theatrical district, was always open and on many occasions I would come home and find people assembled for a late snack. Fats Waller, who was playing in a show on 46th street [*sic*, 44th Street], used to come up and compose on my piano," recalled Murphy.[36] The show Murphy refers to was Waller's Broadway hit *Hot Chocolates*, which opened at the Hudson Theater on 44th Street on June 20, 1929. Johnson was available after the closing of the ill-fated

Messin' Around that preceded it, and with Waller clearly occupied, Johnson was an obvious choice for Murphy. Waller may well have repaid the favor Johnson did him the year before when Johnson suggested him for *Keep Shufflin'*.

Members of the Hall Johnson choir, a mixed-gender chorus of forty voices, play the role of cafe patrons. W. C. Handy and J. Rosamond Johnson arranged the choral parts. James P. Johnson was the musical director and assembled a band containing a few former members of the Fletcher Henderson orchestra. He and the band appear briefly on screen. Jimmy Mordecai plays Bessie's "No Gooder," and she the scorned lover. Isabel Washington plays Bessie's rival. Mordecai gambles with money taken from Bessie and extends his winnings in a crap game with Washington at his side. Mordecai and Washington remove to his room when Smith bursts in. She chases out her rival and proceeds to beg forgiveness of Jimmy who leaves her on the floor clutching a bottle of liquor. In desperation, she begins to sing the famous blues song while the scene transitions to a Harlem club with Bessie at the bar. The band and chorus join in with her. The camera pans across the club with close views of the band members. Johnson is seated with his back to the camera, which quickly passes by, pulling back to a wider view of the club. In his first film appearance (and one of only three known), he is barely visible. His piano, too, is audible only at the opening of the nightclub scene and for a few bars at the end of the picture. Mordecai returns to the club and steals more money from Bessie. Rosamond Johnson's arrangement nods to Gershwin with an interpolation of *Rhapsody in Blue* while Mordecai swaggers out of the club, leaving the snubbed Smith to moan the last few bars of the title song.

Filming took place at the Gramercy studios of RCA Photophone in New York City. There was some advance notice of the film in the Black press.[37] The review in *Variety* focused more on the African American social setting portrayed in the film, rather than the music or Bessie's voice. The title song is referred to as "the champ low-down Colored brethren torch song," and the nightclub scene "produces more local color, with the easy-rider, snake hips, belly-rub and shootin'-from-the-hips type of sensuous AfroAmerican strutting so peculiar to the Harlem blacks [sic]."[38] Murphy took great pains to create an authentic nightclub set, at least as he envisioned it. He said, "I rehearsed the piece in a loft in Harlem and then brought a group . . . from Harlem to our studio. To capture the spirit, I had created a set which was more or less a duplicate of a Harlem nightclub and peopled it with the real people who frequented this Harlem night club."[39] Authentic detail was recreated with the famous dancing waiters from Smalls' Paradise, who spin their serving trays on a fingertip. The Smalls waiters were a cohesive group with their own social club, the "Smalls Waiters Jolly Boys Club."[40] Murphy may have reached out to their organization for recruitment. Of course he was a regular patron himself.

The reception of *St. Louis Blues* in the African American community and in larger American society generated controversy. The *Chicago Defender* and *Pittsburgh Courier* published a few brief advance notices about the film, but after release merely reprinted the review in *Variety*.[41] There is little evidence of widespread distribution to Harlem theaters. The Lafayette was wired for sound pictures by January 1929, but there is no known notice of the film playing there. The Renaissance at Seventh Avenue and 137th Street showed the film between Christmas and New Years.[42] The Alhambra Theater in Harlem, outfitted with sound in March 1930, showed *St. Louis Blues* in April.[43] It was carried over into May "in answer to general public demand."[44] Mainstream newspaper listings indicate frequent showings throughout Pennsylvania, Ohio, Illinois, Michigan, and even as far as Fairbanks, Alaska. The Renaissance revived it in June 1932 as the zeal for movie shorts with all-Black casts reached a peak. Reviewer Vere E. Johns in the *New York Age*, while praising Cab Calloway in *Minnie the Moocher* and Duke Ellington in *Black and Tan* (also directed by Murphy), called Bessie Smith's performance "revolting."[45] While many Black newspapers and Harlem theaters may have been lukewarm or worse in their reception of the film, other outlets embraced it as a worthy celluloid depiction of Harlem entertainment. The African American *Philadelphia Tribune* advertised the full week's showing of the film at the Royal movie house calling Smith "Hotter than Hot," and noting the inclusion of "A Harlem Nite Club Revue including Isabell Washington of Bamboola Fame, Jimmy Johnson's Red Hot Harlem Syncopator's, Jimmy Mordecai Revue."[46] The film reportedly disappeared in the early 1930s, shortly after these last showings, although Chris Albertson insists this was an exaggeration since other prints were known to exist.[47] If they did, few if anyone knew about them, nor were there any further screenings in the United States.

Writer and jazz activist Rudi Blesh undertook a five-year search for the film. Jimmy Ernst, an employee of both Warner Brothers and Blesh's Circle Sound, found a notice in the RKO archives that they had purchased the film from Photophone, and had in turn sold it after resistance to its showing increased. An amusement company in the Southwest purchased it, and was showing it in Mexico and South America.[48] Blesh and Ernst did indeed locate a print in a warehouse in Texas,[49] and Blesh issued music selections on his Circle records label in 1946.[50] Many years after her death, a memorial concert for Bessie Smith was arranged for January 1, 1948, and the film was shown to a group of jazz fans, the first public presentation in the United States in over fifteen years. The depiction of African American social and cultural life in *St. Louis Blues* is a mixed bag of the racist, stereotypical portrayals common to stage shows at the time, but also some aspects of the unique milieu that was Harlem entertainment. Looking past the disturbing depictions, there is much to appreciate nearly a century later. The film is coveted as Bessie Smith's only film appearance.

Her voice bursts out of the grainy screen images, with musical support by the superb choir and Johnson's orchestra. It captures the renowned Smalls' Paradise waiters. In retrospect, it is appreciated as one of Murphy's finest works, which he followed with two other African American–themed productions. *Black and Tan* featured Duke Ellington, and *The Emperor Jones*, with Paul Robeson, gave Murphy another opportunity to call on Johnson.

♪

Johnson ran in the highest circles of African American performing artists and was in high demand for appearances. On August 4, 1929, Johnson participated in an extravaganza at the Alhambra Theater to benefit Lincoln University. Also on the bill were Fats Waller, Charlie Johnson's Smalls' Paradise Band, Cecil Mack's Southland Singers, Bill Bojangles Robinson, Putney Dandridge, Pigmeat Markham, cast members from *Hot Chocolates* including Louis Armstrong and Edith Wilson, and Miller and Lyles. Also in August, Johnson looked to explore perhaps another creative avenue. He applied to the Federal Schools, Inc. of Minneapolis, Extension Division, for their course of practical training in Modern Illustrating, including cartooning. The two-year home study course cost $185 to be paid in monthly $6.00 increments. Johnson paid the first installment, but as the financial crisis worsened he may have dropped the course work as there is no evidence he completed it. His papers include a self-portrait sketch.[51] Shortly after the release of *St. Louis Blues*, Johnson and Smith were reunited in the recording studio. In August and October they recorded eight tunes that were issued. Two tunes from the August session were rejected, and with titles of "My Sportin' Man" and "When My Baby Comes" may have been just too risqué. There were plenty of double entendre blues and popular tunes recorded during this era, though, and Columbia did let a Johnson/Clara Smith pairing recorded in September slip through. Entitled "Oh, Mr. Mitchell," the lyrics by Spencer Williams stand as one of the great double entendre tunes of all time. It was a big seller and Columbia continued to promote it well into 1930.[52] In the spring of 1929, Johnson struck up a songwriting partnership with Stella Unger. Unger had studied with Leopold Godowsky. There has long been a suggestion that Johnson, too, studied with him. However, Johnson never mentions Godowsky in any of his writings, interviews, or grant applications. If he did have any interaction with him, it may have been through Unger. With Saul Bernie, the three produced several tunes, one of which would become one of Johnson's most recorded tunes.

On October 11, Johnson and Smith recorded four tunes; two are blues by Smith, and two are Johnson tunes in standard song form. "You Don't Understand" was composed with Spencer Williams and Clarence Williams. It is a catchy if slightly melodramatic tune with plaintive lyrics that Clarence Williams copyrighted and heavily promoted. The other Johnson tune written with Unger and Bernie, and recorded with Bessie Smith, was "Don't Cry, Baby." After the Smith recording, the tune lay dormant until May 1942, when Erskine Hawkins and his Orchestra recorded it with vocals by Jimmy Mitchell. Their 78 record label erroneously credits Mitchell and Sammy Lowe as composers. Their version slowly percolated through the airwaves, its pace slowed by the recording ban that went into effect that summer. But by the summer of 1943, it reached #1 on the Harlem Hit Parade where it remained for fourteen weeks, and #15 on the pop chart, remaining the most popular #1 song on the Hit Parade for the year.[53] It found its way into the books of Count Basie and Harry James, with vocal versions by Jimmy Rushing and Billy Eckstine. In 1961, the great singer Etta James launched the tune into the rhythm and blues arena with her version that reached #6 on the *Billboard* R&B chart and #39 on the *Billboard* Hot 100. From then on it, became an R&B staple with versions by Aretha Franklin, James Brown, Ray Charles, Tony Bennett, and Madeleine Peyroux, amongst others.

In the fall, Johnson was involved with several productions at the Lafayette Theater. He, along with Duke Ellington and Mercer Cook, assisted Will Marion Cook in a production called *Dust and Dawn*. Rehearsals dragged into the next year and the show seemingly was never produced.[54] The week of November 23, Johnson and Waller provided a sixteen-piece jazz band for Leonard Harper's latest musical comedy at the Lafayette, *Adam and Eve in Harlem*.[55] Another end-of-year stage show produced a tune Johnson would ultimately transform into one of his greatest piano solos.

In June 1929, Miller and Lyles opened in the Vincent Yeomans show *Great Day* and continued with the show until December.[56] The interracial production, set in New Orleans, garnered reasonably good press. After the closing, and after twenty-six years together, Miller and Lyles dissolved their partnership.[57] They would reunite for one more Broadway outing with Johnson two years later, but for the moment, they were on their own. Miller, looking to cash in on the coattails of his recent success with *Great Day*, staged a short-run show with Johnson's music titled *A Great Day in N'Orleans*. Before the opening, Johnson and singers from the show appeared in a benefit for the Florence Mills Theatrical Association at the Schubert Casino Theater on Broadway and 39th Street. Luckey Roberts and his "Entertainers" also donated their services.[58] With fifty singers and dancers, the show opened in Philadelphia at the Pearl Theater on December 30, 1929. It may have then moved on to the vaudeville circuit.[59] Nothing is known of the theatrical content of the show, but it was likely a variety format since its intended destination was a vaudeville tour. One tune included in this otherwise forgotten theatrical footnote became a Johnson masterpiece, but not before a number of failed attempts at finding the right context for presentation.

Johnson was promoting his tune "You Don't Understand" with help from his co-composer Clarence Williams. Numerous recordings were made during a two-month period in a variety of contexts. Bessie Smith, Williams's wife Eva Taylor, a Johnson-led orchestra that included King Oliver and Fats Waller, and two Clarence Williams groups all recorded it. The tune remained dormant until the late fifties and has had periodic play by traditional jazz musicians. Johnson also penned another number, "You've Got to Be Modernistic." It, too, was recorded with his orchestra, and positioned for release on the reverse of the record with his Williams collaboration "You Don't Understand." The arrangement for both tunes includes a vocal chorus by the "Keep Shufflin' Trio," an attempt to capitalize on any remaining familiarity with his popular Broadway show of that name from the year before. "Modernistic" was recorded again by Williams in early December with his Jazz Kings, a larger orchestra that included his wife Eva Taylor singing. In mid-December, the "Great Day New Orleans Singers" recorded it with Johnson's piano as the only backing. Their name derives from the show Johnson and Miller were mounting. They are a large, well-rehearsed group singing a complex arrangement typical of the "Negro" choirs of that time such as those of Hall Johnson and Cecil Mack. They were in the recording studio only a few days after the Florence Mills benefit, an event they attended to promote the show.

Johnson was looking for the right vehicle for this new song. His attempts included these recordings with the large orchestra and different vocal presentations—solo diva, vocal trio, and large choir. He thought he had it with placement in *Great Day in N'Orleans*, but the show fizzled. Another opportunity arose on January 21, 1930. Johnson was in the Brunswick studios to record four piano solos, now considered to be among his best. A pair of moderate tempo, earthy interpretations of standards included "Cryin' for the Carolines" and "What Is This Thing Called Love," one of the earliest renditions of this Cole Porter classic. "Jingles" is an up-tempo, stride/novelty number. The fourth tune was "You've Got to Be Modernistic." This time, Johnson renders it as a tour de force piano solo. This recording is considered by many to be his greatest commercially released solo performance. In the second edition of its Jazz Anthology released in 2011, the Smithsonian Institution chose this recording to represent Johnson's work.[60] Johnson reconfigured his show tune into a dazzling instrumental show piece in which he takes the last chorus through seven variations. He never recorded it again. This recording stands as the authoritative rendition. It continues to intrigue and intimidate pianists. His onetime song from the musical theater found a musical home as a timeless Harlem stride piano solo.

Much has been made of this tune as representative of Johnson's understanding of what constituted modern music of the time. His use of augmented chords, parallel fifths, and whole tone allusions derive from impressionist devices, and were used by other jazz musicians and composers in the 1920s. This sub-genre of "modernistic" music within the popular and jazz sphere bore little relationship to the modernism developing in academic music circles. Furthermore, in the culture to which this music generally appealed, "modernistic" associations meant exoticism (accounting for the popularity of "Oriental" numbers a decade earlier) and mind-altering substances, the latter manifesting as "reefer" tunes.[61] A careful analysis of the music and lyrics of "You've Got to Be Modernistic," both by Johnson, dispel all of these notions underlying his motivations. The lyrics do not contain obtuse or veiled references to drugs or exotica, but rather Johnson's conclusion that the adoption of "modernism" is an external contrivance. The modernistic musical effects he uses are strategically deployed to reflect this message, and not to suggest serious compositional aspirations. The path to modernism is being true to yourself, he contends, and the "modernistic" musical effects become a tongue-in-cheek backdrop to the warning in the lyrics:

> If you want to be modernistic
> Don't be getting too futuristic
> Just keep it up realistic
> Cause it's the one and the only rhythm
> If you want to be modernistic
> Why you got to be optimistic
> Then you're sure to be characteristic
> Modernistic, that's all!

Written just as the stock market crashed in September and October, it is a sobering message from the man who created a musical modernism of his own that fit the times and was now suddenly coming to an end.

1929 and the first few months of 1930 were very busy for Johnson in the recording studio for Columbia, Victor, OKeh, and Brunswick. They all actively promoted his records until the extent of the economic downturn became apparent. He recorded mostly with Clarence Williams, including their remarkable two-piano vaudeville duets on "How Could I be Blue" and "I've Found A New Baby." On the eve of the Great Depression, many performers were doing very well. *Yamekraw* continued to gain notice, and around this time Johnson began broadcasting on radio with Clarence Williams and Eva Taylor on the *Blue Streak Hour* every week on WEAF.[62] Willie "The Lion" Smith recollected that working with Williams in the studio could be a frustrating experience:

> He [Williams] knew he wasn't too great as a piano player so he decided to use two pianos on his wife's show. He got James P. (The Brute) Johnson to

play one and he played the other. But then Williams would push James P. around and get the men in the control room mad at the both of them—Williams for badgering Johnson, and Johnson for letting Williams boss him around. It was The Brute's contention that as long as it was Clarence's show he had a right to have things done the way he wanted.

Well, James Johnson finally did get sick—sick of Clarence's piano playing. He asked me if I would like to substitute for him until he was feeling better—it turned out he never did feel better. He called me on the phone, "Come on, Lion, go on down and make the gig for just this one day."

I stuck out the program for several weeks. James P. had gotten himself real busy and so to get off the hook I recommended young pianist Herman Chittison to finish out the *Dixie Nightingale* series.[63]

James P. Johnson was busy in 1930 as a theater composer. Will Marion Cook was working on another effort for the Lafayette Theater. In addition to Johnson, he recruited Duke Ellington, Porter Grainger, his son Mercer Cook, and Gus Smith.[64] In February, *Variety* reported a revue titled *Sun Down* was on an out-of-town run until March with plans for a Broadway opening. The book was written by Garland Howard and Eddie Hunter. Both men had been staples on the touring Black vaudeville circuit for a decade. Howard had written several other shows in 1929 and 1930, and Hunter was the lead. The music was written by Johnson and Bradford. Nothing is known of the music. It did not open on Broadway.

Smalls' Paradise, at 2294½ Seventh Avenue, had established a formidable following with the downtown clientele since its opening in 1924. Former elevator operator Edwin Smalls came to New York from South Carolina and opened his first club on Fifth Avenue. On October 26, 1925, he moved it to Harlem and it eventually became the largest club there.[65] The floor shows were a big draw for the white clientele coming up to Harlem, dressed in all their finery, to see "exotic" entertainment, but unlike The Cotton Club, Smalls' also admitted Black patrons. John Hammond recalled:

> ... the famous, never-to-be-forgotten Smalls' was in the basement of the Dunbar Bank building. You went downstairs, under a modest marquee, into a standard night-club set up: a room holding about two hundred and fifty persons, with a bar at one end, a bandstand at the other, and banquettes against the wall surrounding a dance floor. Ed had a line of eight girls—dark-skinned; the Cotton Club and Connie's Inn catered to whites and featured light-skinned Negroes—and had original music written for his shows. He served good Chinese food, another plus. Connie's had no kitchen and the Cotton Club menu was bad and expensive.[66]

One of the most popular floor shows ever produced at Small's was *Kitchen Mechanic's Revue*, which opened on March 17, 1930. Johnson collaborated with Andy Razaf who wrote the lyrics. Tim Brymn created the orchestrations which were played by Charlie Johnson's Orchestra, the house band at Small's at the time. Small's management arranged several private showings of the revue. On March 31, special guests and celebrities included Mr. and Mrs. Louis Armstrong, Carl Van Vechten, George Immerman, Revella Hughes, Jean Starr (of *Keep Shufflin'*), Clarence Robinson, and Willie "The Lion" Smith.[67]

Razaf biographer Barry Singer contends the composer and lyricist were attempting to break from the farcical and overtly racist conventions underpinning much African American musical theater of the prior few decades. Of Razaf he writes, "His concept for the show was quite radical: the evening would be a knowing celebration of everyday Negroes at work and at play but mostly at work, in a musical salute to America's favorite racial stereotype." He goes on to note, "Of course, it was only Razaf's implication that it was in any way revolutionary. Though the conceit behind 'Kitchen Mechanic's Revue' definitely was insidious, Razaf's execution was no more than deftly amusing."[68] The less than revolutionary presentation allowed the mixed-race audience to view Razaf's clever combinations of double entendre and cultural cross-references through different lenses. The white theatergoers were entertained by what appeared to be the stereotypes they expected. The Black clientele likely enjoyed the staged expression of their daily existence portrayed in lighthearted fun-poking rather than opprobrious mockery.

On March 14, 1930, eleven tunes written by Johnson and Razaf from the show were copyrighted by the Joe Davis Publishing Co. Since the early 1920s, Davis had had a keen interest in Black music. Two weeks later, two additional tunes by Johnson and Razaf were copyrighted by Davis. All thirteen numbers, some bearing vividly descriptive titles like "Slippery Hips," "Mammy Land," "Bantu Baby," and "Elevator Papa-Switchboard Mama," remained unpublished. The press noted "Go Harlem," "A Porter's Love Song," "Good or Nothin'," and "On the Level" as sure hits.[69] "Elevator Papa-Switchboard Mama" was recorded by the popular comedy duo of Butterbeans and Susie. On May 19, "Porter's Love Song to a Chambermaid" was resubmitted as a published listing. Perhaps more than any other tune from the show, Razaf's lyrics cleverly recast a life of domestic routine into an expression of common humanity. The day-to-day life of household chores becomes the metaphor for aspirational romance. One of Johnson's most popular compositions, it was one of the tunes recorded by Fats Waller at his first session with his group, the "Rhythm," in 1934. Many others have recorded it including Bob Howard, Jimmie Noone, Red Norvo, Hot Lips Page, Ethel Waters, Jimmy Rowles, Willie "The Lion" Smith, Kenny Davern, and Sammy Rimington. It has had crossover appeal with recordings by R&B stylists

Julia Lee and Roy Milton, and vocalists Pearl Bailey and Bobby Short. Johnson recorded it, as well as "Go Harlem," with a group called "Jimmy Johnson and His Orchestra" in March 1931, with Razaf singing. Despite the name, the band was really that of Bingie Madison, an existing orchestra. The arrangements are clearly Johnson's, hinting at techniques he used later in his symphonic pieces.

In April, a show titled *Shuffle Along of 1930* opened at Werba's Flatbush Brooklyn Theater. It was produced by Irvin C. Miller and, according to the program, featured his brother Flournoy Miller and Aubrey Lyles in the starring roles. However, the two comedians who actually played the parts were not Miller and Lyles, but two other men using their names. The Werba's management insisted the comedy duo was to be featured when the show was contracted.[70] This is possible, since Miller and Lyles had dissolved their partnership only the prior November. Irvin may have negotiated the deal before then or promised he could entice his brother to participate with his old partner. The potential draw of the illustrious stars may have been irresistible. The press quickly discovered the hoax and publicized it widely, but not before substantial notice was given highlighting Miller and Lyles as the performers.[71]

The music for the show consisted predominantly of tunes written by Johnson and Fats Waller, almost all of which originally appeared in other productions. "Porter's Love Song to a Chambermaid" and "Go Harlem" were recycled from their recent success in *Kitchen Mechanic's Revue*. Despite the controversy, the one bright spot was the appearance of singer/trumpet player Valaida Snow. She was featured on many of the best Johnson and Waller tunes, including "Porter's Love Song," "Willow Tree," and "Rhythm Man."[72] Snow had just completed the revival of *Keep Shufflin'* at the Lafayette Theater in Harlem, a subpar production also handicapped by Miller and Lyles stand-ins. There were some highly complimentary reviews, noting "The novelty song number 'Just A Porter's Love Song to a Chambermaid' was a high spot on the bill."[73]

Music Week in Harlem commenced on May 5, 1930, under the auspices of the West 135th Street YMCA. W. C. Handy chaired the educational event that featured lectures and musical demonstrations focusing on Black American roots music and the transformation from folk forms to serious composition. Johnson's teacher E. Aldama Jackson chaired the opening day, devoted to the telling of the "Story of Negro Music" from its African roots.[74] "Undeveloped Negro folk music" was discussed by John M. Johnson, president of the S. Coleridge-Taylor Music, Art and Dramatic Club, followed by examples of work songs by the Four Dusty Travelers under the direction of Eva Jessye. J. Rosamond Johnson lectured on the original value and uses of the spiritual with musical demonstrations by the Hallelujah Quartet. On May 8, instrumental syncopation was highlighted, first with W. C. Handy describing and playing the "simple syncopations" of the Coon Songs. James P. Johnson followed, and

The Johnson home in Jamaica, Queens, where he lived from 1930 until his death in 1955. (New York City Department of Records and Information Services, 1940s Tax Department photographs, Collection REC0040 - RG 035, Department of Finance. Courtesy Municipal Archives, City of New York)

played examples of "intricate forms of syncopation," including *Yamekraw*, "Carolina Shout," and a waltz. The evening was completed with J. Lawrence Cook, the piano roll arranging wizard, playing his "concert-jazz" arrangement of "The St Louis Blues."[75] Johnson continued to be sought after as composer for mainstream white theater. He and Stella Unger teamed with popular dance band leader Harold Stern to compose tunes for the Shuberts. These shows included *Three Little Maids*, which included Stern and his orchestra, and *Greenwich Village Follies*, and were followed by tunes for a show featuring versatile dancer/comedian Jim Barton.[76] Another short-lived show titled *Vagabond Love* featured music by Johnson and Unger.[77]

As the year progressed, the impact of the worst economic disaster America has ever known was becoming more apparent. Johnson's roaring twenties was coming to an end. The music business was especially hurt in many respects. With the introduction of sound motion pictures and the growing popularization of radio, musicians who relied on live "accompaniment" jobs were put out of work. The race record market soon dried up. The start of the new decade brought personal tragedy with the premature death of his prolific songwriting partner of the late twenties, Henry Creamer. Creamer had been hospitalized at Mt. Sinai for heart trouble and died on October 14 after a four-week illness. He was fifty-one.[78] James P. Johnson was beginning to be bothered by a sinus condition. With the urging of Clarence Williams, he moved his family out of Manhattan and settled in the more suburban community of Jamaica, Queens. Built in 1920, their detached, three-story, spacious 2,100-square-foot home at 171-38 108th Avenue was across the street from Williams and his wife Eva Taylor, who were at 171-37. Eventually, Shelton Brooks would move down the block at 160-16 108th Avenue.

Johnson recorded very little, and almost exclusively with Clarence Williams. He continued to compose a great deal but also needed income and wouldn't refuse performing opportunities. In late June, Johnson joined his old friend Allie Ross and his Connie's Inn Band for a half week at Loew's Orpheum.[79] Immediately following that, he was back at the Lafayette for a weeklong revue called *Fireworks of 1930* that opened on June 28. It was staged by Leonard Harper, and featured blues icon Mamie Smith and baritone George Dewey Washington, who had created a sensation at the Capital Theater on Broadway. Johnson led the orchestra with Fats Waller.[80] As it turned out, the draw of Harlem for the well-to-do remained strong despite the deepening Great Depression. It was a niche that sustained him for the next five years, and one he enjoyed if not relished.

Chapter 18

CHANGING TASTES, 1931-1935

Your rhythms are magnificent and are your own.[1]
—WILL MARION COOK

The early to mid-1930s is a period erroneously thought of as one of relative inactivity for Johnson. Although he was no longer completely immersed in the hotbed of after-hours musical, gastronomic, and alcoholic carousing, he was by no means a recluse in his home in Jamaica, Queens. The famous cutting contest relayed by Mezz Mezzrow may have been Fats Waller's birthday party of May 21, 1932. Later that year, Johnson helped sponsor a homecoming party for Waller upon his return from France. Johnson and Bud Allen ended up attending to a fully inebriated Waller who, the story goes, passed out on his bedroom floor, only to revive in the predawn hours and insist that his stalwart guests accompany him to Luckey Roberts's apartment for more carousing.[2] *Yamekraw* garnered continued exposure as a concert piece. It was played and broadcast to Germany by the NBC Orchestra under the direction of Erno Rappee on September 6, 1931, as part of the first Dixie Jubilee Program. J. Rosamond Johnson's piece, "An African Drum Dance," and a piece titled simply "Blues" by W. C. Handy, were also featured. The programming of Gershwin's *Rhapsody in Blue* alongside *Yamekraw* acknowledged the musical kinship of both works as a new orchestral genre. The program was reportedly well received in Germany.[3] On November 8, 1931, concert pianist Hazel Harrison (1883–1969) performed a Johnson composition in manuscript titled "Portrait" alongside works by Liszt, Stravinsky, Ravel, and others.[4] Harrison spent much of her time in Europe studying and concertizing. Earlier in the year, she had accepted the position of head of the piano department at the Tuskegee Institute. Nothing is known of a work by this name, and it is interesting to speculate that this might have been an early version of a movement from his *Harlem Symphony*.

Musical styles were beginning to change, including the approach to the piano. Until this time, in New York and beyond, Johnson was still considered king on the keyboard. The arrival of Art Tatum in New York from Toledo, Ohio, in 1932 shook up the Harlem piano community. Pianist Joe Turner claimed it was he who arranged for Tatum to come to New York. Turner, while touring with singer Adelaide Hall, sought out Tatum based on a recommendation from Benny Carter.[5] Carter, who had heard Tatum while on tour through the Midwest and then mentioned him to Turner, may have also himself encouraged Tatum to come east. Reuben Harris[6] and Tatum's biographer James Lester,[7] recount several versions of how the pianist came to travel with Hall to New York. Born in 1909, and despite severely impaired vision, Tatum learned music visually, with braille, and from the full range of aural resources available, including recordings and piano rolls. Of his influences he said, "Pianists who influenced me? Well, there was James P. Johnson and Fats Waller and Lee Sims. . . ."[8] His sister Arlene recalled he studied Johnson's and Waller's piano rolls.[9] Like Johnson and Waller, Tatum listened broadly, and he included Sims as an influence. He was a popular keyboard artist of the day with a highly ornamented style, who also recorded on record and piano roll. Tatum joined Hall, and word of his reputed brilliant technique at the keyboard preceded his arrival, generating great discussion among New York musicians. After a five-month cross-country tour, Adelaide Hall landed in New York to headline at the Lafayette Theater, opening on July 2, 1932.[10] Tatum was unknown to the New York music scene, and he was unidentified by the reviewers who made note of his keyboard prowess backing Hall. "Her already classy act, with two pianos, and beautiful expensive drapes," one reviewer wrote, "has been augmented by a blind piano player from Ohio whose technique, of unusual variety, was on everybody's tongue after the matinee."[11] Talk of that technique of "unusual variety" spread quickly, and shortly thereafter, a first meeting of the reigning piano masters with the newcomer from the Midwest was arranged. A number of stories exist about this first encounter. Maurice Waller and Ed Kirkeby provide detail relayed to them by Fats.[12] He claims to have stopped by the Lafayette Theater unannounced to hear Tatum accompany Hall. In his accompanist role, Tatum displayed nothing earthshaking, so Waller offered to show him around the next night. With Waller as guide, James P. Johnson, Willie "The Lion" Smith, and Lippy Boyette met Tatum at the Lafayette.

They made several stops to break the ice with a few drinks, then landed at a small bar called Morgan's. After some warm-up, Waller encouraged Tatum to play. He soared through "Tea for Two." The astonished Waller, Johnson, and Smith looked on. Johnson played an inspired "Carolina Shout" and "Keep Off the Grass," and Waller his own signature piece "Handful of Keys." Tatum followed with his other dazzler from that time, "Tiger Rag." A final counter by Johnson with his rendition of Chopin's "Revolutionary Etude," a performance Waller recalled as Johnson's most remarkable, did not cause Tatum's retreat, as it had for so many pianists before him. Waller paraphrases Johnson's recollection, who said, "When Tatum played 'Tea for Two' that night I guess that was the first time I ever heard it really played." At the conclusion of perhaps one of the most famous cutting contests of all time, with Tatum crowned the new piano king, Fats insists the four pianists embraced each other affectionately. The group of piano titans made additional rounds at Pod's and Jerry's, Brownie's, and The Nest.[13] Waller's public regard for Tatum is best known from his remark years later when Tatum was in the audience at the Yacht Club. After spotting him, Waller announced, "I just play piano, but God is in the house tonight." Fats Waller, at least when asked, and in social circles, did not demonstrate any bitterness toward Tatum. According to Maurice Waller, in private, he confessed, "That Tatum, he was just too good and it looked like they were running him out of the city. He had too much technique. When that man turns on the powerhouse don't no one play him down."[14] Smith doesn't mention the encounter in his autobiography, and reportedly at other times, refused to play after Tatum, saying, "I don't play after trick pianists."[15] As for Johnson, Joe Turner recalls, "Well, James P. stopped speaking to me for a long time because I had brought Art here. Before Art came, James P. was known as the greatest jazz pianist in the world. That was his reputation! When Art came in 1932, that changed everything."[16] There were those who recognized Johnson was not to be dismissed too easily. Just before Tatum's arrival, as tastes were beginning to change, Chappy Gardner, writing in his regular column for the *Pittsburgh Courier*, had this to say about Johnson and Luckey Roberts:

> Speaking of piano players: The greatest I ever met—Luckeyth Roberts was born in Philadelphia, became famous in New York. Another, Jimmy Johnson, of New York. There two fellows, pioneers, set the pace. None have beaten them—none can. Some get more publicity. These, the distinction of paving the way—and remaining in the lead because of merit. Luckeyth played in the early Harlem cabarets. Wilkins, Barron's, Gib Young's, Connor's. So did Jimmy. Ever hear either play—no! Then you have never heard harmony. It rings from their fingers, no flash, no eccentric move, no put on just harmony, unequaled, unparalleled. Luckeyth plays for America's richest and elite, last week Stuyvesant's of Warrenton, VA and Demarest Lloyd of D.C. In winter, Florida. Jimmy Johnson, writing, arranging numbers for Broadway and playing special

dates in New York. Pianists extraordinary none to excel—few to equal —in a class by themselves.[17]

In the summer of 1931, Johnson was again associated with Miller and Lyles. The comedy team had been estranged since splitting after their work together in mid-1929 in Vincent Yeoman's *Great Day*. Lyles had gone off to Africa for a year, and, when he returned to the United States, the two reconciled with renewed Broadway aspirations. Their first effort was a short-lived musical comedy titled *Lazy Rhythm*. It was staged by Irvin C. Miller, and Miller and Lyles appeared by arrangement with the Columbia Broadcasting Company, who may have aired it live by remote radio hookup from the New Brighton Theater where it opened near the Brooklyn shoreline in mid-August. Johnson's Queens neighbor Shelton Brooks was also a featured performer. The program indicates Johnson and Maceo Pinkard wrote the music and lyrics, although other tunes not written by either composer were included in the first scene titled "Review of Colored Show Song Hits."[18] "Sleepy Time Down South," which had just been published, was singled out in reviews. Miller and Lyles included a poker game sketch, an insurance scam bit, and a familiar parody about Black soldiers lost on the front lines titled "On the Darkest Front," this last an ironic premise given the broadly recognized heroism of African American regiments during WWI.[19] It garnered reasonably good reviews but rather than finding a home across the river on Broadway, Miller and Lyles produced it as a touring show.[20] With Johnson, they began work in early fall on another show with higher hopes for Broadway. *Sugar Hill*, with lyrics written by veteran songwriter and Duke Ellington collaborator Jo Trent, had an out-of-town trial first in Easton, Pennsylvania,[21] then in Philadelphia at the Lincoln Theater (formerly Gibson's) where it opened at the end of November with a "gala" midnight showing December 2. The seventy-five-person company was supplemented by "Jimmy Johnson and his 20 piece orchestra."[22] William Grant Still did many of the orchestrations.[23] Musically, it was a busy few weeks in Philadelphia with stiff competition for the African American entertainment dollar now two years into the Great Depression. Although the show was up against Louis Armstrong, Ethel Waters, Bessie Smith, Mamie Smith, and Bennie Moten and his Orchestra, all playing in town then, Miller and Lyles were the "Talk of Philadelphia" now that they were again appearing together, and the show was held over an extra week.[24] They drew standing-room-only crowds.[25] Johnson's music was also a standout, with reviewers noting, "The able writing of Jimmy Johnson, who is responsible for the score of the show, and Jo Trent, who composed the lyrics, marks one of the most substantial contributions that any music writer of popular numbers has made in a long time. Audiences who visit 'Sugar Hill,' are impressed first of all with the music of the show, and the orchestral rendition of Jimmie Johnson who, besides having written the music for the show, also conducts the orchestra."[26] They moved to the Standard Theater[27] before coming to New York for the Broadway opening on December 25 at the Forrest Theater.

The book, by Charles Tazewell, was subtitled "An Epoch of Negro Life in Harlem." Sugar Hill was the fashionable section of west Harlem located on the hill between Morningside Heights and Harlem proper. The nickname came from the feeling that living in the apartments on the hill required plenty of "sugar," meaning money, to afford the exorbitant rents charged. The set for the show consisted of a deceptively simple single apartment house façade. The staging and lighting, however, were complex. The windows were covered with scrim and backlit so that various apartments could be blacked out while others were lit. All the action took place in either a backlit apartment window or on the sidewalk in front. Set against the singing, dancing, and comedy of Miller and Lyles was a dark-themed plot. The big shot numbers king Gyp Penrose, played by Eubie Blake's one time partner Henry "Broadway" Jones making his dramatic debut, aims to prove himself a tough guy by doing some shooting, but accidentally kills a baby. His girlfriend Cleo covers for him. This gruesome element was based on an actual event. The featured romantic leads were played by the noted vaudeville team of Chappy Chappelle and Juanita Stinnette, who had made their name in Johnson's *Plantation Days*. The featured number, "Fooling Around with Love," was sung by Edna Moten. Harrison Blackburn featured a sand dance and Norton and Ford a tap dance act.

Some reviews of the Broadway opening were very favorable, writing, "The singing and dancing and the choral work are of the highest standard. The wish is that 'Sugar Hill' may remain long at the Forrest Theater."[28] Johnson's music was highlighted, noting, "The show has some catchy song numbers, notably "I Got in Trouble Fooling Around with Love," and "Hot Harlem."[29] Another writer noted, "Things to write home about from Sugar Hill . . . Broadway Jones's dramatic performance throughout and his Hot Harlem number . . . the featuring of "Fooling Around with Love" . . . the comedy of Miller and Lyles (especially the bridge game)."[30] *Billboard* noted, "The score abounds with plenty of hot numbers."[31] *Variety* commented on "Fooling Around with Love" as having popular potential, but observed a number of missed cues, and ironically thought there was too much book and questioned the "taste" of leading off the story with the murder of a baby.[32] The reviewer in *The Stage* was not overly impressed with the production, but commented, "The music, in any case, was at least a cut above the Harlem-Broadway average."[33] Before the opening, a number of the tunes were contracted by the Harms publishing company,[34] and three of the tunes were copyrighted in 1932 and published. Despite the mostly positive reception, the show closed after only eleven performances at the Forrest, but then opened at the Lafayette Theater on January 9, 1932. To salvage what they could, Miller and Lyles then planned an engagement in Boston.[35]

Although the show seemed to have genuine promise for a successful run, once again financial misdealings sank it. Miller and Lyles had gotten themselves into serious trouble with the cast, who reportedly went unpaid for six weeks. When the players cornered the two comedians, an arrangement was struck that ended with the house management advancing the money, relieving the pressure on them for their obligations.[36] Other reports declared that the two had been robbed, and that the backers of the show had pulled support before the show had even reached New York.[37] Miller claimed he took a chance launching the show without solid backing, which he did for the good of his fellow performers, with one report noting, "He went into the show to make it possible for a large number of actors who would have been hopelessly unemployed, to get work. If it had been a success, he said, he would have been a hero, but when it failed he was a scoundrel in their eyes."[38] The show never made it to Boston. After two weeks at the Lafayette, Miller and Lyles recruited several members from the *Sugar Hill* cast for a new show that opened for RKO in Hoboken, New Jersey, around January 20.[39] Debacles were more likely than hits in the rough-and-tumble world of the theatrical business. Undeterred by the failure of *Sugar Hill*, Johnson was already at work on another show titled *Yeah Man*, which was scheduled to open at the Park Lane Theater, formerly Daly's 63rd St Theater, in May. The Black press promoted it as a revue in two acts and twenty-two scenes with book, lyrics, and music all written by Perry Bradford and Jimmy Johnson, and produced by Jesse Wank and Walter Campbell.[40] After four delays, it was scheduled to open May 26.[41] By the time it opened, Bradford and Johnson were no longer associated with the show.[42] The *New York Times* reviewer described it as "a shrill and tuneless farrago."[43] Johnson and Bradford, it seems, were better off having cut and run. After only four performances, it was withdrawn.[44]

During the early to mid-1930s, Johnson filled sporadic local gigs in his home community of Jamaica, Queens, with a pickup orchestra. "Jimmie Johnson and his Stompers" played for the Lebanon Square Club on June 10.[45] The fall of 1933 was especially busy with monthly gigs—"The well-known Jimmy Johnson" furnished music for dancing for the Ajax A. and S. Club lawn party on August 12, 1933;[46] his new unit played on WMCA radio on September 22 from 10:45 to 11:00 PM featuring his "modernistic music";[47] neighbors Arline and Marcell Webb celebrated a birthday and anniversary with fifty guests on October 22 and were entertained by Johnson's orchestra with both Lillie Mae and Arline Webb,[48] and, "Despite the cold weather" noted the press, "everyone was warmed by the mad music of the well-known Jimmie Johnson" at the G. T. Girls pre-Thanksgiving dance November 17, 1933.[49] His orchestra played for dancing for two hundred attendees after a recital of the Jamaica Community Chorus and the Harlem String Trio at Grace Hall in Jamaica on November 14, 1935.[50] Hardly the stuff to draw national attention. Despite the failure of the Broadway efforts *Sugar Hill* and *Yeah Man*, better musical theater opportunities once again opened up for him in established Harlem nightclubs.

In the fall of 1932, George and Connie Immerman opened a new theatrical office downtown. Of this venture, Immerman said: "For ten years I have been proprietor of Connie's Inn, the exclusive night club in Harlem which specializes in colored talent for the amusement of New York City's elite. In connection with the above, I have established offices downtown for the purpose of booking outstanding colored talent, building acts, revues, etc. I am proud to announce in association with my new enterprise the following persons who are acting in technical capacities: Leonard Harper and Ted Blackmon [sic, Blackman], routine and continuity producers. 'Fats' Waller, Andy Razaf and Jimmy Johnson, composers and lyricists. Russell Wooding, orchestrations and arrangements."[51] The first effort out of Immerman's new roster of advisors was a Johnson score for what would become one of his most successful floor show productions, *Harlem Hotcha*. Connie's Inn, along with the Cotton Club and Smalls' Paradise, was still one of the most popular Harlem clubs frequented by the downtown clientele, as Immerman suggested. Others of Immerman's newly appointed technical advisors had a hand in the show: Razaf wrote the lyrics, Blackmon did the staging, and Wooding arranged the tunes. Slighted by the choice of Blackmon for the first assignment of the new team, Johnson's old partner Leonard Harper resigned from his position with Immerman.[52]

The show opened at Connie's Inn on September 25, with Milton Berle appearing in the capacity of master of ceremonies.[53] The show was promoted as "A sizzling riot of sepia fun with the greatest array of Colored Stars ever assembled." The band supporting the show was that of Don Redman and his Orchestra. Redman, one of the most outstanding leader-arrangers in the history of music, was celebrating his one-year anniversary as the house band at Connie's Inn. The hourlong break between the two showings of *Harlem Hotcha* featured dancing by Redman's orchestra. They had been broadcasting on radio over the Columbia Broadcasting Network and continued to do so during the run of the show on Monday and Thursdays from 9:15 to 9:30 p.m. Redman also broadcast over local New York station WMCA ten hours a week. The group was referred to as the "Harlem Hotcha Radio Band." In addition, after the floor show, the Mills Brothers broadcast from Connie's over CBS Tuesdays and Wednesdays from midnight to 12:30 a.m.[54] A week after their very well received opening, the cast and orchestra attended a beefsteak supper tribute at the Alhambra Inn on October 1.[55] A substantial number of tunes from the show were published by Handy Bros. Publishing Company. Handy promoted this new portfolio widely since the show was wildly successful, sending copies to the prominent Los Angeles journalist, editor, social critic, producer, and onetime TOBA performer Harry Levette. Of the effort, Levette wrote, "W. C. Handy, the famous king of the blues, writes that he is sending under separate cover five of his new songs that make 'Harlem Hotcha' famous. Steady! The line forms to the right."[56] Several tunes were recorded, including "There Goes My Headache" by the Mills Brothers and "Aintcha Got Music" by Henry "Red" Allen. In addition to the piano sheet music and band orchestration, Handy orchestrated the latter tune for mixed quartette and male quartette.[57] He reissued "Aintcha Got Music" in his 1944 book, *Unsung Americans Sung*. In reviews of the book, it was singled out from the sixty-five or so tunes in the volume, noting, "'Aintcha Got Music' by Andy Razaf and James Johnson with choral arrangement by Handy, is a gem in lyrics and music. It should have an honored place on choral programs to intersperse with spirituals."[58] Johnson kept it in his active repertoire into the late 1940s. Nearly twenty years later, writer Allan McMillan recalled a conversation with Handy in 1933 during which Handy explained that despite the tremendous financial risk he took publishing Johnson's tunes during those years, he remained dedicated to promoting quality work.[59] The tune *Drums* first appeared in the show. It was described as "the voluptuous and entwining terpsichorean number (in other words, 'cootch dance')." *Drums* was not published by Handy but released back to Johnson. It would metamorphose from a titillating Harlem stage show number in to an orchestrated symphonic tone poem with lyrics added by Langston Hughes to accompany it as an art dance.[60]

The mid-thirties was a transitional time. The primary form of entertainment offered by the famous Harlem venues moved from the stage show features with their mix of vaudeville, burlesque, and musical theater, to the swing dance bands that were gaining favor. The success of Johnson's show transformed the term "Harlem Hotcha" into a general descriptor that was applied to the singing, dancing, and music of other stage shows, breathing a little more life into them. Characterized as "Harlem Hotcha," these productions were used to promote the waning days of the nightclub stage show genre whose venues continued to attract white clientele with the promise of the exotic. Ralph Matthews, in the *Baltimore Afro American*, in explaining the popularity of the Cotton Club in Portland, Oregon, noted, "Harlem Hotcha introduced during the past year, with brown-skinned maidens shaking their shimmy and a band of sepia musicians blasting hot tunes in the true Ellingtonian jungle rhythm is responsible for the arousing of interest on the Oregon capital's dawn patrol."[61] The term was used in conjunction with a number of female entertainers for several years. Harlem Hotcha even became a drink—Crème de Violet, a teaspoon of Triple Sec, a dash of Crème de Cacao, and heavy cream.[62] Following the run at Connie's Inn, *Harlem Hotcha* played at the Lafayette for four weeks in March 1933 with

```
                                                    S Cay
                        The Abyssinian Baptist Church and Community House
                                      132 West 138th Street
    A. CLAYTON POWELL, JR.              New York City
       Director of Activities
                                                    February 14th, 1933.

    My dear Mr. Johnson:

              I want to thank you for your kind cooperation
    of last Saturday night. I deeply appreciate this effort
    on your behalf to help us to help others.

              If I can ever be of any service to you, I shall
    be only too glad to serve.

                                    Yours sincerely,

    ACP r/HF                         A. Clayton Powell, Jr.
```

(Reproduced with permission of Barry Glover, from the James P. Johnson collection [IJS.0111], Institute of Jazz Studies, Rutgers-Newark)

another outstanding band, Luis Russell's orchestra. Blackman restaged the show in March 1937, playing the Club Plantation in Detroit.[63]

Johnson continued to place his "serious" shorter works in performance whenever possible. He and Razaf appeared with Handy at the Carleton Avenue YMCA on November 17, 1932.[64] Johnson played *Yamekraw*. A tune attributed to Johnson titled "Travelling" was performed by tenor Alfred Harrison.[65] This title is otherwise unknown. The tune actually performed may have been "Wandering," a composition written with Henry Creamer in 1926 as part of the musical play *Geechie*. Johnson would feature it ten years later in a similar choral musical presentation. Despite the tourist trade, much of the economy of Harlem, and the financial state of its citizens, was decimated by the Depression. He continued to support charitable events that were even more acutely needed. The year 1933 began with Johnson's involvement in a large fundraiser for Adam Clayton Powell Jr. and the Abyssinian Baptist Church in February. The New York Urban League, in conjunction with the New York Schools of Music, sponsored a concert at Washington Irving High School at 16th Street and Irving Place on September 5, 1933. The proceeds went to the relief department of the League for Harlem's most needy. On the program were Johnson along with Eva Taylor, Clarence Williams, the Southernaires, and baritone George Jones Jr. The *New York Amsterdam News* absorbed all the expenses so that 100 percent of the proceeds went to the charity.[66]

Another film opportunity presented itself. In 1924, Paul Robeson succeeded Charles Gilpin in the lead role of Eugene O'Neill's 1920 play *The Emperor Jones*. The play is a psychological thriller about the fall of the lead character Brutus

Jones, a onetime Pullman porter turned despotic island ruler who becomes a hunted fugitive. His demise, meted out by his brutalized subjects, is hastened by his own psychotic machinations. Like many other white artists of that time, O'Neill gravitated to African American subject matter for his work. And, like so much of the artistic output of that era in this genre, it was then and remains now the subject of controversy for the portrayal of its subject. By the late 1920s, however, it had become something of a classic. Dudley Murphy recognized the cinematic potential of a talking picture treatment, and, while still working on *St. Louis Blues*, sought out O'Neill for the rights to the play. Murphy had sketched out additional scenes. After disappointments with mainstream Hollywood, Murphy resurrected his idea with O'Neill in 1933. O'Neill agreed but stipulated that the lead be played by Robeson. DuBose Heyward, successful author of the 1925 novel turned Broadway play *Porgy*, took Murphy's original outline and developed an expanded narrative. Half or more of the final film was comprised of this new material written by Heyward. *The Emperor Jones* was filmed at the old Paramount studio in Astoria, Queens, then operated by Western Electric. Robeson, by then a star, earned a fee of $18,000. He insisted no shooting be done below the Mason-Dixon Line. Production began May 25, 1933, with all the scenes filmed in the New York area. Murphy returned to Harlem to fill out the cast. He tells the story of an extravagant escapade he orchestrated with a fancifully appointed Rolls Royce he acquired to attract Harlem talent. He said, "I had always had a penchant for glamorous second-hand cars. As I was now casting extras and small parts for the picture, I would go back to Harlem, which I already knew, for types. I rented two suits of purple livery from the costume company and dressed two handsome Negroes, one as chauffeur and the other as a footman to sit on the box and drive my Rolls to Harlem. Needless to say, I created quite an impression."[67] Despite this example of Murphy resorting to a disparaging trope as a recruitment tool, in the context of the time, he was likely thought of as sympathetic to the African American experience. For larger roles in the movie, he attracted Fredi Washington, a very young Harold Nicholas, the dancer George Stamper, who ten years earlier had featured Johnson's "Worried Lonesome Blues" in *Runnin' Wild*, and future comedic icon Jackie "Moms" Mabley. Billie Holiday appears as an extra in the crowd scene. It would have been Murphy's habit as well to seek out talent with whom he had previously worked, so the Hall Johnson Choir, the Smalls' Paradise waiters spinning their trays, and Jimmy Mordechai reappear. J. Rosamond Johnson returned to arrange the vocal score.[68] Frank Tours, a British-born veteran of stage and the newly developing world of film composing, wrote additional music.[69]

Murphy also returned to James P. Johnson, who provides piano background music for sections of the soundtrack and is briefly seen on screen. Susan Delson comments, "As in several of Murphy's previous films, the transitions between sequences offer a rich vein of visual play, usually linked to music. The shoeshine scene on the train ends with a close-up of a shoe being shined; the rhythm of the polishing cloth is picked up by a piano riff (the opening bars of 'St Louis Blues') as the shot cross-fades to a close-up of the pianist in the buffet flat." Filling the frame are Johnson's hands, but as the camera pans out, he is seen only from the back and side. His playing continues through the party. With careful attention, one can see his striding left hand visible behind the main action. He continues playing off screen behind the dialogue of a more intimate parlor scene with Robeson and Washington. Later in the film, he accompanies Mabley singing "Toot It Brother Armstrong" and another blues in a roadhouse scene featuring the requisite crap game. The film was released in September to mostly favorable reviews. It was not without controversy in the Black community as well as in the mainstream. The use of the "N" word angered many in the African American press. Others were hopeful the film, behind Robeson's strong portrayal, would ignite interest in dramatic film roles for African Americans. By contrast, scenes between Robeson and Washington that were considered racy and scenes depicting Black-on-white violence were cut after review by the Hayes office. Delson notes, "Between the cuts mandated by the censors and the footage lost in clipping objectionable language, postproduction edits to *The Emperor Jones* made for a jumpy, discontinuous, and at times unintelligible viewing experience."[70] Thankfully, despite a number of failed restoration attempts, in 2002, the Library of Congress was able to reconstruct nearly all the deleted scenes.

Between 1929 and 1934, mainstream film companies produced a half dozen pictures that engaged African American social issues, including rural/urban conflict, migration tensions, misogyny, and class struggle. Although draped in racially stereotyped imagery and conventions, the films of this five-year period are highly regarded as part of a brief art movement that brought African Americans to the screen in more than only demeaning, stereotypical, minor roles. Three of them—*St. Louis Blues*, *Yamekraw*, and *The Emperor Jones*—included Johnson as bandleader/arranger, composer, and/or pianist. It piqued his interest in work for mainstream Hollywood. The question was whether the large West Coast studios would be as welcoming for African American stage composers who aspired to work in the mainstream film industry as they were for the numerous white songwriters who made their way to California.

Mae West is best remembered for her flamboyant portrayals of sexually liberated women. During the twenties and thirties, she devoted nearly as much creative energy to issues of racial equity. Her 1931 play, *The Constant Sinner*, was banned in some locales including Washington, DC. Its mixed-race cast and plot that revolves around a mixed-race love affair were found objectionable. From her earliest days as a performer, she sought out "Black" tunes not simply for their novelty but for the emotional energy and crossover appeal of the double-entendre lyrics. She was well known for visiting Harlem hot spots[71] and publishers like Perry Bradford in search of material. She may very well have been personally acquainted with James P. Johnson. News reports in 1933 claimed Johnson and Andy Razaf were chosen to do special song numbers for her.[72] Nothing is known of a Johnson/Razaf collaboration for her, but, three years later, Johnson did collaborate with crooner Gene Austin on one tune for West's Paramount film *Klondike Annie*. West wrote the film, and four tunes were specially written for her by Austin that included "Mister Deep Blue Sea," the Johnson collaboration.[73]

Razaf made further efforts to secure film work during this time. Sam Fox of the Fox Movietone Corporation contacted Razaf on December 29 "about you and Jimmy Johnson.... The picture we have in mind will not go into production immediately, and I would like to have you confirm that you will work with Jimmy Johnson should we desire to make a deal." On January 18, 1935, Razaf responded, "I am perfectly willing to work with Jimmie Johnson for said picture. Our associations in the past have been both effective and agreeable."[74] A year later, in January 1936, Fox wrote to Johnson that the proposed film to feature Stepin Fetchit for which Johnson was to contribute music had fallen through. Johnson had inquired of Fox about using other compositions of his in their films. Although it seemed from Fox's earlier letter to Razaf that he had great interest in Johnson's music, by January he seemed much less interested, writing, "Regarding your modern American Compositions that you would like to have me consider, I wish you would take this up with me again in a few weeks as I am very rushed and intend to leave the city in a few days."[75] Johnson was pressing for use of his orchestral work in film as much as for his popular tunes. One year later a press notice reported Leopold Stokowski had arranged to use Johnson's four-movement symphonic suite *St. Louis Blues* as a movie soundtrack.[76] Nothing is known of such a film project. In late July 1936, Razaf and Johnson made their way to Chicago and then on to California for a few weeks' stay in furtherance of film work. On their return, they were to begin work on a musical together.[77] Nothing came of this foray to the coast, nor of a stage show. The question of whether mainstream Hollywood would open a door for African American composers was answered with a "No." For Johnson, the successes of the musical theater, and the brief interest in Black themes in art films, did not translate into expanded opportunity in the film industry at large as it did for so many white stage composers. Their product was for national distribution, and unlike the niche art films made by subsidiaries in New York, mainstream Hollywood would not confront the overtly racist sentiment of most of the country. Many years later, Johnson recalled the barriers that perpetuated the discrimination: "When the sound films came in they hired white people.

There was no room for us. Radio and films changed things, the Negro lost out. When we performed personally in public, the Negro had a chance. When the medium is mechanical and they ship it out all over the country, we don't get a chance. The worst sections of the country pull the whole thing down."[78]

From December 1933 through July 1934, Johnson kept busy in the recording studio with a series of six dates with Clarence Williams. Williams used a variety of names for his groups during the years from the late twenties into the 1930s, many using washboard in the title. The group of records with Johnson were credited to "Clarence Williams and His Orchestra." Subtitled "Novelty Dance" on the records, most included the washboard and are sometimes incorrectly referred to as the washboard band. John Hammond notes that using the designation of "washboard band" allowed the recording companies to skirt paying the musicians union scale, since a washboard band was more akin to a hillbilly designation, and the musicians were not considered "legitimate."[79] It is intriguing to think that Johnson's stature (and likely his own membership in the union) necessitated avoiding the washboard title, and paying at the union rate. Ed Allen, who started playing trumpet with Williams in 1926 and who recorded over a hundred tunes with him, noted rehearsals and sessions were often long and stressful. Williams might change the arrangements or the tunes entirely on the spot. Williams made up some of the tunes in the recording studio. He took credit as composer and eventually published them. The records were intended for distribution in the South, with double entendre and coded titles like "He's a Colonel from Kentucky," "I Got Horses and Got Numbers on My Mind," "Jerry The Junker," and "Chizzlin' Sam" characteristic of the repertoire Johnson recorded with him.[80]

One side in particular turned out to be history making. Singer Chick Bullock was a ubiquitous presence on records during the 1930s, including on many of these sides, adding his straight if not "sweet" vocals. Trumpeter Charlie Gaines had penned a simple tune with what he called some "crazy words." Clarence Williams, whose ear for a hit was still sharp, heard it and immediately paid Gaines a flat fee for it. For the session on March 23, they recorded Gaines's tune "I Can't Dance, I Got Ants in My Pants," but not with Bullock. Louis Jordan, also playing alto saxophone, took the vocal. It was his singing debut on record. The tune is an up-tempo number with a spectacular array of classic vernacular elements including call-and-response vocals, first between Jordan and the band and then with Gaines, Jordan's scat singing, Floyd Casey's swinging washboard, and Gaines's clever double-entendre lyrics. The "novelty" marketing designation presaged Jordan's later marginalization as a novelty vocalist. It became tantamount to an epithet, and his albatross, obscuring his contributions to jazz as an alto player, vocalist, and trend setter in the path he forged toward the hip, blues-based music of the 1940s. Gaines claims the lyrics were so controversial the tune was banned from the radio. This fueled booming sales, and Williams, perhaps uncharacteristically, paid Gaines his share of royalties totaling $500, a nice sum in the depths of the Depression.

The mid-thirties was the nadir for the recording industry, and after the July 1934 session, Johnson would not make another record until 1938. In addition to the recording, Williams invited Johnson to rejoin him and his wife on the radio since they had returned to broadcasting regularly every Wednesday on NBC radio, as well as on the ABC-affiliated WJZ. Johnson joined them on stage as well at the Harlem Opera House in February. He was very close to Williams and his wife Eva Taylor. They had been cross-street neighbors since their last work together on the air in 1930. For Johnson, their warm friendship, and no doubt an opportunity to work, dulled the sharp edges of Williams's musical deficiencies and leadership idiosyncrasies.

Social events and fund raisers continued because of and despite the economic hardships felt disproportionately in the Black community. In late April, Johnson and Williams along with Shelton Brooks, all Jamaica residents, entertained for the St. James Fashion Show's midnight show. They were joined by dancer Bill Robinson.[81] A crowd of five hundred attended a tribute event for Ethel Waters at the Triangle Studios in Harlem at West 131st Street on July 1. The Harlem Congressional League sponsored the affair drawing Harlem's social elite not only to honor Waters but also to further their political agenda of electing a Black woman to Congress. Mistress of Ceremonies Anita Reed was described as a "militant social worker, soloist and singer of extraordinary ability," while the club's president Julia Robinson spoke about "Women in Politics." Other honored guests included Fats Waller and actress Georgette Harvey, who the next year would play Maria in the Broadway production of *Porgy and Bess*.[82] Johnson had completed *Harlem Symphony* and *Jazzamine Concerto*, accomplishments newsworthy enough to warrant notice in syndicated columns in the African American press. The symphony was reportedly played by the Rochester Symphony on several occasions, and word had it that Paul Whiteman was planning to perform it in the fall.[83] Johnson was working diligently composing for the concert hall, but he had not settled into a comfortable retirement to do so. He likely couldn't afford to, but he was also not inclined to shrink from an active musical life. He loved it too much. Despite the grinding desperation of the worsening Depression, Harlem nightspots continued to draw. His next opportunity there drew a rave reception.

In mid-August 1934, Johnson began a highly successful run with an orchestra at Smalls' Paradise. He developed what became an enormously successful nightclub stage show featuring his music called *Mad Manhattan*, which opened October 3, 1934.[84] The show was produced by Howard Elmore and staged by Jean Demeaux, who produced revues at the Ubangi Club. Jo Trent again worked with Johnson on the songs, all copyrighted by Ralph Peer's Southern Music Company. Peer had been a seminal figure as talent scout and executive at OKeh and Victor in the 1920s. He founded Southern in 1928 as his vehicle to bypass the hegemony of the recording companies in maintaining copyrights of the artists with whom he worked. Like most other businessmen in the music industry at the time, his terms were notoriously unfavorable to the artists, especially the African American and Southern white country performers. Peer was unabashed about his racial biases, and frequently expressed them with outright racist comments.[85] Peer had had a modicum of success with a few of Johnson's tunes from several years earlier, in particular "When I Can't Be with You" from 1931, and decided to move on what was from the beginning a successful Harlem stage show. The premiere attracted "the uppercrust of the theatrical and night club world" from uptown and downtown. Theater and gossip column rivals Walter Winchell and Ed Sullivan, future television icon, as well as W. C. Handy and Will Marion Cook attended the premiere,[86] and music publisher Jerry Vogel sent a congratulatory telegram.[87]

The local Harlem press made note of Johnson's prominent role, writing that, "... with the music in the capable hands of James P. (Jimmy) Johnson and his orchestra, the show proves to be a fast-moving, melodious treat and well received by the seasoned audience...."[88] The show starred Marion Hairston, who sang "Whisper Sweet," the Johnson tune that became the highlight.[89] The tune received some exposure with recordings by Bob Howard and Valaida Snow. During the floor show, which had a start time of 12:30 a.m., Johnson conducted the orchestra with Leola Felton at the piano. After the floor show, until nearly 4:00 a.m., Johnson's band played three shows for dancing. The personnel included Audley Smith, Howard Scott, Harry Noisette, trumpets; James Scott, Eric Brown, Trent Harris, saxes; Joe Watts, bass; Yank Porter, drums; and Andy Pendleton, banjo and vocals. Their theme song was "Old Fashioned Love."[90] He was broadcasting locally twice nightly on WNEW at 10:45 p.m. and 12:15 a.m. The band was broadcast at least as far as St. Louis on the ABC radio show *Dance Party*. Johnson received fan mail from Philadelphia, Boston, Evansville and Michigan City, Indiana, St. Louis, Missouri, Ontario, Canada, North Carolina, and Maine.[91] *Variety* noted the revue was on par with what could be found at similar venues downtown. The context remained that of exotic Harlem. With "jungle" type dances, costumes that included "effigies of monkeys," risqué routines, all "Aided by the torrid syncopation of the Johnson orchestra, the show succeeds in being one of the warmest to be found up Harlem way."[92] J. C. Johnson sent a telegram January 25, 1935, asking for a "special favor" for Johnson to plug his "Balcony" song. Johnson always obliged requests from colleagues as well as fans. Emma P. La Freniere thanked him for playing her "Dancing Melody" that was just published. A woman from Boston requested "Solitude," a rendition mentioned by Walter Winchell (who attended the premiere) in his "On Broadway" column, noting, "J. Johnson's crew at Small's [sic], particularly the cornetootier, toying with Ellington's 'Solitude,' a lyric and tune that are really married." A repertoire staple was "Christmas Night in Harlem," a tune Johnson had recorded with Clarence Williams earlier in 1934. A special New Year's Eve celebration was promoted to ring in 1935.[93] The show was so popular patrons were turned away.[94]

Johnson took a night off from Small's on November 22, 1934, to honor W. C. Handy at the Poosepahtuck club at 773 St. Nicholas Avenue. While the club staff provided the entertainment, Johnson was joined by Shelton Brooks, Donald Heywood, Maceo Pinkard, Fats Waller, Edgar Dowell, Alex Hill, J. C. Johnson, Chris Smith, Porter Grainger, Jean Burns, and Clarence Williams at the event billed as "A Night in the Blues."[95] On February 26, 1935, Johnson was one of numerous musical celebrities at the first annual dance of the Bert Hall Rhythm Club held at the Renaissance Casino on 138th Street. Eight hundred people jammed the hall until early morning to hear Adelaide Hall, Bert's wife Josephine Hall (the two had worked with Johnson in *Keep Shufflin'*), Claude Hopkins, Cab Calloway, Teddy Hill, Joyner and Foster, and Fess Williams.[96] Marion Hairston was honored with a party sponsored by the cast, celebrating her sixth month in the starring role of *Mad Manhattan*.[97]

Guitarist friend Ikey Robinson, listening from Chicago, stumbled across the broadcast one evening. In a letter he wrote,

> Hello Jas. P. old pal. Heard your band the other night. Boy you sure have a band. These fellows out here need to listen to you & your boys each and every time. I was just talking about you that afternoon. So while waiting for time to go to work I tuned in on New York & heard this band really swinging & Tressie and I kept on raving & wondering who could it be. We knew it was an eastern band. So all at once he announced Jas. P. Johnson at Smalls. At first Tressie said "they must have made a mistake of the first name. But I kept saying I know Charlie Johnson [sic] band didn't have those kind of arrangements. [Charlie Johnson had the house band at Smalls for many years.] Although he had a good band. But I wanted to hear a solo from you. (line obscured) . . . can make one on it like the old maestro himself Jas. P. Johnson.[98]

Another friend wrote, "Hello Jimmy—Have heard your band several times on the air and it sure sounds good. One night I was very much disappointed as I had several ofay [white] boys waiting to hear you play a piano solo and that night you failed to do so. Glad you are doing good and have a band because you really should have did that long ago."[99] When Johnson played, though, it enthralled, as friend and choral director Eva Jessye observed, noting his "... flexible fingers performing magic tricks in obligato [*sic*], ripples, counter rhythms at the oddest moments, not a two-beat space but what was cleverly filled in the exclusive Johnson style."[100]

The dance bands were becoming as much of a draw as the stage show, and the Lindy Hop of the patrons on the dance floor was the feature rather than the tightly choreographed chorus lines. For seven months, Johnson held forth at one of the top Harlem nightspots with a musical foot in each camp, providing both the music for dancing with a band long in coming, as well as composing and playing the music for the stage show. But several events were about to change the urban dynamic that had maintained Harlem as the center of voyeuristic entertainment. *Mad Manhattan* closed on April 29, 1935, six weeks after the infamous Harlem riot that ensued after a young boy of color was arrested for shoplifting, and rumors swirled about his beating and death. Connie's Inn had closed the year before, a victim of both the financial pressures meted out by the Depression and escalating underworld violence. The former Dutch Schultz mobster Vincent "Mad Dog" Coll had his eye on Connie and George Immerman's still prospering club, creating a deadly rivalry with Coll's old boss. The botched kidnapping of George Immerman by Coll, in an attempt to strong-arm Connie, ended in a shootout in front of the club, hastening its demise.[101] The Cotton Club closed in Harlem in 1936 and moved downtown. Ed Smalls managed to hold on with his club, and, after *Mad Manhattan* closed, Johnson's dance band returned to its ad hoc status, playing primarily for sporadic local affairs until 1939. There were occasional engagements longer than one night at Harlem venues such as when Johnson and his "Paradise Orchestra" played a week at the Harlem Opera House beginning May 17, 1935, in a stage show featuring the great boxer Joe Louis.[102]

Johnson's lack of interest in the life of a bandleader with a regular orchestra, coupled with his inclination to hold in check his prodigious solo ability while broadcasting, were two lost opportunities. Johnson's name failed to gain any further popular acclaim from the general public. Johnson later acknowledged the consequences of avoiding the dance band business: "I had just come out of the period when I was in the show business. I looked down on dance bands. In a dance band you had to work all night. I was making big money and dance bands weren't making big money. Then in Chicago Paul Ash introduced a new form of entertainment—the band on the stage. Well, they began to sell bands for a lot of money after that. I was misplaced. I didn't have an orchestra."[103] Ironically, much of the sound of the burgeoning "swing" bands was developed by a generation of pianists whose rhythmic approach was, at least initially in their careers, modelled from Johnson's innovative transformation of rhythm. Bandleaders well known today whose success bloomed during the "swing era," like Duke

Ellington, Count Basie, Fletcher Henderson, as well as lesser-known figures Cliff Jackson and Claude Hopkins, were all Johnson disciples. With a respectable arsenal of original popular song hits to his credit, Johnson could have toured and recorded with a band of his own, an endeavor that would have increased the likelihood of creating a name for himself as composer and bandleader with the general public. He did not, for a second time. He hadn't done it in the mid-twenties after his success with *Runnin' Wild* and the "Charleston," and didn't again when the swing band became the new focus of entertainment.

Johnson's choices were a complex mix of competing aspirations but driven primarily by his desire to be known as a composer. He was proud of his success in the world of popular music and did not look at this output as a compromise to artistic integrity. In addition to the acclaim he sought alongside his white counterparts like Gershwin, Kern, and Berlin, it was, he thought, more lucrative and less grueling than leading a band. And by the mid-thirties, he was less inclined to take on the taxing life of a touring musician. This was the compromise to commercial music he was not willing to make. It cost him. As the composer of many popular tunes, Johnson should have been better known, but without an orchestral identity to promote his own work, the broad recognition he deserved never really developed. Johnson fell further victim to his restrained nature. During a successful seven-month run with a broadcasting orchestra, he subjugated his talents at the keyboard while playing on the radio, limiting his solo work. His protégé Fats Waller, by contrast, comes booming out of nearly every performance, reflecting their vastly different personalities. While Art Tatum was then taking the world of jazz piano by storm, Johnson did not capitalize on radio exposure for his own pianistic excellence. As the world of the Harlem stage show contracted, Johnson redoubled his efforts exploring opportunities for his symphonic work, his least commercial musical effort. It was a time-consuming venture, and certainly another distraction from the world of commercial music and jazz. Gunther Schuller rightly concludes, ". . . without Johnson ever quite understanding it, both areas, the commercial and jazz, began to pass him by."[104] But at heart Johnson was an optimist. He pressed on with his concert work, and, as a jazz pianist and as composer of popular tunes, he had much more to do.

Chapter 19

THE ORGANIZER, 1935–1940

> I ain't got a thing to lose,
> But those doggone Hongry Blues.
> —LANGSTON HUGHES

Once *Mad Manhattan* concluded, Johnson focused his efforts on his larger, symphonic compositions. He continued to study and seek out teachers. In 1935, Johnson studied instrumentation with Boris Levenson.[1] Levenson was born in 1884 in Akkerman, Bessarabia, a piece of land in Eastern Europe that changed hands repeatedly over the centuries. He studied with Glazunov and Rimsky-Korsakov and saw success conducting in St. Petersburg and Moscow.[2] He immigrated to the United States in 1921,[3] and built a successful career as conductor and composer. Levenson suffered through bitter antisemitism in Russia and, once in the United States, devoted much of his composing to Jewish themes. It was an appropriate model for Johnson, who was also acutely concerned with representation of ethnic and folk material in extended forms. Like Johnson's other teachers, Levenson's work was built on late nineteenth-century compositional principles. In 1936, his old teacher Edward Treumann wrote inviting him to join his upcoming spring and summer master classes.[4] Later that year, Johnson inquired about private instruction in composition from other European musicians.[5] Johnson enjoyed playing the organ for his church and had a pipe organ installed in his home.[6]

Through the mid-1930s, Johnson approached numerous high-profile musicians and society benefactors about performing his symphonic works. His scrapbooks are filled with rejection letters. In September 1935, Fritz Reiner wrote encouragingly to Johnson that he would be glad to examine his scores.[7] Nearly

(Author's collection)

(Author's collection)

two years went by before Fritz Reiner's assistant, in a letter of July 1937, put Johnson off from sending manuscripts until December.[8] A July 1937 news article noted Leopold Stokowski had arranged to use Johnson's four movement symphonic suite *St. Louis Blues* as a movie soundtrack.[9] In September, he was rebuffed by Stokowski.[10] Hans Kindler, conductor of the National Symphony Orchestra wrote on October 2, 1935, "I am sorry, but I cannot look over any music now, because of stress of work of the beginning of the season."[11] In January 1936, he approached Paul Whiteman.[12] He wrote again to Whiteman in December, but was again politely put off.[13] In April 1936, Edwin Franko Goldman, conductor of the Goldman Band in New York, wrote Johnson that no new works could be taken on.[14] The Philharmonic-Symphony Society of New York (better known as the New York Philharmonic) read one of his scores, noted it would be kept in mind for the future, but in May, wrote to Johnson about how he should retrieve it.[15] Leon Barzin of the National Orchestral Association, as with the others, returned Johnson's manuscript of *St. Louis Blues Suite* to him through his assistant, unread.[16] Johnson wrote to Deems Taylor hoping he would include his compositions in Taylor's Serious Music Program for American composers. He reminded Taylor of his popular and musical theater successes, including his work for the prominent white producers, but also highlighted the unique ethnic voice he felt he brings to "serious" music, writing, "I am a negro composer & knowing the work of my brother contemporary composers, I feel I am quite conscious that my work is more truly Negroid & original & less touched by the White Schools [sic] sophistication." In an apologetic conclusion, he hopes Taylor will excuse his personal promotion, assuring him, ". . . I did not wish you to think I was a designing & worrisome amateur."[17] There is no known response from Taylor to Johnson, or whether he included any of Johnson's work, but several years later, Taylor did sign on as a sponsor for Johnson's 1942 concert at the Heckscher Theater that featured his symphonic works.

During the latter part of 1936, Johnson began his quest to obtain a Guggenheim fellowship. In November, he wrote to a number of leading African American figures for support. He was less than veiled about his need for money to further his musical education, and to complete his ambitious works. Johnson was highly deferential to these well-connected, well-educated men with distinguished careers in academia and politics, finding the need to introduce himself to them, thinking they may not associate his name with his notable accomplishments.[18] He sold himself short. James Weldon Johnson, a towering figure as musician, political leader, and writer, wrote back, "Of course I know who you are, and I am familiar with your work." J. W. Johnson had written about J. P. Johnson in his 1930 historical-cultural survey *Black Manhattan*, specifically in reference to his stature as a popular composer. In that book, referring to him as Jimmy Johnson, the more informal name James P.

used to identify his popular and stage work, J. W. includes him in a short list of "outstanding" Black composers writing popular songs at the time.[19] J. W. was very encouraging, providing advice about whom to contact and committed his support as a reference.[20] Johnson wrote to Robert R. Moton, former president of the Tuskegee Institute, for a recommendation.[21] He, too, offered a letter of recommendation when contacted by the Foundation. Lester A. Walton, *New York Age* editor and at the time American Minister to Liberia, not only wrote a letter of recommendation, but sent Johnson a set of lyrics for him to set to music.[22] Johnson wrote to Will Marion Cook in the fall of 1936. Cook, a longtime admirer of Johnson, having declared him the most versatile pianist of their race back in 1923, returned a lengthy letter of encouragement. But he responded as a tired old man, with little energy to actively take up Johnson's cause. He wrote, "I wish I could do something to help along your present ambitions, but I am just a sick and discouraged old man and just manage to eke out an existence."[23] Cook had been diagnosed with tuberculosis in 1915. The disease remained under control for sixteen years, but became active again in the early 1930s, requiring many periods of recuperation.[24] Cook was sixty-seven at the time, and died in 1944. Johnson was rejected for the Guggenheim in March 1937.[25] In November, he was perfunctorily invited to submit his compositions again to the Guggenheim Foundation.[26] He did so in December, but was concerned his manuscripts would not be returned, and may not have completed another application.

In October 1935, the staggering unemployment in the arts world led to the creation of the Federal Theater Project (FTP), a program of the Works Progress Administration. Separate "Negro units" were designated around the country, numbering as many as twenty-two units. The Harlem unit was the largest, and produced the greatest number works during its brief life. John Houseman took over direction of the unit in 1936 and tapped Orson Welles to run the classics division. His charge was to adapt Western classical dramas into productions with an ethnic twist. One of their first productions was *Macbeth*, with the setting transmigrated from Britain to Haiti. A Pan-African spin was layered on with the addition of dancers from Sierra Leone under the direction of Asadata Dafora Horton, swelling the cast to 137. This required a two-level set.[27] The so-called "Voodoo Macbeth" opened on April 14, 1936, at the Lafayette Theater in Harlem to great acclaim and some controversy. Opening night was a glamorous event with floodlights and the Monarch Elks Band playing for the crowd in front of the theater.[28] Johnson's rhapsody *Yamekraw* was used as the overture for the production. After the ten-week run at Lafayette, *Macbeth* moved to the Adelphi Theater on Broadway and then to the Majestic Theater in Brooklyn, where it closed on October 17. A tour was planned but was limited to the Black theater circuit. There were mixed feelings in the Black community about what audience it was best suited for outside of New York. Although the setting of the play was revised from Britain to a voodoo-infused Haitian backdrop, some felt it was such a significant departure from the usual Black stage productions that it should not be restricted only to Black audiences. One reviewer noted the potential for dispelling stereotypes, writing,

> This is one of the first colored productions, to my knowledge, ever created on so elaborate a scale that does not have a patronizing attitude toward the white man's idea of what the colored man is like. There is no black face, slap-stick buffoonery. The production is a high-class artistic creation which depends on excellence of presentation instead of prejudice for its drawing power. No producer, interested only in making money, would attempt such show; he would be too afraid of the old stereotype taboos to risk it. Such a show has been produced at Uncle Sam's expense. It should be used to educate the white citizenry to appreciate the colored performer as an artist instead of a clown.[29]

Others felt differently, cautioning, "We therefore warn downtown visitors that the play is purely for Harlem consumption, and is geared and produced accordingly."[30] The eventual tour included seven cities. The total attendance was 117,244 people, and presumably they all heard Johnson's overture.[31] Johnson contacted the FTP himself in July 1936, but no additional projects were forthcoming for him then.[32]

Johnson undertook a big step in advancing his activities by arranging for a personal representative. In particular, he was looking for performance opportunities for his symphonic works. On February 27, 1937, he signed a contract with George W. Lattimore. For 20 percent commission, the three-year agreement, with allowance for an additional two years, engaged Lattimore to contract for placement of Johnson's compositions as well as arranging for appearances. Lattimore was born in Brooklyn, New York, and made a name initially as a sportswriter and official.[33] After acquiring a law degree, he worked the business side of the entertainment industry beginning in the mid-teens. In the fall of 1918, when Will Marion Cook reorganized the remains of James Reese Europe's orchestra into the New York Syncopated Orchestra after Europe's untimely murder at the hands of his drummer Herbert Wright, Lattimore was engaged as business manager. After a tour of the Northeast and Midwest, the group embarked on a tour of London in May 1919. The name was changed to the Southern Syncopated Orchestra, and for the next two years famously played over 1,200 concerts in Great Britain and France. Despite artistic and popular success, notably introducing Sidney Bechet playing New Orleans–style breaks on the soprano saxophone, his newly adopted instrument, Cook and Lattimore wrangled legally and parted ways, leaving Lattimore to lead the original group as Cook led a splinter orchestra. Both groups ultimately failed financially by December 1920.[34] Lattimore stayed in Europe and continued to build his career as an impresario. While in Paris, he exclusively represented several notable theaters including the Moulin Rouge and the Empire, as well as the opera diva Luisa Tetrazzini. Lattimore returned to the United States in 1935 to represent the prima donna Madame Caterina Jarboro of the Chicago Opera for her world tour.[35] Lattimore was well liked and well respected, and was referred to as "the grand gentleman."[36] Upon his return to the United States, he was welcomed back to the sporting world and one of his first events was as a judge for the first annual Carnival of Sports sponsored by the 369th Regiment Athletic Association and the Boys of Yesteryear at the 142nd Street armory.[37] He produced the opening of what was described at the time as the first art gallery dedicated to African American art, the Augusta Savage Studios. Savage was a commissioned artist for the New York World's Fair for which she produced her sculpture "Lift Every Voice and Sing."[38] He maintained his focus as an international impresario until the eve of World War II, negotiating contracts in Australia and London,[39] and booking Caterina Jarboro abroad for four years.[40] Lattimore seemed to be an excellent choice as publicist for Johnson.

Will Marion Cook, in his 1936 letter to Johnson, emphatically emphasized the need for him to remain original. He told Johnson, "Your rhythms are magnificent and are your own. Don't try to be anybody else. Don't even be influenced by anybody—no matter how great, how popular." In a personal and perhaps paternalistic vein consistent with his nickname "Dad," Cook comments, "You have a good wife. She has stuck to you thru [sic] the 'bitter' and the 'sweet' and its time now for her to take things easy. That you have cut the drinking and the worthless friends makes me very proud of you." Cook expresses his concern about whether Johnson is making enough money to support his family. There was clearly financial impact on Johnson after the Harlem nightclub scene had changed and the Depression worsened. During the twenties, he drove a Cadillac. In 1936 he was driving a Ford Tudor sedan. When his fellowships fell through, he needed to take out yearly loans of $200–$300 in 1936, '37 and '38.[41] Lillie Mae found nonmusical work as a licensed real estate salesperson in 1939 to supplement their income. Cook suggests Johnson return to the popular music market while pursuing his academic ambitions. "Why, just to earn some easy money, don't you try to write a beautiful light but worthy song." He suggests sending some melodies to his son Mercer at Atlanta University.[42] Ultimately, in his letter, Cook offers little to Johnson in the way of tangible assistance. Johnson and Mercer Cook did not collaborate during this time on a "light" song, but several years later collaborated on four songs that became part of Johnson's one-act opera *The Dreamy Kid*.

Johnson had never really left the popular market, but he had had only a handful of tunes copyrighted between 1934 and 1938. "Havin a Ball," with lyrics by Andy Razaf, was copyrighted in 1936 and recorded by Fats Waller in December. While not apparently recorded by him at this time, the sheet music highlights Benny Goodman and His Orchestra featuring the tune. Things picked up for him in 1938. Johnson's portfolio was enhanced somewhat by the tunes that came from his 1938 stage show *Policy Kings*, seven of which were published in late 1938. "You You You" and "Harlem Woogie" were recorded by Les Brown in 1939. Johnson's own 1939 recording of "Harlem Woogie" was released on Vocalion, but his "Havin a Ball" was not. A 1939 newspaper clipping makes notable mention of Johnson's recent songs "The Harlem Woogie" and "You You You" as being popular in Harlem.

♪

Johnson had been contemplating an opera for years. Although there was little support from the musical establishment, in 1936 he pursued this vision in earnest. The finished piece, *The Organizer*, with Johnson's music, included a libretto by Langston Hughes. Before Hughes committed to the work, Johnson sought out other collaborators. In early 1936, he first wrote to writer Edna Ferber, famous as a member of the Algonquin round table, and author of the novel *Showboat* upon which the groundbreaking 1927 musical was based. She demurred, claiming a lack of time and experience as a librettist.[43] Johnson first sought out Hughes in late 1936 or early 1937 to float the idea of a collaboration on an opera. Johnson wrote, "I have one or two subjects and plots of my own I would like to tell you about. Your play *Mulatto* was a distinct success and I was more than glad to witness your success. I am convinced that you and I ought to do a strong Negro Opera." In January 1937, Hughes responded favorably, writing "I was happy to have your letter and would, of course, be glad to work with you on an opera libretto sometime in the future. I have long known and admired your work and once met you some years ago. When we meet, I'd like very much to hear the ideas which you have in mind. I think we could work out something really Negro, modern, and interesting."[44] Since Hughes spent most of 1937 travelling, Johnson pursued other plans, including his thought to base the story line of his projected opera on the John Henry legend. He contacted Howard University professor and poet Sterling A. Brown, whose artistic and political inclinations were similar to that of Hughes. Brown responded in May 1937, "I have heard 'Dad' Cook mention you frequently, and I have been anxious to meet you. He has told me of your fine and distinctive work. I do not see how I will be able to do the project you mention, however, as I am at present head over heels in work."

Johnson wrote to novelist Roark Bradford inquiring about Bradford's 1931 novel *John Henry*. In Bradford's adaptation, the hero is a Mississippi roustabout travelling up and down the Mississippi river rather than the steel-driving man of the original story. Bradford acknowledges his familiarity with Johnson's work but indicates composer Jacques Wolfe has been working on a John Henry opera for nearly two years and expects its imminent completion. Wolfe, who was born in Romania and was a Juilliard graduate, had previously collaborated with Langston Hughes on the song "Sad Song in de Air" published in 1934. Roarke and Wolfe's *John Henry* opera became a Broadway production and opened in January 1940 with Paul Robeson in the title role. The production was under the musical supervision of Leonard De Paur, who just a few months later would lead the choral section of Johnson and Hughes's operatic collaboration. Roarke and Wolfe's *John Henry* closed after only seven performances, with most reviewers citing a weak script. Johnson approached Theodore Browne about his play *Natural Man*. Browne was a playwright involved in the Seattle Negro Repertory Company of the Federal Theater Project, adapting or writing four of the fifteen plays that unit would mount in its three-year existence. *Natural Man* (originally titled *This Ole Hammer*), his most successful play, opened January 28, 1937, at the Seattle Metropolitan Theater. Browne's brother Frank, who lived in New York, responded favorably to Johnson's inquiry. Browne's play, loosely based on the John Henry story, featured some musical sequences with a chorus singing work songs and other popular blues tunes including "Beale Street Blues" and "Careless Love." It was described as a "folk opera," a characterization that resonated with Johnson's own aspirations for such a work.[45] Johnson planned to fully score the work, and contacted Hughes in early 1938, hoping he would set the play in blank verse. Johnson betrays his excitement and ambition, writing, "This will not take you long & I have good promises & chance for production. Besides, I am up for a fellowship this spring & if I get the same this will be my project." Johnson presented to Hughes a contract he had secured with Theodore Browne to do a "grand Opera" on Browne's play. Hughes rejected the contract, which he felt inadequately protected both his and Johnson's interests. Despite the rejections from the preceding two years, Johnson remained optimistic about his prospects for some type of fellowship.

While neither the plan to base the opera on *Natural Man* nor the fellowship came to pass, the John Henry theme held a strong attraction for Johnson. His papers include a sketch for a "John Henry Symphonic Poem," with a principal theme and three subordinate themes depicting "big episodes or pictures of John's wanderings or adventures," as well as a love scene. Johnson inquired of the Institute for Research in Social Science at the University of North Carolina, Chapel Hill, regarding John Henry information. Research Associate Guy B. Johnson responded they had little information, and that a number of old phonograph recordings in their archive were seemingly misplaced.⁴⁶ The idea for an opera must have also lingered in Hughes's mind. He ultimately established the thematic content and story line for the piece, called variously *De Organizer*, *The Organizer*, or on some drafts simply *Organizer*. He wrote the libretto, subtitled "A Blues Opera in One Act," while in Paris in August 1938. It deals directly with the most pressing social issues of the time—capitalism, sharecropping, hunger, race relations, class struggle, and unionization. Hughes had previously written the three-act drama *Blood on the Fields* in 1935, which dealt with attempts to organize California cotton pickers. A year later, the Seattle unit in which Browne was involved produced a play titled *Stevedore* in which a Black union organizer rallies both Black and white longshoremen who are initially at odds. They come together in the concluding scene to fight against the dock bosses. *The Organizer* is based on similar story lines, as were other theatrical works during this time of burgeoning foment for union building. While working with Johnson on the project when he was back in New York, Hughes brought along Ralph Ellison. The three collaborated on a song, "Got to Do It," copyrighted in 1939.⁴⁷

These theatrical works with themes of social protest (like *Stevedore*) were performed by organizations supported by the New Deal Federal Theater Project (FTP). Many had direct ties with socialist or communist sympathizers and organizations, associations that caused concern in the Federal government, eventually leading to the demise of the FTP in 1939 after only three years. *The Organizer* was not a FTP production, but Hughes's communist links were well known. Johnson's associations were not as obvious. David Gelman, who spent many nights with Johnson at the Pied Piper club in 1943 and at his home, recalls Johnson rarely spoke publicly about race, injustice, or other social issues.⁴⁸ However, Willie "The Lion" Smith hinted that Johnson's interest in social reform was more than passing, and that he associated with people who shared his views.⁴⁹ In a rare example of Johnson verbalizing his feelings about race, he responded to Edward Laska, who wrote to Johnson in late 1938 about using his name for a sponsor's committee on a jubilee program organized by W. C. Handy and an interracial committee of music leaders. Laska, who had written the popular "Alcoholic Blues," apparently included in his letter his perceptions of the contributions of African Americans in music which he must have viewed as enlightened. Johnson, however, felt compelled to correct them. In his letter of November 17, 1938, Johnson is unable to contain his angry reaction. He writes, "First of all Negro composers contributed nearly all of the blues written but you must bear in mind, Negro composers have never had the commercial backing & propaganda, & while I [hate] to say so, the non-racial prejudices & barriers & social advantages of the White composers." Johnson did ultimately agree to have his name appear on the sponsor's list for the "Silver Jubilee of

Blues," a national music festival that ran for a week beginning March 2, 1940. The program honored Handy and George Gershwin. George M. Cohan was honorary chairman. Many prominent African American musicians lent their names to the event including Noble Sissle, Louis Armstrong, Buck and Bubbles, Harry T. Burleigh, Duke Ellington, J. Rosamond Johnson, Will Vodery, William Grant Still, writer Alaine Locke, and actress Fredi Washington. Johnson's agent, George W. Lattimore, was also a sponsor.[50]

The subject matter of *The Organizer* was entirely in keeping with Hughes's artistic output. For Johnson, it allowed a significant move away from the vestiges of the minstrel show that pervaded the roles for African Americans in popular music, Hollywood, and especially the musical theater. The contrast of *The Organizer* with his nearly concurrent work on the stage show *Policy Kings* is striking. While Johnson took great pride as a composer for the musical theater, he strove to have his orchestral music tell a different story—that of his race, not only their trials and tribulations but also cultural depth and social accomplishments. *The Organizer* is one of the most important of his works demonstrating this side of his artistic vision.

As Willie "The Lion" Smith intimates, Johnson began more regular associations with left-leaning labor organizations. On February 26, 1939, Johnson took part in the initial concert sponsored by the Labor Club of the American Labor Party titled "Negro Music, Past and Present." It was produced at Labor Stage on West 39th Street, the cultural division of the International Ladies Garment Workers' Union. With interludes written and narrated by playwright Carlton Moss, the program was intended to trace the history of Black music from African dances to the present musical scene. The program was dedicated to Frederick Douglass, and put together by John Velasco, one of the organizers of the Negro Unit of the Federal Theater Project.[51] The performers included dancers Asadata Dafora and Archie Savage portraying African origins, musical director Albert Moss and his choir of twenty voices recollecting the sounds of slavery, and a jump to the twentieth century with the musicians who had recently performed in the "Spirituals to Swing" concert. Ruby Smith was accompanied by Johnson, and Meade Lux Lewis, Albert Ammons, and Leadbelly performed. *The New York Times* reviewer noted, "... the blues came in with Ruby Smith's wonderfully raucous voice and James P. Johnson's fantastic piano."[52] Langdon W. Post, president of the Labor Club, noted, "In presenting this first program depicting the origin and development of Negro music from the African period to the present day, our aim is to draw attention to the fact that one of the main sources of American popular music has been the folk music of the Negro. In the future it is felt that this same folk music will undoubtedly furnish an important basis for so-called classic American music."[53] ILGWU Labor Stage leaders, whose interest was in promoting racial and social tolerance and understanding, played a prominent role in this event. The production was staged by Herbert H. Gordon, director of the ILGWU musical production of *Pins and Needles*. Schaffer Horatio was the producer of Labor Stage. Gordon and Horatio were the ideal audience for Johnson to pitch his opera. This would fulfill their aspiration for "Negro music" to serve as the "basis for so-called classic American music." Two weeks later, on March 12, 1939, *The Organizer* premiered in Harlem at the Harlem Suitcase Theater with Schaffer Horatio in attendance.

Launched by Hughes a year earlier to showcase his work, the Harlem Suitcase Theater was initially sponsored by the Communist-affiliated International Workers Order and used space in their community center. The 1939 performance marked the opening of the new home for the theater in the West 135th Street public library auditorium (now the home of the Schomburg Center branch of the New York Public Library). Johnson played a piano score for this performance. Local media reported interest from the Columbia Broadcasting Company in obtaining radio rights. Schaffer Horatio set in motion an auspicious future for the opera.[54] In August, Hughes wrote to Johnson from Monterey, California, of the opera and other projects on which the two were collaborating. A warm friendship had developed. "Dear Jimmy," wrote Hughes, "The enclosed blues dialogue was sent to Carlton Moss for his Café Society Revue that you remember we spoke of. For the next six weeks I'll be here in the country at the above address, in case there's any news of our opera or anything. Did you get the other lyrics I sent you? Write me. Sincerely, Langston." Earlier that year, Hughes had left New York for Los Angeles where he established the New Negro Theater (NNT), a West Coast equivalent of his Harlem Suitcase Theater. Hughes's play *Don't You Want to Be Free* had inaugurated the initial 1938 Suitcase Theater season, and Hughes also used it to open the NNT. Apparently, Hughes planned for *The Organizer* to follow *Don't You Want to Be Free* at the NNT in 1940, as it had in New York, but this never took place.[55]

There was, however, more exciting news to come for their opera. Schaffer Horatio had arranged for The International Ladies Garment Workers' Union to incorporate *The Organizer* into their annual program. The ILGWU had retained Leonard De Paur to organize a male chorus with the aid of the Harlem Labor Center.[56] The ILGWU Cultural Division, known as Labor Stage, presented its sixth annual program at the Windsor Theater on March 10, 1940. The multi-ethnic program included Jewish, Negro, and Italian "New York Choruses," along with a symphony orchestra and string ensemble. The "Negro Chorus," under the direction of De Paur, performed "Plantin' Plowin' Hoein'" from *The Organizer*. Dorothy Harrison, who played the Organizer's woman in the Suitcase Theater production, was the soloist. The year before, Harrison became the first African American performer featured in the 1939 edition of

Pins and Needles, the Labor Stage musical written by Harold Rome that became a renowned left-leaning production of that time.[57] The full concert version of the opera was performed as part of the ILGWU Convention Festival Concert by the ILGWU Symphony Orchestra and the Negro Chorus, directed by De Paur, in Carnegie Hall on May 31. The members of the Suitcase Theater troupe, which included Dorothy Harrison and Organizer understudy Robert Earl Jones, sang all the parts in this production. De Paur may have been assisted on the vocal arrangements by Eva Jessye, who was a student of Will Marion Cook during the 1920s. Her Original Dixie Jubilee Singers (later the Eva Jessye Choir) appeared in the 1929 King Vidor film *Hallelujah*. She was the choir director for the Gertrude Stein/Virgil Thompson work *Four Saints in Three Acts* and may be best remembered for her role as "unofficial" music director for the original production of *Porgy and Bess*. She is not mentioned on the programs for *The Organizer*, and her possible role did not become apparent until decades later when a copy of the vocal arrangement was discovered among her papers.

The parts include The Organizer, baritone; The Woman, contralto; The Old Man, bass; The Old Woman, soprano; Brother Dosher, tenor; and The Overseer, bass. The Carnegie Hall program includes the following synopsis:

> The scene opens upon the interior of a sharecropper's cabin in the deep south. It is night. A group of sharecroppers is waiting for the Organizer to arrive. They are telling of their hard lives, their "plantin', plowin', hoein'." One cropper sings of his "Hongry Blues." An old woman tells that she "done washed so many clothes her hands is white as snow." The Organizer's woman enters, giving the password, "Jericho," repeated three times, and brings with her leaflets telling about the union.
>
> She sings of her man, the Organizer, and of how lonely she is when he goes away, but "tomorrow he'll be with me and tomorrow we'll be free."
>
> The meeting becomes restless and impatient, waiting for the Organizer. Finally a man's voice is heard giving the password, "Jericho," and the meeting sings, "It's the Organizer, Glory be."
>
> The Organizer tells that when "we got a big strong union, folks, a union of black and white, there'll be more difference in this old South than there is 'twixt day and night."
>
> Suddenly, loud shouts are heard outside, and the Overseer of the plantation comes in. He tells the meeting, "The landlord don't allow no organizin, here."
>
> A scuffle follows, and the Overseer flees. The meeting joins in a final song and shout, "Right, Right, Fight, Fight—we organized a union here tonight . . ."

The "Hungry Blues," sung near the beginning of the first scene by Brother Dosher, establishes the overall themes of choice and self-determination. The lyrics boldly present the notions of poverty, hunger, racism, and the false choices of lying, crying, or dying as the only means of response:

> Just poor sharecroppers, yes!
> But we ain't gonna be always.
> We gonna get together
> And end these hongry days.
> Folks I've got them hongry blues—
> And nothin' in this world to lose.
> People's tellin' me to choose
> 'tween dyin',
> and lyin',
> and keepin' on my cryin'—
> But I's tired o' them hongry blues.
> Listen! Ain't you heard de news?
> There's another thing to choose:
> A brand new world, clean and fine,
> Where nobody's hongry and
> There's no color line!
> A thing like that's worth
> Anybody's dyin'—
> Cause I ain't got a thing to lose
> But them dog-gone hongry blues.[58]

The Organizer's woman enters and introduces the message of fairness and justice for the hard work of the croppers. She sings a lament about her personal sacrifice of being away from her man the Organizer for such long periods. The Organizer arrives, encouraging the group that joining with the union is the only way to ensure justice. He reassures, "De poor white folks is with us. / De rich white folks is mad." Hughes weaves the essence of the John Henry story, including the character of the man, into that of the Organizer as sung by the Organizer's Woman. The struggle between man and machine has become the struggle of race and class as the Organizer "put his hammer down" and "don't drive steel no more,'" instead directing his strength, fearlessness, and honesty toward "organizin' de poor" and to "take this world in hand." Fritz Mahler (his father was cousin to composer Gustave Mahler) was a good choice as conductor of the symphony orchestra playing Johnson's operatic score. Mahler had been musical director of Philadelphia's La Scala Opera Company shortly after immigrating to the United States in 1935, and in 1939 became director of the opera department of the Juilliard summer school. Leonard De Paur had a distinguished career as a choral conductor, arranger, and composer. He first attracted attention as an associate conductor of the Hall Johnson Choir. His De Paur Chorus was organized within the 372nd Infantry Regiment during World War II and toured extensively after the war. There was another man working with ILGWU at the convention who would become one of Johnson's most important patrons a few years later.

In 1929, a company called Radio Labs was established in New York by a struggling radio technician named Moses Asch. He was hoping to find his niche in the newly emerging technology, initially focusing on radio repair. By 1936, Asch developed the more profitable business of sound systems. At that time, he worked primarily for political campaigns and Yiddish organizations. (Asch's father was the noted Yiddish writer Sholem Asch). Soon, the ILGWU began calling on Asch for work. In 1938, the Yiddish radio station WEVD contracted Asch and Radio Labs to build a radio transmitter for their new, larger location at 117 West 46th Street. Given the size of this project, Asch decided to relocate his company to the WEVD building. A new venture emerged with the growing need for noncommercial recordings exclusively for radio broadcast, steering clear of the musicians' union protests about airing commercial recordings. Asch built the first of his legendary recording studios at that location, devoted then to programs for WEVD. Asch provided the sound system for the ILGWU convention of 1940.[59] Given his attraction to socially conscious and ethnic music, his interest was likely high, especially since the Windsor Theater production included the Yiddish Chorus. Asch had dabbled briefly in electric guitars, but except for a brief encounter with Les Paul, up until that time, seemed to have little exposure to jazz. He would soon expand his recording business into folk and ethnic music, spoken word recordings, and jazz.

Asch recorded some of the most important work of James P. Johnson. It is intriguing to speculate that Asch and Johnson may have first crossed paths at the convention, or that Asch had at least first become aware of Johnson there. Johnson's first Asch recordings date from July 1942. Asch would provide a seemingly unencumbered recording opportunity for Johnson and other musicians. Asch allowed Johnson, as well as Mary Lou Williams, to record as piano solos some of their works which would never be considered by the larger, commercial recording companies. Williams described Asch's broadminded recording philosophy: "If you only burped, Moe recorded it."[60] Johnson recorded *Yamekraw*, portions of his *Jassamine* concerto, and the tone poem *Drums*, but he did not memorialize any pieces from *The Organizer* for Asch.

The ILGWU production of *The Organizer* was in rehearsal by October 1939. Johnson wrote to Hughes that he set a new song for the work titled "Glad to See You Again." It does not appear in the extant versions of Hughes's libretto or in Jessye's score, but a draft in Johnson's papers identifies the tune as a duet between The Organizer and The Woman, and where in the piece it is to be included. Professor and jazz pianist James Dapogny, who played a pivotal role in restoring *The Organizer*, states, "I believe that Johnson and Hughes felt that this love duet represented a kind of personal, intimate moment of a sort that their original version had lacked and, following the performance, decided to add the piece."[61]

For nearly sixty years, the only known music from *The Organizer* included two recorded jazz band versions of "Hungry Blues" by Johnson waxed in March and June 1939 for Columbia Records. The tune was not copyrighted by Bregman Vocco and Conn until twenty years later, and never published. The sessions were organized by the legendary (and in some corners controversial) promoter and A&R man John Hammond. Hammond held a deep admiration for Johnson. He frequently cites his early exposure to Johnson's music in the 1920s as epiphanal. He told an interviewer in 1961, "The record that changed my life is still with me. We had a big Victrola in the front parlor, but the Columbia Gramophone that the servants listened to in the back was where I heard my first jazz recording, James P. Johnson's 'Worried and Lonesome [Blues].'"[62] Over the years, he did much to promote Johnson's work. He included him in both of the historic "Spirituals to Swing" concerts of 1938 and '39 and would later write a moving obituary for him. The recordings are small band swing arrangements, the first listed as Jimmy Johnson and his Orchestra, the second as James P. Johnson and his Orchestra.

The instrumental personnel was outstanding and included Henry "Red" Allen, trumpet, J. C. Higginbotham trombone, Fats Waller's tenor man Gene Sedric, and his guitarist Al Casey on the first session, all driven by drummer Big Sid Catlett. Pops Foster played bass on the second session. Anna Robinson, on the first recording, was a new Hammond "discovery" whose voice he thought might rival Billie Holiday. Her career as performer included work at two of Harlem's most noted venues, as a dancer at the Cotton Club and later as a comedic singer at Monroe's Uptown House (previously the site of Barron Wilkin's Club, and, as Monroe's, a bebop incubator like Minton's). Although she was a prolific and clever composer, she was rarely credited on her tunes. Her tumultuous and uninhibited personal life, including a struggle with heroin addiction, led to a violent death.[63] Her two recordings with Johnson, "Harlem Woogie" (two takes) and "Hungry Blues," are her only known commercial recordings. Her voice has elicited strongly opposing impressions. One reviewer at the time was unapologetic, writing, "Nothing is more exasperating than to have an otherwise excellent disk marred by hogcalling disguised as singing. A vocalist should either sing good or else be muzzled by the record companies. I refer specifically to . . . the noise made by Anna Robinson on Vocalion's 'Harlem Woogie' played by

James P. Johnson's band."[64] A more current reviewer commented on her treatment of "Hungry Blues," writing, "Robinson's method of handling this politically outspoken opus was powerful, gutsy and hauntingly bittersweet."[65] The vocalist on the second session is thought to be Ruby Smith, Bessie Smith's niece. Despite a signed contract with Columbia for the June recording and Hammond's support, neither version of the "Hungry Blues" was released at the time.[66] CBS solicited scripts from Hughes for a new dramatic series titled "The Pursuit of Happiness." He sent them *The Organizer*, but CBS rejected it, writing that the material was ". . . too controversial for us to give it an emotional treatment on an essentially dramatic show."[67] As a musical work of social protest, "Hungry Blues" belongs alongside two other notable protest songs of the era, "Black and Blue" and "Strange Fruit," the latter recorded only a month later.

The Organizer was performed several more times over the next two years. The ILGWU included it in a program at the New York World's Fair on September 2, 1940, with selections from *Pins And Needles*,[68] and in four performances at Madison Square Garden in October 1940.[69] Under the direction of Robert H. Gordon, Labor Stage combined "I Hear America Singing," the dance number "Mene, Tekel" featured by Dorothy Harrison in *Pins And Needles*, and *The Organizer* for weekend performances in December.[70] There may have been one additional performance at Labor Stage on April 25, 1942.[71] After that, the score had been presumed lost. The work took on legendary status as a lost collaboration between two luminaries of the Harlem Renaissance until the serendipitous discovery of the vocal score in 1997 by James Dapogny in the papers of Eva Jessye at the University of Michigan.

From 1935 through 1938, Johnson spent considerable time working to gain exposure for his symphonic pieces. But he also had to pay the bills. He continued performance in a variety settings. As the worst of the Depression began to lift, he took the orchestra he had maintained for local gigs in Queens beyond the borough. They were engaged for the season opening of the Hotel Park Lane on May 30, 1936, in Port Jervis, New York.[72] He reunited with Bessie Smith in March 1936, backing her when she sang during a dance contest at the Savoy Ballroom. Also on the bill were her old friend Mildred Bailey, who had encouraged her to participate, and newcomer Ella Fitzgerald, along with the bands of Chick Webb, backing Ella, and Fess Williams.[73] On July 19, 1936, Johnson joined the Elite Social Club at Lottie Joplin's Studio, 212 West 138th Street, for a fund raiser for the Harlem Camp Funds for poor children. Also appearing were W. C. Handy and J. C. Johnson.[74] Most notably, in April, he was leading his band at the Savoy Ballroom,[75] a relationship that likely saw him there several times during this period, because he listed the Savoy as his employer on loan applications. The Brooklyn Urban League held their gala benefit at the Brooklyn Academy of Music on May 8, 1938, in a production titled *Swing to Opera*. It was a star-studded affair with entertainment that included Ivie Anderson, Duke Ellington, Fats Waller, Teddy Wilson, Lionel Hampton, Hazel Scott, Johnson, and many others.[76] Locally in Jamaica, Johnson and his "Rhythm Masters" produced a floor show for the gala opening of the New Rainbow Room of the 99 Inn in November 1938. They then played every Thursday, Saturday, and Sunday through December.[77] His most popular tunes from the decade before, including "Charleston," "Old Fashioned Love," "I Need Lovin'," and "If I Could Be with You" continued to throw off small but regular royalties.[78]

Between all this activity with his orchestra and attention to his symphonic composing, Johnson was continually drawn to the informal night life of Harlem. Pianist Joe Turner recalled that Johnson still frequented many rent parties, despite objections from wife Lillie Mae:

> James P. loved competition. Jam sessions he loved, and for this reason he would go home rather late. We would have our jam session until two or three the next afternoon. He was then living on Long Island, and his wife would come all the way to Harlem, and she would go from street to street until she heard the piano. And she would recognize his style, and then she would go up to the apartment to get him out of there and take him home. He was not the kind of fellow who would look around for women or anything. He just loved to play the piano.[79]

Late-night eating and drinking remained a habit of Johnson and his close friends and associates. Maud Mapp Osborne recalled nights in 1937 when Johnson, Razaf, Waller, Handy, Marion Hairston (of *Mad Manhattan*), Ted Yates, Maurice Dancer, Leonard Harper, and others stayed at Mike's Restaurant (Seventh Avenue and 143rd Street in the cellar) until closing. "We drank seventeen 'shorties' of likker that night, ate twelve orders of spaghetti and Italian Sausage and Ralph Bastone, the manager, who now owns a piece of the 845 Club, there at the time, only charged us $12.70. We all chipped in and paid the bill as those were the good days when everyone knew each other and more often than not, we went dutch on our all night jamborees," she recalled.[80] The Johnsons were often host to many friends at their home in Jamaica, especially the Wallers. Maurice Waller recalled the family visits:

> Some Sundays the family would go out to South Jamaica to visit James P. and Lil Johnson. Their children, James Jr. and Oceola [sic], were the same age as Ronnie and me, so it was a trip we always looked forward to because it gave us the opportunity to play in the "country" with kids our own age. When I was a child I never realized how brilliant a pianist James P. was. A shy, retiring man, he had long ago given up the clamor of

the business. Jimmy had elected to live off of the income from his record and writing royalties. Jimmy Jr. played piano and we'd jam together just like our fathers. Oceola sang and danced and we had a good little act going there. Lil Johnson was one of my favorite women. Outspoken, with a mouth capable of making any man blush, she was also a lovable, generous woman—who more than once belted me across the jaw for talking out of turn or being wild.

Ronnie and I were always excited when Buster [Shepard, a cousin] picked us up to go to the Johnson house. It was a special treat. Clarence Williams and Eva Taylor lived across the street from the Johnsons, so the entire day was a social event. We ran through the backyards and played up a storm. When we were called in there were two pianos to play. We thought the place was paradise.[81]

The slower pace of Long Island also appealed to Fats Waller, who moved his family out of Harlem around 1939. Lillie Mae Johnson recalled how Fats talked his way into the Johnson parlor (as he had done many years earlier) to work out new ideas without disturbing his own family. "I sold Fats his house—just a few blocks from ours, and every once in a while, he'd come in at four or five in the morning to go to bed here. He'd say 'The kids are too noisy over at my house,'" she recalled.[82]

Sometime around late May 1937, Fats Waller bought himself a birthday present—a home disc recorder.[83] To celebrate his thirty-third birthday and try out the new device, he invited his best buddies to his home. His guests included Eubie Blake, James P. Johnson, and Willie "The Lion" Smith, among others. Their itineraries serendipitously had them all in New York at the same time, a rare occurrence. Fats passed around the microphone for comment from each guest. The proceedings are a brief but revealing document of Harlem lore. After a piano introduction by Willie "The Lion," Blake starts off by acknowledging Johnson as his "envy for life" and the "greatest pianist that I have ever known, of our race," with Waller in agreement saying, "Them sentiments is mine, too." Waller hands the microphone to Johnson, who calls him by his nickname, Big Filthy, a name given him by Willie "The Lion" Smith decades earlier. It is a nostalgic reference to their early days romping around Harlem. Waller responds by telling Johnson he'll meet him at the Daisy Chain, the Harlem boardinghouse/bordello run by Hazel Valentine, for whom Waller composed his stride piano instrumental "Valentine Stomp." Johnson responds enthusiastically with "right on!" But Waller may have made the Valentine reference to remind Johnson of the time the pianists and Valentine were joyriding in Johnson's new Cadillac, which, upon arriving back at the Daisy Chain, was promptly repossessed for nonpayment by Johnson.[84] Smith gets his chance to chime in with an extended discourse in Yiddish, and expresses his delight at spending the afternoon with his great friends, extoling their brilliance as pianists. Arranger Ken Macomber jokingly bemoans, "I have to keep a lot of lead in the pencil" to keep up with the complexity of music he is charged with setting down. Eubie Blake recalled the event with fondness:

> We spent much of the day telling stories and recalling the early days. While there was much discussion of the early stride cutting contests, surprisingly, no challenge was given and no attempts to outdo each other at the piano were made. I guess we'd all matured somewhat by that time and were just glad to be able to get together for a private party and enjoy each other's company and companionship. After all, it had been a long time since all of us were able to socialize like that, what with the hectic pace that we had been maintaining in travelling about the country during the 'thirties. This was sort of a grand reunion, and there was much happy conversation and plenty of good food. The day passed all too quickly, and the party broke up at a rather "respectable" hour, with everyone able to navigate themselves home in a sober, or at least near-sober state.[85]

Around the time Waller moved out of the city, Johnson began to surface there more often, beginning what would amount to a second career as interest in traditional jazz increased.

Chapter 20

SPIRITUALS TO SWING, 1938-1939

> From Spirituals to Swing—Hit performers at landmark 1938 concert
> included elegant James P. Johnson.
> —JOHN HAMMOND

In mid-1938, demand for Johnson's music and playing increased. On July 2, he accompanied Fats Waller to the CBS studios for the broadcast of *Saturday Night Swing Club*. They played a remarkable four-hands version of "I Found a New Baby," with Johnson's trademark upper register right hand lacework backing Waller's vocal chorus. Johnson peppers the instrumental chorus that follows with alternating two-handed chords foreshadowing the percussive approach of pianists three decades later. His first studio recording opportunity since 1934 came in August, when Steve Smith, the proprietor of the Hot Record Society Record Shop, called Johnson to take part in a recording session. The Hot Record Society, as the name implies, was an organization of collectors and fans devoted to studying and preserving on records "hot" (traditional) jazz. These were the early days of what became a robust revival of pre–swing era jazz. The personnel recruited for this small group session included a cross-section of jazz styles from New York to New Orleans to Chicago, a session described as chaotic until the musicians measured their particular stylistic inclinations.

In the late fall of 1938, the French jazz authority and record producer Hughes Panassie came to New York to record. The author of the influential *Le Jazz Hot*, published in the United States in 1936 as *Hot Jazz*, Panassie had been anxious to undertake this project for some time, and arranged to record his favorite musicians, so the story goes. One of his favorites was white clarinetist Milton "Mezz" Mezzrow, an impassioned advocate of African American culture, civil rights, and marijuana. The year before Panassie arrived, Mezzrow had attempted to present a mixed-race band on stage at the Harlem Uproar House, which was not in Harlem but in midtown Manhattan at 51st and Broadway. He met only resistance. As the only white member of the band, it seems he ultimately achieved his goal by positioning himself as the leader, rather than as an egalitarian group he had called the Disciples of Swing. His band included Teddy Bunn, guitar, Tommy Ladnier and Sydney De Paris, trumpets, Elmer James, bass, Zutty Singleton, drums, and Willie "The Lion" Smith, piano. Panassie essentially used Mezzrow's working band for the first session on November 21, which appeared under Mezzrow's name. Ernie Anderson, who attended the session, recalled Fats Waller was Panassie's first choice for pianist but was unavailable, so Panassie had to "settle" for Johnson.[1] Although Panassie did not mention Johnson in his book, he held him in high regard. Waller may have been his preference, but he was hardly settling for Johnson. Despite working with nearly all of his usual personnel, Mezzrow recalled that the session did not go smoothly. The plan was to record several tunes with a strong blues feeling. One tune, "Comin' on with the Come On," was recorded in two parts, the first as a slow blues, and the second as an up-tempo number. De Paris insisted on playing modern swing riffs which, according to Mezzrow, did not complement the blues playing of the others. Mezzrow recalled that Johnson and Ladnier became disgusted with the way things were going and began drinking heavily. "Swingin' for Mezz," the last tune, was recorded without piano and second trumpet after Johnson and Ladnier had walked out in a drunken stupor.[2] The records were panned by *Billboard*.[3] "James P. showed up drunker than I've ever seen him before or since," recollected Anderson, also observing, "I found the mood more of an undisciplined rout than a serious musical occasion. Mezz, who dominated proceedings, was at his abysmal worst, according to one critic."[4]

Panassie recorded three additional sessions. Perhaps because of the experience on the first session, Johnson did not participate on the second and third. On January 13, 1939, the last, Johnson played again in a very different band, with trumpeter Frankie Newton and His Orchestra. Mezzrow and Johnson were the only holdovers from the first session. The other musicians were Pete Brown, alto sax, Al Casey, guitar, John Kirby, bass, and Cozy Cole, drums. This grouping clicked. This session received highly favorable reviews. One reviewer noted, "The best of the Hughes Panassie combinations is that headed by Frank Newton, judging by the Bluebird of 'Rosetta' and 'The World Is Waiting for the Sunrise.' This is enticing jazz by any standard, and the solos are exciting, particularly those of Pete Brown on alto sax and James P. Johnson, the pianist who taught Fats Waller."[5] Another reviewer commented, "Here are the last of the Hughes Panassie recordings, and they are just about the best of this Bluebird series. After hearing James P. Johnson romping all over the keyboard on

'Who?,' you realize very few pianists can touch this old master."[6] The session garnered considerable praise from the college scene. The *Barnard Bulletin* noted that despite his long tenure on the jazz scene, Johnson's playing had not lost its swing, observing, "Out of the past also comes another great performer, James P. Johnson (piano), who is outstanding in the records issued by Frankie Newton and his Orchestra."[7] These reviews, while laudatory, frame Johnson as a relic of the past. Johnson had been out of the jazz mainstream for most of the decade. He was, in many ways, newly discovered by this younger generation. If he was a relic, he could still impress, and at the height of the swing era, playing with swing musicians, didn't come across as old fashioned. Johnson was back in the recording studio on February 1, his forty-fifth birthday, this time for Decca, to record behind blues singer Rosetta Crawford with most of Mezzrow's original band, except for Sidney De Paris. Johnson was the titular leader with the group, dubbed the "Hep Cats." When it was finally released in the summer, *Down Beat* included it as one of the best "race records" of the month.[8] In December 1941, Ross Russell, writer, record shop owner, future founder of Dial Records, and producer of seminal recordings of Charlie Parker, wrote a feature article about Johnson for the short-lived magazine *Jazz Information*. About the Crawford sessions, he puts a fine point on Johnson's relevance and freshness, writing [underline emphasis is Russell's]: "The two opening choruses on his Decca 'Stop It, Joe' (Rosetta Crawford) show that here is still the piano with more <u>pure swing</u> than any other in the business, not excepting Hines or Waller—and that with a minimum of effort, with greater economy than ever before. Here is no faded relic or dated exhibit, no tricky musical scholar or effete, meretricious Gershwin. Here literally, freshened by the latest acoustical advances, is the true grandfather."[9] Russell vigorously promoted bebop when it burst forward several years later. But he never lost his affection for Johnson, writing in personal correspondence many years later, "He was a grand person and is one of my favorite players...."[10]

♪

By the late 1930s, John Hammond was a well-known figure in the world of jazz and American music. His ambition was to bring the music of African Americans to a wider audience, and the vehicle he chose was a mammoth concert before an integrated audience in one of America's great concert halls. His goal was achieved with the now legendary "Spirituals to Swing" concerts, produced at Carnegie Hall. For the first concert of December 23, 1938, he presented a lineup of performers representing nearly every phase of American Black music. It was a smashing success, if a little unorganized. Its emphasis was on the blues and was dedicated to the memory of Bessie Smith, who had died tragically in an automobile accident the year before. Hammond had lined up Robert Johnson, but he was killed under mysterious circumstances in August. Count Basie, his recent discovery, was signed on as the headliner. By December 1938, Basie's band had exploded into stratospheric popularity. John Hammond first talked up and wrote about the band in 1936 after hearing their late-night broadcasts on an obscure Kansas City radio station. In January 1938, Hammond coaxed Benny Goodman into featuring Basie and many of his sidemen in Goodman's own historic Carnegie Hall concert. Basie's "economical," rhythmically precise piano style that drove his big band was infectious. Although it was likely invisible to most listeners, he never disavowed his roots in stride piano. Basie told an interviewer only a few months before the first "Spirituals to Swing" concert, "My real ambition is to have my band shouting," just as the piano masters who tutored him did on the keyboard. He acknowledged the interest taken in him by Johnson, Waller, and Willie "The Lion" Smith, from whom he learned how to break up his chords and how to execute.[11] Years later in 2007, at Johnson's induction into the ASCAP Wall of Fame, emcee and bassist John Clayton specifically referenced Basie's personal remark to him about the importance of Johnson's influence on him.

With Basie, Hammond had the perfect combination of blues and swing. And with the affair dedicated to Bessie Smith, Johnson's inclusion was a natural choice for Hammond, bringing to the stage the man who played a pivotal role in the careers of both Basie and Smith. Pre-concert notices highlighted Johnson's historic role as Smith's accompanist. At the concert, Johnson backed Ruby Smith, a niece of Bessie's by marriage, as part of the tribute.[12] Also on the program were Helen Humes, the boogie woogie pianists Albert Ammons, Pete Johnson, and Meade Lux Lewis, blues singer Joe Turner, Sister Rosetta Tharpe, Mitchell's Christian Singers, Sidney Bechet and his New Orleans Feetwarmers, Sonny Terry, and Big Bill Broonzy, who replaced the slain Robert Johnson. Hammond describes the lengths he went to to attract "authentic" gospel and blues musicians from the South.[13] Hammond made good use of Johnson's versatility. In addition to backing Ruby Smith, Johnson played in Bechet's New Orleans group, and was featured on at least one solo, "Carolina Shout." *Down Beat* referred to him as the "Dean of Negro Pianists."[14]

To finance the first concert, Hammond secured support from the Marxist weekly magazine *New Masses* after being turned down by the NAACP and the ILGWU. Hammond was never a member of the communist party but was dedicated to social and racial justice. This would have naturally led to interactions with more serious activists. He insisted, however, that *New Masses*, in promoting the concert, not interject any of their political views. *New Masses* seems to have abided Hammond's request. Although Johnson was beginning to nurture similar associations, especially with his growing friendship with Langston

Hughes, there is no indication his participation in "Spirituals to Swing" was in any way related to these leanings. Hammond supported Johnson's music and musicianship and chose him for both concerts out of this artistic admiration. The concert was oversold. Three hundred attendees were accommodated by seating them on the stage. Master of ceremonies Charles Friedman failed to show, forcing Hammond to assume that responsibility, a new one for him. Hammond had the foresight to have this and the following year's concerts recorded on acetate disc. Years later, while working for Vanguard Records, he convinced them to issue the concerts on LP, which, he claimed, sold more than one hundred thousand copies.[15]

On December 24, 1938, Johnson was interviewed by Alan Lomax, curator of the Folk Music Division of the Library of Congress. Lomax had devoted much of his career to recording the works and reminiscences of folk musicians. Many of his recordings were made in the field, at southern work camps, in small towns, and at prisons. Lomax, who knew Hammond and was aware of the "Spirituals to Swing" concert, arranged to interview and record a number of the performers the next day under the auspices of the WPA. At Haver's studio in New York, Lomax recorded Johnson playing some of his own tunes ("Stop It Joe," "Snowy Morning Blues"), tunes by other pianists ("Bull Diker's Dream," "Pork and Beans") and reminiscing about his early life and other musicians. Always shy and proper in public, Johnson was reluctant to sing the bawdy lyrics to an old-time blues tune. Lomax eventually succeeded in coaxing from Johnson a few of the verses. Johnson would no doubt have preferred to talk about his ambitions as a serious composer. Lomax's focus on the blues while interviewing Johnson have led some to conclude that Lomax may have confused James P. Johnson with Pete Johnson. The catalogue listing for James P. Johnson in the Library of Congress has a notation that the recordings are "by a blues singer from Kansas City," but this is crossed out. Pete Johnson was from Kansas City, and the boogie-woogie trio of Albert Ammons, Meade Lux Lewis, and Pete Johnson was also featured at "Spirituals to Swing," and interviewed and recorded by Lomax on the same day. Joe Turner, the blues singer from Kansas City, also performed at Hammond's concert. The presence of another musician named Johnson, and Turner the blues singer, may have led to the confusion. While Lomax may have known less about James P. Johnson and the jazz tradition of the Northeast, during the interview he asks Johnson about "fast numbers" and inquiries about ragtime. Lomax might have confused the musicians, but the catalogue mislabeling was more likely a clerical error.

The last large-scale stage show of the decade using a Johnson score was produced on Broadway at the dilapidated Nora Bayes Theater. Written and produced by Michael Ashwood, *Policy Kings*, which opened on December 29, 1938, was, from a production standpoint, nearly a complete disaster. The show suffered from preproduction chaos and delay, the nature of which is not entirely clear, but one can guess that *Policy Kings* struggled with more than its share of financial and contractual problems. Johnson and Ashwood had been working on it since the late spring, and managed to put on an early edition for a Harlem Children's Fresh Air Fund fundraiser in June.[16] The book was a comedic treatment about the numbers racket in Harlem, and loosely based on the high-profile trial of numerous mobsters including Dutch Schultz that finally ended during the summer. Ashwood and Johnson may have made additional changes based on the well-publicized trial. A special public preview on December 24 supported the *Amsterdam News* Christmas Fund.[17] The reviews imply the production went off with poorly rehearsed performers of little talent. Of the few aspects praised by the reviews was the fact that the show opened at all. The score, in particular Johnson's music, was the only other bright spot cited almost unanimously:

"Michael Ashwood wrote it and James P. Johnson composed the score. This last is not bad . . . as it [the show] is—well, the music is O.K."[18]

"Despite the fact that a large orchestra appeared to be indulging in a sort of battle royal in the pit, and most of the large chorus preferred to express their own individuality in dancing rather than to be regimented into orderly figures, James P. Johnson's music actually survived those untoward circumstances, and emerged with something of a real swing in it."[19]

"*Policy Kings*, the Harlem musical comedy which opened at the Bayes last night, has a score by James P. Johnson that is worthy of a better fate than to be hitched to *Policy Kings*. There are tunes to set your feet tapping, and tunes for you to hum as you go out. One of the best, a blues song, is named for District Attorney Dewey, and he does not need to feel badly about it either. Many a dance orchestra about town will probably be playing 'You, You, You' too before 1939 is very old."[20]

"Perhaps it would be kinder not to say anything at all about Michael Ashwood's *Policy Kings*, which opened at the Nora Bayes Theater on West Forty-Fourth Street last Friday night, because with the exception of some really catchy tunes by James P. Johnson, there is nothing to recommend it to a discriminating theater-going public."[21]

"Taking its cast from the lesser light of the profession, it had nothing to turn to but the well-written music of J. P. Johnson when acting and plot started to lag and bore."[22]

"James P. Johnson has fashioned a creditable score for the musical. In fact, there are two or three numbers that may yet reach the radio and the records."[23]

Billboard praised acrobatic dancer Irene Cort, singer Cora Green, and Johnson's tunes that it called "catchy and thumping."[24] Dancer and singer Hattie Welch, mother of guitarist Freddie Green's son Alfred Green, was in the show and recalled: "I stayed there [the Black Cat] a long while until I met a woman who was a voice teacher. The next thing I knew she had put me in this show called 'The Policy King.' Kenny Clarke, the drummer who had worked with us at the Black Cat, was also in this show. The money was good because we had to join Equity [actors' union]. Jimmy Johnson wrote beautiful music for the show. We had to rehearse all day on Christmas. I had a hot dog for my Christmas dinner. The next day the show closed and so did my show business career."[25] The publication of most of the production numbers compensated Johnson somewhat for the failure of the show. By the opening, *Policy Kings* was in deep financial trouble and closed after three performances. The self-effacing all-Black musical was on the wane but not dead, and, despite the quality of his work, it remained the predominant stage outlet for Johnson's composing. Comments made in the reviews support the notion that this type of production had run its course. Yet, the public continued to attend such productions expecting the self-parody and stereotypes of the minstrel show. Herbert Drake in the *New York Herald Tribune* remarked, ". . . this newest sepia musical lacks nearly everything shows of its genre are supposed to have." He elaborates, "You expect some fine dancing, at least. . . . the comedians are expected to be uninspiring in a Harlem show. . . ."[26] Herrick Brown's comments in the *New York Sun*, while complimentary of Johnson's music, otherwise rely on blatant stereotypes. He writes, "Not that there aren't some good dusky steppers in *Policy Kings*, for there are. Here again we claim an assist for Mr. Johnson, however, for anybody with rhythm in them—and what Negro hasn't?—could dance to those tunes."[27] John Hammond, in Johnson's obituary, touched upon the overly long-lived prejudices of Broadway and its perpetuation of the minstrel legacy:

> As a writer of show tunes Jimmy was the equal of Gershwin, Youmans, and Kern, but the prejudices of Broadway producers and publishers confined him to the all-Negro musicals, which rarely found favor on Times Square.
>
> He wrote other shows, too, like *Policy Kings*, and *Sugar Hill*, and all of them had librettos that perpetuated every miserable Negro stereotype, with blackface comics rolling eyes and dice, wild shake dancers, and tear-jerking scenes on the old plantation.[28]

Michael Ashwood attempted to revive *Policy Kings* twice. He was encouraged by the popular success of Johnson's music, most notably "You, You, You." He looked for financial backing in August 1939, using a new cast but keeping the script and score.[29] This effort was unsuccessful. In April 1941, Ashwood attempted another revival, this time with a completely rewritten script while still retaining Johnson's score. Clarence Robinson was set to stage the dances, and Joe Jordan to conduct the orchestra.[30] The show was planned for an opening at the Apollo Theater, followed by a tour through Washington, Baltimore, and Philadelphia.[31] This too never materialized.

♪

January 3, 1939, found Johnson among numerous celebrities who came out to the Empire Theater for opening night of the theatrical adaptation of DuBose Heyward's novel *Mamba's Daughters*, featuring the dramatic debut of Ethel Waters. Notables of white and African American theater and society paid homage to Waters. The attendees included Tallulah Bankhead, Arturo Toscanini, Carl Van Vechten, Dorothy Kilgallen, Will Vodery, Mack Stinette, Rev. Adam Clayton Powell, Hazel Scott, Chappy Gardner, Andy Razaf, and R. Cecil McPherson.[32] The acclaimed gangster film *Moon Over Harlem* premiered on June 22 at the Regent Theater in Harlem with great fanfare. The all-Black cast included Johnson stage associate Cora Green and friend Mercedes Gilbert. The occasion provided the first opportunity for the members of the newly established Crescendo Club to congregate at a public event, demonstrating their mission to keep alive the memory of African American composers through community activity.[33] The leadership included J. C. Johnson, president; Charles L. Cook and J. Rosamond Johnson, vice presidents; W. C. Handy, treasurer; Luckey Roberts, assistant treasurer; Henry Troy, secretary; Walter Bishop, assistant secretary; with board of directors including Eubie Blake, Chris Smith, Donald Heywood (who wrote the score for *Moon Over Harlem*), Perry Bradford, Wilbur Sweatman, and Lawrence Deas. Other members included Tim Brymm, R. C. McPherson, Porter Grainger, Joe Jordan, Wen Talbert, Edgar Sampson, Claude Hopkins, Porter Grainger, Joe Gray, Andy Razaf, Clarence Williams, Kay Parker, Will Vodery, Fats Waller, Thomas Chapelle, Fletcher Henderson, Jimmy Lunceford, Don Redman, Arthur Gibbs, Fred Norman, Henry Aroy, Will DeMont Evans, Ford Dabney, Feddie Johnson, Alonzo Govern, Eddie Green, and Jelly Roll Morton. James P. Johnson was chairman of the entertainment committee.[34] On August 20, the Club sponsored a water carnival and dance at the Lido Pool, an effort to lobby for better treatment of African American songwriters.[35] On August 30, Luckey Roberts directed an orchestral program with his Syncopated-Symphonic Orchestra at Carnegie Hall. It was sponsored by the Crescendo Club to benefit "Destitute Negro Songwriters" and the Utopia Children's Fund. The program included Roberts's compositions "Whistling Pete" and "Spanish Fandango," in addition to works by J. C. Johnson, Nathaniel Dett, James Bland, Wen Talbert, and Duke Ellington. Johnson conducted the orchestra in an arrangement of his "Steeplechase Rag" renamed "Over the Bars."[36] He played one piano solo, his signature arrangement of Gershwin's "Liza."[37] During the summer of 1939, Johnson spent a residency at the newly opened Paradise Club in Atlantic City as part of a revue.[38] In mid-September, he played a week of solo piano at Café Society.[39]

To celebrate its Silver Jubilee, ASCAP sponsored a full week of American music at Carnegie Hall, starting October 1, 1939. They empowered W. C. Handy to engage African American members of ASCAP for the "All-Negro" program scheduled for October 2. The so-called Negro Orchestra, conducted by Joe Jordan, at times joined by over one hundred voices of the combined choirs of Juanita Hall, Wen Talbert, and the Abyssinian Baptist Church, performed music ranging from minstrel tunes to symphonies. The ASCAP venture provided Johnson with the opportunity to feature his popular songwriting and orchestral composing. In the first part of the program, after a rousing version of "Lift Every Voice and Sing," excerpts from three symphonies were performed, each conducted by its composer—*Afro-American Symphony* by William Grant Still, incorrectly listed as *American Symphony* on the program; *Sketches of the Deep South*, by Charles L. Cooke; and *Harlem Symphony*, by James P. Johnson.[40] The excerpt he conducted was the second movement listed as "From Harlem," also known as "April in Harlem." The second part of the concert opened with several performances in minstrel-show format performed by members of the Crescendo Club,[41] followed by members presenting their own compositions. Johnson played behind Katherine Handy Lewis and the Wen Talbert Choir for "Charleston" and "Old Fashioned Love." On the program, J. C. Johnson is listed as the composer of "Charleston," and no composer credit is listed at all for the misspelled "Old Fashion [sic] Love." The finale consisted of, as Handy put it, "a wild orgy of blues, jazz, jitterbug and jive, now called swing, in which the following bands participated: Cab Calloway, Noble Sissle, Louis Armstrong, and Claude Hopkins." This event marked the first time Johnson led "his own compositions to victory" on the concert stage.[42] Still's prominence as a composer of symphonic works dominated the reviews of the orchestral pieces, pointing out, "Mr. Still's work was the most finished of the three...."[43] But as was the case at the "Spirituals to Swing" concerts, Johnson is represented by more than one musical genre, the only musician at the ASCAP concert to be represented as both a symphonic and popular composer.

The inclusion of "minstrel show"–inspired performances by a group of esteemed African American composers, whose admirable goal was to acknowledge the music and musicians who made it, might seem out of step at this juncture in the late 1930s. It is a striking reflection of the complex factors that led to the resilience of this archaic format that had, at its essence, a deeply racist conception of African American life and culture. The Crescendo Club was a throwback organization, populated predominantly by an older generation of composers. The minstrel show presentations sparked some controversy among younger writers who also protested that they received no exposure at the event. Johnson was, in fact, one of the youngest in the Crescendo Club, but his association with them cast him as old fashioned. He had worked with many of them over the years and held them in high regard. He seemed to find no inconsistency in abiding a minstrel show performed by his mentors and colleagues, while at the same event, conducting one movement from his symphony. Tolerating the opprobrium of the obsolete stage form might invite criticism, but it reflects Johnson's respect for the past and the quality work of his musical predecessors. He was stalwart in defending their music, and some of his own, despite the association with denigrating presentation formats. Like his admiration for Scott Joplin, which posed fewer conundrums, he was not of a mind to discard the contributions of others despite historically troubling associations. Johnson reconciled this seeming paradox by writing music for a socially conscious opera with Langston Hughes while also for a stereotype-ridden stage show in *Policy Kings*.

Johnson was very active in the recording studio in 1939, waxing twenty-nine tunes and more than thirty-five sides due in large part to the efforts of John Hammond and Perry Bradford. In anticipation of upcoming releases already recorded, the Columbia Phonograph Company announced in July that Johnson would record exclusively for them on the Vocalion label, a deal arranged by Hammond, who had started an official association with the company.[44] His first band sessions were recorded in March and included one instrumental and four vocal numbers. Hammond called on Ruby Smith for two of the vocals. Smith had had a strong reception at the "Spirituals to Swing" concert. One was a cover of her aunt's classic composition from 1927 done then in collaboration with Johnson, "Backwater Blues." Johnson's repeating riff-based orchestral arrangement for this band side is markedly different in character from his piano accompaniment for Bessie. So different, Johnson is credited alone as composer on the record label despite using Bessie's lyrics. Noted jazz writer and producer George Avakian called it "One of the great records of 1939."[45] Avakian also singled out the instrumental "After Tonight" as one of the twenty-five best records of 1939.[46] The other singer was Anna Robinson. The issued records from this date generally did not sell well, and Johnson garnered only a few dollars in royalties from the one cent net royalty contract as composer, including the new arrangement of "Backwater Blues."[47] In June, he was back in the studio for a solo date on the 14th, and another band session on the 16th with mostly the same personnel. Except for the boogie-ish solo "A-Flat Dream," none of these records were issued at the time. By the time they might have been ready for release, the lackluster sales from the first Hammond session likely dissuaded the Columbia executives from releasing them.[48]

Despite the snub from Columbia, Johnson promoted his band as his "Columbia Recording Orchestra of New York City" for performances along the East Coast. His last session for the Columbia-owned Vocalion label featured blues singer Ida Cox. Perhaps to bolster more commercial appeal, and in anticipation of his second "Spirituals to Swing" concert scheduled for Christmas Eve, Hammond tapped members of Benny Goodman's organization for the date including Charlie Christian, Lionel Hampton, and Artie Bernstein. Hammond was credited with rediscovering Cox, who had not made a record in ten years.[49] Hot Lips Page, who had rekindled some notice with his recent gig at the Onyx club, took the trumpet chair, and the unique voice of Edmund Hall was added on clarinet. On October 31, 1939, they produced one coupling for release and one rejected tune. "Deep Sea Blues" and "Death Letter Blues" garnered favorable reviews, citing the "richness and depth" of Cox's voice. Her outstanding band, including Johnson and the Goodman sextet members, "reads like the 'blue book of swing.'"[50] For unclear reasons, an additional four tunes were recorded on this date with the same band but Fletcher Henderson replaces Johnson on piano. It is unlikely there were issues between Johnson and Cox, since he accompanies her again less than two months later in the "Spirituals to Swing" concert.

On October 29, Johnson paired again on radio with Clarence Williams and Eva Taylor for the *Youth on Parade* program sponsored by Famous Furriers. Others on the program included Willie "The Lion" Smith, the Southernaires, Paul Whiteman, and Hugo Mariani and the "Marianettes." Mariani had recorded the soundtrack for the 1930 short *Yamekraw* based on Johnson's piano rhapsody.[51] On November 7, Johnson participated in the first musical event of the season for the left-wing Theater Arts Committee (TAC). The TAC produced a magazine as well as the cabaret. Its executive board included Robert Benchley, Lillian Hellman, John Garfield, and Rex Ingram.[52] The political revue was staged at the Manhattan Center, 34th Street off 8th Avenue.[53] For the program, Johnson set to music "Sweepstake Special," a poem written by the far left/communist writer/editor Solomon Funaroff.[54]

Around this time, Johnson took on the task of rehearsal pianist for a highly anticipated musical theater production titled *Swingin' the Dream*. It was a star-studded affair through and through, with contributions to the book, score, lyrics, choreography, and set design from the likes of Gilbert Seldes, Jimmy Van Heusen, Eddie De Lange, Agnes De Mille, and Walt Disney. Fletcher Henderson added orchestrations. The creation of Erik Charrell, it was a swing adaptation

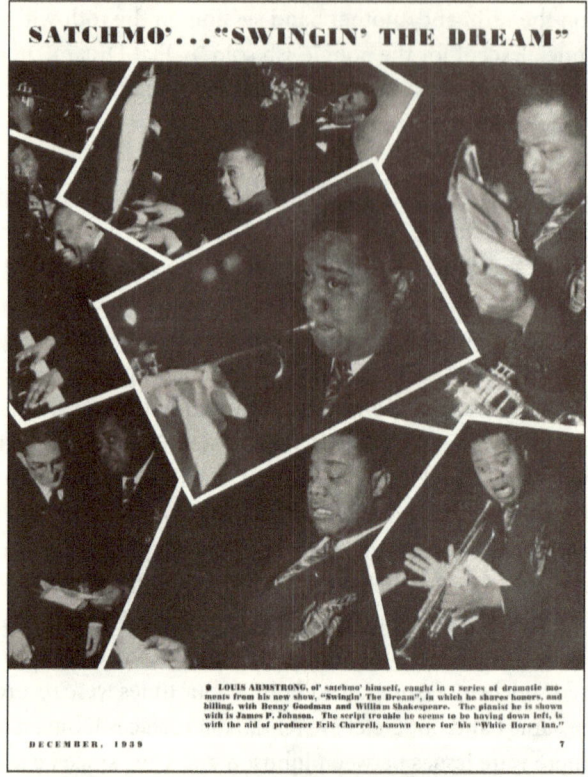

Johnson and Louis Armstrong having fun trading instruments at top left promoting the ill-fated show. (Courtesy of RIPM Jazz Periodicals)

of Shakespeare's *A Mid-Summer Night's Dream*. Set in New Orleans in 1890, it incorporated a mixed-race cast including Dorothy McGuire and Oscar Polk along with Louis Armstrong, Butterfly McQueen, the three Dandridge sisters, Maxine Sullivan, Moms Mabley, and the Savoy Ballroom Lindy Hoppers. The complex musical components included Don Voorhees leading the pit band, with scenes on stage for Bud Freeman and his Summa Cum Laude Orchestra and the Benny Goodman Sextet. As rehearsal pianist, it likely fell to Johnson to help coordinate all this musical activity for the rehearsing actors and musicians. A humorous pictorial spread in a swing music magazine showed Armstrong in various poses working on the script and music. In one, he is standing with his trumpet next to Johnson who is at the piano. In an adjacent photo, Armstrong is at the piano while Johnson stands next to him with the trumpet.[55] The show opened November 29 at the enormous five-thousand-seat Center Theater to disastrous reviews. *Billboard* cited it as "an orgy of wasted talent."[56] It played only thirteen performances before closing. One musical chestnut emerged from the otherwise ill-fated effort, Van Heusen and De Lange's song "Darn That Dream."

Johnson participated in the second "Spirituals to Swing" concert on December 24, 1939. Sponsorship this time came from the left-wing Theater Arts Committee. Sterling Brown, English professor at Howard University, served as master of ceremonies. Many of the musicians from the prior year's successful concert performed again. Benny Goodman's band was added in addition to Count Basie. The boogie woogie piano trio of Pete Johnson, Meade Lux Lewis, and Albert Ammons returned, as did Big Bill Broonzy, Sonny Terry, Sister Rosetta Tharpe, and Helen Humes. The Golden Gate Quartet and Ida Cox were new additions. Johnson was again featured in multiple contexts—playing solos on "Blueberry Rhyme" and "The Mule Walk," accompanying Ida Cox with a small group, and sitting in with the Count Basie Orchestra with Helen Humes singing his tunes "If I Could Be with You" and "Old Fashioned Love." Of Johnson's solos, one reviewer noted, "The discrimination and artistry of James P. Johnson's 'Mule Walk,' and a new composition, 'Blueberry Wine' [sic, Rhyme] were refreshing. The Old Master still rules at the keyboard and is not one bit excited about it. He is so sure he is not even troubled."[57] John Hammond did not feel the 1939 concert was as successful as the first, observing, ". . . it lacked the audience-performer rapport of the earlier concert."[58] In the advertisements, Johnson was billed as the "Grand Old Man of Jazz Piano."[59] He was forty-five.

Johnson was busy again. But whether out of expediency or necessity, Johnson and Lillie Mae as co-owners sold renewal copyrights for his most popular and successful tunes to Music Publishers Holding Corporation. The contract was executed on October 9, 1939, and for the sum of $1.00 and royalties (including an advance of $300), Johnson, his wife, and heirs relinquished control over all compositions published by Harms, M. Witmark, and Jerome Remick.[60] MPHC was formed in 1929 by Warner Brothers, who had already bought controlling interests in the three dominant publishers to serve as a copyright holding company. Many composers had such an arrangement, including the Gershwins. The twenty-one Johnson tunes included his biggest hits—"Charleston," "If I Could Be with You," and "Old Fashioned Love." Warner's interest included the placement of the tunes they held into motion pictures at a deep discount.[61] The former two tunes had more placements in movies in the decade that followed than at any other time, and ultimately Johnson was the beneficiary of the royalties.[62] Johnson took another stab at grant funding by applying to the Rosenwald Foundation, funded by Julius Rosenwald's Sears and Roebuck fortune. Awards to African American artists were one of the fund's priorities. Other recipients included Langston Hughes, W. E. B. Du Bois, James Weldon Johnson, Ralph Ellison, and other artists, but few if any musicians except Marion Anderson. In his application statement which he titled "Plans for Work," Johnson modestly noted, "I have even managed to become a member of the League of Composers . . .,"[63] as if this might be surprising to the selection committee. He tied his hopes to a strong recommendation from John Hammond, who assured Johnson he delivered one in "glowing terms."[64] Johnson did not receive the grant. He may have made another attempt with Rosenwald in 1943, again without success.[65] Musicologist John Howland, who has studied Johnson's orchestra works and the formative elements behind them in detail, draws this conclusion: "Johnson's failure to win an award of this nature by no means reflects poorly on the high quality of his concert works. It says far more about the class, race and cultural barriers of the day that impeded his artistic ambitions. Despite the rather conservative nature of Johnson's formal music studies, his actual compositions are in fact quite up-to-date in their wholehearted embrace of modern popular music in formal structure, idiomatic language, and even aspects of orchestration. This vision sought to bridge American race and class divisions, particularly among the worlds of entertainment and art."[66] Undeterred by the rejection from the gatekeepers of high art, the 1940s would prove to be highly productive, and, in a number of areas of his musical life, very gratifying.

Chapter 21

CAFÉ SOCIETY, 1939–1941

> We were going to be unlike all other nightclubs.
> —BARNEY JOSEPHSON

The "Spirituals to Swing" concerts led to New York nightclub bookings and record dates for many of the performers, most of them promoted by John Hammond. An unlikely figure arose who tapped the musical cornucopia unleashed by Hammond to create one of the legendary jazz performance venues. Barney Josephson, a shoe store owner from Trenton, New Jersey, pursued a new business vision in 1938. He had been thinking about it for a while, ever since visiting Germany in 1931. In that pre-Hitler and post-armistice environment, Josephson was struck by the depth of political commentary presented in German cabarets. Inspired by such venues that fostered serious, free discourse about current affairs, he decided to open a European-style political cafe featuring jazz in the United States. He settled on Sheridan Square in New York's Greenwich Village, where rents were cheap. Looking for talent, he first approached the performers working with the left-wing Theater Arts Committee. He was eventually introduced to artist and photographer Sam Shaw, who suggested he meet John Hammond for direction regarding the music. Hammond was in the thick of rehearsals for the "Spirituals to Swing" concert in 1938, and Josephson took him up on his invitation to attend. After one visit, he remarked to Hammond that he needn't look any further for talent.[1] Hammond and Benny Goodman each put up $5,000 to help bankroll Josephson's club, feeling an affinity for his goals of presenting mixed-race bands for mixed-race audiences.[2] Josephson recalled how Hammond, unbeknownst to him, helped prop up the salary of the musicians by making up the difference they could make from more lucrative engagements.[3]

He called the club Cafe Society Downtown. Josephson took the name for his club from the recommendation of *Vogue* editor Claire Boothe Luce. She knew of Josephson's intent to present political and social satire at the club, and suggested a phrase being used by Hearst columnist Maury Paul (who went by pen name "Cholly Knickerbocker"). In his writing he used the expression "Café Society" to describe New York's nightclub elite. Josephson thought appropriating the designation would be perfectly tongue-in-cheek for his intentions.[4]

The club promoted itself as "The rendezvous of celebs, debs, and plebs," as well as the "Wrong place for the right people." Josephson's brother Leon was a communist party member, and some accounts claim Barney's establishment was a front for party fundraising.[5] There is no question that the club became a favorite watering hole for left-leaning-politically active patrons, including many celebrities. Frequent guests included S. J. Perelman, Paul Robeson, Joe Louis, and Eleanor Roosevelt,[6] and other musicians like Billy Strayhorn, Lena Horne, and Josh White.[7] Café Society had a ten-year run as one of the most successful jazz clubs that spanned the wartime era, and the first where the stated policy did not abide segregation. A flight of stairs down led to the basement club where Josephson invested heavily to have the walls covered with satirical murals by renown artists recommended by Shaw, including Alice Stander, Abe Birnbaum, Stuart Davis, John Groth, Gregor Duncan, William Gropper, Anton Refregier, Syd Hoff, Hugo Gellert, Adolf Dehn, and Adolf Frederick Reinhardt. These were active political cartoonists who had done work for *Esquire*, *The New Yorker*, and *Washington Post*. A dance floor was surrounded by tables, with a small bandstand against one wall. The house band played three shows, with other musical features interspersed. The club was oddly shaped with obstructing pillars adding an element of architectural tension to the heated conversation and music.

James P. Johnson was one of the first musicians to play at the new club. Joe Sullivan led a successful run with his mixed-race band in early 1939 when the club opened, and Johnson led a band and jam session on Mondays, Sullivan's night off. After taking the summer off, these sessions were revived starting in November 1939 and ran until June 1940. They added afternoon jam sessions that included, at various times, Henry Red Allen, Hot Lips Page, Roy Eldridge, Zutty Singleton, Dick Wilson, Don Byas, Eugene Sedric, J. C. Higginbotham, Edmund Hall, Benny Goodman, Bernard Addison, Albert Casey, Pops Foster, Sid Catlett and Vic Dickenson.[8] One particular night in March (although it was probably repeated often), when Johnson's personnel that included Allen, Higginbotham, Sedric, Casey, Foster, and Catlett had just recorded for Vocalion, their performance at the club caught the attention of a critic, who wrote, "The result was really electrifying. All night long these lads let loose with some really stupendous swing."[9] As Hammond put it, this was when "exciting things happen down there."[10] Johnson was also playing with his own band in the evening that included Joe Thomas, trumpet, Bobby Sands, saxophone, and Yank Porter, drums.[11] In mid-September, he played a week of solo piano at Café Society.[12] Just before Christmas in 1939, Josephson promoted a Swing Festival to celebrate the one-year anniversary of the club. Jack Gilford, regular comic at the club, served as master of ceremonies for the program that featured all the regular musicians including Johnson and his band.[13]

Riding the coattails of "Spirituals to Swing," on February 3, 1940, Johnson inaugurated the first in a series of Saturday night concerts at the Park Plaza, 110th Street and 5th Avenue, sponsored by the Theater Arts Committee. Johnson's orchestra played and was followed by a complete floor show at midnight. The events were intended to attract a mixed-race audience.[14] By February, Johnson was promoting his band as the "Café Society Orchestra" and booking local gigs in the tristate area. They played for the Trenton, New Jersey, chapter of the American Institute of Banking on February 10. The next day the band played an afternoon concert for the Hot Club of Trenton at the Ewing riding club. Admission was fifty-five cents. It was to be the inaugural concert in a series of "swing sessions" produced by the club. With his regular bandmates Joe Thomas and George James, and a local rhythm section, they played for four and a half hours.[15] Johnson and his horn players returned on March 3 at the Club Condado with Pops Foster along for the ride. Their third visit to Trenton on March 31 included vocalist Maxine Sullivan, this time with Henry "Red" Allen on trumpet. All three sessions drew well over one hundred fans.[16] The treasurer of the Trenton Hot Club, and one of its founders, was Frank Trolle, who, forty years later, would write the first bio-discography of Johnson.

Johnson appeared solo in a new revue at the Elks Rendezvous cabaret at 133rd and Lenox Avenue starting the end of March 1940.[17] The next week, starting April 7, he fronted his orchestra there for a one-week run as guest band,[18] while Louis Jordan and his band subbed for him on the Monday night spot at Café Society.[19] Another legendary Greenwich Village club called Nick's was the venue chosen by Harry Lim for his Sunday afternoon jam sessions and clambakes. The Java-born Lim had immigrated to the United States the year before and quickly became a highly regarded authority on jazz and friend to jazz musicians. For his session on March 17, the band included Sidney Bechet, Henry "Red" Allen, J. C. Higginbotham, Albert Nicholas, Wellman Braud, and "Big" Sid Catlett. In an extraordinary pairing of pianists, Lim managed to arrange for both Johnson and Jelly Roll Morton for his session, alternating as band and solo pianists.[20] For all the drama during prior matchups between Morton and Johnson, and considering all that has been written about the low regard the stride pianists held for Morton, this one seemed to come off without incident. A year later, Morton would be dead.

The New York Times expectantly reported Johnson would start with his own band regularly at Café Society, and, on June 4, 1940, James P. Johnson replaced Sullivan.[21] His band included Manzie Johnson, drums, Joe Watts, bass, Gene Simon, trombone, Joe Thomas, trumpet, and George James, sax. Hammond was managing them.[22] Also performing were Hazel Scott, the Golden Gate Quartet, and the boogie woogie piano trio of Albert Ammons, Pete Johnson, and Meade Lux Lewis. The *Chicago Defender* commented, after noting Johnson's influence on "many of the top notch artists including Fats Waller," that "Youngsters coming up in the business still regard him as one of the day's greatest keyboard men. According to the manager Barney Josephson, their opening had first nighters applauding for more, which will undoubtedly mean a long stand here."[23] Although not a pianist, one of the "youngsters coming up" was trumpeter Harry "Sweets" Edison, who recalled when Basie introduced him to Johnson. He said, "It was a thrill to meet James P. Johnson and all the people I had read about and admired without thinking I'd ever be shaking hands with them. I met them through Basie. . . ."[24] One Monday night, Johnson led his Columbia Recording Band as an "all-star jam band" at Café Society. This included Henry "Red" Allen, J. C. Higginbotham, Sidney Catlett, Pops Foster, Al Casey, Gene Sedric, and perhaps others.[25]

While opening night for his own band in the featured spot at Café Society might have been a significant enough event to warrant family turnout, Johnson's wife Lillie Mae had plans of her own. The onetime actress attended a gathering honoring actress Hattie McDaniel, who had just won the Academy Award for best supporting actress in *Gone With the Wind*. The party was sponsored by the local chapter of McDaniel's sorority from her days at the University of Denver. The host was Mercedes Gilbert, longtime friend of the Johnsons since the early 1920s. She, too, had moved to Jamaica, Queens.[26] Oddly, the stay for Johnson and his own orchestra was short. For the "summer season," Johnson's band was replaced by Teddy Wilson in early July.[27] He still referred to his band as the Café Society Orchestra when on August 16, the band played a Hudson River cruise for the Omega Phi Psi fraternity annual "Showboat" social event. Their Glee Club, accompanied by Lionel Hampton on piano, the Southernaires, and Johnson's old colleague from *Plantation Days*, the comedian Eddie Green, entertained 2,700 people. July 23 started Negro Week at the World's Fair. Each day was devoted to a different aspect of African American life including the arts. Friday's program, designated swing Friday night, was devoted to recognizing popular and swing music. Master of ceremonies Willie Bryant coordinated the appearances of many members of the Crescendo Club including Johnson, Eubie Blake, Chris Smith, Cecil Mack, Ford Dabney, Tim Brymn, Joe Jordan, and W. C. Handy. Singers Alberta Hunter and Maxine Sullivan also performed, along with the Benny Carter and Tiny Bradshaw Orchestras.[28] Said one reviewer about the event, "And the swing hysteria reached such a point a few minutes later, when James C. [*sic*] Johnson and Louis Jordan rendered 'Old Fashioned Love' and 'If I Could Be with You One Hour Tonight,' that a halt had to be called."[29] The day before, on July 25, Johnson was one of several hundred entertainers who came out to celebrate the thirty-second birthday of Clark Monroe at his renowned Uptown House. Johnson had played there in years past when it was run by Barron Wilkins. Joining him were Billie Holiday, Mezz Mezzrow, Willie Bryant, Benny Carter, Walter Bishop, Al Cooper (leader of the Savoy Sultans), Maurice Dancer, Roy Eldridge, Coleman Hawkins, Louis Armstrong, Tommy Dorsey, Charlie Barnet, and Lucky Millinder, among others.[30]

Barney Josephson planned to open a new club, Café Society Uptown, on 57th Street in October 1940. The boogie woogie trio of Ammons, Pete Johnson, and Lewis, along with Hazel Scott would move to the new location. Josephson planned to reengage Billie Holiday for the Downtown club. She had completed a yearlong run in March. James P. Johnson and his band would also stay on.[31] However, on August 20, shortly after dinner, Johnson suffered the first of what would ultimately be many strokes, precluding his upcoming continuation at Café Society (he would return in 1941). His neighbors Clarence Williams, Shelton Brooks, and Fats Waller visited the next day.[32] Luckey Roberts, while interviewed from his bed in Harlem Hospital about serious injuries he had sustained in a car accident several weeks earlier, made clear that his primary concern was for the readers of the paper be informed about Johnson. He told the interviewer, "Did you know that James P. Johnson, well known orchestra leader, suffered a stroke today?" Alvin Moses, reporter for the Associated Negro Press (ANP), admitted he did not. Roberts continued, "Be sure to say something about it in your column as his many friends throughout the country will be shocked to know of it."[33] Just as Johnson appeared to be making a successful return to visible activity in the music world, he was again removed from public activity, this time to recuperate from his illness. Cliff Jackson filled in for him on his scheduled dates.[34] After the stroke, he attempted to temper his habits. For a while, he gave up all hard liquor in favor of champagne and beer, but after a few years that moderation waned. The Johnsons spent a good deal of time with Lillie Mae's family in the Pocono Mountains region of Pennsylvania. Lillie Mae's older brother William H. Wright, also a musician who played the trap drums, had been staying with them in their Jamaica home.[35] Johnson took up gardening, bird watching, and tended a few chickens. In the winters, when he was feeling up to it, he indulged in a little light skiing and continued his impressive pool playing.[36] His own half siblings, older than he but with whom he had had a close relationship growing up, were also becoming ill or dying. His sister Isabelle's apparent death at age fifty-seven and brother Frank's death at age fifty-nine were unfortunate harbingers of Johnson's own truncated longevity.

Johnson was interviewed on a number of occasions in the early and mid-1940s. One unnamed interviewer observed:

> It would take a full length novel to depict the musical career of Jimmy Johnson, the man who composed the song, "If I Could Be with You" and many other tunes. He stands about five feet five inches and weighs one hundred fifty pounds. His fingers are like those of that celebrated Polish pianist Ignace Paderewski, long and tapering. It is very hard to get him to talk about himself, because he is bashful. But when he sits before the ivory keyboard, all his bashfulness disappears. He is one of the easiest celebrities to talk to. When you meet him you feel as though you have known him for years.[37]

He was probably recovering from his stroke throughout the fall of 1940 but curiously requested a copy of the Directory of Negro Hotels and Guest Houses from the Automobile Club of New York. The Directory had been published the year before by the National Park Service Travel Bureau. On a piece of scrap paper he had listed nearly a dozen cities he planned to visit, suggesting a road tour of some kind, but no performances are known for such a tour.[38] In the 1940 census, Johnson listed his occupation as "composer." It was an expression of what he felt was the ultimate status for a musician. By January 22, 1941, he felt well enough to attend an informal dance of the Crescendo Club at the Renaissance Ballroom with numerous guests from society, stage, radio, and film.

♪

By the early 1940s, the nature of stage entertainment was again changing. In the mid-1930s, big bands had replaced the musical theater/variety stage show. In 1941, enthusiasm for bands on stage was itself waning. The war effort may also have played a role. Producers found it increasingly difficult filling bills with big bands, as so many musicians were in the service. The management of the Apollo Theater decided to "experiment" with a return to tabloid shows, hoping the throwback would appeal to some sense of nostalgia for that format. Johnson teamed with Dan Burley and Jesse Stone to write music for a revived version of the theatrical comedy *On Striver's Row*. The play was written by Abram Hill, a young playwright who, with other writers including Theodore Browne, had formed the American Negro Theater the year before in September 1940. Browne's play *Natural Man*, at one time material Johnson had hoped to use as the basis for his opera *The Organizer*, followed *On Striver's Row* at the ANT after it opened. It was apparently Burley who suggested to Hill he convert his successful play at the American Negro Theater into a musical. Leonard Harper, who had been staging chorus lines to perform along with the band headliners at the Apollo since the mid-1930s, staged the new show, with some contribution in choreography by Bill Robinson. Broadway producer E. Lee La Zaro, shifting his focus from downtown to uptown, was hoping to find potential material he could then turn around for production back on Broadway. Initially, La Zaro sought out Andy Razaf and Leonard Feather (who had already made a name for himself as writer, record producer, and composer) to write the score. Band leader Willie Bryant was being considered for the lead role, "jiving cab driver" Joe Smothers.[39] The Razaf/Feather collaboration didn't materialize, so the music was then provided by Johnson, Burley, and Stone.

On Striver's Row followed Eubie Blake's *Tan Manhattan, Up Harlem Way*, and *Tropicana* as the fourth in the series of book-based shows filling time between stage bands at the Apollo. Each show was planned for a limited one-week run.[40] With four shows daily, *On Striver's Row* ran for a week beginning March 7 at the Apollo, and was then slatted for a road tour through Washington, Baltimore, Richmond, and Philadelphia.[41] The abridged musical version of the Hill play, which ran about ninety minutes, maintained the essence of the comedic plot:

> Ruby Jackson, winner of a $150,000 sweepstakes, is an ordinary working woman whose thoughts are farthest from joining "Striver's Row" and becoming a "dicty." Mr. Van Striver, a destitute realtor who is about to be dropped from the socialite register because of his financial shortcomings, however, has a much different idea for Ruby. He convinces her that he'll "get her in society" for the mere purchase of a few expensive building lots. She and some of her friends attend the Van Striver's coming-out party for their daughter, Cobina, much to the annoyance of most of the self-styled "upper crust" guests. Still, just before the party concludes, the strivers admit it must be much more healthful to lead ordinary lives—simple, respectable lives, similar to the ways of the very Ruby Jackson and her friends whom the socialites had previously despised.[42]

Johnson led the Leon Gross Orchestra in the pit.[43] Rather than Bryant, Louis Jordan, by then a charismatic, popular alto sax player, singer, and bandleader, played the lead character of Joe Smothers, "The Jiver." Jordan had already scored numerous hits with his small band the Tympany Five, which also played in the production.[44] The show seemed to be very successful in the African American community,[45] but the "downtown" clientele was not very receptive. As a satire on upper crust society, *Variety* found it badly lacking, complaining, "'On Striver's Row' misses the boat completely as a satire on the ofay 400; it's overlong and dull for the most part. . . ." The reviewer had no better comment about the music, reporting, "... its music is poor and sadly lacking in the rhythm usually synonymous with colored entertainment." The dancing of Whitey's Lindy Hoppers and the Harlem Swing Highlanders was better received, and the reviewer thought Jordan was the standout with potential as a "novelty maestro."[46] La Zaro, concerned these reviews presaged a poor downtown reception, scuttled his plans for a Broadway run.[47] One wonders how the reviewer could have held such a dim view of the music when considering its composers. Johnson's bona fides were well established, and Burley, Stone, and Jordan went on to cornerstone contributions in the next great musical phenomenon at that time still in its infancy, rock and roll. Dan Burley had made his name first as a sports journalist, and by 1941 was drama editor of the *New York Amsterdam News*. He was also a fine pianist and composer and later in the decade would popularize a hybrid blues style he called skiffle, a progenitor of rock and roll rhythm. Pianist Jesse Stone led a hard-swinging band in Kansas City and the southwest during the 1920s and '30s. In the 1950s, working for Atlantic Records, he composed many rock and roll classics including "Shake, Rattle and Roll," "Money Honey," the first hit for Clyde McPhatter and the Drifters, as well as leading the band on other classic sessions including Chuck Willis's record of "C. C. Rider."[48] Louis Jordan would go on to become a cultural icon of rhythm and blues. None of the music from *On Striver's Row* is known to exist, but considering the pedigree of the composers, it is hard to imagine the music was "poor" and "sadly lacking" in rhythm. More likely, it was ahead of its time, a preview of what would become the lifeblood that shaped the next fifty years of American music, appreciated by the local Harlem community in 1941 but lost on the downtown audience.

From his influential perch at the *Amsterdam News*, Dan Burley had been agitating for more "flesh entertainment in place of ordinary orchestras" for some time. He had his finger on the pulse of the entertainment tastes of his community, and also knew that a large segment of the African American entertainment industry, reeling from the Depression and the domination of the big bands, could use the work. Although the first four musical theater productions of the "new" Apollo policy did not translate to Broadway, they were successful enough for Frank Schiffman, managing director of the theater. From what was initially a strategy to fill in time while big bands could be recruited, Burley's hunch was paying off locally. Schiffman actively promoted the need for entertainers for musical theater productions.[49] Johnson's presence at the Apollo continued, working with Maceo Pinkard. His *Symphonic Fantasy* played a week in Washington and Baltimore before its New York premiere at the Apollo Theater on March 21, 1941. In addition to a score composed by Pinkard, his conception incorporated symphonic orchestral adaptations of Liszt's *Second Hungarian Rhapsody*, Rimsky-Korsakov's *The Flight of the*

Bumble Bee, and Rachmaninoff's *Prelude in C-Sharp Minor*. The symphonic work of three twentieth-century African American composers was also featured. This included Don Redman's orchestration of Pinkard's popular song "Sugar," Johnson's three-movement symphonic treatment of W. C. Handy's "St Louis Blues," which he called *American Symphonic Suite*, and Will Marion Cook's *Swing Along*.[50] Johnson directed the performance of his suite. After the Apollo run, there were plans for a tour through Philadelphia, Baltimore, Washington, Richmond, and Norfolk.[51] Maude Russell, who was the star of the show, was scheduled to play the Troc club on 52nd Street on March 30 with Johnson accompanying her. The appearance was slated for one of the Sunday night jam sessions at the club sponsored by Milt Gabler, but was postponed when Johnson again fell ill.[52] Russell and Johnson were to feature his new tune "Swinga-dilla Street."[53] By the end of May, Johnson was feeling "fully recovered."[54] The tour was stymied by venue problems, but Pinkard arranged for other nearby performances including Carnegie Hall on May 27 and the American Academy of Music in Philadelphia on May 28. In larger venues, like the Westchester County Center in White Plains, New York, on May 26, and the Brooklyn Academy of Music on May 29, Pinkard arranged for "James P. Johnson and his famous Café Society Swing Orchestra" to play for dancing after the formal musical presentation.[55]

Later that year, Pinkard revised the show and planned to add Johnson's new musical comedy sketch *Kitchen Opera*, which he had written with Flournoy Miller. In September, the new version of *Symphonic Fantasy* was still in rehearsal, but it is not known if this edition with *Kitchen Opera* was ever produced.[56] Johnson had hoped for an airing of *Kitchen Opera* on CBS, but nothing seems to have come of this either.[57] Originally titled *Love in the Kitchen*, *Kitchen Opera* was similar in theme to Johnson's highly successful Smalls' Paradise production *Kitchen Mechanics Revue* from 1930. In 1944, Captain Henry Boettcher of the Special Services Division of the Writers' War Board recommended *Kitchen Opera* for the Overseas Soldier Show Entertainment Program. Before and after the war, Boettcher was chairman of the drama department at Carnegie-Mellon University. Miller had been contacted by Dorothy F. Rodgers, wife of songwriter Richard Rodgers and chairman of the Committee on Scripts for Soldier and Sailor Shows, about sending the committee the script and music.[58] There is no evidence the show was produced for the troops. No other productions are known, but Johnson and Miller thought highly of this work. Fourteen tunes were copyrighted by Mills in 1947 with a standard royalty arrangement with the songwriters.[59] In 1950, Johnson and Miller still had hopes for a production.

Johnson continued his run of productions at the Apollo the week of March 28 with a musical comedy revue produced by Irvin C. Miller called *Tan Town Topics*. Miller had just concluded the out-of-town run of his production *Tan*

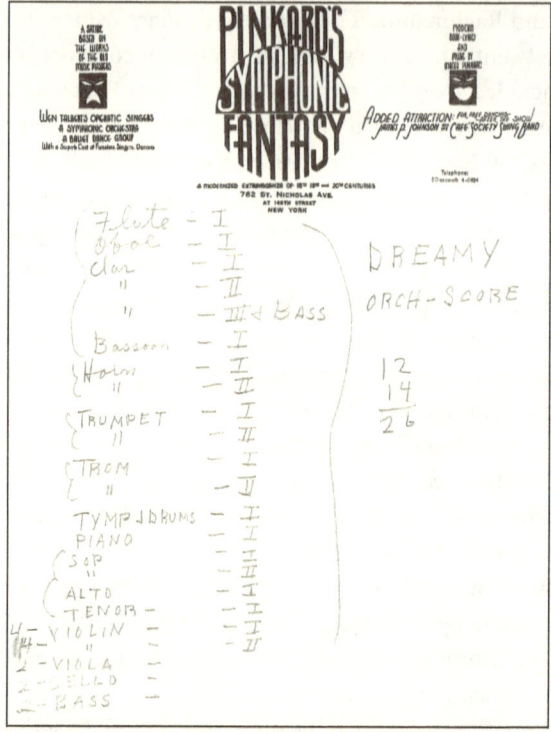

Johnson using a letterhead from Maceo Pinkard's ambitious stage production that notes his dance orchestra to sketch the orchestral parts for his one-act opera *Dreamy Kid*. (Reproduced with permission of Barry Glover, from the James P. Johnson collection [IJS.0111], Institute of Jazz Studies, Rutgers Newark)

Manhattan written by Eubie Blake, Andy Razaf, and his brother Flournoy. *Topics* included four sketches written by Flournoy Miller, including a bit about paying backstage bills. The finale included a musical battle between music of old and the current swing style.[60] The show moved to the Roosevelt Theater on May 25 without Johnson's band, but with Lester Fauntroy's Band in its place.[61]

Johnson continued his participation in numerous tribute and charity events. In May, Johnson had returned to Café Society Uptown playing piano between sets of the Count Basie Orchestra. He was replaced in October 1941 by pianist and singer Connie Berry.[62] Johnson's only trip to the recording studio was with Clarence Williams and Eva Taylor on October 22, 1941, cutting only one tune with them for Victor and released on Bluebird, the patriotic "Uncle Sammy Here I Am." The tune was co-written by Johnson, Williams, and Flournoy Miller. Recorded six weeks before Pearl Harbor, the tune was a prescient "race pride" call to arms for African Americans who already had over 175 years of unparalleled patriotism and proven valor during armed conflict. The undercurrent of the lyrics convey not only patriotism but also a plea to have an opportunity to serve in the military as escape from the amplified devastation of the Depression, still acutely felt by the Black community. By 1941, the entertainment world had largely passed by Williams and his wife Eva Taylor, who trade vocals on the recording. Williams's unabashed vaudeville-style presentation, complete with dialect and malaprops, was badly out of sync with the "jive" that had replaced it by then. Although Taylor is a much more satisfying singer, and she avoids the allusions to demeaning stereotypes, her vocal style was wrought of the early 1920s. *Down Beat* called the coupling (only one side included Johnson on piano) "two sad sides" from, "the old vet who long ago lost his potency as a recording artist . . . a far cry from the memorable classics Williams and Miss Taylor turned out some 15 years ago."[63]

Despite Williams's characteristic promotional efforts, including claims of record-breaking sales and a letter of commendation from President Roosevelt and his wife, the tune didn't catch on.[64] This was Williams's last commercial recording session. After this failed attempt at patriotism wrapped in nostalgia, Williams mostly retired from music and spent his time tending to his antique shop in Harlem. He and his wife led a comfortable life sustained by his royalties and a financial interest in his publishing company. Like Perry Bradford, Williams was responsible for numerous popular and jazz hits, and the publication and recording of many African American musicians during the 1920s and beyond, including during the depths of the Depression. And, like Bradford, he was a shameless self-promoter, attracting his share of controversy. But certainly any shenanigans he perpetrated paled in comparison to the many abusive and outright racist tactics of the white moguls of the mainstream music world. Williams was navigating a rough-and-tumble entertainment culture unfriendly if not dangerous for people of color. Judging by the content, quality, and volume of his output, he was enormously successful. It is not too much to say that jazz as we know it would be very different had there been no Clarence Williams.

♫

Johnson began to take on new students. His most famous was, of course, Fats Waller. But another future musical giant soon entered his studio. In the fall of 1941, an eight-year-old boy returned from summer camp eager to learn to play the piano. He lived in what at the time was called Sunnyside, Queens (now Long Island City), and raised in a liberal-minded Jewish household. He had spent that summer at an interracial summer camp where he heard a fellow camper, an African American boy, play boogie woogie and blues piano. He stood in the corner watching the boy play and was enthralled. A few years later, a neighbor heard him playing and suggested that he knew a man who could really teach him what he wanted to know. The boy was Mike Stoller, who would later achieve fame as part of the songwriting team Lieber and Stoller, and the teacher friend of the neighbor was James P. Johnson. Stoller took the subway out to Jamaica for regular lessons with Johnson at his home. This was a long trip for a ten-year-old, but worth the effort. Johnson taught him the basics of blues structure, and gave him careful exercises to practice. Johnson was quiet and gentle, Stoller recalled, but was sure to correct his fingering when needed. Lillie Mae was very motherly and inviting. Her shock of white hair stood out in his memory sixty years later. At the time, Stoller had only a limited understanding of Johnson's stature, and that he had been Fats Waller's mentor. It wasn't until many years later that he learned about his teacher's pioneering career in music. The songwriter for the Drifters, the Coasters, and Elvis Presley expressed the highest admiration for Johnson, and was eager to talk about his good fortune to have had such a teacher at a formative point in his musical life.[65]

By December 1941, Johnson resumed a professional relationship with his old friend Mercedes Gilbert, performing in her "One Woman Theater" at the Jamaica Presbyterian Church on December 12.[66] Gilbert had been a good friend of both James P. and Lillie Mae since the early 1920s. She had an impressive career, and is thought of as one of the most important women of the Harlem Renaissance, despite her relative obscurity today. Gilbert was accompanied by Grace Dunlap Sevier, who also provided musical interludes. Most of the program was devoted to Gilbert's musical and dramatic presentations. Toward the end of the program, Johnson played three of his most reflective if not haunting tunes, "Harlem Love Song" (the second movement from *Harlem Symphony*), "Blueberry Rhyme," and "Reflections."[67]

One of Johnson's engagements in the new year found him in the company of some of the most prominent independent jazz record producers and writers. On March 28, 1942, The New School for Social Research sponsored a jazz forum and concert to raise awareness for Russian War Relief, the organization tasked with helping our ally against Hitler. Speakers on the panel for the forum included Nesuhi Ertegun, Harry Lim, Robert Goffin, Leonard Feather, Milt Gabler, Ralph Berton, and Charles Edward Smith. The band included Johnson, Sidney Bechet, Sidney de Paris, Pops Foster as a last-minute substitute for Walter Johnson, Claude Jones, and Earl Murphy.[68] Johnson's formal association with John Hammond and Café Society was coming to an end, but new opportunities brought even more public exposure and kept him busier than ever.

Chapter 22

CONCERT HALL REALIZED, 1939–1942

> These are long works with a feeling of breadth and sweep and with a racial pungency that Gershwin missed, and their African rhythms move with a forthright nobility. One feels none of these qualities as borrowed—
> they all reside in the dark, diminutive composer himself.
> —RUDI BLESH

Through the early 1940s, Johnson continued to seek opportunities for his symphonic works. He wrote to Elizabeth Sprague Coolidge, the pianist turned chamber music champion whose quartet performances in the Berkshire Mountains of Massachusetts became the precursor to the world-renowned Tanglewood festivals. Coolidge especially favored ultra-modern music, and so Johnson's request for a performance of his four-movement *Spirit of America* string quartet that he characterized as "typically modern American" with material that included "light 'jazz,' spiritual waltz and fugal jazz rondo" probably made little impact.[1] Johnson intended that his two operas, *The Organizer* and *The Dreamy Kid*, be performed together. This never occurred in his lifetime. Around the same time that John Hammond became an important patron for Johnson in the jazz world, another man arose out of the mountain of rejections who marshalled some of Johnson's most important symphonic pieces into the concert hall.

Paul Kosok was a multitalented, somewhat eccentric man. He had joined Long Island University in the early 1930s as an instructor in history. In addition to his musical talents, an area of special interest was the exploration of ancient methods of irrigation. In particular, he made extensive studies of the pre-Columbian canal systems of coastal Peru, the so-called Nazca Lines. He

(Reproduced with permission of Barry Glover, from the James P. Johnson collection [IJS.0111], Institute of Jazz Studies, Rutgers-Newark)

made field studies there from 1939–1941, and later in the 1940s. How Kosok became aware of Johnson's symphonic work during the late thirties is unclear. But not only did he become aware, he became the music's most important champion. On March 11, 1939, in the Sculpture Court of the Brooklyn Museum, The Brooklyn Civic Orchestra (a community organization "open to all qualified players") sponsored by Long Island University presented their fourth concert of the Schubert Festival. The first half of the concert included only compositions by Franz Schubert. The second half presented all four movements of the *Harlem Symphony*, the first known performance of the complete work. This performance was recorded by the Carnegie Hall Recording Company and was broadcast on WNYC.[2] The first two movements had been premiered by the New York Negro Symphony Orchestra two years earlier. The music director for the NYNS orchestra was pianist, composer, and conductor Wen Talbert, a thoroughly schooled musician from Wilberforce University and Oberlin. He programmed Johnson's music for the inaugural performance of the American Negro Ballet (ANB) on November 21, 1937, at the Lafayette Theater. The American Negro Ballet was the brainchild of Eugene Von Grona, a German-born dancer and choreographer. After immigrating to the United States in the early twenties, he was fascinated by the Harlem Renaissance and began working with African American dancers. On a return trip to Germany in 1934, Von Grona danced his piece *Harlem Impressions* for the new Chancellor of Germany. Hitler stopped the performance when he realized the piece was inspired by African

Americans. After returning to the United States, Von Grona committed more seriously to developing an African American ballet company. He rehearsed his company for three years before their Lafayette debut.

Johnson was guest conductor with the orchestra. The performance was broadcast over WOR. James Weldon Johnson gave an address after intermission. While there was much fanfare at the sold-out opening, most of the reviews were not complimentary. A second performance of the ANB used Johnson's piano rhapsody *Yamekraw* as the overture, with Dean Dixon conducting. In 1941, Dixon became the first African American to conduct the NBC Symphony after Arturo Toscanini's departure. Von Grona attempted to book his company into major concert halls but was rejected. Instead of the Met, he found the only venues available were on the Black vaudeville circuit. He changed the name of the group to Von Grona's Swing Ballet, and the group played the Apollo and was featured in Lew Leslie's *Blackbirds of '39*. The ANB lasted only two years but was one of the first companies of African American dancers intended for formal concert programming. Several ANB dancers joined Agnes De Mille when American Ballet Theatre launched in 1940, as well as joining Katherine Dunham.[3] Later in the 1940s, Dunham and Johnson would perform together.

Shortly after his Brooklyn Museum concert, Kosok left for Peru to pursue his archeological studies. Johnson conducted the second movement of the symphony, "April in Harlem," at the American Society of Composers, Authors and Publishers (ASCAP) Festival of American Music on October 2. While Kosok was in Peru, he found time to indulge his musical interests. By this time he had become a significant champion for Johnson's music. A wire story with dateline from Iquitos, Peru, appearing in the *New York Post* July 27, 1940, and *New York Amsterdam News* around the same time, made note of Kosok's plans for performances of Johnson's music in Lima and perhaps other countries later that winter. According to the article, Kosok had written to Johnson of his plans and the interest generated among music critics in his work. On April 16, 1941, Kosok conducted the National Symphony Orchestra of Peru. In addition to Dvorak, Tchaikovsky, and the works of three Peruvian composers, Kosok included the complete *Harlem Symphony*.[4] J. Mercer Meredith, who attended the concert, provided the following comments in his review of April 19:

> An invasion took place here recently which, unlike others we read about these days, received a tremendous ovation and was in the nature of a triumph for a Negro musician whose work stirred the Peruvians almost to a frenzy.
>
> The occasion was the presentation of James P. Johnson's "Harlem Symphony" by the National Symphony Orchestra of Peru here at an open air concert with an audience of more than fifteen thousand cheering

auditors who acclaimed the creation of the Negro musician which had its premiere at the Academy of Music in Brooklyn and was later heard at Carnegie Hall in New York City.

SINCERE ATTENTION

The eager sea of faces, with eyes riveted on the baton of Dr. Paul Kosok, seemed tensed in thrilling anticipation of an expected treat, and if it to be [sic] presumed that the Peruvians were not disappointed as a thunderous burst of applause came at the conclusion of what the papers here claim to be another great contribution to the Pan-American relations.

Columns of space were devoted to a description of what they called "La Symphonica Harlem," and seldom has such deep appreciation for the work of an American been shown.

Transplanting the scene, if such were possible, to some part of the United States, as thousands milled around in eagerness to voice their appreciation to the great conductor, would spell the making of the modest composer whose ability is unquestioned.[5]

Kosok wrote to Johnson after the concert, confirming these observations as well as his own great admiration for Johnson's music:

I just gave an outdoor concert with the National Symphony Orchestra of Peru before an audience of 15,000 people, and I want to tell you that your symphony was received with a tremendous lot of applause, in fact I had to repeat the Night Club movement. If I give any more concerts in South America I'll try to play it again. In the meantime I would like to know what you are doing and whether you have composed anything new. Also, I'm definitely returning to the USA in July & August. Next fall I would like to put on a program of your music if you can get someone interested in backing up a concert. I am very serious about this. Perhaps you could get a program with the first half orchestral, the second half a short opera, one part of an opera. It ought to be put on in Harlem where there is a mass appeal. However that I will leave to you. Please drop me a line about your plans and whether we can work together next fall. Sincerely yours, Paul Kosok.[6]

Unlike so many others from the musical establishment with broken promises, hollow commitments, and outright rejections, Kosok was a man of his word. On March 8, 1942, the Brooklyn Civic Orchestra, under the direction of Kosok,

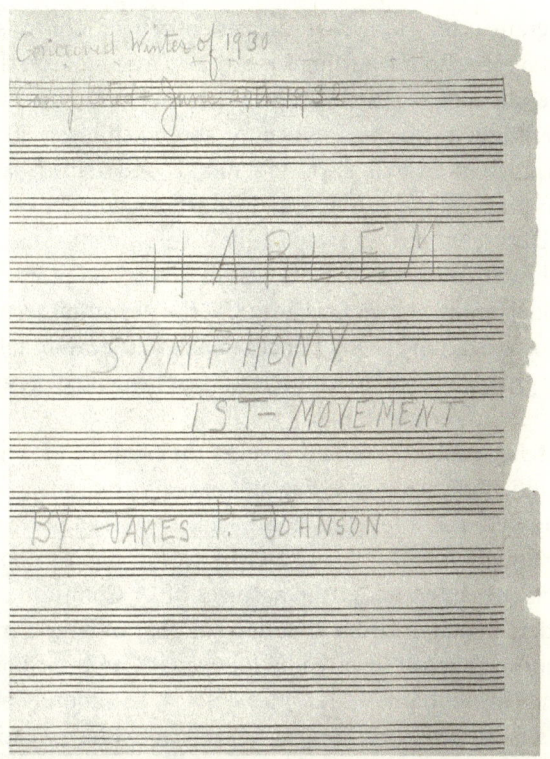

Cover page for *Harlem Symphony* in Johnson's hand. (Reproduced with permission of Barry Glover, from the James P. Johnson collection [IJS.0111], Institute of Jazz Studies, Rutgers-Newark)

de la Orquesta Sinfónica Nacional
LIMA - PERU
DOMINGO 16 DE ABRIL DE 1941
PAUL KOSOK
DIRECTOR

2° CONCIERTO AL AIRE LIBRE — ORUESTA SINFONICA NACIONAL
Director: PAUL KOSOK

— PRIMERA PARTE —

1—ANTON DVORAK : Sinfonia del Nuevo Mundo (4° movimiento)
2—PETER TSCHAIKOWSY : Vals de las Flores (de Casca-Nueces)
3— " " : Capricho Italiano

— SEGUNDA PARTE —

4— James P. Johnson : Sinfonia de Harlem
    a) Un viaje a Harlem
    b) Cancion de amor
    c) Cabaret
    d) En una Mision Bautista

5—THEODORO VALCARCEL : Danza del Combate (de "Suray-Surita")
6—DANIEL A. ROBLES : Kashua "La Huanuquena"
7—E. LOPEZ MINDREAU : Marinera y Tondero

——— From ———
JAMES P. JOHNSON, 171-38 108th Avenue, Jamaica, L. I.

(Reproduced with permission of Barry Glover, from the James P. Johnson collection [IJS.0111], Institute of Jazz Studies, Rutgers-Newark) played a program at the Heckscher Theater entirely of Johnson's symphonic works, including selections from *The Dreamy Kid*. August Heckscher, the mining and real estate mogul and philanthropist, funded the construction of the Heckscher building in 1921 as a refuge for abused children. Its theater was touted for its proscenium arch, thirty-foot murals, and stained glass. The focus was children's productions, and during the thirties a number were sponsored by the FTP. Heckscher passed away the year before Johnson's concert. The Heckscher Theater concert took place just as Kosok had promised. Johnson and his personal representative since 1937, George W. Lattimore, undertook an aggressive sponsorship and promotional campaign. They were able to marshal an impressive group of people to lend at least their name, and presumably some financial support, to the event.

The Heckscher concert program invokes the name of Mayor Fiorello H. LaGuardia as the top patron, chairing an honorary committee that included Mary McLeod Bethune, John Hammond, Langston Hughes, Dr. Adam Clayton Powell Jr., Sigmund Spaeth, and Deems Taylor, eighteen notables in all. The event was presented under the auspices of "A Committee of Friends" whose founders included Bessie Bearden (mother of famed artist Romare Bearden, who was himself inspired by Johnson's "Carolina Shout" in creating a painting by that name), Mercedes Gilbert, Lattimore, Paul Robeson, Thomas "Fats" Waller and wife Anita, Walter White (the executive secretary of the NAACP during this time), Nell Occomy Becker, Carrie Hamer, Ruth A. Handy, Charles W. Joyce, Yetta Kligfeld, Vivian Lawrence, Louise McDonald, the Reverend Adam Clayton Powell Jr., the Reverend Routte, Marcia P. Sterling, and Rose Wyler.[7] The "Friends of James P. Johnson" worked out of an office at 1587 Broadway, and solicited contributions to fund the event. In their fundraising letter, the committee acknowledged Johnson's renown in popular music, but also noted how few people knew of his orchestral works, the focus of this concert. The pitch, appealing to the best connected of Black society as well as the socially conscious in the white music and arts world, framed the event as an expression of American values, proudly noting, "The concert will express our America—its culture and democratic traditions. Only in our America could Mr. Johnson's music have been conceived. Only in a democracy in these troubled times, could one hear these universally appealing symphonies written by a Negro, conducted by a White [sic] and played by a mixed group of artists."[8] A list of over 140 patrons is recognized in the program for their financial support, including Louis Armstrong, Mercer Cook, the Crescendo Club, Joe Glaser, Milt Gabler, W. C. Handy, John Hammond, Professor E. Aldama Jackson (one of Johnson's composition teachers), Barney Josephson, Jack Mills, Ed Smalls, Frank Schiffman, and Walter White. The original date of the concert

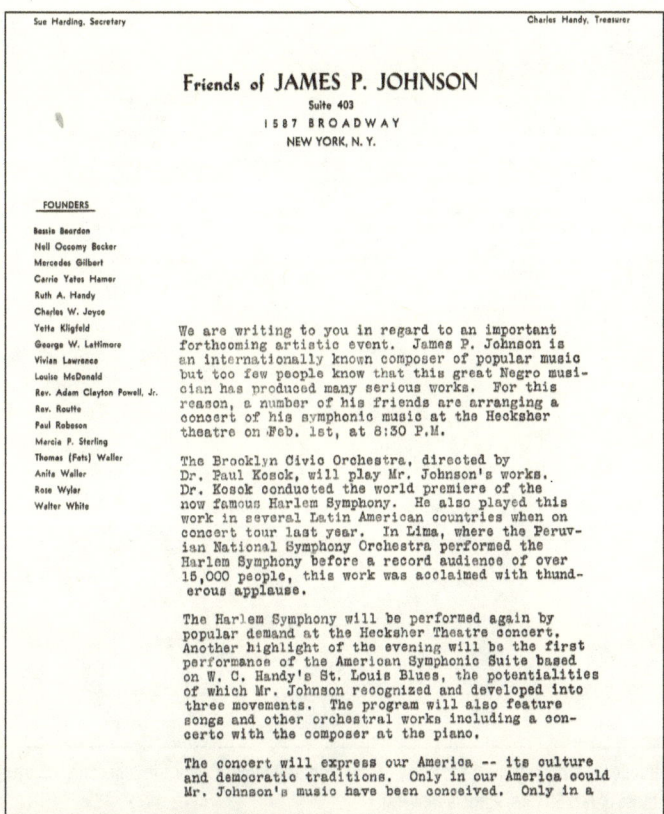

(Reproduced with permission of Barry Glover, from the James P. Johnson collection [IJS.0111], Institute of Jazz Studies, Rutgers-Newark)

was February 1, 1942, but logistical problems necessitated a change to March 8.[9] There was no admission charge for the concert, the costs borne entirely out of patron contributions, which was the expressed purpose of the "Friends of James P. Johnson." The Brooklyn Civic Orchestra was again sponsored by Long Island University. This time, Johnson convinced Kosok to include jazz musicians among the skilled amateurs of the BCO, not for improvising on his carefully scored works, but for their ability to interpret music out of the African American tradition.[10]

The program cover denotes the event as the "First Concert of Symphonic Works by James P. Johnson." Notes inside describe it as "A Dream Realized" and quote Johnson as saying in 1932, "For more than fifteen years it has been my dream to develop the folk material and rich resources of Negro music, and to recast them into symphonic forms." Johnson completed the Harlem Symphony in 1932 but continued to make changes in the score. The program included:

> democracy in these troubled times, could one hear these universally appealing symphonies written by a Negro, conducted by a White and played by a mixed group of artists. There will be no admission charge for this concert. The expenses are to be borne by sponsors whose names will be duly acknowledged on the program and who will receive allotments of complimentary tickets for redistribution. The purpose of this letter is to ask you to serve as a sponsor and to make as large a contribution as possible to defray the expenses of the concert. The enclosed form and return envelope are sent to you for your convenience in remitting your gift.
>
> With appreciation, I am
>
> Sincerely yours,
>
> For the Friends of
>
> James P. Johnson
>
> P.S. Make checks payable to the Friends of James P. Johnson
>
> *Dear Friend Cora, This letter is relative to the concert you promised to help on. Best wishes, Your friend James P. Johnson*

(Reproduced with permission of Barry Glover, from the James P. Johnson collection [IJS.0111], Institute of Jazz Studies, Rutgers-Newark)

Symphony No.1—*Symphony Harlem*

1. A Subway Journey—Penn Station to Harlem
2. Harlem Love Song
3. Night Club
4. Baptist Mission

Second and third movements were played without interruption

American Symphonic Suite—"St. Louis Blues"

First Movement—"Lament"
Third Movement—"Downhearted"

Intermission

Songs—

Dreamy (from *Dreamy Kid*)
Wandering
Sun Will Be Shining for You (from *Dreamy Kid*)
Soloist Lois Jordan
Adagio from First Piano Concerto—*Jazzamine*
Composer at the piano

Symphonic Poem—*African Drums*

From poem by Andy Razaf

The *Harlem Symphony* is designed as a travelogue through Harlem. On the score of the first movement, "Subway Journey," Johnson identifies the location each musical section represents as the train passes by. The journey starts at "Penn Station" and proceeds through "110th Street—the Jewish neighborhood," "116th Street—Spanish neighborhood," "125th Street—Shopping district, lady shoppers gossiping," "135th Street—Negro Neighborhood," "7th Avenue Promenade" and then returning to "Penn Station." The second movement has gone by a number of names—"From Harlem" at the Brooklyn Museum, "Harlem Love Song" at the Heckscher, "Song of Harlem" on his handwritten score, and eventually published in 1944 as a piano solo with the title "April in Harlem." It contains some of Johnson's most beautiful themes. It is the longest of the four movements. For "Night Club," the shortest movement, Johnson relies on early influences. The first two themes are nearly identical to a piece he recorded only once as a piano roll in 1917, "Innovation." The first theme reflects the influence of one of Johnson's (and Gershwin's) mentors, Charles "Luckey" Roberts, borrowing melodic detail from Roberts's tune "Junk Man Rag," published in 1913. Structurally, it sounds like a rag. The fourth movement, "Baptist Mission," builds seven variations on one theme. Rudi Blesh visited Johnson at his home several years later and the composer played it for him. In his book *They All Played Ragtime*, Blesh identifies the material as "a syncopated passacaglia on the hymn 'I Want Jesus to Walk with Me.'"[11]

American Symphonic Suite—"St. Louis Blues," written in three movements and based on W. C. Handy's classic blues song, was completed in 1934. The first movement was titled "Lament" and the third "Downhearted." The second may have been named "Complainin'." Handy had apparently intended to publish the entire work in 1934 or 1935, after its introductory performance at the National Auditions Pageant held in Chicago in connection with the World's Fair called a "Century of Progress." Three Johnson songs were performed, two from his one-act opera *The Dreamy Kid*. The program incorrectly credits Henry Creamer with lyrics for "Dreamy" and Cecil Mack for lyrics to "Sun Will Be Shinin' for

You." Both were written by Mercer Cook for the opera. Cook is incorrectly credited as lyricist for "Wandering," which was written with Henry Creamer. "Wandering" is a Johnson song from the unproduced stage show *Geechie* that Creamer copyrighted in 1926. A number of other tunes from this show were individually copyrighted in the early 1960s by the Creamer estate. The subject matter of *Geechie* is an uplifting story of redemption and vindication. *Jazzamine* piano concerto was copyrighted by Johnson in 1934. The adagio second movement was later published as a piano solo in 1944. Johnson recorded a six-minute solo piano version for Moe Asch in 1945 that was not released until the CD era. An abbreviated version with the fictitious title "Blues for Jimmy" was issued by Asch on LP. It has also been known as *Jassamine, First Piano Concerto*, and *Piano Concerto in A flat*.

African Drums has also been known by several names including simply *Drums* and *Rhythm Drums*. It was originally one of the tunes in the Johnson show *Harlem Hotcha* for which Andy Razaf wrote all the lyrics. Handy Brothers published most of the tunes from the show but released *Drums* back to the composers. The Heckscher Theater program notes the piece is from a poem by Andy Razaf. A different set of unpublished lyrics was written by Langston Hughes. In a handwritten note, Johnson describes the structure of the piece:

> *African Drums*—32 bars of solo drums played by tympany announces or sets the atmosphere and rhythm for a female dancer after which begins an imaginary (?) dance accompanied by the whole orchestra which gives out the dance motive for two bars and is answered by an orchestrated figure depicting the stamping and shouting of the other participants. Then follows a faster and swifter tempo and dance by the other members of the group. This is developed to the solo announcement of the drums again. Then follows the song of Africa and the drums. After this there is a flute solo accompanied by bass violin and tom toms alone depicting the voodoo dance and from here the composition is developed to a grand climax which combines all the themes and drum rhythms with one final announcement of the theme by the orchestra in one triumphant and savage shout and the end.[12]

The New York Amsterdam News reported an overflow audience.[13] Johnson's friend Mercedes Gilbert spoke about Johnson's life and works. Carl Diton, a noted African American composer, pianist, and teacher who had a prominent place in the art music world, praised Johnson's symphony. In particular, he noted Johnson's ability to depart from reliance on dance rhythms, especially in the second movement "April in Harlem." O. V. Clyde noted Johnson's prominent place in jazz as pianist, and that the Heckscher concert "constitutes an historic event whose true significance does not seem to have impressed the musicians of the city." He notes, "Johnson has been trying for years to find a solution for the problem of how to embody the genius of jazz and the blues in larger symphonic forms." He concludes, "In my opinion, Johnson's courageous efforts do not quite succeed simply because I think that he has permitted himself to be too much awed by the teachings of the traditional schools." Clyde goes on, "In the piano concerto, however, where Johnson himself sat down at the piano, the lightnings [sic] of jazz improvisation began to appear in the score, and Johnson, the great jazz pianist, had all he could do to keep from tearing loose from the orchestral moorings in a burst of real licks."[14] Like earlier reviewers of Johnson conducting his stage shows, these observations reinforce Johnson's crescendo of enthusiasm when playing or leading his own music before a crowd. "April in Harlem" and "Baptist Mission" were played again in 1945 as part of Johnson's "Jazzfest and Pop Concert" at Carnegie Hall. Except for the piano rhapsody *Yamekraw*, that was the last orchestral performance of any Johnson extended work for nearly fifty years. He would occasionally play selections of his symphony and concerto as piano solo reductions, but, except for *Yamekraw*, all orchestrations were thought lost until discovered amongst his papers in the early 1990s.

In April 1942, Johnson, Wen Talbert, and Maceo Pinkard announced their intention to form a "Sepia Opera and Symphonic Society."[15] Perhaps encouraged that a concert of his symphonic works had actually come off with some success, Johnson made another failed attempt to secure a Guggenheim fellowship. In his "plan of work" document, he describes his intention to complete a four-movement symphonic suite for orchestra and voices relying on local "private composer teachers" for tutelage. He outlines the theme as a "descriptive historic tale portrayed in music of the part the Negro has played in the creation of our great nation and the fight to preserve it through the most trying periods. I shall endeavor to depict the Negro's loyalty and gallantry from our Country's beginning up to the present time."[16] Each movement is to depict a central African American figure from four great wars—Crispus Attucks from the Revolution, Frederick Douglass from the Civil War, the "Harlem Hellfighters" 15th Regiment from World War I, and Dorie Miller, the hero from Pearl Harbor. With his symphonic projects, Johnson strove to move beyond the plantation- and minstrel-based racist tropes that remained the bedrock of the African American musical stage and film depictions dictated by the wider culture. The "Friends of James P. Johnson" remained active, sponsoring a series of teas and cocktail parties, the first at the home of Mrs. Ruth Handy in Brooklyn on June 6, 1942.[17] After the mostly encouraging performances of *The Organizer* and *Harlem Symphony*, Johnson and his "Friends" were planning more.

Chapter 23

IN DEMAND AGAIN, 1942-1943

> James P. Johnson sounds like a 100-piece orchestra.
> —ROD CLESS

By 1940, in the Northeast at least, racial barriers in the jazz world had begun to melt away. Johnson often participated in interracial bands, both in live performance and on recordings. Johnson's return to very active jazz performance and recording was fostered by a few enthusiastic patrons. During the 1920s, his efforts were advanced primarily by his African American friends and colleagues Clarence Williams, Perry Bradford, W. C. Handy, and Will Marion Cook. From 1938 until the end of his career, a succession of white recording company executives, music publishers, and the newly emerging cadre of jazz critics/writers would keep him visible in the jazz world. In fact, during the 1940s, he was more visible than he had ever been. John Hammond and Hugues Panassie provided the initial springboard into the recording studio, concert stage, and evolving Greenwich Village club scene. Eddie Condon was next to include Johnson in his expanding orbit.

A guitarist of some caliber but rarely heard on his numerous recordings, Condon spent most of his energies as impresario. He was a champion of traditional jazz as it was constituted in the 1940s, bringing together musicians whose musical underpinnings could have been from New Orleans, Chicago, or New York. He organized a regular group of rotating musicians and special guests who were fixtures at his primary venue, the Town Hall in New York. This series of concerts has become legendary as one of the most important showcases for traditional jazz during this time period. Condon served as MC for what he promoted as "jam sessions." With his wry humor, he introduced

Johnson had dabbled with art courses, and made this self-portrait sketch. (Reproduced with permission of Barry Glover, from the James P. Johnson collection [IJS.0111], Institute of Jazz Studies, Rutgers-Newark)

the tunes and players in what often comes off as freewheeling but excellent music. Fortunately, many of these concerts were broadcast and recorded off the air by ardent fans. Johnson began to appear frequently with Condon, first as a special guest at the concert of April 11, 1942, noted to be the fourth concert of the season.[1] There are no known recordings of this event. The program featured Johnson and Dave Bowman on piano, Zutty Singleton and Kansas Fields, drums, Max Kaminsky and Hot Lips Page, cornet, Rod Cless and Pee Wee Russell, clarinet, Benny Morton and J. C. Higginbotham, trombone, Billy Taylor, bass, Condon guitar, Bill Bailey, dancing, and Billie Holiday, vocal. The ensemble played interpretations of tunes associated with the Austin High Gang of Chicago, and Johnson was featured playing "Piano Sketches."[2] He was accompanied by Singleton on "Snowy Morning Blues," "Carolina Shout," a Gershwin tune (with Morton added on trombone), and an improvised "32 bar standard." Holiday sang three tunes.

Dan Burley, in his column for the *New York Amsterdam News*, commented about Johnson's performance, writing, he "laid 'em in the aisles in that final Jazz

Concert at Town Hall Saturday." Burley also reported that Johnson had recently been admitted to the League of Composers, whose only other African American member at that time was William Grant Still.[3] The League was founded in 1923 by Claire Raphael Reis to promote the work of living composers of contemporary music, and included such names as Arnold Schoenberg, Paul Hindemith, and Darius Milhaud. Johnson held memberships in the Song Writers Protective Association and the Dramatists' Guild to protect and promote his interests as a popular and theater composer, not to mention his Local 802 union membership as a performing jazz musician. He was covering all bases. But the League of Composers membership was a true feather in his cap, a privilege of which he was especially proud. Yet, as Johnson was eclipsed by the popularity of his students Ellington and Waller in the commercial music world, he remained in the shadow of William Grant Still in the world of concert music.

His newly initiated association with Eddie Condon paid off with an invitation to be part of a television jazz first. Several years earlier, Fats Waller had appeared on an experimental broadcast while in England. On April 16, 1942, the local CBS television station in New York aired what was hailed as the world's first commercially broadcast jazz concert. Eddie Condon's "Town Hall Jazzopators" appeared in what was billed as a jam session similar in format to his Town Hall concerts. The show replaced the regularly scheduled variety show.[4] The band included Condon, Joe Sullivan, piano, Pee Wee Russell, clarinet, Benny Morton, trombone, Max Kaminsky, trumpet, Billy Taylor, bass, and Zutty Singleton, drums. Hot Lips Page on trumpet and Johnson also played with the band and had special solo spots.[5] Television was in its infancy, and few homes had television sets. Programming was not continuous even during the daytime. And the show was broadcast only on the New York CBS station so as not to risk causing a stir in the largely racially intolerant sections of the country outside of the metro area. While Condon was a known quantity with plenty of connections, it was his silver tongue that likely slipped an integrated band on to the airwaves. Thus, on April 16, 1942, James P. Johnson became the first African American pianist to appear on commercial television. While the occasion was memorialized in still photographs, there are no known recordings of the event, or kinescopes, which had not yet been utilized to archive television broadcasts.

Doing his patriotic duty, Johnson registered for the draft on April 27. The forty-eight-year-old was by then carrying 216 pounds on his 5 foot 6 inch frame.[6] It was hardly likely even the quartermaster corps would have taken him, not two years since his stroke. Another vital relationship was established around this time with record producer Moses Asch. Johnson's first recording date for Moe Asch included three piano solos—"Boogie Woogie Stride," "Impressions," and two takes of "Snowy Morning Blues," all released on the Asch label. These Johnson solos are the first jazz recordings by Asch, whose

Johnson became the first African American jazz pianist to appear on commercial television in the United States with this appearance in April 1942. With him are Zutty Singleton, drums, Oran "Hot Lips" Page, trumpet, and Eddie Condon, guitar. (CBS Photo Archive via Getty Images)

work up until then consisted primarily of Jewish music and the folk recordings he had done with Leadbelly, Woody Guthrie, and Pete Seeger. The session was arranged through the efforts of Charles Edward Smith, but it is unclear who primarily chose Johnson to kick off Asch's legacy of recorded jazz. Smith, probably looking to make amends for leaving Johnson out of his book *Jazzmen*, likely made the suggestion to Asch. Smith claimed the omission was due to a missed deadline, not an overt slight. There had been many opportunities for Asch and Johnson to connect. The two may have become acquainted at the ILGWU concert in 1940 when *The Organizer* was performed and Asch provided the sound system. Café Society was not far from the WEVD building where Asch had his studio, and many of his acquaintances from the political left were meeting there. Asch had also recorded Johnson's good friend Mercedes Gilbert in 1941. Her album *Cavalcade of the American Negro* featured Gilbert reading her script depicting the history of African Americans.[7]

July 2, 1942, has been given for the recording date, but the Asch files reflect October 17, 1943. Asch was a notoriously bad record keeper, but his logs show little activity at all during 1942, even before the American Federation of Musicians recording ban that began at the end of July. The latter date was in the middle of the ban, and discographer and Johnson scholar Robert Hilbert speculates that the October date may have been the mastering date. Asch seemed to be, for the most part, compliant with the ban, but by September 1943, Decca Records had settled with the intractable AFM union leader James Petrillo, and Asch quickly followed. A recording date in October would have been possible. Asch was eager to gear up his activity, but record production was further hampered by wartime shortages of supplies. Finding shellac was a continuing challenge for Asch. Before the recording ban took effect in the summer of 1942, his recording output was not of such volume as to allow him a large allotment, so Asch formed a loose partnership with Herbert Harris, owner of the Stinson Trading Company, who was flush with shellac but few recordings to issue. Harris was a communist party member who specialized in releasing Soviet recordings, but by 1942, the market for that genre in the US was dwindling. Their quasi-partnership began in January 1943. The agreement required all of Asch's recordings to be sold through Harris's Stinson Trading Company, including recordings issued on Asch's own label. The practice continued until the war ended and Asch was able to find his own supply of shellac.[8]

However Asch and Johnson became acquainted, their association proved to be a mutually important one. These initial recordings garnered much praise, favorably launching Asch into the jazz record business and vindicating Johnson as not merely a relic, but capable of producing music of high aesthetic quality and contemporary appeal. They were his first recorded piano solos since his stroke in August 1940. Although the recording quality is a bit anemic, perhaps affected by the poor quality of the wartime shellac, Johnson's playing shows no sign of decline. *Down Beat* announced the release of the Johnson solos in December 1943, in a brief piece titled "Righteous Jazz Rears Its Head on Discs Again." Their February 1944 review was glowing, writing, "'Impressions' is easily the most beautiful piano number pressed in recent years. . . . Too much boogie woogie has been recorded in the last few years, but these two cuttings by Johnson are remarkable exceptions." His version of "Snowy Morning Blues" was highlighted and described as superior to his original recording of 1927. For Asch they concluded, "This album ought to see the Asch firm off to a good start." In their review, *The New York Times* characterized Johnson as "one of the earliest boogie-woogie pianists." Although Johnson's earliest piano rolls, most notably "Arkansas Blues" from 1922, include some of the first recorded examples of boogie woogie left-hand patterns, it is not likely the *Times* reviewers knew this, and more likely their description reflected the domination of boogie woogie in jazz piano at that time. They go on to note more correctly "his style and compositions influenced a host of jazz musicians from Harlem and south of its environs." About the new recordings they conclude, "The music has admirable power and verve and it is written with complete command of the piano. Mr. Johnson's jazz belongs with the best."[9] Even the "Two Deuces," Barry Ulanov and Leonard Feather, editors and record reviewers for *Metronome* who were usually tough graders, praised his first two recordings:

> James P. Johnson is one of the few heroes of the olde [*sic*] time jazz lovers whose music stands up today in open competition. He's a facile pianist, a good musician, and excellent as both on these sides. He does more with the worn out boogie woogie form than you'd expect, concentrating on treble variations rather than endless repetition of the walking bass. The use of the "Hold Tight" riff is an added pleasantry.
>
> "Impressions" is a lovely set of twelve-bar choruses which follows the blues frame but not its modes. It is cast in the whole tone scale, and is, therefore, strongly Debussyan. James P.'s "Impressions" follow the Debussyan manner in mood, too, setting forth some charming, soft, relaxed keyboard speculations.
>
> This is an impressive first attempt for the Asch Recording Co., in the jazz field, good music and excellent reproduction of same.
>
> We look forward with great interest to J.P.'s forthcoming records.[10]

Ulanov and Feather would soon be bitten by the bebop bug, at that time still in its nascent phase. Notably, "Boogie Woogie Stride" and "Impressions" include no stride left hand, which the two critics usually heard as an irrelevant anachronism. In their reviews where Harlem stride dominates Johnson's playing, they were often highly critical. This promising inaugural release was somewhat compromised in its commercial potential because Asch, for unclear reasons, pressed twelve-inch records rather than the ten-inch size that could be played in juke boxes.[11] In their 1944 year-end review, *Down Beat* included "Impressions" and "Boogie Woogie Stride" in their "best of" list for 1944 in the "Hot Discs" section.[12]

The beginning of 1943 saw Johnson playing with "Wild Bill" Davison and his band at the Ken Club in Boston, a cellar club on Tremont Street and the number one venue in the city for small-group jazz. The band, consisting of Davison on cornet, Sandy Williams on trombone, Rod Cless on clarinet, Johnson at the piano, and Kaiser Marshall on drums, opened on February 8. The band caused a stir in town with its "mixed race" personnel.[13] One observer called them "the greatest jazz band ever assembled." He went on, noting, "Man what fine jazz. Two white artists and three colored. They had a Dixieland-Chicago combo that startled the world; and the playingest, drinkingest band in the whole universe."[14] After a five-week run, they played in New York on 52nd Street, which was fast becoming the jazz epicenter in the city. They were first at Jimmy Ryan's (from March 22 to May 15), then at the Onyx Club, after dropping the trombone and drums and adding bassist Al Matthews.[15] Rod Cless beamed about the Davison band and Johnson, telling an interviewer, "This is the best job I ever had. James P. Johnson sounds like a 100-piece orchestra, and after playing all night and rehearsing in the daytime, I feel fine, because the band is such a good kick."[16] Johnson and Mercedes Gilbert appeared in a benefit for the Advisory Committee on Negro Health of the Queensboro Tuberculosis and Health Association on May 16. Johnson played the adagio from his *Jazzamine Concerto*, "Reflections" tone poem, and "Boogey-woogey Runway" [sic].[17] Davison's band did not last much longer at the Onyx, and by the first week in June was replaced by Cozy Cole's trio with stellar pianist Johnny Guarnieri, a Waller/Johnson protégé. Johnson had dropped out of Davison's band at the end of May because of illness,[18] but he returned to Ryan's as solo pianist in early June, around the time Davison left the Onyx. In a front-page notice in *Variety* spotlighting the comeback of 52nd Street, Johnson is described as "one of the outstanding jazz pianists of all time."[19]

Although he was conscious of his health problems and made some attempt to moderate his schedule, relax, and keep the pressure low, Johnson was incorrigibly drawn to musical activity. In August, he attended a mammoth jam session at the studio of *Life* magazine photographer Gjon Mili. From 9:00 p.m. until 4:00 a.m., a succession of New York's greatest jazz musicians assembled in the photographer's cavernous loft to play for an invited audience including notables of the publishing world. Duke Ellington, Billie Holiday, the Mary Lou Williams trio, the Don Redman sextet, Teddy Wilson and his band, and Lee Wiley accompanied by her husband Jess Stacy were among the many musicians who convened from around town after their regular gigs. Eddie Condon served as master of ceremonies, pairing up musicians and selecting tunes. Milt Gabler, by then working for Decca Records, assisted the Army in recording the event for eventual release on V-discs. Unfortunately, the acoustics in Mili's studio were so bad the recordings were unusable. Mili, however, captured the historic gathering on film. His photographs were used in a feature article in *Life* magazine about the event. Johnson, as shown in one of the published photos, plays his "Old Fashioned Love." The caption makes note of Johnson's larger compositional efforts, *The Organizer* and *Harlem Symphony*. As was so often the case at that time, since his name might not have been recognizable to their general readership, it seemed necessary to remind the public he was the teacher of Fats Waller. In another shot, Billie Holiday sings "Fine and Mellow" with her characteristic emotive facial expression with Johnson, not identified, accompanying her along with guitarist Josh White and others.[20]

Johnson was beginning to be visible again. Of his playing, Teddy Wilson had these comments in his autobiography:

What impressed me about Fats was the fact that he had refined and added so much to the James P. Johnson stride style of playing. Perhaps "refined" is the wrong word to use, because James P.'s piano was in its own way flawless and immaculate. He [Fats] also had flawless accuracy, just as James P. and Art Tatum did. There was no such thing as hitting wrong notes with Fats or with the others.

In that stride bass idiom James P. and Fats seem to have stood out head and shoulders above so many of their contemporaries.

I think it was John Hammond who told me the first influence of any kind in jazz music which he experienced was when he was a boy at prep school and he heard records of James P. It seems James P. had made recordings after the First World War, and John Hammond once played me some old 78s he had of him. These recordings were probably made around the early 20s and I believe some of his ideas in his right hand would sound just wonderful if they were orchestrated for the Count Basie Band today. James P.'s ideas in jazz could be perfectly executed by the Basie Band and sound very proper and in place over that number of years. He shared Fats's, Hines's and Tatum's flawless techniques: never a wrong note. His style was very powerful and I heard him play several times in person, in addition to hearing him on recordings.[21]

Even in his later years, when his playing was at times affected by illness, observers remarked over his right-hand inventiveness as much as the power of his left. In a posthumous record review, *New Yorker* critic Whitney Balliett described Johnson's right hand as "brilliantly casual."[22] *Melody Maker* columnist Denis Preston wrote in his obituary of Johnson, "Indeed, the most notable characteristic of his work was its filigree delicacy."[23] Anthropologist Ernest Borneman, who frequently directed his attention to analyses of jazz, its roots, development, and players, attempted to crystallize the essence of good jazz. He wrote, "In jazz, as in all art, the great masterpieces are invariably lucid, serene and perfectly poised. Among the best jazz musicians, this quality is shared by Armstrong . . ., Bechet . . ., Bessie Smith . . ., Teagarden . . . James P. Johnson (above all pianists)."[24]

On July 21, Twentieth Century Fox premiered its highly anticipated musical revue film *Stormy Weather* concurrently on Broadway at the Roxy and in Harlem at the Alhambra Theater. It featured an all-star cast with Lena Horne and Bill "Bojangles" Robinson in the lead roles, along with Fats Waller, Cab Calloway, the Nicholas Brothers, Katherine Dunham, Dooley Wilson, and Flournoy Miller. Miller plays himself, and, with Johnny Lee playing the role of the deceased Aubry Lyles, they give a brief performance of the famous indefinite talk comedy routine that was the lynchpin of their many successful shows two decades earlier. Ada Brown and Zutty Singleton also make appearances. The dances were staged by Clarence Robinson, who had done the same for *Keep Shufflin'*. Music publisher Irving Mills had landed himself the position of assistant to the producer. In so doing, he assured placement in the film of many artists he had managed, and whose tunes he published over the years, including those of Calloway and Waller. The film featured many recognizable hits such as "Ain't Misbehavin'," "I Can't Give You Anything But Love," "Diga Doo," and of course the title song, "Stormy Weather." A new song was slated for inclusion as a feature for Lena Horne. Irving and Jack Mills tapped Johnson, along with Ted Koehler, composer of the title song, to write it. Mills began to promote their tune, "There's No Two Ways About Love," well in advance of the film release. Soundtrack recordings were made as early as February, with arrangements by Benny Carter. *The New York Enquirer* noted, "'There's No Two Ways About Love' is well spotted in the picture and has been selected by Mills for an extensive radio campaign. Already the number has been on the major networks quite a few times."[25] The tune, sung and then reprised by Horne, undergirds the love story between her and Bill Robinson that winds its way through the picture.

The film, and Johnson's tune, garnered excellent reviews:

"Stormy Weather" will have smooth sailing at the b.o. "There's No Two Ways about Love" is a sterling thematic, for intro and finale, which deftly climaxes the romantic relations between the stellar pair.[26]

"Stormy Weather" is a first rate show, just the kind of spirited divertissement that will make you forget all about your own momentary weather troubles. There is so much to choose from, Fox having wisely decided to bury a very thin and trite story line with an abundance of the show world's leading colored talent that "Stormy Weather" has more the appearance of a super vaudeville bill than a motion picture. Musically, too, it is a joy to the ear, especially when Miss Horne digs deep into the depths of romantic despair to put across the classic blues number, after which the picture is titled, in a manner that is distinctive and refreshing even at this late day. She does very well also by "I Can't Give You Anything But Love Baby," "There's No Two Ways About Love," and "Diga Diga Doo" among others.[27]

Mills continued to promote the tune heavily after the release of the movie. *Billboard* identified it as one of the top thirty songs with the most radio plugs in the New York market for most of August and September, and the ads for the film referred to it as Lena Horne's "Big Song."[28] During the same time, Erskine Hawkins was scoring a hit on the Harlem Hit Parade with "Don't Cry, Baby," which reached #1 in July and stayed there for fourteen weeks, remaining on the chart for twenty-nine weeks and hitting #15 on the pop chart.[29] As composer, Johnson could boast two prominent songs in two different markets, one certainly a hit, but one would be hard pressed to find evidence the public knew the composer of either tune. Hawkins vocalist Jimmy Mitchell along with Sammy Lowe were incorrectly credited on the 78 disc as composers of "Don't Cry, Baby," and, although Horne and Carter's soundtrack recording made it onto a V-disc, the tune did not catch on in the popular market despite Mills's promotional efforts. The only commercial recording was made by pianist Teddy Weatherford in Calcutta, India, where he had settled as an expatriate. Johnson's old square dance stride number, "Carolina Balmoral," with lyrics put to it by Langston Hughes, was slated for inclusion in the film, but was deleted for unclear reasons.[30] Instead, "African Dance," written by Hughes, Clarence Muse, and Connie Bemis, became the feature for Bill Robinson in the famous scene where he dances on the drums.[31] Years later, when the soundtrack to the film was released on LP, Horne's segment singing Johnson's tune was not included. It wasn't really a fair fight. The other famous hits of the well-known popular stars like Calloway and Waller consumed the available space.

Johnson did not seem inclined to turn down any gig. He played at the Bushwick Hofbrau in Brooklyn enough times that he listed the establishment as his employer on his 1944 tax return.[32] The Hot Club of Newark, New Jersey, enticed Johnson to participate in one of their jam sessions. Club founder Paul Bacon vividly recalled the session, noting, "The chemistry was explosive, and people talked about that session for years afterward."[33] In October, he appeared with a new band of his own at Smalls' Paradise. November saw him tack on Sunday afternoon jam sessions at Jimmy Ryan's club on 52nd Street sponsored by Milt Gabler. Also in November, Johnson played solo piano on weekend nights at Sperry's Bar and Grill, a local pub in Queens.[34] David Gelman recalled an odd engagement that may have been Sperry's. The piano was often out of tune and had a shortened keyboard. On at least one occasion, the heat was off, and Johnson played wearing his overcoat. The bartender accompanied Johnson on the spoons. One would have thought by this time Johnson was beyond the need for such jobs in such places, playing on bad instruments and accompanied by amateurs. Perhaps he had a personal relationship with the owner of this local establishment. He may have wanted the extra money from any cash jobs available at the time. He had only recently paid off several years of Depression-era debt, albeit relatively low sums, and the Johnsons added a third child, adopted daughter Lillie Mae Jr. in 1943. But his fortunes were improving with recordings and song royalties. By the end of 1944, his reported annual ASCAP and other royalty income was $4,300—not rich by any measure, but above the average salary in 1944 of $2,600. (By 1950, he was reporting $6,500.) In early 1944, the Johnsons purchased property in the vacation community of Amityville on Long Island.[35] The next few years would bring more success and iconic associations.

Chapter 24

RECORDING FLURRY, 1943–1944

> I sure hope I used James P. Johnson's changes on the channel of
> "Honeysuckle Rose." He was the Father.
> —JIMMY ROWLES

The remainder of 1943 and 1944 was Johnson's most productive period in the recording studio. The war was raging and although big bands and singers were still the popular music of the day, there was pent-up demand for jazz of all sorts, especially as interest in older styles grew. Many independent record labels sprung up to provide an outlet for jazz musicians to demonstrate their work in formats other than the big band. Bob Thiele had started his first record label called Signature in 1940 with a recording of Art Hodes. Thiele was known for his unabashed approach of cold calling musicians and introducing himself. In 1943, while serving in the Coast Guard and stationed in Brooklyn, he tracked down Johnson to his Jamaica address, was invited in, and was treated to three hours of Johnson playing solo in his living room.[1] Over the next eight months, Johnson recorded for Thiele with various groups as well as solo, most notably with his moving musical tribute to his best friend Fats Waller, "Blues for Fats," which he recorded three days after Waller's death. Johnson interpolates phrases from Waller's most popular songs, "Ain't Misbehavin'" and "Honeysuckle Rose."

Alfred Lion and Francis Wolff were childhood friends who shared a passion for jazz and had fled Nazi Germany during the 1930s, eventually landing in New York. After attending the 1938 "Spirituals to Swing" concert, Lion became enamored of the exciting boogie woogie of Albert Ammons and Meade Lux Lewis. Two weeks later, on January 6, 1939, he put up the money for a recording and coaxed the two pianists into the studio. Two twelve-inch 78 rpm records

Johnson with three fans. At his right with arm on his shoulder is record producer Bob Thiele. (Otto F. Hess photographs/ Series I: Jazz Artists 1937–1949. Box 5 Folder 11, JPB 17-12. Photo by: Otto F. Hess. Image: [James P. Johnson with 3 fans] © New York Public Library)

were cut, and Blue Note Records was launched. The oversize discs, larger than the usual ten-inch pressings, were made to preserve the music after the recorder ran too long, so the story goes. The larger discs became their standard release. Wolff soon joined Lion, but their venture, at the time an avocational endeavor that served their passion, was interrupted by the war and the recording ban. After Lion was discharged from the army in 1943, the two engaged in the record business full time, establishing their first office at 767 Lexington Avenue, and in so doing created perhaps the most iconic jazz label in history.[2]

Later in life, at the time of the thirtieth anniversary of the Blue Note label, Francis Wolff recalled how their audience perceived their recording philosophy, saying, "I remember though that people used to say, 'Alfred and Frank record only what they like.' That was true."[3] And the two liked James P. Johnson. He was the first musician they sought out to expand their catalogue. On November 17, Johnson recorded four piano solos at Harry Smith Studio—"J. P. Boogie," "Backwater Blues," "Carolina Balmoral," and "Gut Stomp." A second session in December yielded another four solos of similar thematic content: "Improvisations on Pinetop's Boogie-Woogie," "Arkansas Blues," "Caprice Rag," and "Mule Walk"—a boogie, a slow blues, a fast shout, and a moderate tempo stride. It has been suggested that Johnson agreed to include the two boogie woogie tunes as a concession to Lion and Wolff. Johnson was not as vocal a critic of the idiom as was Fats Waller, but, like many of the Harlem musicians, he thought the style was simplistic and repetitive. By the time he made these recordings, he had already recorded "Boogie Woogie Stride" for Asch—an interesting title suggesting mixed idioms, but the piece has no stride in it—and prepared (or at least approved) a folio of five boogie woogie instrumentals published by Mills.[4] Was Johnson, then, simply acquiescing to the requests of his promoters—Lion, Asch, and Mills—who all likely wanted to capitalize on the popularity of the style? Mills had convinced Waller to lend his name to a similar boogie woogie folio two years earlier, and nearly everyone at that time was trying their hand at it. Johnson, himself eager to remain visible, perhaps also saw the public enthusiasm for boogie woogie as one available outlet. Although any popular recognition he had attained was mostly for his popular songs, boogie woogie was the latest popular modality he could work in. But he embraced the sound familiar to the general public only to a degree. He put his own unique stamp on it, much as he had done twenty years earlier in his vocal blues accompaniments and solos.

Johnson's complex blues conception has perennially confounded jazz writers and critics. In 1927, he recorded the solos "Snowy Morning Blues" and "All That I Had Is Gone." One reviewer wrote at the time, "Jimmy Johnson's 'Snowy Morning Blues' and 'All That I Had,' are piano solos, played with a recalcitrant rhythm in the minor chord—the kind that you reject, and accept a moment later. Strange, but that's how impressive it is."[5] Blues and boogie were additional grist for his fertile imagination, and his defiant harmonic and rhythmic expression of it have led generations of critics to question the authenticity of his approach. He challenged the clichés of the style. In effect, no one plays boogie woogie and blues quite like James P. Johnson. Several reviewers commented on the Asch and Blue Note sides when they were released, extolling his reworking of the idiom. One noted, "What is most impressive about Johnson is his wonderful wealth of musical ideas and a complete avoidance of the clichés so common to even the finest pianists in hot jazz. In other words he is one of the truly creative personalities of American jazz, comparable in his own way to the great Duke Ellington."[6] John Lucas, the *Down Beat* record reviewer, who went by the pseudonym Jax, was a Johnson proponent throughout his writing career. Of the Blue Note and Asch solo piano releases, he wrote:

> These four twelve-inch sides immediately place Johnson in the front rank of modern hot pianists. The most amazing thing about them is their utter lack of noticeable dating. Veteran though he is, James P. has kept up with all and ahead of most of his younger contemporaries. Long after he first became recognized as an accomplished, creative keyboard artist, he continued to improve and develop. His newest efforts reveal once again that he has never ceased to progress. Furthermore, each opus

is a real composition, a genuine contribution to hot pianistics and not just another rehashing of antiquated or over-worked material.[7]

Johnson preferred, after all, to be recognized as the "Dean of Jazz Pianists." He had formulated that title as an outgrowth of the numerous descriptions of him at the time as the "grand old man of jazz," "daddy of the piano," and "grandfather of hot piano." Johnson must have been gratified to read not only about his playing but also especially about his composing. On the other hand, Leonard Feather and Barry Ulanov, who had been highly complimentary of Johnson's initial Asch release and overall musicianship, were mostly critical of Johnson's blues on the Blue Note sides, calling it "elementary," "pedestrian," "unbearable monotony," and "indigestible."[8] Later critical and historical writing about Johnson's blues playing was less abrasive, and made attempts to be respectful, but his approach was at best accepted with reservation by some and dismissed by others, a reaction strikingly similar to one that would soon develop regarding the work of an up-and-coming pianist during this same time, one for whom Johnson was a core influence.

In 1957, while listening to a playback of one of his compositions, Thelonious Monk famously commented to his record producer Orin Keepnews, "That sounds like James P. Johnson." Monk, by then an icon of modern jazz, was heavily influenced by the stride style. Many of his unaccompanied solos on standards incorporate large swathes of an undisguised stride bass line and off-the-beat right-hand figures, a return to his roots that is especially notable in his late career playing. But the tune Monk was listening to in the control booth inspiring his famous quote wasn't a stride rendering but rather his slow blues titled "Functional." Monk's piece bears a striking resemblance to Johnson's slow blues from the mid-1940s. Few observers recall Monk in attendance at Johnson gigs or at the same watering spots for musicians. Monk's wife Nellie observed, "Sometimes when he plays the blues, he goes way back to the real old-time pianists, like Jelly Roll Morton and James P. Johnson. I'm always amazed, because I know he hasn't spent a lot of time listening to these pianists, yet it's there in his music."[9] Monk had cut his early musical teeth at the rent parties of Hell's Kitchen in the early 1930s. At that time, the stride pianists were still the mainstays of these events. It is not beyond the realm of possibility Monk encountered Johnson at this time. And Johnson's Asch and Blue Note blues releases more than hint at Monk's approach in "Functional." Certainly Monk's approach was unique, but his broken and rolling left-hand rhythms, occasional loping stride, off-the-beat, angular right-hand figures, and at times illusory suspension of the meter were all reminiscent of Johnson's blues conception. Monk and Johnson were both blues innovators, criticized for challenging popular aesthetics. In 1985, Mosaic records masterfully reissued all of Johnson's Blue Note recordings. Eric Thacker, in the notes, made the pointed observation that Johnson's "... approach to the blues is singular," and reaches a conclusion decades in coming: "... maybe it is high time to accept it as a distinct 'school' of blues pianism, rather than to think of it as a less than successful stab at the 'real thing.'"[10] In that light, Johnson can be thought of as the first "modern" blues pianist.

The stride numbers engendered no such controversy. This was Johnson's own creation. "Gut Stomp," co-written with Willie "The Lion" Smith, is aptly named. It smacks of the gutbucket, stomping feeling of pre–World War I vintage. "Carolina Balmoral" is a piece in a similar vein. He constructs seventeen different variations out of two similar themes, another example of his outstanding improvisational skill that set him apart from his contemporaries. "Mule Walk" may be the one most closely resembling the loping "square and set dances" Johnson grew up with and accompanied at the Jungles Casino. "Caprice Rag," a piece that had only appeared previously on a 1917 piano roll, receives a blistering stride treatment. The eight solo sides, displaying a range of styles, rank among Johnson's finest. Illinois Institute of Technology semantics instructor and future US Senator Samuel Ichiye (S. I.) Hayakawa, a passionate jazz fan, took note of Johnson's Blue Note recordings, writing, "For the past three weeks I have been listening during my moments of leisure to four magnificent 12 inch records of piano solos by James P. Johnson—and I've been having a whale of a good time." A keen observer, he goes on to offer his analysis of Johnson's first four solos, and laments the vicissitudes of society's tastes, observing, "It is said that James P. Johnson's style of piano playing influenced the late Thomas 'Fats' Waller. It is sad that James P. Johnson, 'lost' for many years, had to be 'rediscovered.' Society is like a child; its attention is easily distracted; it forgets and loses its favorites, then whoops with joy when they are found again."[11]

A sad irony surrounds the December solo session. On the same day that Johnson was reaffirming his title as "Dean of Jazz Pianists," Fats Waller, once his protégé and then the man who eventually eclipsed him as popular composer and performer, died of pneumonia on a train nearing Kansas City. It was said Johnson was unable to touch a piano for three days after hearing the news. On that third day, December 18, Johnson paid tribute to his best friend in several ways. He recorded "Blues for Fats." That evening, Johnson participated in another of Eddie Condon's Town Hall concerts. He played several Waller tunes, including "Willow Tree," "Ain't Misbehavin'," and "Honeysuckle Rose," and his own "Carolina Shout." He played "Blues for Fats," described as "a sketch by James P. Johnson written in tribute to the late Fats Waller,"[12] and as "a special piano requiem." He shared the piano that day with Mel Powell and Joe Bushkin.[13] Johnson was one of the honorary pallbearers at Waller's funeral on December 20, along with J. C. Johnson, Bud Allen, Claude Hopkins, Count

Basie, Don Redman, Luckey Roberts, Andy Razaf, Perry Bradford, Clarence Williams, and Duke Ellington.[14] The next day, Barney Josephson sponsored a memorial show for Waller in conjunction with WNEW radio that broadcast the event from Café Society Downtown. The show raised money for the Children's Fund of the *Amsterdam News*. The all-star line up of pianists included Johnson, Count Basie, Art Tatum, Teddy Wilson, Mary Lou Williams, Hazel Scott, Willie "The Lion" Smith, and Eddie Heywood, all playing Waller tunes.[15] Johnson was interviewed by *Time* magazine for their Waller tribute article. Although the jazz world mourned the death of one of its greatest exponents, for Johnson the loss was particularly personal and poignant.

Blue Note wasn't done with Johnson. Over the course of the next year, he was one of a mostly consistent group of musicians whose members included Johnson, clarinet player Edmond Hall, and trumpet player Sidney De Paris. They rotated as leaders of the "Blue Note Jazzmen." Blue Note reissue producer Michael Cuscuna observed it was this group, along with trombone player Vic Dickenson, which led the record label down a path that would become its modus operandi. He notes, "The moniker 'Blue Note Jazzmen' was slapped onto many disparate Sidney Bechet and Art Hodes dates. But there was a group of artists who gave that vague title a meaning and an identity. The four sessions . . . established a very special, cooperative sound. Perhaps this was the beginning of the Blue Note concept of using a repertory company to document top level improvised music."[16] This group of "Blue Note Jazzmen" recorded seventeen titles. Most of the sides included Hall and present a more traditional jazz repertoire with tunes such as "High Society," "Everybody Loves My Baby," and "At the Ball." On Johnson's date of March 4, 1944, Ben Webster, who had recently ended a four-year stint with Duke Ellington, replaces Hall on four masterpieces. Blue Note 32 featured two Johnson compositions. "Victory Stride" is given a contemporary swing feel, although Johnson may have composed it many decades earlier. Johnson's arrangement allows the musicians to shine in extended solos as well as during brief breaks. "Blue Mizz" is another unique Johnson twelve-bar, slow blues. On many band sides, Johnson lays low while others are soloing. On this number, he is heard throughout plying his multifaceted blues licks supporting the other soloists. The pairing of bright swing and sultry blues was a hit, and at least for one week in May was cited by *Billboard* as one of the best-selling record releases nationally.[17] Lorraine Lion (later Gordon), at the time wife of Blue Note founder Alfred, recalled Johnson in the recording studio. "He was like a God, a legend," she said, and Lion and Wolff gave Johnson "free reign" artistically. "Musicians loved him, all loved him," she added, noting how the Blue Note team had become "idol worshippers" of his from their earlier days collecting his records.[18] By the late 1940s, Lion and Wolff began recording the newer jazz styles. But its founders never dismissed their early work. On the fifteenth anniversary of the label, by then synonymous with modern jazz, Alfred Lion reflected, "As I cast a retrospective glance on Blue Note's history, I am happy to observe that our policies stood the test of time and that our early recordings, far from being forgotten, still represent a vital segment of the Blue Note catalogue."[19] Since the passing of the founders, the long legacy of Blue Note records is seen predominantly as the home of modern jazz. In many retrospectives of the label on the occasion of latter-day anniversaries, the focus has been on its bebop days and beyond. A five-CD set, released on its fiftieth anniversary in 1989, included only three pre-bebop tracks, none by Johnson or their own titular "Blue Note Jazzmen."

Johnson continued his regular association with Condon in the Town Hall concert series, appearing on the third concert of the season, February 19, 1944. Condon always featured Johnson as soloist, and on this date he played "The Boogie Woogie Stride," "Gut Stomp," and improvisations on a thirty-two bar standard accompanied by George Wettling. The concerts always concluded with an impromptu ensemble jam.[20] The April 25 concert was reportedly broadcast over local New York station WHN, the only US station that carried the jazz concert series, and aired overseas on the BBC. Transcriptions for airplay were sent to Latin America by the Coordinator of Inter-American Affairs, but these recordings have not been located. Eddie Condon was engaged by the Office of War Information to bring together a group to record for the War Department.[21] The recordings that include Johnson are likely the V-discs made on March 12, 1944. They chose an early Sunday morning, a challenging time to gather jazz musicians, and after several phone calls and taxi rides, a group including Wild Bill Davison, George Lugg, Edmund Hall, Pee Wee Russell, Pops Foster, Kansas Fields, Jimmy Rushing, and Joe Bushkin convened at the Columbia Records studios. The conceit was to simulate a jam session, and Johnson and Bushkin traded off on piano choruses backing Jimmy Rushing on a blues. A Johnson quartet with Hall, Foster, and Fields played "Baby, Won't You Please Come Home," and the two pianists played a duet on Johnson's tune "Old Fashioned Love" after an introduction by Condon, but these two tunes have not been found. An OWI film crew had set up the studio with war-related props and backdrops including images of aircraft. With cameras on cranes roving on dollies, Johnson was captured from many angles.[22] The music was never issued on V-disc, and it is not known if the film was ever shown to the troops.[23] To date, the film has not been located. With the dissolution of the OWI, much of the material they produced, intended as expedient entertainment, was disposed of as scrap.

Waller tributes continued, including a concert sponsored by the American Youth for Democracy (AYD), the newly renamed youth wing of the communist party. On April 2, the AYD invited a remarkable array of pianists to Carnegie

Hall to celebrate their keyboard colleague. Included were Johnson, Willie "The Lion" Smith, Mary Lou Williams, Teddy Wilson and his orchestra, Count Basie and his orchestra, Earl Hines, Pat Flowers, and Duke Ellington.[24] For his brief appearance, Johnson played the lesser-known Waller tunes "Chocolate Bar" and "My Fate Is In Your Hands," selections that Leonard Feather called "unique and intelligent."[25] The next day, the NAACP intended to hold a fundraiser at the Peggy Guggenheim gallery on 57th Street, but the venue was changed at the last minute to the British and American Art Gallery one block away on 56th Street to accommodate a larger crowd. A variety of socially conscious literati sponsored the event, including Carl Van Doren, Olin Downes, Deems Taylor, Robert Goffin, Gilbert Seldes, Julien Levy, Samuel Barlow, and Mrs. John Hammond. Count Basie was tapped to line up the musicians, and, for an admission fee of $2.00, one could enjoy Johnson, Frankie Newton, Bill Coleman, Bobby Hackett, Sid Catlett, Pee Wee Russell, Oscar Pettiford, Joe Bushkin, and Eddie Condon. Basie brought his star lineup with Lester Young, Buck Clayton, Freddy Green, and Dicky Wells.[26]

At two separate sessions in April and two in June, Johnson recorded a series of Waller compositions through World Transcriptions ultimately released on Decca, an opportunity he welcomed. This was his first release on a major label since the October 1941 Clarence Williams session in which he played on only one tune. For World, he first recorded eight Waller tunes as piano solos—"I've Got a Feelin' I'm Fallin'," "My Fate Is in Your Hands," "Ain't Misbehavin'," "Blue Turning Grey Over You," "I'm Gonna Sit Right Down and Write Myself a Letter" (not written by Waller but closely associated with him from his classic recording), "Keepin' Out of Mischief Now," "Squeeze Me," and "Honeysuckle Rose." In June, Johnson recorded the same eight tunes again with accompaniment by drummer Eddie Dougherty, who "could not recall, some three and a half decades later, exactly why a pianist like Johnson needed a drummer to back him."[27] In August and September, he recorded eight of his own tunes with Dougherty—five instrumentals and three standards—that were released the following year.[28]

June continued to be a very active month in the recording studio. Including the numbers for Decca, he recorded twenty-three commercially released sides on Signature, Brunswick, Blue Note, Commodore, and Asch. The Asch album recorded June 12 is titled *New York Jazz*. Charles Edward Smith, in his notes, casts the set of six recordings as an historical survey "tracing the background of Harlem jazz." It is notable for a number of reasons. The cover sports the wonderful artwork of David Stone Martin, who had been introduced to Asch by Mary Lou Williams earlier that year. Martin had been working for the Office of Strategic Services and Office of War Information. The year before, in 1943, one of Martin's paintings was used for Navy recruitment. It was titled "Above and

Beyond the Call of Duty" and featured Dorie Miller. His record cover artwork that started for Asch with *New York Jazz* launched an illustrious career as a jazz album illustrator. There are over five hundred album covers to his credit, and he is renowned for his ability to evoke the feeling of jazz.[29] "The background" for *New York Jazz*, as Smith describes it, is comprised of two tunes that represent early styles, ragtime and the slow drag. Johnson's recording of Scott Joplin's "Euphonic Sounds" is the first commercial recording of this unique composition. Johnson admired Joplin and this piece in particular and thought it very modern. Jess Pickett's "The Dream" epitomizes the multicultural mix of styles that melded the blues, Spanish rhythms, and low country feeling. The second two tunes represent Harlem from the teens through the twenties. In addition to his original instrumental "Four O'clock Groove," the version of W. C. Handy's "Hesitation Blues" includes Johnson's only recorded vocal. The modern era, from "Harlem on Down," is entered with two Johnson originals. "The Boogie Dream" highlights his singular approach to the popular format. "Hot Harlem" comes from his ill-fated 1931 show *Sugar Hill*. At a time when older jazz styles and tunes were beginning to fall out of favor in some corners of the jazz music world, the mainstream press found something refreshing in Johnson's approach. The *New York Herald Tribune* found the music to be "unaffected, straight jazz, suave, not entirely devoid of sophistication (witness 'Four O'clock Groove'), but still without any of the objectionable commercial concessions of the day. They offer good examples of the sort of unselfconscious music so hard to find anywhere around town."[30] The rarely complimentary reviewer for the *New York Times*, Mark A. Schubart, noted, "In this album, Asch presents a comprehensive cross-section of the veteran Harlem pianist's style. Unlike so many jazz pianists, James P. doesn't cut all the tunes he plays down to his size, but accords them varied and ingratiating treatments."[31] Dancer and frequent commentator on jazz Roger Pryor Dodge praised the music and Johnson's conception, especially noting the prescient inclusion of Joplin. He wrote, "Needless to say Johnson is *the* man to play these sides and we can only hope that someone will eventually do an album of ragtime as good as *Euphonic Sounds*."[32]

Frequent work with Condon in May and June further increased the demands on Johnson's schedule. On May 3, NBC's Blue Network arranged a special half hour live broadcast at the Ritz Theater which they recorded, the event supervised by John O'Connor, Fred Waring's manager, and adman Ernie Anderson, who was producing the Town Hall series. The network was considering a commercial release, but the discs from this date remain to be discovered.[33] Despite some hesitation about airing a mixed-race band, the network did begin to broadcast Condon's group regularly beginning May 20, when the Armed Forces Radio Service wanted to record the concerts for the servicemen.[34] On the June 17 date, Condon presented an RCA album of Fats Waller favorites to Johnson as part of the continuing tribute to Waller. Johnson, in his usual featured solo role, played three less well-known tunes of his protégé: "Willow Tree," "Candy Sweets," and "I'm Crazy 'Bout My Baby."[35] He was back with Condon, along with the Lion, for a Monday night concert at Carnegie Hall October 16.[36] Unlike his 1939 recordings, many of which were never released, Johnson's substantial recorded output in 1943 and 1944 was issued and favorably received, with *Down Beat* including him as one of five "hot" (meaning traditional) jazz musicians who excelled in 1944. They especially singled out many of his solos for Blue Note and Asch.[37]

Two recording sessions in 1944 featured Johnson with members of a working band at the time. On September 1, bandmates Rod Cless and Johnson recorded together with a quartet. It was the last session supervised by Perry Bradford. But earlier, on June 22, Johnson recorded with the full front line of the band that included Max Kaminsky, trumpet, Frank Orchard, valve trombone, and Rod Cless, clarinet. They recorded for Commodore under Kaminsky's name, who was leading this group at a newly opened Greenwich Village club called the Pied Piper. No recordings from the club are known to exist, and this session provides the best glimpse of what the band sounded like. The deceptively free-wheeling Chicago-style ensemble sound betrays their excellent musicianship. They opened at the club a few weeks before coming in to the studio and are well-rehearsed on the four tunes that date from the 1920s and earlier.[38] Their energetic synergy would pay off for the new owners of the club and propel their gig into the history books.

Chapter 25

PIED PIPER, 1944–1945

> James P. played with Max Kaminsky's band at the Pied Piper in Greenwich
> Village . . . in a billing that gets more wondrous as the years go by.
> —DICK HYMAN

In early June 1944, James P. Johnson began an engagement that has attained well-deserved legendary status.[1] A Greenwich Village saloon at 15 Barrow Street called La Boheme came under new management when the proprietor sold out to the three owners of the jukebox concession in the bar to whom he owed money. The three neophyte nightclub owners renamed it the Pied Piper. Despite the name, business was slow. The jukebox alone failed to draw enough customers, so a new strategy was required. Through a mutual friend, trumpeter Max Kaminsky was introduced to the owners, who asked him to put together a band. Kaminsky recruited Rod Cless on clarinet, Frank Orchard on valve trombone, Jack Lesberg on bass, Danny Alvin on drums, and James P. Johnson. A few months later, Willie "The Lion" Smith was added. The pay was a meager $55 a week for each man, but the deal included dinner featuring onion soup and fried chicken, and, to the detriment of Cless and Johnson, all the alcohol the musicians wanted. Lesberg recalled one of the owners was an attorney named Feinstein who was a piano buff, and he asked Kaminsky to arrange for a proper instrument for the club.[2]

Kaminsky offered an attractive incentive for Johnson to join him, recalling, "I managed to talk the bosses into investing in a Steinway baby grand, and I took James P. up to 57th Street and turned him loose in the store until he found one that talked back in the right tone of voice."[3] Kaminsky recalled that Johnson was officially the intermission pianist and the Lion the band pianist, but they changed roles as the mood hit them. In addition to the baby grand, there was a fine upright piano, and Johnson and Smith would often perform duets. The twenty-four-year-old Lesberg was newly arrived in town from Boston, and awestruck at his bandmates, marveling, "Willie 'The Lion,' mind you, and James P. there!"[4] With no air conditioning, during the summer, customers would make their way to the sidewalk just outside the door while listening to the two legendary pianists. The Pied Piper became a destination for visiting and local musicians. Kaminsky heavily promoted the engagement:

> Ernie Anderson arranged for me to appear on disc-jockey programs to spread the word about the Pied Piper; The New Yorker magazine gave the club a fine write up; the newspaper columnists gave it enthusiastic plugs; and the place caught on practically overnight. Tim Costello brought the Vanderbilts down, Duke Ellington used to drop in to hear his good friend James P. Johnson, and it wasn't long before the club became a regular musicians' hangout, with all the jazzmen who were still in the service sitting in whenever they were in town, so that instead of six musicians on the stand there was likely to be a dozen or more.[5]

David Gelman was a sixteen-year-old Canadian immigrant who had gotten to know Albert Ammons when he first arrived in New York around 1942. In a true case of mistaken identity, he was eager to see Pete Johnson, who he thought was playing at an upcoming Eddie Condon Town Hall concert. "Pete" must have been a nickname, he thought, for the full name he saw on the ad was James P. Johnson. He immediately learned the difference at the concert, and became an admirer of James P. Johnson. Gelman lived in Greenwich Village, and during the engagement at the Pied Piper, attended nearly every night. He became very close with Johnson and Smith, observing firsthand the goings-on. There was usually a good crowd, Gelman recalls, and, except in bad weather, there would be more fans than regular drinkers and tourists. Gelman recalled visits, and usually a tune or two, by Artie Shaw, Sidney Bechet, Duke Ellington, Mary Lou Williams, Hazel Scott, Eubie Blake, Claude Hopkins, Hank Duncan, Blanche Sewell (Willie "The Lion" Smith's wife), Frankie Newton, and Dick Hyman.[6] Jack Lesberg recalled frequent visits from Art Tatum, Count Basie, Don Frye, and Eddie Condon. The pianists would listen intently to each other, and then play together on the two pianos. Lesberg went on, "Well, the stride school and these guys were fantastic musicians in what they did and the way they did it.... some of these after-hours things were just marvelous things that had happened when Duke or Tatum would come in and play until six in the morning."[7] Feinstein would often close the place to the public at 4:00 a.m. so the musicians could play for themselves. *Down Beat* reported on Tatum's visits while he was playing at the

Pocket calendar advertising the newly opened Pied Piper before Willie the Lion Smith joined the group. (Courtesy of the Maryland Center for History and Culture, Eubie Blake Manuscripts and Ephemera Collection)

Three Deuces on 52nd Street, noting, "Art Tatum spent his night off, listening to James P. Johnson play for him at the Pied Piper. The Great Johnson played all of Tatum's favorites and they knocked each other out."[8] In a photograph taken at the Pied Piper, we can see Bob Haggart and Joe Albany sitting in. In the same photo, Johnson is seen taking a break sitting at a table with legendary jazz writer Walter Schaap, father of jazz scholar Phil Schaap.[9] Dick Wellstood, then a high school senior and soon to become a world-class jazz pianist who fully embraced the stride style like Dick Hyman (who was already in college), was practically kidnapped from his Connecticut home by his buddies to hear Smith and Johnson.[10] Undoubtedly this list of musicians who came to listen and play is incomplete.

Gelman recalled that Johnson was not a big drinker during this time, although Kaminsky had a different memory. He recalled that James P. Johnson Jr. accompanied his father to the club to monitor his alcohol consumption, but not always successfully, as the two would often indulge together. The Lion was not bashful about telling the crowd to keep quiet when he played. Johnson never did. His playing at times could be reserved and reflective, avoiding battle with the audience. Smith and Johnson were the closest of friends, but Smith is often thought of as allowing an apparent arrogance to inflate his abilities, promoting himself as Johnson's equal. In reality, Kaminsky recalls, "Willie the lion was like a lamb around James P., for as great as the lion is and as self-assured as he always acted about himself, he accorded Johnson the highest respect because James P. was the master piano man."[11] Gelman recalled, "When James P. played, the Lion listened." Johnson always played the baby grand. One day a patron offered Smith $50 to play the grand in a duet with Johnson. Smith refused. Both Smith and Ellington referred to

Johnson observing the Lion at the piano, possibly at the Pied Piper. (Author's collection)

Johnson as the master. Most if not all of the visiting pianists demonstrated the same respect for Johnson. Lesberg, too, recalled Smith playing the upright, and the deference accorded Johnson by the other pianists. He noted, "These guys listened to James P."[12]

On occasion, amateur pianists whose livelihoods relied on unseemly businesses such as drugs and prostitution would come in to play. Usually they had very limited repertoire, sometimes only one piece. One night such a man named Bill Pigett (sp?) played his one piece, Johnson's "Caprice Rag." Gelman recalled the more than credible job he did. Asking Pigett about it, he said he practiced it every waking moment. Then Johnson played his piece in what Gelman remembers as one of the most astonishing performances he'd ever heard Johnson play. The record reviewers for a "Hot Jazz" collector's magazine compared Johnson's playing in person versus on record, noting, "We have had the pleasure of hearing Johnson a few times at the Pied Piper club in New York lately and he is tearing the place apart. His rendition of 'Pine Top's Boogie Woogie,' one night, was better than any of his recorded versions."[13] Clarinetist Paul Nossiter was a student of Cless and saw Johnson at the Pied Piper. He recalled, "I went up to James P. while he was playing a wildly fast bit of stride and we carried on a conversation with him looking directly at me. His hands had a life of their own. Incredible!"[14]

The degree of admiration, respect, wonder, and love for Johnson expressed by his bandmates is unqualified. Kaminsky recalled,

When I called up James P. Johnson and Willie the Lion Smith and found out they were interested, I really began to get excited. . . . With James P. Johnson and the lion and a baby grand, how could we go wrong. . . . James P. Johnson, a stocky man with powerful shoulders and great big ham hands, could produce some of the most delicate musical sounds I ever heard. . . . A very modest and reserved man, he was usually serious and concentrated when he played, but when he got really going on the piano he'd have the whole building vibrating. . . . I never tired of trying to let James P. know how much I appreciated him. He not only had such a beautiful way of playing, he had the right way of playing, with nothing corny about it. . . . James P. would produce a hundred different changes in ideas and expression and images. . . .[15]

Jack Lesberg relayed feelings nothing short of reverence when recalling his time playing with him.[16] Shortly after his death, Rod Cless was eulogized by James McGraw in a lengthy article. McGraw recounted how Cless spent intermission at the Pied Piper:

On those hot summer nights you walked in from the street and the atmosphere was so damp and hot and smoke ridden that you found it hard to breathe. The doors were kept closed because the neighbors complained of the "noise" and there was no other ventilation of any kind. You fought your way against the foul surge back to the bandstand. James P. Johnson was playing intermission piano. Rod sat nearby at a table with a drink. He could have taken his drink outside where it was cooler. The other boys in the band were kibitzing out on the stoop or sitting in Mac's car with a jug. But Rod was in that oven listening to Jimmie's hot piano. He had heard it a thousand times. It didn't matter. He wanted to hear it more. Perhaps it was a premonition that soon he would never hear it again on earth.[17]

In August and September, Johnson returned to the studio to record his own tunes after the series of Waller's popular songs for World and Decca. He received some press coverage noting the recordings and his tenure at the Pied Piper.[18] A September 23 Condon Town Hall concert was followed on October 16 by a mammoth Condon concert at Carnegie Hall. Johnson, Smith, Kaminsky, and Lesberg took the night off from the Pied Piper to appear with thirty other musicians.[19] Johnson was featured playing several Waller pieces.[20] No recorded music has surfaced, so we can't know the distinction jazz radio host and writer Ralph Berton was making when he wrote, "Starting the second half, James P.

Johnson played one number in the ornamental style I find I can live without, then, to even the score, came through with *Feeling I'm Falling* in a way which combined everything good he's got, which is plenty."[21] On October 6, Johnson and Smith were featured performers along with Roy Eldridge and others at the inaugural Canteen at Columbia University sponsored by the university radio station. The event was promoted as a benefit for Columbia and Barnard students, especially for those in the military. The item in the school paper made note of their Pied Piper residency.[22] They played two pianos as they were doing downtown. As part of the war effort, the government engaged musicians to support bond drives. The sixth series began November 20 with four half-hour radio programs. Johnson was one of numerous prominent musicians participating in the radio campaign.[23]

The personnel at the Pied Piper began to change. Johnson brought in a band under his leadership on September 12 with Frankie Newton, Wilbur De Paris, George James, Eddie Williams, Joe Brown, and Goldie Lucas to play Tuesday nights. Newton and De Paris traded off on a bass trumpet, most likely at Johnson's urging, indulging his penchant for unusual instrumentation.[24] Johnson continued to play intermission piano on other nights, and trade off with Smith in Kaminsky's band.[25] Starting September 24, Kaminsky took a band into the fraternal clubhouse at 110 West 48th Street for Sunday afternoon jam sessions. Johnson played intermission piano.[26] The Pied Piper engagement began to unwind. Johnson was out in mid-November due to illness, and Rod Cless died on December 8 at age thirty-seven after a fatal fall on his way home from what was already scheduled to be his last night at the Pied Piper.[27] In his memoir, Kaminsky complains about an unnamed musician edging him out as leader in December of 1944. Wilbur De Paris had replaced Frank Orchard in Kaminsky's band in November, and, by December, the band was featured under his leadership.[28] De Paris wanted his brother Sidney to take the trumpet chair, which he did when Wilbur led the band in late November while Johnson was out sick. De Paris's tenure as leader was short-lived. By January 1945, the band was under the direction of James P. Johnson, with the De Paris brothers still on board.[29] Willie "The Lion" Smith led a trio,[30] and Wilbur De Paris led Tuesday night jam sessions on Johnson's night off.[31] The De Paris brothers called their spot the "Swing Soiree."[32]

Johnson undertook his own promotion for the Pied Piper at the urging of his personal representative George W. Lattimore. They had prepared an invitation card with the following statement: "The friends and patrons of the famous pianist, composer and conductor JAMES P. JOHNSON, are cordially invited to hear him with his newly selected group of musicians Every Evening (except Tuesday) from 9:30 P. M. until closing." The card referred to the group as "James P. Johnson and his orchestra," with "Willie Smith (The Lion) Trio."

Lattimore is listed on the invitation as Johnson's personal representative.[33] Johnson and Lattimore were looking for an opportunity to broadcast from the club on local radio, but this likely never came off.[34] By March, Johnson had reduced his own group to a trio with Frankie Newton and Israel Crosby,[35] and shortly after, the Pied Piper closed its doors for good, ending a nearly yearlong magical chapter in jazz history. Johnson's notable presence in Greenwich Village at Café Society, the Pied Piper, and Nick's,[36] was recollected the next year by his friend Langston Hughes, who wrote, "The infectious piano playing of James P. Johnson came back to public attention in a big way by way of Village night spots in recent years."[37] 15 Barrow Street was shuttered as a performance venue, reopening in 1955 as Café Bohemia. For five years, it featured bebop and hard bop jazz legends including the emerging sounds of Miles Davis and John Coltrane until it once again closed.

Although Johnson put substantial energy into his nominal leadership at the Pied Piper, he continued to attend high-profile as well as local engagements. On January 17, 1945, *Esquire* magazine held its second annual All-American Poll-Winners concert—an ambitious program. The first event had taken place at the Metropolitan Opera House in New York, featuring musicians chosen by a panel of experts. The second concert presented the panel's choices in concerts held simultaneously in three cities, each headlined by a great name—Louis Armstrong at the Municipal Auditorium in New Orleans,[38] Duke Ellington in Los Angeles, and Benny Goodman in New York. James P. Johnson was engaged as the pianist in Armstrong's Jazz Foundation Six along with Sidney Bechet, J. C. Higginbotham, and Paul Barbarin. The second half of the concert was broadcast nationally on radio over the Blue Network. Some of the tunes were recorded by the Armed Forces Radio Service (AFRS) and released on transcriptions, including Johnson's solo on "Arkansas Blues." He is introduced with a terse introduction as "one of the great names in jazz piano at the keyboard, James P. Johnson."[39] This was Johnson's first appearance in New Orleans.[40] During the first half, he played "Carolina Shout" and "Snowy Morning Blues." Unfortunately, those performances were not preserved. With locals Paul Barbarin accompanying him on drums and Leon Prima's band, they zipped through "The Evolution of Jazz from the jungle to Basin Street in 5 minutes" for the nearly three-thousand-strong crowd of local VIPs.[41]

It had been over a year since the death of Fats Waller, but his loss was still felt acutely in the jazz and popular music world, and during the week of February 4–11, WNEW broadcast their second annual swing festival dedicated to him. Sometime during that week, perhaps on the first day and more than once, Johnson was in studio for the fifteen-minute segments.[42] On one broadcast, he starts off with a truncated "Old Fashioned Love" when Waller manager Ed Kirkeby interrupts for a scripted segment with Kirkeby and Johnson reminiscing about the old parlor social days with Waller and Willie "The Lion" Smith. Kirkeby suggests Johnson play the "Carolina Shout," which he does, morphing into "Ain't Misbehavin'" with a band of Waller alumni. On another of those dates, Pat Flowers, a brilliant pianist but who is remembered and criticized somewhat unfairly as a Waller clone for his perceived literal adoption of Waller's style, served as MC and coordinator. Johnson plays "Honeysuckle Rose" and "Ain't Misbehavin'" with a band including the Waller alumni and Tommy Dorsey. Flowers and Mildred Bailey each take a vocal chorus. Fortunately, these broadcasts were preserved, providing another example of Johnson's enthralling creativity in live performance playing behind singers as well as with a band. He was continually sought after to participate in charitable and benefit work. After playing several benefit concerts in Brooklyn, the *Pittsburgh Courier* newspaper engaged him to support a project honoring the nineteenth-century African American composer James Bland, who lay in an unmarked grave outside Philadelphia. The goal to raise funds for a proper monument was superseded by plans to create a scholarship in Bland's honor instead.[43] On successive Mondays in April, Condon took his usual roster of Saturday jam session personnel, including Johnson, on the road, first to the Academy of Music in Philadelphia on April 2,[44] and the following week to the Bushnell Memorial in Hartford, Connecticut, on April 9.[45] One year out of college, the future Atlantic Records founder Ahmet Ertegun was producing concerts as the organizer and president of the Washington Jazz Music Society. On April 16, he arranged an eclectic group at Turner's Arena that included Johnson, Ben Webster, Pee Wee Russell, Sid Catlett, Muggsy Spanier, Benny Morton, and Buck Clayton.[46] While Johnson was recording and gigging around, the "Friends of James P. Johnson" had remained active and were about to hand him further realizations as a composer.

Chapter 26

THE SLOW DECLINE, 1945-1946

> All he wanted to do was just play the piano; other things he didn't care about. He just couldn't be bothered by anything that didn't have something to do with playing or composing music.
> —WILLIE "THE LION" SMITH

Johnson's resurgent visibility in the jazz world on record and at the Pied Piper brought him some recognition in Esquire's 1945 *Jazz Book*. In 1944, he received no points from the critics for a place on their All-American Jazz Band. Thanks to advocacy by George Avakian and Charles Edward Smith, in 1945 he was on the board with five, tied with Count Basie and one point behind Nat Cole.[1] Johnson sat for sculptor Esther Zolott. Originally from California, she gained a foothold in the art world through the WPA Farm Security Administration and, by 1935, had works placed in the Art Institute of Chicago. She promised Johnson 20 percent of any copies sold, plus a copy for himself.[2] He tithed half of any proceeds from the sale of the bust, "donated to the cause of Christ our beloved Jesus."[3] As he got older, his faith became more important. He was raised in the African Methodist Episcopal Church, but later in life adopted the Baptist faith of Lillie Mae. He tithed at least $300 a year.[4] Johnson embraced other nontraditional views, such as reincarnation, a topic hotly debated with Willie "The Lion" Smith, who no doubt interjected aspects of Jewish mysticism into the conversation, and Fats Waller, who did not believe in an afterlife.[5]

Johnson was preparing for a concert he hoped would mark the pinnacle of his career as a composer, the presentation of his symphonic works at Carnegie Hall. Jack Lesberg recalled spending time with Johnson rehearsing these works with small string or woodwind groups. Of Johnson's reaction to hearing his concert pieces played, even in rehearsal, "he was like a little kid hearing all this stuff," recalled Lesberg.[6] On May 4, a "Jazzfest and Pop Concert presenting James P. Johnson—composer-pianist" was produced at Carnegie Hall. It was neither the first all-Johnson concert, nor his first appearance at Carnegie Hall, but the feature of his work at the country's most prestigious concert hall he hoped would attract the attention of the serious music world. The concert also showcased the depth and breadth of his contributions to other aspects of American music. In the concert program, George Lattimore succinctly crystalizes Johnson's importance and the scope of the music heard that evening:

> As pianist and composer, James P. Johnson has made one of the most thoroughgoing and decisive contributions to the history of jazz. He has had renown as a pianist for about thirty years, during which time, as a ranking soloist, orchestra leader, and accompanist to such singers as the unforgettable Bessie Smith, his work has helped establish jazz piano style, and has advanced our view of the continuity of jazz. Moreover, this undisputed "dean of jazz pianists" has taught a number of now famous younger men, including the late Fats Waller, while elements of his playing style have been freely absorbed by others. As a composer of popular songs, Johnson has shown that rarest of gifts for the creation of spontaneous melody, and he has written a wonderful series of hit tunes throughout the years. Some of these tunes, which have never lost their familiarity, are on the present program.
>
> Johnson's seriousness, dignity, and critical awareness—qualities that define a rich and mature personality—are felt in his concert compositions on this program. "Harlem Suite," "Yamekraw," and "Ode to Dorie Miller," products of a difficult "after hour" schooling, are rooted in the same mode of feeling that underlies all of Johnson's creative activity.[7]

As composer of extended compositions and popular songs, vocal accompanist, soloist, and "jam session" musician, Johnson was well represented. Baritone William Franklin, soprano Edith Sewell, and guest pianist Bruce Wendell performed in addition to Johnson. Josef Cherniavsky conducted the chorus and orchestra of fifty. Cherniavsky was born in Odessa in 1892 and had studied with the great Leschetizky in Vienna. He had been in the United States since 1916.[8] Perhaps as enticement or compensation for his participation, some of his pieces were included. The concert was highly anticipated, as Lattimore aggressively promoted it, with help from Willie "The Lion" Smith and pianist Sammy Price. Asch, Blue Note, and Decca Records were sponsors. The concert was listed in several issues of the *New York Times*, once with a notice positioned between those for Leonard Bernstein and Eugene Ormandy.[9] Johnson, eagerly anticipating the performance of his symphonic works in America's most noted concert hall, must have been pleased to see his name mentioned alongside these two greats of American concert music.

The first part of the program was dominated by Johnson's orchestral pieces, interspersed with pieces by Cherniavsky, and spirituals sung by Edith Sewell. "April in Harlem" and "Baptist Mission" (excerpts from *Harlem Symphony*) and *Yamekraw* were performed. "Reflections," a tone poem, was listed on the program, but accounts of the concert indicate that it was not performed. The second part of the program featured Johnson and his works almost exclusively. After Cherniavsky's *St. Louis Fantasy*, described as a Russian tribute to W. C. Handy, Johnson accompanied Edith Sewell as she sang "If I Could Be with You" and "Old Fashioned Love." With Johnson still at the piano, William Franklin sang the featured piece of the evening, "Ode to Dorie Miller." The piece, with lyrics by Andy Razaf, is a choral work for male voice and chorus honoring Miller, the twenty-two-year-old African American Navy cook, third class, who was awarded the Navy Cross for heroism at Pearl Harbor. This was its first performance. As one reviewer noted, "plain old jazz didn't get going until 10:10, when Jimmy unloosed [sic] some solo work. The audience had been very happy all evening but now went wild."[10] According to the program, Johnson played "Caprice Rag," "Arkansas Blues," "Boogie Stride," "Impressions," and Fats Waller's "Willow Tree." Perhaps as part of the sponsorship agreement, all the popular and jazz tunes played by Johnson in the second half of the program except for "Willow Tree" had been recorded for his benefactor record labels in the prior few years. Johnson's solos were followed by a "jazz-jamboree" and finale playing Johnson compositions with guest artists listed as Sidney and Wilbur De Paris, Sam [sic, Franz] Jackson, Kaiser Marshall, and Israel Crosby.[11] This part of the performance was supposed to have been recorded, but nothing is known to have survived. Johnson dedicated the concert to Fats Waller.

H. J. Harrison, in his review of the concert in *The Jazz Record*, commented about Johnson's approach to extended composition: "What Jimmy has written is not arranged jazz. It is not jazz with some fancy instruments thrown in to make a big stage show. It isn't string music with some raz-ma-taz stuff added. It's music of itself. The jazz voice is natural to him, and he blends it in with the classical, using both to achieve the expression he wants."[12] Tommy Watkins, in the *New York Amsterdam News*, commented, "James P. Johnson really came through with colors flying at his superb concert staged at Carnegie Hall on Friday nite. He's really in a class of his own." He also praised Johnson's manager George W. Lattimore for his efforts promoting Johnson.[13] David Gelman attended the concert and recalls the turnout was poor, the hall perhaps only a third full. Another reviewer for the *Amsterdam News*, however, noted the turnout was encouraging when considering the concert was presented toward the end of the Carnegie season, and the public was likely saturated with large hall jazz concerts. He commented, "Mr. Johnson is a 'name' in the popular field of music, both as pianist and composer, but he came to Carnegie at the tail end of the season; after the public has been sated with popular concerts. This does not, however, detract from his eminence as a prolific writer who has given the world more than five hundred compositions from 'Hot Piano' to sonatas and symphonies." He felt compelled to point out, however, the frequently cited criticism that Johnson's orchestral works were not true to Western symphonic form. Despite this perceived deficiency, he noted several of the pieces "were well written" and that *Yamekraw* "was particularly interesting."[14]

Sammy Price, who helped with fundraising and promotion, recalled the circumstances that delayed the production and may have contributed to a disappointing turnout—the death of President Franklin D. Roosevelt on April 12. According to Price, the original date of the concert was April 12. He recalled, "So it meant that we had to postpone the thing for a week, [the concert came off three weeks later] and after that the same enthusiasm wasn't there. As a result I don't think we made a profit." Price and Johnson had known each other for many years, running in similar musical circles from Café Society to Eddie Condon's ventures. Their relationship grew deeper after the concert disappointment, with Price noting, "James P. and I became very close, because he knew that I was proud of him as a man and an artist, and he was grateful to me for that until his death." Price, like others, was baffled by Johnson's relative lack of name recognition with the general public and in the commercial music industry. He concluded, "I think the reason he didn't have success with his works was that the Broadway promoters forgot that here was a man that wrote the song *The Charleston*. He should have been able to find financial support for anything he wanted to do."[15]

Other reviewers couldn't see past Johnson as a hot jazz pianist, a perception supported by the response of his well-meaning loyal audience when he came out on stage to play. Harlem's *New York Age* found little reason to include the orchestral musicians in the program, who, they felt, were "distinctly not in the Johnson groove," but the small jazz band ". . . stopped the show," with many encores requested.[16] *Variety* wrote, "A small but enthusiastic (when Johnson appeared) audience was on hand to hear him play the piano. That's what they wanted and that's what they eventually got, late in the evening." The prominent entertainment oracle concluded, "Johnson can return to Carnegie, judging from response, but he would be wise to play more piano and leave the longhairs back at the NBC building."[17] Their suggestion turned out to be sadly prophetic. Except for *Yamekraw*, this was the last orchestral performance of Johnson's symphonic music until it was rediscovered among his personal papers in the early 1990s. It was thought lost for those nearly fifty intervening years. After the

Carnegie Hall disappointment, Johnson mostly abandoned orchestral composing intended for the concert hall, limiting his "serious" work to piano reductions of his orchestral themes, and a number of smaller-scale "tone poems" for piano, some of which were published by Mills over the next several years. In high demand as a jazz musician, new patrons soon emerged to keep him very busy. Although composing for the concert hall was behind him, he turned again to musical theater. If the academy wasn't ready for his approach to reimagining the music of his ancestors, perhaps the popular stage still was.

In late June, Maceo Pinkard was preparing his new show titled *New World Fantasy*. A series of satirical sketches portraying historical events from the eighteenth century to modern times was performed by dancers and operatic singers. The show was staged by Walter Brooks, and described as an "operetta" utilizing excerpts from operas and classical works along with the twenty "historically appointed numbers" composed by Pinkard.[18] Pinkard wanted Johnson to conduct the orchestra of over twenty symphonic musicians when the show had its out-of-town opening, which was planned for either White Plains or Jones Beach.[19] October 1 found Johnson in Hartford, Connecticut, as guest artist with orchestra leader Bill Luckhardt at The Paddock. Part of his appearance was broadcast on WHTD for thirty minutes, from 11:15 to 11:45. *Variety* highlighted the reaction of the standing-room-only audience, noting, "Johnson's playing garnered most of the accolade. His solo ivory tickling far superior to rank and file of house band."[20] Around this time, Johnson planned to venture into radio as host of his own show presenting the history of jazz. Acting as narrator, he called the program *Jazzification*. The script for his first show included playing recent reissues of Jelly Roll Morton's "Sidewalk Blues," Handy's "Saint Louis Blues," Will Marion Cook's "I'm Comin' Virginia," and his own recording of Scott Joplin's "Euphonic Sounds." In his selections, he pays tribute to his good friends and mentors Handy and Cook, and shows his respect for Morton despite the conventional trope that the Harlem musicians had little regard for him. Johnson had been consistent in his admiration for Joplin. For his second show, he planned to explore the "forerunners of ragtime"—the Negro spirituals, quadrilles, work songs, and Negro shouts. The scripts suggest each show ran about fifteen minutes, but there is no evidence it ever aired.[21]

On October 25, Johnson was again the center of attention, this time at a concert at Town Hall. In addition to playing his own works, Johnson emphasized his recollections and interpretations of musicians who he admired and who had influenced him. The concert was promoted in the African American and mainstream press, with the *New York Times* including a picture of him.[22] He was introduced as "the daddy of all jazz pianists," and on the program as "The master of jazz pianists."[23] Ernie Anderson promoted the event as a "jazz piano recital" with his own press releases.[24] Eddie Condon was scheduled to make introductory comments, but he failed to show. Disc jockey Fred Robbins filled in as MC. Johnson opened with a medley of his own compositions, including "If I Could Be with You," "Old Fashioned Love," "Don't Cry Baby," "Charleston," "Carolina Shout," and the second movement of his *Jassamine Concerto*. He followed this with sets highlighting the work of George Gershwin and Fats Waller. In what he characterized as an "Eastern Cycle" and a "Western Cycle," Johnson played his impressions of the styles of other pianists: Jack the Bear, One Leg Willie (Joseph), Luckey Roberts, Willie "The Lion" Smith, and Eubie Blake from the East; Scott Joplin, Jelly Roll Morton, Earl Hines, and Pinetop Smith representing the West. Throughout, Johnson provided brief commentary about the musicians he was acknowledging. Johnson was joined on several numbers by tenor saxophonist Bud Freeman and drummer George Wettling, including an improvised blues to conclude the night.

The *New York Times* reviewer preferred this concert to the earlier Carnegie Hall event. Johnson's style as a pianist was lauded:

> Among jazz musicians, Mr. Johnson is something of an individualist, and his style seems to be strictly his own. It is sturdy, amiable, unhurried and pleasantly calm. His use of rhythm is deft without being frenetic, and embellishments are used for decorative rather than virtuosic purposes. Mr. Johnson obviously admires the tunes he plays, and is refreshingly unafraid to let his audience hear them. Unlike many jazz musicians, Mr. Johnson is not an improviser, and most of his arrangements appear to be carefully worked out. That they do not, as a result, lose any of their spontaneity is eloquent testimony to this artist's sincerity and genuineness.[25]

These observations, while praiseworthy, hint at a moment when Johnson's abilities might have been flagging due to his health. Johnson certainly was a virtuoso at variation, yet the reviewer's impression was of a more careful performance with moderate tempos and less risk taking. Johnson had recovered from the stroke in 1940, but friends and fans from that time recalled he had put on a lot of weight, and, at times, evinced the slightest difficulty speaking. His deficits were subtle, but, by this time, he had periodically missed work. These episodes of illness may have been the result of intermittent, transient neurologic events, what are now known as transient ischemic attacks (TIA). Comparing recordings of Johnson speaking before and after the 1940 stroke, he does not demonstrate to any noticeable degree the characteristic slurring caused by a more significant neurological impairment. His language and word-finding skills also appear well preserved. His speech does sound more pressured and rapid at times, but in all available examples, he can be clearly understood.

On available recordings, only rarely does his playing seem affected, even to the slightest degree. Although he continued to perform, he made no records for a year between mid-1945 and 1946. Johnson's more subdued presentation at Town Hall was also noted by *Variety*, in that he "started slowly with a medley of his own compositions.... His musicianship was best demonstrated in the second movement of his piano concerto 'Jazzamine.'"

He must have, at some point after feeling warmed up, let loose while demonstrating other pianists' styles. The *New York Sun* commented, "What Mr. Johnson has is an invaluable left-hand and a great sense of harmonic orientation." *Variety* noted, "James P. Johnson, the master jazz pianist, had his instrument joyfully singing last night in a way that is definitely off the beaten track for Town Hall.... You had to look to be sure only one piano was functioning."[26] Alfred Lion, who well knew the breadth of Johnson's pianistic capabilities, attended and commented on the performance, observing, "James P. was never in better form. I've heard him play wonderfully, but this was a treat, with every number better than the preceding one. He played like he was a young man again."[27] Barbara Hodgkins, reflecting the "modern" bent of *Metronome*, was less impressed. She described the affair as "pleasant listening," detracted by Johnson's "ever changing tempos and weird ideas." Overall she found his renditions to be "old-fashioned," "old-timey," and that they "all sounded much the same."[28] The *American Jazz Review* headline, with its more traditional jazz leanings, read, "James P. Johnson Wows 'Em!"[29] They cited the concert as a close fourth behind an Eddie Condon production in its poll of 1945 events.[30] The factions of the fragmenting jazz community filtered Johnson's broad-minded program through their own contextual lens. His intention was to showcase his important contributions as composer of popular hits, jazz instrumentals, and serious concert music (if only rendered as a piano solo), as solo and ensemble musician, and as a musical elder statesman devoid of ego and not afraid to demonstrate his affection for his pianist brethren. This latter aspect of his persona was clearly acknowledged by the music community, as "Virtually every name jazz musician in N. Y. showed up at Town Hall" for the concert, observed the reviewer in *Variety*. "In all, it was a neat show, and the nearly filled house loved it," they concluded.[31] Although promoted as the first in a series of concerts by Johnson, no subsequent events are known. He may have hoped to parlay his Town Hall success into a concert tour. The only known city on the itinerary was Washington, DC, where he planned to play at Constitution Hall. Although Marian Anderson had been invited to play there in 1943 by the Daughters of the American Revolution after their racially motivated snub in 1939, Johnson was refused a lease.[32]

In November, Johnson joined Mercedes Gilbert for a reprise of their 1941 association. They toured for a month, including a series of performances in

Richmond, Virginia.[33] They were playing at Historically Black Colleges and Universities, and after a break in December when Johnson was on tour, performed together on January 27, 1946, in New York at New York Times Hall.[34] Blue Note Records sponsored a concert at Town Hall on December 15 to promote their recording artists. Popular radio disc jockey Fred Robbins plugged the *Jamming in Jazz* concert on his *1280 Club* radio show on WOV. Curiously, Johnson was reportedly invited only as a spectator. His last Blue Note records were made only a year and a half earlier. In "the real surprise of the evening," Johnson was called up to the stage, his "sparkling version" of "Liza" was received "especially well" by the capacity crowd.[35]

From December 21 until January 1, Johnson was booked at the Brant Inn in Hamilton, Ontario, Canada. The tour included Toronto and Burlington, Vermont. Ed Kirkeby, Fats Waller's longtime manager, arranged the engagement. Johnson played solo, two sets nightly, and was paid $850 for the twelve-day run in Hamilton. Johnson was still a draw. Kirkeby, long an ardent admirer of Johnson, arranged payment better than scale for him. Lillie Mae accompanied him on the trip. The contract stipulated "Employer to furnish Steinway grand piano (or comparable make) tuned to perfect 440 pitch, and room accommodations for two."[36] On December 22, a solo piano recital was aired on CJBC radio out of Toronto. In the thirty-minute program in which he was introduced as "the dean of modern jazz pianists," he played "If Dreams Come True," "April In Harlem," "Snowy Morning Blues," "Boogie-Woogie—Pine Top," "Dream," "Yancey Special," "Carolina Shout," "Blues for Fats," and "Liza."[37] After returning to New York, Kirkeby planned continued exposure and work for Johnson. Kirkeby planted advance notices in the press of a profile of Johnson in the *New Yorker* magazine, and an operetta titled *The Solid South* that Kirkeby planned to produce for Broadway.[38] Neither came to fruition, as continued health issues required a retreat from activity.

Although few in number, Johnson had his detractors. One was impresario and author Al Rose, who often booked Johnson for his "Journeys Into Jazz" concerts. Rose was opinionated, and often unforgiving regarding the personal foibles of the musicians he knew. Although from New Orleans, Rose had a healthy admiration for Eubie Blake and Luckey Roberts, but not much enthusiasm for the later stride style. By the mid-forties, the dual curses of alcoholism and physical illness frequently compromised Johnson's reliability. Rose acknowledged Johnson's solo keyboard virtuosity, and especially the admiration of his contemporaries, but couldn't abide the absences: "Irrespective, though, of my musical appraisal, I found James P. to be grossly unreliable. When I stopped hiring him it wasn't because of the way he played, but because I couldn't rely on him either to show up or to be in satisfactory condition when he did. But I've been in audiences that included Don Lambert, Luckey, Eubie, and Willie 'the lion'—all mesmerized by James P. at the piano." Johnson at times may have seemed lackadaisical about the seemingly rote parade of staged jazz band jam sessions that was a prominent platform for him. This was betrayed to Rose in a comment he made when the two were talking in Tom Delaney's Harlem club. As Rose recalled it, Johnson told him, "All this jazz business. I always wanted to be a musician—not a jazz musician. Any son-of-a-bitch can play that." Rose, who frequently dismissed Johnson's band playing, missed the point, concluding in his memoir, "I know one son-of-a-bitch who can't."[39] In February, James P. Jr., on leave from the merchant marine, spent some time home with his ailing father.[40] After several more months of rest, Johnson was ready to make what would be his final push as performer and composer.

Chapter 27

NEW PATRONS, 1946–1949

> The most important point that I can see is that the jazz musicians
> of the future will have to be able to play all different kinds of jazz—
> in all its treatments—just like the classical musician who,
> in one concert, might range from Bach to Copland.
> —JAMES P. JOHNSON

Johnson remained as active as possible in 1946, but intermittent illness required him to spend most of the year resting while other pianists substituted for him in his regular jobs. While he was in college in 1946, George Wein recalled a visit he made to Philadelphia to visit a friend, and caught a Max Kaminsky event there. Johnson was the scheduled pianist, but didn't make it, so Kaminsky convinced the young Wein to play piano. H. R. S. continued to promote Johnson's 1938 recordings, although he was no longer recording for them, and the latest additions to their catalogue were decidedly more swing- and bebop-influenced, with pianists such as Billy Taylor and Jimmy Jones. Back in 1938, he had probably recorded for them for a flat fee, but the exposure was welcome.[1] Most of his engagements were one-offs, and despite the cumulative toll of his deteriorating health, he often quickly returned to spectacular soloing. He continued the large-venue concert circuit with Eddie Condon. At Town Hall on May 4, he soloed on "Just Before Daybreak," described as "a beautiful original, beautifully rendered," "Aunt Hagar's Blues," and "Carolina Balmoral."[2] A week later on May 13, Condon's magic formula nearly filled Carnegie Hall in one of their series of "Pops" concerts. Drawing on New Orleans repertoire, Johnson soloed on "Way Down Yonder In New Orleans" and "King Porter Stomp," both "expertly rendered by the venerable pianist-composer...."[3] Neither of these performances are known to have been recorded. On May 26, he played at the Queens Medical Society for a cavalcade of Negro Art sponsored by the Queens Legislative Council. The diverse headliners included Katherine Dunham, Mercedes Gilbert, Josh White, Mary Lou Williams, the Jubilaires, and Pete Johnson.[4] May was a good month, and Johnson felt well enough to travel out of town to play for the Jazz Society of Boston. On May 29, Johnson made his way back to Toronto's Eaton Auditorium to participate in a concert organized by David Gelman, the young Canadian who befriended him at the Pied Piper. Gelman was trying his hand at concert promotion, and this event was his third. It went badly awry as the other featured musicians Sidney Bechet, Budd Johnson, and Sidney De Paris failed to appear. Only Wilbur De Paris and Johnson made good. Johnson's solos on several Waller tunes were well received.[5] Four local musicians were quickly recruited, but the lack of preparation compromised the affair. One of them, tenor sax player Hart Wheeler, whose primary influences were Benny Goodman and Ben Webster, was at that time dabbling in the modern bebop style of Charlie Parker, then exploding on the jazz scene. His playing was well executed but seemed incongruous alongside the more traditional styles of Johnson and De Paris. Hartland "Hart" Wheeler would become one of Canada's most prominent jazz musicians. His one known appearance with Johnson was notable enough to deserve mention in his obituary.[6]

James P. Johnson remained visible in the traditional jazz media. His photo portrait was featured by photographer Bill Gottlieb in the May issue of *The Record Changer*. He appeared on the ABC radio program *Piano Playhouse* in June for a meager fee, with show producer Maggy Fisher writing to him, "You did a wonderful job on *Piano Playhouse*, and I'm looking forward to a return appearance for you very very soon. I hope in the very near future we'll be sponsored so the fee will be higher, but in the meantime it's purely a prestige job."[7] The show had launched the year before and became quite popular, and by 1950 spawned record releases. Milton Cross, more famously known as the voice of the live broadcasts from the Metropolitan Opera, was the announcer. No further performances by Johnson on the show are known, but he continued periodic performances on other live radio programs, including a guest spot with Fred Robbins on WOV's *1280 Club*.[8] In August, at Eddie Condon's Club, he briefly replaced the touring Joe Sullivan before stepping back to rest. Joe Bushkin filled in. When Bushkin left to join Benny Goodman, Johnson was ready to return.[9]

Avid jazz fan Bob Maltz, in his spare time away from his day job working for the city of New York, had ambitious goals for promoting traditional jazz in the city. He envisioned uniting the numerous small jazz societies into one unified entity. He named his newly created organization the New York Jazz Club. Naturally, the rollout of his dream on September 21 needed to launch with a concert at the Town Hall. He gathered the top drawer of esteemed musicians that were the mainstays of the concert hall circuit. Johnson traded piano responsibilities with Art Hodes. Much of the concert was recorded, although it is not clear by whom, and was released on LP years later. Maltz and Hodes welcomed Johnson into their orbit as budding concert promoters and afforded him regular playing opportunities for the remainder of the decade.

One other musical guest was not captured at all on the extant recordings of this concert—Huddie "Leadbelly" Ledbetter, the fabled folk/blues twelve-string guitarist. With Pops Foster, Baby Dodds, and Johnson on piano, Leadbelly sang "Good Morning Blues." After their quartet performance, Johnson gave a brief talk on jazz history, which was then followed by his performances of "Maple Leaf Rag" and "Snowy Morning Blues."[10] His piano features and other ensemble tunes are preserved, but the blues with Ledbetter and his own didactic take on jazz history are lost. The scripts for radio about the history of jazz he had prepared show him to have had a clear conception of the origins and development of the music in line with the prevalent historiography at the time. He includes the place of the blues, ragtime, and the contributions of the geographic centers including the eastern seaboard.[11] He was working on completing a radio project originally conceived by Will Marion Cook, who hoped to "spread a magic carpet" in music over the course of an hour that depicted the history of Black music from West Africa to modern times. Cook's sketches included enough material so that Johnson proposed a series of fifteen- or thirty-minute programs with special guests to include Abbie Mitchell (Cook's widow), Ethel Waters, Jules Bledsoe, and the Southernaires.[12] Unfortunately, we don't get to hear Johnson deliver any of this material himself.

The release of the trio recording with Omer Simeon on clarinet and Pops Foster on bass in the fall of 1946 by Moe Asch on his Disc label was well received in mainstream reviews. Johnson was referred to as "one of the honored old-timers of jazz piano playing and composing."[13] Lattimore continued to promote Johnson for concert tour booking through 1946 and 1947,[14] but illness again sidelined him in November when he was hospitalized at New York's famous Bellevue Hospital, reportedly for, "a tumor on the brain."[15] He was described as "a pretty sick man right now."[16] It may have given him some solace to know that he placed third in the *American Jazz Review* popularity poll of traditional jazz pianists.[17] As had been the case for the prior six years, Johnson once again made a remarkable recovery from this medical setback. As it would turn out, he did not have a brain tumor, but continued to experience neurological deficits from cerebrovascular disease, hardening of the arteries leading to or in the brain, or both. Although these episodes were at times referred to as strokes, his functional recovery was always remarkably good, including his piano playing.

By mid-February 1947, he felt well enough to return to the recording studio with Sidney Bechet and Mezz Mezzrow. On March 1, his endurance must have improved sufficiently so that he could play a double-header. On that day he first participated in Rudi Blesh's weekly *This Is Jazz* radio program, broadcast nationally over the mutual network. Blesh became a prominent new patron for Johnson over the next few years. It was Johnson's first appearance on the show that Blesh had launched in January. Many of these broadcasts, which featured veteran New Orleans musicians like Sidney Bechet, Albert Nicholas, Danny Barker, Pops Foster, and George Brunies, were privately recorded and have been commercially released, including this one. Other than his piano roll versions from twenty years earlier, the extant air check includes the only known recorded performance of Johnson playing the "Charleston." Before the band joins him in what becomes an up-tempo, rousing rendition, Johnson begins with an out-of-tempo solo introduction playing the rarely heard verse. In this brief rendering of the minor key lead-in, his rhapsodization and reharmonization is almost haunting. This and his other solo from the broadcast, "Caprice Rag," along with the band sides, betray none of the effects of the motor dysfunction he could have sustained due to his progressing cerebrovascular disease. After the hourlong commitment (thirty-minute rehearsal and thirty-minute program) in the afternoon, Johnson, along with Bechet and Foster, made the short trip to the Town Hall for the 11:30 p.m. start time of the "Honky Tonk Blues at Midnight" concert, produced by Alan Lomax and People's Songs, an organization dedicated to promoting folk music. On the program were a number of blues musician/singers including Sonny Boy Williamson, Big Bill Broonzy, and Memphis Slim.[18] Bechet and Foster received awards from Lomax for placing first and second respectively in their instrument categories in the *American Jazz Review* poll. Johnson's third-place finish amongst pianists apparently did not warrant an award presentation.[19] Although some of the fervor of the political left had dissipated since the end of the war, the commingling of traditional jazz, blues, and folk music as social statement that had started with the "Spirituals to Swing" concerts and at Café Society was continued with the work of Lomax.

Johnson made appearances on Blesh's radio program in May and June. Although Johnson had been quite ill only six months earlier, the preserved performances from these programs, especially June 14 and June 21, include some of his most inspired and creative playing. Before Johnson laid into "Caprice Rag" for Blesh's radio broadcast, the host provided a brief biographical introduction to the guest pianist. Blesh noted that Johnson had cut "hundreds" of piano rolls. Although the number was inflated well above the fifty-seven known Johnson rolls, the reference to a recording medium that George Avakian called a "near-extinct bar-room curiosity"[20] may have meant little to most of Blesh's audience. Millions of piano rolls representing all genres of music were made in the teens and twenties, but that mode of music reproduction was rapidly rendered obsolete by improved phonograph and radio technology. After a peak in 1927, the roll industry had virtually disappeared by the early years of the Depression.[21] The player piano itself required mechanical upkeep, a luxury few found interest in maintaining when it was easier and cheaper to turn on the radio. Hundreds of thousands of the fragile paper rolls were destroyed. Many sat unplayed in attics. While the large majority of rolls were of non-ragtime or jazz material, from around 1913 to the mid-1920s, the piano roll served as the predominant method to preserve the playing styles of many of the greatest ragtime and early jazz pianists. By the late 1940s, the existence of these performances by revered figures became a long-lost footnote, in many cases characterized as simply rumored. Eventually, musicians, collectors, critics, scholars, and record producers who were part of the 1940s ragtime and early jazz revival stumbled across the piano rolls.

Sam Meltzer, owner of Century Records in the Bronx, New York, specialized in reissuing classic jazz. He was intrigued by an article in the *Jazz Record* from September 1946 noting the discovery of a piano roll presumably played by Scott Joplin. Meltzer himself knew of people who owned rolls but few had ever played them, including a man he tracked down in Tacoma, Washington, who owned rolls by Johnson, Fats Waller, Jelly Roll Morton, and Cliff Jackson. Although there were many questions about authenticity and the quality of the performances, Meltzer was eager to record them and release them on record. Obtaining the rolls went smoothly but recording them was a challenge. He described the tortuous process:

> Right away there were a million problems. We found out that we couldn't use an electric player piano but had to have one of the real old ones that you pump manually. If you think it's easy to find one of those—even in New York, you're nuts. After weeks of looking around in barrooms on Third Avenue, we got a line on one that the composer, Otto Cesana, had in his penthouse studio on West 57th Street. So what did we do?
>
> We had to run a line from the studios of WHOM to Otto's place. From WHOM another line ran to the Majestic recording studios, and a third line, a telephone line, ran from Majestic to Harry Smith's recording studio in the Steinway building where the actual cutting process took place. It sounds complicated as hell, and, believe me it was.[22]

When the music was finally heard, Meltzer's doubts melted away. He issued the tracks of the four pianists, including Johnson's QRS roll of "Make Me A Pallet On The Floor" from 1926.[23] These were the first releases of piano roll transcriptions on phonograph record. Avakian, in his review, noted, "that they are a curiosity of historical and musical interest is undeniable, and the chances are that the Century releases will widen the search for more piano rolls by pioneer jazz pianists in the next few years."[24] Century did indeed issue other piano rolls on record. By 1950, the hunt for rolls was on in earnest by a small but dedicated collecting community, spearheaded by a University of Michigan student by the name of Michael Montgomery. By the time he passed away in 2011, Montgomery was responsible, perhaps more than anyone else, for the collection, preservation, research on, and dissemination of piano roll recordings. Through his dedicated efforts, nearly all of Johnson's rolls have been found, preserved, recut, and recorded.

Jazz and dance have always had a close and symbiotic relationship. Two of Johnson's most famous and important compositions, "Carolina Shout" and "Charleston," were conceived from dance forms. Jazz dancing as participatory entertainment reached its acrobatic peak with the Lindy hop and jitterbug during the 1930s. Dancer Mura Dehn spent her lifetime hoping to transform the popular idiom from the dance floor to the stage as an artistic endeavor. She wrote, "I hope to create a jazz ballet born out of a music rooted in a profound folk tradition. A jazz that gets into your bones. At present I am working with a small group of inspired Savoy Lindy Hoppers."[25] Part of her plan was to find jazz records that provided the necessary elements for a jazz dancer. She auditioned several that were recommended by the staff of the Commodore Music Shop, then run by Jack Crystal after co-founder (and brother-in law) Milt Gabler left to work for Decca Records. She found most of them lacking but had heard Johnson recently on the radio and commented, "A dance record in order to be really good has to have a compelling quality to which you feel that you must dance. When James P. Johnson played 'Charleston' over Rudi Blesh's radio program, This Is Jazz, a few weeks ago, he exemplified this quality. I wish there were a record of this, for James P. certainly lends wings to your feet."[26] On April 13, Johnson, with J. C. Higginbotham, Pops Foster, and Baby Dodds, provided the music for a performance by Dehn and the Jazz Dancers at the auditorium of the ILGWU Local 105 at 100 East 17th Street. The seven performers were billed as "Harlem's greatest dancers." The program consisted of two parts. The first focused on the "Jazz Vocabulary," short pieces based on popular dance steps such as the Charleston, Snake Hips, Lindy, and Shim Sham. The second part featured dance improvisations to blues and jazz tunes.[27]

Three days after her performance with Johnson, Dehn performed with Art Hodes and his band. The concept of popular dance staged as art was poorly received. The reviews of her performance and the productions of others with similar intentions favored the musical accompaniment over the dancers.[28] Others attempting this fusion of music and dance on stage used tightly choreographed material, but Dehn preferred to allow the dancers to improvise. Her efforts were thought to be promising, but ultimately were considered a failure, an outcome attributed to "the ad lib effort that was attempted."[29] Castigating jazz dance for improvising while the music, itself defined as improvisational and widely praised, seems misplaced and ironic. Dehn remained undeterred. Several years later she was validated by Marshall Stearns, who wrote an influential book on jazz dance and invited Dehn to participate in his roundtable inaugurating the Institute of Jazz Studies.[30] Dehn's comment lamenting the unavailability of a Johnson recording of "Charleston" highlighted the irony that he never commercially recorded his most danceable tune.

Traditional jazz was enormously popular with college audiences. In late April or very early May, Rudi Blesh tested the waters for a regular concert series tied in with his Saturday afternoon *This Is Jazz* radio show. He took his all-star roster of musicians that he featured on the air to the Shubert Theater in New Haven, Connecticut, for a two-hour concert to benefit an interracial summer camp. The program intended to trace the history of jazz and, with a lineup of essentially traditional players, presented a "history" in line with his very conservative definition of the genre. Nonetheless, a nearly full house of majority Yale students was treated to the music of Johnson along with Sidney Bechet, Baby Dodds, Albert Nicholas, Marty Marsala, Danny Barker, Pops Foster, and the vaudeville team of Coot Grant and Sox Wilson.[31]

Johnson accompanied pianist Art Hodes and his regulars to Syracuse in April, followed on May 3 by a fundraising concert for the cancer fund at Hamilton College in Clinton, New York. Also on that bill were Max Kaminsky, Miff Mole, Tony Parenti, Jimmy Butts, and Danny Alvin. The college newspaper, *Hamiltonews*, reported on the event before and after. Not since Eddie Condon had played there in 1942 had there been a concert of traditional jazz on campus. The preview article noted, "Between the sets, the far-famed James P. Johnson will entertain on piano, and he will be no mere fill-in. Most people know him as the teacher of the late Thomas 'Fats' Waller and Duke Ellington; few realize how original a pianist he is in his own right."[32] Attendees were expected from surrounding colleges including Cornell, Colgate, Syracuse, and Mohawk, and the Alumni Gymnasium on the night of the performance was filled to capacity. Over eight hundred people attended. W. A. Robbins reviewed the concert. Although he had a few less than stellar remarks about Hodes and Kaminsky, about Johnson he reported, "James P. Johnson showed once more that he is a superb improviser. His solo work, as well as the numbers played with the band and the trio [Parenti on clarinet and Alvin on drums], displayed to advantage how much he has contributed to jazz."[33] A post-concert beer party at Emerson Hall on campus was limited to members of the group or fraternity that sold the most tickets. A private recording of the concert with band, trio, and Johnson

solos, as well as Johnson solos from the post-concert "frat party," have been preserved, and confirm Robbins's observations.

The week of May 18 through 25 was designated the first national annual memorial week honoring Fats Waller. A committee of over one hundred prominent members of the entertainment world was headed by Ed Kirkeby in arranging tributes on radio, in the theaters, and in the press. A special edition of *This Is Jazz* on May 24 focused on Waller.[34] Blesh, the stalwart Johnson patron, brought Johnson to the Steinway building on June 5 to record four piano solos of his own tunes that dated from the teens to the early thirties. Blesh paid Johnson nearly double the usual fee.[35] On two consecutive weekends in June, 6–8 and 13–15, the riverboat SS *Fair Haven* sailed the Hudson from Pier 83 at 42nd Street to Yonkers and back for an evening cruise. For three dollars a ticket, the two to three hundred passengers heard "Jazz on The River" that included Johnson ("the daddy of them all"), Sidney Bechet, Danny Barker, Marty Marsala, Baby Dodds, Albert Nicholas, and Pops Foster—the core of Blesh's usual ensemble. He sponsored the cruises along with Art Hodes.[36] It was perhaps on one of these nights that pianist Ralph Sutton met Johnson. He recalled, "I never met Fats Waller, my favorite composer. I did meet James P. Johnson on a cruise boat on the Hudson River. I introduced myself but was too much in awe to talk with him."[37] On one of the days off the river (June 12), Johnson with Nicholas, Barker, and Foster recorded an album of traditional

Creole tunes for Blesh. As the only non-Louisianan, Johnson does a fine job handling the regional and highly stylized folk material. *Billboard* acknowledged the music was "unquestionably jazz," and that "the total effect is charming," with "a good deal of pleasurable listening," but concluded the music was "strictly for collectors, of course."[38]

While this niche recording may have had limited appeal, Johnson's older recordings and compositions were still selling. H.R.S. sold distribution rights to Empire Records in 1947. They continued to promote his 1938 records as a worthy part of their mainstream jazz catalogue that included others like Sarah Vaughan.[39] His songs continued to find crossover appeal. Kansas City blues and rhythm and blues pianist/singer Julia Lee launched a string of successive hits for the Capital American label with "A Porter's Love Song," Johnson's collaboration with Andy Razaf from the 1930 Smalls' Paradise hit stage show *Kitchen Mechanics Review*. In calling it a "minor classic," *Variety* cited Lee's rendition with her "fine piano" a "best bet," and noted, "'Porter's Love Song' should be a smash in race locations and enjoy a pretty good spin in other spots as well."[40] On June 29, 1947, the Spanish Refugee Appeal sponsored a concert at the Ziegfeld Theater. Rudi Blesh served as master of ceremonies. The year before he had "rediscovered" Bertha "Chippie" Hill, then living in a one-room apartment on Chicago's South Side. She recorded well-received records for Blesh's fledgling Circle record label, and he followed up by featuring her at the concert along with many regulars of his core contingent of musicians including Johnson. Montana Taylor and Brownie McGhee made special appearances. Johnson accompanied Hill on several tunes, which were enthusiastically received by the audience that included Max Gordon, who offered her a regular spot at his legendary club the Village Vanguard.[41]

Johnson had for the most part put aside attempts at large-scale presentations of his orchestral works but continued to study arranging with Maury Deutsch. He instead used these skills to focus again on the musical theater. In June, Johnson had begun work with his old friend Flournoy Miller on a new production. First described as an operetta, *Meet Miss Jones* was the first incarnation of Johnson's last musical theater effort.[42] Diving back into popular stage work prompted Johnson to reinstate his membership in the Dramatists Guild, which he had let lapse in 1937. Johnson and Miller had contracted for a production titled *Hired Husband*, executed September 2, 1947, which may have been a preliminary title for the same show. Current and back dues for the Dramatists Guild were deducted against his advance for this production. *Meet Miss Jones* was conceived as a departure from the usual musical theater format in that all of the dialogue is sung in recitative fashion. Included in the cast was Dorothy Harrison. She had broken ground in the mid-thirties with her role in the ILGWU production of *Pins and Needles* and then performed in

Maury Deutsch, Johnson's last teacher, authored many books on arranging technique. (Reproduced with permission of Barry Glover, from the James P. Johnson collection [IJS.0111], Institute of Jazz Studies, Rutgers-Newark)

The Organizer.[43] The show opened on November 17 at the Experimental Theater, also known as the Elks Theater, on 126th Street in Harlem. It was sponsored by the Negro Musical Comedy Experimental Theater and scheduled to run for only eight performances, closing on November 28.[44] Comedic, farcical plot twists underlie the story that revolves around a love triangle designed to save lead character Rose Jones from marrying gangster playboy Joe.[45] It was favorably received, and there was talk of interest from Lee Shubert in bringing it to Broadway and then mounting a road tour. One review noted, "With music by James P. Johnson and lyrics and book by Flournoy Miller, two capable authors, the show boasts a dozen potential song hits in its two acts. A capable cast more than pleased the opening night audience. Encores were demanded on several numbers which bore the workmanship stamp of Jimmy Johnson."[46] Neither the Broadway run nor a road tour materialized. Three tunes from the show were published by Irving Mills; "Don't Lose Your Head (and Lose Your Gal)," "I've Got to Be Lovely to Harry," and "You're My Rose."

Never far from the performing jazz scene, Johnson was pianist for the final engagement of the New Orleans Stompers, the band featuring Bunk Johnson, which was slated to engage the "Crescent Serenadors" in an "Old Time New Orleans Cutting Contest" at the Caravan Hall Ballroom on East 59th Street between Park Avenue and Lexington Avenue on New York's Upper East Side on October 24. In reality, the personnel for these groups was constantly in flux, exchanging musicians at various times.[47] The tenth anniversary of the death of Bessie Smith was marked by a memorial concert called "Blues for Bessie" at Town Hall January 1, 1948. Bob Maltz produced it as a function of his New York Jazz Club, which by then boasted over a thousand members.[48] The press highlighted the story of the disappearance of her only film, *St. Louis Blues* (and one of only three film appearances of Johnson), and its discovery by Rudi Blesh in a Texas warehouse after a five-year search.[49] The film was shown at the concert. Johnson accompanied Ruby Smith as he had done many times previously and led "Bessie's Blues Boys" which included Baby Dodds, Max Kaminsky, Pops Foster, Jimmy Archey, and Albert Nicholas. Fredi Washington read a Peter Martin script telling of Bessie's rise to stardom. The proceeds benefited the United Negro and Allied Veterans of America.[50]

Johnson never cut the strings that pulled him back to Harlem. Sometime around May, writer Alvin Moses noted the following experience: "Art Tatum and James P. Johnson, just a block apart from each other as I journeyed through the mazes of Harlem with my everready Dawn Patrol Notebook opened. We chatted pleasantly with both of them, two of America's finest piano players and both hale fellows beloved by all who know them intimately."[51] On April 27, pianist Sammy Price organized a tribute to Dan Burley at Tom Delaney's New Jazz Room at 137th Street and Seventh Avenue. Johnson was happy to participate to honor his onetime collaborator and a man who used his position at the *New York Amsterdam News* not only to keep Johnson's name in front of the public, but also that of other Harlem pianists fashion had passed by, including Luckey Roberts and Donald Lambert.[52] Thanks to crossover appeal in the R&B market, Johnson's finances were bolstered by mechanical royalties from hit recordings of "Porter's Love Song" by Julia Lee in mid-1946 and Roy Milton at the end of 1947. In the second quarter of 1948, he made over $600 from these two tunes.[53] The windfall was well timed. Lillie Mae underwent major surgery in November, and the money helped with the medical bills. She recovered well.[54]

Bob Maltz produced a "Jazz Jubilee" that aired on WNYC on Saturday evening, April 17. Maltz was planning a series of thirty-minute programs. This was the first, and it focused on the earliest ragtime-based jazz style. The members of the band included Johnson, Tony Parenti, Danny Barker, and Freddie Moore. They were interviewed by Maltz on the air. The combination of didactics and nostalgia didn't impress the reviewer in *Variety*, who noted the production was "Mildly diverting in a musically historical sort of way."[55] Maltz soon found his niche in a different medium as concert promoter of what he called "jazz sessions." After the unsuccessful radio series, Maltz looked for a regular live performance venue to fit his vision. He first rented space at the Stuyvesant Casino on Second Avenue and 9th Street. By the end of 1948, Maltz moved his productions to a larger hall called the Central Plaza, a few blocks down Second Avenue at 6th Street. The roster of musicians who performed at these now legendary venues included some of the most recognizable names in jazz. From June 1948 through February 1949, Johnson was a regular at these Friday night jazz sessions. Drummer Bob Thompson recalled that the world-class musicians were paid well, and amateurs like himself were encouraged to sit in.[56] Fletcher Henderson biographer Walter C. Allen, who frequented both establishments, recalled, "There has never been anything quite like it in the city, before or since; for a modest admission charge, you could grab a seat at a table, and enjoy a constantly shifting parade of the best jazz musicians around. You could chat with the musicians if so inclined."[57] Admission was a buck, and the crowd was often louder than the music. A young Dan Morgenstern, his distinguished career at *Down Beat* and as the director of the Rutgers Institute of Jazz Studies ahead of him, recalled having to sit under the piano to hear James P. Johnson play. Sidney Bechet, Pee Wee Russell, Miff Mole, Edmond Hall, Wild Bill Davison, Omer Simeon, Bobby Hackett, and singers Ruby Smith, Monette Moore, and Chippie Hill, along with blues pianist Champion Jack Dupree and folk icon Pete Seeger among many other greats shared the bandstand with Johnson during these months. On several occasions Johnson played duets with Joe Sullivan. Maltz sent out reminder postcards to his mailing list that included the lineup for the upcoming Friday night. Next to each musician was a terse, complimentary descriptor, at least once referring to Johnson with his preferred title, "Dean of Jazz Pianists."[58] Eventually the Central Plaza decided to produce their own sessions. Maltz was asked to leave, and he resumed the same format back at the Stuyvesant Casino. Jack Crystal took on similar presentations at the Central Plaza.

Johnson continued to perform at jam sessions and jamborees sponsored by local jazz societies in the tristate area. He backed a Tony Parenti group for weekend night engagements at the Tip Toe Inn in Bridgeport, Connecticut, in September.[59] Bob Harrington worked at the Tip Toe, and in 1970, recalled these Sunday evening jam sessions:

> I remember that I used to get there about an hour before show time and in many ways that hour had a magic charm about it. The barkeep would be busily polishing glasses and getting ready for the evening rush,

Bob Maltz presents

★ **Sidney Bechet** genius of jazz
★ **John Glasel** great young cornetist
★ **Benny Morton** blue note trombone
★ **James P. Johnson** piano king
★ **Bob Casey** dixieland bass
★ **Baby Dodds** new orleans drums
★ **Champion Dupree** boogie & blues

this Fri. Oct. 15th from 8:45 p.m.

AT THE **JAZZ BAND BALL**
STUYVESANT CASINO
140 SECOND AVE. & 9th St., New York City

adm. $1.25   refreshments
NO EXTRA CHARGE FOR TABLES

JAZZ AT THE PLAZA
New Year's Eve
THIS FRIDAY, DEC. 31, FROM 9 P.M. TO 2 A.M.

Bob Maltz presents

★ MUGGSY SPANIER famous cornetist
★ MEZZ MEZZROW king jazz clarinet
★ CHAS. CASTALDO dixieland horn
★ JAMES P. JOHNSON great 88
★ HERB WARD bass stylist
★ GEO. WETTLING drummer deluxe
★ PETE SEEGER banjo and ballads
★ JACK DUPREE party piano
AND MANY OTHER RHYTHM ARTISTS

Admission $1.65 & tax
refreshments, food and party favors

CENTRAL PLAZA
111 SECOND AVE. AT 6TH ST., N.Y.C.

NEW YORK JAZZ CLUB presents

Bunk Johnson

Muggsy Spanier   Georg Brunis

~~Lonnie Johnson~~

Sidney Bechet   Albert Nicholas

James P. Johnson

Wellman Braud   Fred Moore

Brownie McGhee   Nocky Parker   Pops Foster
and other great jazzmen
Johnny Blowers

SAT. SEPT. 27 • 5:30 P.M.
TOWN HALL
123 West 43rd St., N. Y. C.

Tickets Now: $1.20, $1.80 tax incl.
(Box office or mail order)

Bunk Johnson on WNYC Sat. Sept. 20, 10 p.m.

the drummer would be setting up his battery and over in one corner James P. would be softly working over some long forgotten blues. There was shadowy quietness about the room and the pretty passing chords were wistful and warm.

Usually I'd go to the bar, get a couple of glasses sort of half filled with whisky, walk over to James P.'s piano, put one drink atop the piano and say something like, "Jimmy, Berlin came as close to the truth as a white man can—how about playing 'What'll I Do?' till it gets sort of blue?"

James P. would put his constant cigar into a nearby tray, take a few sips of whisky and gently run his short stubby fingers through a few minor chords—and it would happen—that early hour of magic. The barkeep would put down his towel, lean on the bar, mesmerized by the music and the waitresses would lean against a wall, eyes closed, storing up fragments of pleasantness against the soon to be battle of hollering customers.

"What'll I do" changed into "Snowy Morning Blues" and everything was right —this was as hauntingly beautiful as man and piano could ever be—once heard, it would never be forgotten.[60]

For a concert on November 21, Dewey P. Jeanette, chairman of the publicity committee of the Jazz Society of Trenton, arranged for Johnson to bring an all-star band to play at the White Horse Bowling Academy Ballroom, a sprawling, cavernous venue promoted as an "amusement center" that offered not only bowling but a cocktail lounge, pinball, dancing, and fountain service. The band included Buck Clayton, Cecil Scott, Russell Moore, and Freddy Moore.[61] Two months later, Johnson was invited back, but this time as the lone jazz star. Fledgling drummer Irv Kratka[62] brought down his Crescent City Serenaders for a three-hour Sunday afternoon jam session. His band included Bunk Johnson protégé Jerry Blumberg, cornet; Mal Hill, clarinet; Eph Resnick, trombone; Johnny Ellis, bass; and Johnson on piano.[63] Kratka and the band picked up Johnson for the ride down. Kratka, flanking him in the back seat with Resnick, recalled Johnson's patience and kindness in playing with this group of young kids, noting with great admiration, "We were in awe of him."[64]

As he approached fifty years of age in the early 1940s, in what seemed like a renaissance of his music, there were moments when he was on the verge of greater acclaim and admiration from both the commercial and serious music worlds. His tunes were being played and recorded, and, for twenty-five years, he had worked to develop his skills as a composer in an attempt to transcend the ephemeral success of musical trends by casting the fundamental elements of African American music into a timeless, concert form. He continued to be celebrated in the traditional jazz world, but as he entered the twilight of his career, the promise of broader recognition turned out to be a brief tease.

Nearing sixty toward the end of the decade, as illness snapped at his heels, he was fighting against the clock. He had seen the music change dramatically through the years, from ragtime to dixieland to swing, to a newly emerging form called bebop, or rebop, as it was sometimes known then. In 1947, at the request of Art Hodes, Johnson commented on bebop for *The Jazz Record*. At first Johnson demurred about not being an instructor and his lack of knowledge of bebop as a style, although he had discussed bebop with his last teacher Maury Deutsch. Finally, he agreed and confined his comments to the music of Dizzy Gillespie:

> I say that Dizzy makes it sound agreeable and I like it. But that doesn't mean that I like it all. I like anything that's good, and some of it's good just like anything else. It's the old story of it being all according to a person's taste. As far as the big bands are concerned, I like some of the work that the arrangers are doing. A lot of the arrangers write with reason, and that's good, but others write merely for the effect—or simply to astound.
>
> In the classics different scholars have added, from time to time, new, theoretical harmonic effects. Up to very recently that hadn't been done in jazz. What Dizzy and his kind play is simply a new treatment of basic jazz.
>
> I understand that J. C. Heard said in JAZZ RECORD that no one understands rebop and won't understand it for five or ten years. I'm afraid that I have to disagree with him. I think there are quite a few people who understand it now.
>
> As I said, it's just a different treatment of basic jazz and is still jazz. I agree that the music is revolutionary, but it's still the basic thing that counts.

Johnson concluded his statements with an instruction to the next generation of musicians arguing for a performance practice that he hoped would knit together as a cohesive musical tradition what had become stylistic silos more often at odds than at one. He said, "The most important point that I can see is that the jazz musicians of the future will have to be able to play all different kinds of jazz—in all its treatments—just like the classical musician who, in one concert, might range from Bach to Copland."[65]

Yet two years later, Johnson was more acutely aware that this intellectual understanding and comprehension of all aspects of jazz as a unified artistic tradition was not embraced by younger musicians. In 1949, Rudi Blesh spoke with Johnson about musical trends. He was less circumspect in talking with Blesh, who thought him patient rather than bitter, and most of all puzzled by the sad history of racial discrimination and the current state of music. Johnson told him:

The atonal and twelve-tone systems become common and monotonous. I have done six-tone atonal work myself, but they haven't dug to the bottom of the old harmony yet. They've forgotten how to use it—there was a break somewhere—so they think it's all used up. Any harmony is only so many chords unless you have a real melody. And the Schillinger system—you are supposed to have emotional intent by science. This is impossible, because true inspiration is gone. Why do these composers, and the be-boppers, too, try to get away from the melody? It shows a weakness. No melody is in them and they know it.

They're still playing ragtime now, or trying to, but they conceal and cover it up. It's considered certain traditional figures by some, but that's wrong, it's a rhythm that you feel and work with. They're just ashamed of a name.[66]

Although Johnson was not around to hear of it, nearly ten years later, Gillespie would acknowledge the importance of his predecessors, admitting, "If it hadn't been for the Lion and James P. Johnson and Fats Waller, we'd all have been floundering."[67] All his life, Johnson remained a stalwart proponent of the grass-roots heritage of jazz. Although Blesh recalled that Johnson was not bitter as he spoke about his music and how he had adhered to his ideals but his remarks clearly illustrate a sense of frustration. As late as 1948, Johnson continued to study music very seriously. Johnson's youngest daughter Lille Mae recalled how many hours her father spent at the piano experimenting with new ideas. David Gelman never heard Johnson complain or express animosity or derision toward anyone, at least not in public. He would instead talk about overcoming obstacles in one's life since everyone had them. Jazz writer Floyd Levin, who forged a close relationship with Johnson during his stay in Los Angeles in 1949, detected a smoldering resentment. He noted:

In a way, he was a very bitter man—bitter with the knowledge that the world had passed him by. At 58, James P. knew that he possessed a genius recognized by only a few jazz fans. He had learned to accept this situation with a stoic attitude and managed to maintain a rather comfortable life with his adoring wife, Lillie Mae, in their Jamaica, Long Island home. Recent years had brought a moderately affluent position and he pridefully talked about the large pipe organ he had installed in his house—much to the displeasure of the neighbors who complained that the large instrument vibrated the earth and shook pictures from their walls.[68]

He had watched less talented composers gain riches and fame, while many of his own fine tunes had been sold for a few dollars to greedy publishers who, he said, considered them "coon songs." Johnson stoically accepted this situation.[69]

The Johnsons had been a family since 1917, when they married. With their three children, they lived in a well-appointed, comfortable home on Long Island. Lillie Mae Jr. recalled that when her father traveled, he always brought gifts for everyone when he returned. "He was a good father," she said. "My parents never argued in front of us. At home, my mother was the boss, but she would always tell us not to disturb our father when he was studying."[70]

Johnson was a very religious man. He played the organ and piano for the family's congregation and attended church services regularly when he was home. Meanwhile, his life as a performer continued between periods of illness. David Gelman accompanied Willie "The Lion" Smith to Sunday dinner at the Johnsons on a number of occasions in 1943 and 44. Johnson owned a Steinway grand in addition to the pipe organ. They subscribed to the *New York Amsterdam News*. Gelman recalled Lillie Mae ran the home, and insisted he call her Auntie Lil. She was a very good cook, and southern cuisine was her specialty. One night at dinner, she relayed an incident from a New Year's Day of many years past when James P. left and said he would be back that evening. He didn't return for three days. When he finally did, he found the dining room table still set with all the food Lillie Mae had prepared. They all had a good laugh, reminiscing about it those many years later. Johnson adored Lillie Mae and his children. In his letters to his family, there is a somewhat formal but very affectionate tone. He closes his letters with "James" or even "From father James P. Johnson," but begins "My Dear Wife," or "To My Loving Daughter Arceola." He is reassuring about his health and encouraging about things at home. The depths of neglect that could have beaten a lesser man were buffered by the sporadic spikes of appreciation and activity during the 1940s, and his inherently optimistic outlook. By many accounts, Johnson usually reacted to the slights with equanimity. He felt no compulsion to complain as a habit, especially to Blesh, Gelman, and Levin, however much they appreciated him. He had one more significant artistic venture in the works, and he forged ahead with great expectations.

Chapter 28

SUGAR HILL—
THE LAST INNOVATION, 1949-1950

> James P. Johnson, "Dean of the Hot Piana," composed the extra-predomary
> lilting musical score for "Sugar Hill" to be world premiered at
> Las Palmas Theater. He is recognized as being one of the foremost
> factors in influencing the way popular music is played today.
> —*CALIFORNIA EAGLE*, JUNE 30, 1949

In 1948, Johnson and Flournoy Miller pursued plans to produce another large-scale musical theater production. At first they planned to restage *Meet Miss Jones*, but contractual delays scuttled the idea.[1] Using it as framework, the two expanded the book and Johnson added more musical numbers. They sought out well-known producers for their production, first contacting William B. Friedlander, the veteran songwriter and producer of stage shows and film going back to before World War I. The show was renamed *Moneymoon*, and Friedlander, along with Robert Berger, encouraged Johnson and Miller to sign contracts with them and with Mills Music to publish the tunes, with a planned opening on January 20, 1949, in Washington, DC.[2] Paul Schreibman, an entertainment lawyer who seven years later would broker the deal that brought Godzilla to American audiences, and Arnold B. Baranov, also an attorney, owned the Las Palmas Theater in Los Angeles. Miller, who was in Los Angeles, contacted them about producing the show on the West Coast. But the score was under contract with Mills Music, and Jack Mills was reluctant either to work with Schreibman or release the score. The Washington opening never materialized. Schreibman had hoped some of the cast could travel to

Los Angeles after the opening to serve as the nucleus of the company there.[3] Johnson left for Los Angeles at the end of March,[4] followed shortly after by Friedlander.[5] In an impassioned letter to Jack Mills in April 1949 from L.A., Johnson expresses his frustration at Mills's lack of support for the show, and notes the producer's intention of opening the show not only in Los Angeles, but also New York and London. He presses his case for Mills to act.

For nearly three years, Johnson had been refining the concept for what would be his ultimate, large-scale stage production. In the arena of musical theater, he was confident he had something different, telling Mills, "It is truly a departure from the beaten path."[6] Johnson had had a bumpy relationship with Mills over the years, but perhaps not that different from other songwriters and their publishers. In 1945, he had signed a one-year employment agreement with Mills for "the composing and arranging of musical compositions." The terms of the contract stipulated that all product was the sole property of Mills Music, that it was an exclusive agreement, and left to Mills in their sole discretion which compositions they would publish. Johnson was to arrange two compositions for orchestra per month. He was paid a $1,000 advance and the royalty arrangement was 3 cents per copy after 50 percent of net royalties was collected. The deal was not renewed for 1946, but "reinstated" in 1947 with all the same terms except the advance was cut in half.[7] In his effort advocating for the new show, Johnson was persuasive, and Mills relented. Rehearsals began shortly after. With two acts, each initially populated with a hefty twelve songs, *Moneymoon*, was described as "an opera comique." It was scheduled to open at the Las Palmas Theater around June 1.[8] Four additional tunes from the show were contracted with Mills on June 2.[9]

Shortly after rehearsals started, the show was renamed *Sugar Hill*. It opened at the Las Palmas Theater on July 12, 1949. Preproduction notices indicated Johnson would lead a four-piece band in the show with bass, drums, and guitar,[10] but none of the reviews mention this small ensemble and it was likely cut before the opening. It does not seem Johnson played piano at all during the show. The cast was headlined by veteran singer and stage actress Monette Moore, whose career began in the 1920s as a "classic" blues/vaudeville singer, dancer, and comedian. Johnnie Lee, who was Flournoy Miller's on-screen partner in *Stormy Weather*, and *Shuffle Along* veteran Jesse Cryer, who went on to occasional film roles, were also featured. Schriebman and Baranov ran regular ads in the *Los Angeles Times* before the opening and during the run, equal in prominence to other shows running then such as *Showboat*, *Kiss Me Kate*, and *Brigadoon*. Other than including gangster characters, the 1949 *Sugar Hill* bore no resemblance to the Johnson show of the same name from 1931, which ran for only eleven performances. The plot was slightly revised from its progenitor *Meet Miss Jones* and revolves around a love "quadrangle." A wealthy woman

(Rose) discovers her brother is killed by an opposing gang. Her brother's gang boss (Joe) attempts to blackmail Rose, threatening to publicize her brother's gang ties unless she marries him. She hires a deadbeat (Punk) to pose as her husband as an excuse to keep from marrying the gangster, and all the while she is engaged to another man (Harry). Punk's real wife appears, providing a comedic backdrop to an otherwise dark premise. The story ends happily as Rose marries Harry and is the beneficiary of a large life insurance settlement from her brother, Punk gets his wife back, and Joe goes to jail.

Aside from the characteristic farcical shoestring plot, nearly everything else about the production broke with previous stage musical models. Stage director Charles O'Curran combined stage and screen techniques of lighting and staging in such a unique way they were noted by the *Los Angeles Times* to be hitherto untried in this medium.[11] O'Curran had been in Hollywood for many years, and had staged sequences for films including *Riding High* and *Bells of St. Mary's* with Bing Crosby, *If You Knew Susie* with Eddie Cantor, and *Honeymoon* with Shirley Temple.[12] In a further departure, Johnson's score employed the recitative technique, wherein all dialogue is sung. The instrumentation in the pit combined an unusual array of keyboards. There were two pianos, a Hammond organ, and a Novachord, the keyboard instrument manufactured by the Hammond Company for only three years between 1939 and 1942. It is considered perhaps the first all-electronic music synthesizer, constructed of hundreds of vacuum tubes and capacitors. Its many controls produced sounds that in later years were associated with science fiction movies. Nat Finston, who worked at Paramount and MGM studios, and Andre Brummer, who was connected with the New York Philharmonic, were retained to help with the large scale musical production.[13]

Hal Holly's (pseudonym for Charles Emge) review in *Down Beat*, replete with cynicism, castigated the production even before the curtain rose. In condescending manner, he described the glitz of searchlights and celebrities arriving in limousines. He attributed the rousing reception of the audience to white guilt, and also concluded that "everyone at the opening must have had a piece of the show." He went on sarcastically to quote a principal in the production, claiming "The idea of this instrumentation, one of the producers explained, was to avoid the idea 'that Negro music is necessarily jive music.'" Johnson's recitative musical structure challenged most reviewers. They weren't quite sure what to make of it. John L. Scott in the *Los Angeles Times* gave a mixed review and pointed out the pros and cons of uninterrupted singing, namely that individual tunes, in this case numbering twenty, fail to stand out.[14] Holly, continuing with the snide tone of his review, remarked, "'Sugar Hill' is the first musical comedy (if that's what it is) we've ever encountered in which every single last word of 'dialogue' is sung. The entire score, which contains a couple of promising commercial pop songs, is by James P. Johnson, held by many to be quite a figure in that field of music for which we are now trying to find a name."¹⁵ Miller's dialogue was all in rhyme, which further blurred the line between song and storyline. One reviewer assumed Johnson's intentions in *Sugar Hill* must have been similar to his 1920s effort that gave the world the "Charleston," and found them lacking, intimating that the show did not sufficiently focus on catchy dance numbers.¹⁶ The small stage of the Las Palmas Theater allowed little room for high-stepping choreography. Another review noted "six numbers you'll enjoy whistling upon leaving the theater," but even this African American reviewer felt compelled to make comparisons to *Shuffle Along* from nearly thirty years earlier.¹⁷ Overall, as in many of his prior stage shows, Johnson's music redeemed the thin plot. One reviewer noted, "As is true of most musical comedies, the plot was weak, but the catchy tunes of James P. Johnson lift it out of the doldrums. The music should keep the play out of the 'also ran' class." Monette Moore and her feature "Peace Sister Peace" were singled out for praise.¹⁸ *Variety* found the plot to be "wafer thin" but noted "about six of the songs [although they list nine] are excellent and could, with proper plugging, gain large public favor." They, too, couldn't conceptualize a Black stage show as anything other than an unfocused mix of music, dancing, and comedy. They concluded, "James P. Johnson and Flournoy E. Miller should get a good mark for effort on this one, but they made a sorry error in showmanship when they had the dialog [sic] sung as well as the 20 numbers in the show. They aren't Gilbert and Sullivan, and the elements of light opera and lusty humor just don't mix in 'Sugar Hill.'" *Billboard* was overall more enthusiastic, calling it, "excellent entertainment." They particularly noted that the staging and lighting were able to overcome the confines of the cramped Las Palmas Theater. "Johnson's music is tuneful and bouncy," they commented, but the "show's trouble is that the author Flournoy E. Miller and cleffer James P. Johnson never made up their minds as to whether they were doing a musical comedy or light opera." "You Can't Lose A Broken Heart," "Peace, Sister, Peace," and "My Sweet Hunk of Trash" were noted to have commercial potential, the entire production with "a better than even chance of clicking, both here and eventually in New York."¹⁹

The mixed, cynical reviews didn't dissuade the audience. The relatively small 388-seat Las Palmas sold out the first week, grossing an "excellent" $5,200.²⁰ After a sluggish second week, the team reluctantly took the reviews to heart, and after "considerable rewriting and dance restaging," in particular the elimination of some sung dialogue, saw revived capacity crowds taking in $7,200 its third week.²¹ There was reportedly interest from some of the film studios in acquiring rights.²² Plans to sweep cross country to New York seemed to be progressing. By early August, the show was scheduled to open at the Great

Northern Theater in Chicago on Labor Day.[23] After the rewrites, the show gained further in popularity, and Schriebman and Baranov decided to delay the Chicago opening.[24] Former Broadway and stage dancer Eunice Healey came on board with an offer of financing to bring the show directly to New York, but couldn't come to terms with Schriebman and Baranov.[25] Although they couldn't strike a deal with Healey, the two producers continued their search for acceptable theater options in New York as well as San Francisco, even as the show completed its thirteenth and last week in Los Angeles. The final week's $7,000 gross enabled them to keep the cast on stand-by as they attempted to launch the road tour.[26] With an initial preproduction outlay of $15,000, and weekly costs of $4,500, the show had made a modest but solid profit.[27]

Johnson made several radio appearances in L.A. in July to promote the run,[28] and again in August to promote a Broadway opening for the show.[29] Syndicated music writer Owen Callin, who was the International News Service Record Critic, reported meeting Johnson by chance in Los Angeles. Although he described him as "an oldtimer in the music business," Callin acknowledged Johnson's place in creating modern American music, noting, "Jimmy is known as 'Dean of the Hot Piano,' and the 'Father of Stomp and Ragtime.'" The term stride piano had not yet found wide use as the descriptor of Johnson's piano style. Callin noted, "'Sugar Hill' is just about the hottest musical on the Hollywood stages at present."[30] Johnson returned to New York in mid-September, and flew back to L.A. for the final performance on October 8, three months after the opening.[31] Another backer was eager for an opening in San Francisco before Christmas, but he too, could not come to terms with Schriebman and Baranov.[32] Further productions never materialized, and October 8 was the last performance of *Sugar Hill*. The show never made an appearance in Chicago, San Francisco, New York, or London.

In August, Jack Mills, finally convinced of their commercial potential, published nine numbers from the show. Columbia Records recorded and in November released four well-received cast member recordings.[33] "Keep Em Guessing" and "Peace Sister Peace" were recorded by Monette Moore, "You Can't Lose a Broken Heart" was recorded by Johnny Lee and the Ebonaires, and "My Sweet Hunk of Trash" by Dolores Parker. "Four sides from the all-colored revue, 'Sugar Hill,' which closed recently following a smash engagement at the Las Palmas Theater in Hollywood, rate a nod from this reviewer. These are the types of blues rarely heard—zestful, playful, happy-go-lucky blues, and done by some of the greatest entertainers in the profession," noted a local paper.[34] The latter two tunes were recorded in classic duets by Louis Armstrong and Billie Holiday for Decca, and Nat Cole recorded "You Can't Lose A Broken Heart" for Capitol. The sheet music and records came too late. Johnson and O'Curran's experiment in broadening the format of musical comedy went mostly unappreciated. In his review, Hal Holly's final comment might be thought of as either prescient or ignorant, writing, "But we still expect someone to call 'Sugar Hill' James P. Johnson's 'jazz opera' soon."

Johnson was in Los Angeles primarily to promote and supervise his show, but he sought out opportunities to play, and couldn't say no when invited. On May 22, Johnson played a private party at the Hollywood Athletic Club for the fiftieth wedding anniversary of the grandparents of jazz writer, promoter, and enthusiast Floyd Levin. Levin contracted with clarinetist Albert Nicholas to put together a group, and he brought Leonard Bibbs on bass and Louis Gonzales on guitar. The pianist, Gideon Honore, was unable to play at the last minute. Johnson's appearance in the quartet was a surprise to Levin, who recalled the event with clarity and adulation. He reminisced, "James P. Johnson, the world's greatest stride pianist? Playing at my family's private party? I was overjoyed. Shaking hands with James P. Johnson was an unforgettable experience. His huge fist was soft and warm, and it thrilled me to hold the powerful right hand that had produced so much delightful music." Johnson received a rousing reception when he played some of his own tunes, especially the "Charleston." He was renting the home of one of the Mills brothers at 1357 West 37th Place while he was in Los Angeles and they were on tour. On one occasion, Levin recorded Johnson playing the concert grand piano there. Levin spent considerable time with Johnson during the six months he was on the West Coast, noting, "He often visited our home and played with our young son. The great musician moved into our hearts. It was easy to love James P. Johnson."[35] "The warmth of his personality mingled with the happy sounds of his music blend into a truly wonderful memory."[36] For his effort at the anniversary party, the "world's greatest stride pianist" was paid union scale for a sideman, thirteen dollars.[37] He didn't complain.

Sometime between March and June, he substituted for Jess Stacy, who was playing at the St. Francis Room. Trumpeter John Lucas recalled, "We had to get a sub for Jess once, because he went to Cape Girardeau [Stacy's home town in Missouri], and we had James P. Johnson on two different occasions. Johnson was working in an all-black show on Las Palmas. Monette Moore was in it and she was a friend of mine. She said, 'Get James P.' so we did, and that was really exciting."[38] In June, he sat in with Kid Ory's band at the Beverly Cavern, Ory's home base. His band was frequently recorded and broadcast by the Armed Forces Radio Service (AFRS) using their sixteen-inch transcription discs, and one evening with Johnson is preserved. On June 1, Johnson played at the Pasadena Civic Auditorium in a trio with Albert Nicholas and Zutty Singleton alongside the Yerba Buena Jazz Band, one of the foremost bands of the traditional jazz and ragtime revival. The concert was arranged by Nesuhi and Marili Ertegun, who at the time were operating the Jazz Man record shop in Hollywood.[39] Although attendance was below expectations, it was otherwise a successful event. Turk Murphy was leading the Yerba Buena band. Their founder, Lu Watters, was too ill. It was the last performance of the legendary revival group.[40] The review of the event in *Down Beat* sported the headline "Johnson Puts on Great Show at Coast Concert." Once again, reviewer Hal Holly (Charles Emge) is unable to check his sarcasm, at least with regard to Johnson, and observes that Johnson appeared to run into some sort of stylistic conflict with Nicholas over chord changes, and Singleton with regard to the rhythm. Only several weeks earlier, at the more casual affair for Floyd Levin, Johnson and Nicholas seemed to get along just fine. On this occasion, Holly implies, Johnson had more than a little taste, and appeared "just a little more than buoyant." Holly ultimately closes his comments with the following appraisal:

> But the real highlight was Johnson's introduction to one of his own numbers: "Ladies and gentlemen, I shall now play my own original arrangement of 'Who.'" He started with a strain a few of us recognized as the verse of "Hallelujah," then went off into a musical world that was all his own. He should have introduced it as a special arrangement of "What?"
>
> Even so, good old James P. proved himself to be a great musician in that he never really botched it up. We'll gladly take all of our concerts from now on with James P. Johnson just as he was at this one. After all, maybe this was The True Jazz.[41]

It is difficult to know what to make of Holly's assessment. Had James P. too much to drink? Perhaps. The Jerome Kern classic "Who" was a tune with which Johnson was well acquainted. Ten years earlier, before the effects of ill health, he recorded a stunning band version replete with rhythmic complexity, chordal oddities, and melodic variation in two extended solos. On this night, alcohol or infirmity notwithstanding, if Johnson's performance was anything like the "musical world that was all his own" from 1939, Holly would have certainly been correct in his final conclusion.

Chapter 29

FINAL YEARS, 1950–1955

> Jimmy never talked much except about music. He was always
> writing it, playing it, and talking about it.
> —POPS FOSTER

After returning from Los Angeles, Johnson resumed playing at the Central Plaza in November. He also reportedly began having what were described as "silent convulsions."[1] Whether these were true seizures, recurrent small strokes, or some other medical event isn't known, but Johnson's health was clearly deteriorating. Between bouts of illness, he played when he could. On January 28, 1950, Johnson was with Alan Lomax who produced a midnight memorial concert titled *Take This Hammer* at Town Hall to honor Leadbelly, who had passed away the month before. The performers ranged from folk to blues to jazz. The sold-out concert was broadcast over WOV radio.[2] On February 3, 1950, he was advertised with his "jazz trio" that included Edmond Hall and Art Trappier.[3] He played at the Hayloft Restaurant in South Salem on February 11. He continued playing the college circuit. February 1950 found him playing with Max Kaminsky at Cornell University in Ithaca, New York.[4] The last known preserved playing of James P. Johnson is from a Sidney Bechet date on March 5, 1950, at Phi Gamma Delta fraternity's Vernon Hall at Yale University. By this time, Johnson was missing more dates than he was making due to illness. Yet when he did, as evident on the Vernon Hall recordings, he is in remarkably good form. He was at the Stuyvesant Casino several Friday nights in June. On June 9, Alan Lomax was the guest of honor, selling his newly published book *Mister Jelly Roll* about the life of Jelly Roll Morton.[5] Johnson was with Buster Bailey and others on June 23.[6] The *New York Amsterdam News* still counted

Johnson as a master pianist in the company of swing, boogie-woogie, and "modern" players like Thelonious Monk.[7]

While less visible in person, his recordings from the early 1940s were being rereleased. Decca reissued on 78rpm as well as on a ten-inch long-play record the eight sides from 1944 of Johnson tunes with Eddie Dougherty on drums. With "modern" jazz exploding all around, and the "trad" revival losing some steam, the Black and mainstream press commented on the release with high praise. "In his long-playing disc, there are superb examples of the Johnson fertile imagination at work," the *Chicago Defender* noted,[8] and the *Negro News Letter* observed Johnson "played with light fingers and breezy ideas."[9] "A redoubtable old-timer who can still beat out the licks with the best of them is The Daddy of the Piano, James P. Johnson. The least of them can give you a lift with their driving, almost honky-tonk rhythms, and the best are superb examples of a zestful imagination at work" added the *New York Times*.[10] Decca also reissued on LP an Eddie Condon date from 1946 with reviewers noting, "The wonderful piano of James P. Johnson can be heard on two fine sides."[11] Blue Note did the same with his mid-1940s solos and Blue Note Jazzmen sessions. The reviews focus on the timeless nature of his playing, noting, "Yet another important jazz figure whose old records are collected on long-plays from Blue Note is James P. Johnson. His driving rhythms and inventive improvisations are heard solo on Rent Party Piano and he plays with a jump ensemble on 'Jazz Band Ball.'"[12] One review is replete with praising descriptors, including, "Fertile," "Breezy," "Zestful," "Inventive." To keen ears, Johnson's capacity for imaginative improvisation was anything but an anachronism. The review goes on to say, "The style is something exciting and satisfactual [sic]." "It's a fine package: Decca was justified in reissuing same."[13]

Johnson's earliest work was difficult to come by. His first piano solo saw some exposure, albeit on an obscure collector's 78 rpm label. Chicago-based jazz aficionado John Steiner bought the rights to the Paramount name and began issuing music from the 1920s. One of his first releases was the pairing of Johnson's "Harlem Strut" backed by Fletcher Henderson's "Unknown Blues," both piano solos originally issued on the Black Swan label in 1921.[14] About the recording, regular *Record Changer* reviewer Bucklin Moon, admitting he "never was an Eastern Seaboard man," went on to say, "for my money they might just as well have made two sides of 'Harlem Strut' so when I wore out one I could switch over to the other. Not that I mean to slight the Fletcher Henderson number, which is pretty good in itself, but merely that the James P. happens to make me want to get up and yell."[15] Moon's reaction is reminiscent of Ethel Waters's comment about Johnson's ability to ignite a singer's vocalization, which appeared years later in her memoir, *His Eye Is on The Sparrow*. In 1950, Rudi Blesh and Harriet Janis published their seminal work, *They All Played*

Ragtime. This book saved from oblivion the stories of the musicians who played and composed during the last decade of the nineteenth century, and first two decades of the twentieth. Blesh was known to promote what some believed to be a marginalizing purism toward jazz. Yet, he was a stalwart supporter of Johnson not only as performer but also allows a place for Johnson's symphonic constructions in his ragtime treatise. It is from this work that the notion of a "ragtime triumvirate" that includes Scott Joplin, Jelly Roll Morton, and Johnson was established, as reviewer Charles Edward Smith points out: "Yet such defects are of minor importance when the book is judged on its thorough exploration of the ragtime field. We learn not merely of the St. Louis pioneers such as Joplin, James Scott and Tom Turpin, but of Jelly Roll Morton who brought ragtime into jazz, and James P. Johnson, the veteran who within the last few years has played both ragtime and his own concerto with the Brooklyn Symphony Orchestra."[16]

♪

Johnson kept up a regular correspondence with Flournoy Miller. The letters are poignant and open a window into Johnson's personality and life view of a man of otherwise few words. The two had been embroiled in a lawsuit with Schriebman and Baranov, the producers of *Sugar Hill*, for nonpayment of royalties. The result of months of legal wrangling ended without payment for either performer, since there was a discrepancy about the original complaint of nonpayment. Germane to the lawsuit were apparent discrepancies in the gross revenues reported by Baranov in box-office statements to Johnson, as compared to the publicly reported numbers in the trade press. Ironically, Schriebman continued to hold out hope for sufficient backing to restage the show, dangling exaggerated contracts even while he stalled on paying the back royalties.[17] Johnson and Miller continued their own attempts to produce *Sugar Hill*. During the spring of 1950, Miller was working on new lyrics while attending to the lawsuit.[18] Promises from jazz luminaries including Joe Glaser came to naught.[19] CBS sought to include *Sugar Hill* in a handbook on American Opera for the American Composers Alliance,[20] and Flournoy Miller was plugging the show for treatment on television, a prospect Johnson's personal attorney was hopeful would produce some income for the family.[21] In 1957, after Johnson's death, Flournoy Miller made one last attempt to produce a show spotlighting the glory days of Black musical theater. With his daughter Olivette, a noted jazz harpist, and her husband Bert Gibson, she wrote new lyrics to Johnson's tunes from *Runnin' Wild* and the 1949 *Sugar Hill*. The production included the Dyerettes, the Zephyrs, and the Four Tops.[22] Miller again contacted the original producer of *Sugar Hill*, William Friedlander, about a New York production of the original show. Friedlander was enthusiastic but raised a series of concerns that needed to be addressed, not the least of which was the considerable expense of mounting a show. He closed by telling Miller, "We have never lost confidence in this show—and if it gets over here, it will make you a rich man again."[23] *Sugar Hill* never saw another production.

Throughout his correspondence with Miller, Johnson maintains an optimistic outlook about *Sugar Hill* even while fighting poor health. He expresses frustrations about the neglect of his music, but maintains a steady stream of ideas and goals:

> October 5, 1949: "I am not worried. I am confident everything will turn out o.k. & I look forward for the best. Be yourself & best of luck to you & family & friends."
>
> December 7, 1949: "Miller I have been thinking I did not have a fair chance with my 'Smiling Through My Tears' [a tune from *Sugar Hill*] the verse which is a new form of modern music & also the nightmare in 'A Disordered Dream' [tune written with Miller, copyright in 1950] another modern element of music & also no chance which also leaves me the same old antiquated musician of the 1920's & 30's but I have developed since then & for what use."
>
> January 12, 1950: "Things are slow around here now with my sickness caused me to lose about 5 dates."
>
> February 2, 1950: "I am feeling fairly well & looking forward to further progress with the show. I hope the future will turn out better for us. I think you should retain some of the California girls who can remember the routines because I don't. Some of them were strange to me. This is very important musically."
>
> February 6, 1950: "Our case with the lawsuit is now over for the time being. I now feel we should strain our efforts to get the show on with the entire musical score if possible. I have the contracts for *Kitchen Opera*, another play for future use. Tell O'Curran [the director of *Sugar Hill*] to prepare to get a wind and sound effects machine for 'Disordered Dream' & to please study how to use it. I think & plan nothing but *Sugar Hill*."
>
> March 3, 1950: "I would want two weeks to three to finish the music for Horace Heidt & what is the surety of the deal & financial remuneration & can we arrange for the publication or would they. How is the show coming along. You know if the show was playing here the record sale would pick up. Don't forget the show will have to have a rehearsal pianist because I still have that nervous condition yet."
>
> April 7, 1950: "Dear Friend Miller; I hope I haven't hurt your feelings or insulting you by not accepting of your new lyrics to the two songs,

but they don't fit the music very well & I don't like the ideas as well. Realize I don't pretend to know it all, but these two are better lyrics. Have you any new news or propositions. I don't & I have not been feeling so well lately. Well, spring is here again. Well, send me the original two lyrics & let me know all the latest developments & the newest business at hand. Your apologetic friend, James P. Johnson"

April 30, 1950: "I have a new television set a Victor machine & it has occupied our attention the last 2 weeks. What a marvelous & beautiful work the *Kitchen Opera* would be on television. . . ."[24]

Johnson had another stroke on May 9 that required hospitalization,[25] but by May 24, he was back home and picked up his correspondence with Miller.

June 13, 1950: "Dear Flournoy; I received your welcome letter & was very glad to hear from you. No I am not discouraged by the slowness of the show, but I am a little bit interested in possible projects near at hand. I am trying to think of television or other things. We have a lot of material for them."

July 19, 1950: "How is the television prospect coming on. I saw Duke Ellington & band on the television last night on the Dumont Cavalcade of bands show. The show part was very good he just brought back from Europe. I thought the band just ordinary! Maybe I have heard it too much."

September 12, 1950: "I am sorry to take so long answering your letter but I have been at a standstill & in & out owing to conditions & also a slight spell of sickness from which I recovered in a few days. When the show finally goes on I'm afraid I will have forgotten the formula."

January 11, 1951: "Friend Flournoy; A Happy & prosperous New year to you and family. I hope you received my card. I hope that I am not old & decrepit by the time our show goes on. How are you these days. I am only fair & have not been doing anything for about two or three months. I just heard that Fletcher Henderson had a severe stroke & was lying in a coma. I haven't even had a chance to play any piano lately & my left hand seems to have suffered from the layoff. But I'm still hoping for the best luck. Still I'm mighty glad I'm living & doing fairly well. I've seen Eubie and Sissle once . . . [writing trails off to illegibility, then picks up] Disregard this line, I was getting sleepy."

One of his last known gigs, unrecorded, was at the toney Manursing Island Club in Rye, New York, on July 15. As he intimates in his letters, illness precluded all playing by the latter part of 1950. On November 26, 1950, the twenty-fifth anniversary of Smalls' Paradise was marked with a blowout event at the club. There is no indication Johnson attended, but Andy Razaf had flown back from Los Angeles where he had settled, in part to attend. He had bitter recollections of the event. The celebration highlighted one of Smalls's most successful floor shows, the Johnson and Razaf show *Kitchen Mechanic's Revue*. Great praise was afforded Charlie Johnson and his orchestra, who played the music for the production. C. Johnson had a long residency at Smalls, rightly fueling the extra focus on him. The composers of the tunes, however, were not only ignored, but the tunes were incorrectly attributed to Charlie Johnson. In a letter to Ed Smalls, Razaf wrote, "Neither the printed program nor [emcee] Jimmy Mordecai gave a single word of credit to the ones who wrote and staged the original *Kitchen Mechanic's Revue*." Despite his best effort to remain cordial, Razaf went on, "Your research department should have known better. Only my long, sincere friendship for you kept me from filing a protest with ASCAP. I laughed when Charlie Johnson took the bows for writing 'Porter's Love Song.' And had it not been for one thoughtful gentleman there, I never would have been introduced at all."[26] From the known accounts of the evening, neither was James P. Johnson.

On May 3, 1951, he suffered a massive stroke, paralyzing him and putting an end to a career that had stretched over thirty-five years.[27] To stalwart fans of traditional jazz, he was far from forgotten. In that month's issue of *Record Changer*, Johnson ran fifth in their All-Time All-Star jazz poll of pianists, ahead of some forty other pianists.[28] He recovered some, as Lillie wrote to Miller, "Am just writing this to let you know that James P. is holding on thank God he knew me today. I am praying that he lives. He has hardening of the arteries and his blood is too thick. That was the cause of his illness all the time. . . ."[29] He spent the remainder of his life either in the hospital or at home, specially equipped by Lillie Mae to care for her husband, now seriously impaired and unable to care much for himself. Since Johnson rated a B classification with ASCAP, his four-figure quarterly check and royalty payments supported the family. An article that appeared in *Down Beat* in 1953 about Johnson's condition made the following point: "Some of the younger ASCAP writers who are demanding that performance be made the dominant factor in determining classification, thus increasing their current revenue at the sacrifice of later security, might change their reasoning if they could drop in and see Jimmy Johnson."[30] Johnson was now indeed a tragic figure. He lingered through irreversible paralysis only to witness how little attention he received beyond the traditional jazz community. Close friends like Willie "The Lion" Smith were still concerned and visited often, as did other musicians who idolized Johnson, including some not usually associated with his circle, like Eurreal "Little Brother" Montgomery.[31] Upon hearing the news, Hugues Panassie wrote to Lillie Mae, "I was very sorry and upset indeed when I received your letter letting me know about my dear friend

James P. That was a terrible blow on me to hear he was so sick and I want you to know right away how sorry I feel for him and you all. It was bad news also for my friend Mezzrow, who wants me to tell you all also how sorry he feels for James P. I do believe that he made you happy for he is such a kind person. . . . I sympathize deeply with our big sorrow and that we will, over here, never will forget James P."[32]

On September 28, 1953, Smith and other musicians organized a benefit jazz concert for Johnson at Town Hall. His medical bills were mounting, upwards of $800 a year even before his paralyzing event.[33] The list of sponsors, numbering more than fifty, reads like a Who's Who of jazz. Those recognizably associated with Johnson over the years were supporting the event, as were musicians not thought of as a part of his sphere—Lucky Millinder, Bud Powell, Charlie Parker, and Jimmy Mundy—at least gave their name in support.[34] Very few of the illustrious names attended the concert, but Clarence Williams, Luckey Roberts, and Ethel Waters were among those in the audience. Smith recorded an LP of Johnson compositions in August as part of his personal tribute to his friend.[35] *Variety* reported that Johnson's condition was improving,[36] although one is hard pressed to see it in the photo published in *Jet* magazine of the Lion and other musicians visiting a much thinner Johnson lying in his hospital bed at home a few days before the concert. Sadly, the benefit concert was reported as a failure and "at least a disgrace." The reviewer noted, "Willie The Lion Smith worked brilliantly and hard, but there were about 25 people to see and hear him. The only pleasant surprising note was a contribution of $100 mailed in by a Mrs. Jose Ferrer, a singer also known as Rosemary Clooney."[37]

The premature appearance of Johnson's obituary written by George Hoefer in *Down Beat* on May 5, 1954, highlighted the isolation Johnson now suffered. It was retracted in the next issue, and the magazine apologized for its error in having failed to follow up on a false rumor of Johnson's death. When told of the mistake, Lillie Mae Johnson responded, "Usually when they say somebody's passed away who hasn't, it means that he won't."[38] In his typical spiritualistic manner, Willie "The Lion" Smith recalled the last time he saw Johnson, who, he reports, was unconscious and hadn't spoken to anyone for a few weeks. Smith sat down at a piano in Johnson's room and played "Carolina Shout." Johnson was stirred enough to write out a message: "They were too good to the piano players with all that free booze and rich food. It catches up with you."[39] Eubie Blake attributed much of Johnson's serous health issues to his incorrigible alcoholism, including his observations of delirious episodes and a markedly swollen abdomen. Despite Blake's attempts to get his friend to give up the bottle, the damage had been done.[40] Another Johnson tribute concert was held October 22, 1954, at the Paramount Hotel Grand Ballroom.[41] Smith and Johnson were in many ways opposite personalities but maintained

FINAL YEARS, 1950–1955

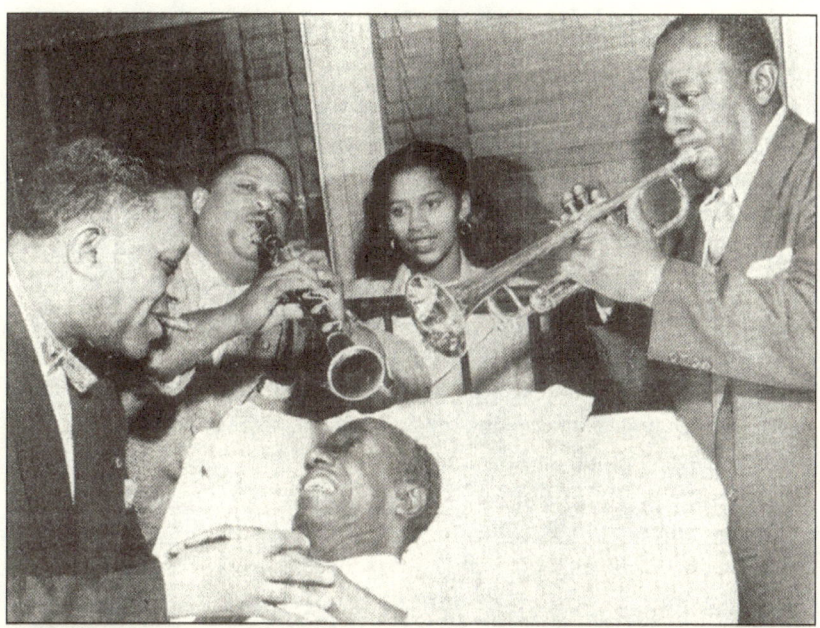

Last known photo of Johnson, bedbound at home with friends visiting him before the 1953 benefit concert. Willie the Lion Smith holding Johnson's hand, Cecil Scott, clarinet, unknown woman, Sidney De Paris, trumpet. (*Jet*, October 15, 1953)

Jazz Concert

FOR THE BENEFIT OF
THE GREAT JAZZ PIANIST AND COMPOSER

JAMES P. Johnson

SPONSORED BY

BLUE CIRCLE RECORD STAR

Willie "The Lion" Smith

AND

HIS MANY FRIENDS

•

MONDAY EVENING, SEPTEMBER 28, 1953
AT 8 P.M.
AT

Town Hall

123 WEST 43rd STREET, NEW YORK, N.Y.

Tickets: $3.60 $3.00 $2.40 $1.80 $1.20

(author's collection)

a close bond of over forty years. In his memoir, Smith perhaps overemphasizes Johnson's personality shortcomings as a doormat, but affectionately relishes his self-proclaimed role as Johnson's keeper, writing:

> He was a worrier and it seemed like he was always getting into trouble over some little thing that didn't mean anything. All he wanted to do was just play the piano; other things he didn't care about. He wasn't much of a showman because if he could manage it he always sat at the piano with his back to the audience. He was soft-spoken Jimmy, rarely talked above a whisper, and he would let people take advantage of him. He just couldn't be bothered by anything that didn't have something to do with playing or composing music. A sort of shy, retiring type that I would have to pump and wind up.[42]

On September 15, 1955, Johnson stopped eating and was hospitalized at Queens General Hospital on September 18, unresponsive. His condition was considered critical.[43] One week before his death, the *New York Age* published a prominent tribute to Johnson noting how underappreciated he was as a composer. They noted he was, ". . . one of the greatest the music profession has known."[44] He lingered for nearly two months in the hospital and died on November 17, 1955, at 3:15 p.m.[45] All the major New York newspapers carried his obituary, but his name probably meant little to the general public. In their headlines and opening paragraphs, they identify Johnson not only as a jazz pianist but also as a prolific composer.[46] It had been a decade since Johnson's orchestral music had been played, but its importance to the Johnson legacy was prominently highlighted at his death. Half of the brief, two-paragraph notice in *Variety* is devoted to Johnson's orchestral efforts.[47] In one of the most pointed summaries of Johnson's enormous contributions, *Billboard* succinctly describes Johnson as a "pioneer jazz pianist and composer of several great standards," and "altho [sic] a student of serious music, is generally credited as one of the founders of the New York jazz piano school and as a prime influence on his pupil, the late Fats Waller, and on Duke Ellington."[48]

In its December 28, 1955, issue, *Down Beat* published a much-improved account. In an obituary that is as much diatribe directed toward the music world and the general public as it is tribute, John Hammond recounted the frustrations of Johnson's career and the neglect of his talents:

> James P. Johnson, one of the great figures in American music, died in New York City on Nov. 17. Two days later, fewer than 75 persons attended the funeral services at University Chapel, in midtown Manhattan.

His enormous talents as composer, pianist, and arranger were as unappreciated in life as now. Although he wrote such tunes as "Charleston," "Old-Fashioned Love," "Porter's Love Song," and "If I Could Be with You," the general public was ignorant of his name. A few musicians may remember such classics as "Carolina Shout," "Worried and Lonesome Blues," and "Snowy Morning Blues," but the sad fact is that Jelly Roll Morton was far better known. Even as a pianist, Jimmy's fame was soon eclipsed by his pupil, Fats Waller.[49]

Hammond further commented on the segregation of the music field, which had confined Johnson to the race record market as a performer and to the all-Black musical as composer. He scorned the disinterest of the music community toward Johnson's serious work, and the "public that never even noticed" Johnson's popular music. After a plea to the record companies to reissue Johnson's early recordings, Hammond concluded, "James P. Johnson was 64 [sic, 61] when he died, and he should have been among the most famous and successful of men. Let us hope that future generations will make up for our lack of appreciation." Bob Harrington, who had seen Johnson play some of his last gigs, in a 1970 article titled, "When James P. Was King," lamented:

> James P. is gone now and other than the musicians who knew of his tremendous talent there are few today who remember him. Maybe someday his greatness will come to full measure.
>
> I think of Jimmy often these days—of what a wonderful person he was. Of the warm smile that would steal over his face.... And I think how very lucky I was to have known and be a friend of so great a man.
>
> The days and years will be long before the likes of James P. Johnson pass this way again.[50]

Many wonderful musicians have come along since James P. was king, but the full measure of Johnson's work, his genius, and the personal character Hammond, Harrington, and many others knew, has yet to be adequately inscribed in the narrative of jazz and American music history.

EPILOGUE

WITH MARK BOROWSKY

On July 1, 1960, Rudi Blesh produced a concert at the Newport Jazz Festival, which he called "Stride Piano All Stars." Among the featured pianists were a seventy-three-year-old Eubie Blake, Willie "The Lion" Smith, and the reclusive New Jersey savant, Donald Lambert. The concert, recorded for posterity by the Voice of America, although not so stated, was an unapologetic tribute to the memory of James P. Johnson. The reverence demonstrated for him by his colleagues was evident in their tune selection—Smith played "Carolina Shout," Blake a rendition of Johnson's "Runnin' Wild Medley," Lambert masterfully recreated Johnson's version of "You Can't Do What My Last Man Did," and the group closed with a performance of "Charleston." Johnson had been dead for nearly five years by that time, and, aside from the Davin interviews, the last of which appeared in print just a few months before, was otherwise a forgotten figure. Since that time, just as Asch, Condon, Hodes, Blesh, and a few others worked to keep Johnson visible in the 1940s, so have the activities of a small but growing coterie of influential Johnson activists advanced important recognition for him and kept stride piano alive.

The *Father of the Stride Piano* LP appeared in 1962 and remained in print for over ten years. It was the only widely available source of Johnson recordings that included unissued late 1930s sessions, as well as some of his seminal sides from the 1920s. A second generation of pianists who had learned the stride language from the masters in the 1940s that included Ralph Sutton, Dick Hyman, Dick Wellstood, Don Ewell, Johnny Guarnieri, and Mike Lipskin (in the 1950s) was keeping the idiom alive in an underground effort while modern jazz was dominating during the 1960s and 1970s. Only the valiant Jaki Byard managed to keep stride piano in front of a broader audience during this time, in part with the encouragement of Charles Mingus who, like Byard, had a deep affection for and understanding of the totality of the jazz tradition. The 1980s saw some resurgence of interest in traditional jazz. A new generation of pianists looked to master the stride style, particularly in France, there spearheaded by Francois Rilhac and Louis Mazetier. In 1981, the Time Life Company released a three-LP box set dedicated to Johnson, one volume in their Giants of Jazz Series. Up to that time, other than the *Father of the Stride Piano* LP, there had been no comprehensive (or even limited) reissue of Johnson's phonograph recordings. They were difficult to find, sporadically included in disparate compilations. The Time Life Johnson set has withstood the test of time as one of the best compilations of his recordings, with Grammy-nominated liner notes by Dick Wellstood, musicologist Willa Rouder, and journalist Frank Kappler.

The monumentally important reissue label Mosaic Records, founded in 1982, issued all of Johnson's Blue Note sessions in 1985, their ninth release. These recordings brought back into clear view Johnson's foundational importance in the creation of the iconic jazz record label, before it became synonymous with modern jazz. The CD format enabled many more reissues, including an eight-CD series issued by the French Classics label between 1992 and 1999, compiling sessions under his name from 1921 to 1947. In 2016, Mosaic released an extensive seven-CD collection of Johnson's commercial recordings from the 1920s and '30s, finally bringing together sessions not only under his name but of others, including the many vocalists he accompanied.

Johnson's underappreciated and understudied piano rolls were for decades the only examples of his solo playing readily available from the transcription recordings that had been released on LP in the 1950s. The critical work of Michael Montgomery in rereleasing many rolls on the Biograph label in the early 1970s maintained their availability, but they have often been derided as mechanically stiff, without much nuance or swing, and adulterated with added notes. Careful listening belies this superficial perception. Dr. Robert Pinsker's printed transcriptions of Johnson's own compositions as he recorded them on piano roll further unravel this concern, and reveal his mastery as player and composer. In recent years, Johnson's astounding renditions are receiving more scholarly attention, as is this forgotten recording medium in general. The noted pianist and scholar Artis Wodehouse is reexamining the rolls themselves, applying the printed instructions in proper foot pumping and use of other player piano devices to enhance expressive elements, a process she calls "pianolizing."

The discovery of the Johnson papers and symphonic scores in 1987 led to other efforts to raise the Johnson profile. Johnson's grandson Barry Glover founded the James P. Johnson Foundation for Music and the Arts as an educational resource for young people to learn about jazz and his grandfather. In 1995, the United States Postal Service issued a Johnson commemorative stamp. Johnson's resting place was unknown until information from his personal papers was pieced together. His gravesite in Mt. Olivet Cemetery in Queens was discovered and found to be unmarked. In 2009, pianist and jazz club owner Michael "Spike" Wilner organized a "rent party" to raise funds for a proper headstone. The *New York Times* and other outlets ran feature stories about Johnson and the event, calling it "the definition of righteous." Over the course of a day at Smalls Jazz Club in Greenwich Village, a dozen pianists paid tribute to Johnson, and an appropriate monument now marks his grave, identifying him as "the Dean of Jazz Pianists." A street sign at the corner of the Van Wyck Expressway and Linden Boulevard in his adopted borough of Queens bears his name and a small photo in tribute.

Johnson's music is perhaps available for performance and study now more than ever. Marin Alsop continues to champion Johnson's music. The scores prepared by her from his handwritten versions found in the family boxes are now available for performance in new engravings at jpjohnsonmusic.com. A serendipitous discovery in the late 1990s by University of Michigan professor and pianist James Dapogny brought to light Johnson's two lost operas. They were reconstructed by him, performed twice at the University of Michigan, and have at this writing just been released on CD. Prominent culture leaders like Wynton Marsalis and Jason Moran have led the effort to support the notion of a jazz tradition and correctly position Johnson within it. The 1921 78 rpm recording of "Carolina Shout" was inducted into the Grammy Hall of Fame by the Recording Academy in 2020, and "Harlem Strut" added to the National Recording Registry of the Library of Congress in 2022, enshrining his earliest works and ensuring their historical importance is recognized. His complex style has been elucidated in excellent transcriptions of his recorded solos by Paul Marcorelles and Riccardo Scivales. But his compositions are living art, and a new generation of musicians is learning the intricacies of the demanding stride piano style. They are demonstrating that Johnson's works and stride piano are not museum pieces or historical relics, but rather music with modern relevance and a timeless vibrancy. These fits and starts of attention have been sporadic steps in the quest to secure for Johnson his rightful place in American music, but the community of jazz critics and writers has yet to adopt a consistent view of Johnson's place "in the tradition." His musical legacy is a deep well of riches to be further explored and enjoyed. Our hope is that his name will be routinely included alongside that of Fats Waller and Jelly Roll Morton, written about in the same company as George Gershwin and Duke Ellington, acknowledged as an innovator on his instrument along with Louis Armstrong and Charlie Parker, and that his tunes and concert pieces are regularly played alongside all the great songwriters and American composers. He deserves no less.

NOTES

INTRODUCTION

1. Ross Russell, "Grandfather of Hot Piano—James P. Johnson," *Jazz Information*, November 1941, 20. "Count Basie Picks the 12 Best Pianists," *Music and Rhythm*, January 1942. Stanley Dance, liner notes to *James P. Johnson—Father of the Stride Piano*, Columbia CL-1780, 1962, LP. Grover Sales, *Jazz—America's Classical Music* (Boston: Da Capo, 1992), 75. David Schiff, "A Composer with Harlem on His Mind," *New York Times*, February 16, 1992, Section 2, 1.

2. Russell, "Grandfather of Hot Piano," 20. While Russell's article correctly outlines the breadth and importance of Johnson's work, there are many factual errors.

3. Michael Steinman, "Jazz Lives—The Triumphs of James P. Johnson," January 7, 2016, https://jazzlives.wordpress.com/2016/01/07/the-triumphs-of-james-p-johnson/, accessed October 9, 2023.

4. Mike Lipskin, "JPJ's Mule Walk," email to stride piano email group@yahoogroups.com, March 1, 2013.

5. Martin Williams, *The Jazz Tradition* (New York: Oxford University Press, 1970), 1, 113.

6. Sales, *Jazz*, 3.

7. Russell, "Grandfather of Hot Piano," 20.

CHAPTER 1. NEW BRUNSWICK, 1894–1902

1. James P. Johnson, insert to *James P. Johnson—Giants of Jazz*, Time-Life Records STL-J18, 1981, LP.

2. Johnson, insert to *James P. Johnson—Giants of Jazz*.

3. 1860 US Federal Census population schedule, South Ward, Petersburg, Virginia, page 324, dwelling 803, family 801, Nathaniel Harrison Household. Petersburg (Virginia) Hustings Court Register of Free Negroes and Mulattoes, 1854, LVA Microfilm 73, Nathl. Harrison entry, document 3. This is the earliest known document in which Nathaniel Harrison appears. He is also listed in the personal property tax book of 1858 in the listing of free Negroes. Virginia Auditor of Public Accounts, Personal Property Tax Books, City of Petersburg, 1857–1859, LVA Microfilm 814, Nat. Harrison, No. 29, Document 6. Petersburg and Colonial Heights Virginia City Directory, 1870/71, Mat (*sic*) Harrison entry, LVA Book F234.P4 A18. Jarratt's Hotel, Petersburg, Virginia. *A guide to the fortifications and battlefields around Petersburg: with a splendid map from actual surveys made by the US Engineer Department*. Petersburg, VA: J. B. Ege's Printing House, 1869.

4. She is likely the Fanny Jones listed in the Register of Free Negroes in 1850. Petersburg (Virginia) Hustings Court Register of Free Negroes and Mulattoes, 1839–1850, LVA Microfilm 73, Jones entries, 1845–1850. 1860 US Federal Census. 1870 US federal Census Population Schedule Ward 6, Petersburg, Virginia, LVA microfilm 213, Page 373A, dwelling 125, family 137, Nathaniel Harrison Household. Josephine's death certificate—New York (New York) Department of Health, Death Certificates (Manhattan, New York), 1919–1948 [Vol. 27–28], Cert. No. 13001. No.14000—lists the cause of death as chronic valvular disease of the heart. She was around seventy-one years old when she died. This is somewhat young for advanced valvular disease due to aging alone as a cause of death. Although possible, it is more likely this was the result of childhood rheumatic fever.

5. Giles R. Wright, *Afro-Americans in New Jersey—A Short History* (Trenton: New Jersey Historical Commission, Department of State, 1988), 19.

6. John P. Wall, Harold E. Pickersgill, *History of Middlesex County, New Jersey 1664–1920* Vol. 1 (New York and Chicago: Lewis Historical Publishing Co., 1921), 288, 27–29, 16, 40.

7. *New Jersey, Abstract of Wills, 1670–1817*. New Jersey State Archives. New Jersey, *Published Archives Series, First Series* (Trenton, NJ: John L. Murphy Publishing Company). Ancestry.com, 2011.

8. Seventh Census of the United States, 1850, Franklin, Somerset, New Jersey; roll: M432; Page 298A; Image: 128.

9. Babcock & Johnson, *New-Brunswick Directory for 1874–'75* (New Brunswick, NJ: Fredonian Office, 1874), 130.

10. New Jersey Department of Health, Bureau of Vital Statistics, marriage certificates, marriage of Richard Nevius and Josephine Harrison, 16 March, 1879, no. N-2 (penned), New Jersey State Archives microfilm 4. 1880 US Federal Census Population Schedule Franklin Somerset County, New Jersey, ED 158, sheet 12, Dwelling 107, family 117, Mary Nevius household.

11. Tom Davin, "Conversations with James P. Johnson," *Jazz Review*, June 1959, 15; New Jersey Department of Health, Bureau of Vital Statistics, Birth certificates and indexes, 1878–1923, birth of William Henry Nevius, December 23, 1879, no. 6 New Jersey State Archives microfilm 18. New Jersey Department of Health, birth of Frank Nevius, October 25, 1881, no. 97 microfilm 34. New Jersey Department of Health, birth of Clifford Nevius, October 15, 1883, no. N54, microfilm 50. 1900 US Federal Census Population schedule New Brunswick Ward 6, Middlesex County New Jersey, ED 47, Sheet 9A, dwelling 145, Family 176, Perry Thompson household. No birth certificate could be found for Isabella.

12. 1885 New Jersey State Census Population schedule, Franklin Somerset County New Jersey, sheet 89, dwelling 522, family 534, George Thompson household. There does not seem to be any relationship with Josephine's future husband Perry Thompson.

13. New Brunswick City Directory, 1890 (New Brunswick, New Jersey: J. Heidingsfield, printer and bookbinder, 1890), 98. Josephine is listed as widow.

14. Johnson, insert to *James P. Johnson—Giants of Jazz*.

15. Documents from his marriage to Josephine and James P.'s birth give most credibility to these dates.

16. New Jersey Dept. of Health, Bureau of Vital Statistics, marriage certificates, marriage of William L. Johnson and Hetty A. Francis, 7 May 1884, New Jersey state archives, microfilm 27. 1885 New Jersey state census population schedule, New Brunswick, Middlesex County, New Jersey, sheet 139, dwelling 234, family 295, William H. Johnson household, New Jersey state archives microfilm 29.

17. New Brunswick Times, *The City of New Brunswick: Its History, Its Homes, and Its Industries* (New Brunswick, NJ: Times Publishing Co., 1909). H. Solomon Hill, *The Negro in New Brunswick, New Jersey—As Revealed by a Study of 100 Families* (master's thesis, Drew University, Madison, NJ, 1942), 8. Wright, *Afro-Americans in New Jersey*, 16, 2.

18. Hill, *Negro in New Brunswick*, 25–28, 26.

19. J. H. Mulholland, compiler, *The New Brunswick City and Business Directory, 1888*, (York Pennsylvania: Evening Dispatch Print, 1888), 140. Mullholland, *New Brunswick City and Business Directory*, 140, 193.

20. Johnson, insert to *James P. Johnson—Giants of Jazz*.

21. Seventh Census of the United States, 1850, Census Place: North Brunswick, Middlesex, New Jersey; roll 455; page 283a.

22. Richard Edwards, *Industries of New Jersey, vol.4* (New York: New York Historical Publishing Co., 1882), 9.

23. US census: 1850; 1870, Census Place: New Brunswick, Middlesex, New Jersey; roll M593_873; page 169B; 1880, Census Place: New Brunswick, Middlesex, New Jersey; roll 789; page 62C; Enumeration District: 122. US Census 1880, Killenberger's New Brunswick city dir., 1877–78.

24. F. Killenberger's New Brunswick City Directory (Julius Heidingsfeld, New Brunswick, New Jersey), 1886; US Census 1880.

25. "Another Called Away—Henry M. Price Closes a Long and Useful Life," *New Brunswick Home News*, January 30, 1889, 3. "The Last Rites—Funeral Services of the Late Henry M. Price," *New Brunswick Home News*, February 2, 1889, 3.

26. Killenberger's, 1886; Killenberger's 1901–1902, 9; Mulholland, 1888, 193; Killenberger's, 1890, 212; Killenberger's 1893, 192; 1896, 25. John P. Wall, *The Chronicles of New Brunswick, New Jersey 1667–1931* (New Brunswick, NJ: Thatcher—Anderson Co., 1931), 290; *Daily Times*, March 30, 1898, 1.

27. Killenberger's, 1891, 23; "Gone to Inspect Water Plants," *Daily Times*, June 7, 1899, 1.

28. Edwards, *Industries of New Jersey*, 9.

29. Killenberger's, 1899–1900, 148.

30. New Jersey Department of Health, Bureau of vital statistics, marriage certificates and indexes: 1878–1940, marriage of William H. H. Smith and Josephine Harrison, 31 December, no. S40, New Jersey state archives microfilm 85. Minutes of the General Assembly of the Presbyterian Church in the United States, Presbyterian Committee of Publication (Richmond, VA: Whittet and Shepperson, 1896). First Reformed Church, New Brunswick, NJ, church register, no. 430, 131.

31. New Jersey Department of Health, Bureau of vital statistics, birth certificates and indexes, 1878–1923, birth of male child of William H. Johnson, 21 February 1893, no. J12, New Jersey state archives microfilm 177. There is no George in the Price, Johnson, or Harrison families, but perhaps the middle name of Joseph was given after William's father, as listed on the earliest possible census record for William. New Jersey Department of Health, Bureau of Vital Statistics, death certificates, 1892–1893, death of George Joseph Johnson, 7 April 1893, no. J142, New Jersey State archives microfilm 132. New Jersey Department of Health, Bureau of vital statistics, birth certificates and indexes, 1878–1923, birth of male child of William H. Johnson, unnamed, no. J40, New Jersey State archives microfilm. Birth dates of 1897 and 1891, often given while Johnson was alive, are incorrect.

32. *Daily Home News*, "A. L. Smith Elected President New Brunswick Board of Health," May 10, 1906, 1.

33. Killenberger's, 1897, 331; Sanborn fire map, 1895.

34. "Horses Wanted," *New Brunswick Daily Times*, December 9, 1896.

35. "Cause for Complaint," *New Brunswick Daily Times*, August 19, 1893, 1.

36. "The Cody Funeral," *Daily News-Times*, May 1, 1894, 1; "John Cody Arrested," *Daily News-Times*, June 16, 1894, 1.

37. *New Brunswick Daily Times*, August 25, 1894, 1.

38. *New Brunswick Daily Times*, November 15, 1897, 1.

39. New Jersey state census, 1895, roll V227_90, p 5, line 20; United States census, 1900, Perry Thompson household; Killenberger's, 1901–1902, 256.

40. Davin, June 1959, 15.

41. There was one other A.M.E. congregation in New Brunswick that by the mid-1890s had essentially disbanded. Hill, *Negro in New Brunswick*, 74.

42. Davin, June 1959, 16.

43. "Concert in Columbia Hall Tonight," *New Brunswick Daily Times*, August 11, 1898, 1.

44. Written in 1869 by Joseph Eastburn Winner. A favorite of Johnson's religious mother, it was ironically a drinking song originally. By the 1890s it was known more as a folk song.

45. Davin, June 1959, 15; Killenberger's, 1899–1900.

46. "Annual Minstrel Show," *New Brunswick Daily Times*, April 2, 1900.

47. "Mirth and Music," *New Brunswick Daily Times*, August 28, 1899.

48. Mark R Jones, *Doin' the Charleston* (Charleston, SC: East Atlantic Publishing, 2013), 19–49.

49. Rudi Blesh and Harriet Janis, *They All Played Ragtime*, 4th ed. (New York: Oak Publications, 1971), 190.

50. Davin, June 1959, 15–16.

51. "Assaulted His Wife," *Daily Times*, April 10, 1900.

52. Lydia Parrish, *Slave Songs of the Georgia Sea Islands* (New York: Creative Age Press, 1942), 54, 234.

53. Reprinted in Bernard Katz, *The Social Implications of Early Negro Music in the United States* (New York: Arno Press, 1969), 4–5.

54. William Francis Allen, Charles Pickard Ware, and Lucy McKim Garrison, *Slave Songs of the United States* (New York: A. Simpson and Co., 1867; reprint New York: Dover, 1995), iv.

55. Stuckey, *Slave Culture*, viii, 57, 63.

56. Allen, Ware, and Garrison, *Slave Songs*, xiv.

57. Davin, June 1959, 16, 15.

CHAPTER 2. JERSEY CITY, 1902–1908

1. Jersey City School Register, School #9 (Trenton: MacCrellish and Quigley, 1902–03). Davin, June 1959, 16.

2. Sanborn map, 1908, 5th ward.

3. "A Well Equipped School," *New York Tribune*, September 14, 1896.

4. Frank Stevens, *Jersey City of Today, Review Special, 1910* (Jersey City: Reprint Bergen Historic Books, Robert D. Griffin, 1996), 3.

5. Jersey City School Register, 1903–04. Boyd's Jersey City and Hoboken Directory, 1905–06 (Jersey City: Boyd's Directory Co.), 1905. Davin, June 1959, 16.

6. Davin, June 1959, 16.

7. Edward Berlin, *King of Ragtime* (New York: Oxford University Press, 2016), 163.

8. Davin, June 1959, 16.

9. Kenneth French, *Images of America: Railroads of Hoboken and Jersey City* (Columbia, SC: Arcadia, 2002).

10. "Golden Jubilee in St. Mark's A.M.E.," *Evening Journal Jersey City*, March 11, 1905.

11. A. P. Miller, *The Black Man's Burden*, 1899, 13.

12. James P. Johnson, "Creative Work—Accomplishments," Guggenheim fellowship application biographical summary, James P. Johnson collection, the Institute of Jazz Studies, Dana Library, Rutgers University at Newark.

13. Davin, July 1959, 10.

14. Davin, July 1959, 16.

15. Davin, July 1959, 16.

16. Davin, June 1959, 16

17. Davin, July 1959, 13.

18. Alan Lomax, *Mister Jelly Roll* (Berkeley: University of California Press, 1950), 62.

19. Edward A. Berlin, "Ragtime and Improvised Piano: Another View," *Journal of Jazz Studies* (Spring/Summer 1977): 8–9.

20. Blesh and Janis, *They All Played Ragtime*, 204.

21. David A. Jasen, *Recorded Ragtime, 1897–1958* (Hamden, CT: Archon Books, 1973), 40.

22. Mark Borowsky, personal communication, 2021.

CHAPTER 3. THE JUNGLES, 1908–1913

1. US Federal Census, 1910, sheet 2B.

2. Davin, July 1959, 11; Ethel Waters, too, recalled the race riots in the Jungles, Ethel Waters with Charles Samuels, *His Eye Is on the Sparrow* (New York: Jove, 1979; originally Doubleday, 1950), 123. Robin Kelley provides a detailed account in Robin D. G. Kelley, *Thelonious Monk* (New York: Free Press, 2009), 15–20.

3. "'San Juan Hill' Has Unique Institutions," *New York Age*, December 26, 1912, 7; "Many Negroes Are In Business," *New York Age*, November 28, 1912, 1.

4. Davin, June 1959, 17.

5. "People's Choral Meeting—Dr. Damrosch to Enlist Interest in the Movement at Cooper Union," *New York Times*, November 8, 1908, 14.

6. "Teachers to Hear Oratorio—Frank Damrosch Arranges for a Special Rehearsal of Elgar's *The Dream of Gerontius*," *New York Times*, March 12, 1903, 8.

7. *New York Times*, February 21, 1909, 55.

8. "Plans for Lincoln Day," *New York Times*, January 24, 1909, 15.

9. *New York Daily Tribune*, December 9, 1908, 6; "Lincoln Day is Celebrated All Over the Nation," *The Evening World*, February 12, 1909, 2.

10. US Federal Census, 1910, sheet 2B.

11. Davin, June 1959, 17.

12. Davin, June 1959, 17.

13. Edgar T. Rouzeau, "StarDust: Jas. P. Johnson, Musician and Songwriter," *Journal and Guide*, undated clipping, JPJC collection, IJS, Newark. Johnson recalls her name as Marie Howell in his Guggenheim Fellowship application biography. His ASCAP biography notes the same name. http://www.traditionalmusic.co.uk/music-search/music-songs-composers%20-%200356.htm, accessed September 2, 2019. An undated, unidentified clipping titled "TinType" by Rosemarie Berry notes the name as Marie Hamell Eely.

14. Davin, June 1959, 17.

15. Davin, July 1959, 11.

16. Davin, July 1959, 11.

17. Marva Griffin Carter, *Swing Along* (New York: Oxford University Press, 2008), 73.

18. Davin, July 1959, 11.

19. James Weldon Johnson, *The Autobiography of an Ex-Colored Man* (New York: Knopf, 1927; Avon Books, 1965), 447.

20. Edward Berlin, *Reflections and Research on Ragtime* (Brooklyn: Brooklyn College Conservatory of Music, 1987), 50.

21. Smith and Hoefer, *Music on My Mind*, 65.

22. Davin, July 1959, 12.

23. Davin, June 1959, 17.

24. Mildred McAdory, "Noted Composer Writes Ode to Hero," *The Worker*, May 3, 1945, 11.

25. Nat Hentoff, "Garvin Bushell and New York Jazz in the 1920s," *Jazz Review*, January 1959, 12.

26. Maurice R. Davie, *Negroes in American Society* (New York: McGraw-Hill, 1949), 94.

27. Hentoff, "Garvin Bushell," 12.

28. Davin, June 1959, 17.

29. Davin, June 1959, 17.

30. Gunther Schuller, *Early Jazz* (New York: Oxford, 1968), 214.

31. Max Harrison, "James P. Johnson: A Jazz Retrospect," reprint from *Jazz Monthly* (Boston: Crescendo Publishing, 1976), 83.

32. Harold Courlander, *Negro Folk Music, USA* (New York: Columbia University Press, 1963), 125.

CHAPTER 4. THE TICKLERS, 1913–1916

1. Blesh and Janis, *They All Played Ragtime*, 191.

2. Smith and Hoefer, *Music on My Mind*, 56.

3. Lynn Abbott and Doug Seroff, *Out of Sight: The Rise of African American Popular Music 1889–1895* (Jackson: University Press of Mississippi, 2002), 455.

4. *Indianapolis Freeman*, June 16, 1900; Smith and Hoefer, *Music on My Mind*, 55.

5. Salem Tutt Whitney, "Jazz Pioneers," *Chicago Defender*, December 5, 1925.

6. Smith and Hoefer, *Music on My Mind*, 56.

7. Davin, July 1959, 12, 10.

8. "The Green Recital," *New York Age*, March 7, 1907, 2.

9. Smith and Hoefer, *Music on My Mind*, 69; Davin, July 1959, 12.

10. "The News of Greater New York," *New York Age*, December 30, 1909, 7.

11. Davin, July 1959, 12.

12. Blesh and Janis, *They All Played Ragtime*, 203.

13. Marcello Piras, "Garibaldi to Syncopation: Bruto Giannini and the Curious Case of Scott Joplin's 'Magnetic Rag,'" *Journal of Jazz Studies* (Winter 2013): 107–77.

14. Rick Benjamin, liner notes to *Treemonisha*, New World Records 80720, 2012, 19, compact disc.

15. James P. Johnson, "Creative Work," Fellowship application, JPJC, IJS; "Jazz Tunes, Blues, Classics Range of this Composer," *Long Island Daily Press*, June 24, 1939.

16. Piras, "Garibaldi," 156.

17. Sue Harding, "We Have with Us," unidentified clipping, November 5, 1938, JPJC, IJS.

18. New York City, Borough of Manhattan death records.

19. Davin, July 1959, 13, 12; Piras theorizes that the Davin transcription mistook Johnson's words, resulting in a misrepresentation of Johnson's attitudes toward Giannini's practice requirements. See Piras, "Garibaldi," 113–14.

20. Davin, July 1959, 12.

21. Davin, March/April 1960, 11.

22. Piras, "Garibaldi," 20.

23. Davin, July 1959, 13.

24. Smith and Hoefer, *Music on My Mind*, 68–69; "Memphis Blues Band at Selwyn Theatre," *New York Age*, April 12, 1919, 6.

25. "Easter Greeting from the Clef Club," *NY Age*, April 20, 1916, 6; "Clef Club Singers and Players of N.Y.," *New York Age*, November 30, 1918, 6.

26. "Memphis Blues at Selwyn Theater Sunday Night," *Chicago Defender*, April 19, 1919, 5; William C. Handy, *Father of the Blues* (New York: Macmillan, 1941; Da Capo, 1969), 194.

27. "Ogden Music Ass'n Prizes Awarded," *New York Amsterdam News*, August 26, 1927, 2.

28. Tim Brooks, *Lost Sounds* (Urbana: University of Illinois Press, 2004), 522; Handy, *Father of the Blues*, 197.

29. Lucien H. White, "Fred M. Bryan, Pianist & Composer, Dies After Four Weeks of Illness," *New York Age*, August 24, 1929.

30. James P. Johnson, note in hand of Johnson, JPJC, IJS.

31. Davin, July 1959, 13.

32. Terry Waldo, *This Is Ragtime* (New York: Hawthorn Books, 1976), 17.

33. Al Rose, *Eubie Blake* (New York: Schirmer, 1979), 45, 147.

34. Waldo, *This Is Ragtime*, 17–18.

35. Mays, William A., personal communication, November 17, 2012.

36. Blesh and Janis, *They All Played Ragtime*, 193; Smith and Hoefer, *Music on My Mind*, 54–55.

37. Smith and Hoefer, *Music on My Mind*, 54–55.

38. Frank Driggs, liner notes to *The Sound of Harlem—Jazz Odyssey Volume III*, Columbia C3L 33, LP; Smith and Hoefer, *Music on My Mind*, 64.

39. Smith and Hoefer, *Music on My Mind*, 88–89, 32.

40. Davin, June 1959, 17.

41. New York State Archives, Albany, New York; State Population Census Schedules, 1925, Election District 46, Assembly District 05, City: New York; County: New York; Page 6.

42. Davin, June 1959, 17.

43. *New York Age*, December 7, 1916, 6.

44. Kelley, *Thelonious Monk*, 27.

45. Ralph Matthews, "Watching the Big Parade—The Rise of the Parlor Social," *Baltimore Afro-American*, September 28, 1940, 4.

46. Mike Lipskin and Len Kunstadt, "This Is William D. Gant," *Record Research*, October 1960, 3, 4, 16.

47. William D. Gant, interview with Mike Lipskin and Len Kunstadt, 1960, Mike Lipskin Collection.

48. William D. Gant, interview with Mike Lipskin and Len Kunstadt, 1960, Mike Lipskin Collection.

49. Davin, June 1959, 17.

50. Blesh and Janis, *They All Played Ragtime*, 200.

51. Waldo, *This Is Ragtime*, 113.

52. Davin, July 1959, 12.

53. John L. Fell and Terkild Vinding, *Stride* (Lanham, MD: Scarecrow Press, 1999), 87.

54. Rose, *Eubie Blake*,148.

55. Rose, *Eubie Blake*, 148.

56. *New York Age*, August 6, 1914, 6.

57. Pennsylvania, Philadelphia marriage index, 1885–1951, Clerk of the Orphans court, Philadelphia, Pennsylvania; Smith and Hoefer, *Music on My Mind*, 35; Waters and Samuels, *His Eye Is on the Sparrow*, 123–24; "Harlem Briefs," *Chicago Defender*, April 10, 1920, 4; Waters and Samuels, *His Eye Is on the Sparrow*, 123–24.

58. "A Note Or Two," *Chicago Defender*, November 21, 1925, 6.

59. Smith and Hoefer, *Music on My Mind*, 36–37.

60. Smith and Hoefer, *Music on My Mind*, 78.

61. Davin, August 1959, 12, 14–15.

62. Davin, July 1959, 13.

63. Davin, June 1959, 17.

64. Davin, July 1959, 12–13. The "Russian Rag" by George L. Cobb was published in 1918.

65. Mark Tucker, *Ellington—The Early Years* (Chicago: University of Illinois Press, 1991), 30.

CHAPTER 5. FIRST PUBLICATIONS AND RECORDINGS, 1916–1917

1. Davin, September 1959, 26.

2. "Musical and Dramatic," *Chicago Defender*, March 7, 1914, 6.

3. James Weldon Johnson, *Black Manhattan* (New York: Atheneum, 1977), 174.

4. "Musical and Dramatic," *Chicago Defender*, March 17, 1914, 6.

5. Johnson, *Black Manhattan*, 174.

6. "Gibson's New Standard Theater," *Philadelphia Tribune*, March 11, 1916, 3.

7. "Hill at Hammerstein's," *New York Age*, June 11, 1914, 6.

8. "Gibson's New Standard Theater," *Philadelphia Tribune*, March 11, 1916, 3.

9. "Amusement Parks," *New York Tribune*, July 9, 1916, C2.

10. Sylvester Russell, "J. Leubrie Hill, Distinguished Star, Actor, Playwright, Stage Producer and Illustrious Song Writer, Passes Away In New York City," undated/unidentified clipping.

11. 1900; Census Place: Bayonne Ward 3, Hudson, New Jersey; Page 3; Enumeration District 0009; FHL microfilm 1240971.

12. "Bill Farrell's Piano Features Club Elegant," *New York Amsterdam News*, December 27, 1947, 11; Dr. Robert Pinsker, personal email communication, February 5, 2012.

13. "Musical and Dramatic," *Chicago Defender*, June 10, 1911, 3.

14. "Musicians Organize Clef Club," *New York Age*, April 28, 1910, 6; Lester A. Walton, "Music and the Stage," *New York Age*, October 27, 1910, 6.

15. "Clef Club Beefsteak," *New York Age*, March 18, 1915, 6.

16. *Chicago Defender*, advertisement, June 17, 1916, 4. "White Rats Last Call," *New York Age*, advertisement, April 13, 1916, 6.

17. *Trow's General Directory of New York City*, RL Polk, publisher, New York, NY, 1916, 1917, 1918. No listing that includes Johnson's name is evident.

18. Davin, July 1959, 13.

19. Smith and Hoefer, *Music on My Mind*, 104.

20. Davin, July 1959, 13.

21. James P. Johnson, "Liberty," score in the hand of James P. Johnson, JPJC, IJS.

22. *Billboard*, August 11, 1917, 73. No recording by Sweatman is known. He was auditioning for Columbia Records in the summer of 1917, but didn't begin his prolific recording association with the label until the next year.

23. *Billboard*, January 12, 1918, 17.

24. *Huntington Herald*, May 6, 1918, advertisement for Emerson Records, 3; *The Daily Courier* (Connellsville, PA), October 18, 1918, advertisement for Columbia Records, 9; QRS hand-played music rolls catalogue, 1918.

25. Davin, September 1959, 26, 27.

26. Vocalstyle Company of Cincinnati, 1916 catalogue title page, Michael Montgomery files.

27. "Say Rolls Help Sheet Music Trade," *Music Trade Indicator*, February 17, 1917, 40.

28. Davin, September 1959, 26.

29. Mike Montgomery, Michigan, to Willa Rouder, May 23, 1979, typewritten transcript, author's collection, from Mike Montgomery files.

30. "AMICA Forum—J. P. Johnson Rolls," Durrell Armstrong, *AMICA Bulletin*, January-February 1980, 5.

31. "Boys of Uncle Sam" was recorded by Standard but not played by Johnson.

32. Brooks, *Lost Sounds*, 522.

33. *Music Trade Indicator*, January 13, 1917, 41; June 30, 1917, 31; August 25, 1917, 27; *Universal Music Rolls, Bulletin for October 1917*, 3–7.

34. Davin, September 1959, 26.

35. *Music Trade Indicator*, May 26, 1917, 67; July 28, 1917, 29; *Universal Music Rolls, Bulletin for October 1917*, 3–7.

36. Michael Montgomery, *George Gershwin Rollography*, text in hand of Michael Montgomery, 1973, author's collection, from Michael Montgomery files.

37. "Tales of Tin Pan Alley—'Swanee' and Its Author," *Along Broadway—The Edison Musical Magazine*, October 1920, 9.

38. Howard Pollack, *George Gershwin: His Life and Work* (Berkeley: University of California Press, 2006), 31.

39. John S. Wilson, "Introduction," in Robert Kimball and Alfred Simon, *The Gershwins* (New York: Atheneum, 1973), xxiii.

40. Artis Wodehouse, "Tracing Gershwin's Piano Rolls," in Wayne Schneider, ed., *The Gershwin Style* (New York: Oxford University Press, 1999), 211.

41. Montgomery, Gershwin Rollography.

42. *Chicago Defender*, advertisement, January 27, 1923, 6.

43. *New York Amsterdam News*, December 27, 1947, 11.

CHAPTER 6. THE GIGGIN' YEARS, 1916-1918

1. Davin, September 1959, 27.

2. "Jack Trotter's New York Notes of Stage and Sport," *Indianapolis Freeman*, unknown date.

3. "Tempo Club Concert," *New York Age*, April 2, 1914, 6.

4. Lester A. Walton, "Philadelphians Hear Clef Club," *New York Age*, April 27, 1918, 6.

5. "Colored Attractions Winning O. K. of Broadway Audiences," *New York Age*, March 22, 1919, 6.

6. "What the Stage Stars Were Doing 10 yrs. Ago," *Afro-American*, February 27, 1932, 8.

7. William E. Clark, "Happy Rhone Runs a Popular Cabaret," *New York Age*, September 16, 1922, 6; Noble Sissle, "Show Business," *New York Age*, October 30, 1948, 15.

8. Davin, September 1959, 26–27. If Johnson was referring to the song "The Sheik of Araby," that tune was not copyrighted until 1921.

9. "Allie Ross, Composer, In Second Orchestral Recital," *New York Age*, January 29, 1921, 5; Davin, March-April 1960, 11; "Allie Ross," 2.

10. Davin, September 1959, 27.

11. Davin, March-April 1960, 11.

12. Davin, March-April 1960, 11.

13. Smith and Hoefer, *Music on My Mind*, 90.

14. Davin, March-April 1960, 11.

15. Davin, March-April 1960, 12.

16. US WWI Draft Registration Cards, 1917–1918. City of Newark, Bureau of vital statistics, record of marriage, certificate No. 5680 6/29/51.

17. Davin, September 1959, 27.

18. Certificate of Death, Bureau of Records and Statistics, Dept of Health, City of New York, cert No. 156-57-411385.

19. Davin March-April 1960, 12.

20. Davin, September 1959, 27.

21. *Variety*, December 7, 1917, 13.

22. *Washington Post*, advert, December 25, 1917, 12; *Boston Daily Globe*, January 6, 1918, 31.

23. Davin, September 1959, 27.

24. *New York Times*, advert, March 3, 1918, 58.

25. "'What's Your Husband Doing' at the Lafayette," *New York Age*, June 14, 1919, 6.

26. Davin, September 1959, 26.

27. "Vaudeville," *New York Tribune*, February 16, 1919, F2.

28. *Variety*, January 18, 1918, 18.

29. Blesh and Janis, *They All Played Ragtime*, 213; *The Sun*, March 17, 1918, 12, advert for Nixon's Victoria; "Tabloid at Victoria," April 2, 1918, 8; "Ben Harney & Co.," *The Evening Public Ledger*, advert for Globe Theater, May 18, 1918.

30. Blesh and Janis, *They All Played Ragtime*, 227.

31. Davin, September 1959, 26.

32. Allan Sutton, *Recording the Twenties* (Denver: Mainspring Press, 2008), 22; "Bankruptcy Sales," *New York Times*, January 24, 1917, 11.

33. Reid Badger, *A Life in Ragtime* (New York: Oxford, 1995), 195.

34. "Smarter Set Co. In 'Darkest Americans,'" *New York Age*, September 28, 1918, 6.

35. "Smarter Set," *Chicago Defender*, July 20, 1918, 6.

36. James Austin, "The Stage-Doings of the Profession," *Philadelphia Tribune*, August 24, 1918, 3.

37. Tony Langston, "Smarter Set Drawing Well at Avenue," *Chicago Defender*, June 28, 1919, 8; *Chicago Defender*, August 3, 1918, advert, 6; Austin, "The Stage," 3; J. H. Gray, "Pennsylvania," *Chicago Defender*, August 31, 1918, 8.

38. Davin, March-April 1960, 12.

39. Davin, March/April 1960, 12. *The Washington Post*, advert, August 25, 1918, 36. *Trenton Evening Times*, advert, September 6, 1918, 15. "Smarter Set Co. In 'Darkest Americans,'" *New York Age*, September 28, 1918, 6. *Harrisburg Telegraph*, October 3, 1918, 12. "Letter," *Chicago Defender*, October 19, 1918, 7. Davin, March/April 1960, 12.

40. The street is incorrectly transcribed by Davin as Carter Street.

41. Waters and Samuels, *His Eye Is on the Sparrow*, 88.

42. Davin, March-April 1960, 12. In the interview, Johnson gives Heywood's home base as the 91 Theater. Ethel Waters recalled Heywood played at the 81. The 81 is also confirmed by research from Michael Montgomery, liner notes to *Eddie Heywood and the Blues Singers*, Document Records DOCD-5380, 1995, CD.

43. *The Indianapolis Star* advert, November 11, 1918, 3; *Logansport Pharos-Tribune*, advert, November 15, 1918, 8.

44. "'Darkest Americans' Scores Big Hit Here," *Logansport Pharos-Tribune*, November 22, 1918, 4.

45. "Smarter Set," *Chicago Defender*, November 23, 1918, 6; *Chicago Defender*, advert, December 7, 1918, 6; "A Note or Two," *Chicago Defender*, February 22, 1919, 14.

CHAPTER 7. TOLEDO, 1919–1920

1. 1920 US Federal Census, Toledo ward 6, Lucas Ohio, roll T625_1408, page 1A; enumeration district 80; Image 1108. Johnson is listed as the head of the household.

2. Bob Dietsche, *Tatum's Town* (Brooklyn, NY: Bobson Press, 2016), 94–95; Herman Rosenberg and Eugene Williams, "June Clark—The Story of a Forgotten Giant," *Jazz Information*, November 1941, 12.

3. Davin, March-April 1960, 13.

4. James Lester, *Too Marvelous for Words—The Life and Genius of Art Tatum* (New York: Oxford University Press, 1994), 19.

5. Ralph Gleason, interview with Earl Hines, Koch Jazz, KOC CD-8565, CD. Originally aired on *Jazz Casual*, February 15, 1963, KQED, San Francisco, California.

6. Stanley Dance, *The World of Earl Hines* (New York: Scribner's, 1977), 133.

7. Davin, March-April 1960, 13, 18.

8. David A. Jasen and Gene Jones, *That American Rag* (New York: Schirmer, 2000), 79–84.

9. William Grant Still, "The Men Behind American Music," *The Crisis*, January 1944, 14.

10. Russ J. Cowans, "Around the Motor City," *Baltimore Afro-American*, February 22, 1936, 14.

11. Phil Pastras, *Dead Man Blues* (Berkeley: University of California Press, 2001), 128. The existence of the Wolverine barbershop was in question until archivist Michael Montgomery discovered an advertisement for it in a 1930s Detroit theatrical program, cited in Jon Milan, *Images of America—Detroit* (Charleston, SC: Arcadia, 2009), 64.

12. Robert Pinsker, personal communication email, April 21, 2007; WWI draft registration card.

13. Davin, March-April 1960, 13.

14. Dance, *The World of Earl Hines*, 18; Dietsche, *Tatum's Town*, 20.

15. Blesh and Janis, *They All Played Ragtime*, 261. Charles Payne Rogers, "Charles Thompson," *Record Changer*, May 1950, 13.

16. Trebor Tichener, liner notes to "Charles Thompson—The Neglected Professor," Delmark Euphonic Series 738, c 2000.

17. "John C. Cotter, *The Negro in Music in St. Louis* (Master of Arts thesis, Washington University, St. Louis, MO, June 1959), 302–4.

18. Paul Affeldt, Interview with Brun, on *Brun Campbell—Joplin's Disciple*, Delmark 753, 2001, compact disc.

19. Frank E. Percival, "Foresight of One Man Put Toledo's Music Teaching on Business Basis," *Musical America*, March 13, 1915; Bradford Mills, "Going Was Tough in the Old Days," *Toledo Blade*, February 18, 1951.

20. "Toledo Conservatory of Music—An Institution of Which Toledo Is Proud," *Toledo Blade*, August 6, 1910, 2.

21. William D. Speck, *Images of America—Toledo: A History in Architecture 1890–1914* (Charleston, SC: Arcadia, 2002), 86.

22. Toledo Conservatory of Music and Dramatic Art Prospectus, 1920, 6.

23. 1930 US Federal Census, York, DuPage, Illinois; roll 511, page 18A; Enumeration district 6; Image: 306.0; FHL microfilm.

24. "Jan Chiapusso," *Neosho Daily News*, October 12, 1942, 2.

25. Toledo Conservatory Prospectus, 6.

26. "Jan Chiapusso, Pianist," Advertisement, *Detroit Free Press*, September 14, 1919, 21.

27. "Chiapusso, Pianist, Plays," *New York Times*, March 19, 1919; "Jan Chiapusso, Pianist, Reappears," *New York Times*, April 7, 1920.

28. "Chiapusso gives a Piano Recital at Kimball Hall," *Chicago Tribune*, November 22, 1920, 21.

29. *Tone Picture Recitals*, flier for lecture and piano recitals by Jan Chiapusso, undated.

30. Jan Chiappuso, *Bach's World* (Bloomington: Indiana University Press, 1968).

31. New York City directory, 1918, 1921–22, Moses L. Boyd.

32. Waters and Samuels, *His Eye Is on the Sparrow*, 124.

33. Davin, March-April 1960, 13.

34. Waters and Samuels, *His Eye Is on the Sparrow*, 125.

35. Davin, March-April 1960, 13.

36. Ronald Clifford Foreman Jr., *Jazz and Race Records, 1920–1932* (dissertation, University of Illinois, 1969), 40.

37. Nathan Irvin Huggins, *Harlem Renaissance* (New York: Oxford University Press, 1971), 9–11.

38. Johnson claimed Bradford based this tune on his composition "Mamma's and Pappa's Blues."

CHAPTER 8. NEW YORK BREAKOUT YEAR, 1921

1. Bob Berkman, Draft QRS history for the Billings Rollography, 1995, author's collection, from Michael Montgomery files.

2. Jim Kidd, Montreal, to Michael Montgomery, Detroit, typewritten letter, February 8, 1966, author's collection, from Michael Montgomery files; Brian Dolan, *Inventing Entertainment* (Lanham, MD: Rowman and Littlefield, 2009), 131; *QRS Dealers' Complete Reference Catalogue*, complete to June 30, 1922, The Q.R.S. Music Company, Chicago, Illinois.

3. *Crain's Market Data Book and Directory*, 2nd ed. (Chicago: G. D. Crain, Jr., 1922), 319.

4. Q.R.S. contract, January 10, 1921, JPJC, IJS.

5. J. Russel Robinson as told to Ralph Auf Der Heide, "Dixieland Piano," *Record Changer*, August 1947, 8.

6. Davin, September 1959, 26.

7. *The Bystander* (Kansas City, MO), February 17, 1921.

8. *Chicago Defender*, advertisement, January 29, 1921.

9. G. James Fleming, "Player Pianos, Versatility Not Passé, And Thus This Story About J. L. Cook," *New York Amsterdam News*, January 30, 1937, 11.

10. Edward Murrain, "His Monopoly in Music Wins 29 Years of Fame," *New York Age*, November 22, 1952, 4.

11. Edward Murrain, "His Monopoly in Music Wins 29 Years of Fame," *New York Age*, November 22, 1952, 4.

12. Glenn Thomas, *The AMICA Bulletin*, July–August 2021, 32, 33; *Baltimore Afro-American*, advertisement, March 17, 1922, 3; "The Player Piano Department," *Music Trade Review*, April 1, 1922, 43.

13. "The Player Piano Department," 43.

14. Johnson, "Creative Work—accomplishments," fellowship draft application, JPJC, IJS.

15. Armstrong, *AMICA Forum*, 5.

16. Robert Pinsker, *James P. Johnson—The Piano Rolls of His Own Compositions, 1917–1927* (Riverside, CA: James P. Johnson Foundation, 2003).

17. "Taste of Clerks in Music Roll Selections Too Often Sole Guidance of Roll Buyers," *Music Trade Review*, February 20, 1926, 29.

18. "New York City Briefs," *Chicago Defender*, April 2, 1921, 9.

19. "Here and There Among the Folks," *Billboard*, May 7, 1921, 45.

20. "Elks to Give Dance," *Chicago Defender*, June 4, 1921, 9; "New York City Briefs," *Chicago Defender*, June 18, 1921, 9.

21. "Breaks into Winter Garden," *Billboard*, July 2, 1921, 61.

22. Certificate of Award, Conservatory of Musical Art, JPJC, IJS.

23. *New York Age*, advertisement, July 23, 1921, 6.

24. "The Dressing Room Club," *Billboard*, August 6, 1921, 65.

25. Davin, March-April 1960, 12.

26. Lynn Abbott and Doug Seroff, *The Original Blues* (Jackson: University Press of Mississippi, 2017), 215, citation from *Indianapolis Freeman*.

27. *New York Age*, August 13, 1914, 6; *New York Age*, December 14, 1914, 6; "A Note Or Two," *Chicago Defender*, March 18, 1916, 3.

28. Sutton, *Race Records*, 24–29.

29. It is possible some of the arrangements were done by H. Qualli Clark, who at this time had arranged other Johnson numbers for publication.

30. Gus Smith, "Theatrical Jottings," *New York Age*, May 3, 1930, 6; "Send Get Well Cards," *New York Age*, November 10, 1945, 4.

31. Sutton, *Recording the Twenties*, 32, 38.

32. Davin, March–April 1960, 12.

33. Kappler, Wellstood, and Rouder, 28.

34. This characterization has been suggested by scholar Marcello Piras.

35. David Gilbert, *The Product of Our Souls* (Chapel Hill: University of North Carolina Press, 2015), 159.

36. Allan Sutton, *Race Records and the American Recording Industry, 1919–1945* (Denver, CO: Mainspring Press, 2016), 30.

37. Discographies list the recording date as October, but the record was being advertised for sale as early as September 24 in *The Music Trade Review*. It is paired in the ad with "You'll Think of Me Blues" on Arto 9096 that was recorded in August with Alice Leslie Carter.

38. "Musician Kills Self with Leap From 4th Floor Window of Harlem Hospital—Lands on Picket Fence," *New York Age*, December 3, 1932, 1.

39. *The Billboard*, advertisement, November 5, 1921, 38.

40. *Chicago Defender*, advertisement, November 5, 1921.

41. Mark Tucker, *Ellington—The Early Years* (Urbana: University of Illinois Press, 1991), 74.

42. Duke Ellington, liner notes to *James P. Johnson—Father of the Stride Piano*, Columbia Records, CL 1780, 1962, LP; reprinted in *Music Is My Mistress*, 1973.

43. "J. A. Jackson's Page," *Billboard*, January 14, 1922, 47.

44. Gant, interview with Lipskin and Kunstadt.

45. *New York Age*, advertisement, January 21, 1922, 6.

46. *Chicago Defender*, January 14, 1922, 9.

47. "The Golden Age of Blues Recording," *Record Research*, January–February 1957, 3, 4.

48. *Chicago Defender*, January 28, 1922, 5.

CHAPTER 9. HARLEM STRIDE PIANO

1. Dick Wellstood, liner notes to *Donald Lambert—Harlem Stride Classics*, Pumpkin Productions 104, 1977, LP.

2. Smith and Hoefer, *Music on My Mind*, 3.

3. Ralph Matthews, "Watching the Big Parade," *Baltimore Afro American*, September 28, 1940, 4.

4. Fats Waller and His Rhythm, "I Got Rhythm," HMV (Swi) HE2902, 1935, 78 rpm recording initially issued only in Sweden.

5. "Joe Turner: American Blues in Paris," *New York Amsterdam News*, May 24, 1980, 36.

6. Dan Burley, *Dan Burley's Original Handbook of Harlem Jive* (New York: D. Burley, 1944), 148; "Record Reviews—Freddy Slack," *Metronome*, February 1944, 23; "Record Reviews—James P. Johnson," *Metronome*, March 1944, 21.

7. Inez M. Cavanaugh, "Reminiscing in Tempo," *Metronome*, November 1944, 17.

8. Herbie Nichols, "Jazz Milieu," *Music Dial*, August 1944, 24.

9. "'Boston'—Stop Time Chorus," first violin part, manuscript, JPJC, IJS.

10. *Harlem Symphony—Night Club*, score in hand of James P. Johnson, JPJC, IJS.

11. John S. Wilson, "The Jazz Panorama," *Hi-Fi Review Supplement*, April 1959.

12. Whitney Balliett, "Supreme Tickler," *The New Yorker*, May 11, 1963, 153–56.

13. Smith and Hoefer, *Music on My Mind*, 85.

14. Mike Lipskin, http://www.mikelipskinjazz.com/stridepiano.htm, accessed September 16, 2019.

15. Blesh and Janis, *They All Played Ragtime*, 187. These distinctions between ragtime and stride have at times fostered value judgments about the music, a predilection of writers that colors the assessment of the music's "evolution" through many eras. The equivalence of new with better quality is an unfortunate artifact of some critical and scholarly writing. In noting the distinctions, Blesh avoided this trap but always placed stride more in the ragtime camp than jazz.

16. The void is somewhat filled by the many piano rolls made during this time by both white and Black pianists.

17. Humphrey Lyttleton, *The Best of Jazz—From Basin Street to Harlem* (New York: Taplinger, 1973), 33.

18. Wellstood, liner notes to *Donald Lambert—Harlem Stride Classics*.

19. Louis Mazetier, personal email communication, January 9, 2022.

20. Joan M. Wildman, "The Function of the Left Hand in the Evolution of Jazz Piano," *Journal of Jazz Studies*, Spring/Summer 1979, 33.

21. Henry Francis, "Musical Aspects of Stride Piano," *Storyville*, August-September 1972, 213.

22. Wellstood, liner notes to *Lambert*.

23. Francis, "Musical Aspects," 214, 213.

24. Schuller, *Early Jazz*, 219.

25. Wellstood, liner notes to *Lambert*.

26. Schuller, *Early Jazz*, 215.

27. Eli H. Newberger, "The Transition from Ragtime to Improvised Piano Style," *Journal of Jazz Studies*, Spring 1976, 15.

28. Kappler, Wellstood, and Rouder, 37.

29. Dick Wellstood, "Reviews: Recordings—W. C. Handy Blues acc. By James P. Johnson," *Jazz Review*, December 1958, 34.

30. Henry Martin, "Balancing Composition and Improvisation in James P. Johnson's 'Carolina Shout,'" *Journal of Music Theory*, Fall 2005, 277–99.

31. Isaac Goldberg, *Tin Pan Alley* (New York: Frederick Unger, 1930), 14.

32. Blesh and Janis, *They All Played Ragtime*, 206.

33. Nat Hentoff, "Garvin Bushell and New York Jazz in the 1920s," *Jazz Review*, January 1959, 13.

34. Joe Turner, "The Pianists in My Life," *Melody Maker*, April 25, 1953, 2.

35. Pops Foster and Tom Stoddard, *Pops Foster* (Berkeley: University of California Press, 1971), 97, 153.

36. Hentoff, "Garvin Bushell," 13.

37. Sharon A. Pease, "Fats Pichon a Video Star Now," *Down Beat*, December 1, 1950, 12.

38. Waters and Samuels, *His Eye Is on the Sparrow*, 145, 147.

39. John S. Wilson, "Tuning in on a Teddy Wilson Lecture," *New York Times*, February 16, 1975, NJ103.

40. Stanley Dance, liner notes to Johnny Hodges and Earl Hines *Stride Right*, Verve V/VG-8647, 1966, LP.

41. Max Harrison, *A Jazz Retrospect*, Boston: Crescendo Publishing, 1976), reprint of "James P. Johnson," *Jazz Monthly*, 84.

42. Fell and Vinding, *Stride*, 180–81.

43. Don Gold, "Billy Taylor," *Down Beat*, January 9, 1958, 16.

44. Schuller, *Early Jazz*, 214.

CHAPTER 10. JAMES P. AND FATS WALLER

1. Kirkeby, *Ain't Misbehavin'*, 37.

2. Maurice Waller and Anthony Calabrese, *Fats Waller* (New York: Schirmer, 1977), 26.

3. Laurie Wright, *"Fats" in Fact* (Essex, UK: Storyville Publications, 1992), 8.

4. Waller and Calabrese, *Fats Waller*, 27.

5. Ernie Anderson, "An Ernie Anderson Memoir," in Wright, *"Fats" in Fact*, 321.

6. Waller and Calabrese, *Fats Waller*, 27.

7. Seymour Peck, "PM Visits: The Dean of Jazz Pianists," *PM*, April 27, 1945, 20.

8. Waller and Calabrese, *Fats Waller*, 28–29.

9. Shapiro and Hentoff, *Hear Me Talkin' to Ya*, 253.

10. Kirkeby, *Ain't Misbehavin'*, 41.

11. George Hoefer, liner notes to *The Sound of Harlem*, Columbia Records, Jazz Odyssey, vol III C3L-33, 1964, LP; Laurie Wright indicates the contest took place at the Regal Theater, Wright, 12. No primary or contemporaneous verification has been found.

12. Waller and Calabrese, *Fats Waller*, 38.

13. Smith and Hoefer, *Music on My Mind*, 99.

14. Peck, "PM Visits," 20.

15. Barry Singer, *Black and Blue: The Life and Lyrics of Andy Razaf* (New York: Schirmer, 1992), 121.

16. Wright, 13.

17. Michael Montgomery, liner notes to *Thomas (Fats) Waller, 1923–1924*, Biograph BLP-1002Q, 1970, LP.

18. *Chicago Defender*, January 16, 1926, 7.

19. Kirkeby, *Ain't Misbehavin'*, 96.

20. Smith and Hoefer, *Music on My Mind*, 258–59.

21. Wellstood, "Reviews: Recordings—W. C. Handy Blues acc. By James P. Johnson," 34.

22. Rose, *Eubie Blake*, 148–49.

23. Joel Vance, *Fats Waller: His Life and Times* (Chicago: Contemporary Books, 1977), 111, 156.

24. Robert Bagar, "Showed Gershwin How to Play Syncopation," *Pittsburgh Press*, June 7, 1942.

25. Kirkeby, 53; Johnson is heard referring to Waller as "Big Filthy" on the 1937 Fats Waller home recordings, Ristic 22/23.

26. Smith and Hoefer, *Music on My Mind*, 257.

CHAPTER 11. PLANTATION DAYS, 1922–1923

1. "Trixie Smith Now a Black Swan Artist," *New York Age*, February 4, 1922, 6.
2. "A Scrumptuous Time," *New York Age*, March 18, 1922, 6.
3. Grant Harper Reid, *Rhythm for Sale* (North Charleston, SC: CreateSpace, 2013), 16–18.
4. *New York Age*, advertisement, May 12, 1922, 6.
5. "Plantation Days," *Chicago Defender*, June 24, 1922, 7.
6. "Harper & Blanks," *Chicago Defender*, July 1, 1922, 7.
7. Bill Egan, *Florence Mills: Harlem Jazz Queen* (Lanham, MD: Scarecrow Press, 2004), 64–68.
8. "Manhattan Y.W.C.A.," *New York Age*, May 20, 1922, 7.
9. *Chicago Daily Tribune*, advertisement, July 16, 1922, G2.
10. "Beg Your Pardon," *Chicago Daily Tribune*, July 3, 1922, 13.
11. "Chicago," *Variety*, October 13, 1922, 26.
12. "Plantation Days," *Chicago Defender*, June 24, 1922, 7; "Harper and Blank" (*sic*), *Chicago Defender*, July 1, 1922, 7.
13. *Billboard*, July 8, 1922, 9.
14. "Plantation Days," *Chicago Daily Tribune*, June 22, 1922.
15. *Chicago Defender*, advertisement, August 12, 1922, 7.
16. "To Have Dance," *Chicago Defender*, August 12, 1922.
17. "Information Notice," *Chicago Defender*, September 16, 1922, 9. On that location now is a public housing project.
18. "Held Over," *Chicago Defender*, September 16, 1922, 7.
19. "Chicago," *Variety*, October 13, 1922, 26.
20. "Gets Us Told," *Chicago Defender*, October 14, 1922, 7.
21. *Bandanna Land* program, undated, JPJC, IJS.
22. Tony Langston, "'Bandanna Land' Opens at Avenue; Vaudeville at Grand and Monogram," *Chicago Defender*, October 14, 1922, 6.
23. "Cabaret and Smoker at the Appomattox Club," *Broad Ax*, September 30, 1922, 3.
24. "'Plantation Days' Turns 'Em Away," *Afro-American*, March 16, 1923.
25. Len G. Shaw, "The Theater," *Detroit Free Press*, October 23, 1922, 6; *Detroit Free Press* advertisement, October 25, 1922, 19.
26. "Murat—'Plantation Days,'" *Indianapolis Star*, November 7, 1922, 11; "Notes of the Stage," *Indianapolis Star*, November 10, 1922, 10; *Plantation Days* program, JPJC, IJS.
27. *Indianapolis Ledger*, advertisement, October 28, 1922, 8.
28. *Cleveland Plain Dealer*, advert, November 9, 1922, 4.
29. Art Hodes and Chadwick Hansen, *Selections from the Gutter* (Berkeley: University of California Press, 1977), 5.

30. G. M. W., "'Plantation Days' Is Carnival of Jazz," *Toledo Blade*, December 18, 1922.

31. *Cleveland Gazette*, advertisement, December 9, 1922, 1; *Cleveland Gazette*, December 30, 1922, 1.

32. "Two of 'Plantation Days' Troupe Entertaining at Carlton Terrace," *Cleveland Plain Dealer*, December 31, 1922, 59.

33. "Plantation Days," *Chicago Defender*, February 3, 1923, 8; "Plantation Days," *Billboard*, January 27, 1923, 50.

34. Kirkeby, *Ain't Misbehavin'*, 37.

35. Johnson, "Creative Work—Accomplishments," grant application, undated, JPJC, IJS.

36. Gene Lees, *Leader of the Band: The Life of Woody Herman* (New York: Oxford University Press, 1995), 38; Roy Gibbons, "Jazz King Makes $800,000 In Five Years," *Logansport Pharos-Tribune*, June 23, 1922, 7.

37. Richard Sudhalter, *Lost Chords* (New York: Oxford University Press, 1999), 91–92.

38. Sudhalter, *Lost Chords*, 765, fn.

39. Gibbons, *Logansport Pharos-Tribune*, 7; Sudhalter, 95–96.

40. *Fort Wayne Sentinel*, advertisement, March 12, 1922, 26.

41. *The Times of India*, advertisement, August 18, 1923, 2; *Rockford Morning Star*, advertisement, January 5, 1923, 6.

42. Michael Montgomery, liner notes to *The Greatest Jazz, Blues, and Ragtime of the Century*, Biograph BCD 116 DDD, Compact Disc, referencing Ed Sprenkle's opinion that Johnson may have recorded the last chorus.

43. "Sleuth Acting for 'Shuffle Along' Spike 'Plantation,'" *New York Amsterdam News*, February 28, 1923.

44. "Review A Hit," *Chicago Defender*, August 12, 1922, 7.

45. *Plantation Days* program, Shubert Murat Theater, Indianapolis, November 5, 1922, JPJC, IJS; Undated, unidentified theater program with Chicago printing address, JPJC, IJS.

46. *New York Amsterdam News*, February 28, 1923.

47. Plantation Days program, undated, unidentified theater program with Chicago printing address, JPJC, IJS; Robert Kimball and William Bolcom, *Reminiscing with Sissle and Blake* (New York: Viking Press, 1973), 127, 241.

48. J. A. Jackson, "'Plantation Days' Off to London," *Baltimore Afro American*, March 16, 1923, 15.

49. Plantation Days program, New Dunbar Theater, February 12, 1923, JPJC, IJS.

50. "Stage News," *Chicago Defender*, February 24, 1923, 8.

51. "'Plantation Days' Colored Revue at Grand Three Days," *Sunday Repository* (Canton, Ohio), December 10, 1922, 32.

52. *New York Age*, March 3, 1923, 6; James P. Johnson, US passport, British passport control stamp March 3, 1923, JPJC, IJS; "'Plantation Days' Off to London," *Afro-American*, March 16, 1923, 15; *New York Age*, April 27, 1923, 6.

53. Edward Jablonski and Lawrence D. Stewart, *The Gershwin Years* (Garden City, NY: Doubleday, 1973), 81–82.

54. Reid, *Rhythm for Sale*, 29.

55. Reid, *Rhythm for Sale*, 28.

56. Warren B. Wells, "Many Protests in British Capital Over Invasion of Colored Players," *New York Tribune*, April 1, 1923.

57. "Sir Alfred Butt Defends Colored Artists," *Pittsburgh Courier*, April 14, 1923, 8.

58. Wells, April 1, 1923.

59. Waters and Samuels, *His Eye Is on the Sparrow*, 159.

60. "'Plantation' Title Not Prevented in London—Court Decides Against Cochran in Butt Injunction Matter," *Variety*, March 22, 1923.

61. Hannen Swaffer, "The Scandal of Negro Revues," *Daily Graphic—London*, March 6, 1923.

62. "Negro Artists Not Wanted in London," *Baltimore Afro American*, April 6, 1923.

63. Jablonski and Stewart, *The Gershwin Years*, 81–82.

64. "On Foreign Stages," *New York Times*, April 8, 1923, X1.

65. Bob Thomas, *Astaire: The Man, The Dancer* (New York: St. Martin's Press, 1984), 45.

66. H. G., "The Rainbow," *London Observer*, April 8, 1923; "The Negro 'Plantation' Turn," *Sunday Times of London*, April 8, 1923.

67. Reid, *Rhythm for Sale*, 31–32.

68. Jones, *Doin' the Charleston*, 59, 155.

69. Edmund Jenkins, London, to James P. Johnson, London, May 15, 1923, typewritten manuscript, JPJC, IJS.

70. Pollack, 283.

71. "'Plantation Days' Back from Abroad," *Baltimore Afro American*, June 15, 1923, 5.

72. New York passenger lists, 1820–1957, ancestry.com.

73. "'Plantation Days' Producer Assembling Talent for Show," *Pittsburgh Courier*, July 7, 1923, 11.

74. "Plantation Days," unidentified advertisement, March 15, 1924; "Discovering a Colored Star," *Chicago Sunday Herald and Examiner*, March 23, 1924.

75. Kennard Williams, "In the Spotlight," *Baltimore Afro American*, May 2, 1924, 4.

76. "Symphony Music," *New York Amsterdam News*, December 11, 1937, 13.

77. "Cab with Plantation Days," *Baltimore Afro American*, March 19, 1927, 11; "Cab Calloway Spurned Law Study for Career on Stage," *Baltimore Afro American*, February 8, 1930, 8.

78. "Plantation Days Is Attraction at Palace Theater," *Rockford Morning Star*, December 16, 1926, 12.

79. "Blanche Calloway Is Actress and Wife," *Baltimore Afro American*, December 24, 1927, 8.

80. Floyd G. Snelson, "Theatrical Comment," *Pittsburgh Courier*, December 20, 1924, 9.

81. Ivorey Cobb, "Ida Cox, Famed Blues Singer, Headed for New Comeback," *Chicago Defender*, January 20, 1940, 20. Cox's *Raisin' Cain* was not the Johnson show of the same name.

82. "In the Realm of Music," *Baltimore Afro American*, March 5, 1927, 9.

83. *Chicago Defender*, advertisement, July 19, 1924, 7.

CHAPTER 12. RUNNING WILD, 1923

1. Singer, *Black and Blue*, 133.

2. *Times-Picayune*, advertisement, September 20, 1923, 11.

3. *Macon Telegraph*, advertisement, February 9, 1924, 5.

4. "Radio Program Tonight," *Bellingham Herald*, September 21, 1923, 14; "Today's Radio Program," *Seattle Daily Times*, October 12, 1923, 21.

5. Abel, "Review of Disc Records," *New York Clipper*, October 19, 1923, 22.

6. Marva Griffin Carter, *Swing Along* (New York: Oxford University Press, 2008), 73–74.
7. Henry T. Sampson, "Blacks in Blackface," Lanham, MD: Scarecrow Press, 2014, 72.
8. Rose, *Eubie Blake*, 71.
9. Kimball and Bolcom, 101.
10. *Billboard*, August 11, 1923, 7.
11. Singer, *Black and Blue*, 112.
12. "White to Sponsor New Colored Revue," *Billboard*, July 21, 1923, 8.
13. *Chicago Defender*, March 17, 1923, 8.
14. Carter, 107.
15. James A. Jackson, "Recent Blues Craze Bringing Another Big Publishing House to the Fore," *New York Amsterdam News*, July 11, 1923, entertainment section.
16. "'Runnin' Wild,'" *Chicago Defender*, September 8, 1923, 6.
17. Meakin, "Plays Produced Outside New York City," *Variety*, August 30, 1923.
18. Jonesy, "Runnin' Wild," *Billboard*, September 8, 1923.
19. "'Runnin' Wild,'" *New York Amsterdam News*, September 5, 1923.
20. "'Runnin' Wild,'" *Chicago Defender*, September 8, 1923, 6.
21. Jonesy, *Billboard*, September 8, 1923.
22. "New Colored Show did $8,000 Weekly," *Variety*, August 30, 1923, 13.
23. *Billboard*, September 15, 1923, 119.
24. *Variety*, September 20, 1923, 14.
25. *Boston Globe*, undated uncredited clipping, JPJC, IJS; "'Runnin Wild' Melange of Dusky Class," *Boston Telegram*, undated clipping, JPJC, IJS; "'Runnin Wild' at The Selwyn—New Miller and Lyles Musical comedy Is A Hit," *The Traveler*, undated clipping, JPJC, IJS; Don Carle Gillette, "Boston Plays," *Billboard*, September 15, 1923, 89.
26. "Some Hits and Disappointments Among Boston's Newest Shows," *Variety*, September 13, 1923, 18.
27. *Variety*, October 11, 1923, 15, 54; *Variety*, October 18, 1923, 15.
28. *Variety*, October 25, 1923, 16; *Billboard*, October 27, 1923, 32.
29. Nicholas Van Hoogstraten, *Lost Broadway Theaters* (New York: Princeton Architectural Press, 1997), 91–93.
30. *Variety*, October 18, 1923, 12.
31. *Billboard*, November 11, 1923, 56; *Billboard*, October 27, 1923, 57.
32. "John Hammond, Hep-Cat Executive, Works Hard to Help Musicians," *Philadelphia Tribune*, March 20, 1941, 14.
33. Miller and Lyles Record Argument," *Baltimore Afro American*, November 23, 1923, A5.
34. "*Variety*, November 1, 1923, 13, 16.
35. *Billboard*, November 10, 1923, 36.
36. Alan Dale, *New York American*, October 31, 1923.
37. *Billboard*, November 22, 1923, 56.
38. *The Stage*, November 15, 1923, 27; "Runnin' Wild," *Variety*, November 1, 1923, 20.
39. *Baltimore Afro American*, November 23, 1923, A5; OKeh Series 4000 Numerical listing, pt. 2, OKeh 4727, recorded October 1922, http://www.78discography.com/OK4500.html, accessed April 12, 2015.
40. "'Runnin' Wild' Is Bright," *New York Times*, October 30, 1923, 17.
41. "Gossip of the Rialto," *New York Times*, November 11, 1923, X1.

42. "9,000 Guests Invited to a Colored Wedding," *New York Times*, November 22, 1923, 19.

43. Kimball and Bolcolm, *Reminiscing*, 86.

44. *Billboard*, November 17, 1923, 56.

45. "In Old New York," *Baltimore Afro American*, February 8, 1924, A10.

46. Yuval Taylor and Jake Austen, *Darkest America* (New York: W. W. Norton, 2012), 291–96.

47. *New York Times*, October 30, 1923, 17.

48. *Globe and Sun*, October 31, 1923.

49. M.A.G., *New York Tribune*, October 30, 1923.

50. N.J., *Brooklyn Daily Eagle*, October 30, 1923, 10.

51. *Billboard*, December 22, 1923, 23.

52. Meakin, "Plays Produced Outside New York City," *Variety*, August 30, 1923.

53. "White to Sponsor New Colored Revue," *Billboard*, July 21, 1923, 8.

54. *Variety*, February 21, 1924, 11–12.

55. *New York Age*, advertisement, January 19, 1921, 6.

56. *Billboard*, December 15, 1923, 68.

57. *Variety*, February 28, 1924, 11.

58. *Variety*, March 26, 1924, 14.

59. "The New York Symphony," *New York Times*, March 24, 1924, 12.

60. "Spring Editions," *Brooklyn Daily Eagle*, March 25, 1924, 8.

61. *Billboard*, March 29, 1924, 7.

62. "Drawing Color Line with 'Runnin' Wild,'" *New York Age*, March 29, 1924, 1.

63. "Snappy Gossip from Gotham," *Town Talk* (Alexandria, Louisiana), April 2, 1924, 6.

64. *Variety*, April 2, 1924, 14; April 9, 1924, 13; April 23, 1924, 14.

65. "Benefit for Tuskegee," *Brooklyn Daily Eagle*, April 27, 1924, 69; *Billboard*, May 10, 1924, 29.

66. J. A. Jackson, "Real Negro Art by and with Negro Artists," *Billboard*, February 23, 1924, 50.

67. J. A. Jackson, "Picked Up by the Page," *Billboard*, January 26, 1924, 52.

68. "Will Marion Cook's Letter," *Chicago Defender*, March 22, 1924, 7.

69. *New York Age*, advert, January 19, 1924, 6; "Sunday Concerts to Be Presented by Colored Artists on Broadway," *New York Age*, January 29, 1924, 6.

70. Jones, *Doin' the Charleston*, 249.

71. *Billboard*, February 16, 1924, 53.

72. "'Negro Nuances' is Coming Here," *Baltimore Afro American*, February 22, 1924, 10.

73. J. A. Jackson, "Real Negro Art by and with Negro Artists," *Billboard*, February 23, 1924, 50.

74. "Will Marion Cook's Letter," *Chicago Defender*, March 22, 1924, 7.

75. *Billboard*, November 10, 1923, 17.

76. *Variety*, February 14, 1924, 3. Abel, "Review of Disc Records," *New York Clipper*, November 9, 1923, 22.

77. *Billboard*, December 15, 1923.

78. Reid, *Rhythm for Sale*, 84.

79. Tucker, 98.

80. Reid, *Rhythm for Sale*, 84.

81. John Edward Hasse, *Beyond Category: The Life and Genius of Duke Ellington* (New York: Da Capo, 1993), 73–79.

82. Mark Berresford, *That's Got 'Em! The Life and Music of Wilbur Sweatman* (Jackson: University Press of Mississippi, 2010), 146.

83. Sidney Bechet, *Treat It Gentle* (New York: Twayne Publishers, 1960), 140–41.

84. *New York Clipper*, April 24, 1924, 19.

85. "Runnin' Wild: Miller and Lyles Show Stirs Mirth in Newark," *Chicago Defender*, June 14, 1924, 6.

86. *Pittsburgh Courier*, September 20, 1924.

87. Floyd G. Snelson, "'Runnin' Wild' Makes Big Hit in Far North," *Pittsburgh Courier*, September 13, 1924, 10.

88. "At the Play in Brooklyn," *Brooklyn Daily Eagle*, February 15, 1925, 62.

89. "I Ain't Gonna Play No Second Fiddle," Sheet music cover, Perry Bradford Music Company.

90. "Stage Notes," *Pittsburgh Courier*, February 6, 1926, 10.

91. "Dance Test of Skill Fine for Reducing," *Kenosha Evening News*, August 11, 1925, 4; Davin, July 1959, 12.

92. Abel, "Disc Reviews," *Variety*, May 13, 1925, 48.

93. "Marvin Lee Chicago Representative for Harms," *Music Trade Review*, July 4, 1925, 45.

94. Tom Lord, *The Jazz Discography*, https://lordisco.com/tjd/TuneIndex?title=charleston&action2=Search&search=title&dest=TuneDetail&select=true, accessed January 8, 2022.

95. "Real Negro Comedy Features 'Runnin' Wild' at Colonial," *New York Age*, January 5, 1924, 2; "'Runnin' Wild' Co. to appear at Presentation," *Pittsburgh Courier*, May 17, 1924, 14.

96. Harms, Mechanical Royalty Statement, three months ending December 31, 1925, JPJC, IJS.

CHAPTER 13. THE RENT PARTY

1. Isabel Wilkerson, *The Warmth of Other Suns* (New York: Vantage Books, 2010).

2. Smith and Hoefer, *Music on My Mind*, 152.

3. Mait Edey, liner notes to *Boogie-Woogie Rarities, 1927–1932*, Milestone Records, MLP 2009, 1969, LP. Players like Blythe and C. Johnson also soon incorporated James P. Johnson's rhythmic innovations after 1921. This transformation can be heard in their own piano rolls.

4. Dan Burley, "Dan Burley's Back Door Stuff," *New York Amsterdam News*, April 19, 1947, 19.

5. Ellington, liner notes.

6. Smith and Hoefer, *Music on My Mind*, 156.

7. Peck, "PM Visits," 20.

8. Singer, 151–52; Kirkeby, *Ain't Misbehavin'*, 78.

9. Jervis Anderson, *This Was Harlem* (New York: Farrar, Straus and Giroux, 1982), 152.

10. Gilbert Osofsky, *Harlem: The Making of a Ghetto* (Chicago: Ivan R. Dee, 1996; originally HarperCollins, 1966), 139, from the *New York Herald Tribune*, February 12, 13, 1930.

11. Smith and Hoefer, *Music on My Mind*, 153; Waller and Calabrese, *Fats Waller*, 37.

12. Wallace Thurman, *The Blacker the Berry* (New York: Macmillan, 1970; originally Macaulay, 1929), 152–54.

13. Smith and Hoefer, *Music on My Mind*, 155.

14. Ellington, liner notes.
15. Hentoff, "Garvin Bushell," 10.
16. Stanley Dance, *The World of Duke Ellington* (New York: Da Capo, 1970), 47.
17. Chris Albertson, liner notes to *Backwater Blues*, Riverside Records RLP 151, 1961, LP.
18. Shapiro and Hentoff, *Hear Me Talkin' to Ya*, 174.
19. Dance, *Ellington*, 63–64.
20. Duke Ellington and His Orchestra, *In Europe*, 1965, Jazz-Club JC-124, LP.
21. David Hajdu, *Lush Life: A Biography of Billy Strayhorn* (New York: Farrar, Straus and Giroux, 1996), 253.
22. Eddie Condon, *We Called It Music* (New York: Da Capo, 1992), 18, 181–82.
23. Jim Kidd, "Louis Hooper," *Record Research*, June 1966, 4.
24. Rex Stewart, *Jazz Masters of the 30s* (New York: Da Capo, 1972), 145–46.
25. Milton "Mezz" Mezzrow, *Really the Blues* (New York: Random House, 1946), 231–32.
26. Smith and Hoefer, *Music on My Mind*, 156.
27. Kelley, *Thelonious Monk*, 35.
28. *Monk Alone: The Complete Solo Studio Recordings: 1962–1968*, Columbia C2K 65495; *The Complete Black Lion and Vogue Recordings of Thelonious Monk*, Mosaic MD3-112.
29. Smith and Hoefer, *Music on My Mind*, 225.
30. Kirkeby, *Ain't Misbehavin'*, 96.

CHAPTER 14. ON STAGE, 1924–1926

1. "Mother Dies," *Chicago Defender*, July 5, 1924, 7.
2. New York Department of Health, death certificates (Manhattan, New York), 1919–1948 [Vol. 27–28], certificate no. 13659; Bayview-New York Bay Cemetery grave 7, row 15, H No.
3. *Daily Record* (Long Branch, NJ), advertisement, June 14, 1924, 4.
4. "Hollywood Follies," *Chicago Defender*, July 5, 1924, 7.
5. "'Hollywood Follies' Offers Gayety," *Omaha Daily News*, August 17, 1924, 8; "Hollywood Follies Is This Week's Burlesque," *The Journal* (Meridian, CT), January 12, 1925, 9.
6. *Daily News*, advertisement, June 22, 1924, 81.
7. *Asbury Park Press*, June 18, 1924, 17.
8. *Daily Times* (Davenport, IA), advertisement, August 23, 1924, 12.
9. *Daily News*, advertisement, July 20, 1924, 73.
10. "'Hollywood Follies' Big Hit at Gayety," *Buffalo Times*, September 30, 1924, 2.
11. "Gayety Offering Has Notable Cast," *Buffalo Courier*, October 5, 1924, 77.
12. "Theaters," *Dayton Daily News*, April 6, 1925, 8.
13. *Philadelphia Inquirer*, February 10, 1925, 20.
14. *Boston Herald*, November 9, 1924, 49.
15. *Billboard*, August 16, 1924, 72; Reid, *Rhythm for Sale*, 103.
16. "New Revue," *Daily News*, July 16, 1924, 16; "Theater Notes, *Daily News*, August 1, 1924, 20.
17. "Morrissey Does Not Plan to Quit," *Daily News*, August 9, 1924, 40.
18. "Harry Steppe," Wikipedia, http://en.wikipedia.org/wiki/Harry_Steppe, accessed May 9, 1915.

19. "Miner's Empire," *Jewish Chronicle* (Newark, NJ), October 10, 1924, 110.

20. "Gayety Theatre Next Week," *Webster News-Times* (Webster Groves, MO), February 20, 1925, 3.

21. Grand Theater, Unidentified advertisement, December 6, 1924.

22. *Pittsburgh Courier*, November 8, 1924, 17.

23. Tony Langston, "'Cottonland' Gains Favor at Grand," *Chicago Defender*, December 13, 1924; Floyd G. Snelson, "'Joy Makers' Shine at the Monogram," *Pittsburgh Courier*, December 6, 1924, 10.

24. "'Cottonland' in St. Louis," *Baltimore Afro American*, January 3, 1925.

25. 1910 United States Federal Census; Census Place: Brooklyn Ward 30, Kings, New York; Roll T624_985, Page 9A, Enumeration District 1411; Image: FHL microfilm: 1374998.

26. Cesar Saerchinger, *International Who's Who in Music and Musical Gazetteer* (New York: Current Literature Publishing, 1918), 648.

27. *New York Amsterdam News*, advertisement, September 23, 1925, 5.

28. Frances Moss Mann, "Music News," *New York Amsterdam News*, March 9, 1935, 5.

29. "St. Mark's Choir Concert," *Chicago Defender*, June 7, 1919, 4.

30. Nora Holt, "Music," *New York Amsterdam News*, July 23, 1949, 22.

31. *New York Age*, advertisement, July 1, 1915, 6.

32. *Chicago Defender*, advertisement, April 29, 1922, 9.

33. Cleveland G. Allen, "Music," *Chicago Defender*, July 14, 1928, 11.

34. Johnson, Guggenheim application, JPJC, IJS.

35. L. H. White, "Concert at Carnegie Hall," *New York Age*, February 20, 1913, 6.

36. *New York Age*, July 1, 1915, 6.

37. "Creative Work—accomplishments," typewritten note by James P. Johnson, JPJC, IJS. John Howland, in *Ellington Uptown: Duke Ellington, James P. Johnson, and the Birth of Concert Jazz*, identifies the source material for Johnson's references to his studies of Western music, and analyzes Johnson's *Harlem Symphony* with regard to these influences.

38. Kirkeby, *Ain't Misbehavin'*, 104.

39. "Mrs. Stella Unger, Lyricist, Dies at 65," *New York Times*, February 16, 1970, 37.

40. "Don't Need Nobody to Tell Me I'm in Bad," © July 1923; "Don't Never Tell Nobody What Your Good Man Can Do," © July 1923; "You Just Can't Have No One Man By Yourself," © June 1924.

41. *Billboard*, June 28, 1924, 46.

42. Sammy 'Dolled Up,'" *Baltimore Afro American*, August 1, 1925, A5.

43. "Stars That Shine," *Pittsburgh Courier*, August 15, 1925, 10.

44. *Billboard*, August 28, 1925, 28.

45. "'Sunshine Sammy' at Head of Splendid Show," *New York Amsterdam News*, September 9, 1925, 6; "Sunshine Sammy to Star in New Show," *Chicago Defender*, September 12, 1925, 7.

46. "New Road Show," *Chicago Defender*, September 26, 1925, 7; "Sunshine Sammy's Show," *Baltimore Afro American*, October 3, 1925, 9.

47. "Sunshine Sammy Here Next Monday," *Baltimore Afro American*, November 21, 1925.

48. "Pierce's Letter," *Chicago Defender*, October 3, 1925, 6.

49. "Hittin' Here And There," *Chicago Defender*, December 5, 1925, 6.

50. "They're 'Moochin Along' at the Lafayette Theater All This Week," *New York Amsterdam News*, December 9, 1925, 5.

51. "Hittin' Here And There," *Chicago Defender*, December 19, 1925, 7.

52. "Musical at Howard," *Baltimore Afro American*, December 19, 1925, 5.

53. "Royal," *Baltimore Afro American*, December 19, 1925, 5.

54. "'Moochin Along' Closed," *Chicago Defender*, January 23, 1926, 6; *Pittsburgh Courier*, February 20, 1926, 10.

55. Walter C. Allen, "Hendersonia: The Music of Fletcher Henderson and His Musicians," (Highland Park, NJ: Walter C. Allen, 1973), 164.

56. *Billboard*, advertisement, April 3, 1926, 3.

57. "Negro Players Organize," *New York Age*, May 1, 1913, 6.

58. David A. Jason and Gene Jones, *Speadin' Rhythm Around* (New York: Schirmer, 1998), 360–72.

59. "Two Openings," *Daily News*, February 28, 1926, 42.

60. *Creole Follies*, program, JPJC, IJS.

61. "Creole Follies," *Daily News*, April 12, 1926, 20.

62. *Billboard*, July 31, 1926, 19; *Billboard*, September 4, 1926, 9.

63. *Variety*, August 25, 1926, 46.

64. *Pittsburgh Courier*, September 4, 1926, 10; "Theatre History," *Baltimore Afro American*, August 28, 1926.

65. *Catalog of Copyright Entries*, Copyright Office, The Library of Congress, Third Series, 1953, 143.

66. "Whitney Benefit at Lafayette a Success Despite Bad Weather," *New York Amsterdam News*, November 17, 1926, 10; *Pittsburgh Courier*, November 13, 1926, A3.

CHAPTER 15. YAMEKRAW, 1927

1. Perry Bradford, *Born with the Blues* (New York: Oak Publications, 1965), 131.

2. Kirkeby, *Ain't Misbehavin'*, 99–101.

3. Bradford, *Born with the Blues*, 132. Johnson would later write a tune for one of Mae West's movies. "He May Be Your Man but He Comes to See Me Sometimes" was copyrighted in 1922 by the obscure but excellent pianist Lemuel Fowler. He was a QRS pianist, and his tune was widely recorded.

4. "Stage Artists Give Charity Benefit," *Baltimore Afro American*, January 15, 1927, 10.

5. *Chicago Defender*, April 19, 1927, 6.

6. Perry Bradford and Noble Sissle, liner notes to *Yamekraw—Negro Rhapsody*, Folkways Records, FJ 2842, 1962, LP.

7. James P. Johnson, *Yamekraw—Negro Rhapsody*, Perry Bradford, Inc., 1927.

8. Gilbert, *Product*, 43.

9. Bradford and Sissle, liner notes.

10. Robert Pinsker, personal communication, January 31, 2001.

11. Howland, *Ellington Uptown*, 69–78.

12. *Variety*, August 17, 1927, 55; "Around New York," *Baltimore Afro American*, July 16, 1927, 12.

13. Andy Razaf, "Our Lighter Side," *New York Amsterdam News*, August 10, 1927, 11.

14. Dave Peyton, "The Musical Bunch," *Chicago Defender*, December 10, 1927, 6.

15. "Stars That Shine," *Pittsburgh Courier*, December 24, 1927, 16.

16. Billy Jones, "Stars That Shine," *Chicago Defender*, December 3, 1927, 9.
17. "Yamekraw," *Talking Machine World*, June 1928, 172.
18. "Yamekraw Heard Over Big Network," *Talking Machine World*, July 1928.
19. *Billboard*, advertisement, Orchestra Music Supply Co., December 22, 1928, 2.
20. "James P. Johnson Screens 'Yamekraw,'" *Chicago Defender*, July 26, 1930, 5.
21. "Yamekraw," movie program, week of August 1, 1930, JPJC, IJS.
22. "At the Lafayette Theater," *New York Age*, August 30, 1930, 7.
23. *The Evening Independent* (Massillon, OH), June 26, 1930, 11; Palace Theater advertisement, *Harrisburg Telegraph*, June 7, 1930, 20.
24. "Sound Shorts," *Billboard*, May 10, 1930, 41.
25. "At the Lafayette Theater," *New York Age*, August 30, 1930, 7.
26. Ryan Jay Friedman, *Hollywood's African American Films: The Transition to Sound*, (New Brunswick, NJ: Rutgers University Press, 2011), 86.
27. Robert Pinsker, personal communication, January 31, 2001.
28. *Freeport Journal-Standard* (Freeport, IL), February 5, 1933, 3.
29. Waldo, *This Is Ragtime*, 117.

CHAPTER 16. KEEP SHUFFLIN', 1928

1. *Pittsburgh Courier*, October 1, 1927, 15.
2. "'Rang Tang' Not Paying Full Salaries, Report," *Pittsburgh Courier*, October 22, 1927, 14.
3. *New York Age*, November 19, 1927, 7.
4. Mark Hellinger, "About Broadway," *Atlanta Constitution*, June 16, 1929, E11.
5. David Pietrusza, *Rothstein* (New York: Basic Books, 2011), 100.
6. Jerome Charyn, *Gangsters and Gold Diggers* (New York: Thunder's Mouth Press, 2003), 10, 80–83.
7. Pietrusza, *Rothstein*, 98, 99–101.
8. *Billboard*, February 25, 1928, 25.
9. Bradford, *Born with the Blues*, 135–38.
10. Pollack, *George Gershwin*, 377.
11. Bradford, *Born with the Blues*, 135–38.
12. Bradford, *Born with the Blues*, 137.
13. "Aubrey Lyles of Miller & Lyles Files Bankruptcy Plea in US Court, Southern N. Y. Dist.," *New York Age*, December 12, 1925, 3.
14. Waller and Calabrese, *Fats Waller*, 72.
15. Kirkeby, *Ain't Misbehavin'*, 112–33.
16. Columbia Recording Co., royalty statement, JPJC, IJS. 3753 copies of "Lock and Key," and 12,994 copies of "Sweet Mistreater" were sold from October through December 1927. The contract allowed for the then standard 90 percent of one cent for each copy sold, half to go to Henry Creamer, who was also paid $75.00.
17. Bradford, *Born with the Blues*, 137–38.
18. *New York Age*, October 1, 1927.
19. "Miller and Lyles Head 'Keep Shufflin,' Coming to Gibson Theater Next Week," *Pittsburgh Courier*, February 11, 1928, 10; "Rialto Gossip," *New York Times*, February 19, 1928, 109.

20. "New Song Hit Is Written By Gershwin," *Pittsburgh Courier*, February 18, 1928, 14.

21. Pollack, *George Gershwin*, 329.

22. "'Keep Shufflin' New Hit at the Gibson Theater," *Pittsburgh Courier*, February 25, 1928, A3.

23. Singer, 189–90.

24. Van Hoogstraten, *Lost Broadway Theaters*, 123.

25. Bide Dudley, *New York Evening World*, February 28, 1928.

26. "Club Chats," *New York Amsterdam News*, January 25, 1928, 6.

27. Percival Outram, "Activities Among Union Musicians," *New York Age*, March 31, 1928, 7; Percival Outram, "Activities Among Union Musicians," *New York Age*, April 28, 1928, 7.

28. *The Stage*, March 29, 1928.

29. W. Rollo Wilson, "Keep Shufflin' New Hit at the Gibson Theater," *Pittsburgh Courier*, February 25, 1928, A3.

30. Owen Coyle, "Jabbo Smith—His Horn Is Hot Again," *Mississippi Rag*, July 1976, 2.

31. Mike Joyce, "Cladys 'Jabbo' Smith: Personal Interview," *Cadence*, May 1982.

32. "'Battle Axe' Kenny Is Host to Miller & Lyles," *New York Age*, April 14, 1928, 6.

33. Hoefer and Driggs, liner notes to *The Sound of Harlem*.

34. Geraldyne Dismond, "Bert Hall Balt. Musician, Dies in New York," *Baltimore Afro American*, March 5, 1932.

35. Garvin Bushell, *Jazz from the Beginning* (New York: Da Capo, 1998), 50.

36. Clarissa and Marion Cumbo, "In Retrospect—The Symphony of the New World," *Black Perspective in Music* (Autumn 1975): 312.

37. "Capital spotlight," *Baltimore Afro American*, April 10, 1937, 5.

38. D. Antoinette Handy, *Black Women in American Bands and Orchestras* (Lanham, MD: Scarecrow Press, 1981), 98.

39. Samuel C. Allen Scholarship foundation website, http://www.samallenfoundation.com/samallen.html, accessed 12/20/02; Tom Lord, "The Jazz Discography," Lord Music reference, Inc., Chilliwack, BC, Canada, online discography, accessed 2016.

40. "'Keep Shufflin'' Saved By Music," *Baltimore Afro American*, February 25, 1928, 8.

41. *Variety*, March 7, 1928.

42. "'Give Me Sunshine' Joyous Song Hit of 'Keep Shufflin,'" *New York Herald Tribune*, February 28, 1928, 14.

43. "'Keep Shufflin'' New Hit at the Gibson Theater," *Pittsburgh Courier*, February 25, 1928, A3.

44. Orrin C. Evans, "Catchy Songs Stop the Show at Gibson's," *Philadelphia Tribune*, February 16, 1928, 6.

45. Bushell, *Jazz from the Beginning*, 74.

46. Fell and Vinding, *Stride*, 152 fn, suggest that the tune may be a reference to a well-known Harlem personality known as Sippi. He was an ex-prizefighter and hansom cab driver who would, at times, break into song and dance wearing a signature battered top hat. The lyrics of the song, however, refer to Mississippi River imagery and not an urban adaptation of any sort.

47. A. F. Rosemond, "News of Paris," *New York Amsterdam News*, May 2, 1928, 6.

48. Bushell, *Jazz from the Beginning*, 74.

49. Waller, 74.

50. Kirkeby, *Ain't Misbehavin'*, 74.

51. Gant, interview with Lipskin and Kunstadt.

52. James P. Johnson to Flournoy Miller, Los Angeles, October 15, 1950, transcript in the hand of James P. Johnson, Flournoy Miller collection, Schomburg Center for Research in Black Culture, New York Public Library.

53. Alyn Shipton, *Fats Waller—His Life and Times* (New York: Universe Books, 1988), 37.

54. Ben Kragting Jr. and Harry Coster, "Victor's Church Studio, Camden (1918–1935): Lost and Found?" *VJM's Jazz and Blues Mart*, Winter/Spring 2010, 3–11.

55. Wright, *Afro-Americans*, 43.

56. Paul S. Machlin, *Stride: The Music of Fats Waller* (Boston: Twayne, 1985), 111 fn.

57. Bushell, *Jazz from the Beginning*, 74.

58. Shipton, *Fats Waller*, 36–37, 38.

59. Wright, *Afro-Americans*, 42–43.

60. Machlin, *Stride*, 68, 66, 66, 68, 69.

61. "'Battle Axe' Kenny Is Host to Miller & Lyles," *New York Age*, April 14, 1928, 6.

62. *New York Amsterdam News*, April 4, 1928, 9.

63. "Miller and Lyles Get Big Reception," *Chicago Defender*, April 28, 1928, 6.

64. *Chicago Defender*, photo caption, April 21, 1928, A10.

65. "3,000 Shuffle at Miller-Lyles Harlem Jubilee," *New York Herald Tribune*, April 16, 1928, 32.

66. "Annual Rainbow Ball to Be Given Tonight," *New York Times*, April 21, 1928, 9; "Gay Colors Rule at Rainbow Ball," *New York Times*, April 22, 1928, 38.

67. *Variety*, April 18, 1928.

68. Handy, *Black Women*, 219.

69. "Millionaire Playboy Becomes Poet Laureate of the Village," *Milwaukee Journal*, July 18, 1935, 22.

70. Handy, *Black Women*, 212–13.

71. Handy, *Black Women*, 213.

72. Waller and Calabrese, *Fats Waller*, 75–76; Kirkeby, *Ain't Misbehavin'*, 117–18.

73. Waller and Calabrese, *Fats Waller*, 75–76.

74. "W. C. Handy's Concert," *Variety*, May 2, 1928, 63.

75. Lucien H. White, "Wm. C. Handy Presented Orchestra and Singers in Program of Blues and Spirituals at Carnegie Hall," *New York Age*, May 5, 1928, 7

76. Lawrence W. Levine, "Jazz and American Culture," *Journal of American Folklore* (January–March 1989): 12–13.

77. "Around New York," *Baltimore Afro American*, July 16, 1927, 12.

78. "Mrs. Peach Goodridge Celebrates her Birthday," *New York Age*, June 2, 1928, 10.

79. *Brooklyn Daily Eagle*, May 21, 1928, 34.

80. Burns Mantle, from the *Daily News*, "Bojangles Robinson's Dancing Featured in 'Blackbirds of 1928,'" *New York Age*, May 19, 1928, 6.

81. "'Keep Shufflin' Gives Up Ghost," *Baltimore Afro American*, June 2, 1928, 9.

82. "Seek to Oust 'Keep Shufflin,'" *New York Times*, April 26, 1928, 30.

83. "'Keep Shufflin' to Stay," *New York Times*, May 1, 1928, 40.

84. "The High Hatters," http://www.playbillvault.com/Show/Detail/6293/The-High-Hatters, accessed July 31, 2014.

85. "'Muddy Waters' Author May Write 'Alimony Blues' in Seclusion of Jail," *New York Amsterdam News*, April 11, 1928, 1.

86. "Hill's Social Club 'Ragamuffin' Ball Goes Big Despite Weather," *New York Age*, June 30, 1928, 10.

87. "'Fats' Waller Released." *Pittsburgh Courier*, December 1, 1928, 15.

88. *Variety*, July 11, 1928, 26.

89. "8:45—Fats Waller and Jimmy Johnson, WPCH Manhattan," *Brooklyn Daily Eagle*, radio listings, June 14, 1928, 30.

90. Joseph l. Wootten, "The Disc—Review of Records," *Philadelphia Tribune*, August 9, 1928, 6.

91. Harrison Smith, *Record Research*, August 1955, 7.

92. "'Keep Shufflin' Arrives at the Boulevard Theater," *Brooklyn Daily Eagle*, September 11, 1928, 36; "Werba's Has 'Keep Shufflin'—Other Local Attractions," *Brooklyn Daily Eagle*, September 16, 1928, 64.

93. "'Keep Shufflin' Give Untiring Entertainment," *Indianapolis News*, October 23, 1928, 5.

94. "Shubert-Pitt to Feature 'Keep Shufflin,'" *Pittsburgh Courier*, October 27, 1928.

95. "'Keep Shufflin' Hit at Pittsburgh House," *Baltimore Afro American*, November 17, 1928, 8.

96. Bushell, *Jazz from the Beginning*, 75.

97. George D. Tyler, "In Chicago Theaters," *Baltimore Afro American*, November 10, 1928, 8.

98. Dave Peyton, "The Musical Bunch," *Chicago Defender*, November 24, 1928, 6.

99. "At the Lafayette Theater," *New York Age*, April 5, 1930.

CHAPTER 17. ST. LOUIS BLUES, 1929-1930

1. Kappler, Wellstood, and Rouder, 32.

2. Foster and Stoddard, *Pops Foster*, 150–51, 152.

3. Roger Prior Dodge, *Hot Jazz and Jazz Dance*, 40.

4. Dodge, *Hot Jazz and Jazz Dance*, 7.

5. Sammy Price, *What Do They Want? A Jazz Autobiography* (Urbana: University of Illinois Press, 1990), 34.

6. Frank Driggs and Chuck Haddix, *Kansas City Jazz* (New York: Oxford University Press, 2005), 161.

7. Albertson, *Bessie*, 146, 155.

8. *New York Amsterdam News*, December 19, 1928, 12.

9. Chappy Gardner, "Along the Rialto," *Pittsburgh Courier*, January 12, 1929, B2.

10. Bob Slater, "Theatrical Jottings," *New York Age*, March 30, 1929, 6.

11. "At the Embassy Next Week," *Baltimore Afro American*, April 13, 1929, 38.

12. Maurice Dancer, "'Messin' Around' Co. Opens in Baltimore," *Pittsburgh Courier*, April 20, 1929, A4.

13. Van Hoogstraten, *Lost Broadway Theaters*, 67; "Major Butt gave Up Life to Save Others," *The Post-Star* (Glen Falls, NY), April 20, 1921, 1.

14. "'Messin' Around' Presents a Novelty," *New York Times*, April 23, 1929, 24.

15. *Billboard*, May 4, 1929, 35.

16. William G. King, "Messin' Around," *New York Evening Post*, April 23, 1929.

17. *Variety*, April 24, 1929, 52.

18. Charles Brackett, *The New Yorker*, May 4, 1929, 30.

19. Richard Watts Jr., *Herald Tribune*, April 23, 1929.

20. Watts, *Herald Tribune*, April 23, 1929.

21. "'Messin' Around' Opens at the Hudson Theater," *New York Age*, April 27, 1929, 6.

22. "'Messin' Around' Makes Debut—New Musical Comedy Faces Fire of Gotham Critics; Johnson's Music Lauded—Monette Moore in Cast," *Pittsburgh Courier*, May 4, 1929, 3.

23. Maurice Dancer, "Stage Gossip," *Philadelphia Tribune*, May 23, 1929, 6.

24. *New York Age*, May 4, 1929, 7.

25. Maurice Dancer, "'Messin Around' in Legal Tangle Over New York Times Review," *Pittsburgh Courier*, May 25, 1929, B3.

26. *Variety*, April 24, 1929, 52; "Too Many Plain Girls in N. Y. Show, Critic Says," *Baltimore Afro American*, May 11, 1929, 9.

27. "Too Many Plain Girls in N. Y. Show, Critic Says," *Baltimore Afro American*, May 11, 1929, 9.

28. "Show Ends through Misunderstanding," *Chicago Defender*, June 1, 1929, 7.

29. "Down Broadway," *Pittsburgh Courier*, June 15, 1929, A3.

30. "Revamp Failure," *Daily News*, June 17, 1929, 27.

31. Van Hoogstraten, *Lost Broadway Theaters*, 67.

32. Susan Delson, *Dudley Murphy, Hollywood Wildcard* (Minneapolis: University of Minnesota Press, 2006), ix, x, 45, 61.

33. Handy, *Black Women*, 224.

34. Delson, *Dudley Murphy*, 88.

35. Albertson, *Bessie*, 159.

36. Delson, *Dudley Murphy*, 101.

37. "'St Louis Blues' Is Featured by RCA in a Two-Reel Short," *Chicago Defender*, July 6, 1929, 7.

38. *Variety*, September 10, 1929.

39. Delson, *Dudley Murphy*, 89.

40. "Hill's Social Club 'Ragamuffin' Ball Goes Big Despite Weather," *New York Age*, June 30, 1928, 10.

41. *Chicago Defender*, June 29, 1929, 6; July 6, 1929, 15; July 6, 1929, 7; "Blues Dramatized," *Pittsburgh Courier*, July 6, 1929, 15.

42. *New York Age*, advertisement, December 28, 1929.

43. *New York Amsterdam News*, advertisement, April 30, 1930, 10.

44. "At the Alhambra Theatre," *New York Age*, May 10, 1930, 6.

45. Vere E. Johns, "Radio: Drama," *New York Age*, July 9, 1932, 6.

46. *Philadelphia Tribune*, advertisement, October 10, 1929, 6.

47. Albertson, *Bessie*, 160.

48. "Bessie Smith," *Record Changer*, March 1948, 6.

49. "Present Long Lost Bessie Smith Picture on Broadway," *Chicago Defender*, January 10, 1948, 8.

50. Circle J1016, Circle J1017.

51. James P. Johnson self-portrait pencil sketch, JPJC, IJS.

52. *New York Amsterdam News*, advertisement, July 19, 1930, 9.

53. Joel Whitburn, *Top R&B Singles, 1942–1999* (Menomonee Falls: Record Research, 2000), 183.

54. Bob Slater, "Theatrical Jottings," *New York Age*, January 4, 1930, 6; January 18, 1930, 6.

55. *New York Age*, November 23, 1929, 6.

56. "Hits and Bits," *Chicago Defender*, November 9, 1929, 6.

57. "They Agree to Disagree," *Baltimore Afro American*, December 7, 1929, 9.

58. S. Tutt Whitney, "Appreciation," *New York Amsterdam News*, December 18, 1929, 8; "Benefit for Florence Mills Association Is a Big Success," *New York Age*, December 21, 1929.

59. Salem Tutt Whitney, "Timely Topics—Hit and Miss," *Chicago Defender* (national edition), January 4, 1930, 6.

60. Johnson is also represented accompanying Bessie Smith on "Backwater Blues" in the set.

61. David Schiff, *Gershwin: Rhapsody in Blue* (Cambridge: Cambridge University Press, 1997), 37–38.

62. "With Our Song Writers Along Tin Pan Alley," *New York Amsterdam News*, March 26, 1930, 9.

63. Smith and Hoefer, *Music on My Mind*, 208–9. The Dixie Nightingale was Eva Taylor's sobriquet.

64. *New York Age*, January 4, 1930.

65. "Smalls' Paradise to Observe 4th Anniversary," *New York Age*, October 19, 1929, 7.

66. John Hammond, *John Hammond on Record* (New York: Ridge Press, 1977), 55.

67. Floyd G. Snelson Jr., "New Floor Revue at Small's [sic]," *Pittsburgh Courier*, April 5, 1930, 6A.

68. Singer, *Black and Blue*, 238–39.

69. "With Our Song Writers Along Tin Pan Alley," *New York Amsterdam News*, March 26, 1930, 9.

70. Arthur Pollock, "Plays and Things," *Brooklyn Daily Eagle*, April 27, 1930, 60.

71. "Belated Discovery Made That Miller and Lyles Did Not Head Brooklyn Show," *New York Amsterdam News*, April 30, 1930; "In Local Playhouses," *Brooklyn Daily Eagle*, April 30, 1930, 60.

72. Bernard L. Peterson, *A Century of Musicals in Black and White* (Westport, CT: Greenwood Press, 1993), 314.

73. "Stage Review—Shuffle Along," *Baltimore Afro American*, May 24, 1930, A11.

74. Cora Gary Illidge, "Music News," *New York Amsterdam News*, May 7, 1930, 12.

75. Cora Gary Illidge, "Music News," *New York Amsterdam News*, May 14, 1930, 10.

76. *Billboard*, March 8, 1930, 27; *Variety*, March 26, 1930, 73.

77. *Billboard*, April 5, 1930, 27.

78. "Death Robs Stage and Musical World of Two Leaders," *New York Amsterdam News*, October 22, 1930, 1.

79. *New York Age*, June 21, 1930, 6.

80. *New York Amsterdam News*, advertisement, June 25, 1930; "At the Lafayette Theater," *New York Age*, July 5, 1930, 6.

CHAPTER 18. CHANGING TASTES, 1931–1935

1. Will Marion Cook to James P. Johnson, November 25, 1936, transcript in the hand of WM Cook, JPJC, IJS.
2. Kirkeby, *Ain't Misbehavin'*, 152–53, 159.
3. "Germans enjoy melodies given by Southernaires," *Chicago Defender*, September 12, 1931, 2.
4. Piano recital by Hazel Harrison, Roerich Hall, concert program, November 8, 1931, JPJC, IJS.
5. Jon Pareles, "Joe Turner at Cookery: Half Century of Jazz Piano," *New York Times*, October 21, 1983, C23; James Renel Burden, "Conversation with Joe Turner: Last of the Stride Pianists," *Black Perspective in Music* (1981): 189.
6. Waller, 97.
7. Lester, *Too Marvelous*, 69–72.
8. Ralph J. Gleason, "Look, Ma, No Left Hands," *Down Beat*, January 28, 1953, 14.
9. Dietsche, *Tatum's Town*, 1.
10. "Adelaide Hall to Head Show," *New York Amsterdam News*, June 29, 1932, 7.
11. Chappy Gardner, "Adelaide Hall Is a Hit at Lafayette," *Pittsburgh Courier*, July 9, 1932, A6.
12. Waller, 96–98; Kirkeby, *Ain't Misbehavin'*, 145–49.
13. Kirkeby, *Ain't Misbehavin'*, 149.
14. Waller, 99.
15. Mike Lipskin, personal communication.
16. Burden, "Conversation with Joe Turner," 189.
17. Chappy Gardner, "Along the Rialto," *Pittsburgh Courier*, March 5, 1932, A6.
18. *Lazy Rhythm*, New Brighton Theater Program, August 17, 1931, JPJC, IJS.
19. Arthur Pollock, "The Theaters," *Brooklyn Daily Eagle*, August 18, 1931, 19.
20. Peterson, *Century of Musicals*, 214.
21. "'Sugar Hill' Comes to New York Soon," *Chicago Defender*, October 10, 1931, 8.
22. *Philadelphia Tribune*, advertisement, November 26, 1931, 6.
23. *New York Age*, November 28, 1931, 6. Some of his orchestrations exist in the Johnson papers, JPJC, IJS.
24. *Philadelphia Tribune*, advertisement, December 3, 1931, 6.
25. L. A. S. Bellinger, "Howard-Lincoln Sidelights," *Pittsburgh Courier*, December 5, 1931, A5.
26. "At the Theaters," *Philadelphia Tribune*, December 3, 1931, 6.
27. "'Sugar Hill' for Broadway on Dec. 25th," *Baltimore Afro American*, December 26, 1931, 20.
28. "F. Miller, Lyle in Broadway's Spotlight Now," *Chicago Defender*, January 2, 1932, 5.
29. "Sugar Hill Comes to Broadway," *Pittsburgh Courier*, January 2, 1932, A7.
30. "Behind the Curtain," *Baltimore Afro American*, January 9, 1932, 9.
31. Eugene Barr, *Billboard*, January 2, 1932, 19
32. "Sugar Hill," *Variety*, December 29, 1931, 34.
33. *The Stage*, January 21, 1932, 13.
34. "Miller, Lyles Show Ready," *Chicago Defender*, October 31, 1931, 5.
35. "Sugar Hill to Be Here Soon," *New York Amsterdam News*, January 6, 1932, 10.
36. "Miller-Lyles Kept Prisoners 8 Hours By Cast," *Baltimore Afro American*, January 23, 1932, 21.

37. Ralph Matthews, "Looking at the Stars," *Baltimore Afro American*, January 30, 1932, 13.
38. Ralph Matthews, "Looking at the Stars," *Baltimore Afro American*, February 6, 1932, 9.
39. "New Reviews," *Baltimore Afro American*, January 30, 1932, 5.
40. "Yeah Man to Be Given in Harlem Soon," *Chicago Defender*, May 21, 1932, 5; "New revue to open here," *New York Amsterdam News*, May 11, 1932, 7.
41. "B'Way Openings," *Chicago Daily Tribune*, May 22, 1932, F9; *New York Times*, advertisement, May 21, 1932, 6; "Theatrical notes," *New York Times*, May 23, 1932, 18.
42. "Theatrical notes," *New York Times*, May 26, 1932, 31.
43. "The play," *New York Times*, May 27, 1932, 27.
44. "Theatrical notes," *New York Times*, May 31, 1932, 15.
45. "Jamaica Clubs," *New York Age*, June 18, 1932, 9.
46. "Long Island News Notes and Social Items," *New York Age*, August 19, 1933, 8.
47. "New York City and Vicinity," *Philadelphia Tribune*, September 28, 1933, 8.
48. *New York Amsterdam News*, October 25, 1933, 11.
49. Ernestine Waddy, "Jamaica Juniors," *New York Age*, November 25, 1933, 7.
50. *New York Amsterdam News*, November 9, 1935, 5; "200 concert lovers go to joint recital," *New York Amsterdam News*, November 23, 1935, 5.
51. "Connie booking big acts in N.Y.," *Baltimore Afro American*, October 22, 1932, 10; "Immermans open new theatrical office," *New York Amsterdam News*, October 12, 1932, 8.
52. Reid, *Rhythm for Sale*, 178–79.
53. "Connie's Inn to Present Show Sunday Night," *Chicago Defender*, September 24, 1932; "N. Y. Raves Over Show at Connies," *Chicago Defender*, October 8, 1932, 5.
54. Floyd G. Snelson, "Broadway Bound," *Pittsburgh Courier*, October 22, 1932, A1.
55. Maurice Dancer, "Harlem Night by Night" *Pittsburgh Courier*, October 1, 1932, A6.
56. "Coast Codgings as Doped by Harry Levette," *Chicago Defender*, November 19, 1932.
57. "Published Song Hit," *New York Amsterdam News*, November 9, 1932, 11A.
58. "Music by Nora Holt," *New York Amsterdam News*, September 16, 1944, 9A.
59. Allan McMillan, "Allan's Alley," *New York Amsterdam News*, August 11, 1951, 25.
60. James P. Johnson, handwritten description, JPJC, IJS; James P. Johnson and Langston Hughes, "Can't You Hear Those Drums," typewritten lyric sheet, JPJC, IJS.
61. Ralph Matthews, "Black and Tan Craze Sweeps Portland; Lumbar Jacks Fall Hard for Harlem Hotcha," *Baltimore Afro American*, March 24, 1934, 5.
62. Ted Yates, "Believe Me," *Baltimore Afro American*, August 10, 1935, 5.
63. "Earl Morris Finds Teddy Blackman's Harlem Hotcha Revue Worthy of Its Name," *Pittsburgh Courier*, May 22, 1937, 21.
64. *New York Amsterdam News*, November 23, 1932, 10.
65. "Music News," *New York Amsterdam News*, November 30, 1932, 7.
66. "Eva Taylor Will Sing on Benefit for Needy," *New York Amsterdam News*, September 6, 1933, 1.
67. Delson, *Dudley Murphy*, 125–28, 133–34.
68. *The Emperor Jones*, Exhibitor's Campaign Book, United Artists, 1933.
69. Robert Pinsker, "James P. Johnson in the film *The Emperor Jones*," www.sandiegoragtime.com, accessed September 12, 2021.
70. Delson, *Dudley Murphy*, 136 fn, 140–48. Delson was not aware Johnson is the pianist.
71. Smith and Hoefer, *Music on My Mind*, 172.

72. "Mae West Comes to Harlem," *Pittsburgh Courier*, April 29, 1933, A6. Later that year, West's film *I'm No Angel* was released with lyrics by African American writer Ben Ellison.

73. *Atlanta Daily World*, March 11, 1936, 3.

74. Singer, *Black and Blue*, 376–77.

75. Sam Fox, Los Angeles, to James P. Johnson, Jamaica, NY, typewritten letter, January 11, 1936, JPJC, IJS.

76. Rosemarie Berry, "Negro Composer's Symphony Is Accepted for Motion Pictures," *Pittsburgh Courier*, July 31, 1937, 12.

77. J. Wayne Burrell, "Harlem Social Whirl," *Baltimore Afro American*, August 31, 1936, 20.

78. Blesh and Janis, *They All Played Ragtime*, 205.

79. Hammond, *John Hammond*, 119.

80. Herbie Friedwald, Ed Allen interview, January 14, 1961, Hogan Jazz Archive.

81. "Flying Around Jamaica Picking Up the Gossip," *New York Age*, May 5, 1934, 8.

82. "Ethel Waters Honored by Harlem Club Woman," *New York Age*, July 7, 1934, 34.

83. "Jimmy Johnson Successful as Song Creator," *Baltimore Afro American*, May 5, 1934, 8; Ivan L. Harry, "Rambling Around Jamaica," *Baltimore Afro American*, August 4, 1934, 6, and August 11, 1934, 6.

84. *New York Age*, August 18, 1934, 4.

85. Sutton, "Recording the Twenties," 206, 210.

86. "New Show Launched at Small's [sic] Paradise," *New York Amsterdam News*, October 6, 1934, 7.

87. Jerry Vogel to James P. Johnson, telegram, date unknown.

88. Marcus Wright, "The Talk of the Town," *New York Age*, October 13, 1934, 4.

89. Maurice Dancer, "Harlem in Bloom," *Pittsburgh Courier*, October 13, 1934, A9.

90. Eva Jessye, "Radio Revue," *Baltimore Afro American*, September 8, 1934, 9.

91. Letters to James P. Johnson, JPJC, IJS.

92. *Variety*, "Small's [sic] Paradise, N.Y.," October 9, 1934, 65.

93. *New York Amsterdam News*, advertisement, December 22, 1934, A12.

94. "Smalls' Paradise," *New York Age*, January 5, 1935, 2.

95. *Chicago Defender*, November 24, 1934, 9.

96. "Rhythm Club Holds First Annual Dance," *New York Amsterdam News*, March 2, 1935, 3.

97. "Johnson to Return to Small's [sic] Paradise," *New York Amsterdam News*, April 20, 1935, 10.

98. Ikey Robinson to James P. Johnson, transcript in the hand of Ikey Robinson, January 10, 1935, JPJC, IJS.

99. George Howe to James P. Johnson, transcript in the hand of George Howe, undated, JPJC, IJS.

100. Eva Jessye, "Radio Revue," *Baltimore Afro American*, September 8, 1934, 9.

101. Kirkeby, *Ain't Misbehavin'*, 143–44; Damon Runyon, "The Brighter Side," *San Francisco Examiner*, December 13, 1938, 18.

102. *New York Amsterdam News*, advertisement, May 18, 1935, 10.

103. Peck, "PM Visits," 20.

104. Schuller, *Early Jazz*, 223.

CHAPTER 19. THE ORGANIZER, 1935-1940

1. "Creative Work—accomplishments," typewritten note by James P. Johnson, JPJC, IJS.
2. Macy Nulman, *Concise Encyclopedia of Jewish Music* (New York: McGraw-Hill, 1975), 151.
3. 1930 US federal census, Manhattan, New York, New York, Roll 1553; page 38A, enumeration district 393, image 807.0, FHL microfilm 2341288; Passenger and crew lists of vessels arriving at New York, New York, 1921 microfilm serial T715; microfilm roll 2998, line 18, page 40.
4. Edward E. Treumann to James P. Johnson, New York, March 25, 1936, transcript in the hand of Edward E. Treumann, JPJC, IJS.
5. James P. Johnson to Maurice Immesuif, December 17, 1936, transcript in hand of James P. Johnson, JPJC, IJS.
6. R. P. Mathews, district manager, Wicks Pipe Organ Co. to James P. Johnson, March 2, 1937, typed transcript, JPJC, IJS.
7. Fritz Reiner to James P. Johnson, September 29, 1935, typed transcript, JPJC, IJS.
8. Jane Perkins to James P. Johnson, July 20, 1937, typed transcript, JPJC, IJS.
9. Rosemarie Berry, "Negro Composer's Symphony Is Accepted for Motion Pictures," *Pittsburgh Courier*, July 31, 1937, 12.
10. Natalie Disston, assistant to Mr. Stokowski, to James P. Johnson, September 21, 1937, typed transcript, JPJC, IJS.
11. Hans Kindler to James P. Johnson, October 2, 1935, typed transcript, JPJC, IJS.
12. Adolph Deutsch to James P. Johnson, January 22, 1936, typed transcript, JPJC, IJS.
13. Freda Coan [sp?] to James P. Johnson, December 9, 1936, typed transcript, JPJC, IJS.
14. Ella Palow to James P. Johnson, April 7, 1936, typed transcript, JPJC, IJS.
15. The Philharmonic-Symphony Society of New York to James P. Johnson, May 26, 1936, typed transcript, JPJC, IJS, signature illegible.
16. Hope Harvey to James P. Johnson, December 18, 1936, typed transcript, JPJC, IJS.
17. James P. Johnson, New York, to Deems Taylor, undated, transcript in hand of James P. Johnson, James P. Johnson collection, IJS.
18. James P. Johnson to James Weldon Johnson, undated, transcript in the hand of James P. Johnson, JPJC, IJS.
19. Johnson, *Black Manhattan*, 115.
20. James Weldon Johnson to James P. Johnson, November 11, 1936, letter in the hand of J. W. Johnson, JPJC, IJS.
21. R. R. Moton Jr. to James P. Johnson, December 9, 1936, typewritten letter, JPJC, IJS.
22. Lester A. Walton, Monrovia, Liberia, to James P. Johnson, March 8, 1937, typewritten letter, JPJC, IJS.
23. Will Marion Cook to James P. Johnson, November 25, 1936, transcript in the hand of W. M. Cook, JPJC, IJS.
24. Carter, *Swing Along*, 109.
25. Henry Allen Moe, secretary, from John Simon Guggenheim Memorial Foundation to James P. Johnson, March 16, 1937, typewritten transcript, JPJC, IJS.
26. Henry Allen Moe, secretary, from John Simon Guggenheim Memorial Foundation to James P. Johnson, November 29, 1937, typewritten transcript, JPJC, IJS.

27. Errol G. Hill and James V. Hatch, *A History of African American Theater* (Cambridge: Cambridge University Press, 2008), 315–17.

28. "Crowds Jam Streets As 'Macbeth' Opens," *New York Times*, April 15, 1936, 25.

29. Ralph Matthews, "Looking at the Stars," *Baltimore Afro American*, June 13, 1936, 10.

30. Roy Ottley, "Harlem's Lord and Lady Macbeth in Full Regalia," *New York Amsterdam News*, April 18, 1936, 8.

31. "'Macbeth' Scores Major Triumph in Year's Presentations of Federal Theater Project," *Pittsburgh Courier*, January 16, 1937, A6.

32. Philip W. Barber to James P. Johnson, July 1, 1936, typewritten transcript, JPJC, IJS.

33. Romeo L. Dougherty, "Sports Whirl," *New York Amsterdam News*, June 8, 1935, 14.

34. Carter, *Swing Along*, 101–6.

35. "MME Jarboro to Make New World's Tour," *Chicago Defender*, June 1, 1935, 7.

36. *New York Age*, June 8, 1935, 8.

37. "Thompson, San Romani Top Armory Track Meet," *New York Amsterdam News*, April 9, 1938, 19.

38. "Artists Get Inspiration from Augusta Savage Who Opens Gallery to Sell Their Work to the Public," *Chicago Defender*, June 10, 1939, 13.

39. "Star Acts to make Big Trip," *New York Amsterdam News*, September 24, 1938, 20.

40. "Plans Concert Tour," *New York Amsterdam News*, July 29, 1939, 19.

41. Confidential Personal Loan Co., Inc., assignment of salary, wages, commissions, and other compensation for services, executed April 13, 1937, in the amount of $300, JPJC, IJS. Johnson is listed as in the employ of the Savoy Ballroom. All debts were repaid by 1942.

42. Will Marion Cook to James P. Johnson, November 25, 1936, transcript in the hand of W. M. Cook, JPJC, IJS.

43. Edna Ferber to James P. Johnson, April 8, 1936, typewritten transcript, JPJC, IJS.

44. Langston Hughes to James P. Johnson, January 24, 1937, transcript in the hand of Langston Hughes, JPJC, IJS.

45. "Famous 'John Henry' Tramps Boards Again," February 26, 1937, unidentified newspaper clipping, JPJC, IJS.

46. Guy B. Johnson to James P. Johnson, date unknown, typewritten transcript, JPJC, IJS.

47. Arnold Rampersad, *Ralph Ellison: A Biography* (New York: Vintage Books, 2008), 123.

48. Gelman, who is white, admitted that this may have hindered Johnson's comfort being forthright about such issues.

49. Smith and Hoefer, *Music on My Mind*, 236.

50. "Silver Jubilee of Blues to Honor Handy, Gershwin," *Atlanta Daily World*, November 27, 1939, 2.

51. "Negro Concerts," *New York Times*, February 5, 1939, 7; "Programs of the Week—Series of Negro Concerts at Labor Stage," *New York Times*, February 12, 1939, 134.

52. "Negro Music Sung in Tableaux," *New York Times*, February 27, 1939, 10.

53. "Langdon W. Post Sees Negro Folk Music as Main Source of American Popular Music," *New York Amsterdam News*, February 25, 1939, 16.

54. "Jimmy Johnston [sic] to Produce Symphony," *Chicago Defender*, April 1, 1939, 18.

55. Hill and Hatch, *History of African American Theater*, 358.

56. "New Male Chorus," *Chicago Defender*, March 16, 1940, 21.

57. "Dorothy Harrison, 'Pins and Needles' Star, on Workers' Concert Bill," *New York Amsterdam News*, March 9, 1940, 21.

58. Langston Hughes, libretto, undated, Schomburg Center, NYPL.

59. Peter D. Goldsmith, *Making People's Music: Moe Asch* (Washington, DC: Smithsonian Institution Press, 1998), 67, 76, 89.

60. Richard Carlin, *Worlds of Sound: The Story of Smithsonian Folkways* (New York: HarperCollins, 2008), 5.

61. James Dapogny, interview with the author, December 2002.

62. Charles Graham, "Meet the A&R man John Hammond," *Down Beat*, October 12, 1961, 23.

63. Milt Hinton, David G Berger, and Holly Maxson, *Playing the Changes* (Nashville, TN: Vanderbilt University Press, 2008), 50–53.

64. Frank Marshall Davis, "Rating the Records," *New York Amsterdam News*, May 13, 1939, 21. Davis, who also had unfriendly comments about Lionel Hampton's voice, commented that Johnson's instrumental coupling "After Tonight," without Robinson's vocal, made fine listening.

65. Arwulf Arwulf, "Anna Robinson Biography," *All Music Guide*, https://www.allmusic.com/artist/anna-robinson-mn0000575783/biography, accessed September 13, 2021.

66. The March recording, first released on *James P. Johnson—Father of the Stride Piano*, CL 1780, Columbia, 1962, LP, remained in print for almost fifteen years. The June recording remained obscure until it was issued by the Meritt Record Society, a small specialty collector's label, in a limited edition series in 1979, *Red Allen & James P. Johnson, Meritt #5*. This reissue incorrectly credits Anna Robinson as the vocalist.

67. Arnold Rampersad, *The Life of Langston Hughes* (New York: Oxford University Press, 1986), 384.

68. "Program for Today at the World's Fair," *New York Times*, September 2, 1940, 18.

69. "News and Gossip of the Rialto," *New York Times*, June 16, 1940, X1.

70. "Gossip of the Rialto," *New York Times*, October 27, 1940, 129.

71. "Dan Burley's Back Door Stuff," *New York Amsterdam News*, April 18, 1942, 16.

72. *Middletown Times Herald*, advertisement, May 29, 1936, 16.

73. Albertson, *Bessie*, 245.

74. "Club Chats," *New York Amsterdam News*, July 18, 1936, 11.

75. John W. Schaum, "Piano Pointers," *Metronome*, April 1937, 58.

76. *New York Age*, advertisement, April 23, 1938, 10.

77. *New York Amsterdam News*, advertisement, November 5, 1938, 21; *New York Amsterdam News*, advertisement, December 3, 1938, 21.

78. Royalty statements, 1937–1939, from Remick Music Corporation and Harms, Inc., JPJC, IJS.

79. Kappler, Wellstood, and Rouder, 24.

80. Allan McMillan, "Back Door Stuff," *New York Amsterdam News*, February 5, 1949, 27; Allan McMillan, "Allan's Alley," *New York Amsterdam News*, May 14, 1949, 25.

81. Waller and Calabrese, *Fats Waller*, 168.

82. Vance, *Fats Waller*, 121.

83. The date and locations of these recordings is not precisely known. They were likely made in Waller's home in Manhattan, since he didn't move out to Queens until 1938 or '39.

84. Vance, *Fats Waller*, 74.

85. Wright, *Afro-Americans*, 135–36.

CHAPTER 20. SPIRITUALS TO SWING, 1938–1939

1. Wright, *Afro-Americans*, 326.
2. Mezzrow, *Really the Blues*, 361.
3. M. H. Orodenker, "Off the Records," *Billboard*, February 18, 1939, 15.
4. Wright, *Afro-Americans*, 326.
5. Frank Marshall Davis, "Rating the Record," *Atlanta Daily World* April 17, 1939, 2.
6. Unidentified and undated clipping, JPJC, IJS.
7. *Barnard Bulletin*, May 16, 1939, 1.
8. "Race Records," *Down Beat*, August 1939, 21.
9. Russell, *Jazz Information*, 24.
10. Ross Russell, Escondido, to Michael Montgomery, Detroit, July 10, 1970, typewritten transcript, Collection of Scott Brown from the Michael Montgomery files.
11. "Wants Band to Shout," *New York Amsterdam News*, October 29, 1938.
12. "Negro Music Night at Carnegie Hall," *Variety*, December 7, 1938, 51. This notice incorrectly referred to Ruby Smith as Bessie's daughter, a common error. She was born Ruby Walker and changed her name to Smith after Bessie's death.
13. Hammond, *John Hammond*, 200–202.
14. "Count Basie Invades Carnegie Hall," *Down Beat*, December 1938, 2.
15. Hammond, *John Hammond*, 200, 311, 339.
16. "Harlem Benefit," *Daily News*, May 28, 1938, 22.
17. "Benefit Preview," *Daily News*, December 24, 1928, 23.
18. L.N., "The Play," *New York Times*, December 31, 1938, 6.
19. S.W., *New York World Telegram*, December 31, 1938.
20. Herrick Brown, "'Policy Kings' Has Premiere at Nora Bayes Theater," *New York Sun*, December 31, 1938.
21. "Comedy Is Flop—Jimmy Johnson Music Best Thing in Show," *New York Amsterdam News*, January 7, 1939, 17.
22. "'Policy Kings' Closes," *Pittsburgh Courier*, January 14, 1939, 21.
23. Robert Coleman, *Daily Mirror*.
24. "Policy Kings," *Billboard*, January 14, 1939, 16.
25. Alfred Green, *Rhythm Is My Beat: Jazz Guitar Great Freddie Green and the Count Basie Sound* (Lanham, MD: Rowman and Littlefield, 2015), 63.
26. Herbert Drake, *New York Herald Tribune*, December 31, 1938.
27. Brown, December 31, 1938.
28. John Hammond, "Talents of James P. Johnson Went Unappreciated," *Down Beat*, December 28, 1955, 12.
29. "'Policy Kings' to Be Revived This Fall," *Chicago Defender*, August 26, 1939, 20.
30. "'Policy Kings' in Production," *New York Amsterdam News*, April 6, 1941, 20.
31. "'Policy Kings' Will Attempt a Revival," *Chicago Defender*, April 26, 1941, 21.
32. "Harlemites, Park Ave. Rub Elbows at Play's Opening," *New York Amsterdam News*, January 7, 1939, 12.
33. "Moon Over Harlem Has Premiere," *New York Amsterdam News*, June 24, 1939, 17.
34. "What's ASCAP," *Chicago Defender*, January 11, 1941, 20.
35. "Crescendo Club Plans Carnival," *New York Amsterdam News*, August 5, 1939, 16.

36. "Benefit Concerts Given," *New York Times*, August 31, 1939, 21; "When Luckey Roberts Went Park Ave," *New York Amsterdam News*, September 9, 1939, 16.

37. "Incidental Notes," *Jazz Information*, September 8, 1939, 3.

38. Billy Jones, "Stars That Shine," *Chicago Defender*, July 8, 1939, 9.

39. "The Bandwagon," *Jazz Information*, September 19, 1939, 2.

40. ASCAP Festival of American Music concert program, JPJC, IJS.

41. "ASCAP Anniversary Features Race Music," *Chicago Defender*, October 7, 1939, 21; Howard Taubman, "Negro Music Given at ASCAP Recital," *New York Times*, October 3, 1939, 26.

42. ASCAP Silver Jubilee concert program, October 2, 1939, JPJC, IJS.

43. *New York Sun*, October 3, 1939.

44. "Columbia Record Co. Signs James Johnson," *Chicago Defender*, July 29, 1939, 7.

45. George Avakian, "The Collector's Corner," *Tempo*, May 1939, 9.

46. George Avakian, "25 Best Record Sides of 1939," *Tempo*, January 1940, 11.

47. Columbia Recording Corporation statement of royalties for the three-month period ending September 30, 1939, JPJC, IJS.

48. "A-Flat Dream" was likely issued to capitalize on the emerging craze for boogie woogie.

49. "Ida Cox, Former Blues Singer, Rediscovered by Columbia; Signed," *Pittsburgh Courier*, November 11, 1939, 21.

50. Ven-Der, "Recordings," *Chicago Defender*, February 3, 1940, 21.

51. *Chicago Defender*, November 4, 1939.

52. Theater Arts Committee letterhead, JPJC, IJS.

53. "TAC Cabaret to Open Nov. 7," *New York Times*, October 19, 1939, 31.

54. "TAC Cabarets Start Nov. 7," *Brooklyn Daily Eagle*, October 15, 1939, 33.

55. "Satchmo—'Swingin' the Dream,'" *Swing—The Guide to Modern Music*, December 1939, 7.

56. *Billboard*, December 9, 1939.

57. J. D. Smith, "From Spirituals to Swing," December 29, 1939, 2.

58. Hammond, *John Hammond*, 232.

59. *New York Amsterdam News*, advertisement, December 23, 1939, 21.

60. Music Publishers Holding Corporation Contract, October 9, 1939, JPJC, IJS.

61. Mike Lipskin, personal communication, June 2016.

62. Royalty statements, JPJC, IJS.

63. "Plans for Work," page III, JPJC, IJS.

64. John Hammond to James P. Johnson, typewritten letter, February 1, 1940, JPJC, IJS.

65. Julius Rosenwald Fund Fellowship application instructions, 1943, JPJC, IJS.

66. Howland, *Ellington Uptown*, 211.

CHAPTER 21. CAFÉ SOCIETY, 1939–1941

1. Barney Josephson and Terry Trilling-Josephson, *Café Society* (Chicago: University of Illinois Press, 2009), 19–20, 13. Despite Johnson's regular appearances at Café Society, the only reference to him in the book specific to his playing at the Café is in Dan Morgenstern's introduction and photograph.

2. Hammond, *John Hammond*, 207.

3. Josephson, 16–17.

4. Hammond, *John Hammond*, 206–7; Josephson, 27.

5. Singer, *Black and Blue*, 110; Hammond, *John Hammond*, 207.

6. Peter J. Silvester, *A Left Hand Like God* (New York: Da Capo, 1989), 159.

7. Linda Dahl, *Morning Glory* (New York: Pantheon Books, 1999), 141.

8. "Café Society Monday Jam Sessions Directed by James P. Johnson," *Jazz Information*, December 8, 1939, 1.

9. "Another Great All-Star Band," *Metronome*, April 1939, 23.

10. John Hammond, "John Hammond Says," *Metronome*, April 1939, 26.

11. "Ida Cox Joins Café Society Show; Big Bill, Sonny Terry Also There," *Jazz Information*, December 22, 1939, 1.

12. "The Bandwagon," *Jazz Information*, September 19, 1939, 2.

13. "First Year for Café Society," *Swing—The Guide to Modern Music*, January 1940, 39.

14. "Cabaret TAC Moves Uptown Feb 3 to Park Plaza," *New York Amsterdam News*, January 27, 1940, 20.

15. "Hot Club Formed in Trenton," *Jazz Information*, February 23, 1940, 1.

16. "Second Jam Session in Trenton," *Jazz Information*, March 1940, 12; "Hot Club Throws Bash in Trenton," *Down Beat*, April 1940, 15.

17. "New Elk's Rendezvous Show Surpasses All Others in Fun," *New York Amsterdam News*, March 30, 1940, 16.

18. "Where to Go, What to Do," *New York Amsterdam News*, April 6, 1940, 20.

19. "Jimmy Johnson Working at Elks," *Jazz Information*, March 29, 1940, 1.

20. "Nick's Session Features Old Timers," *Jazz Information*, March 15, 1940, 1.

21. "News of Night Clubs," *New York Times*, June 2, 1940, 122.

22. "The Brand New Band at Café Society," *Pittsburgh Courier*, June 22, 1940; "Café Society—Johnson's Band Is Tops at Spot," *Chicago Defender*, June 22, 1940, 21.

23. "'Society Jimmy' Says Harlem of Jimmy Johnson Taking Ork to Café Society," *Chicago Defender*, June 15, 1940, 20.

24. Stanley Dance, *The World of Count Basie* (New York: Scribner's, 1980), 104.

25. Unidentified clipping, JPJC, IJS.

26. "Tender Fete for Actress in Jamaica," *New York Amsterdam News*, June 22, 1940, 16.

27. "News of Night Clubs," *New York Times*, June 30, 1940, 109; "Stars by Billy Jones," *Chicago Defender*, July 20, 1940, 20.

28. "Harlem's Day," *Chicago Defender*, August 3, 1940, 20; St. Clair Bourne, "Program Runs Rest of Week," *New York Amsterdam News*, July 27, 1940, 1.

29. Ted Poston, "Jitterbugs at Fair Defy Rain," undated, unidentified clipping, JPJC, IJS.

30. "Stage Stars Honor Harlem Cabaret Man," *Chicago Defender*, July 27, 1940, 21.

31. "Hazel Scott to Café Society," *Chicago Defender*, August 24, 1940, 21.

32. "James P. Johnson, Musician-Songwriter, Is Stricken," *Chicago Defender*, August 24, 1940, 21.

33. Alvin Moses, "Footlite Flickers," *Atlanta Daily World*, September 2, 1940, 2.

34. "Jackson for Johnson," *Down Beat*, September 1940, 2.

35. 1940 US federal census, Queens, New York, roll T627_2743, page 62B; enumeration district 41-1206.

36. *Time*, December 27, 1943.
37. "Jimmy Johnson Successful as Song Creator," unidentified, undated clipping, JPJC, IJS.
38. Rose DiFillippe to James P. Johnson, typewritten letter, November 4, 1940, JPJC, IJS.
39. "'Striver's Row' Rumored for Broadway," *New York Amsterdam News*, December 7, 1940, 20.
40. Brooks Atkinson, "The Play," *New York Times*, March 6, 1941, 24.
41. "'Striver's Row' Musical Version, Now Rehearsing for Opening in Harlem and Then on the Road," *New York Amsterdam News*, March 1, 1941, 20; "'On Striver's Row' Opens Apollo Run," *New York Amsterdam News*, March 8, 1941, 21.
42. Morgen S. Jensen, "'On Striver's Row' Draws Crowd to Apollo Theater," *Pittsburgh Courier*, March 15, 1941, 20.
43. "'Striver's Row' Comedy Scores Hit as Musical," *New York Amsterdam News*, March 15, 1941, 20.
44. Morgen S. Jensen, "'On Striver's Row' Draws Crowds to Apollo Theater," *Pittsburgh Courier*, March 15, 1941, 20.
45. Jensen, "'On Striver's Row,'" 20; "Stage Notes," *New York Amsterdam News*, March 15, 1941, 21.
46. *Variety*, "House Reviews—Apollo, N.Y.," March 12, 1941, 47.
47. "Burr Production Here on April 10," *New York Times*, March 3, 1941, 11.
48. Charlie Gillett, *The Sound of the City* (New York: Dell Publishing, 1972), 30, 83, 168.
49. Cephus Jones, "Nationwide Talent Hunt Inaugurated by Apollo," *Atlanta Daily World*, March 24, 1941, 2.
50. "'Symphonic Fantasy' to make debut; 65 in cast," *Baltimore Afro American*, January 25, 1941.
51. "Pinkard Show Has Maude Russell, Betty Voorhees," *Baltimore Afro American*, March 15, 1941, 13.
52. "Stage Notes," *New York Amsterdam News*, April 12, 1941, 20.
53. "Stage Notes," *New York Amsterdam News*, March 22, 1941, 20.
54. "James P. Johnson Is Feeling Ok," *Down Beat*, June 15, 1941, 5.
55. "Things Perk Up for Pinkard Fantasy; Gets Broadway Band," *Chicago Defender*, May 10, 1941, 20.
56. "J.P.'s New Sketch," *New York Amsterdam News*, September 20, 1941, 21.
57. "Stage Notes," *New York Amsterdam News*, December 6, 1941, 20.
58. Dorothy F. Rodgers to Flournoy Miller, typewritten letter, June 15, 1944, Flournoy Miller collection, Schomburg Center.
59. 1947 revised Uniform Popular Songwriters Contract, March 6, 1947, Flournoy Miller Collection, Schomburg Center.
60. "Apollo Stages Miller Revue," *New York Amsterdam News*, March 29, 1941, 21.
61. *Pittsburgh Courier*, advertisement, May 24, 1941, 21.
62. "Connie Berry Stars at Café Society," *Chicago Defender*, October 11, 1941, 20.
63. "Williams Blue Five," *Down Beat*, December 15, 1941, 15.
64. *Chicago Defender*, October 25, 1941, 20; "Clarence Williams Blue Five Records 2 Numbers," *Chicago Defender*, January 17, 1942, 21; *New York Age*, January 31, 1942, 10.
65. Mike Stoller, interview with the author.
66. Bessye J. Bearden, "New York Society," *Chicago Defender*, November 22, 1941, 18.

67. Bessye J. Bearden, "New York Society," *Chicago Defender*, November 22, 1941, 18. "Mercedes Gilbert Gives Solo Show," *New York Amsterdam News*, December 20,1941, 19; Jamaica Debut—Mercedes Gilbert "One Woman Theater," Presbyterian Church House, December 12, 1941, concert program, JPJC, IJS.

68. "Jazz Players to Aid Russians," *New York Times*, March 28, 1942, 11.

CHAPTER 22. CONCERT HALL REALIZED, 1939-1942

1. James P. Johnson to Mrs. Sprague Coolidge, letter in the hand of Johnson, undated, JPJC, IJS.
2. Unidentified clipping, JPJC; promotional post card, JPJC; Dr. Paul Kosok, director of Brooklyn Civic Orchestra, *Symphonie Harlem*, Carnegie Hall Recording Company, March 11, 1939, 78 rpm recordings.
3. "Pioneer Negro American Ballet at Riverside," *New York Amsterdam News*, December 5, 1981, 30.
4. de la Orquestra Sinfonica Nacional, Lima, Peru, April 16, 1941, concert program, JPJC, IJS.
5. J. Mercer Meredith, *New York Amsterdam News*, April 19, 1941.
6. Paul Kosok to James P. Johnson, letter in the hand of Paul Kosok, JPJC, IJS.
7. "Johnson's Works to Be Played," *Pittsburgh Courier*, December 27, 1941, 20.
8. Friends of James P. Johnson, typewritten form letter, undated, JPJC, IJS.
9. "Concert Date of Johnson Changes," *New York Amsterdam News*, February 7, 1942, 17.
10. Charles Edward Smith, "The Jazz Years," *Metronome*, April 1961, 12.
11. Blesh and Janis, *They All Played Ragtime*, 204.
12. James P. Johnson, handwritten note, JPJC, IJS.
13. *New York Amsterdam News*, March 14, 1942.
14. Unidentified newspaper clipping, March 12, 1942, JPJC, IJS.
15. "Billy Rowe's Notebook," *Pittsburgh Courier*, April 18, 1942, 20.
16. James P Johnson, Plan-Of Work, typewritten manuscript, JPJC, IJS.
17. "Socially Speaking," *New York Amsterdam News*, June 6, 1942, 9.

CHAPTER 23. IN DEMAND AGAIN, 1942-1943

1. *Eddie Condon Presents—A Jazz Concert*, The Town Hall, April 11, 1942, JPJC, IJS.
2. *New York Amsterdam News*, advertisement, April 4, 1942, 17; "Bill Bailey Dances at Town Hall with Eddie Condon Program," *New York Amsterdam News*, April 18, 1942, 17; "Jam Concerts Successful; Booked Ahead Next Year," *Pittsburgh Courier*, April 11, 1942, 21; "Programs of the Week," *New York Times*, April 5, 1942, X6.
3. "Dan Burley's Back Door Stuff," *New York Amsterdam News*, April 18, 1942, 16.
4. "Jam Concerts Successful; Booked Ahead Next Year," 21.
5. *Metronome*, May 1942, 8.
6. World War II registration card, JPJC, IJS.
7. Goldsmith, *Making People's Music*, 110, 102, 127.
8. Goldsmith, *Making People's Music*, 109-10.
9. "Records: New Sonata by Howard Taubman," *New York Times*, January 23, 1944, X5.

10. Two Deuces, "Record Reviews," *Metronome*, January 1944, 32.

11. Goldsmith, *Making People's Music*, 129.

12. "Hot Discs," *Down Beat*, January 1945.

13. "Davison Wakes Up Boston," *Jazz Record*, February 15, 1943, 3.

14. George "Cuz" Falkener, "The Boston Jazz Scene," *Good Diggin'*, December 1948, 9.

15. "What the Musicians Are Doing," *Jazz Record*, May 15, 1943, 2.

16. "Boston Is Jumping," *Jazz Record*, March 1, 1943, 2.

17. Advisory Committee on Negro Health of the Queensboro Tuberculosis and Health Association, Musicale and Programme, Lost Battalion Memorial Hall, Elmhurst, N.Y., May 16, 1943, concert program, JPJC, IJS.

18. "What the Musicians Are Doing," *Jazz Record*, June 1, 1943, 2.

19. "N.Y.'s Swing Street in the Groove Again," *Variety*, June 9, 1943, 1.

20. "Jam Session," *Life*, October 11, 1943, 117–24.

21. Teddy Wilson, Arie Ligthart, and Humphrey Van Loo, *Teddy Wilson Talks Jazz* (New York: Continuum, 2001), 101, 106.

22. Whitney Balliett, "Supreme Tickler," *The New Yorker*, May 11, 1963, 158–59.

23. Denis Preston, "James P.—They Called Him 'The Brute,'" *Melody Maker*, December 3, 1955.

24. Ernest Borneman, "The Anthropologist Looks at Jazz," *Record Changer*, May 1944, 38.

25. "Jack Mills Presents 'There's No Two Ways About Love,'" *New York Enquirer*, June 28, 1943.

26. "Stormy Weather," *Variety*, June 2, 1943, 8.

27. "'Stormy Weather' Negro Musical with Bill Robinson at the Roxy," *New York Times*, July 22, 1943, 15.

28. "Songs with Most Radio Plugs," *Billboard*, September 25, 1943, 12; *Billboard*, advertisement, September 25, 1943, 12.

29. Whitburn, *Top R&B Singles, 1942–1999*, 183.

30. James P. Johnson, New York, to Flournoy Miller, Los Angeles, May 24, 1950, transcript in the hand of James P. Johnson, Flournoy Miller collection, Schomburg Center.

31. Morroe Berger, Edward Berger, and James Patrick, *Benny Carter: A Life in American Music* (Lanham, MD: Scarecrow Press, 2002), 251.

32. 1944 Federal tax return, JPJC, IJS.

33. Frank Driggs and Harris Lewine, *Black Beauty, White Heat* (New York: William Morrow, 1982), 13.

34. "I Thought I Heard," *Jazz Record*, November 1943, 2.

35. Lee Siegel, New York, to Mr. and Mrs. James P. Johnson, New York, January 8, 1944, and February 5, 1944, typewritten letters, JPJC, IJS.

CHAPTER 24. RECORDING FLURRY, 1943–1944

1. Joe H. Klee, "Speaking for the Record," *Mississippi Rag*, February 1975, 10.

2. Michael Cuscuna, *The Blue Note Years* (New York: Rizzoli International Publications, 1995), 15–17.

3. Cuscuna, *The Blue Note Years*, 18.

4. "Jimmy Johnson's Boogie Woogie original piano solos," Mills Music, New York, 1943.

5. Joseph L. Wootton, "The Disc—Review of Records," *Philadelphia Tribune*, June 14, 1928, 6.

6. "Jazz Pianist Extraordinary," *Shackleton's Review of Recorded Music*, February 1944, 9.

7. Jax (John Lucas), "Diggin' the Discs," *Down Beat*, February 15, 1944, 8.

8. Leonard Feather and Barry Ulanov, "Johnson on Wax—1944," *Jazz Times Bulletin*, 1944, 12–13.

9. Frank London Brown, "More Man Than Myth, Monk Has Emerged from the Shadows," *Down Beat*, October 30, 1958, 13.

10. Eric Thacker, liner notes to *The Complete Edmond Hall/James P. Johnson/Sidney De Paris/Vic Dickenson Blue Note Sessions*, Mosaic Records, MR6-109, 1985, LP.

11. "Second Thoughts by S. I. Hayakawa," *Chicago Defender*, April 29, 1944, 13.

12. "Condon to Give Concert," *New York Times*, December 17, 1943, 23.

13. "Jazz Concert Series Begun," *Pittsburgh Courier*, December 25, 1943, 15.

14. "Music World Honors Fats Waller in Final Tribute," *Chicago Defender*, December 25, 1943, 1; "Police Hold Huge Crowd in Check at Composer's Rites," *Pittsburgh Courier*, December 25, 1943, 15.

15. "Show Honors Fats Waller," *New York Times*, December 22, 1943, 26.

16. Michael Cuscuna, producer's note in *The Complete Edmond Hall/James P. Johnson/Sidney De Paris/Vic Dickenson Blue Note Sessions*, Mosaic Records, MR6–109, 1985, LP.

17. "Popular Record Releases, May 4 through May 11," *Billboard*, May 13, 1944, 18.

18. Lorraine Gordon, telephone interview with Scott E. Brown, September 7, 2012.

19. Alfred Lion, "Blue Note," *Metronome*, August 1954, 14.

20. "Opera and Concert Programs of Week," *New York Times*, February 13, 1944, X5; "Jazz Concert Given Here," *New York Times*, February 20, 1944, 34.

21. "Jazz Concerts to Broadcast," *Pittsburgh Courier*, April 15, 1944, 13.

22. Frederick Ramsey Jr., "Those Washington D.C. Blues," *Record Changer*, September 1945, 4–7.

23. Several but not all of the tunes played were issued on LP—Aircheck Records, Aircheck 31—in 1981. Johnson's name is not listed as one of the musicians, but his presence has been verified by Frederick Ramsey Jr. and by aural identification.

24. *Esquire's 1945 Jazz Book* (New York: A. S. Barnes, 1945), 117.

25. Leonard Feather, "Waller Concert Good Go Despite Politico," *Metronome*, May 1944, 33.

26. Pat Richardson, *Jazz Record*, May 1944, 10; "NAACP Gains in Jazz Recital," *Pittsburgh Courier*, April 8, 1944, 13; "Jazz to Benefit NCAP [sic]," *Variety*, March 29, 1944, 29.

27. Kappler, Wellstood, and Rouder, 50.

28. "James P. Does Fats Album for Decca," *Billboard*, December 23, 1944, 15.

29. Goldsmith, *Making People's Music*, 133.

30. *NY Herald Tribune*, February 11, 1945, 5.

31. "Records: Bach Album," *New York Times*, May 11, 1945, X5.

32. Roger Pryor Dodge, "On the Labels," *Record Changer*, October 1945, 33.

33. "Hot Jazz Series Mulled by Blue," *Variety*, May 10, 1944, 19.

34. Ernie Anderson, liner notes to *Eddie Condon—The Town Hall Concerts, Volume One*, Jazzology Records, JCECD-1001/1002, 1988, compact disc.

35. "In Honor of the Grand Old Master," *Baltimore Afro American*, July 1, 1944, 8.

36. "Condon Jive Invades Carnegie Hall, Likes It and Books 3 More Dates," *Variety*, October 18, 1944, 39.

37. Jax [John Lucas], "Best Hot Discs of 1944," *Down Beat*, January 1, 1945, 11.

38. Max Kaminsky and His Band, "Love Nest"/"Everybody Loves My Baby," Commodore 595, 78 rpm, and "Eccentric"/"Guess Who's in Town," Commodore 560, 78 rpm.

CHAPTER 25. PIED PIPER, 1944–1945

1. "I Thought I Heard," *Jazz Record*, June 1944, 2.
2. Bob Rusch, "Jack Lesberg," *Cadence*, June 1987, 11.
3. Max Kaminsky, *My Life in Jazz* (New York: Harper and Row, 1963), 157.
4. Rusch, "Jack Lesberg," 16.
5. Kaminsky, *My Life in Jazz*, 157–58.
6. David Gelman, interview with Mike Lipskin and Mark Borowsky, October 15, 2005.
7. Rusch, "Jack Lesberg," 16.
8. Ruth Reinhardt, "Random Ramblings from Rhythm Row," *Down Beat*, September 15, 1944, 2.
9. Orrin Keepnews and Bill Grauer Jr., *A Pictoral History of Jazz* (New York: Crown, 1955), 201.
10. Peggy Hart, "Dick Wellstood," *American Jazz Review*, March 1947, 3.
11. Kaminsky, *My Life in Jazz*, 158.
12. Rusch, "Jack Lesberg," 16.
13. "Hot Jazz on Record," *The Needle*, September 1944, 24.
14. Paul Nossiter to Michael Steinman, email note, February 1, 2012.
15. Kaminsky, *My Life in Jazz*, 156–62.
16. Jack Lesberg, to Scott Brown, personal communication, IAJRC convention, Rochelle Park, New Jersey, 1983.
17. James McGraw, "Remembering Rod Cless," *Jazz Record*, January 1945, 11.
18. "Jas P. Johnson Cuts for Decca," *Baltimore Afro American*, October 7, 1944, 8.
19. "Programs of the Week," *New York Times*, October 15, 1944, X5.
20. "Jazz at Carnegie Hall," *New York Times*, October 17, 1944, 19.
21. Ralph Berton, "Condon at Carnegie," *Jazz Record*, November 1944, 13.
22. "In Gala Earl Hall Opening Tonight at 7:30," *Columbia Daily Spectator*, October 6, 1944.
23. "Our Composers' Works Kick Off 6th War Loan," *Pittsburgh Courier*, November 18, 1944, 13.
24. Herman Rosenberg, "Manhattan Mélange," *Record Changer*, October 1944, 73.
25. "The Pied Piper" advertisement, *The Needle*, November 1944, 12.
26. Rosenberg, "Manhattan Mélange," 72.
27. "Rod Cless Passes Away," Editorial, *Jazz Session*, January–February 1945, 5; *Record Changer*, January 1945, 61.
28. "I Thought I Heard," *Jazz Record*, December 1944, 2.
29. "I Thought I Heard," *Jazz Record*, January 1945, 2; Carlton Brown, "On Records," unidentified clipping, February 27, 1945, 41.
30. *Record Changer*, January 1945, 61.
31. "Jam in Village," *Down Beat*, January 15, 1945, 4.
32. *New York Amsterdam News*, advertisement, January 20, 1945, 23.

33. Pied Piper invitation advertising card, JPJC, IJS.

34. "Jam in Village," *Down Beat*, January 15, 1945, 4.

35. *Record Changer*, March 1945, 29.

36. "Jazz and the Village Loses a Colorful Figure," *Down Beat*, August 12, 1946, 2.

37. Langston Hughes, "Here to Yonder—Greenwich Village Negroes," *Chicago Defender*, October 19, 1946, 14.

38. *New Orleans Times-Picayune*, January 7, 1945, 66, noted the concert was presented by the National Jazz Foundation.

39. Tony Middleton, introduction announcement, *The Second Esquire Concert*, Saga Records, SAGA 6924, 1974, LP.

40. Jean Knall, "Jazz Kings Top Second Concert," *New Orleans Times-Picayune*, January 18, 1945, 13.

41. "Concert with Armstrong," *Basin Street*, March 1945, 1–2.

42. "WNEW Lines up Stars for 'Swing Festival,'" *Variety*, January 31, 1945, 22.

43. "Show World Acts to Aid Bland Fund," *Pittsburgh Courier*, February 24, 1945, 21.

44. "'Le Jazz Hot' Makes Debut at Academy," *Philadelphia Tribune*, April 7, 1945, 15.

45. "Off the Cuff," *Billboard*, April 14, 1945, 24.

46. "Jazz Concert," *Evening Star*, April 15, 1945, 44.

CHAPTER 26. THE SLOW DECLINE, 1945–1946

1. *Esquire's 1945 Jazz Book*, 96.

2. Ester Zolott, to James P. Johnson, typewritten letter, July 23, 1945, JPJC, IJS.

3. The whereabouts of this bust are unknown. James P. Johnson, handwritten note, undated, JPJC, IIJS.

4. Federal tax returns, 1943, 1944, 1948, 1949, JPJC, IJS.

5. Smith and Hoefer, *Music on My Mind*, 233.

6. Rusch, "Jack Lesberg," 17.

7. George Lattimore, Carnegie Hall concert program, *Jazzfest and Pop Concert*, May 4, 1945.

8. Saerchinger, *International Who's Who in Music and Musical Gazetteer*, 115.

9. "Events and Happenings in the World of Music," *New York Times*, April 8, 1945, 43.

10. H. J. Harrison, *Jazz Record*, June 1945, 5–6.

11. "James P. Johnson Plays Piano at Carnegie Hall," *Variety*, May 9, 1945, 35.

12. Harrison, *Jazz Record*, 5–6.

13. "Escapading in Brooklyn with Tommy Watkins," *New York Amsterdam News*, May 12, 1945, B3.

14. "James Johnson 'Pop' Concert Is Mixed Music," *New York Amsterdam News*, May 12, 1945, A4.

15. Price, *What Do They Want*, 59.

16. Chauncey Northern, "In the Realm of Music," *New York Age*, May 12, 1954, 10.

17. "James P. Johnson Plays Piano at Carnegie Hall," *Variety*, May 9, 1945, 35.

18. "Pinkard Preps New Operetta," *Pittsburgh Courier*, July 14, 1945, 13.

19. "New Maceo Pinkard Play to Open Soon," *New York Amsterdam News*, June 23, 1945, 7B.
20. "Radio Reviews," *Variety*, October 3, 1945, 48.
21. James P. Johnson, undated typewritten script for radio broadcast, JPJC, IJS.
22. "Opera and Concert Programs," *New York Times*, October 21, 1945.
23. George W. Lattimore, "James P. Johnson Now Booking 1946–47 Concert Tour," promotional brochure.
24. Ernest Anderson, "The Master Jazz Pianist James P. Johnson," typewritten letter press release, undated, JPJC, IJS.
25. "James P. Johnson, Jazz Pianist, Heard," *New York Times*, October 26, 1945, 17.
26. Lattimore, promotional brochure.
27. Lewis Eaton, "James P. Johnson at Town Hall," *Jazz Record*, November 1945, 12.
28. Barbara Hodgkins, "Indefatigable Condon and J. P. Give Concerts Again," *Metronome*, December 1945, 58.
29. "James P. Johnson Wows 'Em!," *American Jazz Review*, November 1945, 1.
30. "Concert Poll," *American Jazz Review*, April 1946, 7.
31. "James P. Johnson Hit in N. Y. Jazz Concert," *Variety*, October 31, 1945, 48.
32. *New York Age*, October 27, 1945, 10.
33. "Gilbert-Johnson Team," *Chicago Defender*, November 17, 1945, 16; Negro Actors Guild of America newsletter, December 1, 1945, 3.
34. "Another Talent," *Negro Star*, December 7, 1945, 1.
35. "Blue Note Makes Concert History," *American Jazz Review*, January 1946, 5; "Blue Note at Town Hall," *Jazz Record*, January 1946, 18.
36. Brant Inn contract, JPJC, IJC.
37. Radio script, JPJC, IJS.
38. "New Yorker Mag Spots Jazz Pianist," *Pittsburgh Courier*, January 19, 1946, 19; "James P. Johnson to Be New-Yorkerized," *Los Angeles Tribune*, January 19, 1946, 19.
39. Al Rose, *I Remember Jazz* (Baton Rouge: Louisiana State University Press, 1987), 68, 70.
40. Billy Austin, "Society in Jamaica," *New York Amsterdam News*, February 9, 1946, 18.

CHAPTER 27. NEW PATRONS, 1946–1949

1. *Billboard*, advertisement, March 9, 1946, 34.
2. "Krupa Jazz Trio Makes Town Hall Jump for Condon," *American Jazz Review*, May 1946, 7.
3. "Carnegie 'Pops' Condon Excites Record Crowd," *American Jazz Review*, May 1946, 1.
4. "Negro Art Cavalcade Sunday in New York," *Chicago Defender*, May 25, 1946, 4.
5. Buller, "Toronto," *Metronome*, July 1946, 43.
6. "Harland (Hart) Wheeler," Toronto Musicians Association website, tma149.ca, accessed May 23, 2020.
7. Maggy Fisher to James P. Johnson, typewritten note, July 2, 1946, JPJC, IJS.
8. *Variety*, advertisement, August 7, 1946, 44.
9. "Around the Town," *Jazz Record*, August 1946, 17.
10. Peggy Hart, "N. Y. Jazz Club Holds 1st Bash," *American Jazz Review*, October 1946, 1.

11. Johnson, handwritten notes for radio programs, JPJC, IJS.

12. Will Marion Cook, "Masterpieces of Negro Songs," developed by James P. Johnson, typewritten outline, undated, JPJC, IJS.

13. Howard Taubman, "Records: From Italy," *New York Times*, November 3, 1946, 71.

14. Lattimore, promotional brochure.

15. "James P. Stricken, Condition Improving," *Down Beat*, November 18, 1946, 8.

16. "I Ran Into," *Jazz Record*, November 1946, 2.

17. "Popularity Poll," *American Jazz Review*, January 1947, 4.

18. "Jazzmen for March 1 Bash at Town Hall," *Down Beat*, February 26, 1947, 4.

19. "Bechet, Foster to Get Awards at T.H.," *American Jazz Review*, March 1947, 4.

20. George Avakian, *Jazz Record*, April 1947, 7.

21. Dolan, *Inventing Entertainment*, 157.

22. Sam Meltzer, *Jazz Record*, April 1947, 23.

23. Century 4001, 78 rpm.

24. Avakian, *Jazz Record*, 34.

25. Mura Dehn, "A Few Words," *Jazz Record*, February 1947, 22.

26. Mura Dehn, "Record Dance Guide," *Jazz Record*, May 1947, 33.

27. "Mura Dehn's Jazz Dance Concert," *Jazz Record*, April 1947, 25.

28. "Dizzy Plays for Dance Recital," *Down Beat*, May 7, 1947, 1.

29. "To Unite Dance-Jazz on Concert Stage," *Down Beat*, June 18, 1947, 15.

30. Marshall Stearns, "The Institute of Jazz Studies," *Record Changer*, July-August 1953, 7.

31. "Inside Stuff-Radio," *Variety*, May 7, 1947, 48.

32. "Concert—Chicago and Clinton," *Hamiltonews*, May 1, 1947, 1, 3.

33. W. A. Robbins, "Jazz in Retrospect," *Hamiltonews*, May 8, 1947, 7.

34. "Fats Waller Memorial Week Opens on May 18," *Pittsburgh Courier*, May 17, 1947, 16.

35. Associated Musicians of Greater New York contract, June 2, 1947, JPJC, IJS.

36. "A Jazz-Boat on the Hudson River," *New York Times*, June 1, 1947; "Rebirth of Basin Street Jazz—In Starlight on the Hudson," *The Sun*, June 9, 1947, 3.

37. Fell and Vinding, *Stride*, 190.

38. "Album Reviews," *Billboard*, October 30, 1948, 36.

39. *Billboard*, advertisement, January 24, 1948.

40. George Frazier, "Jocks, Jukes and Discs," *Variety*, June 18, 1947, 40.

41. Bob Arthur, "Let the Good Times Roll—An Impression of Chippie Hill," *Playback*, February 1950, 4.

42. Al Monroe, "Swinging the News," *Chicago Defender*, June 21, 1947, 10.

43. "'Meet Miss Jones' with Star Cast Is Slated for Broadway This Fall," *Chicago Defender*, October 4, 1947, 17.

44. "'Meet Miss Jones' Amusing Musical at Elks Theater," advertisement, *New York Amsterdam News*, November 15, 1947, 23.

45. *New York Age*, November 29, 1947, 5.

46. "Broadway's 'Meet Miss Jones' Another 'Lucasta,'" *Chicago Defender*, December 6, 1947, 18.

47. Swedish Bunk Johnson Society, http://www.fellers.se/Bunk/Welcome.html, accessed February 26, 2019.

48. "Bessie 'Salute' for January 1," *Down Beat*, December 17, 1947, 1.
49. "Present Long Lost Bessie Smith Picture on Broadway," *Chicago Defender*, January 10, 1948, 8.
50. "Blues for Bessie Due at Town Hall," *New York Amsterdam News*, December 27, 1947, 11; "Programs of the Week," *New York Times*, December 28, 1947, X8; "Memorial Concert Honors Bessie Smith," *New York Times*, January 2, 1948, 14.
51. "Broadway to Harlem Notes," *Chicago Defender*, May 8, 1948, 8.
52. "Sam Price to Honor Columnist April 27," *New York Amsterdam News*, April 17, 1948, 25.
53. Mayfair Music Corporation, statement of royalties, period ending June 30, 1948, JPJC, IJS.
54. "Jamaica Notes by Billy Austin," *New York Amsterdam News*, November 27, 1948, 25.
55. "Jazz Jubilee," *Variety*, April 21, 1948, 29.
56. Todd Bryant Weeks, "A Drummer Speaks: Bob Thompson's Musical Memories," *Allegro*, Vol. CVIII, No. 4, Internet Archive, accessed February 19, 2018.
57. Allen, *Hendersonia*, 461.
58. Central Plaza and Stuyvesant Casino post cards, 1948–1949, collection of Scott Brown.
59. "Jazz Parade," *Record Changer*, September 1948, 4.
60. Bob Harrington, "When James P. Was King," *After Beat*, January 1971, 5.
61. *Trenton Evening Times*, Advertisement for Jazz Society of Trenton, November 19, 1948, 28; "Jazz Society's Program Sunday Features Clayton," *Trenton Evening Times*, November 17, 1948, 28.
62. In 1950 Kratka started the groundbreaking Music Minus One series of recordings that allowed musicians to play along with a recorded band minus their instrument. He also later founded other labels including Inner City and Classic Jazz.
63. "Program Sunday By Jazz Society," *Trenton Evening Times*, January 12, 1949, 3.
64. Irv Kratka, phone interview with Scott Brown, August 23, 2015.
65. Johnson, *Jazz Record*, 13–14.
66. Blesh and Janis, *They All Played Ragtime*, 205.
67. "Jazz Pianist Feted—Dixieland Concert Given for Willie (The Lion) Smith," *New York Times*, November 26, 1956, 55.
68. Floyd Levin, "I Remember James P.," *RagTimes*, November 1970, 4–6.
69. Floyd Levin, *Classic Jazz* (Berkeley: University of California Press, 2000), 101.
70. Lillie Mae Johnson McIntyre, interview with Scott Brown, November 1981.

CHAPTER 28. *SUGAR HILL*—THE LAST INNOVATION, 1949–1950

1. Luise M. Sillcox to Walter Brooks and Annemarie Kantz, typewritten letter, December 24, 1947, Flournoy Miller Collection, Schomberg Center.
2. Robert B. Berger, Teaneck, to Flournoy Miller, Los Angeles, December 3, 1948, typewritten transcript, Miller Collection, Schomberg Center.
3. Flournoy Miller, Los Angeles, to William Friedlander, New York, undated, Miller collection.
4. James P. Johnson, to Flournoy Miller, Los Angeles, telegram, Miller collection.

5. Robert D. Berger, to Flournoy Miller, telegram, Miller collection.

6. James P. Johnson, to Jack Mills, transcript in the hand of James P. Johnson, April 18, 1949, JPJC, IJS.

7. Mills Music contract with James P. Johnson, JPJC, IJS.

8. "'Moneymoon' in Rehearsal," *Pittsburgh Courier*, April 30, 1949, 19.

9. Mills Music, contract with James P. Johnson and Flournoy Miller, JPJC, IJS.

10. "Negro Revue to Bow June 29 in H' Wood," *Variety*, June 15, 1949, 51.

11. "'Sugar Hill' Handling Novel," *Los Angeles Times*, July 7, 1949.

12. "The Playgoer," *Sugar Hill*, Las Palmas Theater program.

13. "'Sugar Hill' Holds Prem," *Pittsburgh Courier*, July 16, 1949, 18.

14. John L. Scott, "'Sugar Hill' Novel Stage Musical Offering at Las Palmas Theater," *Los Angeles Times*, July 14, 1949.

15. Hal Holly, "'Sugar Hill' Draws Raves but Leaves Holly Chilled," *Down Beat*, August 26, 1949, 8.

16. Paul V. Coates, "'Sugar Hill' Not Too Rich," *Mirror News*, July 13, 1949, 34.

17. "'Sugar Hill' Has Music Comedy and Ultra Class," *Chicago Defender*, July 16, 1949, 25.

18. Harry Levette, "'Sugar Hill' Play Is Called 'Fine Package,'" *New York Amsterdam News* July 30, 1949, 19.

19. "Out of Town Review," *Billboard*, July 23, 1949, 40.

20. "Estimates for Last Week," *Variety*, July 20, 1949, 51.

21. Las Palmas Theater box office statement, week ending July 23, 1949, JPJC, IJS; "'Kate' Continues to Soar in LA, 541/2G; 'Hill' 7G," *Variety*, August 3, 1949, 50.

22. Mike Molony, "Cinemeandering," *Chateaugay Record*, August 5, 1949, 6.

23. "'Sugar Hill' Set to Open in Chicago," *Variety*, August 3, 1949, 49.

24. "'Sugar Hill' Delays Skedded Chi Start," *Variety*, August 24, 1949, 57.

25. "Miss Healey May Bring 'Sugar Hill' to B'Way," *Variety*, August 31, 1949, 57.

26. "'Finian's' $40,600, 'Sugar' 7G, L.A.," *Variety*, October 12, 1949, 57.

27. "Negro Revue to Bow June 29 in H' Wood," *Variety*, June 15, 1949, 51.

28. Dave Dexter, "Vine at Sunset," *Capital News*, August 1949, 13.

29. "Billy Rowe's Notebook," *Pittsburgh Courier*, August 20, 1949, 18.

30. Owen Callin, "Record Rendezvous," *Bakersfield Californian*, August 27, 1949, 8.

31. "'Sugar Hill' Is Extended to Sat., Oct. 8th," *Los Angeles Sentinel*, September 29, 1949, B6.

32. Unsigned, undated letter, Flournoy Miller collection.

33. "CRC Isn't Missing One Original—Cast Show Bet," *Variety*, August 17, 1949, 47.

34. "Record Reviews from Bach to Bop," *Los Angeles Sentinel*, November 10, 1949, B4.

35. Levin, *Classic Jazz*, 99, 101.

36. Levin, *RagTimes*, 4–6.

37. American Federation of Musicians contract, Floyd Levin, employer, and Albert Nicholas, May 21, 1949, JPJC, IJS.

38. Derek Coller, *Jess Stacy: The Quiet Man of Jazz* (New Orleans: Jazzology Press, 1997), 135.

39. "Ertegun Concert to Spot Watters," *Down Beat*, June 17, 1949, 3.

40. "On the West Coast," *Playback*, July 1949, 9.

41. Hal Holly, "Johnson Puts on Great Show at Coast Concert," *Down Beat*, July 15, 1949, 9.

CHAPTER 29. FINAL YEARS, 1950-1955

1. "Jas. P. Johnson Suffers Attack," *New York Age*, September 24, 1955, 4.
2. "Programs of the Week," *New York Times*, January 22, 1950, 6X; Dan Burley, "Clothesline," *New York Age*, February 4, 1950, 5.
3. Central Plaza advertisement card.
4. Rea and Payson Clark, to James P. Johnson, July 7, 1951, transcript in hand of Rea Clark, JPJC, IJS.
5. Bob Maltz Presents post card, Stuyvesant Casino, June 9, 1950.
6. "Music Notes," *New York Times*, June 23, 1950, 37.
7. Julius J. Adams, "Men Piano Players Rate High in Talent," *New York Amsterdam News*, October 15, 1949, 27.
8. "'Daddy' of the Piano on Disc," *Chicago Defender*, May 27, 1950, 21.
9. *Negro News Letter*, Washington, DC, December 10, 1951, 1.
10. Carter Harman, "Records: Jazz—Revival of Interest in Dixieland Style and Swing Noted in Current Trend," *New York Times*, May 14, 1950, 116.
11. David C. Whitney, "Music on Records," *Rockford Register-Republic*, August 15, 1950, 14. This review was syndicated.
12. "Records: Mahler," *New York Times*, August 5, 1951, 82.
13. "With Rowe," *Richmond Times-Dispatch*, July 9, 1950, D-9.
14. The 1949 78rpm Paramount release is confused often as an original Paramount release from the 1920s. Johnson never recorded for the original Paramount label.
15. Bucklin Moon, "Records Noted," *Record Changer*, September 1949, 17.
16. Charles Edward Smith, "That Ragtime Time," *New York Times*, October 15, 1950, BR4.
17. Paul P. Schriebman, Hollywood, California, to Flournoy E. Miller, Los Angeles, typewritten letter, January 3, 1952, Miller Collection.
18. Flournoy Miller to James P. Johnson, telegram, March 25, 1950, Miller Collection.
19. Joe Glaser to Flournoy Miller, typewritten letter, September 5, 1950, Miller Collection.
20. Julius Mattfeld, New York, to Flournoy Miller, Los Angeles, February 2, 1953, typewritten letter, Miller Collection.
21. Samuel M. Ostroff, New York, to Flournoy Miller, Los Angeles, typewritten letter, June 23, 1953, Miller Collection.
22. "Louis Jordan Sounds Thrill 800 in Chicago," *Chicago Defender*, April 6, 1957, 8.
23. William B. Friedlander, New York, typewritten letter to Flournoy E. Miller, Los Angeles, August 28, 1957, Miller Collection.
24. All letters James P. Johnson to Flournoy Miller, in the hand of Johnson, Miller Collection.
25. Lillie Johnson, New York, to Flournoy and Bessie Miller, Los Angeles, May 16, 1950, transcript in hand of Lillie Johnson, Miller Collection.
26. Singer, *Black and Blue*, 325–26.
27. Lillie Mae Johnson to Prof. Johnson, transcript in hand of Lillie Mae Johnson, September 9, 1951, JPJC, IJS; *Down Beat*, June 29, 1951, 13.
28. "Louis Wins Again," *Record Changer*, May 1951, 3–5.

29. Lillie Johnson, New York, to Flournoy Miller, Los Angeles, May 19, 1951, transcript in the hand of Lillie Johnson, Miller collection.

30. Sharon A. Pease, "Johnson, Now Ailing, Sustained by Royalties," *Down Beat*, May 20, 1953, 20.

31. Paige VanVorst, "Little Brother Montgomery," *Jazz Beat*, January 2007, 30.

32. Hugues Panassie to Lillie Mae Johnson, typewritten letter, October 15, 1951, JPJC, IJS.

33. James P. Johnson tax return, undated, probably from around 1950, JPJC, IJS.

34. "Jazz Concert," flier, JPJC, IJS.

35. "Willie 'The Lion' Smith Plays Musical Compositions by James P. Johnson," Blue Circle Records, 1500–33, 10" LP.

36. "Town Hall, N.Y., Benefit Set for James P. Johnson," *Variety*, September 16, 1953, 43.

37. "Benny Frenchie," *Record Changer*, December 1953, 16.

38. "James P. Johnson Alive; Report of Death Regretted," *Down Beat*, May 19, 1954, 1.

39. Smith and Hoefer, *Music on My Mind*, 257.

40. Lawrence T. Carter, *Eubie Blake* (Detroit: Balamp Publishing, 1979), 71.

41. "Music Notes," *New York Times*, October 22, 1954, 23.

42. Smith and Hoefer, *Music on My Mind*, 257.

43. "Jas. P. Johnson Suffers Attack," *New York Age*, September 24, 1955, 4.

44. Rob Roy, "James Johnson, Unsung Great of Songwriting, Scribe Says," *New York Age*, November 12, 1955, 9.

45. City of New York, Department of Health, Bureau of Records and Statistics, certificate of death, no. 156-55411375, November 23, 1955.

46. "James P. Johnson, Jazz Pianist Dies—Well-Known Performer on Radio and Records Was a Prolific Composer," *New York Times*, November 18, 1955, 25.

47. "Obituaries—James P. Johnson," *Variety*, November 23, 1955, 63.

48. "J. P. Johnson dies in N.Y.," *Billboard*, November 26, 1955, 17.

49. Hammond, *Down Beat*, 12.

50. Harrington, "When James P. Was King," 5.

BIBLIOGRAPHY

ARCHIVAL DOCUMENTS

Babcock and Johnson, *New-Brunswick Directory for 1874-'75* (New Brunswick, NJ: Fredonian Office, 1874) 130.

Bayview—New York Bay Cemetery grave 7, row 15, H No.

Boyd's Jersey City and Hoboken Directory, 1905-6 (Jersey City, NJ: Boyd's Directory, 1905).

Certificate of Death, Bureau of Records and Statistics, Dept of Health, City of New York, cert. No. 156-57-411385.

City of Newark, Bureau of vital statistics, record of marriage, certificate No. 5680, June 29, 1951.

Crains' Market Data Book and Directory, 2nd Ed. (Chicago: G. D. Crain, Jr., 1922), 319.

F. Killenberger's New Brunswick City Directory (New Brunswick, NJ: Julius Heidingsfeld), 1877-78, 1886, 1890, 1891, 1893, 1896, 1897, 1899-1900, 1901-1902.

First Reformed Church, New Brunswick, NJ, church register, no.430, 131.

Giles R. Wright, *Afro-Americans in New Jersey—A Short History* (Trenton: New Jersey Historical Commission, Department of State, 1988), 19.

J. H. Mulholland, compiler, *New Brunswick City and Business Directory, 1888* (York, PA: Evening Dispatch Print, 1888), 140.

James P. Johnson, US passport, British passport control stamp March 3, 1923.

Jarratt's Hotel, Petersburg, Virginia. *A guide to the fortifications and battlefields around Petersburg: with a splendid map from actual surveys made by the US Engineer Department.* Petersburg, VA: J. B. Ege's Printing House, 1869.

Jersey City School Register, School #9 (Trenton: MacCrellish and Quigley, 1902-03, 1903-04).

Josephine Thompson, New York (New York) Department of Health, Death Certificates (Manhattan, New York), 1919-1948 [Vol. 27-28], Cert. No. 13001-14000.

Library of Congress, *Catalog of Copyright Entries*.

Minutes of the General Assembly of the Presbyterian Church in the United States, Presbyterian Committee of Publication (Richmond, VA: Whittet and Shepperson, 1896).

New Brunswick City Directory, 1890 (New Brunswick, NJ: J. Heidingsfield, printer and bookbinder, 1890).

New Brunswick Times, *The City of New Brunswick: Its History, Its Homes, and Its Industries* (New Brunswick, NJ: Times Publishing, 1909).

New Jersey Department of Health, Bureau of Vital Statistics.

New Jersey state census population schedule, 1885, 1895.

New Jersey, Abstract of Wills, 1670–1817, New Jersey State Archives, New Jersey, Published Archives Series, First Series (Trenton, NJ: John L. Murphy).

New York Department of Health, death certificates (Manhattan, New York), 1919–1948, [Vol. 27–28], cert no. 13001–14000, certificate no. 13659.

New York passenger lists, 1820–1957, ancestry.com.

New York State Archives, Albany, State Population Census Schedules, 1925; Election District: 46; Assembly District: 05; City: New York; County: New York; Page: 6.

Pennsylvania, Philadelphia marriage index, 1885–1951, Clerk of the Orphans court, Philadelphia, Pennsylvania.

Petersburg (Virginia) Hustings Court Register of Free Negroes and Mulattoes, 1854, LVA Microfilm 73, Nathl. Harrison entry, document 3.

Petersburg (Virginia) Hustings Court Register of Free Negroes and Mulattoes,1839–1850, LVA Microfilm 73, Jones entries, 1845–1850.

Petersburg and Colonial Heights Virginia City Directory, 1870/71, Mat [sic] Harrison entry, LVA Book F234.P4 A18.

QRS Dealers' Complete Reference Catalogue, complete to June 30, 1922, The QRS Music Company, Chicago, IL.

QRS hand-played music rolls catalogue, 1918.

Richard Edwards, *Industries of New Jersey*, vol. 4 (New York: New York Historical Publishing Co., 1882), 9.

Sanborn fire map, New Brunswick, New Jersey, 1895.

Sanborn map, Jersey City, New Jersey, 1908, 5th ward.

Seventh Census of the United States, 1850, Census Place: North Brunswick, Middlesex, New Jersey; Roll 455; Page 283a.

Toledo Conservatory of Music and Dramatic Art Prospectus, 1920.

Tone Picture Recitals, flier for lecture and piano recitals by Jan Chiapusso, undated.

Trow's General Directory of New York City (New York: R. L. Polk and Co., 1916, 1917, 1918, 1921–1922).

Universal Music Rolls, Bulletin for October 1917, 3–7.

US Federal Census population schedule, 1850, 1860, 1870, 1880, 1900, 1910, 1920, 1930, 1940.

US WWI Draft Registration Cards, 1917–1918.

Virginia Auditor of Public Accounts, Personal Property Tax Books, City of Petersburg, 1857–1859, LVA Microfilm 814, Nat. Harrison, No. 29, Document 6.

Vocalstyle Company of Cincinnati, 1916 catalogue title page.

BOOKS

Abbott, Lynn, and Doug Seroff. *The Original Blues*. Jackson: University Press of Mississippi, 2017.

Abbott, Lynn, and Doug Seroff. *Out of Sight: The Rise of African American Popular Music 1889–1895*. Jackson: University Press of Mississippi, 2002.

Albertson, Chris. *Bessie*. New Haven, CT: Yale University Press, 2003.

Allen, Walter C. *Hendersonia: The Music of Fletcher Henderson and His Musicians*. Highland Park, NJ: Walter C. Allen, 1973.

Allen, William Francis, Charles Pickard Ware, and Lucy McKim Garrison. *Slave Songs of the United States*. New York: A. Simpson and Co., 1867; reprint, New York: Dover, 1995.

Anderson, Jervis. *This Was Harlem*. New York: Farrar, Straus and Giroux, 1982.

Badger, Reid. *A Life in Ragtime*. New York: Oxford, 1995.

Baldwin, James. *Go Tell It on the Mountain*. 1952; reprint, New York: Vintage, 2013.

Bechet, Sidney. *Treat It Gentle*. New York: Twayne Publishers, 1960.

Berlin, Edward. *King of Ragtime*. New York: Oxford University Press, 2016.

Berlin, Edward. *Reflections and Research on Ragtime*. Brooklyn: Brooklyn College Conservatory of Music, 1987.

Berresford, Mark. *That's Got 'Em!—The Life and Music of Wilbur Sweatman*. Jackson: University Press of Mississippi, 2010.

Blesh, Rudi, and Harriet Janis. *They All Played Ragtime*. 4th ed. New York: Oak Publications, 1971.

Bradford, Perry. *Born with the Blues*. New York: Oak Publications, 1965.

Brooks, Tim. *Lost Sounds*. Urbana: University of Illinois Press, 2004.

Burley, Dan. *Dan Burley's Original Handbook of Harlem Jive*. New York: D. Burley, 1944.

Bushell, Garvin. *Jazz from the Beginning*. New York: Da Capo, 1998.

Carter, Marva Griffin. *Swing Along*. New York: Oxford University Press, 2008.

Charyn, Jerome. *Gangsters and Gold Diggers*. New York: Thunder's Mouth Press, 2003.

Condon, Eddie. *We Called It Music*. New York: Da Capo, 1992.

Cotter, John C. *The Negro in Music in St. Louis*. Masters thesis, Washington University, Department of Music, St. Louis, MO, June 1959.

Courlander, Harold. *Negro Folk Music, USA*. New York: Columbia University Press, 1963.

Dance, Stanley. Liner notes to *James P. Johnson—Father of the Stride Piano*. Columbia CL-1780, 1962, LP.

Dance Stanley. *The World of Duke Ellington*. New York: Da Capo, 1970.

Dance, Stanley. *The World of Earl Hines*. New York: Scribner's, 1977.

Davie, Maurice R. *Negroes in American Society*. New York: McGraw-Hill, 1949.

Dietsche, Bob. *Tatum's Town*. Brooklyn, NY: Bobson Press, 2016.

Dodge, Roger Prior. *Hot Jazz and Jazz Dance*. New York: Oxford University Press, 1995.

Dolan, Brian. *Inventing Entertainment*. Lanham, MD: Rowman and Littlefield, 2009.

Egan, Bill. *Florence Mills: Harlem Jazz Queen*. Lanham, MD: Scarecrow Press, 2004.

Epstein, Dena J. *Sinful Tunes and Spirituals*. Urbana: University of Illinois Press, 2003 [1977].

Fell, John L., and Terkild Vinding. *Stride*. Lanham, MD: Scarecrow Press, 1999.

Foreman, Ronald Clifford, Jr. *Jazz and Race Records, 1920–1932*. PhD dissertation, University of Illinois, 1969.

Foster, Pops, and Tom Stoddard. *Pops Foster*. Berkeley: University of California Press, 1971.

French, Kenneth. *Images of America: Railroads of Hoboken and Jersey City*. Columbia, SC: Arcadia, 2002.

Friedman, Ryan Jay. *Hollywood's African American Films: The Transition to Sound*. New Brunswick, NJ: Rutgers University Press, 2011.

Gannett, William Channing. *Educational Commission for Freedmen—1st Annual Report*. In Epstein.

Gilbert, David. *The Product of Our Souls*. Chapel Hill: University of North Carolina Press, 2015.
Goldberg, Isaac. *Tin Pan Alley*. New York: Frederick Unger, 1930.
Green, Alfred. *Rhythm Is My Beat: Jazz Guitar Great Freddie Green and the Count Basie Sound*. Lanham, MD: Rowman and Littlefield, 2015.
Hadlock, Richard. *Jazz Masters of the Twenties*. New York: Macmillan, 1965.
Hajdu, David. *Lush Life: A Biography of Billy Strayhorn*. New York: Farrar, Straus and Giroux, 1996.
Handy, D. Antoinette. *Black Women in American Bands and Orchestras*. Lanham, MD: Scarecrow Press, 1981.
Handy, William C. *Father of the Blues*. New York: Macmillan, 1941; Da Capo, 1969.
Harrison, Max. *A Jazz Retrospect*. Boston: Crescendo Publishing, 1976. Reprint of "James P. Johnson" from *Jazz Monthly*.
Haslam, Gerald W., and Janice E. Haslam. *In Thought and Action: The Enigmatic Life of S. I. Hayakawa*. Lincoln, NE: UNP-Bison Books, 2011.
Hasse, John Edward. *Beyond Category: The Life and Genius of Duke Ellington*. New York: Da Capo, 1993.
Hill, Constance Valis. *Brotherhood in Rhythm: The Jazz Tap Dancing of the Nicholas Brothers*. New York: Oxford University Press, 2000.
Hill, H. Solomon. *The Negro in New Brunswick, New Jersey—As Revealed by a Study of 100 Families*. Master's thesis, Drew University, Madison, NJ, 1942.
Hodes, Art, and Chadwick Hansen. *Selections from the Gutter*. Berkeley: University of California Press, 1977.
Howland, John. *Ellington Uptown: Duke Ellington, James P. Johnson, and the Birth of Concert Jazz*. Ann Arbor: University of Michigan Press, 2009.
Huggins, Nathan Irvin. *Harlem Renaissance*. New York: Oxford University Press, 1971.
Hughes, Langston. *The Big Sea*. New York: Hill and Wang, 1940.
Jablonski, Edward, and Lawrence D. Stewart. *The Gershwin Years*. Garden City, NY: Doubleday, 1973.
Jasen, David A. *Recorded Ragtime, 1897–1958*. Hamden, CT: Archon Books, 1973.
Jasen, David A., and Gene Jones. *Speadin' Rhythm Around*. New York: Schirmer, 1998.
Jasen, David A., and Gene Jones. *That American Rag*. New York: Schirmer, 2000.
Jasen, David A., and Trebor Jay Tichenor. *Rags and Ragtime: A Musical History*. New York: Seabury Press, 1978.
Johnson, James Weldon. *The Autobiography of an Ex-Colored Man*. New York: Knopf, 1927; Avon Books, 1965.
Johnson, James Weldon. *Black Manhattan*. New York: Atheneum, 1977. Originally James Weldon Johnson, 1930.
Johnson, James Weldon. *The Book of American Negro Spirituals*. New York: Viking Press, 1925.
Jones, Mark R. *Doin' the Charleston*. Charleston, SC: East Atlantic Publishing, 2013.
Katz, Bernard. *The Social Implications of Early Negro Music in the United States*. New York: Arno Press, 1969.
Kelley, Robin D. G. *Thelonious Monk*. New York: Free Press, 2009.
Keepnews, Orrin, and Bill Grauer, Jr. *A Pictoral History of Jazz*. New York: Crown, 1955.

Kimball, Robert, and William Bolcom. *Reminiscing with Sissle and Blake*. New York: Viking Press, 1973.
Kirkeby, Ed. *Ain't Misbehavin'*. New York: Dodd, Mead, 1966.
Knowles, Mark. *The Wicked Waltz and Other Scandalous Dances*. Jefferson, NC: McFarland, 2009.
Lees, Gene. *Leader of the Band: The Life of Woody Herman*. New York: Oxford University Press, 1995.
Lester, James. *Too Marvelous for Words: The Life and Genius of Art Tatum*. New York: Oxford University Press, 1994.
Lomax, Alan. *Mister Jelly Roll*. Berkeley: University of California Press, 1950.
Lyttleton, Humphrey. *The Best of Jazz: From Basin Street to Harlem*. New York: Taplinger, 1973.
Machlin, Paul S. *Stride: The Music of Fats Waller*. Boston: Twayne Publisher, 1985.
Mezzrow, Milton "Mezz." *Really the Blues*. New York: Random House, 1946.
Milan, Jon. *Images of America: Detroit*. Charleston, SC: Arcadia, 2009.
Miller, A. P. *The Black Man's Burden*. 1899.
Osofsky, Gilbert. *Harlem: The Making of a Ghetto*. Chicago: Ivan R. Dee, 1996; originally HarperCollins, 1966.
Parrish, Lydia. *Slave Songs of the Georgia Sea Islands*. New York: Creative Age Press, 1942.
Pastras, Phil. *Dead Man Blues*. Berkeley: University of California Press, 2001.
Pietrusza, David. *Rothstein*. New York: Basic Books, 2011.
Pinsker, Robert. *James P. Johnson: The Piano Rolls of His Own Compositions, 1917–1927*. Riverside, CA: James P. Johnson Foundation, 2003.
Pollack, Howard. *George Gershwin: His Life and Work*. Berkeley: University of California Press, 2006.
Pollitzer, William S. *The Gullah People and Their African Heritage*. Athens: University of Georgia Press, 1999.
Reid, Grant Harper. *Rhythm for Sale*. North Charleston, SC: CreateSpace, 2013.
Rogers, J. A. "Jazz at Home." In *The New Negro*, Alain Locke, ed. New York: Atheneum, 1977. © originally Albert and Charles Boni, 1925.
Rose, Al. *Eubie Blake*. New York: Schirmer, 1979.
Rosenbaum, Art. *Shout Because You're Free*. Athens: University of Georgia Press, 1998.
Saerchinger, Cesar. *International Who's Who in Music and Musical Gazetteer*. New York: Current Literature Publishing, 1918.
Sales, Grover. *Jazz: America's Classical Music*. Boston: Da Capo, 1992.
Sampson, Henry T. *Blacks in Blackface*. Lanham, MD: Scarecrow Press, 2014.
Schafer, William J., and Johannnes Riedel. *The Art of Ragtime*. New York: Da Capo, 1977.
Schuller, Gunther. *Early Jazz*. New York: Oxford University Press, 1968.
Shapiro, Nat, and Nat Hentoff. *Hear Me Talkin' to Ya*. New York: Dover Publications, 1966. Originally Rinehart and Company, 1955.
Shipton, Alyn. *Fats Waller: His Life and Times*. New York: Universe Books, 1988.
Singer, Barry. *Black and Blue: The Life and Lyrics of Andy Razaf*. New York: Schirmer, 1992.
Smith, Charles Edward. *Jazz* (First Series), June 1942.
Smith, Willie "The Lion," and George Hoefer. *Music on My Mind*. New York: Da Capo, 1964.

Southern, Eileen. *The Music of Black Americans*. New York: Norton, 1971.

Speck, William D. *Images of America: Toledo: A History in Architecture 1890–1914*. Charleston, SC: Arcadia, 2002.

Stearns, Marshall. *The Story of Jazz*. London: Oxford, 1958.

Stearns, Marshall, and Jean Sterns. *Jazz Dance: The Story of American Vernacular Dance*. New York: Da Capo, 1994.

Stevens, Frank. *Jersey City of Today*. Review Special, 1910. Jersey City: reprint, Bergen Historic Books, Robert D. Griffin, 1996.

Stewart, Rex. *Jazz Masters of the 30s*. New York: Da Capo, 1972.

Stuckey, Sterling. *Slave Culture*. New York: Oxford University Press, 1987.

Sudhalter, Richard. *Lost Chords*. New York: Oxford University Press, 1999.

Sutton, Allan. *Race Records and the American Recording Industry, 1919–1945*. Denver, CO: Mainspring Press, 2016.

Sutton, Allan. *Recording the Twenties*. Denver: Mainspring Press, 2008.

Taylor, Yuval, and Jake Austen. *Darkest America*. New York: W. W. Norton, 2012.

Thomas, Bob. *Astaire: The Man, The Dancer*. New York: St. Martin's Press, 1984.

Thurman, Wallace. *The Blacker the Berry*. New York: Macmillan, 1970; originally Macaulay, 1929.

Tichener, Trebor Jay. *Ragtime Rarities: Complete Original Music for 63 Piano Rags*. New York: Dover, 1975.

Tucker, Mark. *Ellington: The Early Years*. Chicago: University of Illinois Press, 1991.

Vance, Joel. *Fats Waller: His Life and Times*. Chicago: Contemporary Books, 1977.

Van Hoogstraten, Nicholas. *Lost Broadway Theaters*. New York: Princeton Architectural Press, 1997.

Waldo, Terry. *This Is Ragtime*. New York: Hawthorn Books, 1976.

Wall, John P. *The Chronicles of New Brunswick, New Jersey 1667–1931*. New Brunswick, NJ: Thatcher-Anderson, 1931.

Wall, John P., and Harold E. Pickersgill. *History of Middlesex County, New Jersey 1664–1920*. Vol 1. New York and Chicago: Lewis Historical Publishing, 1921.

Waller, Maurice, and Anthony Calabrese. *Fats Waller*. New York: Schirmer, 1977.

Waters, Ethel, with Charles Samuels. *His Eye Is on the Sparrow*. New York: Jove, 1979, originally Doubleday, 1950.

Wilkerson, Isabel. *The Warmth of Other Suns*. New York: Vantage Books, 2010.

Wilson, John S. "Introduction." In Robert Kimball and Alfred Simon, *The Gershwins*. New York: Atheneum, 1973.

Wodehouse, Artis. "Tracing Gershwin's Piano Rolls." In Wayne Schneider, ed., *The Gershwin Style*. New York: Oxford University Press, 1999.

Wright, Laurie. *"Fats" in Fact*. Essex, UK: Storyville Publications, 1992.

PERIODICALS

GENERAL

Asbury Park Press
Atlanta Constitution
Baltimore Afro American
Boston Daily Globe
Boston Herald
Broad Ax (Chicago)
Brooklyn Daily Eagle
Buffalo Courier
Buffalo Times
Chicago Daily Tribune
Chicago Defender
Chicago Sunday Herald and Examiner
Chicago Tribune
Cleveland Gazette
Cleveland Plain Dealer
Courier-Post (Camden, NJ)
Daily Graphic—London
Daily News
Daily People
Dayton Daily News
Florence Morning News (Florence, SC)
Freeport Journal-Standard (Freeport, IL)
Harrisburg Telegraph
Hartford Courant
Indianapolis Freeman
Indianapolis Star
Jewish Chronicle (Newark, NJ)
Journal and Guide
Logansport Pharos-Tribune
London Observer
Long Island Daily Press
Los Angeles Times
Macon Telegraph
Messenger-Inquirer (Owensboro, KY)
New Brunswick Daily Times
New Brunswick Home News
New York American
New York Amsterdam News
New York Clipper
New York Daily Tribune

New York Tribune
Oakland Tribune
Philadelphia Tribune
Pittsburgh Courier
PM
Springfield Missouri Republican
Sunday Times of London
The Bellingham Herald
The Boston Telegram
The Bridgeport Telegram
The Bystander (Kansas City, MO)
The Daily Courier (Connellsville, PA)
The Daily News-Times
The Daily Record (Long Branch, NJ)
The Daily Republican (Monongahela, PA)
The Daily Times (Davenport, IA)
The Detroit Free Press
The Englewood Times (Chicago)
The Evening Independent (Massillon, OH)
The Evening Journal (Jersey City, NJ)
The Evening Public Ledger
The Evening World
The Fort Wayne Sentinel
The Huntington Herald
The Indianapolis News
The Journal (Meridian, CT)
The Malone Farmer
The Montgomery Advertiser (Montgomery, AL)
The Neosho Daily News
The New York Age
The New Yorker
The New York Times
The Ogden Standard-Examiner (Ogden, UT)
The Omaha Daily News
The Philadelphia Inquirer
The Pittsburgh Press
The Republican-Journal (Ogdensburg, NY)
The Rockford Morning Star
The Seattle Daily Times
The Standard Union (Brooklyn, NY)
The Sun
The Sunday Repository (Canton, OH)
The Times of India
The Traveler
The Worker

Times-Picayune
Toledo Blade
Trenton Evening Times
Washington Post
Webster News-Times (Webster Groves, MO)

TRADE

Billboard
Down Beat
Hi-Fi Review Supplement
Jazz Information
Jazz Journal
Jazz Monthly
Jazz Quarterly
Jazz Review
Journal of American Folklore
Journal of Jazz Studies
Journal of Music Theory
Le Jazz Hot
Melody Maker
Musical America
Music and Rhythm
Music Dial
Music Trade Indicator
Record Changer
Record Research
Storyville
The AMICA Bulletin
The Crisis
The Edison Musical Magazine
The Music Trade Review
The Stage
Variety
VJM's Jazz and Blues Mart

GENERAL INDEX

Page numbers in **bold** indicate an illustration.

52nd Street, 311, 312, 315
81 Theater, 80
91 Decatur, 80
101 Ranch, 74
100th Street Hall (McFarland's), 34

Abyssinian Baptist Church, 114, 174, 240
Aeolian Company, 64, 65, 66, 69, 70
Afro-American Symphony, 277
"After Tonight" (Farrell), 65, 66
"Ain't Misbehavin'," 317, 321, 324, 333
Albany, Joe, 329
Albertson, Chris, 212, 220, 222
"Alcoholic Blues," 258
Alfred Music, 195
Alhambra Theater, 222, 223, 238
"All That I Had Is Gone," 319
Allan, Jim, 35, 41, 47, 53, 57
Allen, Bud, 232, 321
Allen, Ed, 244
Allen, Henry "Red," 239, 264, 284, 285, 286
Allen, Samuel C., 200
Allen, Walter C., 355
Alsop, Marin, 380
Alvin, Danny, 327, 350
American Federation of Musicians (AFM), 309, 310
American Jazz Review, 341, 346, 347
American Labor Party, 259
American Negro Ballet (ANB), 296
American Piano Company, 65
American Society of Composers, Authors and Publishers (ASCAP), 179, 183, 192, 272, 277, 297, 298, 316, 373, 386n13
Ammons, Albert, 259, 281, 286, 287, 317, 328
Anderson, Ernie, 115, 116, 270, 325, 328, 339
Anderson, Marian, 72, 281, 341
Apollo Theater, 6, 155, 276, 288, 289, 290, 291, 297
Archey, Jimmy, 354
"Arkansas Blues," 310, 333, 337
Armed Forces Radio Service (AFRS), 325, 326, 333, 366
Armstrong, Louis, 5, 178, 180, 195, 198, 223, 228, 235, 277, **280**, 287, 300, 313, 333, 365, 380
Artempo Record Rolls, 64, 66, 67, **68**
Arto (records), 96, 99
Asch, Moses, 263, 304, 308, 309, 310, 311, 319, 320, 324, 325, 326, 336, 346, 378
Ash, Paul, 248
Ashwood, Michael, 273, 274, 276
Astaire, Fred and Adele, 134, 138
"(At) Jazz Band Ball," 369
"At the Ball, That's All," 60, 322
Attucks, Crispus, 305
"Aunt Hagar's Blues," 344
Austin, Gene, 243
Autobiography of an Ex-Colored Man, The, 35
Avakian, George, 278, 335, 347, 349

"Baby, Get That Towel Wet," 62, 63
"Baby, Let Your Drawers Hang Low," 24
"Baby, Won't You Please Come Home," 323
"Backwater Blues," 213, 214, 215, 278, 318
Bailey, Buster, 368
Bailey, Charles P., 80
Bailey, Mildred, 334
Bailey, Pearl, 228
Bailey's 81 Theater, 80
Ballet Mecanique, 219, 220
Balliett, Whitney, 313
"Ballin' The Jack," 60
Band Box, 88
Baranov, Arnold B., 361, 362, 365, 370
Barbarin, Paul, 333
Bargy, Roy, 82, 83, 169
Barker, Danny, 347, 350, 351, 354
Barnard College, 332
Barron Wilkins's Exclusive Club, 34, 42, 49, 51, 57, 287
Barzin, Leon, 252
Basie, William "Count," 3, 5, 182, 224, 249, 272, 281, 292, 322, 324, 328, 335
Bayes, Nora, 72
Bayview-New York Bay Cemetery, 34
Baxter, Lee, 81
Bearden, Bessie, 300
Bearden, Romare, 300
Bebop, 3, 264, 271, 311, 323, 333, 344, 345, 358
Bechet, Sidney, 151, 154, 155, 272, 285, 294, 313, 322, 328, 333, 345, 347, 350, 351, 355, 368
Bennett, Robert Russell, 153
Bennett and White, 64
Benny Goldstein's Cabaret, 81
Berger, Robert, 361
Berle, Milton, 238
Berlin, Irving, 128, 193
Bernard, Mike, 49
Bernie, Saul, 223, 224
Bernstein, Artie, 279
Berry, Connie, 292
Bert Hall Rhythm Club, Inc., 199, 247
Berton, Ralph, 294, 331
Bestry, Harry, 148, 172

Bethune, Mary McLeod, 300
Beverly Cavern, 366
Bibbs, Leonard, 366
Biograph label, 379
Bishop, Walter, 287
"Black and Blue," 265
Black and Tan (film), 189, 222, 223
"Black Bottom" (dance), 196
Black Manhattan, 252
Black Man's Burden, The, 26
Black Swan Phonograph Company, 98, 111, 121, 369
Blackbirds of 1928, 73, 208, 216
Blacker the Berry, The, 162
Blackman, Ted, 238, 240
Blake, Eubie, 52, 53; Al Rose relationship, 342; compares Johnson and Waller, 120; composing style, 66; Crescendo Club, 276, 286; first meets Johnson, 52; humor, 147; influence on Johnson, 97, 112, 157; Johnson playing in style of, 340; Johnson's health, 372, 374; "Keep Off the Grass" origin, 99; at Lottie Joplin's, 74; Newport Jazz Festival, 378; at Pied Piper, 328, **329**; recalls Gershwin, 69, 70; recalls "One Leg" Willie, 48; recalls Luckey Roberts, 51; *Shuffle Along*, 153; Sissle and Blake, 140, 212; style, 104, 108, 110; *Tan Manhattan*, 289, 292; Tickler, 53; Waller birthday party, 236, 267, 268
Bland, James, 334
Blanks, Oceola, 122, 123, 126
Bledsoe, Jules, 346
"Bleeding Hearted Blues," 139
Blesh, Rudi, 53, 106, 110, 222, 295, 303, 347, 350, **351**, 352, 354, 358, 369, 378
Blood on the Fields (Hughes), 258
Bloom, Rube, 187
"Blue Note Jazzmen," 322, 323
Blue Note Records, 318, 320, 322, 324, 326, 336, 342, 369, 379
Blue Streak Hour, 226
"Blue Turning Grey Over You," 324
Blumberg, Jerry, 357

Body and Soul (film), 175, **176**, 177
boogie woogie, 38, 47, 49, 105, 110, 160, 272, 273, 279, 281, 286, 287, 293, 308, 310, 311, 317, 318, 319, 323, 325, 330, 337, 342, 369, 419n48
Boone, Blind, 65
Borneman, Ernest, 313
Borowsky, Mark, 29, 378
"Boston" (piano style), 105, 106
Boyette, Raymond "Lippy," 50, 118, 162, 233
Bradford, Perry: composer, 69, 139, 152, 156, 178, 195, 202, 219, 227, 237; Crescendo Club, 276; and *Keep Shufflin'*, 193–96; producer/publisher, 49, 89, 181, 182, 185, 200, 202, 209, 211, 215, 243, 278, 293, 306, 326; Waller funeral, 322; and *Yamekraw*, 186, 187, 188, 195
Bradford, Roark, 257
Bradshaw, Tiny, 286
Brant Inn, 342
Braud, Wellman, 126, 285
Bregman, Vocco and Conn, 264
Brooklyn Civic Orchestra, 296, 298, 301
Brooks, Russell, 50, 115, 116, 117, 118
Brooks, Shelton, 231, 235, 245, 247, 287
Brooks, Walter, 339
Broonzy, Big Bill, 272, 281, 347
Brown, Pete, 270
Brown, Sterling A., 256, 281
Browne, Theodore, 257, 288
Brownie's (club), 234
Brownskin Models, 180
Brummer, Andre, 363
Brunies, George, 347
Brunswick records, 127, 225, 226, 324
Bryan, Frederick M., 46, **47**, 65, 71, 207
Bryant, Willie, 286, 287, 289
Brymm, Tim, 35, 228, 286
Buck and Bubbles, 142, 259
"Buddy's Habits," 66
Bullock, Chick, 244
Burley, Dan, 105, 160, 288, 289, 290, 307, 354
Bushell, Garvin, 37, 38, 110, 111, 164, 199, 200, 201, 202, 203, 204, 209, 210, 211
Bushkin, Joe, 321, 323, 324, 345

Bushwick Hofbrau, 315
Butt, Sir Alfred, 129, 132, 133, 134, 136
Butterbeans and Susie, 228
Butts, Jimmy, 350
Byard, Jaki, 378

Café Bohemia, 333
Café Society, 260, 283, 292, 294, 309, 322, 333, 338, 347
Callin, Owen, 365
Calloway, Blanche, 137, 180, 211
Calloway, Cab, 137, 222, 247, 277, 313, 314, 315
Campbell, S. Brunson, 84
"Candy Sweets," 326
Capitol Records, 365
Carnegie Hall, 32, 43, 148, 174, 206, 261, 277, 291, 298, 305, 323, 326, 331, 335, 336, 337, 338, 339, 340, 344; recording company, **296**
"Carolina Fox Trot," 66
Carroll, Earl, 6
Carter, Alice Leslie, 96, 97, 99, 102
Carter, Benny, 154, 233, 286, 287, 314, 315
Casey, Al, 264, 286
Casey, Floyd, 244
Castle, Irene, 71, 102
Castle, Vernon, 71
Catagonia Club, 166
Catlett, Big Sid, 264, 285, 286, 324, 334
Cavalcade of the American Negro (Gilbert), 309
Central Plaza, 355, **356**, 368
Century Records, 348, 349
Chappelle and Stinnette, 137, 236
"Charleston" (dance), 88, 177, 178, 219
"Charlie, My Back Door Man," 200
Cherniavsky, Josef, 336, 337
Chiapusso, Jan Joseph, 85, **86**, 87
"Chicago Blues," 209
"Chili Pepper," 185
Chittison, Herman, 227
"Chizzlin' Sam," 244
"Chocolate Bar," 324
Christian, Charlie, 279
"Christmas Night in Harlem," 247

Circle Records, 222
Ciro's, 180
City Alley (New Brunswick, NJ), 9, 14, 16, 17
Clairmont, Robert, 206
Clark, H. Qualli, 99, **100**, 129, 394n29
Clark, June, 79, 81, 88
Clark, Melville, 91, 92
Clark Monroe's Uptown House, 287
Clarke, Kenny, 275
Clayton, Buck, 324, 334, 357
Clef Club, 34, 46, **47**, 50, 52, 56, 62, 68, 71, 73, 87, **93**, 96–99, 119, 142, 170
Cless, Rod, 306, 311, 312, 326, 327, 330, 331, 332
Clooney, Rosemary, 374
Cochran, Charles B., 133, 134
Cohan, George M., 259
Cole, Nat, 335, 365
Coleman, Bill, 324
Collingwood Hall, 84
Colonial Theater, 144, 145, 150
Colored Vaudeville Benevolent Association, 62, 122
Coltrane, John, 333
Columbia Broadcasting Company, 235, 238, 260, 265, 269, 308, 370
Columbia Records, 153, 209, 210, 226, 264, 265, 277, 279, 323, 365
Comedy Club, 165
"Comin' on with the Come On," 270
Commodore Music Shop, 349
Commodore Records, 324, 326
Condon, Eddie, 166, 306, 308, **309**, 312, 321, 323, 324, 325, 326, 328, 331, 334, 338, 339, 341, 344, 345, 350, 369, 378
Connie's Inn, 6, 73, 88, 216, 238, 239, 248
Conrad, Con, 192, 195, 196, 197, 198, 205, 207, 208, 209, 210
Conservatory of Musical Art, 95
Constitution Hall, 341
Cook, Jean Lawrence, 94, **113**, 230
Cook, Mercer, 224, 227, 255, 300, 304
Cook, Will Marion, 35, 48, 91, 140, 142, 143, 145, 150–52, 174, 177, 183, 185, 186, 207, 224, 227, 232, 246, 253, 254, 255, 261, 291, 306, 339, 346

Cooke, Charles L., 276, 277
Cool Off, 34
Coolidge, Elizabeth Sprague, 295
Cooper, Al, 287
Copeland, Martha, 74, 209
Coterie of Friends, 135
Cotton Club, 88, 173, 193, 227, 248
Courlander, Harold, 39
Cowans, Russ J., 83
Cox, Ida, 137, 279, 281
Crawford, Rosetta, 271
"Crazy Blues," 62
Creamer, Henry, 126, 179, 180, 183, 184, 193, 197, 201, 202, 210, 230, 231, 240, 303, 304, 406n16
Creation, 31, 32
Crescendo Club, 276–78, 286, 288, 300
Crescent Theater, 71
Crosby, Israel, 333, 337
Cross, Milton, 345
Cryer, Jesse, 362
"Cryin' for My Used to Be," 119
"Cryin' for the Carolines," 225
Crystal, Jack, 349, 355
Cumbo, Marion, 200
Cuscuna, Michael, 322

Dabney, Ford, 73, 191, 207, 276, 286
Daisy Chain (brothel), 182, 267
Daly's 63rd Street Theatre, 196, 237
Damrosch, Frank, 31, 32, 174
Dance, Stanley, 3
Dapogny, James, 264, 265, 380
"Darn That Dream," 280
Davin, Tom, 17, 22, 25, 31, 33, 47, 68, 69, 77, 83, 90, 378
Davis, Joe, 228
Davis, Miles, 333
Davison, "Wild Bill," 311, 323, 355
De Courville, Albert, 129
De Paris, Sydney, 270, 294, 322, 332, 337, 345, **375**
De Paris, Wilbur, 332, 337, 345
De Paur, Leonard, 257, 260, 261, 263
Deas, Lawrence, 41, 122, 124, 130, 136, 276

"Death Letter Blues," 279
Decca Records, 271, 310, 312, 324, 331, 336, 349, 365, 369
"Deep Sea Blues," 279
Dehn, Mura, 349, 350
Deppe, Lois, 82
Deutsch, Maury, 352, **353**, 358
Dickenson, Vic, 322
Diton, Carl, 304
Dixon, Dean, 297
"Do What You Did Last Night," 210
"Doctor Jazzes Raz-Ma-Taz," 94, 95
Dodds, Baby, 346, 349, 350, 351, 354
Dodge, Roger Pryor, 214, 325
"Don't Hit That Lady (Dressed in Green)," 24
"Don't Tell Your Monkey Man," 145
Dorsey, Tommy, 287, 334
Dougherty, Eddie, 324, 369
Douglas, Louis, 151
Douglas, Marion, 151
Douglass, Frederick, 259, 305
Down Beat, 167, 271, 272, 293, 310, 311, 319, 326, 328, 355, 363, 367, 373, 374, 376
Doyle, Freddie, 34
Drake's dancing class (Jungles Casino), 36
Dramatists' Guild, 308, 352
"Dream, The" ("The Ladies Dream," "Digah's Stomp," "Digah's Dream," "The Bowdiger's Dream," "The Bull Diker's Dream"), 35, 40, 41, 273, 325, 342
Dressing Room Club, 96
Dudley, Sherman S., 78
Duncan, Hank, 105, 328
Duncan, Ina, 145
Dunham, Katherine, 297, 313, 345
Dupree, Champion Jack, 355
Dupree, Reece, 71
Dyerettes, 370

Ebonaires, 365
Eckstine, Billy, 224
Edison, Harry "Sweets," 286
Eldridge, Roy, 287, 332
Elgar's Syncopated band, 124, 126
Elk's Café, 46

Elk's Experimental Theater, 353
Ellington, Duke, 5, 7, 100, 101, 111, 114, 154, 159, 161, 164, 165, 166, 178, 189, 198, 209, 210, 222, 223, 224, 227, 235, 248, 249, 308, 322, 324, 328, 329, 333, 350, 372, 376, 380
Ellis, Johnny, 357
Ellison, Ralph, 258, 281
Eltinge Theatre, 206
Emperor Jones, The, 223, 240, 241, 242
Empire Records, 352
Ertegun, Ahmet, 334
Ertegun, Nesuhi, 294, 366
Esquire magazine, 333, 335
Etting, Ruth, 180
"Euphonic Sounds," 29, 40, 325, 339
Europe, James Reese, 34, 38, 52, 56, 63, 72, 78, 101, 140, 142, 146, 183, 254
Evans, Roy, 209, 210, 215
"Every Time I Feel the Spirit Moving in My Heart," 186
"Everybody Loves My Baby," 322
Ewell, Don, 378

Farrell, William H., 62, **63**, 70, 77, 95, 137
Father of the Stride Piano (LP), 378, 379
Feather, Leonard, 289, 294, 311, 320, 324
Federal Theater Project (FTP), 189, 253, 254, 257, 258
Ferber, Edna, 256
Fields, Kansas, 323
"Fine and Mellow," 312
Finley, Dude, 34
Finston, Nat, 363
Flowers, Pat, 324, 334
Foster, Pops, 111, 169, 212, 264, 286, 294, 323, 346, 347, 349, 350, 351, 354, 368
Four Tops, 370
Fowler, Lemuel, 405n3
Fox, Richard K., 49
Fox, Sam, 243
Francis, Henry, 107
Franklin, William, 336, 337
Freeman, Bud, 280, 340
French Classics (record label), 379
Friedlander, William B., 361, 362, 370

"Friends of James P. Johnson," 300, **301, 302**, 305, 334
Frogs, The, 56
"Frogs Legs Rag," 49
From Dover Street to Dixie, 133
Frye, Don, 328
Funaroff, Solomon, 279
"Functional," 320

Gabler, Milt, 291, 294, 300, 312, 315, 349
Gaiety Building, 161, 181
Gaines, Charlie, 244
Gant, Willie, 50, 68, 74, 97, 101, 167, 201, 202
Geechies, 37, 67, 156
Gelman, David, 258, 315, 328, 329, 330, 337, 345, 359, 360, 416n48
General Phonograph Company, 98. *See also* OKeh Records
George White's *Scandals*, 193
"Georgia's Always on My Mind," 210
Gershwin, George, 51, 66, 68, 69, 70, 129, 131, 134, 141, 161, 169, 186, 187, 190, 193, 194, 196, 211, 221, 232, 259, 271, 281, 307, 340, 380
Giannini, Bruto, 42, **44**, 45, 46, 85, 174
Gilbert, Mercedes, **176**, 177, 276, 286, 294, 300, 304, 309, 310, 341, 342, 345
Gilford, Jack, 285
Gillespie, Dizzy, 358, 359
Gilpin, Charles, 147, 240
Glaser, Joe, 300, 370
Glover (Johnson), Arceola, 215, 266, 267
Glover, Barry, 379
Godowsky, Leopold, 175, 223
Goffin, Robert, 294
Golden Gate Quartet, 286
Goldman, Edwin Franko, 252
Gonzales, Louis, 366
"Good Morning Blues," 346
Goodman, Benny, 256, 272, 279, 280, 281, 283, 333, 345
Gordon, Bob, 47
Gordon, Lorraine (Lion), 322
Gordon, Max, 352
Gordon, Sam, 46
Gotham and Attucks, 35

Gottlieb, Bill, 345
Gould, Walter "One-Leg Shadow," 88
Grainger, Porter, 150, 155, 227, 247
Grammy Hall of Fame, 380
Gray, Eddie, 97, 98
Great Day, 224
Great Day New Orleans Singers, 225
Great Migration, 12, 38, 159
Green, Eddie, 123, 131, 136, 180, 276, 286
Green, Freddy, 324
Green Mill Gardens, 123, 125
Greene, Alma T. Jupiter, 42, 43
Greene, Ernest, 41, 42, 43, 49
Greer, Sonny, 165
Grew, Claude, 27
Guarnieri, Johnny, 112, 312, 378
"Guess Who's in Town," 210
Guggenheim fellowship, 252, 253, 305
Gullahs, 37, 67, 156

H. M. Prices Sons, 13, 14, **15**
Hackett, Bobby, 324, 355
Haggart, Bob, 329
Hairston, Marion, 246, 247, 266
Hall, Adelaide, 74, 142, 145, 208, 233, 247
Hall, Bert, 126, 131, 199, 211, 215, 247
Hall, Edmund, 279, 322, 323, 355, 368
Hall, Josephine, 199, 207, 216, 218, 247
Hall Johnson choir, 221, 241, 263
Hallie Anderson's Orchestra, 34
Hamilton College, 350
Hammond, John, 145, 161, 244, 264, 271, 272, 275, 278, 282, 283, 284, 286, 294, 300, 306, 313, 376
Hampton, Lionel, 279, 286
"Handful of Keys," 234
Handy, Katherine, 206, 277
Handy, Lucille, 151
Handy, Ruth, 305
Handy, W. C., 37, 46, 78, 96, 181, 183, 186, 193, 206, 207, 220, 221, 229, 232, 238, 240, 246, 247, 258, 259, 266, 276, 277, 286, 300, 306, 337
"Harlem Hellfighters," 305
"Harlem Hotcha" (drink), 239

"Harlem Hotcha" (expression), 239
Harlem Renaissance, 6, 7, 36, 89, 162, 177, 185, 187, 197, 265, 294, 296
Harlem stride piano, 4, 5, 84, 98, 104–13, 117, 167, 225, 311
Harlem Suitcase Theater, 260, 261
Harlem Uproar House, 270
Harms (music publisher), 152, 153, 154, 157, 200, 236, 281
Harney, Ben, 77
Harper, Leonard: *Adam and Eve in Harlem*, 224; and Connie Immerman, 238; *Dark Secrets*, 180; *Fireworks of 1930*, 231; *Harper and Blanks Revue*, 122; *Harper's Dixie Revue*, 154; *Harry Steppe and His Big Show*, 173; *Hollywood Follies*, 171; Hollywood Inn, 155; *Keep Shufflin'*, 196; late-night feasting, 266; *Negro Nuances*, 151; *On Striver's Row*, 288, 289; *Plantation Days*, 123–26, 129–33, 135–38; *Step on It*, 172; *Sunshine Sammy* (*Whirl of Dixie*), 177
Harper and Blanks, 122, 123–26, 129, 131, 136
Harper's Dixie Revue, 154
Harrington, Bob, 355, 377
Harris, Fats, 47
Harris, Herbert, 310
Harrison, Dorothy, 260, 261, 265, 352
Harrison, Hazel, 232
Harrison, Jimmy, 81, 88
Harrison, Josephine (Johnson, Thompson), 10, 11, 12, 14, 16, 17, 20, 23, 26, 27, 33, 171
Harrison, Max, 39
Harrison, Nathaniel, 10
Harry Smith Studio, 318
Harvey, Georgette, 245
Haviland, F. B., 62, 63, 64
Hawkins, Bob, 49
Hawkins, Coleman, 287
Hawkins, Erskine, 224
Hayakawa, Samuel Ichiye (S. I.), 321
Hayes office, 242
"He Took It Away from Me," 98
Healey, Eunice, 365
Heard, J. C., 358
"Heart Breakin' Joe," 155

Heckscher Theater, 252, 300, 304, 305
Hegamin, Lucille, 96, 99, 102
Heidt, Horace, 371
Heineman, Otto, 78
Hell's Kitchen, 30, **31**, 34, 35, 41, 67, 105, 115, 320
Henderson, Fletcher, 81, 111, 178, 205, 221, 249, 276, 279, 355, 369, 372
Henry, John (legend of), 256, 262
Here, There, and Everywhere (Hill and Rogers), 60
Herman's (cabaret), 81
"He's a Colonel from Kentucky," 244
"Hesitation Blues," 40, 325
Heyward, DuBose, 208, 241, 276
Heywood, Eddie, 322
Heywood, Eddie, Sr., 80
Higginbotham, J. C., 264, 284, 285, 286, 307, 333, 349
"High Society," 322
Hilbert, Robert, 309
Hill, Abram, 288
Hill, Alex, 247
Hill, Bertha "Chippie," 352
Hill, J. Leubrie, 38, 47, 54, 59, 60, 61, 146
Hill, Mal, 357
Hines, Earl "Fatha," 82, 112, 313, 324, 340
Hite, Mattie, 88, 96
Hobart, George V., 76
Hodes, Art, 317, 322, 346, 349, 350, **351**, 358, 378
Hoefer, George, 54, 276, 374
Hole in the Wall, 74, 164
Holiday, Billie, 241, 287, 307, 312, 365
Holly, Hal (Charles Emge), 363, 365, 367
Hollywood Inn (Palais De Dance), 154, 155
"Honeysuckle Rose," 317, 321, 324, 334
"Honky Tonk Blues at Midnight," 347
Honore, Gideon, 366
Hoofer's Club, 166, 167
Hooper, Louis, 166
Hopkins, Claude, 165, 247, 249, 277, 321, 328
Horatio, Schaffer, 260
Horne, Lena, 313, 315
Horsley, Gus, 215
Hot Chocolates (Waller and Razaf), 211, 220

Hot Club of Newark, 315
Hot Club of Trenton, 285
Hot Record Society Record Shop, 269
Houseman, John, 253
"How Could I be Blue," 226
"How Jazz Was Born," 200
Howard, I. Wesley, 200
Howell, Marie, 33
Howland, John, 187, 189, 282
H. R. S. records, 344, 352
Hudson Theater, 216, 219
Huff, Dickie, 49
Hughes, Langston, 239, 250, 256, 257, 258, 260, 277, 281, 300, 315, 333
Hughes, Lillie Mae, 75. *See also* Wright, Lillie Mae; Johnson, Lillie Mae
Hull, Harry, 200
Humes, Helen, 281
Hunter, Alberta, 151, 286
Hupfeld, Herman, 184
Hurston, Zora Neale, 197
Hurtig, Jules, 6, 155, 172
Hurtig and Seamon, 155, 171, 178
"Hydrant Love," 156
Hyman, Dick, 327, 328, 329, 378

"I Ain't Gonna Play No Second Fiddle," 156, 178
"I Can't Dance, I Got Ants in My Pants," 244
"I Got Horses and Got Numbers on My Mind," 244
"I Got Rhythm," 70, 105
"I Want Jesus to Walk with Me," 303
"If Dreams Come True," 342
"If I Were Your Daddy," 98
"I'm Comin' Virginia," 399
"I'm Crazy 'Bout My Baby," 326
"I'm Gonna Sit Right Down and Write Myself a Letter," 324
"I'm Just Wild About Harry," 52
"I'm Looking for That Birdie," 18
Immerman, Connie, 248
Immerman, George, 228, 238, 248
indefinite talk, 147, 313
Institute of Jazz Studies, 240, 292, 296, 299, 301, 302, 307, 350, 353, 355

International Ladies Garment Workers' Union (ILGWU), 259, 260, 261, 263, 265, 272, 309, 349, 352
International Workers Order, 260
Isquith, Louis, 208, 216, 218
"I've (I) Found A New Baby," 226, 269
"I've Got a Feelin' I'm Fallin'," 324

Jack the Bear (John Wilson), 35, 40, 41, 340
Jackson, Bee, 182
Jackson, Cliff, 164, 165, 249, 287, 348
Jackson, E. (Eugene) Aldama, 73, 94, 174, **176**, 229, 300
Jackson, Franz, 337
Jackson, Mike, 49
Jackson, Sadie, 180
Jackson School of Composition and Music, 174
James, Etta, 224
James, George, 286
James, Harry, 224
James P. Johnson Foundation for Music and the Arts, 379
Janis, Harriet, 369
Jarratt's Hotel, 10
"Jazz on The River," **351**
Jazz Record, The, 337, 348, 358
Jazz Society of Boston, 345
Jazz Society of Trenton, 357
"Jazzapation—A Study in Jazz by the Masters," 185
"Jazzfest and Pop Concert," 305
Jazzmen, 3, 309
Jenkins, Daniel, 19, 151
Jenkins, Edmund Thornton, 135, 136, 151
Jenkins Orphanage Band, 19, 198
"Jerry The Junker," 244
Jessye, Eva, 229, 248, 261, 265
Jet magazine, 374
Jimmy Ryan's, 311, 312, 315
John Henry (novel), 257
John Henry (opera), 257
John T. Gibson's New Standard Theater, 79
John T. Ricks' Orchestra, 145
Johnson (McIntyre), Lillie Mae, Jr., 315, 359, 360

Johnson, Budd, 345
Johnson, Bunk, 354, 357
Johnson, Charlie, 223, 228, 247, 373
Johnson, Edmund, 57, 87
Johnson, Hall, 225
Johnson, Herb, 199, 200
Johnson, J. C., 210, 246, 247, 276, 321
Johnson, J. Rosamond, 56, 186, 206, 221, 229, 232, 241, 276
Johnson, James P., **113**, **144**, **169**, **280**, **307**, **318**, **330**; birth, 16; burlesque, 171, 172; commercial television, 308, **309**; dance, 4, 19, 22, 36, 37, 89, 106, 135, 142, 144, 153, 156, 157, 158, 180, 211, 217, 239, 304, 315, 349, 350, 364; "Dean of Jazz Pianists," 9, 320, 321, 336, 342, 355, 380; Harlem home, **125**; innovator, 5, 6, 50, 66, 70, 112, 214, 352, 361, 363, 380; Jamaica, Queens, 168, **230**, 231, 232, 237, 238, 245, 266, 286, 287, 294, 317, 359; obscurity 3, 4, 7, 366, 377; piano rolls, 64–70, 91–95, 98, 110, **113**, 116, 119, 129, 153, 158, 173, 179, 180, 187, 303, 321, 347–49, 379; postage stamp, 379; practice technique, 45, 55, 57, 387n19; P.S. 69, 30; radio scripts, 339, 345, 346, 347; San Juan Hill home, **31**; stroke, 287, 288, 310, 340, 346, 368, 372, 373; teachers, 33, 41–46, 57, 69, 73, 75, 84, 85–87, 94, 96, 173, 174, **175**, **176**, 229, 300, **353**, 386n13
Johnson, James P., Jr., 180, 266, 267, 329, 343
Johnson, James Weldon, 35, 59, 60, 183, 252, 253, 281, 297
Johnson, Lillie Mae, 75, **76**, 80, 81, 117, 118, 123, 131, 175, **176**, 255, 266, 267, 281, 286, 287, 294, 342, 359, 360, 373, 374
Johnson, Manzie, 286
Johnson, Pete, 273, 281, 286, 287, 328, 345
Johnson, William H., 12, 13, 14, 16, 17
Joint Is Jumpin', The (film), 168
Jones, Byron, 210
Jones, Claude, 294
Jones, Francis, 10
Jones, Henry "Broadway," 236
Jones, Isham, 127–29
Jones, Robert Earl, 261
Jones, Shrimp, 72

Joplin, Lottie, 74, 265
Joplin, Scott, 27, 29, 35, 40, 43, 46, 57, 65, 84, 109, 110, 111, 206, 325, 339, 340, 348, 370
Jordan, Joe, 35, 180, 189, 196, 197, 276, 277, 286
Jordan, Louis, 244, 285, 287, 289, 290
Joseph, "One-Leg" Willie, 48, 49, 340
Josephson, Barney, 283, 286, 300, 322
"Joy Club," 181, 182, 201
Jubilaires, 345
Jungles Casino, 36, 37, 47, 57, 67, 156, 321
"Junk Man Rag," 51, 303

Kaminsky, Max, 308, 326, 329, 330, 331, 332, 334, 350, 354, 368
Kappler, Frank, 379
Keep Shufflin' Trio, 225
"Keepin' Out of Mischief Now," 324
Keepnews, Orin, 320
Kenny, "Battle Axe," 205
Kentucky Club (Club Kentucky), 154. *See also* Hollywood Inn
Keppard, Floyd, 27
Kincaid, Nelson, 72
Kindler, Hans, 252
"King Porter Stomp," 344
Kirkeby, Ed, 114, 117, 119, 170, 182, 195, 201, 207, 333, 342, 351
Kitchen Tom (Eddie Bosso), 47
Klondike Annie, 243
Koehler, Ted, 314
Kortlander, Max, 92
Kosok, Paul, 295, 297, 298, **299**
Kratka, Irv, 357, 429n62

La Boheme (club), 327. *See also* Pied Piper
La Guardia, Fiorello H., 103, 300
La Zaro, E. Lee, 289, 290
Labor Stage, 259, 260, 265
Ladnier, Tommy, 270
Lady, Be Good (show), 196
Lafayette Theater, 6, 71, 122, 129, 131, 142, 166, 177, 178, 180, 183, 189, 195, 208, 211, 215, 222, 224, 227, 231, 233, 237, 239, 253, 296, 297
Lambert, Donald, 75, 342, 354, 378
Las Palmas Theater, 361, 362, 364, 366

Laska, Edward, 258
Lattimore, George W., 254, 255, 259, 300, 332, 333, 336, 337, 346
Layton, Turner, 150
Le Jazz Hot, 3, 269
League of Composers, 281, 308
Ledbetter, Huddie "Leadbelly," 259, 309, 346, 368
Lee, Canada, 218
Lee, George, 41
Lee, Johnny, 313, 362, 365
Lee, Julia, 352, 354
"Left Her on the Railroad Track," 25, 62, 63
Leroy Wilkins's Café, 53, 57, 88, 118, 199, 200
Lesberg, Jack, 327, 328, 330, 331, 335, 336
Leslie, Lew, 73, 122, 133, 136, 208, 216
Levenson, Boris, 250, **251**
Levette, Harry, 239
Levin, Floyd, 359, 360, 366, 367
Lewis, John, 5
Lewis, Meade Lux, 259, 281, 286, 287, 317
"Lift Every Voice and Sing," 277
Lim, Harry, 285, 294
Lincoln, Abraham, birth centennial, 32
Lincoln Center, 3
Lincoln Square Arcade, 43, **44**
Lincoln Theater, 89
Lincoln University, 223
Lion, Alfred, 317, 318, 319, 322, 323, 341
Lion, Lorraine, 322
Lion's Jaw, 81
Lipskin, Michael, 5, 106, 378
"Little Brown Jug," 18, 27
"Little Rock Getaway," 66
Livia (club), 74
Liza (show), 196
"Liza" (song) 277, 342
Local 802, 308
Locke, Alain, 6
Loesser, Frank, 6
Lomax, Alan, 273, 347, 368
"Lonesome Swallow," 210
Long Island University, 295, 296, 301
Longshaw, Fred, 185
Louis, Joe, 248
Louisiana Sugar Babes, 202, 204, 208
"Love Will Find a Way," 140

"Loveless Love," 93, 94, 95
Lucas, John, 366
"Lucy Long," 156, 178
Lugg, George, 323
Luna Park, **61**
Lyles, Aubrey, 140, 146, 194, 197, 211, 229, 313

M. Witmark and Sons, 219
Mabley, Jackie "Moms," 241, 242, 280
Machlin, Paul S., 204
Mack, Cecil (Richard C. McPherson), 35, 56, 142, **144**, 158, 172, 177, 178, 183, 223, 225, 286, 303
Macomber, Ken, 189, 268
Madison, Bingie, 229
Mahler, Fritz, 262
"Make Me a Pallet on the Floor," 348
Maltz, Bob, 345, 354, 355, **356**
"Man I Love, The," 196
"Maori," 35
"Maple Leaf Rag," 49, 95, 206, 346
Marcorelles, Paul, 380
Mariani, Hugo, 188, 279
Marsala, Marty, 350, 351
Marsalis, Wynton, 380
Marshall, Kaiser, 337
Martin, Daisy, 102
Martin, David Stone, 324
Martin, Henry, 110
Mayor of Dixie, The (Miller and Lyles), 140, 146
Mazetier, Louis, 107, 378
McDaniel, Hattie, 286
McFarlands (100th St. Hall), 34
McGhee, Brownie, 352
McGowan, Russ, 83
McKinney's Cotton Pickers, 180
McLean, Richard "Abba Labba," 48, 51, 57
McShann, Jay, 214
Mediterraneans, The 188
Meltzer, Sam, 348
"Memphis Blues," 206
Meritt Record Society, 417n66
Metcalf, Louis, 212
Metro-Goldwyn-Mayer, 143
Metronome, 311, 341
"Metropolitan Glide, The," 36

Mezzrow, Milton "Mezz," 167, 168, 232, 269, 270, 287, 347, 374
Micheaux, Oscar, 175, 177
Mili, Gjon, 312
Miller, A. P., 26
Miller, Dorie, 305, 325
Miller, Flournoy, 146, 147, 179, 194, 198, 201, 211, 224, 229, 237, 291, 292, 313, 352, 353, 361, 363, 364, 370, 371, 372, 373
Miller, Irvin C., 148, 156, 180, 194, 229, 235, 291
Miller, Olivette, 370
Miller and Lyles: dissolve partnership, 224; first meeting, 76; *Great Day*, 224; *Keep Shufflin'*, 191, 192, 193, 194, 195, 197, **199**, 205, 207, 208, 210; Lafayette Christmas show, 215; *Lazy Rhythm*, 235; Lincoln University benefit, 223; *Rang Tang*, 191, 192, 197; *Runnin' Wild*, 139, 140, 142, 143, 144, 146, 147, 148, **149**, 150, 151, 155, 156; Sissle and Blake, 52; *Shuffle Along of 1930*, 229; stage show structure, 216; *Sugar Hill* (1931), 235–37. *See also* Lyles, Aubrey; Miller, Flournoy
Millinder, Lucky, 374
Mills, Bradford, 84, 87
Mills, Florence, 35, 74, 123, 133, 134, 135, 136, 137, 171, 224, 225
Mills, Irving, 314, 353
Mills, Jack, 139, 157, 300, 314, 362, 365
Mills Brothers, 238, 239, 366
Mills music, 291, 319, 361
Milton, Roy, 354
Mingus, Charles, 378
Mitchell, Abbie, 151, 346
Mole, Miff, 350, 355
Monk, Nellie, 320
Monk, Thelonious, 5, 50, 105, 168, 169, 320, 369
Montgomery, Eurreal "Little Brother," 373
Montgomery, Frank, 59, 61, 152
Montgomery, Michael, 349, 379
Moon, Bucklin, 369
Moore, Freddie, 354, 357
Moore, Monette, 216, 217, 362, 365, 366
Moore, Russell, 357
Moran, Jason, 380
Mordecai, Jimmy, 188, 221, 222, 241, 373

Morgenstern, Dan, 355
Morrison, Ernest (Sunshine Sammy) 177
Morrissey, Will, 172, 177
Morton, Benny, 334
Morton, "Jelly Roll," 5, 28, 34, 40, 66, 83, 111, 126, 127, 167, 178, 276, 285, 320, 339, 340, 348, 368, 370, 377, 380
Mosaic Records, 320, 379
Moss, Carlton, 259, 260
Most Happy Fella, The (Loesser), 6
Moten, Bennie, 235
Moton, Robert R., 253
"Mournful Tho'ts," 209
Mt. Olivet Cemetery, 380
Mt. Zion African Methodist Episcopal Church, 12, 17, **18**, 19
Mundy, Jimmy, 374
Murphy, Dudley, 161, 188, 189, 219, 220, 221, 241
Murphy, Earl, 294
Murphy, Turk, 367
Music Publishers Holding Corporation, 281
"My Fate Is in Your Hands," 324
My Friend from Kentucky, 59
"My Handy Man," 210
"My Sportin' Man," 223

National Association for the Advancement of Colored People (NAACP), 272, 324
National Association of Negro Musicians, 89
National Blues Singing Championship, 101, **102**, 103
National Recording Registry of the Library of Congress, 380
National Symphony Orchestra of Peru, 297
Natural Man (This Ole Hammer), 257
Negro Folk Music and Drama Society, 151
Nest Club, 200, 234
Nevius, Clifford, 11, 17, 33
Nevius, Frank, 11, 17, 287
Nevius, Isabella (Bella), 11, 17, 18, 33, 87, 171, 287
Nevius, John, 11
Nevius, Petrus, Sr., 11
Nevius, Richard, 11, 12
Nevius, William Henry, 11, 17, 33
New Amsterdam Orchestra, 34, 73

New Masses, 272
New School for Social Research, 294
New World Fantasy, 339
New York Jazz Club, 345, 354, **356**
New York Negro Symphony Orchestra, 296
New York Orchestra, 40
New York Philharmonic, 252
New York Syncopated Orchestra, 254. *See also* Southern Syncopated Orchestra
New York Times Hall, 342
New York Urban League, 240
New York World's Fair (1940), 265
Newport Jazz Festival, 378
Newton, Frankie, 270, 324, 328, 332, 333
Nicholas, Albert, 285, 347, 350, 351, 354, 366, 367
Nicholas, Harold, 241
Nicholas Brothers, 146, 313
Nichols, Herbie, 105
Nick's (club), 285, 333
Nossiter, Paul, 330

O'Curran, Charles, 363, 365, 371
Office of War Information (OWI), 323, 324
"Oh, Mr. Mitchell," 223
"Oh, You Drummer," 47
OKeh Records, 89, 98, 99, 139, 146, 185, 226
Oliver, Joe "King," 66, 128, 225
O'Neal, Jimmy, 122, 173
O'Neill, Eugene, 240, 241
Onyx Club, 311, 312
Orchard, Frank, 326, 327, 332
Orient, The (Jerry Preston's), 88, 166
Original Dixieland Jazz Band, 73
Original Spring Revue, 123
Ory, Kid, 366
Osborne, Maud Mapp, 266
Our Gang, 177

Pace, Harry, 98, 111, 181
Pace and Handy Music Company, 47, 98, 99
Pace Phonograph Corporation, 98
Page, Hot Lips, 279, 308
Panassie, Hughes, 3, 269, 306, 373
Paramount Records, 369
Paramount Studio, 241

Parenti, Tony, 350, 354, 355
Parker, Charlie, 374, 380
Parker, Dolores, 365
Pasadena Civic Auditorium, 366
Pastor, Tony, 49, 77
Pathé, 97
"Peculiar Rag," 35
Peer, Ralph, 245
Pekin Theater, 140
Perfect (record label), 98
"Perfect Rag," 66
Perry, George, 27
"Persian Rug," 204
Petersburg, Virginia, 10
Pettiford, Oscar, 324
Peyton, Dave, 187
Piano Playhouse, 345
Pichon, Walter "Fats," 111
Pickett, Jess, 40, 325
Pied Piper, 326–34, **329**
Pigett, Bill, 330
"Pine Top's Boogie Woogie," 330, 342
Pinkard, Maceo, 180, 183, 235, 247, 290, 305, 339
Pins and Needles, 261, 265, 352
Pinsker, Robert, 83, 187, 379
Piras, Marcello, 42, 46
Plantation Revue, 123, 133
Pod's and Jerry's, 166, 234
Police Gazette, 49
Porgy, 208, 241
Porgy and Bess, 245, 261
"Pork and Beans," 51, 273
Port Royal Experiment, 21, 22
Porter, Arthur, 142, 145, 216
Porter, Cole, 196
Powell, Adam Clayton, Jr., **240**, 300
Powell, Bud, 5, 374
Powell, Mel, 321
"Preachin' the Blues," 213
Preston, "West Indian Jerry," 166
Price, Caleb, 13
Price, Henry C., 13, 14
Price, Henry M., 13
Price, William H., 13, 14
Price, Sammy, 214, 336, 338, 354

Queens General Hospital, 376
QRS Music Company, 64, 69, 91, 92, **93**, 94, 95, 99, **113**, 118, 121, 129, 158, 165

racism, 7, 69, 122, 123, 132, 134, 135, 147, 150, 189, 198, 243, 244, 246
ragtime, 4, 5, 27, 28, 33, 37, 38, 104, 108, 109, 206, 325
Randolph's (Lewis's Saloon), 53
Rang Tang, 191, 192, 197
Razaf, Andy: *Brownskin Models*, 180; Crescendo Club, 276; *Drums*, 303, 304; film work, 243; *Harlem Hotcha*, 238, 239; "Havin' a Ball," 256; Joy Club, 181; *Keep Shufflin'*, 196, 197, 200; *Kitchen Mechanics Revue*, 228, 229, 352; late night feasting, 266; *Mamba's Daughters*, 276; "My Handy Man," 210; *Ode to Dorie Miller*, 337; *On Striver's Row*, 289; Smalls Paradise 25th anniversary, 373; *Tan Manhattan*, 292; with W. C. Handy, 240; Waller funeral, 322; West Indian accent, 161; *Yamekraw*, 187
Really the Blues, 167, 168
Record Changer, 345, 369, 373
Rector, Eddie, 216
Redman, Don, 178, 238, 276, 291, 322
Reiner, Fritz, 250, 252
rent party, 27, 41, 118, 159–70, 320
Resnick, Eph, 357
"Revolutionary Etude," 234
Rhapsody in Blue, 169, 188, 221, 232
Rhone, Arthur "Happy," 71, **72**, 95, 99, 124
Rhythm Club, 167
"Rhythm Man," 229
Rhythmodik, 64
Rilhac, Francois, 378
ring shout, 4, 19, 20, 21, 22, 39, 67, 109, 110, 156
Robbins, Fred, 340, 342, 345
Roberts, Charles Luckeyeth "Luckey": Al Rose, 342; Barron Wilkins, 42, 49; biography, 51, 52; compositional style, 66, 110; *Cotton Blossoms*, 142; Crescendo Club, 276, 277; Dan Burley tribute, 354; *Darkest Americans*, 79, 121; Florence Mills Theatrical Association, 224; Gershwin, impression of, 70; influence on Johnson, 97, 112, 120, 303; introduction to Johnson, 51; Johnson benefit concert, 374; Johnson plays his style, 340; Johnson's stroke, 287; *My People*, 78; "One-Leg" Willie Joseph recollection, 48; playing style, 57, 104, 161, 166, 234; QRS, 93, **113**, 115; society orchestra, 56, 72; Waller funeral, 322; Waller homecoming party, 232
Robeson, Paul, 151, 175, 176, 240–42, 257, 300
Robinson, Anna, 264, 278
Robinson, Bill "Bojangles," 208, 223, 245, 289, 313, 314
Robinson, Clarence, 196, 228, 276, 313
Robinson, Ikey, 247
Robinson, J. Russel, 92, 93, 97, 129, 192
Robinson, Madame, **176**
Rock, The (The Garden of Joy), 74
"Rock Me in the Cradle of Love," 60
Rogers, Alex, 56, 60, 128, 142, 179
Rollini, Adrian, 203
Rosalie, 196
Rose, Al, 342
Rosenwald Foundation, 281, 282
Ross, Allie, 73, 174, 231
Roth, Murray, 188
Rothstein, Arnold, 192, 195, 208, 211
Rouder, Willa, 379
"Roumania," 95
Rowles, Jimmy, 228, 317
"Runnin' Wild" (song), 141
Runyon, Damon, 193
Rushing, Jimmy, 224, 323
Russell, Luis, 239
Russell, Maude, 291
Russell, Pee Wee, 307, 308, 323, 324, 334, 355
Russell, Ross, 3, 4, 271
Rutgers Institute of Jazz Studies, 240, 292, 296, 299, 301, 302, 307, 350, 353, 355

Sales, Grover, 3
"Sam Jones Done Snagged His Britches," 186
San Juan Hill, 30, **31**
Saturday Night Swing Club, 269
Saunders, Gertrude, 74, 95, 151, 171, 173, 178

Savoy Ballroom, 265
Schaap, Phil, 329
Schaap, Walter, 329
Schiff, David, 3
Schiffman, Frank, 290, 300
Schillinger system, 359
Schomburg Center, 260
Schreibman, Paul, 361, 362, 365, 370
Schuller, Gunther, 39, 109, 113, 249
Scivales, Riccardo, 380
Scott, Cecil, 357, **375**
Scott, Hazel, 286, 287, 322, 328
Seamon, Harry, 155
Sears, Al, 200
Sedric, Gene, 264, 286
Seeger, Pete, 309, 355
Selwyn, Archibald "Arch," 143, 145, 148, 155
Selwyn's Theater, 143, 172
Seminole, Paul, 199
"Sepia Opera and Symphonic Society," 305
Sewell, Blanche, 328
Sewell, Edith, 336, 337
Shaw, Artie, 328
"She Got Good Booty," 24
Shilkret, Nat, 188, 203
Shipp, Jesse A., 56, 177, 178
Short, Bobby, 228
Show of Shows, 219
Shubert Brothers, 6, 122, 230, 353
Shuffle Along, 41, 52, 101, 122, 124, 130, 140, 141, 143, 144, 145, 148, 150, 153, 155, 171, 172, 196, 197, 200, 362, 364
"Sidewalk Blues," 339
Signature Records, 317, 324
Simeon, Omer, 346, 355
Simmons, Alberta, 49, 50, 105
Simon, Gene, 286
Sims, Lee, 233
Singleton, Freddie, 47
Singleton, Zutty, 366, 367
Sissle, Noble, 52, 101, 121, 140, 185, 277, 372
Sketches of the Deep South, 277
Slack, Freddy, 105
Slave Songs of the United States, 21
Slim, Memphis, 347
Smalls, Edwin A., 88, 227, 248, 300, 373

Smalls' Paradise, 6, 88, 198, 220, 221, 227, 241, 245, 247, 291, 315, 352, 373
Smalls' Sugar Cane Club, 88
Smart (Smarter) Set, 78
Smith, Arthur Leland, 16
Smith, Bessie, 5, 74, 80, 188, 195, 202, 212, 213, 214, 219, 220, 221, 222, 225, 235, 265, 271, 272, 313, 354
Smith, Charles Edward, 3, 23, 294, 309, 324, 335, 370
Smith, Chris, 183, 247, 276, 286
Smith, Clara, 223
Smith, Harrison, 209, 210
Smith, Jabbo, 198, 202, 203
Smith, Mamie, 53, 54, 89, 199, 231, 235
Smith, Pinetop, 340
Smith, Ruby, 259, 265, 272, 278, 354, 355
Smith, Steve, 269
Smith, Trixie, 98, 102, 121
Smith, Willie "The Lion," 54, 55, **330**; admiration of Johnson, 342; Basie, influence on, 272; benefit concert for Johnson, 374, **375**; "Crazy Blues" and "Mama's Blues," 62; dinner at Johnson's home, 360; Gillespie admiration for, 359; "Gut Stomp," 321; Harlem clubs, 74, 166; Harlem stride piano, 104, 106, 107, 110, 111, 112, 117, 161; "Jazzfest and Pop Concert," 336; Johnson and music, 335, 119, 169, 170; Johnson first meeting, 53, 54; Johnson, impression of style, 340; Joy Club, 181; Jungles Casino, 36; *Kitchen Mechanics Revue* preview, 228; leftist leanings of Johnson, 258, 259; Mezzrow band, 270; nicknames, 120; Pied Piper, 327–33, **330**; playing style, 75; radio with Clarence Williams, 226, 279; recordings of Johnson tunes, 228, 374; rent party/cutting contest, 161, 162, 163, 167, 168; sickbed visits, 373, **375**; sporting house tunes, 24; "Stride Piano All Stars," 378; Tatum meeting, 233, 234; Ticklers, impression of, 41, 42, 46, 49, 53; Waller first meeting, 118; Waller home recording, 267; Waller tributes, 322, 324, 326
Smithsonian Institution, 225
Snow, Valaida, 211, 229, 246

Snowden, Elmer, 154
"Solitude," 247
Song Writers Protective Association, 308
Southern Syncopated Orchestra, 151, 254
Southernaires, 240, 279, 286, 346
Spaeth, Sigmund, 300
Spanier, Muggsy, 334
Spaulding, Henry George, 20
Sperry's Bar and Grill, 315
Sphinx Music Publishing Company, 99, 125, 129
"Spirituals to Swing," 259, 264, 271, 272, 273, 277, 278, 279, 281, 283, 285, 317
Spitalny, Phil, 188
"Squeeze Me," 324
St. Cyprian Episcopal Church, 30
St. Louis Blues (film), 188, 189, 219, 220, 221, 222, 223, 241, 242, 354
"St. Louis Blues" (song), 206, 230, 242, 339
St. Louis 1916 ragtime contest, 84
St. Mark's African Methodist Episcopal Zion Church, 26, 174
Stacy, Jess, 366
Stamper, George, 124, 131, 137, 146, 151, 152, 155, 241
Standard Music Roll Company, 64, 96
Stearns, Marshall, 350
Steiner, John, 369
Stepner, Abraham, 173
Stevedore, 258
Stevens, Josephine, 88
Stewart, Rex, 167
Stewart, Sammy, 152
Still, William Grant, 82, 106, 180, 186, 188, 195, 207, 235, 277, 308
Stinson Trading Company, 310
Stern, Harold, 230
Stokowski, Leopold, 243, 252
Stoller, Mike, 293, 294
Stone, Jesse, 288, 289, 290
Stormy Weather (film), 313, 362
"Strange Fruit," 265
Stransky, Josef, 33
"Stride Piano All Stars," 378
Strike Up the Band (show), 196
Stuyvesant Casino, 355, **356**, 368

Sugar Hill (neighborhood), 236
Sullivan, Ed, 246
Sullivan, Joe (Black), 166
Sullivan, Joe (white), 66, 284, 286, 308, 345, 355
Sullivan, Maxine, 280, 285, 286
"Sunflower Slow Drag," 49
Sutton, Ralph, 351, 378
Swaffer, Hannen, 134
Sweatman, Wilbur, 64, 78
Swing Along (Cook), 291
"Swingin' at the Daisy Chain," 182
"Swingin' for Mezz," 270

Talbert, Wen, 137, 276, 277, 296, 305
Tan Manhattan (Blake), 291
Tatum, Art, 8, 46, 81, 83, 126, 170, 233, 234, 249, 313, 322, 328, 329, 354
Taylor, Billy, 112
Taylor, Deems, 252, 300
Taylor, Eva, 213, 225, 226, 240, 267, 279, 292, 293
Taylor, Montana, 352
Tazewell, Charles, 236
"Tea for Two," 233
Teagarden, Jack, 313
Tempo Club, 56
Theater Arts Committee (TAC), 279, 281, 283, 285
"There'll be a Hot Time in the Old Town Tonight," 18
They All Played Ragtime, 53, 303, 369, 370
Thiele, Bob, 317, **318**
This Is Jazz, 347, 349–51
Thomas, Joe, 286
Thompson, Bob, 355
Thompson, Charles, 68, 83, 84
Thompson, Perry, 17, 20, 21, 23, 30, 33, 34, 171
"Thou Swell," 204
"Tiger Rag," 234
Time Life Company, 379
Tip Toe Inn, 355
Tisdale, Clarence, 72
Todd, Clarence, 197
Toledo Conservatory of Music, 84, 85, **86**, 87
"Tomato Sauce," 185

"Toot It Brother Armstrong," 242
Tours, Frank, 241
Town Hall, 306, 308, 323, 331, 339, 341, 342, 346, 347, 354, 368, 374
Trappier, Art, 368
Treemonisha, 43
Trent, Jo, 155, 183, 191, 235, 245
Treumann, Edward E., 43, 173, **175**, 250
"Trixie's Blues," 121
Trolle, Frank, 285
"Troublesome Ivories," 52
Tucker, Sophie, 64
Tunstall, Fred, 53, 131
Turk, Roy, 180
Turner, Joe (pianist), 105, 111, 164, 165, 233, 266
Turner, Joe (singer), 273
Turner, Lavinia, 97, 98
Turpin, Tom, 84
Tuskegee Institute, 150, 253
Tutt, J. Homer, 78, 79, 80, 121, 146

Ulanov, Barry, 311, 320
Underneath the Harlem Moon (film), 168
Unger, Stella, 175, 223, 224, 230
Union Baptist Church, 30
Universal Music Company, 64
University of Michigan, 265
"Unknown Blues," 369
Unsung Americans Sung, 239

Valentine, Hazel, 182, 267
"Valentine Stomp," 182, 267
Vaughan, Sarah, 352
V-discs, 312, 323
Vechten, Carl Van, 161, 220, 228
Vernon Hall, 368
Victor Records, 202, 203, 205, 226, 292
Vitaphone, 188
Vocalion, 278
Vocalstyle Company, 64
Vodery, Will, 38, 66, 99, 101, 133, 135, 185, 196, 197, 276
Voice of America, 378
Von Grona, Eugene, 296, 297
Voorhees, Don, 188

Walker, Madame C. J. (granddaughter), 146
Waller, Anita, 207
Waller, Maurice, 81, 116, 195, 201, 266
Waller, Thomas "Fats": *Adam and Eve in Harlem*, 224; afterlife, 335; benefit concerts, 223, 245, 247, 266; boogie woogie, 318, 319; Connie's Inn, 238; Count Basie, influence on, 272; Crescendo Club, 276; death/tributes, 223, 317, 321, 322, 323, 324, 325, 326, 333, 334, 337, 351; *Fireworks of 1930*, 231; "Friends of James P. Johnson," 300; Harlem establishments, 74, 89, 182; home recording, 267; *Hot Chocolates*, 216, 219; Johnson performances of tunes, 321, 322, 324, 331, 340, 345; Johnson recordings of tunes, 324; Johnson teaching and influence, 46, 50, 111, 114–20, 164, 286, 293, 312, 321, 336, 350, 376; Johnson tunes recorded, 228, 256; Joy Club, 181; *Keep Shufflin'*, 191, 195–98, 200–205, 207–9, 211; Lafayette Theater Christmas show, 215; late night feasts, 266; Long Island, 268, 287; Panassie recordings, 270; piano rolls, 94, **113**, 180, 348; playing style, 78, 249, 271; popularity/influence, 5, 7, 112, 308, 312, 359, 377, 380; radio with Johnson, 209; recording studio in, 212; recordings with Johnson, 202–5, 209, 225; rent party/cutting contests, 161, 162, 166, 167, 168, 232; *Rhapsody in Blue* party, 169; Saturday Night Swing Club, 269; *Shuffle Along of 1930*, 229; St. Louis Blues, 220, 221; *Stormy Weather*, 313–15; stride piano, 105; Tatum meeting, 233, 234; television, 308; West Indian accent, 170
Walton, Lester A., 253
Washington, Fredi, 241, 242, 354
Washington, Isabel, 221, 222
Washington Jazz Music Society, 334
"Watch Me Go," 97
Waters, Ethel, 5, 53, 74, 79, 83, 88, 111, 124, 126, 133, 137, 171, 199, 209, 210, 228, 235, 245, 276, 346, 369, 374
Waters (Watters, Walters), Johnny, 82, 83
Watkins, Phil, 41

Watters, Lu, 367
Watts, Joe, 286
"Way Down Yonder In New Orleans," 344
Weatherford, Teddy, 315
Webb, Lyda (Elida), 157
Webster, Ben, 322, 334, 345
Wein, George, 344
Welch, Hattie, 275
Welles, Orson, 189, 253
Wells, Dicky, 324
Wellstood, Dick, 105, 108, 109, 119, 120, 329, 378, 379
Wendell, Bruce, 336
Wendling, Pete, 64, 92
West, Mae, 182, 183, 196, 242, 243
Wettling, George, 323, 340
Whaley, Tom, 164
"What Is This Thing Called Love," 225
"What's The Use of Being Alone," 202
Wheeler, Hartland "Hart," 345
"When It's Cherry Time in Tokio [sic]," 65
"When My Baby Comes," 223
"When the Rain Turns into Snow," 98
Whetsol, Arthur, 210
"Whistling Seath," 88
White, Dan, 156
White, George, 6, 141, 142, 143, 144, 145, 148, 150, 155
White, Josh, 184, 312, 345
White, Lucien H., 207
White, Walter, 300
White Rats Actors' Union, 62
Whiteman, Paul, 129, 135, 245, 252, 279
Whitney, Salem Tutt, 41, 78, 79, 121, 146, 180
"Who?," 270, 367
"Wild Cherries Rag," 66
Wilkes, Mattie, 146
Wilkinson, Thad "Snowball," 49
Williams, "Cootie," 209
Williams, Clarence, **113**, 179, 183, 201, 207, 209, 215, 223, 224, 225, 226, 231, 240, 244, 245, 247, 267, 276, 279, 287, 292, 293, 306, 322, 374
Williams, Corky, 167

Williams, Martin, 5
Williams, Mary Lou, 263, 322, 324, 328, 345
Williams, Spencer, 223
Williamson, Sonny Boy, 347
"Willow Tree," 200, 204, 205, 229, 321, 326, 337
Wilner, Michael "Spike," 380
Wilson, Edith, 151, 223
Williams, Bert, 35, 78, **93**, 102, 155, 206
Williams, Corky, 51, 118
Williams, Dan, 35
Williams, Spencer, 223
Wilson, Edwin E., 66, 69
Wilson, Teddy, 112, 266, 286, 312, 322, 324
Winchell, Walter, 246, 247
Windsor Theater, 260
Wodehouse, Artis, 379
Wolfe, Jacques, 257
Wolff, Francis, 317, 318, 322, 323
Wolverine (barbershop), 83
Wooding, Russell, 180, 238
Wooding, Sam, 131, 199, 200, 203
Woods, Tommy, 146
World Transcriptions, 324, 331
Wright, Herbert, 254
Wright, Lillie Mae, 53, 75. *See also* Johnson, Lillie Mae
Wright, William J., 175, 287

Yale University, 368
"Yancey Special," 342
"Yellow Dog Blues," 206
Yerba Buena Jazz Band, 366, 367
"You Can Read My Letters, But You Can't Read My Mind," 186
"You Can't Do What My Last Man Did," 139, 378
"You Never Miss a Good Thing Till It's Gone," 97
Young, Lester, 324

Zephyrs, 370
Ziegfeld, Florenz, 60
Ziegfeld Follies, 60, 141, 180, 196
Zolott, Esther, 335

SHOW INDEX

A la Carte, 184, 195
Adam and Eve in Harlem, 224
American Negro Ballet, 296, 297

Bandanna Land, 125
Brownskin Models, 180

Chicago Loop: Musical Comedy in Two Acts, 179
Cotton Blossoms, 142
Cottonland, 173
Creole Follies, 180

Dark Secrets, 180
Darkest Americans, 79, 80, 81, 121, 213
Darktown Follies, 59, 60, **61**, 121, 152
Dreamy Kid, The, 255, 295, 300, 303
Dust and Dawn, 224

Fireworks of 1930, 231
From Speedville to Broadway, 61

Geechie: Dusky Romance in Three Acts, 179, 202, 240, 304
Great Day In N'Orleans, A, 224, 225
Greenwich Village Follies, 230

Harlem Hotcha, 238, 239, 240, 304
Harlem Opera House production featuring Joe Louis, 248
Harper and Blanks Revue, 122, 123
Harry Steppe and His Big Show, 172, 173
Hired Husband, 352
Hollywood Follies, 171, 172

Keep Shufflin', 193–211, **199**, 215, 216, 221, 229, 314
Kitchen Mechanic's Revue, 228, 291, 352, 373
Kitchen Opera (Love in the Kitchen), 291, 371, 372

Lazy Rhythm, 235

Macbeth, 189, 253
Mad Manhattan, 245, 248, 250

Meet Miss Jones, 352, 361, 362
Messin' Around, 195, 215–19
Moneymoon, 361, 362
Mooching Along, 158, 177, 178

Negro Nuances, 150–52

On Striver's Row, 288, 289, 290
Organizer, The, 256–65, 278, 288, 305, 309, 312, 352

Paradise Club revue (Atlantic City), 277
Pinkard's Symphonic Fantasy, 290, 291, **292**
Plantation Days, 82, 122–38, 142, 151, 152, 155, 171, 178, 236
Policy Kings, 256, 259, 273, 274–76, 278

Rainbow, The, 131, 136
Raisin' Cain—A Cyclonic Musical Comedy, 142
Runnin' Wild, 139–58, **144**, **149**, **158**, 172, 173, 174, 178, 194, 197, 216, 241, 249, 370

Shuffle Along of 1930, 229
Solid South, The, 342
Step on It, 172
Stoppin' Traffic, 219
Sugar Hill (1931), 105, 106, 235, 236, 237, 238, 325
Sugar Hill (1949), 362–66, 370, 371
Sun Down, 227
Sunshine Sammy (Whirl of Dixie), 177
Swingin' the Dream, 180, 279, 280

Tan Town Topics, 291
Three Little Maids, 230

Vagabond Love, 230
Vanities (Carroll), 180

Watch Out, 172
What's Your Husband Doing, 76, 77

Yeah Man, 237, 238

TUNE INDEX

"A-Flat Dream," 279
African Drums, 303, 304
"After Hours," 96, 187
"After Tonight," 278, 417n64
"Aintcha Got Music," 239
"Alabama Stomp," 180
American Symphonic Suite—"St. Louis Blues," 243, 252, 291, 302, 303
"April in Harlem" ("From Harlem," "Harlem Love Song," "Song of Harlem"), 277, 294, 297, 304, 337, 342

"Bantu Baby," 228
"Baptist Mission" (from *Harlem Symphony*), 305, 337
"Blue Mizz," 322
"Blueberry Rhyme," 281, 294
"Blues for Fats," 317, 321, 342
"Boogey-woogey Runway," 312
"Boogie Dream, The," 325
"Boogie Woogie Stride," 308, 311, 319, 323, 337
"Boston," 106
"Boys of Uncle Sam," 63
"Broadway Glide," 124
"Brothers and Sisters," 186

Can't You Hear Those Drums, 413n60
"Caprice Rag," 65, 78, 98, 187, 321, 330, 337, 347
"Carolina Balmoral," 22, 315, 318, 321, 344
"Carolina Shout," 66, 67, **68**, 84, 98, 99, **100**, 101, 109, 110, 112, 114, 116, 117, 118, 129, 130, 164, 165, 166, 179, 230, 233, 234, 272, 300, 307, 321, 333, 334, 340, 342, 349, 374, 377, 378
"Charleston," 6, 8, 37, 135, 142, 144, 152, 153, 154, 156, 157, **158**, 172, 174, 178, 180, 194, 196, 249, 266, 277, 281, 338, 340, 347, 349, 364, 366, 377, 378
"Charleston Dance, The," 157
"Charlestonovitch," 180
"Chicago Stomp Down," 180
"Cotton Pickin'," 184

"Desperate Blues," 121, 125, 129, 173
"Disordered Dream, A," 371

"Dixieland Echoes," 184, 185, 187
"Don't Cry Baby," 6, 224, 315, 340
"Don't Lose Your Head (and Lose Your Gal)," 353
"Downhearted," 303
"Dreamy" (from *Dreamy Kid*), 303
"Drums," 239, 263, 304

"Eccentricity," 66, 95, 179
"Echoes of Ole Dixieland," 184
"Elevator Papa-Switchboard Mama," 228
"Everybody's Doin' the Charleston Now," 158, 179
"Exhortation," 210

"Fascination," 66, 69
"Feelin' Blue," 215
"Fooling Around with Love," 236
"Four O'clock Groove," 325

"Get Away From My Window," 217
"Ginger Brown," 144, 152, 153
"Give Me the Sunshine," 196, 200, 210, 211
"Glad to See You Again" (from *The Organizer*), 263
"Go Harlem," 228, 229
"Good or Nothin'," 228
"Got to Do It," 258
"Gut Stomp," 37, 318, 321, 323

"Harlem Strut," 98, 164, 165, 369
Harlem Symphony, 66, 106, 137, 233, 245, 277, **296**, 297, **299**, 301, 302, 303, 305, 312, 336, 337
"Harlem Woogie," 256, 264
"Havin' a Ball," 256
"Honey," 184
"Hot Curves," 189
"Hot Diggity Dog," 126
"Hot Harlem," 236, 325
"Hungry Blues," 262, 264, 265

"I Need Lovin'," 180, 266
"If I Could Be With You," 6, 119, 126, 180, 195, 266, 281, 287, 288, 337, 340, 377

"I'm Stepping Out with Lulu," 184
"Impressions," 308, 310, 311, 337
"Improvisations on Pinetop's Boogie-Woogie," 318
"Imitator's Rag," 28, 58
"Innovation," 66, 70, 303
"International Vampire Babes," 124
"It Takes Love to Cure the Heart's Disease," 95
"I've Got to Be Lovely to Harry," 353
"Ivy, Cling to Me," 127, 128

"J. P. Boogie," 318
Jazzamine Concerto (*Piano Concerto in A flat*), 245, 263, 303, 304, 312, 340, 341
"Jingles," 179, 225
John Henry Symphonic Poem, 257
"Juba Dance," 142
"Just Before Daybreak," 344

"Keep Em Guessing," 365
"Keep Off the Grass," 98, 99, 179, 233, 234

"Lament," 303
"Land of Jazz, The," 151
"Liberty," 63
"Liza Jane's Weddin'," 184
"Lock and Key," 195, 215
"Log Cabin Days," 144
"Love Bug," 152, 153, 173
"Love I Crave, The," 173

"Mamma's Blues" ("Mama and Papa Blues," "Mama's Blues," "Mamma's and Pappa's Blues"), 25, 66, 69, 127
"Mammy Land," 228
Mississippi Moan: Symphonic Poem, 185
"Mississippi River Flood," 184
"Mississippi Roustabouts," 186
"Mister Deep Blue Sea," 243
"Mule Walk," 37, 281, 318, 321
"My Sweet Hunk of Trash," 364, 365

"Night Club," 298
"Night-time in Dixieland," 53

"Ode to Dorie Miller," 336, 337
"Old Fashioned Love," 142, 143, 144, 145, 146, 152, 153, 157, 246, 266, 277, 281, 287, 312, 323, 333, 337, 340, 377
"On the Level," 228
"Open Your Heart," 144, 146, 152, 153, 155
Organizer, The, 258, 259, 260
"Over the Bars" (Steeplechase Rag), 53

"Peace Sister Peace," 364, 365
"Plantin' Plowin' Hoein'" (from *The Organizer*), 260
"Porter's Love Song, A," 228
"Porter's Love Song to a Chambermaid," 228, 229, 352, 354, 373, 377
"Portrait," 232
"Put Your Mind Right on It," 215, 217

"Reflections," 294, 312, 337
Rhythm Drums, 304
"Riffs," 215
"Runnin' Wild Medley," 378

"Scalin' the Blues," 179
"Scouting Around," 139, 185
"Shout On," 217
"Sippi," 201, 204, 205, 210, 211
"Skiddle-De Scow," 195, 211, 217
"Slippery Hips," 228
"Smiling Through My Tears," 371
"Snowy Morning Blues," 215, 273, 307, 308, 310, 319, 333, 342, 346, 355, 377
"Sorry" ("So Sorry"), 215
Spirit of America, 295
"Steeplechase Rag" ("Over the Bars") 53, 65, 277
"Stop It" ("Stop It, Joe"), 63, 88, 127, 187, 270, 273
"Strut in with Jerry," 124
"Subway Journey" (from *Harlem Symphony*), **296**
"Sun Kist Rose," 156
"Sun Will Be Shining for You" (from *Dreamy Kid*), 303–4

"Sweepstake Special," 279
"Sweet Mistreater," 195, 215
"Swinga-dilla Street," 291

"There Goes My Headache," 239
"There's No Two Ways About Love," 314
"Toddlin'" ("Toddlin' Home"), 139, 185
"Travelling," 240
"Twilight Rag," 53

"Ukulele Blues," 124, 126, 129, 131
"Uncle Sammy Here I Am," 292

"Victory Stride," 322

"Wandering," 240, 303, 304
"We Are Leaving for Yamekraw," 186, 187
"Weeping Blues," 52
"When I Can't Be with You," 246
"Whisper Sweet," 246
"Worried and Lonesome Blues" ("Worried Lonesome Blues"), 152, 241, 264, 377

Yamekraw, 181, 185–90, 202, 207, 208, 210, 211, 217, 226, 230, 232, 240, 242, 253, 263, 297, 305, 336, 338
"Yamekraw Blues," 189
"You Can't Lose A Broken Heart," 364, 365
"You Don't Understand," 223, 225
"You Said You Wouldn't But You Done It," 126
"You You You," 256, 274, 276
"Your Love Is All I Crave," 216, 217, 218, 219
"You're My Rose," 353
"You've Got to Be Modernistic" ("Modernistic"), 225, 226

ABOUT THE AUTHOR

Photo courtesy of the author

SCOTT E. BROWN is an independent jazz researcher. He has written two books on James P. Johnson and has published several articles and lectured widely about jazz. He is a practicing physician and holds a master's degree in jazz history and research.

www.ingramcontent.com/pod-product-compliance
Lightning Source LLC
Chambersburg PA
CBHW030559230426
43661CB00053B/1780